MEASUREMENT AND EVALUATION IN PSYCHOLOGY AND EDUCATION

SEVENTH EDITION

Robert M. Thorndike
Western Washington University

Upper Saddle River, New Jersey
Columbus, Ohio

Library of Congress Cataloging-in-Publication Data

Thorndike, Robert M.
    Measurement and evaluation in psychology and education/Robert M.
Thorndike. — 7th ed.
        p. cm.
    Includes bibliographical references and indexes.
    ISBN 0-13-019998-2
    1.   Educational tests and measurements. 2.   Psychological tests for children. I. Title.

LB1131.M433 2005
371.26—dc22

2004007704

Vice President and Executive Publisher: Jeffery W. Johnston
Publisher: Kevin M. Davis
Editorial Assistant: Amanda King
Production Editor: Mary Harlan
Production Coordinator: Penny Walker, *The GTS Companies*/York, PA Campus
Design Coordinator: Diane C. Lorenzo
Text Design and Illustrations: *The GTS Companies*/York, PA Campus
Cover Design: Jeff Vanik
Cover Image: Superstock
Production Manager: Laura Messerly
Director of Marketing: Ann Castel Davis
Marketing Manager: Autumn Purdy
Marketing Coordinator: Tyra Poole

This book was set in Berkeley Book by *The GTS Companies*/York, PA Campus. It was printed and bound by R. R. Donnelley & Sons Company. The cover was printed by The Lehigh Press, Inc.

Pearson Education Ltd.
Pearson Education Singapore Pte. Ltd.
Pearson Education Canada, Ltd.
Pearson Education–Japan

Pearson Education Australia Pty. Limited
Pearson Education North Asia Ltd.
Pearson Educación de Mexico, S.A. de C.V.
Pearson Education Malaysia Pte. Ltd.

10 9 8 7 6 5 4 3 2 1
ISBN: 0-13-019998-2

Preface

When the first edition of this book was published in 1955, I was 12 years old and made minimal contributions, although I did serve as a guinea pig for some of my father's testing experiments. The second and third editions were also published without any substantive input from me, but I started using the third edition for my own classes in measurement in 1970. My father, Robert L. Thorndike, and I discussed many measurement issues once I became psychometrically literate, so my reactions to the third edition had some indirect influence on the fourth, which was published just after my father retired. With the fifth edition, I took over many of my father's responsibilities, although he continued to have a significant influence on the revisions. Throughout these first five editions of the book, Elizabeth Hagen provided a healthy dose of applied educational material, although much of her role was assumed by George Cunningham for the fifth edition. With the sixth edition, I brought in my daughter, Tracy Thorndike-Christ, an educational psychologist, as a contributor for some of the applied material. Clinical awareness was added by Max and Arleen Lewis, who prepared the revision of the chapter on personality testing, and Richard F. Ittenbach, who revised the chapter on exceptional children and the one on ethics and issues in assessment. As this seventh edition goes to press, my father has been dead for 14 years, but his influence is still clearly present, both in parts of the text that retain his unique flair for language and in the profound influence he has had on my own thinking and professional development. Thanks, Pop.

During the five decades since the first edition, there have been major changes in educational and psychometric theory and practice. Concern for the rights of all individuals without regard to color, gender, disability, or any number of other characteristics has become a central issue that has led to attempts to provide optimal educational experiences for all children. Society at large has been pressured to assure that every individual be given equal opportunity for access to higher education and to desirable employment. But even with these changes (and perhaps because of them), the need remains for objective, dependable, and relevant information as a basis for making decisions. Tests provided much of that information in 1955, and they are, if anything, an even more essential source of information at the dawn of the 21st century.

The first six editions of this book helped three generations of educators and psychologists develop the skills to use test information wisely; this seventh edition is intended to continue providing that service. To that end, specialists in various areas of measurement theory were again asked to revise selected chapters. Once again, Max and Arleen Lewis have lent their clinical expertise to the revision of Chapter 11 on the measurement of personality, interests, and adjustment. Arleen teamed with her father, Glendon W. Casto, to prepare the revisions of Chapter 13, Assessment of Children with Disabilities. Finally, K. Dayle Jones revised Chapter 14, Ethics and Issues in Assessment.

This seventh edition continues our tradition of treating tests as sources of information that can serve as useful aids in decision making. We emphasize that tests exist to help people make decisions and that the quality of those decisions depends on a knowledgeable use of test information. Many of the problems that have been attributed to tests are as much a consequence of improper test use as of poorly constructed tests. Our purpose is to provide test users with the information and skills needed to avoid making mistakes in using and interpreting tests.

Changes in the Seventh Edition

Users of previous editions of the book will notice two primary changes in the seventh edition. First, the chapter on special topics in measurement has been eliminated. Item response theory approaches to measurement and test development have been moved to the chapters on reliability and giving meaning to test scores (Chapters 3 and 4), and computer-assisted test administration has been integrated into the main text in appropriate places. Meta-analysis and validity generalization have been moved to the validity chapter (Chapter 5). Second, the "by hand" computation of various statistics in the sixth edition's Appendix 1 has been eliminated, and procedures for using SPSS and EXCEL to perform needed computations have been incorporated into the main text, particularly in Chapter 2, but elsewhere as appropriate. Numerous other changes have been made, many in response to comments from users of the sixth edition. For example, use of Internet resources to locate information about particular tests has been expanded in Chapter 6 and publisher websites are given in later chapters for many of the specific tests covered. Because there is so much material available on the websites of test publishers, the appendices listing characteristics of particular tests and giving addresses for test publishers have been eliminated.

The general organization of the book into three parts remains unchanged. The first part, Chapters 1 through 6, provides a general overview of the issues in testing with which any user of test information should be familiar. It includes a chapter setting out our basic theme, followed by a chapter on necessary quantitative concepts, one on frames of reference (normative, ipsative, criterion, and latent trait), moves on to chapters on reliability and validity of measurement procedures, and concludes with a chapter on practical issues, including a discussion of where to get information on specific tests. Item response theory material has been added to Chapters 3 and 4, and the validity chapter (Chapter 5) has been expanded to include meta-analysis and validity generalization.

The second part of the book, Chapters 7 through 12, provides measurement procedures for specific applications. Chapter 7 covers the kinds of decisions that must be made in educational settings and what kinds of information are needed for each kind of decision. Chapter 8, Aptitude Tests, has been updated with discussions of the latest revisions of the Woodcock-Johnson, Raven's Progressive Matrices, and Stanford-Binet, and some newer brief intelligence tests. Chapter 9, Standardized Achievement Tests, describes both group and individually administered tests of achievement. Chapter 10 introduces rubrics for scoring essays and other methods for appraising behavior "on the fly" in nonstandardized settings. Chapter 11 introduces the major instruments for measuring interests, personality, and adjustment. Finally, Chapter 12 reviews methods for measuring attitudes and for constructing rating scales and checklists.

The third part of the book has three chapters. Chapter 13 covers testing exceptional children and includes a discussion of historical and legal issues as well as practical issues in such assessment. Chapter 14 reviews the legal and ethical responsibilities of test users and test takers. The final chapter discusses the process of test construction with a primary focus on achievement testing. Guidelines for writing objective test items and procedures for item analysis form the major portion of the chapter, but suggestions for writing and scoring essay tests are also included.

Acknowledgments

I would like to thank the following colleagues who provided helpful and insightful reviews: Jeffrey L. Lorentz, University of Houston; William C. Prattella, Mercy College; Kip Tellez, University of Houston; Robert Terry, University of Oklahoma; and Marty Tombari, University of Denver. I am thankful to them all, as well as to my wife, Elva, who has now been through the process of authorship and production seven times and who continues to offer support and understanding.

Robert M. Thorndike

EDUCATOR LEARNING CENTER:
AN INVALUABLE ONLINE RESOURCE

Merrill Education and the Association for Supervision and Curriculum Development (ASCD) invite you to take advantage of a new online resource, one that provides access to the top research and proven strategies associated with ASCD and Merrill—the Educator Learning Center. At **www.EducatorLearningCenter.com** you will find resources that will enhance your students' understanding of course topics and of current educational issues, in addition to being invaluable for further research.

How the Educator Learning Center Will Help Your Students Become Better Teachers

With the combined resources of Merrill Education and ASCD, you and your students will find a wealth of tools and materials to better prepare them for the classroom.

Research
- More than 600 articles from the ASCD journal *Educational Leadership* discuss everyday issues faced by practicing teachers.
- A direct link on the site to Research Navigator™ gives students access to many of the leading education journals, as well as extensive content detailing the research process.
- Excerpts from Merrill Education texts give your students insights on important topics of instructional methods, diverse populations, assessment, classroom management, technology, and refining classroom practice.

Classroom Practice
- Hundreds of lesson plans and teaching strategies are categorized by content area and age range.
- Case studies and classroom video footage provide virtual field experience for student reflection.
- Computer simulations and other electronic tools keep your students abreast of today's classrooms and current technologies.

Look into the Value of Educator Learning Center Yourself

A four-month subscription to Educator Learning Center is $25 but is **FREE** when used in conjunction with this text. To obtain free passcodes for your students, simply contact your local Merrill/Prentice Hall sales representative, and your representative will give you a special ISBN to give your bookstore when ordering your textbooks. To preview the value of this website to you and your students, please go to **www.EducatorLearningCenter.com** and click on "Demo."

Brief Contents

PART ONE   TECHNICAL ISSUES

CHAPTER 1   Fundamental Issues in Measurement   1
CHAPTER 2   Measurement and Numbers   22
CHAPTER 3   Giving Meaning to Scores   58
CHAPTER 4   Qualities Desired in Any Measurement Procedure: Reliability   109
CHAPTER 5   Qualities Desired in Any Measurement Procedure: Validity   145
CHAPTER 6   Practical Issues Related to Testing   197

PART TWO   TESTING AND MEASUREMENT DEVICES

CHAPTER 7   Assessment and Educational Decisions   218
CHAPTER 8   Aptitude Tests   238
CHAPTER 9   Standardized Achievement Tests   288
CHAPTER 10   Performance and Product Evaluation   307
CHAPTER 11   Interests, Personality, and Adjustment   326
CHAPTER 12   Attitudes and Rating Scales   363

PART THREE   SPECIAL TOPICS IN TESTING

CHAPTER 13   Assessment of Children with Disabilities   399
CHAPTER 14   Ethics and Issues in Assessment   416
CHAPTER 15   Principles of Test Development   439
Appendix: Percent of Cases Falling Below Selected Values on the Normal Curve   481
References   483
Author Index   495
Subject Index   499

Contents

PART ONE

TECHNICAL ISSUES

CHAPTER 1

Fundamental Issues in
Measurement   1

Introduction   1
A Little History   2
 The Early Period   3
 The Boom Period   4
 The First Period of Criticism   5
 The Battery Period   5
 The Second Period of Criticism   6
 The Age of Accountability   6
Types of Decisions   7
Measurement and Decisions   8
 The Role of Values in Decision Making   8
Steps in the Measurement Process   9
 Identifying and Defining the Attribute   10
 *Determining Operations to Isolate and Display the
  Attribute*   11
 Quantifying the Attribute   13
 *Problems Relating to the Measurement
  Process*   14
Some Current Issues in Measurement   15
 Testing Minority Individuals   16
 Invasion of Privacy   17
 The Use of Normative Comparisons   17

 Other Factors That Influence Scores   18
 Rights and Responsibilites of Test Takers   18
SUMMARY   19
QUESTIONS AND EXERCISES   20
SUGGESTED READINGS   21

CHAPTER 2

Measurement and Numbers   22

Questions to Ask About Test Scores   22
Scales of Measurement   25
Preparation of a Frequency Distribution   27
 Grouped Frequency Distributions   28
 Cumulative Frequency Distributions   33
Graphic Representation   34
Measures of Central Tendency   36
 The Mode   37
 The Median   37
 Percentiles   39
 The Arithmetic Mean   40
 *Central Tendency and the Shape of the
  Distribution*   42
Measures of Variability   43
 The Range   44
 The Semi-Interquartile Range   44
 The Standard Deviation   45
Interpreting the Standard Deviation   47
Interpreting the Score of an Individual   49
Measures of Relationship   50

SUMMARY   55
QUESTIONS AND EXERCISES   56
SUGGESTED READINGS   57

CHAPTER 3

Giving Meaning to Scores   58

The Nature of a Score   58
   Frames of Reference   59
   Domains in Criterion- and Norm-Referenced
      Tests   61
Criterion-Referenced Evaluation   62
Norm-Referenced Evaluation   64
   Grade Norms   65
   Age Norms   69
   Percentile Norms   70
   Standard Score Norms   76
   Normalizing Transformations   79
   Stanines   82
Interchangeability of Different Types of
   Norms   84
Quotients   87
Profiles   88
Criterion-Referenced Reports   92
Norms for School Averages   97
Cautions in Using Norms   98
A Third Frame of Reference: Item Response
   Theory   100
SUMMARY   106
QUESTIONS AND EXERCISES   107
SUGGESTED READINGS   108

CHAPTER 4

Qualities Desired in Any Measurement
Procedure: Reliability   109

Introduction   109
Reliability as Consistency   110
   Sources of Inconsistency   111
Two Ways to Express Reliability   112
   Standard Error of Measurement   112
   Reliability Coefficient   112
Ways to Assess Reliability   113
   Retesting with the Same Test   114
   Testing with Parallel Forms   115
   Single-Administration Methods   116
   Comparison of Methods   121

Interpretation of Reliability Data   122
   Standard Error of Measurement   122
   Reliability Coefficient   124
Factors Affecting Reliability   125
   Variability of the Group   125
   Level of the Group on the Trait   125
   Length of the Test   127
   Operations Used for Estimating
      Reliability   128
   Practical versus Theoretical Reliability   128
Minimum Level of Reliability   130
Reliability of Difference Scores   131
Effects of Unreliability on Correlation Between
   Variables   134
Reliability of Criterion-Referenced Tests   135
Reliability of Computer Adaptive Tests   139
SUMMARY   143
QUESTIONS AND EXERCISES   143
SUGGESTED READINGS   144

CHAPTER 5

Qualities Desired in Any Measurement
Procedure: Validity   145

Introduction   145
Content-Related Evidence of Validity   147
   Preparing a Test Blueprint   147
   Content Validity for Measures of Aptitude and
      Typical Performance   156
Criterion-Related Evidence of Validity   157
   Face Validity   157
   Empirical Validity   157
Construct-Related Evidence of Validity   174
   Predictions About Correlations   176
   Predictions About Group Differences   178
   Predictions About Responses to Experimental
      Treatments or Interventions   178
The Unified View of Validity   179
   Validation as a Scientific Enterprise   179
   Construct Validity as the Whole of Validity   181
   Messick's Unified Theory of Validity   185
   Beyond Messick: Refinements and Shifts in
      Focus   189
Validity Theory and Test Bias   190
Overlap of Reliability and Validity   191
Validity for Criterion-Referenced Tests   192
Meta-Analysis and Validity Generalization   193

SUMMARY   194
QUESTIONS AND EXERCISES   194
SUGGESTED READINGS   195

CHAPTER 6

Practical Issues Related to Testing   197

Factors Making for Practicality in Routine
  Test Use   197
    Economy   197
    Features Facilitating Test Administration   200
    Features Facilitating Interpretation and Use of
      Scores   201
    E-Testing   203
Guide for Evaluating a Test   204
    General Identifying Information   204
    Information About the Test   205
    Aids to Interpreting Test Results   205
    Validity   205
    Reliability   206
    Administration and Scoring   206
    Scales and Norms   207
Getting Information About Specific Tests   207
    What Tests Exist?   207
    Exactly What Is Test X Like?   209
    What Do Critics Think of Test X?   211
    What Research Has Been Conducted on
      Test X?   212
SUMMARY   214
QUESTIONS AND EXERCISES   214
SOURCES OF TEST INFORMATION   215

PART TWO

TESTING AND MEASUREMENT DEVICES

CHAPTER 7

Assessment and Educational
Decisions   218

Introduction   218
Values and Decisions   219
Placement Decisions   219
    Issues Related to Mainstreaming   220
    How Placement Decisions Are Made   221
Classroom Instructional Decisions   222
    The Use of Objectives   223
    Types of Assessment Instruments   223

Day-by-Day Instructional Decisions   225
Reporting Academic Progress   227
    Performance in Relation to Perfection   228
    Performance in Relation to Par   228
    Performance in Relation to Potential   229
    Assigning Grades   230
    Importance of Grades   230
Planning Educational Futures   231
    Selection Decisions   232
    Curricular Decisions   233
    Public and Political Decisions   234
SUMMARY   235
QUESTIONS AND EXERCISES   236
SUGGESTED READINGS   236

CHAPTER 8

Aptitude Tests   238

Introduction   238
Theories of Cognitive Abilities   239
    Binet's Theory   239
    Spearman's g   240
    Thurstone's Primary Mental Abilities   240
    Theories of Jensen and Wechsler   241
    Cattell-Horn G_f-G_c Theory   243
    Carroll's Three-Stratum Theory   244
    Sternberg's Triarchic Theory   244
    Das-Naglieri PASS Model   245
    Gardner's Proposal   246
Individual General-Ability Tests   246
    Stanford-Binet Intelligence Scale, Fourth
      Edition   247
    Stanford-Binet Intelligence Scale,
      Fifth Edition   253
    Wechsler Scales   255
    Woodcock-Johnson Psycho-Educational
      Battery–Third Edition   259
    Das-Naglieri Cognitive Assessment
      System   259
    Nonverbal Measures of Cognitive Ability   262
    Abbreviated Individual Tests   265
Group General-Ability Tests   266
Tests of Multiple Abilities   273
    Differential Aptitude Test Battery   273
    General Aptitude Test Battery   276
Role of General Cognitive Ability: The Bell
  Curve   280

SUMMARY   284
QUESTIONS AND EXERCISES   285
SUGGESTED READINGS   286

CHAPTER 9

Standardized Achievement Tests   288

Introduction   288
Distinctive Features of Standardized Achievement
  Tests   288
Uses of Standardized Achievement Tests   290
Types of Standardized Achievement Tests   290
Group Standardized Achievement Tests   291
Individually Administered Achievement
  Tests   294
Secondary-School and College-Level Achievement
  Tests   295
Problems with Statewide Administration of
  Achievement Test Batteries: The "Lake
  Wobegon Effect"   298
Interpreting Standardized Achievement Test
  Batteries   300
Diagnostic Achievement Tests   302
Criterion-Referenced Standardized Achievement
  Tests   303
  *Examples of Criterion-Referenced Standardized
    Achievement Tests*   304
  *Problems with Criterion-Referenced Standardized
    Achievement Tests*   304
SUMMARY   305
QUESTIONS AND EXERCISES   305
SUGGESTED READINGS   306

CHAPTER 10

Performance and Product Evaluation   307

Introduction   307
Artificiality of Conventional Cognitive
  Tests   307
Conventional Cognitive Tests   308
Assessing Products   309
Applying Performance and Product Evaluation
  to Cognitive Tasks   310
  Scoring Performance Tests   310
Assessing Processes   313

  Using Checklists   313
  Using Rating Scales   314
Assessing Products and Performances   315
  Advantages of Multiple Observers   316
  *Reliability or Agreement for Multiple
    Observers*   316
Systematic Observation   318
  *Conducting the Systematic
    Observation*   319
  *Advantages and Disadvantages of Systematic
    Observation*   322
SUMMARY   324
QUESTIONS AND EXERCISES   325
SUGGESTED READINGS   325

CHAPTER 11

Interests, Personality, and Adjustment   326

Introduction   326
Interest Measurement   327
  Strong Interest Inventory   327
  Career Assessment Inventory   336
  Self-Directed Search   336
Personality and Adjustment Assessment   337
  Dynamic Approaches   338
  Trait Approaches   341
  *Humanistic Approaches: Personality as
    Self-Perception*   351
  Behavioral Approaches   352
Problems with Personality and Interest
  Measures   358
Computerized Scoring and Interpretation   360
  Advantages   360
  Disadvantages   360
SUMMARY   361
QUESTIONS AND EXERCISES   361
SUGGESTED READINGS   362

CHAPTER 12

Attitudes and Rating Scales   363

Introduction   363
Learning About Personality from Others   364
  Letters of Recommendation   364
  Rating Scales   366

Problems in Obtaining Sound Ratings 367
Improving the Effectiveness of Ratings 374
Improving the Accuracy of Ratings 379
Rating Procedures for Special Situations 383
Measuring Attitudes 386
Summative Attitude Scales 388
Single-Item Scales 389
Example of an Attitude Rating Scale 390
Alternative Formats 393
SUMMARY 395
QUESTIONS AND EXERCISES 396
SUGGESTED READINGS 397

PART THREE

SPECIAL TOPICS IN TESTING

CHAPTER 13

Assessment of Children with Disabilities 399

Introduction 399
Summary of Major Legislation and
Litigation 401
Influential Legislation 401
Influential Litigation 402
Assessment Processes 403
Referral to Placement Sequence 403
Major Domains of Involvement 405
Intelligence and Cognitive Functioning 405
Adaptive Behavior and Self-Help Skills 406
Behavioral and Socioemotional
Functioning 407
Neuropsychological Functioning 408
Traditional Academic Functioning 409
Reading, Math, and Written-Language
Assessment 409
Curriculum-Based Assessment 410
Ecological Assessment 411
Current and Emerging Issues 412
Minimum Competency Testing 412
Outcomes-Based Assessment 414
SUMMARY 414
QUESTIONS AND EXERCISES 415
SUGGESTED READINGS 415

CHAPTER 14

Ethics and Issues in Assessment 416

Introduction 416
Professional Training and Competence 417
Professional Training 417
Professional Competence 419
Validity of Clinical Opinion 420
Professional and Scientific Responsibility 421
Standards for Educational and Psychological
Testing 421
Respect for the Rights and Dignity of
Others 423
Privacy and Confidentiality 423
Autonomy and Self-Determination 425
Beneficence 427
Social Responsibility 427
Distributive Justice 428
Social Benefits of Testing 428
Maximizing the Positive 430
Controversial Issues in Testing 432
Test Bias 432
Truth in Testing 434
High-Stakes Testing 435
Internet-Based Psychological Testing 436
SUMMARY 437
QUESTIONS AND EXERCISES 438
SUGGESTED READINGS 438

CHAPTER 15

Principles of Test Development 439

Introduction 439
Suggestions for Writing Objective Test
Items 440
General Principles for Objective Items 440
Writing True–False Items 443
Writing Multiple-Choice Items 448
Writing Matching Items 459
Preparing the Objective Test for Use 462
Scoring the Objective Test 465
Correction for Guessing 465
Using Item Analysis to Improve Objective
Tests 468
Simplified Procedures for Conducting Item
Analyses 468

More Formal Item Analysis Procedures   471
Writing Essay Test Items   473
  Writing Essay Questions   474
  Preparing the Essay Test   476
  Scoring Essay Items   477
SUMMARY   478
QUESTIONS AND EXERCISES   479
SUGGESTED READINGS   480

Appendix: Percent of Cases Falling Below
Selected Values on the Normal Curve   481

References   483

Author Index   495

Subject Index   499

Part One

Technical Issues

CHAPTER 1

Fundamental Issues in Measurement

Introduction
A Little History
 The Early Period
 The Boom Period
 The First Period of Criticism
 The Battery Period
 The Second Period of Criticism
 The Age of Accountability
Types of Decisions
Measurement and Decisions
 The Role of Values in Decision Making
Steps in the Measurement Process
 Identifying and Defining the Attribute

Determining Operations to Isolate and Display
 the Attribute
 Quantifying the Attribute
 Problems Relating to the Measurement Process
Some Current Issues in Measurement
 Testing Minority Individuals
 Invasion of Privacy
 The Use of Normative Comparisons
 Other Factors That Influence Scores
 Rights and Responsibilities of Test Takers
Summary
Questions and Exercises
Suggested Readings

INTRODUCTION

Societies and individuals have always had to make decisions. Making decisions is a requirement of daily life for everyone. We all decide when to get up in the morning, what to have for breakfast, and what to wear; we make some kinds of decisions with such regularity that we hardly think about the process. Other decisions that we make less frequently require careful thought and analysis: Which college should I attend? What should I major in? Should I accept a job with XYZ Enterprises? Decisions of this kind are best made based on information about the alternative choices and their consequences: Am I interested in a particular college? What job prospects will it open for me? What are the chances that I will succeed? What are the benefits and working conditions at XYZ Enterprises?

Other decisions are made by individuals acting for the larger society. Daily, teachers must make decisions about the best educational experiences to provide for students, based on an assessment of their students' current knowledge and abilities. A school psychologist may have to decide whether to recommend a special educational experience for a child who is having difficulty in reading or mathematics. School, district, and state educational administrators must make decisions about educational policy and often have to produce evidence for state and local school boards and state legislatures on the achievement of students. Employers must decide which job applicants to hire and which positions they should fill. A college counselor must decide what action to take with a student who is having difficulty adjusting to the personal freedom that a college environment provides. The list of decisions that people must make is as long as the list of human interactions.

We generally assume that the more people know about the factors involved in their decisions, the better their decisions are likely to be. That is, more and better information is likely to lead to better decisions. Of course, merely having information is no guarantee that it will be used to the best advantage. The information must be appropriate for the decision to be made, and the decision maker must also know how best to use the information and what inferences it does and does not support. Our purpose in this book is to present some of the basic concepts, practices, and methods that have been developed in education and psychology to aid in the decision-making process. With these methods, potential decision makers will be better prepared to obtain and use the information needed to make sound decisions.

A LITTLE HISTORY

Although educational measurement has gained considerable prominence in recent decades, the formal evaluation of educational achievement and the use of this information to make decisions has been going on for centuries. As far back as the dawn of the common era, the Chinese used competitive examinations to select individuals for civil service positions (DuBois, 1970; R. M. Thorndike, 1990a). Over the centuries, they developed a system of checks and controls to eliminate possible bias in their testing—procedures that in many ways resembled the best of modern practice. For example, examinees were isolated to prevent possible cheating, compositions were copied by trained scribes to eliminate the chance that differences in penmanship might affect scores, and each examination was evaluated by a pair of graders, with differences being resolved by a third judge. Testing sessions were extremely rigorous, lasting up to 3 days. Rates of passing were low, usually less than 10%. In a number of ways, Chinese practice served as a model for developing civil service examinations in western Europe and America during the 1800s.

Formal measurement procedures began to appear in Western educational practice during the 19th century. For several centuries, secondary schools and universities had been using essay and oral examinations to evaluate student achievement, but in 1897, Joseph M. Rice used some of the first uniform written examinations to test spelling achievement of students in the public schools of Boston. Rice wanted the schools to make room in the curriculum for teaching science and argued that some of the time spent on spelling drills could be used for that purpose. He demonstrated that the amount of time devoted to spelling drills was not related to achievement in spelling and concluded that this time could be reduced, thus making time to teach science. His study represents one of the first times tests were used to help make a curricular decision.

Throughout the latter half of the 19th century, pioneering work in the infant science of psychology involved developing new ways to measure human behavior and experience. Many measurement advances came from laboratory studies such as those of Hermann Ebbinghaus, who in 1896 introduced the completion test (fill in the blanks) as a way to measure mental fatigue in students. The work of Ernst Weber and Gustav Fechner on the measurement of sensory processes laid the logical foundation for psychological and educational measurement. Other important advances, such as the development of the correlation coefficient by Sir Francis Galton and Karl Pearson, were made in the service of research on the distribution and causes of human differences. The late 1800s have been characterized by DuBois (1970) as the *laboratory period* in the history of psychological measurement. This period has also been called the *era of brass instrument psychology* because mechanical devices were often used to collect measurements of physical or sensory characteristics.

Increasing interest in measuring human characteristics in the second half of the 19th century can be traced to the need to make decisions in three contexts. First, enactment of mandatory school attendance laws resulted in a growing demand for objectivity and accountability in assessing student performance in the public schools. These laws brought into the schools for the first time a large number of students who were of middle or lower socioeconomic background and were unfamiliar with formal education. Many of these children performed poorly and were considered by some educators of the time to be "feebleminded" and unable to learn. The development of accurate measurement methods and instruments was seen as a way to differentiate children with true mental handicaps from those who suffered from disadvantaged backgrounds. Second, the medical community was in the process of refining its ideas about abnormal behavior. Behavioral measurements were seen as a way to classify and diagnose patients. Third, government agencies began to replace patronage systems for filling government jobs with competitive examinations to assess prospective employees' abilities. Tests began to be used as the basis of employee selection.

Not until the first years of the 20th century did well-developed prototypes of modern educational and psychological measurements begin to appear. Although it is difficult to identify a single critical event, the 1905 publication of the Binet-Simon scales of mental ability is often considered to be the beginning of the modern era in behavioral measurement. The Binet-Simon scales, originally published in French but soon translated into English and other languages, have been hailed as the first successful attempt to measure complex mental processes with a standard set of tasks of graded complexity. These scales were designed to help educators identify students whose mental ability was insufficient for them to benefit from standard public education. On the basis of the mental measurement, a decision was then made whether to place these students in special classes. Subsequent editions of the scales, published in 1908 and 1911, contained tasks that spanned the full range of abilities for school-age children and could be used to identify students at either extreme of the ability continuum. (See R. M. Thorndike, 1990a, for a more complete description of these scales.)

At the same time that Binet and Simon were developing the first measures of intelligence, E. L. Thorndike and his students at Teachers College of Columbia University were tackling problems related to measuring school abilities. Their work ranged from theoretical developments on the nature of the measurement process to the creation of scales to assess classroom learning in reading and arithmetic and also level of skill development in tasks such as handwriting. The era of mental testing had begun.

It is convenient to divide the history of mental testing in the 20th century into six periods: an early period, a boom period, a first period of criticism, a battery period, a second period of criticism, and a period of accountability.

The Early Period

The *early period,* which comprises the years before American entry into World War I, was a period of tentative exploration and theory development. The Binet-Simon scales, revised twice by Binet, were brought to the United States by several pioneers in measurement. The most influential of these was Lewis Terman of Stanford University. In 1916, Terman published the first version of a test that is still one of the standards by which measures of intelligence are judged: the Stanford-Binet Intelligence Scale. (As a new century dawns, a fifth edition of the Stanford-Binet has just been released.) Working with Terman, Arthur Otis began to explore the possibility of testing the mental ability of children and adults in groups. In Australia, S. D. Porteus prepared a maze test of intelligence for use with people with hearing or language handicaps.

In 1904 Charles Spearman published two important theories relating to the measurement of human abilities. The first was a statistical theory that proposed to describe and account for the inconsistency in measurements of human behavior. The second theory claimed to account for the fact that different measures of cognitive ability showed substantial consistency in the ways in which they ranked people. The statistical theory to describe inconsistency has developed into the concept of reliability that we will discuss in Chapter 4. Spearman's second theory, that there is a single dimension of ability underlying most human performance, played a major role in determining the direction that measures of ability took for many years and is still influential in theories of human cognitive abilities. Spearman proposed that the consistency of people's performance on different ability measures was the result of the level of general intelligence that they possessed. We will discuss modern descendants of this theory and the tests that have been developed to measure intelligence in Chapter 8.

The Boom Period

American involvement in World War I created a need to expand the army very quickly. For the first time, the new science of psychology was called on to play a part in a military situation. This event started a 15-year *boom period* during which many advances and innovations were made in the field of testing and measurement. As part of the war effort, a group of psychologists led by Robert Yerkes expanded Otis's work to develop and implement the first large-scale group testing of ability with the Army Alpha (a verbal test) and the Army Beta (a test using mazes and puzzles similar to Porteus's that required no spoken or written language). The Army Alpha was the first widely distributed test to use the multiple-choice item form. The first objective measure of personality, the Woodworth Personal Data Sheet, was also developed for the army to help identify those emotionally unfit for military service. The Alpha and Beta tests were used to select officer trainees and to remove those with intellectual handicaps from military service.

In the 12 years following the war, the variety of behaviors that were subjected to measurement continued to expand rapidly. E. K. Strong and his students began to measure vocational interests to help college students choose majors and careers consistent with their interests. Measurements of personality and ability were developed and refined, and the use of standardized tests for educational decisions became more widespread. In 1929, L. L. Thurstone proposed ways to scale and measure attitudes and values. Many people considered it only a matter of a few years before accurate measurement and prediction of all types of human behavior would be achieved.

The period immediately following World War I was also a low point for the mental testing movement. High expectations about what test scores could tell us about people's abilities and character led test developers and users to place far too much reliance on the correctness of test scores. The results of the U.S. Army testing program revealed large score differences between White American examinees and those having different ethnic backgrounds. Low test scores for African Americans and immigrants from southern and eastern Europe were interpreted as revealing an intellectual hierarchy, with people of northern European ancestry ("Nordics") at the top.

Members of the lowest scoring ethnic groups, particularly those of African ancestry, were labeled "feebleminded." A number of critics, most notably Walter Lippmann, questioned both the tests themselves and the conclusions drawn from the test scores.

The First Period of Criticism

The 1930s saw a crash not only in the stock market but also in the expectations for mental measurement. This time covered a *period of criticism* and *consolidation*. To be sure, new tests were published, most notably the original Kuder scales of vocational interests, the Minnesota Multiphasic Personality Inventory, and the first serious competitor for the Stanford-Binet, the Wechsler-Bellevue Intelligence Scale. Major advances were also made in the mathematical theory underlying tests, particularly L. L. Thurstone's refinements of a statistical procedure known as factor analysis. However, it was becoming clear that the problems of measuring human behavior had not all been solved and were much more difficult than they had appeared to be in the heady years of the 1920s.

The rapid expansion in the variety of tests being produced, the increasing use of test scores for decision making, and the criticisms of testing in the press led a young psychologist named Oscar Buros to call on the professional psychological and educational testing community to police itself. Buros observed that many tests had little or no objective evidence to support the uses to which they were being put. In 1935 he initiated the *Mental Measurements Yearbook (MMY)* as a place where critical reviews of tests and testing practices could be published. His objective was to obtain reviews of tests from the leading experts in testing that would cause test producers to provide better tests and more evidence supporting specific uses of tests. As we shall see in Chapter 6, the *MMY* publications remain one of the best sources of information about tests.

The Battery Period

In the 1940s, psychological measurement was once again called on for use in the military service. As part of the war effort, batteries of tests were developed that measured several different abilities. Based on the theory developed by Thurstone and others that there were several distinct types or dimensions of abilities, these test batteries were used to place military recruits in the positions for which they were best suited. The success of this approach in reducing failure rates in various military training programs led the measurement field into a period of emphasis on test batteries and factor analysis. For 25 years, until about 1965, efforts were directed toward analyzing the dimensions of human behavior by developing an increasing variety of tests of ability and personality. Taxonomies of ability, such as those of Bloom (1956) and Guilford (1985), were offered to describe the range of mental functioning.

During the 1950s, educational and psychological testing grew into a big business. The use of nationally normed, commercially prepared tests to assess student progress became a common feature of school life. The Scholastic Aptitude Tests (SAT, now called the Scholastic Assessment Tests) or the American College Testing Program (ACT Assessment) became almost universally required as part of a college admissions portfolio. Business, industry, and the civil service system made increasing use of measurements of attitudes and personality, as well as ability, in hiring and promotion decisions. The General Aptitude Test Battery (GATB) was developed by the U.S. Employment Service, and other test batteries were developed by private testing companies to assist individuals and organizations in making career and hiring decisions. Patients in mental institutions were routinely assessed through a variety of measures of personality and adjustment.

In 1954, led by the American Psychological Association, the professional testing community published a set of guidelines for educational and psychological tests to provide public standards for good testing practice. Testing became part of the American way of life. The widespread use—and misuse—of tests brought about a new wave of protests.

The Second Period of Criticism

The beginning of a *second period of criticism* was signaled in 1965 by a series of congressional hearings on testing as an invasion of privacy. The 1960s was also a time when the civil rights movement was in full swing and women were reacting against what they perceived to be a male-dominated society. Because the ability test scores of Blacks were generally lower than those of Whites, and the scores of women were lower than those of men in some areas, tests were excoriated as biased tools of White male oppression. Since that time, debate has continued over the use of ability and personality testing in public education and employment. A major concern has been the possible use of tests to discriminate, intentionally or otherwise, against women or members of minority groups in education and employment. As a result of this concern, the tests themselves have been very carefully scrutinized for biased content, certain types of testing practices have been eliminated or changed, and much more attention has been given to the rights of individuals. The testing industry responded vigorously to the desire to make tests fair to all who take them, but this has not been sufficient to forestall both legislation and administrative and court decisions restricting the use of tests. A recent example is the proposal to eliminate performance on the SAT as a tool in making admissions decisions at institutions in the University of California system.

This situation is unfortunate because it deprives decision makers of some of the best information on which to base their actions. In effect, we may have thrown out the baby with the bath water in our efforts to eliminate bias from the practice of testing. In Chapters 13 and 14 we will take a closer look at the controversies surrounding educational and psychological uses of tests.

The Age of Accountability

At the same time that public criticism of testing was on the rise, governments were putting greater faith in testing as a way to determine whether government programs were achieving their objectives. With passage of the 1965 Elementary and Secondary Education Act, federally funded education initiatives began to include a requirement that programs report some form of assessment, often in the form of standardized test results. In recent years most states have enacted laws requiring students to pass standardized tests in order to earn a high school diploma. The Washington Assessment of Student Learning, for example, is used to test students at selected points in their school career. State standards of minimum performance have been developed, and the performance of public schools is compared on the basis of test scores. Some funding decisions are based on schools' or districts' average test scores. The legislation calls for all students to achieve at least a minimum level of performance on these tests to qualify for high school graduation by 2008. Other states, including Texas and Florida, have similar laws for student testing, and a few states also require teachers to pass standardized tests to earn certification. Thus, at the same time that widespread criticism of tests, particularly standardized tests used to make educational decisions, has arisen, there has been a move to increase the role of such tests in the name of ensuring that schools are accountable for the learning of their students.

TYPES OF DECISIONS

Educational and psychological evaluation and measurement have evolved to help people make decisions related to people, individually or in groups. Teachers, counselors, school administrators, and psychologists in business and industry, for example, are continuously involved in making decisions about people or in helping people make decisions for and about themselves. The role of measurement procedures is to provide information that will permit these decisions to be as informed and appropriate as possible.

Some decisions are *instructional;* many decisions made by teachers and school psychologists are of this sort. An instructional decision may relate to a class as a whole: For example, should class time be spent reviewing "carrying" in addition? Or does most of the class have adequate competency in this skill? Other decisions relate to specific students: For example, what reading materials are likely to be suitable for Mary, in view of her interests and level of reading skill? If such decisions are to be made wisely, it is important to know, in the first case, the overall level of skill of the class in "carrying" and, in the second, how competent a reader Mary is.

Some decisions are *curricular*. A school may be considering a curricular change such as introducing computer-assisted instruction (CAI) to teach the principles of multiplying fractions or a web-based module on African geography. Should the change be made? A wise decision hinges on finding out how well students progress in learning to multiply fractions using CAI or African geography from web materials rather than the conventional approaches. The evidence of progress can only be as good as the measures of mathematics competence or geography knowledge we use to assess the outcomes of the alternative instructional programs.

Some decisions are *selection* ones made by an employer or a decision maker in an educational institution. A popular college must decide which applicants to admit to its freshman class. Criteria for admission are likely to be complex, but one criterion will usually be that the admitted student is judged likely to be able to complete successfully the academic work that the college requires. When combined with other sources such as high school grades, standardized tests of academic ability such as the SAT can add useful information about who is most likely to succeed at the college. Selection decisions also arise in employment. The employer, seeking to identify the potentially more effective employees from an applicant pool, may find that performance in a controlled testing situation provides information that can improve the accuracy and objectivity of hiring decisions, resulting in improved productivity and greater employee satisfaction.

Sometimes decisions are *placement,* or *classification,* decisions. A high school may have to decide whether a freshman should be put in the advanced placement section in mathematics or in the regular section. An army personnel technician may have to decide whether a recruit should be assigned to the school for electronic technicians or the school for cooks and bakers. A family doctor makes a classification decision when he or she diagnoses a backache to be the result of muscle strain or a pinched nerve. For placement decisions, the decision maker needs information to help predict how much the individual will learn from or how successful the candidate will be in each of the alternative programs. Information helps the person making a classification decision to identify the group to which the individual most likely or properly belongs.

Finally, many decisions can best be called *personal* decisions. They are choices that each individual makes at the many crossroads of life. Should I plan to go on for a master's degree or to some other type of postcollege training? Or should I seek a job at the end of college? If a job, what kind of job? In light of this decision, what sort of program should I take in college? Guidance counselors frequently use standardized tests to help young adults make decisions like these. The more information people have about their own interests and abilities, the more informed personal decisions they can make.

MEASUREMENT AND DECISIONS

Educational and psychological measurement techniques can help people make better decisions by providing more and better information. Throughout this book, we will identify and describe properties that measurement devices must have if they are to help people make sound decisions. We will show the form in which test results should be presented if they are to be most helpful to the decision maker. As we look at each type of assessment technique, we will ask "For what types of decisions can the particular technique contribute valuable information?" We must be concerned with a variety of factors, including poor motivation, emotional upset, inadequate schooling, or atypical linguistic or cultural background, all of which can distort the information provided by a test, questionnaire, or other assessment procedure. We will also consider precautions that need to be observed in using the information for decision making.

The Role of Values in Decision Making

Measurement procedures do not make decisions; *people* make decisions. At most, measurement procedures can provide information on some of the factors that are relevant to the decision. The SAT can provide an indication of how well Grace is likely to do in college-level work. Combined with information about how academically demanding the engineering program is at Siwash University, the test score can be used to make a specific estimate of how well Grace is likely to do in that program. However, only Grace can decide whether she should go to Siwash and whether she should study engineering. Is she interested in engineering? Does she have a personal reason for wanting to go to Siwash rather than to some other university? Are economic factors of concern? What role does Grace aspire to play in society? Maybe she has no interest in further education and would rather be a beachcomber.

This example should make it clear that decisions about courses of action to take involve *values* as well as facts. The SAT produces a score that is a *fact,* and that fact may lead to a prediction that Grace has five chances in six of being admitted to Siwash and only one chance in six of being admitted to Stanford. But, if she considers Stanford to be 10 times more desirable than Siwash, it still might be a sensible decision for her to apply to Stanford despite her radically lower chance of being admitted. The test score provides no information about the domain of values. This information must be supplied from other sources before Grace can make a sensible decision.

The issue of values affects institutional decision makers as well as individuals. An aptitude test may permit an estimate of the probability of success for a Black or a Hispanic student, in comparison with the probability of success for a White or Asian student, in some types of academic or professional training. However, an admission decision would have to include, explicitly or implicitly, some judgment about the relative value to society of adding more White or Asian individuals to a profession in comparison with the value of having increased Black or Hispanic representation.

Issues of value are always complex and often controversial, but they are frequently deeply involved in decision making. Very few decisions are value neutral. It is important that this fact be recognized, and it is also important that assessment procedures that can supply better information not be blamed for the ambiguities or conflicts that may be found in our value system. We should not kill the messenger who brings us news we do not want to hear. Rather, we should consider policies and procedures that might change the unwelcome facts.

As we suggested at the beginning of this chapter, all aspects of human behavior involve making decisions. We *must* make decisions. Even taking no action in a situation is a decision. In most cases, people weigh the evidence on the likelihood of various outcomes and the positive and negative consequences of each possible outcome. The role of educational and psychological assessment procedures can be no more than to provide some of the information on which certain kinds of decisions may be based. The evidence suggests that, when properly used, these procedures can provide useful information that is more accurate than that provided by alternate approaches. The study of educational and psychological assessment should yield an understanding of the tools and techniques available for obtaining the kinds of information about people that these measures can yield. Beyond that, such study should provide criteria for evaluating the information that these tools offer, for judging the degree of confidence that can be placed in the information, and for sensing the limitations inherent in that information.

After voters in the state of California voted to end the use of ethnic identity as a factor in university admissions, state education officials proposed to eliminate the use of SAT scores in admissions decisions. The apparent reason for the decision not to use the test scores is that White and Asian Americans typically earn higher scores on these tests than do Black and Hispanic Americans, thereby giving them a better chance of admission to the state's universities. If proportional representation by all ethnic groups is a valued objective for system administrators, then using test scores has negative value because it would tend to produce unequal admissions rates. On the other hand, legislators in Washington State wished to be able to reward schools and districts whose students showed higher than average achievement of the state's educational objectives, as measured by the state's assessment tests. Like the SAT, the Washington State tests also show different levels of achievement for different ethnic groups, but the high value placed on rewarding achievement outweighed the negative outcome of revealing ethnic differences. The two state education establishments reached contradictory conclusions about the use of standardized tests due to the different values each was trying to satisfy.

So far, we have considered practical decisions leading to action. Measurement is also important in providing information to guide theoretical decisions. In these cases, the desired result is not action but, instead, understanding. Do girls read better than boys do? A reading test is needed to obtain the information on which to base a decision. Do students who are anxious about tests perform less well on them than students who are not anxious? A questionnaire on "test anxiety" and a test of academic achievement could be used to obtain information helpful in reaching a decision on this issue. Even a question as basic as whether the size of reward a rat receives for running through a maze affects the rat's running speed requires that the investigator make measurements. Measurement is fundamental to answering nearly all the questions that science asks, not only in the physical sciences but also in the behavioral and biological sciences. The questions we choose to ask, however, are guided and limited by our values.

STEPS IN THE MEASUREMENT PROCESS

In this book, we discuss the measurement of human abilities, interests, and personality traits. We need to pause for a moment to look at what is implied by measurement and what requirements must be met if we are legitimately to claim that a measurement has been made. We also need to ask how well the available techniques for measuring the human characteristics of interest do in fact meet these requirements.

Measurement in any field involves three common steps: (1) identifying and defining the quality or the attribute that is to be measured, (2) determining the set of operations by which the attribute may be isolated and displayed for observation, and (3) establishing a set of procedures or definitions for translating our observations into quantitative statements of degree or amount. An understanding of these steps and of the difficulties that each presents provides a sound foundation for understanding the procedures and problems of measurement in psychology and education.

Identifying and Defining the Attribute

We never measure a thing or a person. We always measure a **quality** or an **attribute** of the thing or person. We measure, for example, the *length* of a table, the *temperature* of a blast furnace, the *durability* of an automobile tire, the *flavor* of a soft drink, the *intelligence* of a schoolchild, or the *emotional maturity* of an adolescent. Psychologists and educators frequently use the term **construct** to refer to the more abstract and difficult-to-observe properties of people, such as their intelligence or personality.

When we deal with simple physical attributes, such as length, it rarely occurs to us to wonder about the meaning or definition of the attribute. A clear meaning for length was established long ago in the history of both the species and the individual. The units for expressing length and the operations for making the property manifest have changed over the years (we no longer speak of palms or cubits); however, the underlying concepts have not. Although mastery of the concepts of *long* and *short* may represent significant accomplishments in the life of a preschool child, they are automatic in adult society. We all know what we mean by *length*.

The construct of length is one about which there is little disagreement, and the operations by which length can be determined are well known. However, this level of construct agreement and clarity of definition do not exist for all physical attributes. What do we mean by durability in an automobile tire? Do we mean resistance to wear and abrasion from contact with the road? Do we mean resistance to puncture by pointed objects? Do we mean resistance to deterioration or decay with the passage of time or exposure to sunlight? Or do we mean some combination of these three and possibly other factors? Until we can reach some agreement on what we mean by durability, we can make no progress toward measuring it. To the extent that we disagree on what durability means (i.e., on a definition of the construct), we will disagree on what procedures are appropriate for measuring it. If we use different procedures, we are likely to get different results from our measurements, and we will disagree on the value that we obtain to represent the durability of a particular brand of tire.

The problem of agreeing on what a given construct means is even more acute when we start to consider those attributes of concern to the psychologist or educator. What do we mean by *intelligence?* What kinds of behavior shall we characterize as intelligent? Shall we define the construct primarily in terms of dealing with ideas and abstract concepts? Or will it include dealing with things—with concrete objects? Will it refer primarily to behavior in novel situations? Or will it include responses in familiar and habitual settings? Will it refer to speed and fluency of response or to level of complexity of the response without regard to time? Will it include skill in social interactions? What kinds of products result from the exercise of intelligence: a theory about atomic structures, a ballet, or a snowman? We all have a general idea of what we mean when we characterize behavior as intelligent, but there are many specific points on which we may disagree as we try to make our definition sufficiently precise to allow measurement. This problem of precisely defining the attribute is present for all psychological constructs—more for some than for others. The first problem that psychologists or educators face as they try to measure attributes is arriving at clear, precise, and generally accepted definitions of those attributes.

Of course, we must answer another question before we face the problem of defining the attribute. We must decide which attributes are relevant and important to measure if our description is to be useful. A description may fail to be useful for the need at hand because the chosen features are irrelevant. For example, in describing a painting, we might report its height, breadth, and weight with great precision and reach high agreement about the amount of each property the painting possesses. If our concern were to crate the picture for shipment, these might be just the items of information that we would need. However, if our purpose were to characterize the painting as a work of art, our description would be useless; the attributes of the painting we just described would be irrelevant to its quality as a work of art.

Similarly, a description of a person may be of little value for our purpose if we choose the wrong attributes to describe. A company selecting employees to become truck drivers might test their verbal comprehension and ability to solve quantitative problems, getting very accurate measures of these functions. Information on these factors, however, is likely to be of little help in identifying people who have low accident records and would be steady and dependable on the job. Other factors, such as eye–hand coordination, depth perception, and freedom from uncontrolled aggressive impulses, might prove much more relevant to the tasks and pressures that a truck driver faces.

Consider a high school music teacher who thoroughly tested the pupils' knowledge of such facts as who wrote the "Emperor Concerto" and whether andante is faster than allegro. The teacher would obtain a dependable appraisal of the students' knowledge about music and musicians without presenting them with a single note of actual music, a single theme or melody, a single interpretation or appraisal of living music. As an appraisal of musical appreciation, such a test seems almost worthless because it uses bits of factual knowledge *about* music and composers in place of information that would indicate progress in appreciation of the music itself. One of the pitfalls to which psychologists and educators occasionally are prone is to elect to measure some attribute because it is easy to measure rather than because it provides the most relevant information for making the decision at hand. It is important to measure traits that are relevant to the decisions to be made rather than merely to measure traits that are easy to assess. We will discuss the issue of relevance again when we cover validity in Chapter 5.

Determining Operations to Isolate and Display the Attribute

The second step in developing a measurement procedure is finding or inventing a set of operations that will isolate the attribute of interest and display it. The operations for measuring the length of an object such as a table have been essentially unchanged for many centuries. We convey them to the child early in elementary school. The ruler, the meter stick, and the tape measure are uniformly accepted as appropriate instruments, and laying one of them along an object is an appropriate procedure for displaying to the eye the length of the table, desk, or other object. But the operations for measuring length, or distance, are not always that simple. By what operations do we measure the distance from New York to Chicago? From the earth to the sun? From our solar system to the giant spiral galaxy in Andromeda? How shall we measure the length of a tuberculosis bacillus or the diameter of a neutron? Physical science has progressed by developing both instruments that extend the capabilities of our senses and indirect procedures that make accessible to us amounts too great or too small for the simple, direct approach of laying a measuring stick along the object. Some operations for measuring length, or distance, have become indirect, elaborate, and increasingly precise. These less intuitive methods (such as the shift of certain wavelengths of light toward the red end of the spectrum) are accepted because they give results that are consistent, verifiable, and useful.

Returning to the example of the durability of the automobile tire, we can see that the operations for eliciting or displaying that attribute will depend on and interact with the definition that we have accepted for the construct. If our definition is in terms of resistance to abrasion, we need to develop some standard and uniform procedure for applying an abrasive force to a specimen and gauging the rate at which the rubber wears away, that is, a standardized simulated road test. If we have indicated puncture resistance as the central concept, we need a way of applying graduated puncturing forces. If our definition is in terms of resistance to deterioration from sun, oil, and other destructive agents, our procedure must expose the samples to these agents and provide some index of the resulting loss of strength or resilience. A definition that incorporates more than one aspect will require an assessment of each, with appropriate weight, and combine the aspects in an appropriate way; that is, if our definition of durability, for example, includes resistance to abrasion, punctures, and deterioration, then a measure of durability must assess all of these properties and combine them in some way to give a single index of durability. Many of the constructs we wish to measure in education and psychology are similar to our construct of durability in that the global construct includes a combination of more or less independent simpler constructs. How to combine a person's ability to answer questions that require reasoning with unfamiliar material, their short-term memory, their knowledge of culturally salient facts, and many other relatively narrowly defined constructs into a global construct of intelligence, or whether to combine them at all, is a hotly debated topic in both psychology and education.

The definition of an attribute and the operations for eliciting it interact. On the one hand, the definition we have set up determines what we will accept as relevant and reasonable operations. Conversely, the operations that we can devise to elicit or display the attribute constitute in a very practical sense the definition of that attribute. An attribute defined by how it is measured is said to have an **operational definition.** The set of procedures we are willing (or forced by our lack of ingenuity) to accept as showing the durability of an automobile tire become the operational definition of durability for us and may limit what we can say about it.

The history of psychological and educational measurement during the 20th century has largely been the history of the invention of instruments and procedures for eliciting, in a standard way and under uniform conditions, the behaviors that serve as indicators of the relevant attributes of people. The series of tasks devised by Binet and his successors constitute operations for eliciting behavior that is indicative of intelligence, and the Stanford-Binet and other tests have come to provide operational definitions of intelligence. The fact that there is no single, universally accepted test and that different tests vary somewhat in the tasks they include and the order in which they rank people on the trait are evidence that we do not have complete consensus on what intelligence is or on what the appropriate procedures are for eliciting it. This lack of consensus is generally characteristic of the state of the art in psychological and educational measurement. There is enough ambiguity in our definitions and enough variety in the instruments we have devised to elicit the relevant behaviors that different measures of what is alleged to be the same trait may rank people quite differently. This fact requires that we be very careful not to overgeneralize or overinterpret the results of our measurements.

The problem of developing an operational definition for the characteristic of interest is also present in the classroom. Teachers regularly face the problem of assessing student performance, but what we will call *performance* is closely linked with the way we assess it. Only to the extent that teachers agree on their operational definitions of student achievement will their assessments have comparable meaning. If one teacher emphasizes quick recall of facts in his assessments and another looks for application of principles in hers, they are, to some undetermined extent, evaluating different traits, and the grades they give their students will mean different things. Here, we do not suggest that this difference in emphasis is inappropriate, only that it is a fact of which educators should be aware. This variability in definitions also provides a major impetus for standardized achievement tests, because such tests are seen as providing a common definition of the attribute to be measured and the method of measurement. The definition provided by the test may not exactly represent what either teacher means by achievement in Subject X, but such definitions usually are developed to provide an adequate fit to the definitions most teachers espouse.

Quantifying the Attribute

The third step in the measurement process, once we have accepted a set of operations for eliciting an attribute, is to express the result of those operations in quantitative terms. Measurement has sometimes been defined as *assigning numbers to objects or people according to a set of rules*. The numbers represent how much of the attribute is present in the person or thing.

Using numbers has several advantages, two of which concern us. First, quantification makes communication more efficient and precise. We know much more from the statement that Ralph is 6 feet tall and weighs 175 pounds than we could learn from an attempt to describe Ralph's size in nonquantitative terms. We will see in Chapter 3 that much of the meaning that numbers have comes from the context in which the measurements are made (that is, the rules used to guide the assignment), but, given that context, information in quantitative form is more compact, more easily understood, and generally more accurate than is the same information in other forms, such as verbal descriptions or photographs. In fact, we are so accustomed to communicating some types of information, such as temperature or age, in quantitative terms that we would have difficulty using another framework.

A second major advantage of quantification is that we can apply the power of mathematics to our observations to reveal broader levels of meaning. Consider, for example, trying to describe the performance of a class on a reading test or the accomplishments of a batter in baseball. In either case, we are accustomed to using the average as a summary of several individual performances. For many purposes, it is useful to be able to add, subtract, multiply, or divide to bring out the full meaning that a set of information may have. Some of the mathematical operations that are useful to educators and psychologists in summarizing their quantitative information are described in Chapter 2.

The critical initial step in quantification is to use a set of rules for assigning numbers that allows us answer the question "How many?" or "How much?" The set of rules is called a **scale.** In the case of the length of a table the question becomes "How many inches?" The inch, or the meter, represents the basic unit, and the set of rules includes the measuring instrument itself and the act of laying the instrument along the object to be measured.

We can demonstrate that any inch equals any other inch by laying two inch-long objects side by side and seeing their equality. Such a demonstration is direct and straightforward proof of equality that is sufficient for some of the simplest physical measures. For measuring devices such as the thermometer, units are equal by *definition*. Thus, we define equal increases in temperature to correspond to equal amounts of expansion of a volume of mercury. One degree centigrade is *defined as* 1/100 of the difference between the freezing and boiling points of water. Long experience with this definition has shown it to be useful because it gives results that relate in an orderly and meaningful way to many other physical measures. (Beyond a certain point—the boiling point of mercury— this particular definition breaks down. However, other procedures that can be used outside this range can be shown to yield results equal to those of the mercury thermometer. The same principle allows educators to use a graded series of tests to assess student progress over several years.)

None of our psychological attributes have units whose equality can be demonstrated by direct comparison in the way that the equality of inches or pounds can. How will we demonstrate that arithmetic Problem X is equal, in amount of arithmetic ability that it represents, to arithmetic Problem Y? How can we show that one symptom of anxiety is equal to another anxiety indicator? For the qualities of concern to the psychologist or educator, we always have to fall back on a somewhat arbitrary definition to provide units and quantification. Most frequently, we consider one task successfully completed—a word defined, an arithmetic problem solved, an analogy completed, or an attitude statement endorsed—equal to any other task in the series and then use the total number of successes or endorsements for an individual as the value representing the person on the particular attribute. This count of tasks successfully completed, or of choices of a certain type, provides a plausible and manageable definition of amount, but we have no adequate evidence of the equivalence of different test tasks or different questionnaire responses. By what right or evidence do we treat a number series item such as "1, 3, 6, 10, 15, ___?___, ___?___" as showing the same amount of intellectual ability as, for example, a verbal analogies item such as "Hot is to cold as wet is to ___?___?"

The definition of equivalent tasks and, consequently, of units for psychological tests is shaky at best. When we have to deal with a teacher's rating of a student's cooperativeness or a supervisor's evaluation of an employee's initiative, for example, where a set of categories such as "superior," "very good," "good," "satisfactory," and "unsatisfactory" is used, the meaningfulness of the units in which these ratings are expressed is even more suspect. We discuss ways to report the results of measurements that yield approximately equal units in Chapter 3.

Problems Relating to the Measurement Process

In psychological and educational measurement, we encounter problems in relation to each of the three steps just described.

First, we have problems in selecting the attributes of concern and in defining them clearly, unequivocally, and in mutually agreeable terms. Even for something as straightforward as reading ability, we can get a range of interpretations. To what extent should a definition include each of the following abilities?

1. Reads quickly
2. Converts visual symbols to sounds
3. Obtains direct literal meanings from the text
4. Draws inferences that go beyond what is directly stated
5. Is aware of the author's bias or point of view.

As we deal with more complex and intangible concepts such as cooperativeness, anxiety, adjustment, or rigidity, we may expect even more diversity in definition.

Second, we encounter problems in devising procedures to elicit the relevant attributes. For some attributes, we have been fairly successful in setting up operations that call on the individual to display the attribute and permit us to observe it under uniform and standardized conditions. We have had this success primarily in the domain of abilities, where standardized tests have been assembled in which the examinee is called on, for instance, to read with understanding, to perceive quantitative relationships, or to identify correct forms of expression. However, with many attributes we clearly have been less successful. By what standard operations can we elicit, in a form in which we can assess it, a potential employee's initiative, a client's anxiety, or a soldier's suitability for combat duty? With continued research and with more ingenuity, we may hope to devise improved operations for making certain of these attributes or qualities manifest, but identifying suitable measurement operations for many psychological attributes will remain a problem.

Finally, even our best psychological units of measure leave much to be desired. Units are set equal by definition; the definition may have a certain plausibility, but the equality of units cannot be established in any fundamental sense. For this reason, the addition, subtraction, and comparison of scores will always be somewhat suspect. Furthermore, the precision with which the attribute is assessed—the consistency from one occasion to another or from one appraiser to another—is often discouragingly low.

In spite of the problems involved in developing educational and psychological measuring devices, the task has proved to be worthwhile. The procedures now available have developed a record of usefulness in helping individuals make decisions in a wide variety of human contexts. Efficiency of education and equality of opportunity are enhanced by the proper use and interpretation of tests. Use of interest and personality inventories has led to people having greater self-understanding and reduced psychological discomfort. Measures of human abilities have been used to provide access to educational and occupational positions without regard to ethnic or racial background.

Critics of testing are quick to point out that inequalities in test performance still exist, but, in the last 25 years, the users of tests have become much more cautious in their interpretations and much more sensitive to the rights of the test taker. Generally, the information provided by tests is more accurate than that available from other sources. When we acknowledge that decisions *must* be made and that accurate information coupled with a clear understanding of our values generally leads to the best decisions, we will find continuing growth in the importance of measurement and assessment processes in psychology and education.

SOME CURRENT ISSUES IN MEASUREMENT

Educational and psychological assessments are far from perfect. Since the earliest attempts to develop measurement techniques in a systematic way, the procedures have been a target for a wide spectrum of critics. Much of this criticism has been a justified response to the naive enthusiasm of measurement proponents and some of their ill-conceived applications and interpretations of measurement results. In subsequent chapters in our discussion of test interpretation and use, we will try to be sensitive to earlier criticisms and to the more technical questions that arise concerning the reliability and validity of test results. At this point, however, we will identify and comment briefly on some of the issues that have been of special concern.

Testing Minority Individuals

For many years, the use and interpretation of tests within minority and other groups whose experiences and cultures differ from that typical of the general population for which a test was designed have received a great deal of attention. There are, of course, all sorts of subgroups in American society, differing from one another in a variety of ways. Ethnic and linguistic minorities are probably the most clear-cut of these; they are the ones for whom the appropriateness of tests and questionnaires designed to reflect the values and experiences of the typical middle-class, White Americans are most open to question. In recent years the number of Americans for whom English is not the preferred language has increased to the point where many ability and achievement tests are available in a Spanish translation. Additionally, feminist groups complain that test material is often male oriented. Major test publishers now go to considerable lengths to ensure that their test items do not present an unfair challenge to women or to members of ethnic or linguistic minority groups.

Some questions arise concerning achievement tests that attempt to assess what a student has *learned* to do. In part, these questions center on the degree to which the same educational objectives hold for groups from minority cultures. Is the ability to read standard English with understanding an important goal for African American, Hispanic, or Native American children? Is knowledge about the U.S. Constitution as relevant for these groups as for the middle-class, White eighth grader? One senses that as far as the basic skills of dealing with language and numbers are concerned, many of the same objectives would apply but that as one moves into the content areas of history and literature more divergence might be seen.

In part, the questions focus on the specific materials through which basic skills are exhibited. Is the same reading passage about the life of the Zulu appropriate in a reading test for a Hispanic or a Native American youngster as it would be for a child of White middle-class background? Or should test materials, and perhaps instructional materials as well, be specifically tailored to the life and experiences of each ethnic group? We know too little about the importance of factors of specific content on performance in areas such as reading comprehension and need to do further research to make informed decisions.

The motivation of minority groups to do well on tests in school is also an issue. Some minority groups, such as recent immigrants from Southeast Asia, place great emphasis on individual academic achievement. Others, such as some Native American groups, place much more value on communal accomplishments and group identity. In many cases of academic difficulty, we must ask whether unfortunate experiences with testing in school have soured students on the whole enterprise, so that they withdraw from the task and do not try. It is perhaps a challenge to the whole pattern of education, not just to the choice of testing instruments, to provide a reasonable mixture of satisfying and success-enhancing experiences in school with all types of school tasks. As far as possible, tasks and tests should be adapted to the present capabilities and concerns of the individual student.

Many more questions—perhaps more serious ones—are raised when tests are used as a basis for deciding what an individual *can learn to do,* that is, as aptitude measures. An inference from a test score obtained at Time 1 concerning what a person can learn to do by Time 2 is clearly a more questionable inference than one that merely states what that person can do at Time 1. There are many intervening events that can throw the prediction off—and there are correspondingly more possibilities of biasing factors coming in to distort systematically the prediction for minority group members. Present facts that imply one prediction for the majority group may imply a different prediction for a minority group member whose experiences before testing were far from typical. Remembering that decisions must be made, the problem is to learn what types of inferences *can* appropriately be made for individuals with differing backgrounds and what types of adjustments or modifications need to be built into the system to permit the most accurate and equitable inferences and decisions for all people.

Invasion of Privacy

A second concern often expressed involves invasion of privacy. What kind of information is it reasonable to require individuals to give about themselves and under what circumstances? This issue arises not only in relation to testing, but also in relation to all types of information from and about a person. What types of records should appropriately be kept? And to whom should they be made available? At one end of the spectrum are tests of job knowledge or skill, such as clerical tests, to which few would object when the skill is clearly and directly relevant to the position for which the person is applying and access is limited to potential employers. It is hard to argue that a test of the ability to use a word processor should not be used to select the best candidate for a job where the chief duties will involve word processing. At the other end of the spectrum are self-descriptive instruments that lead to inferences about emotional stability or a scattering of tests that try to assess honesty under temptation to lie or steal; in these latter tests, individuals are led to give information about themselves without being aware of what information they are giving or how it will be interpreted. The use of these instruments seems most open to question. In between are instruments that involve varying degrees of self-revelation and that appear to have varying degrees of immediate relevance to a decision.

The issue is not only what information is being obtained, but also the purpose for which it is being obtained. Is the information being obtained at the individual's request to provide help with personal or vocational problems or for use in a counseling relationship? The fact that the person has come for help implies a willingness on his or her part to provide the information needed for help to be given; here, invasion of privacy becomes a matter of relatively minor concern. However, when the information is obtained to further institutional objectives—that is, those of an employer, of an educational institution, or of "science"—then concern for the individual's right to privacy mounts, and some equitable balance must be struck between individual values and rights and social ones. For example, more students were willing to allow the use of a questionnaire to verify the emotional stability of an airline pilot, who is responsible for many lives, than to verify that of a bank clerk (75% vs. 34%). The rights of the individual are not absolute, but the feeling is often expressed that these rights have received too little consideration in the past.

To an increasing extent, the courts are taking a role in deciding what information is allowable. Several court cases have required a demonstration of the validity or relevance of test scores or personality profiles to job performance before such instruments can be used for employee selection. These court decisions have affected the type of information that may be collected and who may have access to that information.

The Use of Normative Comparisons

A somewhat different type of issue has been raised concerning the emphasis, in test interpretation, on comparing the performance of one person with norms representing the typical performance of a national, or sometimes a local, sample of people. The point being made with increasing fervor is that many of the decisions for which tests are used, especially instructional ones, do not call for—and are only confused by—comparisons with other people. The essential information is whether the person can perform a specified task; this information should guide decisions on what should be taught or what tasks should be undertaken next. Of course, there are settings in which comparison with others is essential to sound judgment and decision: Is the latest applicant at the personnel office a good keyboard operator? How do we define "good keyboard operator" except in terms of the performance of other job applicants? A rate of 60 words per minute with two errors per minute is meaningless unless we know that the average graduate from a commercial school can enter about 70 words per minute with perhaps one error per minute. The employer wants an employee who comes up to a standard of typical performance, and that standard is set by the performance of others. In the same way, a school system trying to evaluate the reading achievement of its sixth graders as "good," "satisfactory," or "needing improvement" needs some benchmark against which to compare its own performance. No absolute standard of reading performance exists. Whether it is reasonable to expect the sixth graders in Centerville to read and understand a particular article in *Reader's Digest* can only be judged by knowing whether representative groups of sixth graders nationwide are able to read and understand the same or similar articles.

In the past, normative comparisons with an outside reference group have often been used to guide decisions for which they had little or no relevance. Greater emphasis is now being given to criterion-referenced and mastery tests and to performance assessments. These procedures have an important place in making some sorts of decisions, but not all. We need to know which type of comparison is useful for which situation. When should we ask if a student can satisfactorily perform a specific task? And when should we ask how that student compares in relation to other students? This issue is discussed in more detail in Chapter 3.

Other Factors That Influence Scores

An issue that has concerned measurement professionals and consumers for many years is the effect of extraneous factors on performance. One such factor that has received considerable study is the effect of anxiety. Does anxiety raise or lower performance on achievement tests? Are some groups more prone to this effect than others? If test anxiety does have a systematic effect, what can or should the teacher or examiner do to minimize the effect?

Other factors, such as the nutritional status of students or their ability to concentrate on the tasks at hand, may also affect scores. Two particular factors that have received considerable theoretical attention are (1) the racial, ethnic, or gender relationship between examiner and examinee and (2) the effect of coaching on test performance. Although the effects of these extraneous factors are not clear, public concern over their possible effects has prompted educators and measurement professionals to give them increasing attention.

Rights and Responsibilities of Test Takers

Researchers in all areas of science where living organisms are used in research, including psychologists and educational researchers, have grown increasingly sensitive to the rights of their research participants. Psychologists and counselors in professional practice have also developed a greater awareness of their responsibilities toward their clients. On the research side, this trend has led to the development of institutional research boards at universities and funding agencies that review planned research on humans and animals to make sure that the rights of the study participants are respected.

In the area of educational and psychological measurement, the awareness of the rights of examinees has found voice in several publications by the professional organizations most concerned with tests and testing practice. The most influential publication has been a series of sets of guidelines for educational and psychological tests that was first developed by the American Psychological Association in 1954. Since then, the guidelines have been revised four times. The most recent edition, published in 1999 as a joint project of the American Educational Research Association (AERA), the American Psychological Association (APA), and the National Council on Measurement in Education (NCME), and titled *Standards for Educational and Psychological Testing (Standards)*, explains the current standards for the practice of test construction, administration, and interpretation to protect the rights of test takers.

The APA maintains a web page devoted to issues in the fair use and interpretation of tests at http://www.apa.org/science/testing.html. Here one can read the APA statement on "Rights and Responsibilities of Test Takers," a statement that points out that both the person giving the test and the test taker have obligations in a testing situation. For example, the test taker has the right to an explanation of the procedures he or she will encounter and how they will be used, but test takers also have a responsibility to ask questions about aspects of the testing session they do not understand and to participate responsibly in the testing enterprise. This site has links to a wide array of resources about testing and provides an order form to obtain a copy of the current version of the *Standards*.

The AERA has published a statement on high-stakes testing (testing in which the outcome will have important life consequences for the examinees) in pre-K–12 public education that may be accessed at the AERA web site (http://www.aera.net/about/policy/stakes.html). Other organizations, such as the American Counseling Association, the National Association of School Psychologists, the NCME, and the Society for Industrial and Organizational Psychology also maintain web sites that may from time to time contain information about tests and testing. Links to all of these web sites from the APA web site mentioned in the preceding paragraph can be found under the heading "links to other testing-related sites." A particularly useful site that we will visit in more detail in Chapter 6 is maintained by the Buros Institute of Mental Measurements.

SUMMARY

The objective of this book is to improve the knowledge and understanding of decision makers by giving them a better basis for evaluating different measurement procedures and for knowing what each signifies and how much confidence can be placed in each. To this end, we will describe the process of preparing test exercises, develop the general criteria of validity and reliability by which all types of measures are evaluated, provide a familiarity with the different ways of reporting test scores, and describe and evaluate a number of the techniques and instruments commonly used for appraising human characteristics. Our success will be measured by the extent to which our readers use measurement results with wisdom and restraint in their decision making.

QUESTIONS AND EXERCISES

1. List some instances, preferably recent, of decisions you made about yourself or others made about you in which results from some kind of educational or psychological measurement played a part. Classify each decision as (1) instructional, (2) selection, (3) placement or classification, or (4) personal.

2. From your personal experience of a decision made, describe one or more instances for which an educational or psychological measurement could have been helpful but was unavailable. On what basis was the decision actually made?

3. What are some alternatives to educational or psychological measurements as guides for each of the following decisions?
   a. How much time should be spent on phonics in the first-grade reading program?
   b. Which 5 of 15 applicants should be hired as computer programmers?
   c. Should Charles Turner be encouraged to realize his desire to go to college and law school and to become a lawyer?

4. What are the advantages of the alternatives you proposed in Question 3, in comparison with some type of test or questionnaire? What are the disadvantages?

5. To what extent and in what way might *values* be involved in each of the decisions stated in Question 3?

6. Give an example of each of the following types of tests:
   a. A criterion-referenced achievement test
   b. A norm-referenced achievement test
   c. An aptitude test
   d. A measure of likes and preferences
   e. A measure of personality or adjustment
   f. A measure of a trait or construct

7. For one of the attributes listed here, describe how you might (1) define the attribute, (2) set up procedures to make that attribute observable, and (3) quantify the attribute.

a. Critical thinking
b. Friendliness
c. "Good citizenship" in an elementary school pupil
d. Competence as an automobile driver

8. The usefulness of tests for making decisions involving minority group members depends on the type of decision involved. For what sorts of decisions would a standardized test be most defensible? For what sorts would one be most questionable?

9. Which of the following practices would you consider acceptable? Which would you consider to be an invasion of privacy? What factors influence your opinion?
   a. Requiring medical school applicants (1) to take an achievement test in chemistry, (2) to fill out a questionnaire designed to assess emotional stability, or (3) to take a scale of attitudes toward socialized medicine
   b. Requiring applicants for a secretarial job (1) to take a test of general intelligence, (2) to take a test of keyboarding speed and accuracy, or (3) to fill out a questionnaire designed to appraise dependability
   c. Giving a 10-year-old boy whose reading achievement is at the 8-year-old level (1) a nonverbal test of intellectual ability, (2) an interview focused on the conditions in his home, or (3) a series of diagnostic tests of specific reading skills

10. Why is it important for test users to know and adhere to professional recommendations for appropriate test use?

11. Write down some rights or responsibilities that you believe test users and test takers have. Go to the American Psychological Association web site (http://www.apa.org/science/testing.html) and read the rights and responsibilities statement mentioned earlier in this chapter. Are factors listed that were not on your list? Did you include any factors that the statement did not mention?

SUGGESTED READINGS

Alexander, L., & James, H. T. (1987). *The nation's report card: Improving the assessment of student achievement.* Washington, DC: National Academy of Education.

American Educational Research Association, American Psychological Association, & National Council on Measurement in Education. (1999). *Standards for educational and psychological testing.* Washington, DC: American Psychological Association.

Anastasi, A., & Urbina, S. (1997). *Psychological testing* (7th ed.). Upper Saddle River, NJ: Prentice Hall.

Cohen, R. J., & Swerdlik, M. E. (1999). *Psychological testing and assessment: An introduction to tests and measurements* (4th ed.). Mountain View, CA: Mayfield.

Cronbach, L. J. (1975). Five decades of public controversy over mental testing. *American Psychologist, 30,* 1–14.

DuBois, P. H. (1970). *A history of psychological testing.* Boston: Allyn and Bacon.

Gottfredson, L. S., & Sharf, J. C. (1988). *Fairness in employment testing: A special issue of the Journal of Vocational Behavior, 33*(3). Duluth, MN: Academic Press.

Gregory, R. J. (1996). *Psychological testing: History, principles, and applications.* (2nd ed.) Boston: Allyn & Bacon.

Haney, W. (1981). Validity, vaudeville, and values: A short history of social concerns over standardized testing. *American Psychologist, 36,* 1021–1034.

Hartigan, J. A., & Wigdor, A. K. (Eds.). (1989). *Fairness in employment testing: Validity generalization, minority issues, and the General Aptitude Test Battery.* Washington, DC: National Academy Press.

Howard, G. S. (1985). The role of values in the science of psychology. *American Psychologist, 40,* 255–265.

Jones, L. V. (1971). The nature of measurement. In R. L. Thorndike (Ed.), *Educational measurement* (2nd ed., pp. 335–355). Washington, DC: American Council on Education.

Linn, R. L. (1989). Current perspectives and future directions. In R. L. Linn (Ed.), *Educational measurement* (3rd ed., pp. 1–12). New York: Macmillan.

Murphy, K. R., & Davidshofer, C. O. (2001). *Psychological testing: Principles and applications* (5th ed.). Upper Saddle River, NJ: Prentice Hall.

Rogers, T. B. (1995). *The psychological testing enterprise.* Pacific Grove, CA: Brooks/Cole.

Thorndike, R. M. (1990). *A century of ability testing.* Chicago: Riverside.

Vold, D. J. (1985). The roots of teacher testing in America. *Educational Measurement: Issues and Practice, 4*(3), 5–8.

Wigdor, A. K., & Garner, W. R. (Eds.). (1982). *Ability testing: Uses, consequences, and controversies: Pt. 1. Report of the committee.* Washington, DC: National Academy Press.

CHAPTER 2

Measurement and Numbers

Questions to Ask About Test Scores
Scales of Measurement
Preparation of a Frequency Distribution
    Grouped Frequency Distributions
    Cumulative Frequency Distributions
Graphic Representation
Measures of Central Tendency
    The Mode
    The Median
    Percentiles
    The Arithmetic Mean

Central Tendency and the Shape of the Distribution
Measures of Variability
    The Range
    The Semi-Interquartile Range
    The Standard Deviation
Interpreting the Standard Deviation
Interpreting the Score of an Individual
Measures of Relationship
Summary
Questions and Exercises
Suggested Readings

QUESTIONS TO ASK ABOUT TEST SCORES

Catherine Johnson and Peter Cordero wanted to gather information about achievement levels in their two sixth-grade classes. They gave their students a 45-item reading test provided in their current reading series, a 65-item review test from the mathematics book, and a dictation spelling test of 80 items based on the words their classes had been studying during the past 6 weeks. They marked the papers, counted the number of correct answers on each, and recorded the scores. Then they made up a joint class list that showed the three scores for each student. In addition, they recorded which class each student was in (1 for Ms. Johnson's class, 2 for Mr. Cordero's) and each student's gender (1 for boys, 2 for girls). With five pieces of information for each of 52 students, they wondered what they should do with all those numbers.

Tests *do* produce scores, and scores *are* numbers. So, if we are to think about and use test scores, we must be prepared to think about and work with numbers. The numbers that represent test scores can be organized to provide the answers to a range of questions, but first we must know what kinds of questions to ask. Once we have the questions in mind, we can begin to ask how the numbers can be arranged to provide the answers.

Look at the numbers (scores) shown in Table 2–1 for the sixth graders in the two classes. What kinds of questions might the two teachers ask about this set of numbers? What questions can *you*

Table 2–1
Scores for 52 Sixth-Grade Students on Tests of Reading, Spelling, and Mathematics

First Name	Last Name	Gender	Class	Reading (45)*	Spelling (80)	Math (65)
Aaron	Andrews	1	1	32	64	43
Byron	Biggs	1	1	40	64	37
Charles	Cowen	1	1	36	60	38
Donna	Davis	2	1	41	74	40
Erin	Edwards	2	1	36	69	28
Fernando	Franco	1	1	41	67	42
Gail	Galaraga	2	1	40	71	37
Harpo	Henry	1	1	30	51	34
Irrida	Ignacio	2	1	37	68	35
Jack	Johanson	1	1	26	56	26
Kleven	Klipsch	1	1	28	51	25
Laverne	Lappenski	2	1	36	57	53
Mary	Madison	2	1	39	68	37
Nathan	Natts	1	1	22	47	22
Oprah	Oates	2	1	36	59	33
Petula	Peters	2	1	32	64	33
Quadra	Quickly	2	1	21	44	19
Rahim	Roberts	1	1	29	64	43
Salim	Salik	1	1	41	76	33
Thomas	Tank	1	1	35	65	38
Usaka	Urban	2	1	41	65	38
Victor	Vasquez	1	1	37	68	40
Wakana	Watanabe	2	1	25	53	21
Xenum	Xerxes	1	1	25	54	31
Yuan	Young	1	1	32	59	24
Zebulon	Zibberits	1	1	42	73	44
Angela	Ash	2	2	43	64	52
Bellinda	Brown	2	2	33	38	41
Charlotta	Cowen	2	2	33	47	50
Dominik	Dubrow	1	2	39	66	34
Erik	Eriksen	1	2	39	55	47
Francis	French	2	2	38	59	49
Guido	Garcia	1	2	31	52	29
Hillary	Huan	2	2	38	61	48

(continued)

Table 2–1   *Continued*

First Name	Last Name	Gender	Class	Reading (45)*	Spelling (80)	Math (65)
Igor	Ivanovich	1	2	33	53	43
Jill	Johanson	2	2	42	61	45
Kaleen	Knowles	2	2	35	55	51
Larry	Lewis	1	2	29	40	34
Moe	Mastrioni	1	2	36	58	39
Nancy	Nowits	2	2	28	44	44
Orden	Orford	1	2	35	53	38
Petre	Popovich	1	2	36	52	53
Quincy	Quirn	1	2	33	48	33
Rhonda	Rostropovich	2	2	31	50	31
Sally	Stebbens	2	2	33	51	32
Thelma	Thwaites	2	2	38	43	45
Uriah	Urdahl	1	2	42	61	60
Velma	Vauter	2	2	29	49	36
William	Westerbeke	1	2	33	54	33
Xena	Xerxes	2	2	30	57	37
Yannita	Younts	2	2	44	63	49
Zephina	Zoro	2	2	30	47	38

*Maximum score in parentheses.

ask? Before reading further, study the sets of scores and jot down the questions that come to your mind in connection with these scores. See how many of the question types you can anticipate.

Each student has five numbers assigned to him or her, but we might want to inquire whether each of these numbers actually conveys quantitative information. Do the numbers that are assigned to represent gender and class have the same kind of meaning as the test scores? This is a question of the *scale* the numbers represent.

A second, rather general type of question that we might ask is, what is the basic pattern of the set of scores? How do they "run"? What do they "look like"? How can we get a picture of the set of math scores, for example, so that we can get an impression of the group as a whole? To answer this type of question, we will need to consider simple ways of tabulating and graphing a set of scores.

A third type of question that will almost certainly arise is, what is this group like, on the average? In general, have they done as well on the test as some other sixth-grade group? What is the typical level of performance in the group? All these questions call for some single number to represent the group as a whole, some measure of where the *middle* of the group lies. To answer this type of question, we will need to become acquainted with statistics developed to represent the average, or typical, score.

Fourth, to describe the group, we might feel a need to describe the extent to which the scores spread out away from the average value. Have all the children in the group made about the same progress, or do they show a wide range of achievement? How does this group compare with other classes, with respect to the *spread* of scores, and do the students show the same spread of achievement on all three tests? This type of question calls for a study of measures of variability.

Fifth, we might ask how a particular individual stands on one of the tests. We might want to know whether Aaron Andrews did well or poorly on the mathematics test. And if we decide that his score is a good one, we might want some way of saying just how good it is. We might ask whether Aaron did better in reading or in mathematics. To answer this question, we will need a *common yardstick* on which to express performance in two quite different areas. One need, then, is for some uniform way of expressing and interpreting the performance of an individual, independent of the particular test. How does this person stand relative to the group?

A sixth query is of the following type: To what extent do those who excel in reading also excel in mathematics? To what extent do these two abilities go together in the same individuals? Is the individual who is superior in one area likely to be superior in the other? To express this *association* between two measurements, we will need to become acquainted with indices of correlation.

Many other questions may arise with respect to a set of scores. The most important ones concern the drawing of general conclusions from data on a limited group. For example, the 26 girls in this group have an average reading score of 35.0, and the 26 boys have an average score of 33.9. These are *descriptive* facts about this testing of these particular girls and boys. But these children might be considered to represent a larger population, such as all students in this school district. From the results in these two classes, we might want to make an estimate or best guess of the average level of reading achievement in the larger group. We also might want to know whether we can safely conclude that the total population of girls from which this sample is drawn would surpass the total population of boys on this same test. These problems are of **inference.** Problems of statistical inference make up the bulk of advanced statistical work. For a detailed description of the principles and applications of statistical inference, see Thorndike and Dinnel (2001) or any other book on statistical methods. They do not enter into the basic interpretation of test scores for an individual or a group and we will not consider them further here.

The routines developed for organizing numbers to answer these and other questions constitute the field called **statistics.** This name and, in fact, the very prospect of working with numbers seem a bit scary to some people. Fortunately, much of the mechanics of working with numbers can now be performed on a pocket calculator or personal computer, so we can concentrate on the questions to ask and on the ways in which the numbers are arranged to answer them, rather than worry about computational details. As we discuss ways to answer each of the six types of questions mentioned above, we will introduce easy-to-use computer programs to perform the necessary computations. Two very widely available programs will be presented, the package of statistical programs known as SPSS and the data analysis routines included in the Microsoft Excel spreadsheet program. Both programs have some shortcomings, but both are relatively easy to use once you get used to them.

SCALES OF MEASUREMENT

One way to define measurement is *the assignment of numbers to objects according to a set of rules.* The set of rules is called a **scale.** Knowing the scale that has been used to make a measurement is critical to proper interpretation of the measurement. For example, Ms. Johnson and Mr. Cordero assigned the number 1 to their male students and the number 2 to their female students, but what information do these numbers contain? Feminist ideology aside, does the number 2 mean that the girls possess more of the trait of gender than the boys do? Obviously not; in this case the numbers do not convey information about *amount* of anything. The number 1 has been substituted for the label "boy" and the number 2 has been substituted for "girl," but we could just as well have used the numbers 163 and 27. Each number takes on the meaning of a verbal label. When numbers are used in this way, the scale is called a **nominal scale.** The numbers take the place of names. Your student number represents a "score" on a nominal scale, as do the numbers on the backs of athletes. When numbers do not contain information about amount of a trait, it is not appropriate to treat them like numbers. In general, you cannot add them or perform any other arithmetic operations and obtain a meaningful result.

Sometimes numbers are assigned to represent the order of individuals on a trait. None of the numbers in Table 2–1 are of this kind, but suppose Mr. Cordero decided to rank order his students on the basis of their spelling test scores with the student who earned the highest score, Dominik Dubrow, getting a rank of 1, second highest, Angela Ash, ranked 2, and so forth. What kind of information would these numbers represent?

A set of ranks conveys information about the order in which the students stand on the trait, but the ranks do not contain information about amount. More importantly, the differences between numbers do not have a constant meaning. The difference between a rank of 1 and a rank of 5 is not necessarily the same as the difference between a rank of 11 and one of 15. Both differ by four units, but four units of rank usually cover a greater portion of the trait at the extremes than in the middle. A scale that tells us the order in which people stand, who has more of the trait, but not how much more, is called an **ordinal scale.** Several common ways of reporting test score information that we will describe in Chapter 3 produce ordinal scales.

Tests that are scored like those in Table 2–1 treat each item as equal to every other item. Getting 10 items correct yields a score of 10, getting 20 items correct yields a score of 20, and getting 30 items correct would give you a score of 30. Because each item is assumed equal in amount of the trait it measures, equal differences in scores are treated as equal differences in the trait. Although this assumption is somewhat tenuous when measuring human abilities, it represents the same basic kind of measurement as the centigrade or Fahrenheit temperature scales. Equal numerical differences in score represent equal differences in the property being measured. When we can make this assumption, the scale is called an **interval scale.** Most of the computations that are done with test scores require that we assume the scale of measurement is an interval scale.

Suppose Zebulon Zibberits tries his hardest, but still cannot spell any of the words in Mr. Cordero's list correctly. Does this mean that Zebulon has zero spelling ability? Probably not. The scale of spelling ability represented by this test starts at a point well above zero, so a score of zero on the test does not mean zero ability. Very few scales used in psychology and education are constructed such that a score of zero means exactly none of the trait or property in question. Exceptions would be scales like those for height, weight, and duration of time. When the scale is constructed so a score of zero means exactly none of the trait, it is called a **ratio scale.** Scales like this allow us to conclude not only that the size of the unit is the same everywhere along the scale, but also that a score that is numerically twice another score means exactly twice as much of the trait. Someone who takes 10 minutes to solve a problem takes twice as long as someone who takes 5 minutes, and the person who takes 20 minutes to solve the problem takes twice as long as the 10-minute person and four times as long as the 5-minute person.

Ratio scales allow us to make proportional statements like these. Very few ratio scales exist in the fields of education and psychology, but fortunately interval scales allow us to perform most of the analyses we need.

PREPARATION OF A FREQUENCY DISTRIBUTION

In Table 2–1, we showed a record sheet on which test scores for 52 sixth graders were recorded. Let us look at the scores in the Math column and consider how they can be rearranged to give a clearer picture of how the pupils have performed on the math test. The simplest rearrangement is merely to list the scores in order from highest to lowest, as follows:

60	49	44	41	38	37	33	31	24
53	49	44	40	38	36	33	31	22
53	48	43	40	38	35	33	29	21
52	47	43	39	37	34	33	28	19
51	45	43	38	37	34	33	26	
50	45	42	38	37	34	32	25	

This arrangement gives a somewhat better picture of the way the scores fall than does Table 2–1. We can see the highest (60) and lowest (19) scores at a glance. It is also easy to see that the middle person in the group falls somewhere in the mid-30s. We can see by inspection that most of the scores fall between 30 and 45. But this simple rearrangement of scores still has too much detail for us to see the general pattern clearly. We need to condense the data into a more compact form.

Often, the first step in organizing scores for presentation is to prepare a display called a **frequency distribution,** a table that shows how often each score has occurred. Each score value is listed, and the number of times it occurs is shown. A portion of the frequency distribution for the math test is shown in Table 2–2. However, Table 2–2 is still not a very good form for reporting the facts. The table is too long and spread out. We have shown only part of it; the whole table would take 42 lines, almost as many as the original listing of scores. It would have a number of zero entries, and there would be marked variations in the Frequency column from one score to the next.

MAKING THE COMPUTER DO IT

Frequency Distributions

Excel is not designed to provide a frequency distribution like the one we have just described. Rather, it will prepare a grouped frequency distribution as described in the next section. SPSS will produce a frequency distribution, but you must be careful when reading it because score values with zero frequency are omitted from the list of scores. To prepare a frequency distribution using SPSS of the data from Table 2–1, start the program, enter the data from Table 2–1, click on the <u>A</u>nalyze button in the menu at the top of the screen, and select De<u>s</u>criptive Statistics. The screen should look like the one shown on page 28:

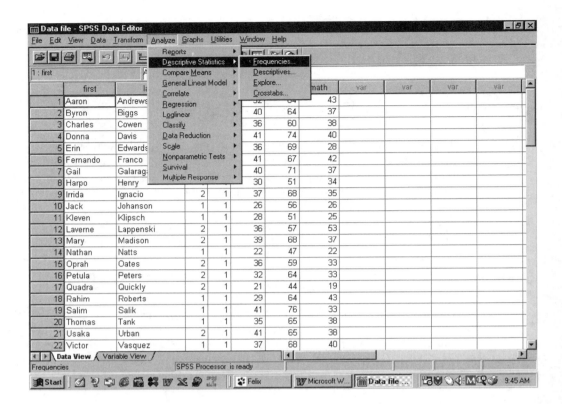

Select Frequencies and you will see a dialogue box in which you can select the variables to be analyzed. Highlight the name of the variable you want by clicking on it, then click on the arrow button to move the variable into the Variables window. If you use the data from Table 2–1 and select the Math variable, you should get the complete frequency distribution, part of which we showed you in Table 2–2. You can get other reports from this program, but we will wait to describe them until we have covered those topics.

Grouped Frequency Distributions

Scores are often *grouped* into broader categories to further improve the clarity of presentation. We discard some detail in the data to make it easier to grasp the picture presented by the entire set of scores. In our example, we will group three adjacent scores, so that each grouping *interval* includes three points of score. The entire range of scores from 19 to 60 is represented by 14 intervals. When this is done, the set of scores is represented as shown in Table 2–3, a fairly compact table illustrating how many people there are in each **score interval.** Thus, for example, we have two people in interval 19–21. We do not know how many of them got 19s, 20s, or 21s; we have lost this information in the grouping. *We assume that they are evenly spread throughout the interval.* In most cases, there is no reason to believe that one score will occur more often than any other, and this assumption is a sound one, so the gains in compactness and convenience of presentation more than make

Table 2–2
Frequency Distribution of Scores on the Mathematics Test for
52 Students

Score (X)	Frequency
60	1
59	0
58	0
57	0
56	0
55	0
54	0
53	1
52	1
.	.
.	.
.	.
40	2
39	1
38	5
37	4
.	.
.	.
.	.
28	1
27	0
26	1
25	1
24	1
23	0
22	1
21	1
20	0
19	1

up for any slight inaccuracy introduced by the groupings. (In some special applications, such as reports of family income, certain values are more likely than others, for example, $10,000, $18,000, $25,000. Special precautions are required when grouping material of this type. An effort should be made to place the most popular values near the middle of an interval to reduce distortion.)

Table 2–3
Grouped Frequency Distribution of Scores from 52 Students on a
Math Test Using an Interval of 3

Interval	Frequency
19–21	2
22–24	2
25–27	2
28–30	2
31–33	8
34–36	5
37–39	10
40–42	4
43–45	7
46–48	2
49–51	4
52–54	3
55–57	0
58–60	1

In practical situations, we always face the problem of deciding how broad the groupings should be, that is, whether to group by 3, 5, 10, or some other number of points of score. The decision is a compromise between (1) losing detail from our data and (2) obtaining a convenient, compact, and smooth representation of the results. The use of broader intervals results in losing more detail, but condenses the data into a more compact picture. A practical rule of thumb is to choose an interval that will divide the total score range into roughly 10 to 20 groups. In our example, the highest score is 60, and the lowest is 19. The range of scores is 60 to 19, giving a range of 41 points. Dividing 41 by 15, we get 2.7. The nearest whole number is 3, so we group the data by 3s. In addition to the "rule of 15," we also find that intervals of 5, 10, and multiples of 10 make convenient groupings. Because the purpose of grouping scores is to arrive at a convenient and clear representation, factors of convenience become a major consideration.

In cases where graphs are going to be prepared using the scores in their grouped form, it is also convenient to use an interval that includes an odd number of score points, for example, 3, 5, or 7, because it is sometimes necessary to use the midpoint of the score interval to represent all scores in the interval. If the interval has an even number of score values, this midpoint will be halfway between two actual scores, but if an odd number is used for the interval width, the midpoint will be a whole score value, making for a more attractive graph.

Note also that sometimes there is no need to group the data into broader categories. If the original scores cover a range of no more than about 20 points, grouping may not be required. Also, with modern computing equipment it is usually easier to compute the statistical indices, described later in the chapter, from the original set of scores unless the data come to you as a grouped frequency distribution. In that case, most programs require special procedures that are beyond our scope.

MAKING THE COMPUTER DO IT

Grouped Frequency Distributions

Excel is designed to produce grouped frequency distributions, but you must follow a particular sequence of steps that can at times be frustrating until you become used to them. After you have opened the file containing the data you wish to analyze, the first step is to decide on the number of intervals. Excel calls these intervals *bins*. Using our set of scores for the math test, the easiest way to determine how many bins to use is to sort the scores to find the range they cover. Click on any score in the Math column, then click on one of the sort icons. The scores will now be in order, so you can determine the highest and lowest. Finding the range to be 41 and applying our "rule of 15," we again decide to use bins of 3.

You must now set up your bins. Bins are specified by giving the highest score that is to fall in each bin. Therefore, if we want to use a bin size of 3, our first bin should have 19, 20, or 21 specified as its value. Excel sorts scores into bins in ascending order. That is, the program looks at all the scores and puts those that are less than or equal to the bin limit in the first bin. If we start with a bin limit that is below the lowest score, it will have a frequency of zero, but if we start with a bin limit that is more than our chosen interval above the lowest score, the lowest interval will be too wide. Any of the three values given here will produce a proper set of bins.

After deciding on the first bin limit, set each additional bin limit one interval above the one below it. If we start with a limit of 21, then the other bin limits would be 24, 27, 30, . . . 54, 57, 60. *The bins must be arranged with the lowest at the top of its column.* In a column to the right of your data (for instance, column I), type the word *bins* in the first row. Then type in the bin limits, starting with the lowest, in the cells under the "bins" heading. If we use 19 for our first bin limit, the remaining limits would be 22, 25, . . . 58, 61.

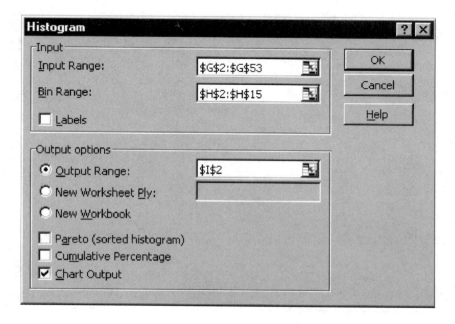

The Excel frequency distribution routine is part of the Histogram program in the Data Analysis group of programs that are included in the Tools menu. (Histograms are discussed in the next section.) Click on Tools, then on Data Analysis. A dialogue box will appear that includes many data analysis options. Click on Histogram and click OK. You should see a screen that looks like the one on the previous page imposed over your data.

Excel works by specifying areas of the data table to be included in the analysis. The scores for the math test are listed in column G with a label in the first row and data in cells G2 to G53. Click on the Input Range window in the Histogram pop-up dialogue box. Then in the main screen highlight the cells containing the math test scores. The cell references G2 and G53 will appear in the pop-up box window. Next, click in the Bin Range window of the pop-up box. Then, again on the main screen, highlight the bin limits you placed in the column under "bins." The cell references for these cells will appear in the window. Finally, click the Output Range button on the pop-up box to activate that window and *click in the window*. Then click in a cell where you would like the grouped frequency distribution to start (usually just to the right of your bins column, in this case I2). If you are using the data from Table 2–1 and have followed the directions as we have outlined them, your screen should look like this:

	A	B	C	D	E	F	G	H	I	J	K
1	First	Last	Gender	Class	Reading	Spelling	Math	bins	Bin	Frequency	
2	Quadra	Quickly	2	1	21	44	19	21	21	2	
3	Nathan	Natts	1	1	22	47	22	24	24	2	
4	Wakana	Watanabe	2	1	25	53	21	27	27	2	
5	Xenum	Xerxes	1	1	25	54	31	30	30	2	
6	Jack	Johanson	1	1	26	56	26	33	33	8	
7	Kleven	Klipsch	1	1	28	51	25	36	36	5	
8	Nancy	Nowits	2	2	28	44	44	39	39	10	
9	Rahim	Roberts	1	1	29	64	43	42	42	4	
10	Larry	Lewis	1	2	29	40	34	45	45	7	
11	Velma	Vauter	2	2	29	49	36	48	48	2	
12	Harpo	Henry	1	1	30	51	34	51	51	4	
13	Xena	Xerxes	2	2	30	57	37	54	54	3	
14	Zephina	Zoro	2	2	30	47	38	57	57	0	
15	Guido	Garcia	1	2	31	52	29	60	60	1	
16	Rhonda	Rostropovich	2	2	31	50	31		More	0	
17	Aaron	Andrews	1	1	32	64	43				
18	Petula	Peters	2	1	32	64	33				
19	Yuan	Young	1	1	32	59	24				
20	Bellinda	Brown	2	2	33	38	41				
21	Charlotta	Cowen	2	2	33	47	50				
22	Igor	Ivanovich	1	2	33	53	43				
23	Quincy	Quirn	1	2	33	48	33				
24	Sally	Stebbens	2	2	33	51	32				

The row labeled "More" is used to take care of any scores that are above the highest bin limit you listed. SPSS does not have a program for producing grouped frequency distributions.

Cumulative Frequency Distributions

We often want to know how many people got scores below some particular value. The most direct way to answer this question is with a **cumulative frequency distribution,** which lists each score or interval and the number of scores falling *in or below* the score or interval. A cumulative frequency distribution is easily prepared from the frequency distribution or grouped frequency distribution, as shown in Table 2–4, which presents the **cumulative frequency,** as well as the frequency in each interval. Each entry in the column labeled "Cumulative Frequency" shows the total number of individuals having a score equal to or less than the highest score in that interval; that is, there are 2 students scoring *at or below* 21, (2 + 2) = 4 students scoring at or below 24, (4 + 2) = 6 scoring at or below 27, (6 + 2) = 8 scoring at or below 30, (8 + 8) = 16 scoring at or below 33, and so forth. The cumulative frequency distribution is especially useful for determining some expressions of relative position, which we will discuss in Chapter 3. Unfortunately, neither SPSS nor Excel has a routine for providing cumulative frequency distributions, but both will give you cumulative percents; that is, each frequency distribution program has the ability to output the values equal to

$$\text{Cumulative percent} = \frac{\text{cumulative frequency}}{\text{total number of cases}}$$

These values are included in Table 2–4. The cumulative percents are given whenever you request a frequency distribution from SPSS. With Excel you must click on the Cumulative Percentages box in the Histogram dialogue box.

Table 2–4
Cumulative Frequency Distribution of Scores from 52 Students on a Math Test Using an Interval of 3

Interval	Frequency	Cumulative Frequency	Cumulative Percent
19–21	2	2	4
22–24	2	4	8
25–27	2	6	12
28–30	2	8	15
31–33	8	16	31
34–36	5	21	40
37–39	10	31	60
40–42	4	35	67
43–45	7	42	81
46–48	2	44	85
49–51	4	48	92
52–54	3	51	98
55–57	0	51	98
58–60	1	52	100

Figure 2–1
Histogram of 52 mathematics scores.

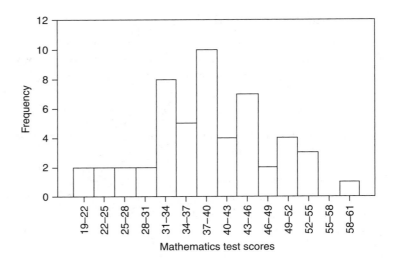

GRAPHIC REPRESENTATION

It is often helpful to translate the facts of a table like Table 2–3 into a pictorial representation. A common type of graphic representation, called a **histogram,** is shown in Figure 2–1. This type of graph can be thought of, somewhat grimly, as "piling up the bodies." The score intervals for the mathematics test scores that we used in Table 2–3 are shown along the baseline (the **abscissa**), and the vertical height of the pile (the **ordinate**) represents the number of people whose scores fall in that interval. The diagram shows that there are two "bodies" piled up in interval 19–21, two in interval 22–24, and so forth. This figure gives a clear picture of how the scores pile up, with most of them in the 30 to 45 range and long, low "tails" running out to the extreme low and high scores.

MAKING THE COMPUTER DO IT

Histograms

Both SPSS and Excel will prepare graphs of grouped frequency distributions, but they do it in very different ways. Excel's procedure is by far the simpler one, but from the technical point of view, the graph it produces is properly called a **bar graph,** not a histogram because the bars are separated from each other. Unfortunately, the way the intervals are labeled can lead to difficulty in reading the graph as well. Note that in the example in Figure 2–2, taken from the frequency distribution in Table 2–3, the labels appear to apply to the wrong categories. A second drawback with Excel is that there is very little you can do to edit the graph other than change the proportions and the axis labels. The lesson in this example is that you have to look at computer output with caution because the choices made by the programmer who wrote the program may not give you the picture you expect or want.

Figure 2–2

Graph of a grouped frequency distribution from Excel.

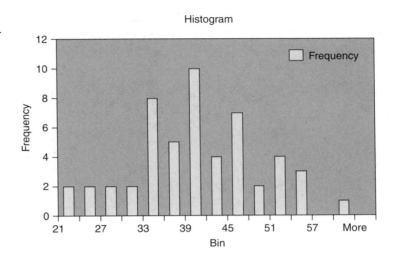

SPSS automatically groups the data to produce a graph with about 10 categories (the default for our example yields 9). The result is a proper histogram (the bars touch each other), but you will probably want to edit the graph to improve its appearance. If you double-click on the output of the graph, you can edit it. The graph in Figure 2–1 is an edited version of the graph from SPSS where we have changed the number of intervals to correspond to Table 2–3 and have modified other aspects of the graph. You may want to experiment with the graph editor to see if you can get your histogram output to look like ours.

We can use a similar procedure to provide a graphic representation of the cumulative frequency distribution. This graph, known as the **cumulative frequency curve** (also sometimes called an **ogive**), is prepared by placing values of the cumulative frequency on the ordinate, and scores or score intervals on the abscissa. A *point* representing the cumulative frequency for each score or interval is then plotted, and the points are connected, forming a graph such as the one shown in Figure 2–3. Note that the cumulative frequency curve never drops back toward the abscissa.

MAKING THE COMPUTER DO IT

Cumulative Frequency Curves

Excel will prepare a graph of the cumulative percentage distribution if you select both Cumulative Percentage and Chart Output. To obtain a graph of cumulative frequency or cumulative percentage from SPSS, click on the Graphs menu and select Line. Click on Define, select the variable you wish to graph, and place it in the Category Axis window. Select "Cum n of cases," then click OK. You can also graph the cumulative percentages

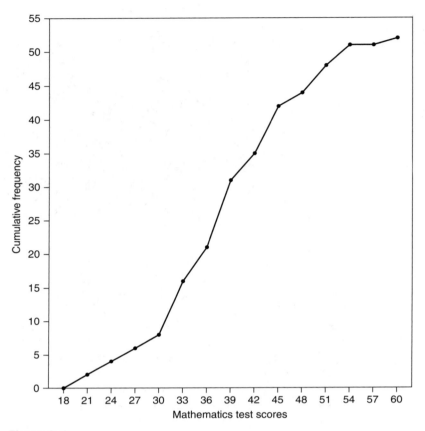

Figure 2–3
Cumulative frequency curve of 52 mathematics scores.

by selecting "Cum % of cases." If there are more than about 20 discrete score values, the program will group the data. With fewer than 20 score values, however, the program will produce a cumulative frequency curve from the program's cumulative frequency distribution. This means that the graph will omit values of the variable that have zero frequency in the same way that the frequency distribution itself does. Again, this requires caution in interpreting the graph because there is no warning that the program has omitted some values.

MEASURES OF CENTRAL TENDENCY

We often need a statistic to represent the typical, or average or middle, score of a group of scores. We present three such statistics, each of which defines the center in a different way and conveys slightly different information.

The Mode

A very simple way of identifying the typical score is to pick the one that occurs most frequently. This score is called the **mode** and corresponds to the highest point in the histogram. If you examine the array of math scores in the tabulation in the Preparation of a Frequency Distribution section, you will find that the scores 33 and 38 each occur five times. A unique value for the mode does not exist with these data. If one of the students who scored 37 had instead scored 38, the mode would be 38. If one of the 34s had been a 33, then 33 would have been the mode. The mode is sensitive to such minor changes in the data and is therefore a crude and often not very useful indicator of the typical score. In Table 2–3, the grouped frequency distribution, the **modal interval** is 37–39. When the scores are grouped in this way, we can call the midpoint of the modal interval, 38, the *mode*.

Our two computer programs approach determination of the mode in the same way. Both look for the score value in the raw data that has the greatest frequency. When, as is often the case, two or more scores occur with the same frequency, the smaller value is reported as the mode. Thus, both programs report the mode for our set of math test scores as 33, even though the score 38 also had a frequency of five. SPSS reports that there are multiple modes, but Excel does not. When we compare this result with the highest point in our grouped frequency distribution, we get quite a discrepancy. In Table 2–3 the mode clearly fell in the interval 37–39, yielding a mode at the midpoint of the interval, or 38.

The Median

A much more useful way of representing the typical, or average, score is to find *the value on the score scale that separates the top half of the group from the bottom half*. This value is called the **median.** In our example, with 52 cases, this means separating the top 26 students from the bottom 26. The required value for our mathematics scores can be found by placing the scores in order of magnitude the way we did earlier or by using the Sort command in Excel. We want to identify the point below which 50% of the cases fall. Because 50% of 52 is 26, we must identify the point below which 26 pupils fall. Starting with the lowest score, we count up until we have the necessary 26 cases.

Counting just the scores in a table such as the one shown earlier, the 26th score is one of the scores of 38. Using Excel, the 25th case is Gail Galaraga, whose score is 37. We need to include 1 more case to obtain the required 26 cases. The next score value (38) is shared by five individuals. *We require only one fifth of these individuals.* Now how shall we think of these cases being spread out over the score value of 38? As noted earlier in this chapter, a reasonable assumption is that they are spread out evenly over the interval. Then to include one fifth of the scores, we would have to go one fifth of the way from the bottom of the interval toward the top.

At this point, we must define what we mean by a score of 38. First, let us note that although test scores go by jumps (or discrete increments) of one unit (37, 38, and 39), we consider the underlying ability that the test measures to have a continuous distribution that takes in all the intermediate values between two scores. We might liken the situation to a digital clock. Although time is continuous, the recording instrument runs by jumps, with one jump every time the basic unit of 1 minute is passed.

Figure 2–4 illustrates this point. The bottom line represents the continuum of ability. We define *38* as the interval on the continuum that is closer to point 38 than to either 37 or 39. Thus, in Figure 2–4, 38 is represented as a slice extending from 37.5 to 38.5. Although somewhat arbitrary, this definition of a score is a reasonable one and is accepted by most authorities. The score interval 37–39 is really to be thought of as extending from 36.5 to 39.5 on the underlying continuum, as is shown in the figure. We do not get scores lying *between* 37 and 38 or between 38

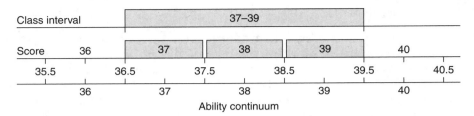

Figure 2–4
Relation between scores and ability continuum.

and 39—not because those levels of the trait do not exist, but because our measuring instrument does not register any values between 37 and 38 or between 38 and 39.

Because we require one fifth of the cases in interval 37.5–38.5, we must go one fifth of the way from 37.5 to 38.5; that is, we have

$$1/5(38.15 - 37.5) = 1/5(1) = .2$$

This is how far we must go through the interval represented by the score 38 to include one of the five people in the interval and find the point below which 26 people fall. We must add .2 to the value 37.5, which is the lower limit of the score interval that contains the median. Therefore, the median for this set of scores is

$$37.5 + .2 = 37.7$$

Note that the median need not be a whole score value.

MAKING THE COMPUTER DO IT

The Median

Most computer programs, including SPSS and Excel, define the median as the score obtained by the middle person, regardless of how many people got the same score. The programs look at the cumulative percent of cases for each score interval and select as the median the score corresponding to the first interval where the cumulative percent exceeds 50%. In our example, the interval for a score of 38 is the first interval with a cumulative percentage above 50 (it is actually 57.7). Both programs report 38 as the median. Because the differences found in computing the median by this approach and the one described above are usually small, they are not likely to be important to test users. However, when working with grouped data, the differences can be substantial. SPSS has a way to handle grouped data and produce results essentially identical to what we found here, but Excel does not. In the special case where the median falls exactly between two individuals who have different scores, the proper course to take is to find the point halfway between the two people's scores. For example, if we have 100 individuals where the 50th person's score is 30 and the 51st person's score is 32, the appropriate value for the median is halfway between the scores or 31. Both Excel and SPSS will produce this result.

Percentiles

The same steps used to compute the median can be used to find the score below which any other percentage of the group falls. These values are called **percentiles.** The median is the 50th percentile, that is, the point on the score scale below which 50% of the individuals fall. If we want to find the 25th percentile, we must find the point on the score scale below which 25% of the cases fall; 25% of 52 is 13. For our set of 52 mathematics scores, 13 cases take us through the score value 32 ($cf = 11$), and include two of the five cases with a score of 33. So, the 25th percentile is located in the interval 32.5–33.5 and is computed to be $32.5 + (2/5) = 32.9$.

As another illustration, consider the 85th percentile. We have $(.85)(52) = 44.2$ people making up the bottom 85% of our group. Because 44 cases carry us to the top of interval 45.5–48.5, and there are 2 cases in the next interval, for the 85th percentile, we need $.2/2 = .1$ of the interval and the 85th percentile is $48.5 + .1 = 48.6$. Other percentiles can be found in the same way. Percentiles have many uses, especially in connection with test norms and the interpretation of scores. We will encounter them again in Chapter 3.

MAKING THE COMPUTER DO IT

Percentiles

Excel computes percentiles using a different program function than we have discussed so far. On the Insert menu (and also as a button on the toolbar next to the sort icons) you can place a *function* (f_X) in a cell of the spreadsheet. First select a cell in which you wish the percentile to appear. Then click on the f_X symbol and a series of function types such as "Math and Trig" and "Statistical" will appear. If you select the Statistical group you will be presented with a wide variety of options, one of which is "Percentile." You can use this approach to compute any percentile you wish and most of the other descriptive statistics we will be discussing. After selecting Statistical, select Percentile and you will see a screen like this:

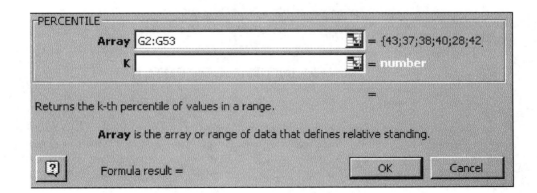

Select the cells containing the data you wish to include in the analysis (here the scores for our 52 students' math scores are in cells G2 to G53). Then click in the **K** cell and enter the percentile you wish (.50 for the median). Click OK and the desired percentile will appear in the selected cell.

Excel uses the same approach to find percentiles that it uses to find the median. That is, the program compares the specified percentile with the array of cumulative percentages and reports as the pth percentile (for example, the 17th) the first score value where the cumulative percentage is greater than p. The result is not as precise as the one described on page 39 (the same score may be reported as corresponding to several different percentiles), but it is usually accurate enough. We describe how to compute percentiles with SPSS in the next section.

The Arithmetic Mean

Another frequently used statistic for representing the middle of a group is the familiar average of everyday experience. Because statisticians speak of many measures of central tendency as averages, they identify this one as the **arithmetic mean (M)**. It is computed as the sum of a set of scores divided by the total number of scores. Thus, the arithmetic mean of the scores 4, 6, and 7 is

$$(4 + 6 + 7)/3 = 17/3 = 5.67$$

In our example of scores on the mathematics test, we can add the scores of all 52 individuals in the group, giving us 1,985. Dividing by 52, we get $M = 38.17$ for the average, or arithmetic mean, for this group.

We can express the process for computing the mean using a simple formula. Statisticians use the capital Greek letter sigma (Σ) to stand for the process of summation. If we use the letter X to stand for a variable, such as math test scores, then the expression ΣX tells us to sum the values of X. Because the mean requires that we divide this sum by the number of scores (N), an expression for the mean is

$$M = \frac{\Sigma X}{N} = \frac{1,985}{52} = 38.17$$

We will have many occasions to use this formula and other similar ones.

MAKING THE COMPUTER DO IT

The Arithmetic Mean

Excel and SPSS both have programs to compute the mean and several other measures that describe distributions of scores. In Excel, there is a program in the Data Analysis package called "Descriptive Statistics." Click on that program, then click OK and you will see a screen like this:

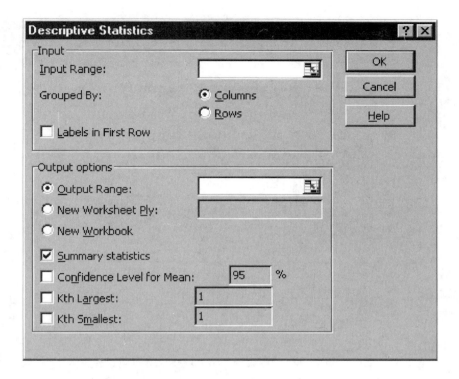

Click in the Input Range window on the pop-up box, then on the main screen highlight the scores to be included in computing the mean. If you are using the data from Table 2–1, the math test scores are in column G, rows 2–53. Next click in the "Output Range" window of a pop-up box. Then click on a cell in the spreadsheet where you would like the output to start, such as column I, row 1. Finally, make sure there is a check in the "Summary statistics" box, then click OK. The program will produce the three measures of central tendency we have described, plus 10 other statistics, some of which we will discuss shortly. Make sure you look at the "count" statistic to be sure you have included the correct number of scores in your computations. You can also use the statistical function (f) method (see the preceding box on percentiles) to obtain just the arithmetic mean. It is listed as the Average function.

If you are using SPSS to compute your descriptive statistics, you can get everything you need at the same time that you are preparing your frequency distribution. After opening the Frequencies program and selecting the variables you wish to analyze, click on the Statistics button to obtain the following screen:

Click in the boxes next to the statistics you wish to compute. Here we have selected the mean, median, mode, and sum; three particular percentiles (10, 27, and 46); and three measures of variability to be described shortly. Placing a check mark in the "Values are group midpoints" box will cause SPSS to compute the median and percentiles as we have described them in this chapter. Failing to check that box will cause the program to take the

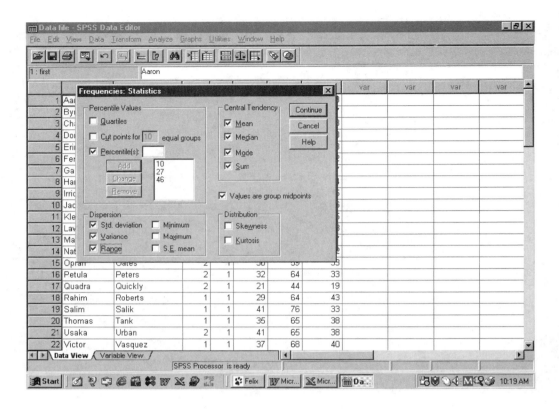

first score value whose cumulative percentage exceeds the specified value. Click 'Continue,' then 'OK' to obtain your summary statistics.

Central Tendency and the Shape of the Distribution

The mode, arithmetic mean, and median seldom have exactly the same value, but usually they do not differ greatly. In our example, the values of the median and mean are 37.7 and 38.17, respectively, and one alternative for the mode is 38. The three statistics will differ substantially only when the set of scores is *skewed* greatly, that is, when there is a piling up of scores at one end and a long, thin tail at the other. Figure 2–5 shows three distributions that differ in the amount and direction of skewness. The top figure is positively skewed; that is, it has a tail running up to the high scores. We might get a distribution like this for income in the United States, because there are many people with small and moderate incomes and only a few with very large incomes. The center figure in Figure 2–5 is negatively skewed. A distribution like this would result if a class were given a very easy test that resulted in a piling up of perfect and near-perfect scores. The bottom figure is symmetrical and is not skewed in either direction. Many psychological and educational variables give such a symmetrical distribution.

Excel and SPSS both provide an index of skewness as part of their descriptive statistics package. The index will yield a positive number if the distribution looks like Figure 2–5a, a negative

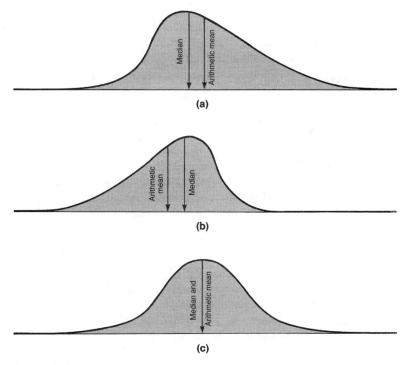

Figure 2–5
Frequency distributions differing in skewness: (a) positively skewed, (b) negatively skewed, and (c) symmetrical.

value if the graph looks like Figure 2–5b, and a value near zero for a distribution that is approximately symmetric.

In the distributions that are approximately symmetrical, either the mean or the median will represent the average of the group equally well, but with skewed distributions, the median generally seems preferable because it is affected less by a few cases out in the long tail. The mean is more often used when the distribution is symmetrical for reasons that will become clear later in this chapter when we discuss the normal distribution. The mode is used less often because, although it is easy to obtain, it is less stable than the mean and median, as we have seen in our example. Also, the mode is not related to other statistics we may wish to obtain.

MEASURES OF VARIABILITY

It is often significant, when describing a set of scores, to report how *variable* the scores are—that is, how much they spread out from high to low. For example, two groups of children, each with a median age of 10 years, would represent quite different educational situations if one group had a spread of ages from 9 to 11 and the other group ranged from 6 to 14. A measure of this spread is an important statistic for describing a group.

The Range

A simple measure of variability is the **range** of scores in the group, which is simply the difference between the highest and the lowest scores. In our math test example, the spread of scores is from 60 to 19, giving a range of 41 points. However, the range depends only on the two extreme cases in the total group. This fact makes the range quite undependable because it can be changed quite a bit by the addition or omission of a single extreme case. If Uriah Urdahl had not taken the math test, the range would have been 19 to 53, or 34 rather than 41.

The Semi-Interquartile Range

A better measure of variability is the range of scores that includes a specified part of the total group—usually the middle 50%. The middle 50% of the cases in the group are the cases lying between the 25th and the 75th percentiles. We can compute these two percentiles, following the procedures outlined earlier. For our example, the 25th percentile was computed to be 32.9. If you calculate the 75th percentile using these procedures, you will find that it is 44.0. The distance between the 25th and 75th percentiles is thus 11.1 points of score and contains the scores of the middle 50% of the distribution or 26 students.

The 25th and 75th percentiles are called the **quartiles,** because they cut off the bottom quarter and the top quarter of the group, respectively. The score distance between them is called the **interquartile range.** A statistic that is often reported as a measure of variability is the **semi-interquartile range** (Q), which is half of the interquartile range. It is the *average* distance from the median to the two quartiles; that is, it tells how far the quartile points lie from the median on the average. In our example, the semi-interquartile range is

$$Q = \frac{44.0 - 32.9}{2} = 5.55$$

If the middle 26 scores spread out twice as far, Q would be twice as large; if they spread out only half as far, Q would be half as large. Two distributions that have the same mean, the same total number of cases, and the same general form and that differ only in that one has a variability twice as large as the other are shown in Figure 2–6.

MAKING THE COMPUTER DO IT

Quartiles

SPSS will compute the quartiles for you in the Frequencies routine. Click on the box labeled "Quartiles" and be sure you tell the program to treat the data values as group midpoints. For our student math achievement data, we get a very small discrepancy from that obtained above in computing the 25th percentile because SPSS uses a formula that is very general, but the answers will be the same within .01. You must compute the interquartile range and Q for yourself. You can use the Percentile function in Excel to get the 25th and 75th percentiles, but they will be whole points of score because of the way Excel determines percentiles. The quartiles are then used to compute Q.

Figure 2–6
Two distributions differing only in
variability: (a) large variability and
(b) small variability.

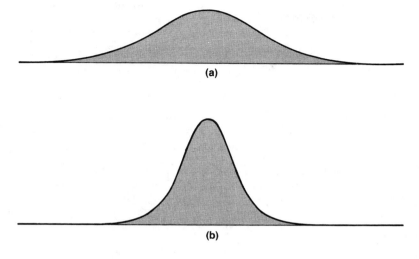

(a)

(b)

The Standard Deviation

The semi-interquartile range belongs to the same family of statistics as the median. Both are special cases of the more general concept of percentiles. There are also measures of variability that belong to the family of the arithmetic mean and are based on score deviations from the mean. The most commonly used is called the **standard deviation.** Let us take a look at it.

Suppose we had four scores: 4, 5, 6, and 7. Adding these scores and dividing by the total number of scores, we find the arithmetic mean to be

$$(4 + 5 + 6 + 7)/4 = 5.5$$

But now we ask how widely these scores spread out around that mean value. Suppose we find the difference between each score and the mean; that is, we subtract 5.5 from each score. We then have -1.5, -0.5, 0.5, and 1.5. These values represent **deviations** of the four scores from the mean. The bigger the deviations, the more widely the set of scores spreads out around the mean. If our scores were 2, 5, 6, and 9, the mean would still be 5.5, but the deviations would be -3.5, -0.5, 0.5, and 3.5. What we require as an index of the variability, or spread, present in the data is some type of average of these deviations.

If we simply add the four deviation values for either case in the preceding paragraph, we find that they add up to zero. The positive deviations exactly balance the negative ones. This outcome will always be true because one of the definitions of the arithmetic mean is that it is the point around which the sum of deviations is zero. We will have to do something else to get an index of the amount of spread. The procedure that statisticians have devised for handling the plus (positive) and the minus (negative) signs is to square all the deviations, thus getting only positive values. (A minus times a minus is a plus.) An average of these squared deviations is obtained by adding them and dividing by the total number of cases. This value is called the **variance.** This statistic is widely used in more advanced statistical procedures. The variance is defined as the *mean* of the *squared* deviations from the mean.

To compensate for having squared the individual deviations, we must then compute the square root of this average value. The resulting statistic is called the **standard deviation (SD).**

It is the square root of the average of the squared deviations from the mean. (With most calculators, you need only press the designated key to get the square root of a number.) For the first set of scores used in the preceding example, calculations are as follows:

$$SD = \sqrt{\frac{(-1.5)^2 + (-.5)^2 + (.5)^2 + (1.5)^2}{4}}$$

$$SD = \sqrt{\frac{2.25 + 0.25 + 0.25 + 2.25}{4}}$$

$$SD = \sqrt{1.25} = 1.12$$

The variance of this set of scores is 1.25; the standard deviation is 1.12. The standard deviation of the second, more variable set of scores is

$$SD = \sqrt{\frac{(-3.5)^2 + (-0.5)^2 + (.5)^2 + (3.5)^2}{4}} = \sqrt{\frac{25}{4}} = 2.5$$

A comparison of the two standard deviations tells us that the second set of scores spreads out more widely around its mean than the first does.

Using the same notation that we encountered with the mean, we can write the following formula for the standard deviation:

$$SD = \sqrt{\frac{\Sigma(X - M)^2}{N}}$$

This formula tells us to do the following:

1. Subtract the mean from each score to obtain deviations (e.g., 2 − 5.5 = −3.5).
2. Square each deviation.
3. Sum the squared deviations.
4. Divide the sum of the squared deviations by the number of cases (N).
5. Take the square root of the result.

There is one factor in computing the standard deviation that may cause your calculator or computer to give results that are different from what you would get using the formula given above or that are obtained by a classmate when you are both working with the same set of data. Earlier in the chapter, we mentioned that **statistical inference** was the term applied when using the data from a sample to estimate a characteristic of a larger group (called a **population**). This distinction does not affect the mean (the same value serves as a description of the sample and as an estimate for the population), but it does affect the standard deviation. In the standard deviation that is used to describe the variability of the sample, the sum of the squared deviations from the mean is divided by the number of members of the sample (N). However, the best estimate (from the sample data) of the standard deviation of the population from which the sample comes is found by dividing the sum of squared deviations from the sample mean by $N - 1$ rather than N. Using $N - 1$ in the denominator has the effect of making the population estimate slightly larger than the sample value. The difference is not of practical importance for most measurement applications, but it can cause some confusion when people compare their answers to a problem. You may want to check the manual for your calculator to see which version it uses (many will give you either one) so that you will not get frustrated if you obtain slightly different answers from the ones we provide. For a discussion of why this difference exists and for computing formulas for hand calculators, see Thorndike and Dinnel (2001) or another introductory statistics book.

MAKING THE COMPUTER DO IT

Standard Deviation

Most calculators and all computer spreadsheet and statistics packages include a program that will calculate the standard deviation for a set of data. Both Excel and SPSS provide the variance and standard deviation as optional output from several programs. With SPSS, all you have to do is click on the Standard Deviation button in the Statistics section of Frequencies. If you select the SPSS Descriptives program, the standard deviation is part of the standard output. Excel produces both the standard deviation and variance as part of the output from its Descriptive Statistics routine.

SPSS does not provide an option for which standard deviation you get, it always uses $N - 1$, but Excel does allow you to get the sample standard deviation if you use the f_X approach. The function list includes both STDEV (which uses $N - 1$) and STDEVP (which uses N). The difference is minimal unless N is quite small, but knowing that it exists can explain some inconsistencies between summaries of the same data.

INTERPRETING THE STANDARD DEVIATION

It is almost impossible to say in simple terms what the standard deviation is or what it corresponds to in pictorial or geometric terms. Primarily, it is a statistic that characterizes the spread of a distribution of scores. It increases in direct proportion to the scores spreading out more widely around the mean. The larger the standard deviation, the greater the variability among the individuals. A student sometimes asks, but what is a small standard deviation? What is a large one? There is really no answer to either question. Suppose that for some group the standard deviation of weights is 10. Is this value large or small? It depends on whether we are talking about ounces, pounds, or kilograms and on whether we are dealing with the weights of mice, men, or mammoths.

The standard deviation gets its most clear-cut meaning for one type of distribution of scores, the **normal distribution,** or **normal curve.** This distribution is defined by a particular mathematical equation, but to the everyday user, it is defined approximately by its pictorial qualities. The normal curve is a symmetrical curve having a bell-like shape. In fact, it is sometimes called the **bell curve.** Most of the cases pile up in the middle score values; going away from the middle in either direction, the pile drops off, first slowly and then more rapidly and then slowly again as the cases trail out into relatively long tails at each end. An illustration of a typical normal curve is shown in Figure 2–7. This curve is the normal curve that best fits the math test data taken from Table 2–1. It has the same mean, standard deviation, and total area (number of cases) as the math test data. The histogram of mathematics test scores (Figure 2–1) appears as well and reveals how the ideal curve fits the actual test scores. Because the normal curve is symmetrical, the mean, median, and mode all have the same value.

Figure 2–7

Normal distribution (bell curve) superimposed on the histogram of 52 mathematics test scores.

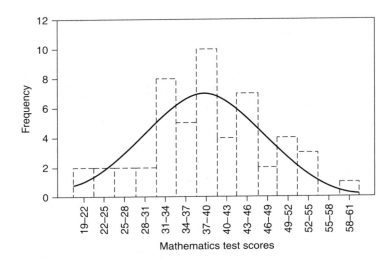

Think back to what the bars of the histogram tell us. Each bar is the same width and its height is equal to the frequency of scores in the interval covered by the bar. Therefore, the area covered by each bar is proportional to the number of cases in its interval. This means that we can think of the area covered by a part of a graph as equal to the proportion of the scores in our group that fall within the interval. There are 5 + 10 = 15 individuals falling in the two score intervals 34–36 and 37–39, so there are 15 individuals in this part of the graph. Because there are 52 students in the total group, we can say that .29 or 29% of them fall in the interval between 34 and 39.

For the normal curve, there is an exact mathematical relationship between the standard deviation and the proportion of cases. The same proportion of cases will always be found within the same standard deviation limits. This relationship is shown in Table 2–5. From this table, we can see that in any normal curve about two thirds (68.2%) of the cases fall in the range between +1.0 and −1.0 SD from the mean. Thus, if the mean is 50 and the standard deviation is 10, about 68% of the cases will fall in the range from a score of 40 to a score of 60 (34% between 40 and 50 and 34% between 50 and 60). Approximately 95% (actually, 95.4%) will fall between +2.0 and −2.0 SD from the mean, and nearly all the cases will fall between +3.0 and −3.0 SD from the mean.

Table 2–5

Proportion of Cases Falling Within Certain Specified Standard Deviation (SD) Limits for a Normal Distribution

Limits Within Which Cases Lie	% of Cases
Between the mean and *either* +1.0 SD or −1.0 SD	34.1
Between the mean and *either* +2.0 SD or −2.0 SD	47.7
Between the mean and *either* +3.0 SD or −3.0 SD	49.9
Between +1.0 SD and −1.0 SD	68.2
Between +2.0 SD and −2.0 SD	95.4
Between +3.0 SD and −3.0 SD	99.8

Because of this constant relationship between the standard deviation and the proportion of cases, we know that in a normal distribution, an individual who gets a score 1 *SD* above the mean will surpass 84% of the group—the 50% who fall below the mean and the 34% who fall between the mean and +1.0 standard deviation.

This unvarying relationship of the standard deviation unit to the arrangement of scores in the normal distribution gives the standard deviation a type of *standard* meaning as a unit of score. It becomes a yardstick in terms of which groups may be compared or the status of a given individual on different traits expressed. For example, if John's score in reading is 1 *SD* above the mean and his score in mathematics is 2 *SD*s above the mean, then his performance in mathematics is better than his performance in reading. (The use of the standard deviation and the normal distribution for expressing relative performance will be discussed in Chapter 3.) Although the relationship of the standard deviation unit to the score distribution does not hold *exactly* in distributions other than the theoretical normal distribution, frequently the distributions of test scores and other measures approach the normal distribution closely enough for the standard deviation to continue to have nearly the same meaning.

In summary, the statistics most used to describe the variability of a set of scores are the semi-interquartile range and the standard deviation. The semi-interquartile range is based on percentiles—specifically, the 25th and 75th percentiles—and is commonly used when the median is being used as a measure of the middle of the group. The standard deviation is a measure of variability that goes with the arithmetic mean. It is useful in the field of testing primarily because it provides a standard unit of measure having comparable meaning from one test to another.

INTERPRETING THE SCORE OF AN INDIVIDUAL

When the scores of individuals in a group are expressed in standard deviation units, they are called **standard scores** or **Z-scores.** A person's Z-score is the distance between his or her raw score and the mean, divided by the standard deviation. Using X_i to represent the raw score of a person on variable X (for example, the mathematics test), the person's Z-score is

$$Z_X = \frac{X_i - M_X}{SD_X}$$

The same person's Z-score on the reading test (which we will call variable Y) would be found by

$$Z_Y = \frac{Y_i - M_Y}{SD_Y}$$

If we know that $M_X = 38.17$, $M_Y = 34.44$, $SD_X = 8.93$, and $SD_Y = 5.55$, then Aaron Andrews' Z-scores on these two variables are

$$Z_X = \frac{43 - 38.17}{8.93} = +0.54$$

$$Z_Y = \frac{32 - 34.44}{5.55} = -0.44$$

(Aaron's raw scores were 43 and 32, respectively.) What these two Z-scores tell us is that Aaron is about one-half standard deviation above the mean in math and about one-half standard deviation below the mean in reading.

The problems of interpreting the score of an individual will be treated more fully in Chapter 3, where we turn to test norms and units of measure. It will suffice now to indicate that the two sorts of measures we have just been considering—percentiles and standard scores—provide a framework with which we can view the performance of a specific person. Both provide a way to view the person's performance relative to a specific *reference group*. Percentile information tells us what point in the score distribution just exceeds a specified fraction of the scores for the group; the standard deviation provides a common unit of distance from the mean of the group. The individual's score can then be expressed as a distance above or below the mean in these common units. In this way it is possible to give a meaningful answer to questions such as "Are you taller than you are heavy?"

MEASURES OF RELATIONSHIP

We look now for a statistic to express the relationship between two sets of scores. For example, in Table 2–1, for each pupil we have scores for reading, mathematics, and spelling. To what extent did those pupils who scored well in mathematics also score well on the reading test? In this case, we have two scores for each individual. We can picture these scores using a graph in two dimensions, one dimension for each test. Such a graph is shown in Figure 2–8 and is called a **scatterplot.** The first person listed in Table 2–1, Aaron Andrews, had a reading test score of 32 and a mathematics test score of 43. His scores are represented by the *X* in Figure 2–8, plotted at 32 on the vertical, or reading, scale and at 43 on the horizontal, or mathematics, scale. The dots in the figure each represent one of the other 51 pupils' paired scores.

The vertical and horizontal lines drawn through the scatterplot are the means of the two variables and divide the plot into four parts or **quadrants.** When a person who does well in reading

Figure 2–8
Scatterplot of reading and mathematics scores.

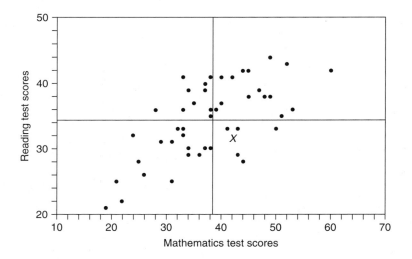

(above the mean) also does well in mathematics, the dot representing that pair of scores falls in the upper right-hand quadrant. The dot for one who does poorly (below the mean) on both tests falls in the lower left quadrant. Where a good score on one test is paired with a poor score on the other, we find the points falling in the other quadrants, that is, the upper left and the lower right. Children who score in the middle on both tests are represented by points in the center of the plot. Inspection of Figure 2–8 reveals some tendency for the scores to scatter in the lower left to the upper right direction, from low reading and low mathematics to high reading and high mathematics, but there are many exceptions. The relationship is far from perfect; it is a matter of degree. We need some type of index to express this degree of relationship.

As an index of degree of relationship, a statistic known as the **correlation coefficient** can be computed. (The symbol r is used to designate this coefficient.) Looking at the formula for r will help us understand why the coefficient has the properties it does. The correlation coefficient is defined as

$$r = \frac{\sum Z_X Z_Y}{N}$$

where Z_X and Z_Y are the pair of standard scores for an individual (such as the $+0.54$ and -0.44 scores for Aaron Andrews). What the formula tells us to do is multiply each person's standard score on one variable by their standard score on the other, sum the products across all cases, and divide the result by the number of people in our sample.

Now think about those pairs of standard scores. If a person's Z-score is above the mean, it will have a positive sign; if it is below the mean, the sign will be negative. When both Z-scores are above the mean, the product will be positive. Likewise, when both scores are below the mean, the product will also be positive. However, if one score is above the mean and the other is below the mean, the product will be negative. When we add these products across all the people in our sample, the result will be positive if people tend, on average, to have scores on the same side of the mean on both variables. Conversely, the sum will be negative if people who score above the mean on one variable tend to score below the mean on the other, and vice versa. Dividing by N simply adjusts the resulting sum for the number of people in the group.

The correlation coefficient can take values ranging from $+1.0$ through zero to -1.0. A correlation of $+1.0$ signifies a perfect positive relationship between the two variables. It means that the person with the highest Z-score on one test also had the highest Z-score on the other, the next highest on one was the second highest on the other, and so forth, exactly parallel through the whole group. A scatterplot of data like this would form a straight line of dots running from the lower left quadrant to the upper right quadrant. A correlation of -1.0 means that the scores on one test go in exactly the reverse direction from the scores on the other. The person highest on one test is the lowest on the other, the second highest on one is the second lowest on the other, and so forth. The scatterplot in this case would be a line of dots running from the upper left to the lower right. A zero correlation represents a complete lack of relationship; that is, there is no tendency for people who score high on one test to be either above or below average on the other (the positive products balance out the negative ones). The pattern is essentially random and the scatterplot will look like a circle. In-between values of the correlation coefficient represent tendencies for a relationship to exist, but with discrepancies, as in the case shown in Figure 2–8.

Every correlation coefficient contains two pieces of information. One is the *sign* of the correlation, which tells whether the two variables tend to rank people in the same order (plus) or in the reverse order (minus). The second piece of information is the *magnitude* of the correlation, which tells how strong the relationship is. The correlations +.50 and −.50 indicate the same strength of relationship, but the first reveals that there is some tendency for people to be in the same rank order on both variables; the second shows some tendency for people with the highest scores on one variable to have the lowest scores on the other. Figure 2–9 illustrates four different

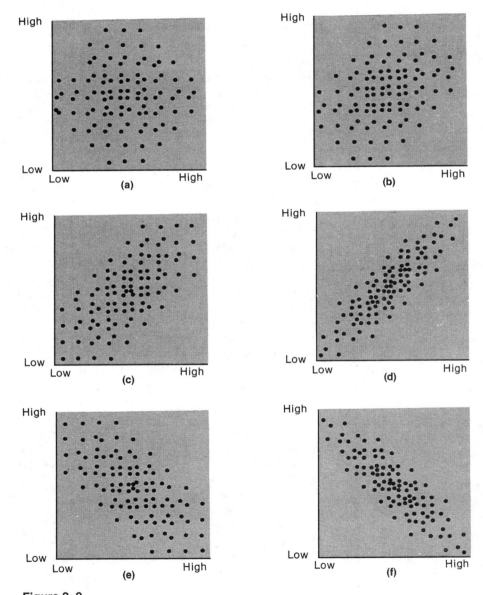

Figure 2–9
Distribution of scores for representative values of correlation coefficient: (a) correlation of 0.00, (b) correlation of +.30, (c) correlation of +.60, (d) correlation of +.90, (e) correlation of −.60, and (f) correlation of −.90.

levels of relationships. In Figure 2–9a, the correlation is zero, and the points scatter in a pattern that is almost circular. All combinations are found equally: high–high, low–low, high–low, and low–high. Figure 2–9b corresponds to a correlation of +.30. You can see a slight trend for the points to group in the low–low and high–high direction. This tendency is more marked in Figure 2–9c, which represents a correlation of +.60. In Figure 2–9d, which portrays a correlation of +.90, the trend is much more pronounced. Note that when the correlation is −.60 (Figure 2–9e) or −.90 (Figure 2–9f), the scattering of the points is the same, but the swarm of dots falls along the opposite diagonal from that of Figures 2–9c and 2–9d—from the upper left-hand corner to the lower right-hand corner. But even with as high a correlation as +.90, the scores spread out quite a bit and do not all lie directly on the line from low–low to high–high. The scores plotted in Figure 2–8 correspond to a correlation coefficient of +.62, which is fairly high for most relationships between variables found in education and psychology.

As is the case for the standard deviation, many modern pocket calculators include a program to compute the correlation coefficient. Likewise, spreadsheet and statistics packages will always have programs to compute correlations, although they may be listed under the heading of *regression*, a closely related topic that we will discuss in Chapter 5.

MAKING THE COMPUTER DO IT

Correlation Coefficients

Both SPSS and Excel have convenient routines for computing the correlations among several variables at the same time. SPSS has a Correlate program under the Analyze menu. Clicking on this program, you will be asked which of three types of correlation you wish to compute. Select "Bivariate." You will then be presented with a dialogue box that allows you to specify the variables to be correlated. Move each of the variables you want to find correlations for into the Variables box. The Pearson correlation, which is the one we have been discussing, is the one you want, so click OK. The output will include a square table in which each entry is the correlation of the variable in the row with the variable in the column. The values in the diagonal of the table will be 1.0, which says that the correlation of any variable with itself is perfect. Each cell of the table also includes the number of cases used to compute the correlation and the statistical significance ("Sig") test for the correlation.

In Excel you simply select the Correlation option from the Data Analysis menu. A dialogue box will appear asking you for the Input Range. You must highlight all of the scores to be included in the analysis, or specify the upper left cell and the lower right cell of the part of the table containing the scores you want to analyze. Then click on the "Output Range" button in the dialogue box, click in the "Output Range" box, and click in an empty cell where you wish the upper left corner of the correlation table to go. The output will be the lower half of the table you would get from SPSS, including the ones in the diagonal. Excel also has a Correl function on the f_X menu that you can use to find the correlation between a pair of variables. Highlight the scores on one variable for Array 1, then highlight the scores on the other variable for Array 2. Click OK, and the correlation will appear in the cell into which you have pasted the function.

You will encounter correlation coefficients in connection with testing and measurement in three important settings. The first situation is one in which we are trying to determine how precise and consistent a measurement procedure is. Thus, if we want to know how consistent a measure of speed we can expect to get from runners doing a 50-meter dash, we can have each person run the distance twice, perhaps on successive days. Correlating the two sets of scores will give information on the stability, or **reliability,** of this measure of running speed. The second situation is one in which we are studying the relationship between two different measures to evaluate one as a ***predictor*** of the other. Thus, we might want to study a scholastic achievement test from high school as a predictor of college grades. The correlation of the test scores with grades would give an indication of the test's usefulness as a predictor. These two uses of the correlation coefficient will be described more fully in Chapters 4 and 5.

The third situation in which we encounter correlation coefficients is more purely descriptive. We often are interested in the relationships between variables, simply to understand better how behavior is organized. What correlations do we find between measures of verbal and quantitative abilities? How close is the relationship between interest in mechanical jobs and comprehension of mechanical devices? Is rate of physical development related to rate of intellectual development? Many research problems in human behavior can best—or perhaps only—be studied by observing relationships as they develop in a natural setting, and these relationships are expressed with correlation coefficients.

We face the problem, in each case, of evaluating the correlation we obtain. Suppose the two sets of 50-meter dash scores yield a correlation of +.80. Is this satisfactory? Suppose the achievement test scores correlate +.60 with college grades. Should we be pleased or discouraged? (The wording of this question implies that we want correlations to be high. When a correlation expresses the reliability, or consistency, of a test, or its accuracy in predicting an outcome of interest to us, it is certainly true that the higher the correlation, the more pleased we are. In other contexts, however, "bigness" does not necessarily correspond to "goodness," and we may not have a preference on the size of a correlation—or may even prefer a low one.)

The answer to the third question lies in part in the plots of Figure 2–9. Clearly, the higher the correlation, the more closely scores on one variable agree with scores on the other. If we think of discrepancies away from the diagonal line, from low–low to high–high, as "errors," the errors become smaller as the correlation becomes larger. If we think of the *standard deviation of scores on test Y* as the errors we would make in predicting people's scores without test X, then the correlation coefficient between X and Y tells us how much our errors will be reduced by using test X as a predictor of variable Y. The square of the correlation coefficient (r^2) tells us how much our errors in estimating people's test Y scores are reduced using test X over what those errors would be without the test. But these discrepancies are still discouragingly large for even rather substantial correlation coefficients, for example, for those shown in Figure 2–8. We must always be aware of these discrepancies and realize that with a correlation such as +.60 between achievement test scores and school grades (which is about as high as correlations between these measures usually get), there will be a number of children whose school performance will differ a good deal from the best prediction we can make from the test. We will discuss these issues in more detail in Chapter 5.

However, everything is relative, and any given correlation coefficient must be interpreted in comparison with values that are commonly obtained. Table 2–6 contains a number of correlations that have been reported for different types of variables. The nature of the scores being correlated is described, and the coefficient is reported. An examination of this table will provide some initial background for interpreting correlation coefficients. The correlation coefficient will gradually

Table 2–6
Correlations Between Selected Variables

Variable	Correlation Coefficient
Heights of identical twins	.95
Intelligence test scores of identical twins	.88
Reading test scores in Grade 3 versus Grade 6	.80
Rank in high school class versus teacher's rating of work habits	.73
Height versus weight in 10-year-olds	.60
Arithmetic computation test score versus nonverbal intelligence test (Grade 8)	.54
Height of brothers (adjusted for age)	.50
Intelligence test score versus parents' occupational level	.30
Strength of grip versus running speed	.16
Height versus intelligence test score	.06
Ratio of head length to width versus intelligence test score	.01
Armed Forces Qualification Test scores of recruits versus number of school grades repeated	−.27
Artist interest score versus banker interest score	−.64

take on added meaning as you encounter coefficients of different sizes in your reading and as you work with tests.

SUMMARY

All measurements produce numbers. It is usually desirable to summarize the numbers that result from measurements so that we can both answer specific questions about the people we have measured and draw general conclusions. We have focused on six basic types of questions.

1. *What type of scale does our measurement represent?*
Different uses of numbers allow us to do different things with the resulting data. In nominal scales, numbers substitute for labels. Ordinal scales are usually in the form of ranks. Interval and ratio scales allow us to find means and standard deviations.

2. *What does the general array of numbers "look like"? Or how do they arrange themselves?*

The answer to this question involves sorting the scores into a frequency distribution (Table 2–2) or a grouped frequency distribution (Table 2–3). Histograms (Figure 2–1) can also provide a picture of the data.

3. *What does the typical individual look like? Or where is the middle of the group?*
The mode, median (or 50th percentile), and mean are indices of where the middle of the group falls. The mean, or arithmetic average, is the most commonly used measure of the center of the group.

4. *How widely do the scores spread out around their center? Or what is their spread?*
The spread of scores can be represented by the range, the semi-interquartile range (half the

distance between the 25th and the 75th percentiles), and the standard deviation, which is a measure of how far scores deviate, on the average, from the mean.

5. *How should we interpret the score of any individual?* We will discuss this topic in Chapter 3.

6. *To what extent do the scores from two measurements "go together"? Or what is the degree of relationship between the two sets of scores?* Generally, the most useful measurement of relationships is the correlation coefficient. This index runs from $+1.0$, indicating a perfect positive relationship or exact agreement, through zero, indicating no association between the sets of scores, to -1.00, indicating a perfect negative relationship, or exact disagreement, on the order of individuals on the two traits. The correlation coefficient is important as an index of stability of measurement and as a measure of how well one trait can be predicted from another.

QUESTIONS AND EXERCISES

1. For each of the following sets of scores, select the most suitable score interval and set up a form for tallying the scores:

Test	Number of Cases	Range of Scores
Mathematics	103	15–65
Reading Comprehension	60	60–140
Interest Inventory	582	65–248

2. In each of the following distributions, indicate the size of the score interval, the midpoints of the intervals shown, and the real limits of the intervals (i.e., the dividing points between them):

a.	b.	c.
4–7	17–19	60–69
8–11	20–22	70–79
12–15	23–25	80–89
.	.	.
.	.	.

3. Using the spelling scores given in Table 2–1, make a frequency distribution and a histogram. Compute the median and the upper and lower quartiles. Also, compute the arithmetic mean and the standard deviation from the original scores.

4. The Bureau of Census uses the median in reporting average income. Why is this index used rather than the mean?

5. A 50-item mathematics test was given to the 150 students in five classes at Sunnyside School. Scores ranged from 16 to 50, with 93 of the students getting scores above 40. What would this score distribution look like? What could you say about the suitability of this test for this group? What measures of central tendency and variability would be most suitable? Why?

6. A high school teacher gave two sections of a biology class the same test. The results were as follows:

	Section A	Section B
Median	74.6	74.3
Mean	75.0	73.2
75th percentile	79.0	80.0
25th percentile	71.0	64.4
Standard deviation	6.0	10.5

From these data, what can you say about these two classes? What implications do the test results have for teaching the two groups?

7. A test in history given to 2,500 10th-grade students had a mean of 52 and a standard deviation of 10.5. How many standard deviations above or below the mean would the following students fall?

Heather	48	Rob	60	Marc	31
Krista	56	Tina	36	Bill	84

8. If the distribution in Question 7 was approximately normal, what percentage of the group would Heather, Krista, Rob, Tina, Marc, and Bill each surpass?

9. Assuming that a set of scores is normally distributed with a mean of 82 and a standard deviation of 12, what percent of the distribution would each of the following scores exceed?
   a. 74
   b. 85
   c. 99

10. Explain the meaning of each of the following correlation coefficients:
   a. The correlation between scores on a reading test and scores on a group test of general intellectual ability is +0.78.
   b. Ratings of students on good citizenship and on aggressiveness show a correlation of −0.56.
   c. The correlation between weight and sociability is +0.02.

SUGGESTED READINGS

Dretzke, B. J., & Heilman, K. A. (1998). *Statistics with Microsoft Excel*. Upper Saddle River, NJ: Prentice Hall.

Heiman, G. W. (2000). *Basic statistics for the behavioral sciences* (3rd ed.). Boston: Houghton Mifflin.

Kirk, R. E. (1999). *Statistics: An introduction* (4th ed.). Fort Worth, TX: Harcourt Brace.

Runyon, R. P., Coleman, K. A., & Pittenger, D. J. (2000). *Fundamentals of behavioral statistics* (9th ed.). New York: McGraw-Hill.

Sweet, S. A. (1999). *Data analysis with SPSS*. Needham Heights, MA: Allyn & Bacon.

Thorndike, R. M., & Dinnel, D. L. (2001) *Basic statistics for the behavioral sciences*. Upper Saddle River, NJ: Merrill/Prentice Hall.

CHAPTER 3

Giving Meaning to Scores

The Nature of a Score
    Frames of Reference
    Domains in Criterion- and Norm-Referenced Tests
Criterion-Referenced Evaluation
Norm-Referenced Evaluation
    Grade Norms
    Age Norms
    Percentile Norms
    Standard Score Norms
    Normalizing Transformations
    Stanines

Interchangeability of Different Types of Norms
Quotients
Profiles
Criterion-Referenced Reports
Norms for School Averages
Cautions in Using Norms
A Third Frame of Reference: Item Response Theory
Summary
Questions and Exercises
Suggested Readings

THE NATURE OF A SCORE

Quadra Quickly got a score of 44 on her spelling test. What does this score mean, and how should we interpret it?

Standing alone, the number has no meaning at all and is completely uninterpretable. At the most superficial level, we do not even know whether this number represents a perfect score of 44 out of 44 or a very low percentage of the possible score, such as 44 out of 100. Even if we do know that the score is 44 out of 80, or 55%, what then?

Consider the two 20-word spelling tests in Table 3–1. A score of 15 on Test A would have a vastly different meaning from the same score on Test B. A person who gets only 15 correct on Test A would not be outstanding in a second- or third-grade class. Have a few friends or classmates take Test B. You will probably find that not many of them can spell 15 of these words correctly. When this test was given to a class of graduate students, only 22% spelled 15 or more of the words correctly. A score of 15 on Test B is a good score among graduate students of education or psychology.

As it stands, then, knowing that Quadra spelled 44 words correctly, or even that she spelled 55% correctly, has no direct meaning or significance. The score has meaning only when we have some standard with which to compare it.

Table 3–1
Two 20-Word Spelling Tests

Test A	Test A	Test B	Test B
bar	feet	baroque	feasible
cat	act	catarrh	accommodation
form	rate	formaldehyde	inaugurate
jar	inch	jardiniere	insignia
nap	rent	naphtha	deterrent
dish	lip	discernible	eucalyptus
fat	air	fatiguing	questionnaire
sack	rim	sacrilegious	rhythm
rich	must	ricochet	ignoramus
sit	red	citrus	accrued

Frames of Reference

The way that we derive meaning from a test score depends on the context or frame of reference in which we wish to interpret it. This frame of reference may be described using three basic dimensions. First, there is what we might call a temporal dimension: Is the focus of our concern what a person can do now or what that person is likely to do in the future? Are we interested in describing the current state or in forecasting the future?

A second dimension involves the contrast between what people *can* do and what they would *like* to do or would *normally* do. When we assess a person's capacity, we determine *maximum performance,* and when we ask about a person's preferences or habits, we assess *typical performance.* Maximum performance implies a set of tasks that can be judged for correctness; there is a "right" answer. With typical performance there is not a right answer, but we may ask whether one individual's responses are like those of most people or are unusual in some way.

A third dimension is the nature of the standard against which we compare a person's behavior. In some cases, the content of the test itself may provide the standard; in some cases, it is the person's own behavior in other situations or on other tests that provides the standard; and in still other instances, it is the person's behavior in comparison with the behavior of other people. Thus, a given measurement is interpreted as being either oriented in the present or oriented in the future; as measuring either maximum or typical performance; and as relating the person's performance to a standard defined by the test itself, to the person's own scores on this or other measures, or to the performance of other people.

Many instructional decisions in schools call for information about what a student or group of students can do now. Wakana Watanabe is making a good many mistakes in her oral reading. To develop an instructional strategy that will help her overcome this difficulty, we need to determine the cause of her problem. One question we might ask is whether she can match words with their initial consonant sounds. A brief test focused on this specific skill, perhaps presented by the teacher to Wakana individually while the other students work on other tasks, can help to determine whether a deficiency in this particular skill is part of her problem.

Table 3–2
A Focused Test

Test on Capitalizing Proper Nouns

Directions: Read the paragraph. The punctuation is correct, and the words that begin a sentence have been capitalized. No other words have been capitalized. Some need to be. Draw a line under *each word* that should begin with a capital.

We saw mary yesterday. She said she had gone to chicago, illinois, to see her aunt helen. Her aunt took her for a drive along the shore of lake michigan. On the way they passed the conrad hilton hotel, where mary's uncle joseph works. Mary said she had enjoyed the trip, but she was glad to be back home with her own friends.

We might also want to know how many children in Wakana's class have mastery of the rule on capitalizing proper nouns. A focused test such as the one in Table 3–2 can provide evidence to guide a decision on whether further teaching of this skill is needed. At a broader level, we may ask whether the current program in mathematics in the Centerville school district is producing satisfactory achievement. Administration of a survey mathematics test with national or regional norms can permit a comparison of Centerville's students with students in the rest of the country, and this comparison can be combined with other information about Centerville's students and its schools to make a decision on whether progress is satisfactory.

Whenever we ask questions about how much a person can do, we also face the issue of the purpose of our evaluation. There are two fundamental purposes for evaluating capacity in an educational context. One is to reach a summary statement of the person's accomplishments to date, such as teachers do at the end of each marking period. Evaluation for this purpose is called **summative evaluation.** It provides a summary of student achievement. By contrast, teachers and counselors are often interested in using tests to determine their students' strengths and weaknesses, the areas where they are doing well and those where they are doing poorly. Assessment for this purpose, to guide future instruction, is called **formative evaluation.** Test results are used to inform or to shape the course of instruction.

The type of maximum performance test that describes what a person *has learned to do* is called an **achievement test.** The oral reading test given to Wakana, the capitalization test in Table 3–2, and the mathematics test given to the students in Centerville are illustrations of sharply contrasting types of achievement tests. The test on initial consonant sounds is concerned with mastery of one specific skill by one student, and no question is raised as to whether Wakana's skill in this area is better or worse than that of any other student. The only question is, can she perform this task well enough so that we can rule out deficiency in this skill as a cause of her difficulty with oral reading?

Similarly, Wakana's teacher is concerned with the level of mastery, *within* this class, of a specific skill in English usage. Tests concerned with level of mastery of such defined skills are often called **domain-referenced** or **criterion-referenced tests** because the focus is solely on reaching a standard of performance on a specific skill called for by the test exercises. The test itself and the domain of content it represents provide the standard. Many, perhaps most, assessments needed for instructional decisions are of this sort.

We may contrast these tests with the mathematics survey test given to appraise mathematics achievement in Centerville. Here, the concern is whether Centerville's students are showing satisfactory achievement *when compared with the students in other towns and school systems like Centerville.*

Performance is evaluated not in relation to the set of tasks per se, but in relation to the perform-ance of some more general reference group. A test used in this way is spoken of as a **norm-referenced test,** because the quality of the performance is defined by comparison with the behavior of others. A norm-referenced test may appropriately be used in many situations calling for curricular, guidance, or research decisions. Occasionally throughout this book, we will com-pare and contrast criterion-referenced and norm-referenced achievement tests with respect to their construction, desired characteristics, and use.

Some decisions that we need to make require information on what a person *can learn to do.* Will Helen be able to master the techniques of computer programming? How readily will Rahim assim-ilate calculus? Selection and placement decisions typically involve predictions about future learning or performance, based on the present characteristics of the individual. A test that is used in this way as a predictor of future learning is called an **aptitude test.** Aptitude tests are usually norm referenced.

In some situations, our decision calls for an estimate of what a person *is likely to do.* The selec-tion of bus drivers, police officers, and candidates for many other jobs is best made with an eye to aspects of the person's personality or temperament. We would not want to select someone with a high level of aggression to drive a large vehicle on confined city streets. Nor would we want peo-ple who have difficulty controlling their tempers carrying firearms and serving as keepers of the peace. A measure of typical performance can serve as a useful aid in such situations, and these measures usually are also norm referenced.

Note that some of the most effective predictors of future learning or behavior are measures of past learning or behavior. Thus, for both computer programming and calculus, an effective pre-dictor might be a test measuring competence in high school algebra. Such a test would measure previously learned knowledge and skills, but we would be using that achievement measure to pre-dict future learning. Any test, whatever it is called, assesses a person's present characteristics. We cannot directly measure a person's hypothetical "native" or "inborn" qualities. All we can meas-ure is what that person is able and willing to do in the here and now. That information can then be used to evaluate past learning, as when an algebra test is used to decide whether Roxanne should get an A in her algebra course, or to predict future learning, as when a counselor must decide whether Roxanne has a reasonable probability of successfully completing calculus. The distinction between an aptitude and an achievement test often lies more in the purpose for which the test results are used than in the nature or content of the test itself.

Domains in Criterion- and Norm-Referenced Tests

It is important to realize that all achievement tests (in fact, all tests) relate to a specified domain of content. The mathematics survey test covers a fairly broad array of topics, while the test on the rules for capitalization is restricted to a narrowly defined set of behaviors. Thus, it is not really appropriate to differentiate between criterion-referenced and norm-referenced tests by saying that the former derive their meaning from a precisely specified domain, while the latter do not. A well-constructed, norm-referenced achievement test will represent a very carefully defined domain, but the domain is generally more diverse than that of a criterion-referenced test and it has only a small number of items covering a given topic or instructional objective. The criterion-referenced achievement test will represent a narrowly defined domain and will therefore cover its referent content more thoroughly than will a norm-referenced test of the same length.

There is a second dimension to using information from an achievement test. In addition to the traditional distinction between criterion-referenced and norm-referenced tests on the breadth of the domain they cover, the second dimension relates to the way that the level, or altitude, of performance is represented or used in reaching decisions. A test score from either type of test gets its content meaning from the domain of content that the test represents, but the kind of inference that a teacher or counselor draws from the score can be either absolute or relative. The teacher makes a judgment on the basis of the test score. If the judgment is that when a student or group of students have gained a particular level of proficiency with respect to the content the test represents, they have mastered the material, then the judgment is an absolute, *mastery–nonmastery* one. The decision reached is either that the students have mastered the material or that they have not; degree of mastery is not an issue. Decisions of this type are called **mastery decisions.** The usual definition of a criterion-referenced test is a test that covers a narrow domain and is used for mastery decisions.

By contrast, teachers can also use tests to judge relative achievement of objectives. Relative mastery involves estimating the percentage of the domain that students have mastered. For example, the teacher may decide that students have mastered an objective relating to spelling when they can spell correctly 19 out of 20 words from the domain. But the same teacher might use the information that the average student got a score of 14 on the spelling test to indicate that the students had achieved about 70% mastery of the domain. We refer to decisions of this kind as **relative achievement decisions,** but the frame of reference is still the domain of content without regard to the performance of anyone other than the current examinees.

The typical norm-referenced test uses neither of these ways to represent the level of performance. Rather, level is referenced to a larger group called a **norm group,** or norm sample. A normative interpretation of a score could lead to the conclusion that the individual was performing at a very high level compared with an appropriate reference group, but the same performance might fall far below mastery from the criterion-referenced perspective. Conversely, a ninth grader who has achieved mastery of multiplication facts at the level of 95% accuracy ordinarily would not show a high level of performance when compared with other ninth graders.

CRITERION-REFERENCED EVALUATION

We can approach the problem of a frame of reference for interpreting test results from the two rather different points of view mentioned earlier. One, criterion-referenced evaluation, discussed here, focuses on the tasks themselves, while the other, norm-referenced testing, focuses on the performance of typical people. Consider the 20 spelling words in Test A of Table 3–1. If we knew that these had been chosen from the words taught in a third-grade spelling program and if we had agreed on some grounds (at this point unspecified) that 80% correct represented an acceptable standard for performance in spelling when words are presented by dictation, with illustrative sentences, then we could interpret Ellen's score of 18 correct on the test as indicating that she had reached the criterion of mastery of the words taught in third-grade spelling and Peter's score of 12 correct as indicating that he had not. Here, we have test content selected from a narrowly defined domain and we have a mastery test interpretation. The test is criterion referenced in that (1) the tasks are drawn from and related to a specific instructional domain, (2) the form of presentation of the tasks and the response to them is set in accordance with the defined objective, and (3) a level of performance acceptable for mastery, with which the performance of each student is compared, is defined in advance. That is, criterion-referenced tests relate to a carefully defined domain of content, they focus on achievement of behavioral objectives, and the results are often (but not necessarily) used for mastery judgments.

The "mastery" frame of reference is an appropriate one for some types of educational decisions. For example, decisions on what materials and methods should be used for additional instruction in spelling with Ellen and Peter might revolve around the question of whether they had reached the specified criterion of mastery of the third-grade spelling words. More crucially, in a sequential subject such as mathematics, the decision on whether to begin a unit involving borrowing in subtraction might depend on whether students had reached a criterion of mastery on a test of two-place subtraction that did not require borrowing.

Although the two topics of domain referencing of test content and mastery–nonmastery decisions about achievement historically have been linked, it is important to realize that they are quite different and independent ideas that have come to be treated together. It is also important to realize that both exist in a sociopolitical context that invests them with normative meaning. What, for example, should a third grader be expected to know about multiplication or spelling? The answer to this question depends on what is expected of second and fourth graders, and these expectations put norm-referenced boundaries on what is taught in the third grade. Professional judgment and many years of experience combine to define the reasonable domain of content and a reasonable level of performance. A test is then constructed to represent this content at this level.

Given a test that is designed to represent a particular domain of content, the scores from that test may be interpreted strictly with respect to that content, or they may be interpreted in a normative framework by comparing one person's performance with that of others. Domain-referenced interpretation means that the degree of achievement is assessed relative to the test itself and the instructional objectives that gave rise to the test. The evaluation may result in a dichotomous judgment that the person has mastered the material and is ready for further instruction, for certification or licensure, or for whatever decision is the object of the measurement. Or, the evaluation may result in a judgment of degree of mastery. The latter approximates what teachers do when they assign grades, while the former is similar to a pass/fail decision or a decision to begin new material.

For the group of tests that are typically called criterion referenced, the standard, then, is provided by the definition of the specific objectives that the test is designed to measure. When the type of decision to be made is a mastery decision, this description of the content, together with the level of performance that the teacher, school, or school system has agreed on as representing an acceptable level of mastery of that objective, provides an absolute standard. Thus, the illustrative domain-referenced test of capitalization of proper nouns in Table 3–2 is presumed to provide a representative sample of tasks calling for this specific competence. If we accept the sample of tasks as representative and if we agree that 80% accuracy in performing this task is the minimum acceptable performance, then a score of 10 out of 13 words correctly underlined defines the standard in an absolute sense.

Even the dichotomous or mastery judgment is made in a sociopolitical, hence normative, context. The teacher or school has to decide what constitutes mastery, and there are some not-so-subtle social pressures that affect such decisions. Most teachers define the level of achievement necessary for mastery in such a way that an "appropriate" minimum number of students are identified as masters. In practice, this means that over a period of time the teacher develops a fairly accurate idea of how typical students will perform on his or her tests covering a course of instruction. The tests, grading practices, or passing standards are adjusted so that, in the long run, the right number of students pass, which makes the setting of passing standards basically a normative decision! (See Shepard, 1984, for a discussion of setting standards in criterion-referenced testing and Jaeger, 1989, for a discussion of standard-setting methods generally.)

In the usual classroom test used for summative evaluation, such a standard operates indirectly and imperfectly, partly through the teacher's choice of tasks to make up the test and partly through his or her standards for evaluating the responses. Thus, to make up their tests, teachers pick tasks that they consider appropriate to represent the learnings of their students. No conscientious teacher would give spelling Test A in Table 3–1 to an ordinary high school group or Test B to third graders. When the responses vary in quality, as in essay examinations, teachers set standards for grading that correspond to what they consider is reasonable to expect from students like theirs. We would expect quite different answers to the question "What were the causes of the War of 1812?" from a ninth grader and from a college history major.

However, the inner standard of the individual teacher tends to be subjective and unstable. Furthermore, it provides no basis for comparing different classes or different areas of ability. Such a yardstick can give no answers to such questions as "Are the children in School A better in reading than those in School B?" "Is Mary better in reading than in mathematics?" "Is Johnny doing as well in algebra as most ninth graders?" We need some broader, more uniform, objective, and stable standard of reference if we are to be able to interpret those psychological and educational measurements that undertake to appraise some trait or to survey competence in some broad area of the school curriculum. Most of this chapter is devoted to describing and evaluating several normative reference frames that have been used to give a standard meaning to test scores.

NORM-REFERENCED EVALUATION

The most commonly used frame of reference for interpreting test performance is based not on a somewhat arbitrary standard defined by a particular selection of content and interpreted as representing mastery of that content domain, but rather is based on the performance of other people. This represents a norm-referenced interpretation. Thus, the scores of Charlotta Cowen (47) and Gail Galaraga (71) on the 80-item spelling test from Table 2–1 can be viewed in relation to the performance of a large reference group of typical sixth graders or of students in different school grades. Their performance is viewed not in terms of mastery versus nonmastery or in terms of relative mastery of the subject matter, but instead as above average, average, or below average compared to the reference group; we need ways to refine that scale of relative performance so that all positions on the trait can be expressed in quantitative terms.

In seeking a scale to represent the amount of the trait a person possesses, we would like to report results in units that have the following properties:

1. Uniform meaning from test to test, so that a basis of comparison is provided through which we can compare different tests—for example, different reading tests, a reading test with an arithmetic test, or an achievement test with a scholastic aptitude test.
2. Units of uniform size, so that a change of 10 points on one part of the scale signifies the same thing as a change of 10 points on any other part of the scale.
3. A true-zero point of *just none of* the quality in question, so that we can legitimately think of scores as representing *twice as much as* or *two-thirds as much as*.

The different types of norm-referenced scales that have been developed for tests represent marked progress toward the first two of these objectives and thus satisfy the requirements for an interval scale. The third, which is the mark of a ratio scale, can probably never be reached for the traits with which we are concerned in psychological and educational measurement. We can put five 1-lb loaves of bread on one side of a pair of scales, and they will balance the contents of one 5-lb bag of flour placed on the other side. "No weight" is *truly* "no weight," and units of weight can be

Table 3–3
Main Types of Norms for Educational and Psychological Tests

Type of Norm	Type of Comparison	Type of Group
Grade norms	Individual matched to group whose performance he or she equals	Successive grade groups
Age norms	Same as above	Successive age groups
Percentile norms	Percentage of group surpassed by individual	Single age or grade group to which individual belongs
Standard score norms	Number of standard deviations individual falls above or below average of group	Same as above

added so that 2 lb is twice 1 lb. But we do not have that type of zero point or that type of adding in the case of educational and psychological measurement. If you put together two below-average students, you will not get a genius, and a pair of bad spellers cannot jointly win a spelling bee. In some cases, this deficit is the result of the particular way we have chosen to measure the trait, but for many psychological and educational traits, the deficit is a result of how we conceptualize the trait itself.

Basically, a raw point score on a test is given normative meaning only by referring it to some type of group or groups called *norm groups*. A score on the typical test is not high or low or good or bad in any absolute sense; it is higher or lower or better or worse than other scores. We can relate one person's score to a more general normative framework in two general ways. One way is to compare the person with a graded series of groups to see which one he or she matches. Each group in the series usually represents a particular school grade or a particular chronological age. A variant on this approach is to prepare a graded set of work samples such as samples of handwriting or responses to an essay question. Each person's product is then compared to the standard set of samples and given the score of the sample it most closely matches.

The second way to set a normative standard is to find where in a particular group the person falls in terms of the percentage of the group surpassed or in terms of position relative to the group's mean and standard deviation. These two approaches produce four main patterns for interpreting the score of an individual, which are shown schematically in Table 3–3. We next consider each in turn, evaluating its advantages and disadvantages. At the end of the chapter we examine a third way to give quantitative meaning to scores, a method based on the probability that the examinee will respond in a particular way. This method has been given the label *item response theory* or IRT.

Grade Norms

For any trait that shows a progressive and relatively uniform increase from one school grade to the next, we can prepare a set of **grade norms** or **grade equivalents.** The norm for any grade, in this sense, is the average score obtained by individuals in that grade. Because school participation and the related cognitive growth are both more or less continuous, grade norms typically are expressed with one decimal place. The whole number gives the grade, and the decimal is the month within the grade. Thus, a grade equivalent of 5.4 is read as performance corresponding to that of the average child in the fourth month of fifth grade.

In simplest outline, the process of establishing grade norms involves giving the test to a representative sample of pupils in each of a number of consecutive grades, calculating the average score at each level, and then establishing grade equivalents for the in-between scores. Thus, a reading comprehension test, such as that from the Iowa Tests of Basic Skills (ITBS)–Form J, Level 9, might be given in November to pupils in grades 2, 3, 4, and 5, with the following results:

Grade Level	Average Raw Score
2.3	13
3.3	22
4.3	31
5.3	37

The testing establishes grade equivalents for raw scores of 13, 22, 31, and 37. However, grade equivalents are also needed for the in-between scores. These are usually determined arithmetically by interpolation, although sometimes intermediate points may be established by actually testing at other times during the school year. After interpolation, we have the following table*:

Raw Score	Grade Equivalent	Raw Score	Grade Equivalent
10	1.9	24	3.5
11	2.0	25	3.6
12	2.2	26	3.7
13	2.3	27	3.8
14	2.5	28	3.9
15	2.6	29	4.0
16	2.8	30	4.1
17	2.9	31	4.3
18	3.0	32	4.4
19	3.1	33	4.5
20	3.2	34	4.7
21	3.2	35	4.9
22	3.3	36	5.1
23	3.4	37	5.3

*Note: Copyright © 1993 by The University of Iowa. Reproduced from *Iowa Tests of Basic Skills, Interpretive Guide for Teachers and Counselors, Form J.* Reproduced by permission of the publisher, The Riverside Publishing Company. The most recent forms of this test series calculate Developmental Standard Scores (see following section) first and derive grade equivalent scores from these.

Because raw scores on this particular test can range from 0 to 49, some way is needed to establish grade equivalents for the more extreme scores. Establishing such grade equivalents is often done by equating scores on the level of the test on which we are working with scores from lower and higher levels of the same test series, forms that have been given to earlier and later grades. In this way, grade equivalents can be extended down as low as the first month of kindergarten (denoted K.1) and up as high as the end of the first year in college (denoted 13.9), and a complete table to translate raw scores to grade equivalents can be prepared. (The reading test of this particular edition of the ITBS actually is a multilevel test that uses six overlapping sets of passages and items in a single booklet. In this way, some of the same items are used for three different levels of the test, and the projection of grade equivalents is simplified and made more accurate.)

If Jennifer got a raw score of 28 on this test, it would give her a grade equivalent of 3.9, and this score could be translated as "performing as well on this test as the average child who has completed 9 months of third grade." Such an interpretation has the advantage of connecting the test score to familiar milestones of educational development. However, this seductively simple interpretation of a child's performance has a number of drawbacks as well.

A first major question about grade norms is whether we can think of them as providing precisely or even approximately equal units. In what sense is the growth in ability in paragraph reading from grade 3.2 to 4.2 equal to the growth from grade 6.2 to 7.2? Grounds for assuming equality are clearly tenuous. When the skill is one that has been taught throughout the school years, there may be some reason to expect a year's learning at one level to be about equal to a year's learning at some other. And there is evidence that during elementary school (and possibly middle school or junior high), grade-equivalent units are near enough to equal to be serviceable. However, even in this range and for areas where instruction has been continuous, the equality is only approximate. If, on the other hand, we are concerned with a subject like Spanish, in which instruction typically does not begin until secondary school, or in something like biology, for which instruction is concentrated in a single grade, grade equivalents become completely meaningless. In addition, instruction in many skills, such as the basic skills in reading and in arithmetic computation, tapers off and largely stops by high school, so grade units have little or no meaning at this level. For this reason many achievement batteries show a grade equivalent of 10.0+ or 11.0+ as representing the whole upper range of scores. When grade equivalents such as 12.5 are reported, these do not really represent the average performance of students tested in the middle of the 12th grade, but rather they are an artificial and fictitious extrapolation of the score scale, used to provide some converted score to be reported for the most capable 8th and 9th graders.

A further note of caution must be introduced with respect to the interpretation of grade norms. Consider a bright and educationally advanced child in the third grade. Suppose we find that on a standardized mathematics test this child gets a score with the grade equivalent of 5.9. This score does *not* mean that this child has a mastery of the mathematics taught in the fifth grade. The *score* is as high as that earned by the average child at the end of fifth grade, but this higher score almost certainly has been obtained in large part by superior mastery of third-grade work. The average child falls well short of a perfect score on the topics that have been taught at his or her own grade level. The able child can get a number of additional points (and consequently a higher grade equivalent) merely by complete mastery of this "at-grade" material. *This warning is worth remembering.* The fact that a third-grade child has a grade equivalent of 5.9 does not mean that the child is ready to move ahead into sixth-grade work. The grade equivalent is only the reflection of a score and does not tell in what way that score was obtained. Reference to the content of the questions the child answered correctly would be needed to reach a judgment that the child had sufficient mastery of fifth-grade material to be able to move into the sixth grade. Thus, grade equivalents should not be used to make mastery decisions.

Finally, there is reason to question the comparability of grade equivalents from one school subject to another. Does being a year ahead (or behind) one's grade level in language usage represent the same amount of advancement (or retardation) as the same deviation in arithmetic concepts? A good deal of evidence exists, which we consider later in this chapter, that it does not. Growth in different school subjects proceeds at different rates, depending on in-school emphasis and out-of-school learning. For this reason, the glib comparison of a pupil's grade equivalent in different school subjects can result in quite misleading conclusions.

To summarize, grade norms, which relate the performance of an individual to that of the average child at each grade level, are useful primarily in providing a framework for interpreting the academic accomplishment of children in the elementary school. For this purpose, they are relatively convenient and popular, even though we cannot place great confidence in the equality of grade units or their exact equivalence from one subject to another.

Grade norms are relatively easy to determine because they are based on the administrative groups already established in the school organization. In the directly academic areas of achievement, the concept of grade level is perhaps more meaningful than is age level, for it is in relation to grade placement that a child's performance is likely to be interpreted and acted on. Outside the school setting, grade norms have little meaning.

Developmental Standard Scores

We have noted several problems with grade equivalents as normative representations of a child's performance, particularly that there is an implicit assumption that the amount of growth in the ability being tested is equal from one year to the next. Because this assumption clearly is violated for many abilities, test publishers have developed a type of score scale that is anchored to school grades but provides a better approximation to an equal interval scale, the *Developmental Standard Score Scale*.

Developmental standard scores (DSSs or SSs) are based on normalized score distributions within each grade (see the discussion of normalizing transformations later in this chapter). Scale values for two grades are chosen arbitrarily to define the scale metric, and the within-grade means and standard deviations are then used to locate other grade equivalents on this scale. For example, the Iowa Tests of Basic Skills authors have chosen to fix a scale value of 200 as equivalent to the median performance of fourth graders and a value of 250 for eighth graders tested in the spring. The relationship between grade equivalents and DSSs reported in the test manual is as follows:

Grade	K	1	2	3	4	5	6	7	8	9	10	11	12
DSS	130	150	168	185	200	214	227	239	250	260	268	275	280

One fact is quite clear from comparing grade equivalents and DSSs: Equal changes in grade equivalents do not correspond to equal changes in DSS. The DSS scale is constructed to have equal intervals (a 10-unit change has the same meaning everywhere on the scale). The comparison shows that there is a bigger change from year to year during the early years of school than there is in later years, 18 points from first to second grade, 10 points from eighth to ninth.

The main drawback of DSSs is that, unlike grade equivalents, they have no inherent meaning. The values chosen for the anchor points are quite arbitrary. Meaning is given only by their relationship to the grade-equivalent scale. It would be appropriate, for example, to say that a student who received a DSS of 255 was performing at the level of students in about December of their ninth-grade year. Because of their complexity and lack of obvious meaning, developmental standard scores are hard to interpret correctly and should be used with caution, even though they are reported by many test publishers. Test publishers who provide DSSs always offer normative information in other formats as well. For example, the process for reporting norm-referenced scores for the ITBS determines DSSs first because of their interval-scale properties, and then provides tables for converting the DSSs to the other types of normative scores described in this chapter (with the exception of age norms).

Age Norms

If a trait is one that may be expected to show continuous and relatively uniform growth with age, it may be appropriate to convert the raw score into an **age score,** or **age equivalent,** as a type of common score scale. During childhood we can observe continuous growth in height and weight, in various indices of anatomical maturity, and in a wide range of perceptual, motor, and cognitive performances. It makes a crude type of sense to describe an 8-year-old as being as tall as the average 10-year-old and having the strength of grip of the average 9-year-old, as well as the speaking vocabulary of the average 6-year-old. In the early development of intelligence and aptitude tests, raw scores were typically converted into age equivalents, and the term *mental age* was added to the vocabulary of the mental tester and the general public alike, with occasionally unfortunate consequences.

An age equivalent is, of course, the average score earned by individuals of a given age and is obtained by testing representative samples of 8-year-olds, 9-year-olds, 10-year-olds, and so forth. In this respect, it parallels the grade equivalent described earlier. And, as in the case of grade equivalents, a major issue is whether we can reasonably think of a year's growth as representing a standard and uniform unit. Is growth from age 5 to age 6 equal to growth from age 10 to age 11? And is growth in any 1 year equivalent to growth in any other year on our scale? As we move up the age scale, we soon reach a point where we see that the year's growth unit is clearly not appropriate. There comes a point, some time in the teens or early 20s, when growth in almost any trait that we can measure slows down and finally stops. In Figure 3–1, which illustrates the normal growth of height for girls, the slowdown takes place quite abruptly after age 14. A year's change in height after age 14 seems clearly to be much less than a year's change earlier on the scale. At about age 14 or 15, the concept of height-age ceases to have any meaning. The same problem of a flattening growth curve is found, varying only in the age at which it occurs—and in abruptness, for any trait that we can measure.

The problem introduced by the flattening growth curve is most apparent when we consider the individual who falls far above average. What age equivalent shall we assign to a girl who is 5 ft 10 in. (70 in.) tall? The average woman *never* gets that tall at any age. If we are to assign any age value, we must invent some hypothetical extension of our growth curve, such as the dashed line in Figure 3–1. This line assumes that growth after age 14 continues at about the same rate that was typical up to age 14. On this extrapolated curve, the height of 5 ft 10 in. would be assigned a height-age of about 16 years and 6 months. But this is a completely artificial and arbitrary age equivalent. It does *not* correspond to the average height of $16\frac{1}{2}$-year-olds. It does not correspond to the average height at *any* age. It merely signifies "taller than average." Unfortunately, there is no cue to be gotten from these extrapolated age equivalents that suggests their arbitrary nature. The problem is even more severe here than it is with extrapolated grade equivalents.

Figure 3–1
Girls' age norms for height.

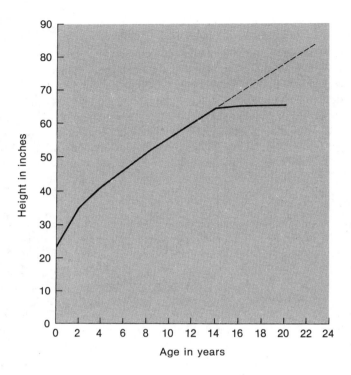

Age norms, which are based on the characteristics of the average person at each age level, provide a readily comprehended framework for interpreting the status of a particular individual. However, the equality of age units is open to serious question, and as one goes up to adolescence and adulthood, age ceases to have any meaning as a unit in which to express level of performance. Age norms are most appropriate for infancy and childhood and for characteristics that grow as a part of the general development of the individual, such as height, weight, or dentition. General mental development, such as the cognitive characteristics embodied in the concept of mental age, shows a sufficiently universal pattern to be a useful normative indicator of status, but, in general, age norms should not be used for cognitive characteristics beyond the elementary school years, because the patterns of growth of these functions depend too heavily on formal school experiences or have not been found to show the pattern of growth necessary for age norms to be appropriate.

Percentile Norms

We have just seen that in the case of age and grade norms, meaning is given to the individual's score by determining the age or grade group in which the person would be exactly average. But, often such a comparison group is inappropriate or some other group would be more useful. For example, we are frequently concerned with the performance of people who are no longer in the elementary grades where grade norms have meaning. Or, we may be interested in personality or attitude characteristics for which age or grade norms are wholly unusable. Or, the type of information that we seek may require that we specify the group of interest more narrowly than is practical for age or grade norms. For example, we may be interested in people who are all the same age or are all in the same grade.

Each individual belongs to many different groups. An individual who is 18 years old belongs to some of the following groups, but not to others: all 18-year-olds, 18-year-olds in the 12th grade, 18-year-olds applying to college, 18-year-olds not applying to college, 18-year-olds applying to Ivy League colleges, 18-year-olds attending public (or parochial) schools, and 18-year-olds attending school in California. For some purposes it is desirable or necessary to define the comparison group more narrowly than is possible with grade or age norms. One universally applicable system of norms is the percentile norm system.

The typical percentile norm, or **percentile rank,** uses the same information that we used to compute percentiles in Chapter 2, but the procedure is slightly different. *Percentile ranks are calculated to correspond to obtainable score values.* If a test has 10 items, it can yield 11 different raw scores, the whole numbers from 0 to 10. There are only 11 possible values that percentile ranks could assume for this test, one for each obtainable score, but it would still be possible to calculate any number of percentiles. For example, one could compute, using the procedures described in Chapter 2, the 67.4th percentile as well as the 67th and 68th. But only the 11 obtainable scores would have corresponding percentile ranks. The normative interpretation of test scores more often uses percentile ranks than percentiles, because test results come in a limited number of whole score units.

The procedure for determining percentile ranks starts with a frequency distribution such as the one shown in Table 3–4. We assume, as we did for percentiles, that (1) the underlying trait the test measures is continuous, (2) each observable score falls at the midpoint of an interval on this continuum, and (3) the people who obtained a given raw score are spread evenly throughout the interval. Because each raw score falls at the middle of an interval, half of the people in the interval are considered to be below the midpoint and half above. Even if only one person falls into a particular interval, we assume that half of that person falls above the midpoint of the interval and half falls below.

Table 3–4
Determining Percentile Ranks for a 10-Item Test

Raw Score	Frequency	Cumulative Frequency	Percentile Rank
10	1	60	99
9	3	59	96
8	5	56	89
7	12	51	75
6	15	39	52
5	9	24	32
4	7	15	19
3	4	8	10
2	2	4	5
1	1	2	2
0	1	1	1

To find the percentile rank of a raw score, we count the number of people who are below that score and divide by the total number of people. The number of people below a raw score value includes all of the people who obtained lower scores plus half of the people who received the score in question (the latter group because they are assumed to be in the bottom half of the interval and, therefore, below the raw score). For example, to calculate the percentile rank of a raw score of 4 in Table 3–4, we would take the eight people who got scores below 4 and half of the seven people at 4. The result is $(8 + 3.5)/60 = 11.5/60 = 0.1917$. In reporting percentile ranks it is conventional to round the answer to two decimal places and multiply by 100 to remove the decimal point except at the extremes of the scale. The percentile rank that corresponds to a raw score of 4 is therefore 19.

The major procedural difference between calculating percentiles, such as the median, and percentile ranks, such as those in Table 3–4, is where one starts. To calculate **percentiles,** we *specify a percent of interest,* such as the 25th or 60th, and determine the answer, a point on the continuous score scale, by the procedures described in Chapter 2. The values that correspond to these percentages need not be, and seldom are, whole points of score. When calculating **percentile ranks,** we start with *a point on the score scale,* an obtainable score value, and find as the answer the percentage of the group that falls below the chosen score.

Percentile ranks are very widely adaptable and applicable. They can be used wherever an appropriate normative group can be obtained to serve as a yardstick. They are appropriate for young and old and for educational, counseling, or industrial situations. To surpass 90% of a reference comparison group signifies a comparable degree of excellence whether the function being measured is how rapidly one can solve simultaneous equations or how far one can spit. Percentile ranks are widely used and their meaning is readily understood. Were it not for the two points we next consider, they would provide a framework very nearly ideal for interpreting test scores.

The first issue that faces us in the case of percentile ranks is specifying the norming group. On what type of group should the norms be based? Clearly, we will need different norm groups for different ages and grades in the population. A 9-year-old must be evaluated in terms of 9-year-old norms; a sixth grader, in terms of sixth-grade norms; an applicant for a job as real estate agent, in terms of norms for real estate agent applicants. The appropriate norm group is in every case the relevant group to which the individual belongs and in terms of which his or her status is to be evaluated. It makes no sense, for example, to evaluate the performance of medical school applicants on a biology test by comparing their scores with norms based on high school seniors. If the test is to be used by a medical school, the user must find or develop norms for medical school applicants.

Hence, if percentile ranks are to be used, multiple sets of norms are usually needed. There must be norms appropriate for each distinct type of group or situation in which the test is to be used. This requirement is recognized by the better test publishers, and they provide norms not only for age and grade groups but also for special types of educational or occupational populations. However, there are limits to the number of distinct populations for which a test publisher can produce norms, so published percentile ranks will often need to be supplemented by the test user, who can build norm groups particularly suited to local needs. Thus, a given school system will often find it valuable to develop local percentile norms for its own pupils. (Most test publishers will assist school districts with the development of local norms.) Such norms will permit scores for individual pupils to be interpreted in relation to the local group, a comparison that may be more significant for local decisions than is comparison with national, regional, or state norms. Likewise, an employer who uses a test with a particular category of job applicant may well find it useful to accumulate results over a period of time and prepare norms for this particular group

MAKING THE COMPUTER DO IT

Percentile Ranks

Both SPSS and Excel claim to compute approximate percentile ranks for a set of raw scores, although the process is easier and more accurate with SPSS. Unfortunately, the programs define percentile ranks in different ways. SPSS determines the *rank* of each score in the set of data and divides the rank by the total number of cases. When there is an odd number of cases with a given rank, this introduces a small error due to the fact that the middle case is not divided in half, but the error is of little consequence. We mention it only to make you aware that you may get small differences when doing the computations by hand.

To obtain percentile ranks with SPSS you must use the Rank Cases option on the Transformation menu. You will see a screen like this:

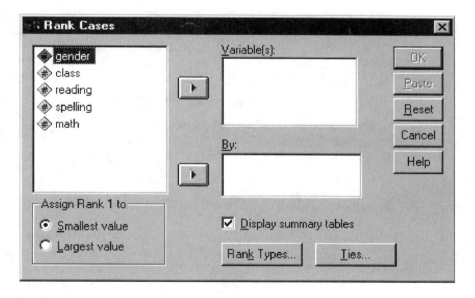

Transfer the variables for which you wish to get percentile ranks into the Variable(s) window, then click on Rank Types. You will see this screen:

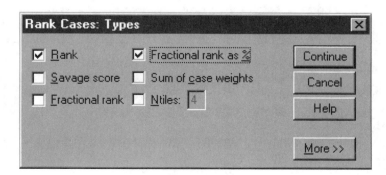

Click on the box for "Fractional rank as %," click Continue, then click OK. The program will create two new variables in your data file, one giving the rank of each score, the other giving the percentile rank, but with the error noted above. The program creates two new variables for each variable analyzed. Each new variable will have the same name as the original variable, but preceded by an *r* for ranks and a *p* for percentile ranks. If your variable name has eight characters, the last character will be dropped.

To obtain percentile ranks using Excel, you must use the "function" option (f_x). One of the functions in the statistics list is called PERCENTRANK. If you select this function you will get a dialog box like the one shown below superimposed on your data. You must supply the portion of the data table to be included and the score value for which the percentile rank is to be computed. Here we have selected the 52 scores (rows 2–53) for the variable in column G (Math score) and requested the percentile rank of a score of 33. The program tells us that the percentile rank of this score is 0.215.

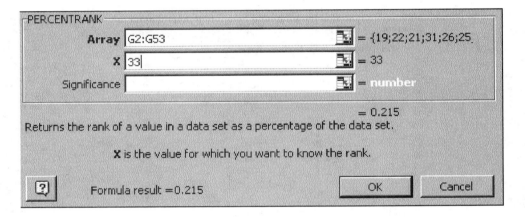

Unfortunately, the results provided by Excel are systematically in error by a substantial amount if you use the program according to the instructions. The values returned by the program are *approximately* equivalent to the ones returned by SPSS *for the score below the one you enter,* but this is not a reliable way to correct the error. For example, the correct percentile rank for a score of 33 in the data we have been using is 25.96 (13.5/52). The value returned by SPSS is 26.92 (14/52). As we have seen, Excel produces a value of 0.215 for a percentile rank of 21.5. This is approximately the correct value for the score 32. Because Excel produces incorrect results that cannot easily be corrected, we cannot recommend using it to compute percentile ranks.

of people. These strictly local norms will greatly facilitate the evaluation of new applicants. Thus, the possibility of specifying many different norm groups for different uses of a test constitutes both a problem, in the sense of greater complexity, and a strength, in that more accurate comparisons can be made.

The second percentile rank issue relates to the question of equality of units. Can we think of five percentile points as representing the same amount of the trait throughout the percentile

Figure 3–2
Normal curve, showing selected
percentile points.

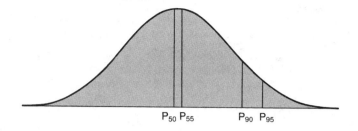

$$P_{50}\ P_{55}\qquad P_{90}\ P_{95}$$

scale? Is the difference between the 50th and 55th percentile equivalent to the difference between the 90th and 95th? To answer this question, we must notice the way in which the test scores for a group of people usually pile up. We saw one histogram of scores in Figure 2–1 of Chapter 2. This picture is fairly representative of the way the scores fall in many situations. Cases pile up around the middle score values and tail off at either end. The ideal model of this type of score distribution, the normal curve, was also considered in connection with the standard deviation in Chapter 2 (see Table 2–5 and Figure 2–6) and is shown in Figure 3–2. The exact normal curve is an idealized mathematical model, but many types of test results distribute themselves in a manner that approximates a normal curve. You will notice the piling up of most cases in the middle, the tailing off at both ends, and the generally symmetrical pattern.

In Figure 3–2, four points have been marked: the 50th, 55th, 90th, and 95th percentiles. The baseline represents a trait that has been measured in a scale with equal units. The units could be items correct on a test. Note that near the median, 5% of the cases (the 5% lying between the 50th and 55th percentiles) fall in a tall narrow pile. Toward the tail of the distribution, 5% of cases (the 5% between the 90th and 95th percentiles) make a relatively broad low bar. In the second instance, 5% of the cases spread out over a considerably wider range of the trait than in the first. The same number of percentile points corresponds to about three times as much of the score scale when we are around the 90th–95th percentiles as when we are near the median. The farther out in the tail we go, the more extreme the situation becomes.

Thus, percentile units are typically and systematically unequal, relative to the raw score units. The difference between being first or second in a group of 100 is many times as great as the difference between being 50th and 51st. Equal percentile differences do not, in general, represent equal differences in amount of the trait in question. Any interpretation of percentile ranks must take into account the fact that such a scale has been pulled out at both ends and squeezed in the middle. Mary, who falls at the 45th percentile in arithmetic and at the 55th in reading, shows a trivial difference in these two abilities, whereas Alice, with respective percentiles of 85 and 95, shows a larger difference, one that may be important for decision making.

The fact that units on the percentile scale are systematically uneven means that this is an ordinal scale. Larger numbers mean more of the trait, but equal differences in percentile rank do not mean equal differences in the trait. Percentile ranks do not solve the equality of units problem that we encountered with age and grade equivalents.

One of the consequences of this inequality of units in the percentile scale is that percentiles cannot be treated with many of the procedures of mathematics. For example, we cannot add two percentile ranks together and get a meaningful result. The sum or average of the percentile ranks of two raw scores will not yield the same result as determining the percentile rank of the sum or average of the two raw scores directly. A separate table of percentile equivalents would be needed for every combination of raw scores that we might wish to use. Again, the better test publishers provide percentile rank conversion tables for all of the combinations of subtest scores that they recommend as well as for the subtests themselves.

Standard Score Norms

Because the units of a score system based on percentile ranks are so clearly unequal, we are led to look for some other unit that does have the same meaning throughout its whole range of values. **Standard score scales** have been developed to serve this purpose.

In Chapter 2 we became acquainted with the standard deviation (SD) as a measure of the spread, or scatter, of a group of scores and standard scores or Z-scores as a way to express the relative position of a single score in a distribution. The standard deviation is a function of the deviations of individual scores away from the mean. Any score may be expressed in terms of the number of standard deviations it is away from the mean. The mean *mathematics* score for ninth graders on the Tests of Achievement and Proficiency is 24.1 and the standard deviation is 9.8, so a person who gets a score of 30 falls

$$\frac{30 - 24.1}{9.8} = 0.60$$

SD units above the mean. A score of 15 would be 0.93 SD units *below* the mean. In standard deviation units, or Z-scores, we would call these scores +0.60 and −0.93, respectively.

A Z-score can be found in any score distribution by first subtracting the group mean (M) from the raw score (X) of interest and then dividing this deviation by the standard deviation:

$$Z = \frac{X - M}{SD}$$

If this is done for every score in the original distribution, the new distribution of Z-scores will have a mean of zero, and the standard deviation of the new distribution will be 1.0. About half of the Z-scores will be negative, indicating that the people with these scores fell below the mean, and about half will be positive. Most of the Z-scores (about 99%) will fall between −3.0 and +3.0.

Suppose we have given the Tests of Achievement and Proficiency—Form G during the fall to the pupils in a ninth-grade class, and two pupils have the following scores on mathematics and reading comprehension:

Pupil	Mathematics	Reading Comprehension
Henry	30	48
Joe	37	42

Let us see how we can use standard scores to compare performance of an individual on two tests or the performance of the two individuals on a single test.

The mean and standard deviation for the mathematics and reading comprehension tests are as follows:

	Mathematics	Reading Comprehension
Mean	22.7	33.8
SD	9.4	11.1

On mathematics, Henry is 7.3 points above the mean. His Z-score is $7.3/9.4 = +0.78$. On reading comprehension, he is 14.2 points above the mean, or $Z = 14.2/11.1 = +1.28$. Henry is about one-half of a standard deviation better in reading comprehension relative to the norm group than in mathematics. For Joe, the corresponding calculations for mathematics give

$$(37 - 22.7)/9.4 = +1.52$$

and for reading comprehension give

$$(42 - 33.8)/11.1 = +0.74$$

Thus, Henry has done about as well on mathematics as Joe has done on reading comprehension, while Joe's mathematics score is about one-quarter of a standard deviation better than Henry's score on reading comprehension.

Each pupil's level of excellence is expressed as a number of standard deviation units above or below the mean of the comparison group. The Z-scores provide a standard unit of measure having essentially the same meaning from one test to another. For aid in interpreting the degree of excellence represented by a standard score, see Table 2–5.

Converted Standard Scores

All in all, Z-scores are quite satisfactory except for two matters of convenience: (1) They require use of plus and minus signs, which may be miscopied or overlooked, and (2) they get us involved with decimal points, which may be misplaced. Also, people do not generally like to think of themselves as negative or fractional quantities. We can get rid of the need to use decimal points by multiplying every Z-score by some convenient constant, such as 10, and we can get rid of minus signs by adding a convenient constant amount, such as 50. Then, for Henry's scores on mathematics and reading comprehension we would have

	Mathematics	Reading Comprehension
Mean of distribution of scores	22.7	33.8
SD of distribution	9.4	11.1
Henry's raw score	30	48
Henry's Z-score	+0.78	+1.28
Z-score $\times$ 10	8	13
Plus a constant amount (50)	58	63

MAKING THE COMPUTER DO IT

Standard Scores

You can use either SPSS or Excel to compute Z-scores, but again the process is much easier using SPSS because the program will compute a new standard score variable for each person in the distribution and save the new variable in your data file. To create a new standard score variable with SPSS, simply select the Descriptives option from the Analysis menu. The following dialog box will appear:

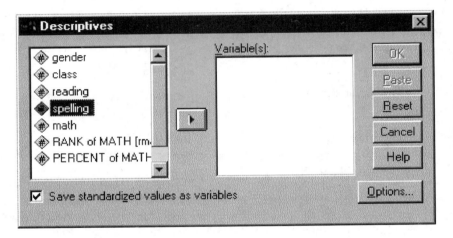

Select the variables for which you wish standard scores, then click on the "Save standardized values as variables" box. A new variable with the original variable name prefixed by Z will be created in your data file. The only problem with this program is that it uses the population estimate of the standard deviation in computing the Z-scores rather than the sample value. This results in Z-scores that are slightly too small, but the error is consistent across individuals and variables and for reasonably large groups is not large enough to worry about.

Excel requires that you first compute the mean and standard deviation of the distribution. You must then use the function option (f_x) and select Standardize from the statistics list. You will then be prompted to enter a score, the mean, and the standard deviation. The Z-score for the selected score will be displayed. The advantage of Excel is that you can use the proper standard deviation, but the disadvantage is that you must compute each Z-score separately. We will describe an alternative way to obtain Z-scores in the next box.

(The convention is to round such converted scores to the nearest whole number, consistent with the objective of making them easy to use.) Because we have converted Henry's scores on the two tests to a common scale ($M = 50, SD = 10$) we can compare them directly and see that Henry is somewhat better in reading comprehension than he is in mathematics. However, as we discuss in more detail later, this comparison requires the tests to have been normed on comparable groups.

Converted standard scores are based on a simple equation that changes the size of the units and the location of the mean. In symbolic form, the equation for the above transformation is

$$C = 10(Z) + 50$$

where Z is the standard score defined earlier and C is the converted standard score. The general formula is

$$C = SD_A(Z) + M_A$$

where SD_A and M_A are any arbitrary standard deviation and any arbitrary mean, respectively, selected for convenience.

The use of 50 and 10 for the mean and the standard deviation, respectively, is an arbitrary decision. We could have used values other than 50 and 10 in setting up the conversion into convenient standard scores. The army has used a standard score scale with a mean of 100 and a standard deviation of 20 for reporting its test results. The College Entrance Examination Board has long used a scale with a mean of 500 and a standard deviation of 100 for reporting scores on the SAT, the Graduate Record Examination, and other tests produced under its auspices. The navy has used the 50 and 10 system; intelligence tests generally use a mean of 100 and a standard deviation of 15.

The scale of scores following a conversion such as this one is stretched out or squeezed together (depending on whether the original standard deviation is smaller or larger than the new one), but the stretching is uniform all along the scale. The *size* of the units is changed, but it is changed uniformly throughout the score scale. If the raw score scale represented equal units to begin with, the new scale still does, but nothing has been done to make unequal units more nearly equal. Because the above equation is an equation for a straight line, this type of transformation of scores is called a **linear conversion,** or a **linear transformation.** (It is necessary here to add a note on terminology. We use the symbol Z to stand for standard scores in their original form and C to stand for *any* linear transformation of a Z-score. The symbol T is often used for the special case of a linear transformation using a mean of 50 and a standard deviation of 10.)

Normalizing Transformations

Area Normalizing Transformation

Frequently, standard score scales are developed by combining the percentile ranks corresponding to the raw scores with a linear transformation of the Z-scores that are associated with those percentile ranks in the normal distribution, making the assumption that the trait being measured has a normal distribution. (This is called an **area conversion** of scores. Because the complete transformation cannot be expressed by a straight line, or linear equation, it is also called a **nonlinear transformation.**) Thus, in the mathematics test, we found that the percentile rank of a score of 33 for the data in Table 2–1 was 26. In the table of the normal distribution (provided in the Appendix), the Z-score below which 26% of the cases fall is -0.64. If the distribution of mathematics scores were exactly normal, this is what the Z-score of a raw score of 33 would be. Consequently, to create an area-normalized version of this raw score we would *assign* a standard score of -0.64 to a raw score of 33. Expressing this result on a scale in which the standard deviation is to be 10 and the mean 50, we have

$$T = 10(-0.64) + 50 = -6 + 50 = 44$$

The complete process of preparing a normalized standard score scale by the area conversion method involves finding the percentile rank for each obtainable raw score. The Z-score below which the specified percentage of the normal distribution falls is then substituted for the raw

MAKING THE COMPUTER DO IT

Linear Transformations

It is quite simple to get either SPSS or Excel to perform any linear transformation of a set of standard scores. The easiest way to do it in SPSS is to use the Compute procedure in the Transform menu. You must first create the standard score variable as described in the preceding box. Then put the name you wish to use for the transformed variable in the Target Variable box and enter the transformation equation in the box labeled Numeric Expression. Click OK and the new variable will be added to your data file. The box below shows how to compute a new variable called "treading" (*T*-reading), which has an SD of 10 and a mean of 50, from the reading test scores. Note that we first created the *Z*-score variable "zreading" (*Z*-reading).

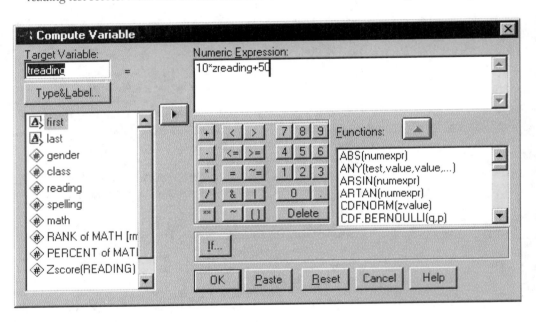

The procedure for transforming variables in Excel is quite similar. First, you must create the standard score variable, then compute the transformed variable. The easiest way to do this is to determine the mean and standard deviation of the variable to be transformed, then write a function that will compute the *Z*-scores as described earlier. For example, the mean and *SD* of the math scores for our 52 students in Table 2–1 are 38.17 and 8.84, respectively. The following screen shows the function for computing the *Z*-score for Quadra Quickly. Her math score is in cell G2, so the function "$=(G2-38.17)/8.84$" placed in cell H2 computes her *Z*-score of -2.17. Scores for the other students can be found by highlighting the remaining cells in column H, clicking on the Edit menu, the Fill command, and the Down selection. (Ctrl+D will accomplish the same result.) This places the same function in all cells of column H. Once you have computed the *Z*-scores, you can use the same procedure to obtain any other linear transformation and put the *C*-scores in column I. For example, to convert the *Z*-scores in column H into scores using the scale commonly used for IQ scores, we would insert the function "=(H2*15)+100" in cell I2. Again using the Fill command with the Down selection, we would get the desired transformed standard scores for all pupils in column I.

score, resulting in a set of Z-scores that yield a normal distribution for the group on which we have obtained our data. These Z-scores can then be subjected to a linear transformation using whatever mean and standard deviation are desired.

Normal Curve Equivalents

A second type of normalized standard score gaining popularity in education is the scale of **normal curve equivalents,** or the NCE scale. This scale is developed using the normalizing procedures described above and the same mean that the T scale uses, but the standard deviation is set at 21.06 rather than at 10. The reason for choosing this particular standard deviation is that it gives a scale in which a score of 1 corresponds to a percentile rank of 1 and a score of 99 corresponds to a percentile rank of 99. The relationship between NCEs and percentile ranks (PRs) is shown in the first two columns of Table 3–5. Most major publishers of educational achievement tests provide tables of NCE scores, thus allowing for comparison of relative performance on different tests. As these publishers note, however, the tests differ in content, so a common score scale does not imply that one test could be substituted for another. Also, the norm groups may not be comparable, so unless you know that two tests were normed on the same or comparable groups, NCEs from different tests should be compared with caution.

Table 3–5
Relationship Between Normal Curve Equivalents, Percentile Ranks, and Stanines

NCE	PR	Stanine	PR
99	99	9	≥96+
90	97	8	89–95
80	92	7	77–88
70	83	6	60–76
60	65	5	40–59
50	50	4	23–39
40	32	3	11–22
30	17	2	4–10
20	8	1	3≤
10	3		
1	1		

We have now identified two ways to develop standard score scales based on an arbitrary mean and standard deviation. In one, the *linear transformation method,* Z-scores are *computed* from the observed mean and standard deviation and the resulting Z-scores may be further transformed by first being multiplied by an arbitrary new standard deviation and then added to an arbitrary new mean. This method does not change the relative distances between scores and leaves the shape of the score distribution unchanged. In the other method, the *area or normalizing transformation,* percentile ranks are used to *assign* Z-scores to raw scores, based on the percentage of the normal distribution that falls below the Z-score. These assigned Z-scores are then transformed with an arbitrary standard deviation and mean to a desired scale. The resulting scores will form a normal distribution, regardless of the shape of the distribution of the raw scores.

Normalized standard scores make sense whenever it seems likely that the group is a complete one that has not been curtailed by systematic selection at the upper or lower ends. Furthermore, they make sense whenever it seems likely that the original raw score scale does not represent a scale of equal units but the underlying trait could reasonably be assumed to have a normal distribution. Many test makers systematically plan to include in their tests many items of medium difficulty and few easy or hard items. The effect of this practice is to produce tests that spread out and make fine discriminations among the middle 80% or 90% of test takers, while making coarser discriminations at the extremes. That is, the raw score units in the middle of the distribution correspond to smaller true increments in the ability being measured than do raw score units at the extremes. The "true" distribution of ability is pulled out into a flat-topped distribution of scores. The operation of normalizing the distribution reverses this process.

Stanines

A type of normalized standard score that has become quite popular for educational tests is the **stanine** (a condensation of the phrase *standard nine-point scale*) score. The stanine scale has a mean of 5, and stanine units each represent half of a standard deviation on the basic trait dimension. Stanines tend to play down small differences in score and to express performance in broader categories, so that attention tends to be focused on differences that are large enough to matter. The relationship between the stanine scale and the percentile rank scale is shown in the last two columns of Table 3–5.

The relationships between a number of the different standard score scales (after normalization) and the relationship of each to percentiles and to the normal distribution are shown in Figure 3–3. This figure presents the model of the normal curve, and beneath the normal

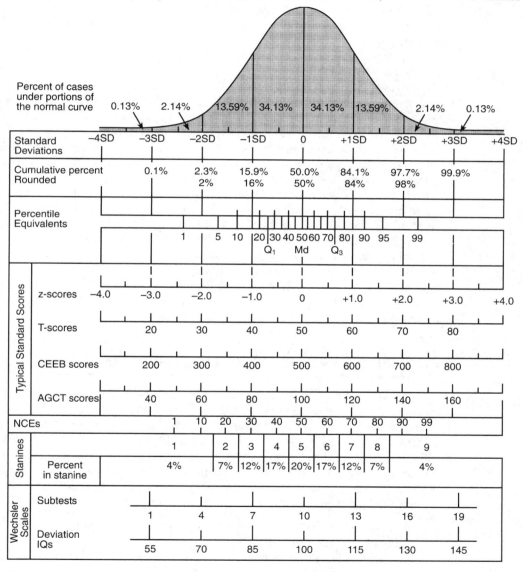

Figure 3–3
Various types of standard score scales in relation to percentiles and the normal curve.
Sample items similar to those in the Differential Aptitude Tests: Fourth Edition. Copyright © 1990 by The Psychological Corporation, a Harcourt Assessment Company. Reproduced by permission. All rights reserved. *Differential Aptitude Tests* and *DAT* are trademarks of The Psychological Corporation registered in the United States of America and/or other jurisdictions.

curve are a scale of percentiles and several of the common standard score scales. This figure illustrates the equivalence of scores in the different systems. Thus, a College Entrance Examination Board (CEEB) standard score of 600 would represent the same level of excellence (in relation to some common reference group) as an Army standard score (or AGCT) of 120, a Navy standard score (or T-score) of 60, a stanine score of 7, a percentile rank of 84, an NCE of 71, or a Wechsler IQ of 115. The particular choice of score scale is arbitrary and a matter of convenience. It is unfortunate that all testing agencies have not been able to agree on a common score unit. However, the important thing is that the same score scale and comparable norming groups be used for all tests in a given organization, so that results from different tests may be directly comparable.

Earlier, we discussed the importance of identifying an appropriate norm group, to allow interpretation of a raw score using percentile norms. The same requirement applies with equal force when we wish to express a person's characteristics within a standard score framework. The conversion from raw to standard score must be based on a relevant group of which the individual with whom we are concerned can be considered a member. It makes no more sense to determine an engineering graduate student's standard score on norm data obtained from high school physics students than it does to express the same comparison in percentiles.

In summary, standard scores, like percentile ranks, base the interpretation of the individual's score on his or her performance in relation to a particular reference group. They differ from percentile ranks in that they are expressed in units that are presumed to be equal, hence they represent an interval scale. The basic unit is the standard deviation of the reference group, and the individual's score is expressed as a number of standard deviation units above or below the mean of the group. Standard score scales may be based on either a linear or an area (normalizing) conversion of the original scores. Different numerical standard score scales have been used by different testing agencies. Standard score scales share with percentile ranks the problem of defining an appropriate reference group.

INTERCHANGEABILITY OF DIFFERENT TYPES OF NORMS

Whichever type of normative scale is used, a table of norms will be prepared by the test publisher. This table will show the different possible raw scores on the test, together with the corresponding score equivalents in the system of norms being used. Many publishers provide tables giving more than one type of score equivalent. Table 3–6 gives an example, which shows the fall testing norms for the vocabulary test of the ITBS–Form A, Level 9 (grade 3). Five types of norms are shown. The developmental standard scores (standard scores in this publisher's terminology) are based on a group tested early in the third grade. The NCE score scale assigns a mean of 50 and a standard deviation of 21.06 to an early third-grade group. Thus, a boy with a raw score of 21 can be characterized as follows:

1. Having a DSS of 191 (200 is the mean for fourth graders tested in the spring)
2. Having a grade equivalent of 4.2
3. Falling at the 78th percentile in the third-grade group
4. Receiving an NCE of 66
5. Receiving a stanine of 7.

From Table 3–6, it is easy to see that the different systems of norms are different ways of expressing the same thing. We can translate from one to another, moving back and forth. Thus,

Table 3–6
Vocabulary Norms for the Iowa Tests of Basic Skills–Form A, Level 9, Grade 3 Fall Norms

Raw Score	Standard Score	Grade Equivalent	Percentile Rank	Normal Curve Equivalent	Stanine
0	121	K.2	1	1	1
1	124	K.4	1	1	1
2	128	K.6	1	1	1
3	132	K.9	2	7	1
4	136	1.1	4	13	1
5	141	1.4	6	17	2
6	147	1.7	9	22	2
7	152	1.9	13	26	3
8	157	2.1	19	32	3
9	161	2.4	24	35	4
10	164	2.6	29	38	4
11	167	2.7	34	41	4
12	170	2.9	39	44	4
13	172	3.0	43	46	5
14	174	3.1	47	48	5
15	177	3.3	54	52	5
16	179	3.5	58	54	5
17	181	3.6	61	56	6
18	183	3.7	65	58	6
19	185	3.8	68	60	6
20	188	4.0	73	63	6
21	191	4.2	78	66	7
22	194	4.4	82	69	7
23	197	4.6	86	73	7
24	200	4.8	89	76	8
25	204	5.1	92	80	8
26	209	5.5	95	85	8
27	216	6.0	97	90	9
28	226	6.7	99	99	9
29	240	7.9	99	99	9

Source: Copyright 2003 by The University of Iowa. *ITBS Norms and Score Conversions, Form A, Levels 5–14*. Reproduced by permission of the publisher, The Riverside Publishing Company.

Table 3–7
Comparison of Developmental Standard Scores, Grade Equivalents, and Percentiles

Type of Score	Reading Comprehension			Mathematics Computation		
	John	Henry	Will	John	Henry	Will
DSS	210	223	235	210	223	226
Grade equivalent	5.5	6.5	7.5	5.5	6.5	6.7
Percentile rank	50	65	77	53	74	77

a child who receives an NCE of 66 in the third-grade group tested in October has a grade equivalent of 4.2. A grade equivalent of 4.0 corresponds to a percentile rank of 73 and a stanine of 6. The different systems of interpretation support one another for different purposes.

However, the different norm systems are not entirely consistent as we shift from one school subject or trait to another. This inconsistency occurs because some functions mature or change more rapidly from one year to the next, relative to the spread of scores at a given age or grade level. This can be seen most dramatically by comparing subjects like reading comprehension and mathematics. The phenomenon is illustrated by the pairs of scores shown in Table 3–7, based on the ITBS. It is assumed that the three boys were tested at the end of 5 months in the fifth grade (midyear norms). John received scores on both tests that were just average. His grade equivalent was 5.5, and he was close to the 50th percentile for pupils tested after 5 months in the fifth grade. Henry shows superior performance, but how does he compare in the two subjects? From one point of view, he does equally well in both; he is just 1 full year ahead in grade equivalent. But in terms of percentiles he is better in mathematics than in reading, that is, at the 74th percentile in mathematics compared with the 65th percentile in reading. Will, on the other hand, falls at just the same percentile in both reading and mathematics. However, in his case the grade equivalent for reading is 7.5, and for mathematics, it is 6.7.

The discrepancies that appear in this example result from the differences in the variability of performance and rate of growth in reading and mathematics. Reading shows a *wide* spread within a single grade group, relative to the mean change from grade to grade. Some fifth graders read better than the average eighth or ninth grader, so a reading grade equivalent of 8.0 or even 9.0 is not unheard of for fifth graders. In fact, a grade equivalent of 9.0 corresponds to the 89th percentile for pupils at grade 5.5 in this particular test series. By contrast, a fifth grader almost never does as well in mathematics as an eighth or ninth grader—in part because the fifth grader has not encountered or been taught many of the topics that will be presented in the sixth, seventh, and eighth grades and included in a test for those grade levels. All the basic skills that are involved in reading usually have been developed by fifth grade, so changes in reading performance result largely from greater mastery of those processes. With mathematics the case is quite different. Eighth graders are not doing better the same things fifth graders do; eighth graders are doing different things. For example, fifth graders are likely to be working with whole numbers and relatively simple fractions, whereas eighth graders will be studying decimals, complex fractions, and geometry. A fifth grader might well be able to read and understand an eighth-grade history book, but very few could do eighth-grade mathematics. Thus, fifth graders are more homogeneous with respect to mathematics than to reading skills.

The preceding point must always be kept in mind, particularly when comparing grade equivalents for different subjects. A bright child will often appear most advanced in reading and language and least so in mathematics and spelling, when the results are reported in grade equivalents. This difference may result, in whole or in part, simply from the differences in the growth functions for the subjects and need not imply a genuinely uneven pattern of progress for the child. For this reason most testing specialists are quite critical of grade equivalents and express a strong preference for percentile ranks or some type of standard score. However, because they *appear* to have a simple and direct meaning in the school context, grade equivalents continue to be popular with school personnel and are provided by most test publishers.

QUOTIENTS

In the early days of mental testing, after age norms had been used for a few years, it became apparent that there was a need to convert the age score into an index that would express rate of progress. The 8-year-old who had an age equivalent of $10\frac{1}{2}$ years was obviously better than average, but how much better? Some index was needed to take account of chronological age (actual time lived), as well as the age equivalent on the test (score level reached).

One response to the need was the expedient of dividing a person's test age equivalent by his or her chronological age to yield a quotient. This procedure was applied most extensively with tests of intelligence, where the age equivalent on the test was called a **mental age** and the corresponding quotient was an **intelligence quotient** (IQ). In the 1920s it became common practice to multiply this fraction by 100 (to eliminate decimals), thus giving rise to the general form of the scale that is now so well known in education and psychology (see Chapter 8). However, quotients are subject to the same problems that beset the age equivalent scores from which they are computed, and when growth stops, the quotient starts to decline because chronological age continues to increase at a constant rate.

The notion of the IQ is deeply embedded in the history of psychological and educational testing and, in fact, in contemporary American language and culture. The expression *IQ test* has become part of our common speech. We are probably stuck with the term. But the way that the IQ is defined has changed. IQs have become, in almost every case, normalized standard scores with a mean of 100 and a standard deviation of 15, and we should think of them and use them in this way. These scores are sometimes referred to as *deviation intelligence quotients,* or deviation IQs, because they are basically standard scores expressed as a deviation above or below a mean of 100. The 1986 revision of the Stanford-Binet Intelligence Scale substituted the term *standard age score* for IQ to reflect more accurately the true nature of the scores, and many other tests have followed suit in dropping references to IQ.

Unfortunately, the score scale for reporting IQs does not have *exactly* the same meaning from test to test. The Wechsler test series is based on a mean of 100 and a standard deviation of 15, whereas the Stanford-Binet and some group tests have used a mean of 100 and a standard deviation of 16 (*this has changed to 100 and 15 with* the most recent revisions of these tests). Furthermore, tests are normed at different points in time and use different sampling procedures. These differences in procedure also lead to some variation in the norms and, consequently, in the distribution of IQs they yield for any given school or community. A series of studies by Flynn (1984,

1998) also suggests that there has been a long-term rise in IQs worldwide, dating at least to the mid-1930s, which would mean that norms that are 15 to 20 years old are probably not appropriate for use today. Such a change in mean performance makes it difficult to compare results over time or between successive test forms. We discuss issues related to intelligence and tests used to measure it in Chapter 8.

PROFILES

The various types of normative frames of reference we have been considering provide a way of expressing scores from quite different tests in common units, so that the scores can be meaningfully compared. No direct way exists to compare a score of 30 words correctly spelled with a score of 20 arithmetic problems solved correctly. But, if both are expressed in terms of the grade level to which they correspond or in terms of the percentage of some defined common group that gets scores below that point, then a meaningful comparison is possible. A set of different test scores for an individual, expressed in a common unit of measure, is called a **score profile.** The separate scores may be presented for comparison in tabular form by listing the converted score values. A record showing such converted scores for several pupils is given in Figure 3–4. The comparison of different subareas of performance is made pictorially clearer by a graphic presentation of the profile. Two ways of plotting profiles are shown in Figures 3–5 and 3–6.

Figures 3–4 and 3–5 show part of a class record form and an individual profile chart for the ITBS, respectively. The class record illustrates the form in which the data are reported back to the schools by the test publisher's computerized test scoring service. (The precise form that the reporting of results takes differs from one scoring service to another.) Four norm-referenced scores are reported for each pupil on each test (see Figure 3–4). The first row of the report for each student contains developmental standard scores (called *SS*s in this publisher's materials) for the 13 subtests and eight composites. The second row of scores are grade equivalents (GEs), and because the tests were given after the pupils had spent 8 months in the third grade, average performance for the country as a whole would be 3.8. The last two rows for each student contain stanines (NS) and percentile ranks (NPR) based on the spring 2000 national norm group. Looking at the scores for Eliot Johnson on the reading total score, we can see that the four score systems give an essentially equivalent picture of his performance. His reading total grade equivalent of 2.5 is below average average, and this is also reflected in his stanine and NPR scores of 3 and 18, respectively. The standard scale score of 164 is also consistent with below-average performance in the spring of third grade. All four reference systems show him to be well below average in reading. Eliot's performance is noticeably better in language skills, where he comes in at grade level.

Figure 3–5 shows data for testings of a student in two successive years (fifth and sixth grades). The so-called "developmental scale" referred to toward the left is actually a scale of grade equivalents (GEs). Thus, this pupil had a vocabulary grade equivalent of 3.7 when she was tested the first time. By the next year her grade equivalent on this test was 4.6. Similar growth of approximately one GE is shown for each of the other subtests, although the level of performance in either year shows considerable variation from one subject to another.

The results show her scores generally to have been at or above the national average. An examination of her profile for the fifth-grade test indicates that she was strongest in capitalization,

THE IOWA TESTS

LIST OF STUDENT SCORES
Iowa Tests of Basic Skills® (ITBS®)

Class/Group: Ness
School: Longfellow
District: Dalen Community
Order No.: 002-A7000028-0-002

Test Date: 04/2002
Report Date: 04/26/02
Norms: Spring 2000
Page: 1
Grade: 3

Column key: STUDENT NAME / I.D. Number / Calc. / F-1 F-2 F-3 / Code / A B C D E F G H I J K L M N O P Z — Birth Date / Level (Gender) / Age / Program / Form

STUDENT NAME		Vocabulary	Comprehension	Reading TOTAL	Word Analysis	Listening	Spelling	Capitalization	Punctuation	Usage/Express.	Language TOTAL	Conceptual Estimate	Problems/Interp.	Computation	Math TOTAL	Core TOTAL	Social Studies	Science	Maps/Diagrams	Ref. Materials	Sources TOTAL	Composite
Andrews, Jamie (F) 09/92, 09-06, AB, GT, Level 9	SS	204	188	196	196	179	203	214	196	215	207	182	193	172	188	196	179	186	204	228	216	197
0000141452	GE	5.0	4.0	4.5	4.5	3.4	5.1	5.8	4.5	5.8	5.3	3.6	4.4	3.2	4.0	4.5	3.4	3.9	5.0	6.9	5.9	4.5
	NS	7	5	6	6	4	7	7	6	8	7	5	6	5	5	6	4	5	7	9	8	6
	NPR	81	55	67	64	39	82	83	67	82	81	44	63	22	55	68	39	51	79	97	91	69
Benevides, Alicia (F) 03/93, 09-01, A, Level 9	SS	172	198	185	172	198	182	147	184	180	173	175	189	176	182	180	188	183	193	190	192	184
0000157073	GE	3.0	4.6	3.8	3.0	4.6	3.6	1.7	3.7	3.5	3.1	3.3	4.1	3.4	3.7	3.4	4.0	3.6	4.2	4.1	4.2	3.7
	NS	4	6	5	4	6	5	2	5	5	4	4	5	5	5	4	5	5	5	6	5	4
	NPR	31	71	53	31	71	48	9	52	44	30	35	59	35	48	42	58	49	67	63	65	50
Catts, Jim (M) 11/92, 09-04, A, Level 9	SS	o152	o147	o150	o146	o147	152	o155	o181	o146	o158	o146	o134	o159	o140	o149	o165	o150	o157	o163	o160	o154
0000146255	GE	1.8	1.7	1.8	1.5	1.7	1.9	2.1	3.6	1.7	2.2	1.5	1.0	2.5	1.2	1.7	2.6	1.8	2.2	2.6	2.4	1.9
	NS	o2	o2	o2	o1	o2	2	o3	o5	o2	o3	o1	o1	o5	o1	o1	o3	o2	o3	o3	o3	o2
	NPR	o8	o4	o5	o1	o4	5	o15	o46	o6	o10	o2	o1	o8	o1	o3	o19	o6	o12	o13	o12	o4
Easterday, Ona (F) 11/92, 09-04, A, Level 9	SS	157	#		168	142	150	178	154	142	158	158	169	168	164		159	139	151	181	166	166
0000173431	GE	2.1	#		2.8	1.3	2.3	3.5	2.0	1.3	2.2	2.3	2.9	2.8	2.6		2.4	1.2	1.8	3.5	2.7	2.7
	NS	3	#		3	2	3	4	2	2	2	2	4	3	2		3	1	2	5	3	3
	NPR	11	#		20	4	10	42	10	4	10	10	26	20	17		12	1	8	46	19	19
Fossil, Graham (M) 09/92, 09-06, A, Level 9	SS	152	160	156	151	165	159	147	165	174	161	179	173	182	176	164	168	163	151	175	163	164
0000146937	GE	1.8	2.3	2.1	1.8	2.6	2.3	1.7	2.6	3.2	2.4	3.4	3.1	3.5	3.3	2.6	2.8	2.5	1.8	3.4	2.5	2.5
	NS	2	3	2	2	3	3	2	3	4	3	4	4	5	4	3	4	3	2	4	3	3
	NPR	8	15	9	8	21	10	9	21	34	14	43	33	49	37	15	24	19	8	34	15	14
Friday, Leticia (F) 07/93, 08-08, A, Level 8	SS	132	167	150	158	153	150				151	153	158	155	156	152	159	163			154	156
0000143196	GE	K.9	2.8	1.8	2.2	2.0	1.8				1.8	2.0	2.2	2.3	2.3	1.9	2.4	2.5			2.0	2.0
	NS	1	4	2	3	2	2				2	2	2	2	2	1	3	3			2	2
	NPR	1	24	5	13	6	4				5	6	13	4	8	3	12	19			6	5
Hernandez, Claire (F) 03/93, 09-01, A, Level 9	SS	218	232	225	224	214	192	214	215	260	220	224	250	199	237	227	220	202	249	235	242	224
0000163173	GE	6.1	7.3	6.9	6.9	5.8	4.2	5.8	5.9	9.8	6.3	6.6	8.8	4.7	7.6	6.8	6.2	4.9	8.7	7.5	8.2	6.4
	NS	8	9	9	9	7	6	7	7	9	8	8	9	9	9	9	8	9	9	9	9	9
	NPR	95	96	96	98	85	69	85	86	99	93	98	99	84	99	99	95	77	99	99	99	98
Johnson, Eliot (M) 03/93, 09-01, A, Level 9	SS	180	147	164	147	180	185	193	196	178	188	177	185	180	181	178	165	163	168	170	169	172
0000145652	GE	3.5	1.7	2.5	1.7	3.5	3.8	4.3	4.5	3.4	4.0	3.4	3.8	3.5	3.6	3.3	2.6	2.5	2.8	2.9	2.8	3.0
	NS	5	2	3	2	5	5	6	6	4	5	4	5	5	4	4	3	3	3	4	3	3
	NPR	45	4	18	4	45	54	65	70	40	57	38	53	44	46	38	19	19	22	26	23	27
Lee, Adam (M) 09/92, 09-07, A, GT, Level 9	SS	210	194	202	197	197	188	188	235	250	232	180	197	186	188	207	192	183	189	190	190	198
0000157073	GE	5.4	4.3	5.0	4.6	4.6	4.0	4.0	7.5	8.8	7.3	3.5	4.6	3.9	4.0	5.3	4.3	3.6	4.0	4.1	4.1	4.6
	NS	8	6	6	6	6	6	6	8	9	9	4	6	5	5	7	6	5	6	6	6	6
	NPR	89	66	78	72	72	61	61	94	98	98	45	72	59	59	85	64	49	61	63	61	74
Mondavi, Kara (F) 11/92, 09-04, A, GT, Level 9	SS	183	194	188	228	215	201	214	235	215	216	237	213	203	225	210	192	186	204	228	216	204
0000157074	GE	3.7	4.3	4.0	6.9	5.8	4.9	5.8	7.5	5.8	5.9	7.7	5.7	5.2	6.9	5.5	4.3	3.9	5.0	6.9	5.9	4.9
	NS	6	6	6	9	7	7	7	8	7	8	9	7	8	9	7	6	5	7	9	8	7
	NPR	50	66	58	98	84	82	85	94	84	91	99	87	89	98	89	64	51	81	98	92	82

Figure 3–4 List report of student scores. Copyright © 2001 by The Riverside Publishing Company. All rights reserved. Reproduced from the *Iowa Test of Basic Skills® (ITBS®)*. No part of this work may be reproduced or transmitted in any form or by any means, electronic or mechanical, including photocopying and recording or by any information storage or retrieval system without the proper written permission of The Riverside Publishing Company unless such copying is expressly permitted by federal copyright law. Address inquiries to Permissions Department, The Riverside Publishing Company, 425 Spring Lake Drive, Itasca, Illinois 60143-2079.

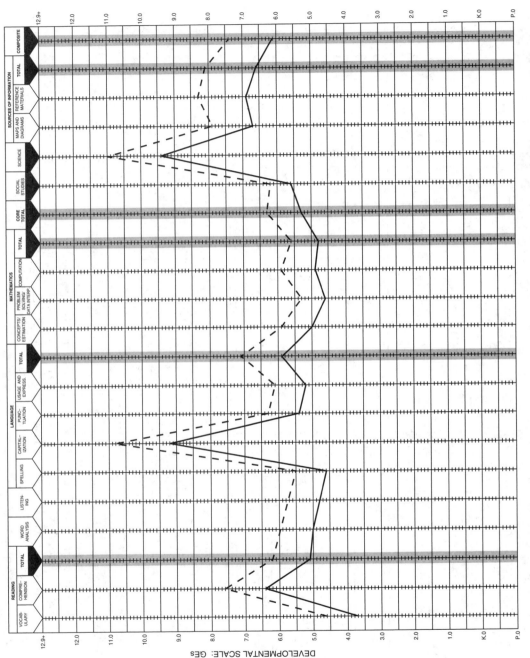

Figure 3–5 Student profile chart. Copyright © 2001 by The Riverside Publishing Company. All rights reserved. Reproduced from the *Iowa Test of Basic Skills® (ITBS®)*. No part of this work may be reproduced or transmitted in any form or by any means, electronic or mechanical, including photocopying and recording or by any information storage or retrieval system without the proper written permission of The Riverside Publishing Company unless such copying is expressly permitted by federal copyright law. Address inquiries to Permissions Department, The Riverside Publishing Company, 425 Spring Lake Drive, Itasca, Illinois 60143-2079.

science, and reading comprehension skills and weakest in vocabulary and spelling. Some of the hazards of paying a great deal of attention to small ups and downs in a profile can be seen in a comparison of her performance on successive testings. Although the profile shows a relatively consistent pattern of highs and lows over the years, relative superiority changes somewhat from one year to the next.

Figure 3–6 shows a second type of profile chart for the ITBS. Here, the scores for Eliot Johnson (see Figure 3–4) are shown for each of the separate subtests of the battery. Note that in this case the different tests are represented by separate bars rather than by points connected by a line. The scale used in this case is a percentile rank scale, but in plotting percentile values, appropriate adjustments in the scale have been made to compensate for the inequality of percentile units. That is, the percentile points have been spaced in the same way that they are in a normal curve, being more widely spaced at the upper and lower extremes than in the middle range. This percentile scale corresponds to the scale called Percentile Equivalents in Figure 3–3. By this adjustment, the

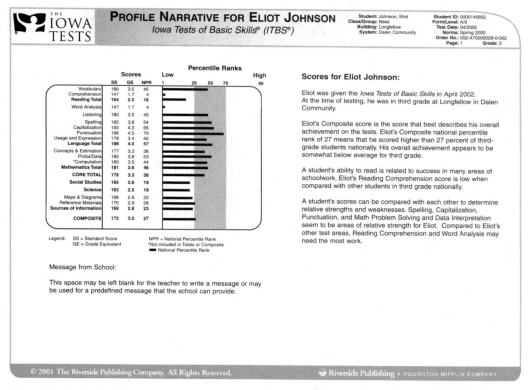

Figure 3–6 Profile narrative report—parent copy. Copyright © 2001 by The Riverside Publishing Company. All rights reserved. Reproduced from the *Iowa Test of Basic Skills® (ITBS®)*. No part of this work may be reproduced or transmitted in any form or by any means, electronic or mechanical, including photocopying and recording or by any information storage or retrieval system without the proper written permission of The Riverside Publishing Company unless such copying is expressly permitted by federal copyright law. Address inquiries to Permissions Department, The Riverside Publishing Company, 425 Spring Lake Drive, Itasca, Illinois 60143-2079.

percentile values for an individual are plotted on an equal unit scale. A given linear distance can reasonably be thought to represent the same difference in amount of ability, whether it lies high in the scale, low in the scale, or near the middle of the scale. By the same token, the same distance can be considered equivalent from one test to another.

In the profile in Figure 3–6, the middle 50% is shaded to indicate a band of average performance for the norm group. The scores of this student have been plotted as bars that extend from the left side of the chart. For this type of norm, the average of the group constitutes the anchor point of the scale, and the individual scores can be referred to this base level. This type of figure brings out the individual's strengths and weaknesses quite clearly. Note also that the numerical values for this student's percentile ranks in the national norm group are given to the left of the profile. In addition, this particular test publisher's scoring service provides a narrative interpretation of the profile. Such an interpretation can also help draw the attention of teachers and parents to noteworthy features of the student's performance. Because this profile is intended to serve as a report to parents, there is also space for teacher comments.

The profile chart is a very effective way of representing an individual's scores, but profiles must be interpreted with caution. First, procedures for plotting profiles assume that the norms for the tests are comparable. For this to be true, age, grade, or percentile scores must be based on equivalent groups for all the tests. We usually find this to be the case for the subtests of a test battery. Norms for all the subtests are established at the same time, on the basis of testing the same group. This guarantee of comparability of norms for the different component tests is one of the most attractive features of an integrated test battery. If separately developed tests are plotted in a profile, we can usually only hope that the groups on which the norms were established were comparable and that the profile is an unbiased picture of relative achievement in different fields. When it is necessary to use tests from several different sources, one way to be sure of having equivalent norm groups is to develop local norms on a common population and to plot individual profiles in terms of those local norms.

A second problem in interpreting profiles is that of deciding how much attention to pay to the ups and downs in the profile. Not all the differences that appear in a profile are meaningful, either in a statistical or in a practical sense. We must decide which of the differences deserve some attention on our part and which do not. This problem arises because no test score is completely exact. No magic size exists at which a score difference suddenly becomes worthy of attention, and any rule of thumb is at best a rough guide. But, differences must be big enough so that we can be reasonably sure (1) that they would still be there if the person were tested again and (2) that they make a practical difference in terms of what they imply for performance, before we start to interpret them and base action on them. We will return to this topic during our discussion of reliability in Chapter 4.

CRITERION-REFERENCED REPORTS

Interest in criterion-referenced interpretations of test scores has led test publishers to produce a profile of student performance based on specific item content. A well-designed test will include items that tap various aspects of skill or knowledge development. Modern test scoring and computer technology have made it possible to report a student's performance on subsets of items that are homogeneous with respect to a particular kind of content. An example of such a report for the ITBS is shown in Figure 3–7.

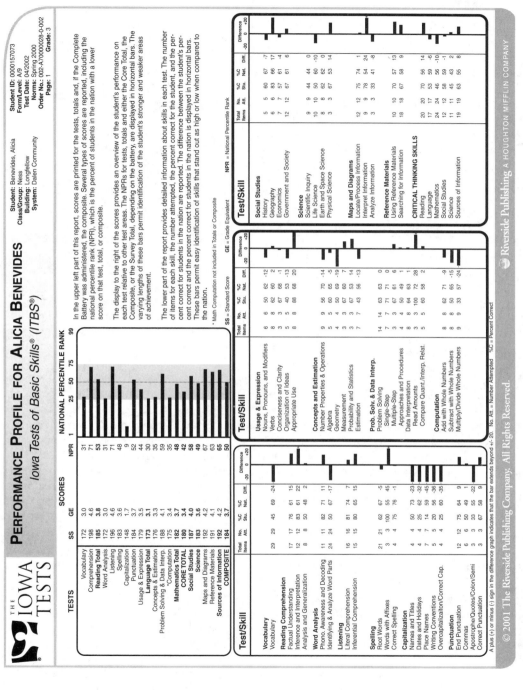

Figure 3–7 Student criterion-referenced skills analysis. Copyright © 2001 by The Riverside Publishing Company. All rights reserved. Reproduced from the *Iowa Test of Basic Skills* (*ITBS*). No part of this work may be reproduced or transmitted in any form or by any means, electronic or mechanical, including photocopying and recording or by any information storage or retrieval system without the proper written permission of The Riverside Publishing Company unless such copying is expressly permitted by federal copyright law. Address inquiries to Permissions Department, The Riverside Publishing Company, 425 Spring Lake Drive, Itasca, Illinois 60143-2079.

The report presented in Figure 3–7 lists each subtopic for each test of the ITBS, along with the number of items assessing that skill. The number of items the student attempted, the percentage of items correct for the student, the percentage correct for the nation, and the difference in percent correct for this student from the national norm group are also given. This report allows the teacher to identify specific strengths and weaknesses at a more fine-grained level than is possible with the ordinary norm-referenced report. For example, this student seems to have particular problems with the use of apostrophes, quotes, and colons, although her overall punctuation performance is average. Although each subskill is measured by too few items to yield a very reliable assessment, the information can be valuable to the classroom teacher in designing the instructional program for the individual student. Skills marked with a plus (+) represent areas of relative strength for the student, while those marked with a minus (−) are areas of relative weakness.

An even more detailed description of this student's performance can be provided in an individual item analysis such as that illustrated in Figure 3–8, which shows part of the class results for math concepts and estimation. Each column represents a student and each row corresponds to an item. The item numbers are given, organized by the skill they measure, and the student's response to the item is indicated if it was incorrect (a solid dot indicates the student got the item correct and an open dot indicates an omission). From the information on this chart the teacher can see that eight students got item 23 correct, one student omitted the item, seven chose alternative A, two chose alternative C, and one chose alternative D. By looking for commonly made errors such as alternative A, the teacher can diagnose particular skill areas where the students need extra work. For comparison purposes, percentages correct are given for each item for the national norm group and the school system as well as this particular class.

Figure 3–8 gives student-by-student detail, but for examining the strengths and weaknesses of the class as a whole, information such as that provided in Figure 3–9 may be more useful. This report compares the performance of this class with that of the national norm group, the building, and the school system. The results, shown item by item in terms of percent correct, are displayed both numerically and graphically. The two vertical lines indicate when the difference is less than 10% and, therefore, probably too small to be of interest. The results for this class show a broad pattern of performance above the norm group in problem solving and approaches and procedures with performance in other areas near the national norm. (Note that the complete table for the class would contain similar information about items covering other skills and knowledge areas.)

Figure 3–7 illustrates quite clearly the way content-based and norm-based frames of reference can coexist in the same test and can supplement each other in score interpretation. The report shows this student's performance, by content area, with reference to the number of items covering that content, the average performance of her class, and the average performance of the grade-equivalent national norm group. Additional reports are available that show, for example, the performance of the class on each item relative to national, system, and building norms (school performance) or that summarize the individual information in Figure 3–7 for the entire class. The publisher's catalog for this test lists more than 30 forms of reports that are available. However, it is important to keep in mind that criterion-referenced interpretations of standardized tests are based on very small numbers of items (one or two in some cases) for each content area or objective. Therefore, any conclusions based on such data must be tentative and should be confirmed using other sources of information.

THE IOWA TESTS

CLASS ITEM RESPONSE RECORD
Iowa Tests of Basic Skills® (ITBS®)

Class/Group: Ness
Building: Longfellow
System: Dalen Community

Form/Level: A/9
Test Date: 04/2003
Norms: Spring 2000
Order No.: 002-A70000028-0-002
Page: 1
Grade: 3

MATH CONCEPTS AND ESTIMATION

Number Tested = 25 Number Included = 250

Item No.	No. Items	Avg. %C Nation	Avg. %C System	Avg. %C Class
Math Concept & Est. 31		63	59	61
Number Properties	9	70	66	70
1 Compare Numbers		87	81	85
2 Order Numbers		78	76	80
3 Represent Numbers		81	74	78
9 Apply Properties		66	63	67
6 Classify Divisibility		61	53	57
15 Classify Divisibility		69	62	66
19 Perform Operations		68	66	70
23 Perform Operations		51	48	52
12 Write Expanded Form		73	68	72
Algebra	5	65	59	63
4 Operational Symbols		86	76	80
16 Solve Equations		82	75	79
20 Use Expression to Model		47	46	50
11 Explore Numerical Patterns		72	61	65
22 Explore Numerical Patterns		40	37	41
Geometry	4	69	61	65
5 Identify Geometric Figure		84	78	82
21 Identify Geometric Figure		50	41	45
18 Describe Patterns		56	47	51
7 Apply Concept of Area		84	76	80
Measurement	3	60	53	57
13 Measure Time		74	68	72
24 Estimate with Precision		51	46	50
8 Identify Approp Units		54	44	48
Probability	3	53	43	47
10 Apply Concepts		55	44	48

%C = Percent Correct

Legend: ● = Correct Response ○ = No Response ✳ = Multiple Responses Alpha = Incorrect Response

Riverside Publishing A HOUGHTON MIFFLIN COMPANY

Figure 3–8 Individual item analysis. Copyright © 2001 by The Riverside Publishing Company. All rights reserved. Reproduced from the *Iowa Test of Basic Skills®* (*ITBS®*). No part of this work may be reproduced or transmitted in any form or by any means, electronic or mechanical, including photocopying and recording or by any information storage or retrieval system without the proper written permission of The Riverside Publishing Company unless such copying is expressly permitted by federal copyright law. Address inquiries to Permissions Department, The Riverside Publishing Company, 425 Spring Lake Drive, Itasca, Illinois 60143-2079.

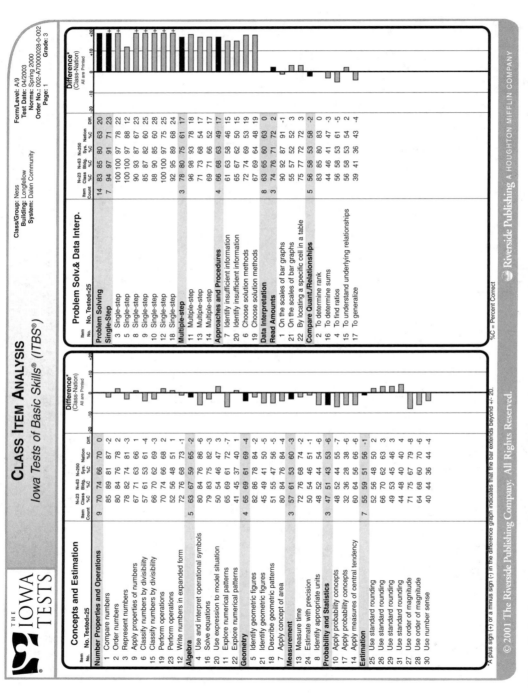

Figure 3–9 Group item analysis. Copyright © 2001 by The Riverside Publishing Company. All rights reserved. Reproduced from the *Iowa Test of Basic Skills* (*ITBS*). No part of this work may be reproduced or transmitted in any form or by any means, electronic or mechanical, including photocopying and recording or by any information storage or retrieval system without the proper written permission of The Riverside Publishing Company unless such copying is expressly permitted by federal copyright law. Address inquiries to Permissions Department, The Riverside Publishing Company, 425 Spring Lake Drive, Itasca, Illinois 60143-2079.

NORMS FOR SCHOOL AVERAGES

Up to this point, we have asked how we can interpret an individual's standing on a test. Sometimes a question arises about the relative performance of a class, a school, a school district, or even the schools of a whole state. The current emphasis on accountability in education provides ample reason for educators to be concerned about evaluating the performance of students taken as groups. When evaluating the achievement of a school in relation to other schools, it is necessary to have norms for school averages.

It should be clear that the variation from school to school in average ability or achievement will be much less than the variation from pupil to pupil. No school average comes even close to reaching the level of its ablest student, and no average drops anywhere near the performance of the least able. Thus, a single pupil at the beginning of fifth grade who gets a reading grade equivalent of 6.2 might fall at the 75th percentile, whereas a school whose *average* reading grade equivalent of beginning fifth graders is 6.2 might fall at about the 94th percentile of schools. The relationship between norms for individuals and groups is illustrated more fully in Table 3–8. The two distributions center at about the same point, but the greater variation among individuals quickly becomes apparent. On this test, an individual grade equivalent of 6.6 ranks at the 79th percentile, but a school in which the average performance is a grade equivalent of 6.6 is at the 92th percentile. The same effect is found for performances that are below average.

Table 3–8
Individual and School Average Norms for the Iowa Tests of Basic Skills–Form A, Fall Norms for Grade 5 Vocabulary Test

Grade Equivalent	Percentile Rank for Individual	Percentile Rank for School Averages
9.4	99	99
7.2	87	97
7.0	83	96
6.6	79	92
5.7	61	67
5.5	58	62
5.2	50	48
5.0	46	43
4.4	34	23
4.0	24	11
3.6	16	5
3.5	14	4
2.4	5	1
1.0	1	1

Source: Copyright © 2003 by The University of Iowa. *ITBS Norms and Score Conversions, Form A, Levels 5–14.* Reproduced by permission of the publisher, The Riverside Publishing Company.

When a school principal or an administrator in a central office is concerned with interpreting the average performance in a school, norms for school averages are the appropriate ones to use, and it is reasonable to expect the test publisher to provide them. The better test publishers will also provide item analyses and criterion-referenced reports at the level of the class, building, district, and state.

CAUTIONS IN USING NORMS

For a test that assesses standing on some trait or competence in some area of knowledge, norms provide a basis for interpreting the scores of an individual or a group. Converting the score for any test taken singly into an age or grade equivalent, percentile rank, or standard score permits an interpretation of the level at which the individual is functioning on that particular test. Bringing together the set of scores for an individual in a common unit of measure, and perhaps expressing these scores in a profile, brings out the relative level of performance of the individual in different areas.

The average performance for a class, a grade group in a school, or the children in the same grade throughout a school system may be reported similarly. We can then see the average level of performance within the group on some single function or the relative performance of the group in each of several areas. Norms provide a frame of reference within which the picture may be viewed and bring all parts of the picture into a common focus. Now, what does the picture mean, and what should we do about it?

Obviously, it is not possible, in a few pages, to provide a ready-made interpretation for each set of scores that may be obtained in a practical testing situation. However, we can lay out a few general guidelines and principles that may help to forestall some unwise interpretations of test results.

The most general point to keep in mind is that test results, presented in any normative scale, are a *description of what is,* not a *prescription of what should be* or a statement of what will be (although they may give an indication of probable future performance). The results make it possible to compare an individual or a class with other individuals and classes with respect to one or more aspects of accomplishment or personality, but they do not in any absolute sense tell us whether the individual is doing "well" or "poorly." They do not provide this information for several reasons.

Normative Scores Give Relative Rather Than Absolute Information. They tell whether an individual pupil's achievement is as high as that of other pupils or whether a class scores as high as other classes. But they do not tell us whether the basic concepts of the number system are being mastered or whether the pupils read well enough to comprehend the instructions for filling out an income tax return. Furthermore, they give us little guidance on how much improvement we might expect from *all* pupils if our educational system operated throughout at higher efficiency.

Remember that by the very nature of relative scores, there will be as many people below average as above. When "the norm" means the average of a reference group, it is a statistical necessity that about half of the group be, to a greater or lesser degree, below average. There has been an enormous amount of foolishness—both in single schools and in statewide legislation—about bringing all pupils "up to the grade norm." This might conceivably be done temporarily if we had a sudden and enormous improvement in educational effectiveness; however, the next time new norms were established for the test it would take a higher absolute level of performance to, say, read at the sixth-grade level. So we would be back again with half of the pupils falling at or below average. And if the effectiveness of the schools were to return to the former level, we would be faced with the unhappy prospect of more than half of the students testing "below grade level."

The relative nature of norms has been recognized in the criterion-referenced test movement. When a teacher or a school is concerned with appraising mastery of some *specific* instructional objective, it may be more useful to develop test exercises that appraise that objective, to agree on some standard as representing an acceptable level of mastery, and to determine which students do and which do not have mastery of that specific objective than it would be to know how the students from this school perform relative to those from other schools. In the context described, it is possible for all students to achieve mastery, but some will get there faster than others. Even in a criterion-referenced framework there will still be differences among individuals in their levels of accomplishment.

Output Must Be Evaluated Relative to Input.   Test results typically give a picture of output—of the individual or of the group as it exists at the time of testing, after a period of exposure to educational effort. But what of the input? Where did the group start?

The notion of input is a complex and rather subtle one. Our conception of input should include not only earlier status on the particular ability being measured and individual potential for learning, as far as we are able to appraise this, but also the familial circumstances and environmental supports that make it easier for some children to learn than for others. Parental aspirations for the child, parental skills at teaching and guidance of learning, parental discipline and control, linguistic patterns, and cultural resources in the home are part of the input just as truly as are the biological characteristics of the young organism. Furthermore, peer group and community attitudes are an additional real, though possibly modifiable, part of the input as far as the prospects for learning for a given child are concerned. We must recognize that the adequate appraisal of input is no simple matter, and that, correspondingly, the appraisal of output as "satisfactory" or "unsatisfactory" is something we can do with only modest confidence.

Output Must Be Evaluated Relative to Objectives.   The design, content, and norms for published standardized tests are based on their authors' perceptions of common national curricular objectives. The topics included, their relative emphasis, and the levels at which they are introduced reflect that perceived general national pattern. To the extent, then, that a given school system deviates in its objectives and curricular emphases from the national pattern, as interpreted by the test maker, its output at a given grade level can be expected to deviate from the national norms. If computational skills receive little emphasis, it is reasonable to find that computational facility will be underdeveloped. If map reading has been delayed beyond the grade level at which it is introduced into the test, it is reasonable to find that relative standing on that part of the test will suffer. Unevenness of the local profile, in relation to national norms, should always lead one to inquire whether the low spots represent failures of the local program to achieve its objectives or a planned deviation of emphasis from what is more typical of schools nationally. Low performance that results from conscious curricular decisions would be much less cause for alarm than a similar level of performance would be in an area of curricular emphasis. Which of these conditions obtained will no doubt influence what is done with the finding.

To the extent that individual states have uniform objectives for all districts within their boundaries, well-designed standardized tests measuring achievement of these objectives often are available through contract arrangements with test publishers. Several states now contract with organizations that specialize in test development to have tests constructed according to specifications provided by the state board of education. Such tests usually are intended to be used at particular points in the educational program, such as the transitions from elementary school to middle school, middle school to high school, and near the end of high school.

If these considerations and some of the caveats discussed in the next two chapters are borne in mind, the teacher, principal, superintendent, or school board will be able to interpret the reported test results with increased wisdom and restraint.

A THIRD FRAME OF REFERENCE: ITEM RESPONSE THEORY

Many of the recent developments in testing stem from what has come to be called **item response theory** (IRT), or **latent trait theory.** (We will use the terms more or less interchangeably.) The origins of this approach go back before 1910, and the basic logic of the theory was pretty well worked out by E. L. Thorndike and L. L. Thurstone in the 1920s (see R. M. Thorndike, 1999a), but the practical application of this theory has depended on the availability of computers. IRT itself has in turn shaped the ways in which computers are used in testing. Let us look at the set of interlocking developments that stem from the interactions of the theoretical models and the availability of computers to implement them. Our discussion will be in terms of cognitive abilities, but item response theory can be applied equally well to personality measures and measures of other psychological traits.

Latent trait theory assumes the existence of a relatively unified underlying trait, or characteristic, that determines an individual's ability to succeed with some particular type of cognitive task. Possible attributes might be *knowledge of word meanings, arithmetical reasoning,* or *spatial visualizing.* We can represent the trait as a linear scale (as shown in Figure 3–10) on which both tasks and people can be placed in an ordered sequence. The tasks in this example are words to be defined, and the trait is knowledge of word meanings. A given test may contain items measuring several such dimensions, but each item should be a relatively pure measure of only one trait.

For the *tasks,* the scale can be thought of as a scale of difficulty (we could also think of this as the ability requirement of the item), so the words in the illustration go from very easy on the left to quite difficult on the right. *The difficulty of an item is defined as the ability level at which half of the examinees will get the item correct.* For any single item, the point on the scale where the probability of a correct response is 50% is called b. Thus, the five words to be defined have five different b-values.

For *people,* the scale can be thought of as a scale of ability. A person's ability level is defined by the tasks that that person *can just about do*—that is, the difficulty level at which the examinee would get half of the items correct. Thus, Joe can most likely define *borrow* because his ability

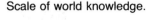

Scale of world knowledge.

Figure 3–10
Scale of word knowledge.

exceeds the difficulty of the item, but he is unlikely to be able to define *incision* because its diffi-culty exceeds his ability. The likelihood that Billy can correctly define *borrow* is relatively low. It is the joint ordering of the people and the tasks which defines the scale. The term used to refer to a person's ability level is the Greek letter theta (θ). Billy has a relatively low value of θ, Joe and Mr. Jones have intermediate values, and Dr. Thompson's θ-value is quite high.

It is important to note that in this model, a person's ability level is subject to change over time. That is, if Billy is 6 years old, we can expect that his position on the scale of ability, his θ, will change as he matures. Conversely, we would expect the *b*-values, the relative difficulty of the words in a large and representative sample from the population, to remain nearly constant for long periods of time. The stability of the difficulty scale is what gives meaning to the ability scale.

The ability/difficulty scale is an arbitrary one, just as the Fahrenheit scale of temperature is. We could use a scale with different-sized units (for example, Celsius) or a different zero point (for example, Celsius or Kelvin). But, for a given scale, the units are presumably equal throughout the scale and the *relative* position of a person or task does not depend either on the size of the units or on the placement of the zero point. As an example of our temperature-scale analogy, consider that a summer day may be warmer than a winter day, and this fact does not depend on whether the summer temperature is expressed as 20 °C or 68 °F and the winter temperature is 0 °C or 32 °F. The relative positions of the two days are the same in either scale, and a spring day of 10 °C or 50 °F would be halfway between them on the scale. Likewise, a heat greater than 100 °C (212 °F) has the ability to cause water to boil (at standard atmospheric pressure) and a heat below this point does not.

The relationship between ability level and passing an item of a given difficulty is not an all-or-none matter but, instead, is a question of probability. The form of the relationship between ability and the probability of passing an item is shown in Figure 3–11. The graph in this figure is called the **item characteristic curve,** or **item trace line,** and there is one such curve for every item. The item characteristic curve shows that for an item of a given difficulty, the proba-bility that a person will pass the item increases as their ability level goes up. Thus, if we include

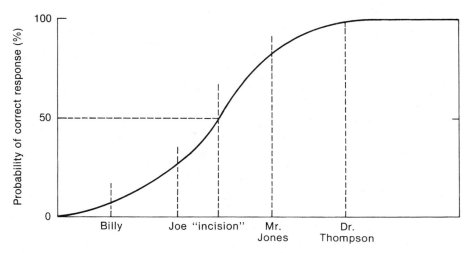

Figure 3–11
Item characteristic curve for the meaning of the word *incision*.

the word *incision* on a test given to a group of people at Joe's level of ability, about 25% would be able to define the word, while among those at Mr. Jones' level, about 85% would be able to provide a correct definition. Turning things around, Joe could define about 25% of the words whose difficulty was the same as *incision's,* while Mr. Jones could provide correct definitions for about 85% of such words.

As we see from Figure 3–11, the probability of a person's passing an item as a function of ability level is expressed by a curve that is quite flat at the two extremes but rises steeply around the level that matches the difficulty of the item. The test item differentiates most effectively between those whose abilities are somewhat above and those whose abilities are somewhat below the difficulty level of the task but provides very little differentiation among those whose abilities are very high or very low. Dr. Thompson and other people at her ability level would pass almost all the items at the difficulty level represented by *incision,* and we would know that she had high verbal ability, but we would not know *how* high. We would need words in the difficulty range from *prologue* to *tenet* (see Figure 3–10) in order to locate Dr. Thompson's ability with any precision, because these words are sufficiently difficult that she would not get all of them correct.

The trace line of an item is a characteristic of the item that does not depend on the people taking the test, but our ability to reveal the entire curve depends on applying the item to a sufficiently heterogeneous group that people over the full range of ability are represented. If we gave items like *incision* only to people like Joe and Mr. Jones, we could only see that part of the curve that falls between them. Because this range covers the difficulty level of the item (the point on the ability dimension where 50% of the examinees would get it correct), the result would not be too serious, but if only people like Billy or like Dr. Thompson were included, we would be able to tell very little about the item.

Each item has its own characteristic curve that is defined by its *difficulty level* (the 50% point, which is called its *b* parameter) and its *discrimination*. **Discrimination** is the ability of the item to separate those of higher ability from those of lower ability. A widely used index of item discrimination is the correlation between score on the single item and score on the entire set of items that measure the dimension. The ability of an item to allow for discrimination of different levels of ability is a function of the rate at which the probability of getting the item correct changes with ability. Graphically, this rate of change can be seen as the *slope of the item characteristic curve.* The label given to the slope of the curve is *a. The a parameter is the slope of the curve at the 50% point.* Figure 3–12 shows curves representing two items that differ in difficulty but are equal in discrimination. The shapes of the two curves are the same, but their *b* parameters, the ability levels required to have a 50% chance of getting the item correct, are different.

Figure 3–13 shows two items that are of the same difficulty but differ in discrimination. The *a* parameter, or rate of change in the probability of getting the item correct, is much steeper for Item 1 than for Item 2. There is a higher correlation between item score and test score. More discriminating items are more sensitive to differences in the ability levels of examinees. To illustrate this point, look at the two people who are plotted on the ability continuum. On Item 1, Joshua has a probability of about .25 of getting the item correct and Jacob has a probability of about .75 of correctly answering the item. However, on Item 2 the probabilities are much closer together. Because the slope of the item characteristic curve, and hence the correlation of the item with ability level, is lower, the difference in probability of a correct response is only about 20% instead of 50%. The item does not differentiate between the two examinees as well. (However, Item 2 does provide some information over a wider range of ability levels.)

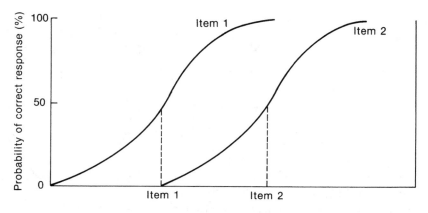

Two items of equal discrimination that differ in difficulty

Figure 3–12
Item characteristic curves for items that differ in difficulty.

For items where examinees choose their answers from a set of given alternatives (true–false, multiple choice, and similar item forms called *select-response items*), the curve has a third feature, the probability of getting the item correct by chance, or guessing. This effect is seen when the curve flattens out at some probability greater than zero. The probability value at which the curve flattens out is called the *c* parameter or the guessing parameter. Figure 3–14 provides an example of such a curve. This is different from the situation for Item 2 in Figure 3–13. In the latter case, although the graph does not go down far enough for the trace line to reach zero, the curve is still descending. If people of extremely low ability had been included in the sample, we should find an ability level where examinees have zero chance of getting the item correct. This occurs

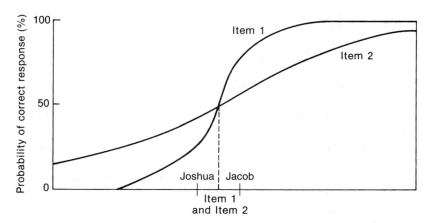

Two items of equal difficulty that differ in discrimination

Figure 3–13
Item characteristic curves for two items of equal difficulty that differ in discrimination.

Figure 3–14
Effect of guessing on the item characteristic curve.

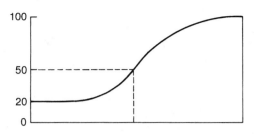

when examinees must produce their own answers for the items, such as writing definitions of words rather than selecting the definition from a list of alternatives. Item trace lines for items where the examinees produce their own responses, such as short answer and definition items, can always reach zero; those for select-response items never can.

Practical measurement using the IRT framework requires that we be able to give each person the items most appropriate for people at their ability level. It is this feature for which a computer is essential, and the technology for selecting which items to administer is known as **computer adaptive testing** or CAT. The rapid development and widespread availability of computers has combined with item response theory to lead to the development of CAT. By adaptive testing, we mean the rapid adjustment of the difficulty level of the test tasks to the ability level of the person being tested. As we indicated earlier, tasks that are much too difficult or much too easy give little new information about the ability level of an examinee. For example, our knowing that an examinee who is an applicant for college admission could define the word *dig* would tell us essentially nothing about whether the applicant was a promising candidate. *Dig* is a word that *any* high school senior could be expected to know. We would also learn relatively little if the examinee failed on *fracedinous*. Probably not one high school senior in 100,000 would know the meaning of the word. (*Webster's Unabridged Dictionary* defines it as "producing heat by putrefaction [obsolete].") We gain useful information by testing with tasks on which we *do not* know in advance whether the examinee will succeed.

Ideally, in adaptive testing, we start at a difficulty level at which we are *most uncertain* whether the examinee can pass the item. This point would usually be at an item of about 50% difficulty for that age or grade group, because in the absence of any special information, this is our best guess of the person's ability level. Each correct response raises our estimate of the person's ability level somewhat and makes it appropriate to present next a somewhat more difficult item. As long as the examinee continues to get items correct, we continue to raise our estimate of the ability level and to raise the difficulty level of the next item presented. If our initial guess was accurate, and thus our starting level was close to the examinee's ability level, the examinee should quickly get an item incorrect, and we would lower our estimate slightly and drop back to a slightly easier item. With a sequence of passes and failures, we would soon zero in with items near the examinee's ability level, and the record of passes and failures would give a good final estimate of this ability.

Any given level of precision in the estimate can be achieved by well-designed adaptive testing, using perhaps half as many test items as would be required in a conventional test designed for use with a complete age or grade group. This is because in conventional tests, in order to include items that are appropriate for people of differing abilities, it is necessary to include items that are too easy or too hard for a given examinee. In conventional tests, only a relatively small proportion of the items are at the correct level for a particular person. We will discuss how precise our estimates are in Chapter 4.

A truly effective procedure for adaptive testing must entail searching the pool of items and finding one item that is of most appropriate difficulty, given our current estimate of the examinee's ability level. This searching is something that only a computer can do efficiently and rapidly enough for effective testing. The complete pool of items can be stored on a disk, coded by difficulty level and, if need be, by discrimination level and content category. The computer can be programmed to adjust its estimate of the examinee's ability level by an appropriate amount after each pass or failure and to seek out the yet unused item that best matches that new estimate. An ongoing record is maintained of the examinee's estimated ability level and of the precision of that estimate. The computer can be programmed to terminate testing either after a specified number of items has been administered or when a specified precision of estimate has been reached. This approach is almost universally used for testing programs that are administered by computer, such as the Scholastic Assessment Test (SAT) and Graduate Record Exams. See Wainer (1990) for a discussion of how to implement computer adaptive testing.

One feature of adaptive testing is that within any given group, no two individuals are likely to take exactly the same test, because each unique pattern of right and wrong answers produces a different test. A person with very consistent performance would take a short test because the process would focus in on the ability level quite quickly. On the other hand, a person showing variable performance, that is, passing some quite hard items while missing some relatively easy ones, would require a much longer test in order to reach the same level of precision in the ability estimate.

One of the interesting potential applications of item response theory and adaptive testing is the linking of grading procedures between classes or sections of a course. One of the motivating forces that led to the creation of standardized tests such as the SAT was the desire for comparable information for students from different schools. If some items that had been calibrated by IRT methods were included in locally developed tests in different schools or in different sections of a course where, for example, ability grouping had been used, the tests could be equated and the relative performance of pupils in different classes assessed on a common scale. The different levels of the Cognitive Abilities Test use item response theory to achieve a common scale, called a *universal scale score,* for the different levels of the test. The American College Testing Program also uses IRT to create a common scale for several different tests that have no items in common but have been given to a common group of examinees.

If we have determined the difficulty values on a common scale for a sufficient pool of items, we can use items from that pool to do a number of useful and interesting things. We outline some of them here.

1. *Estimating ability level from any set of items.* If the difficulty scale values are available for a large pool of items measuring a common trait, an unbiased estimate (unbiased in a statistical sense, not in the social policy sense discussed in Chapter 5) of a person's ability level on that trait can be obtained from *any* set of items drawn from that pool. The precision of the estimate will depend on the number of items, increasing in precision as the number of items increases. It will also depend on how closely the difficulty of the items matches the ability level of the person, with accuracy increasing with the closeness of the match. But there will be no systematic error in the estimate in any case, assuming the probability of a correct response is not zero (or chance level for select-response items) or 1.0. In these two cases, the item gives no information about the person's ability.

2. *Preparing equivalent test forms.* By drawing from the pool sets of items having the same average difficulty value, the same spread of difficulty values, and the same average discrimination, we can prepare test forms that are equivalent in the sense that any given raw score signifies the

same level of examinee ability, irrespective of the test form on which it is based. We could use the test forms to measure gains from instruction, giving one form before some instructional period, and another after. Or, in situations in which test security or examinee copying is likely to be a problem, different forms could be given to individuals in alternating seats. If, for some reason, one test were invalidated for a person, an alternate, equivalent form could be administered.

3. *Matrix sampling in testing.* At times, a researcher may wish to cover very completely some domain of content and may not be interested in making decisions about specific individuals but, instead, in assessing the performance level of a class, a school, or a school system. It is then not necessary that every test item be administered to every person. Each person can be given a fraction of the items, as long as each item has been given to some of the people. The investigator can then think of the class or school or school system as a composite "person." Upon determining the proportion of items passed at known difficulty scale values, the researcher can estimate an ability level for the group, either with respect to the complete domain or with respect to specific limited segments of that domain. This approach makes it possible to hold testing time within reasonable limits and yet to cover completely the domain of content in which the investigator is interested.

SUMMARY

A raw score, taken by itself, rarely has meaning. A score may be given meaning by a consideration of the domain of instructional content that the test items represent. The performance of individuals or groups can then be assessed either in terms of the percentage of the domain they have mastered or relative to a standard of performance set before the test is administered. These methods of giving meaning to a raw score are called criterion-referenced interpretations. They are appropriate for tests that focus on one or a small number of carefully defined objectives and for which standards of performance can be either empirically or logically derived.

Because many tests are designed to appraise several objectives, and because meaningful absolute standards of performance are not available for most tests, a raw score is generally given meaning by comparison with some reference group or groups. This method of giving a raw score meaning is called norm-referenced interpretation. The comparison may be with

1. A series of grade groups (grade norms)
2. A series of age groups (age norms)
3. A single group, in which performance is indicated by what percentage of that group the score surpassed (percentile norms)
4. A single group, in which performance is indicated by the number of standard deviations the score is

above or below the group mean (standard score norms). (Norms of this type may be subjected to a linear conversion to eliminate decimal points and negative values or to nonlinear transformations to normalize the score distribution.)

Each alternative has certain advantages and certain limitations.

Quotients such as the IQ were developed to get a single index to express the degree to which individuals deviated from their age group. Because of their various limitations, quotients have been replaced by standard scores, and the term *IQ* is no longer technically appropriate.

If the norms available for a number of different tests are of the same kind and are based on comparable groups, all the tests can be expressed in comparable terms. The results can then be shown pictorially in the form of a profile. Profiles emphasize score differences within the individual. When profiles are used, we must take care not to overinterpret their minor ups and downs.

Norms represent a descriptive framework for interpreting the score of an individual, a class group, or some larger aggregation. However, before a judgment can be made on whether an individual or group is doing well or poorly, allowance must be made for ability level, cultural background, and curricular emphases. The norm is merely an average and not a straitjacket into which everyone can be forced to fit. It describes the person's current performance, relative to some specified comparison group.

An alternative to traditional methods of giving meaning to test scores is provided by item response theory and computer adaptive testing. IRT determines the difficulty level of each item and places the items on a continuum of difficulty. Examinees are placed on the same continuum in terms of their ability level. CAT is then used to select the most appropriate next item for an examinee, based on his or her pattern of past successes and failures.

QUESTIONS AND EXERCISES

1. Why does the frame of reference used to interpret a test score make a difference?

2. Can the same test be interpreted in both a criterion-referenced and a norm-referenced manner? If so, how would the two interpretations differ?

3. A pupil in the sixth grade received a raw score of 25 on the Level 12 Reading Test (Form J) of the Iowa Tests of Basic Skills. What additional information would be needed to interpret this score?

4. Why do standardized tests designed for use with high school students almost never use age or grade norms?

5. What limitations would national norms have for use by a county school system in rural West Virginia? What might the local school system do about the limitations?

6. What assumptions lie behind developing and using age norms? Grade norms? Normalized standard scores?

7. In Figure 3–3, why are the standard scores evenly spaced, while the percentile scores are unevenly spaced?

8. State A gives a battery of achievement tests each May in the 4th, 8th, and 11th grades. The median grade level in each subject in each district in the state is reported to the state board of education. Should these results be reported? If so, what else should be included in the report? In what ways might the board use the results to promote better education? What uses should the board avoid?

9. Ms. P takes pride in the fact that each year she has gotten at least 85% of her fourth-grade class "up to the norm" in each subject. How desirable is this as an educational objective? What limitations or dangers do you see in it?

10. School F has a policy of assigning transfer students to a grade on the basis of their average grade equivalent on an achievement battery. Thus, a boy with an average grade equivalent of 5.3 would be assigned to the fifth grade, no matter what his age or his grade in his previous school. What are the values and limitations of such a practice?

11. The superintendent of schools in Riverview, Iowa, noted that Springdale Elementary School fell consistently about a half grade below national norms on an achievement battery. He was distressed because this performance was the lowest of any school in the city. How justified is his dissatisfaction? Do you need other information to answer this question? If so, what?

12. The board of education in East Centerville noted that the fourth and fifth grades in their community fell substantially below national norms in mathematics, although they scored at or above average in all other subjects. They propose to study this situation further. What additional information do they need?

13. The third-grade teachers in Bigcity school district have prepared a 30-item test to assess mastery of the basic multiplication facts. What score should they accept as demonstrating

"mastery" of these facts? How should such a score be determined?

14. What are the advantages of reporting test performance in terms of stanines? In terms of normal curve equivalents? What problems arise from using each of these forms of normative report?

15. Obtain the manual for some test, and study the information given about norms.
    a. How adequate is the norming population? Is sufficient information given for you to make a judgment?
    b. Calculate the chance score (i.e., the score to be expected from blind guessing) for the test, and note its grade equivalent. What limitations does this suggest for using the test?
    c. What limitations are there on the usefulness of the test at the upper end of its range?
    d. How many raw score points correspond to 1 full year on the grade-equivalent scale? Is this number of points of score the same throughout the range of the test?

16. Have you ever taken a computer adaptive test? If you have, how did you find the experience different from that of taking an ordinary paper-and-pencil test? If you have not taken a test using CAT, can you think of ways this testing format might affect your performance?

SUGGESTED READINGS

Angoff, W. H. (1971). Scales, norms, and equivalent scores. In R. L. Thorndike (Ed.), *Educational measurement* (2nd ed., pp. 508–600). Washington, DC: American Council on Education.

Flynn, J. R. (1998). WAIS-III and WISC-III gains in the United States from 1972 to 1995: How to compensate for obsolete norms. *Perceptual & Motor Skills, 86,* 1231–1239.

Holland, P. W., & Rubin, D. B. (Eds.). (1982). *Test equating.* New York: Academic Press.

Hoover, H. D. (1984). The most appropriate scores for measuring educational development in the elementary schools: GE's. *Educational Measurement: Issues and Practices, 3,* 8–14.

Jaeger, R. M. (1989). Certification of student competence. In R. L. Linn (Ed.), *Educational measurement* (3rd ed., pp. 485–514). New York: Macmillan.

Kolen, M. J. (1988). Defining score scales in relation to measurement error. *Journal of Educational Measurement, 25,* 97–110.

Livingston, S. A., & Zieky, M. J. (1982). *Passing scores: A manual for setting standards of performance on educational and occupational tests.* Princeton, NJ: Educational Testing Service.

Michell, J. (1986). Measurement scales and statistics: A clash of paradigms. *Psychological Bulletin, 3,* 398–407.

Nitko, A. J. (1984). Defining "criterion-referenced test." In R. A. Berk (Ed.), *A guide to criterion-referenced test construction* (pp. 8–28). Baltimore: Johns Hopkins University Press.

Petersen, N. S., Kolen, M. J., & Hoover, H. D. (1989). Scaling, norming, and equating. In R. L. Linn (Ed.), *Educational measurement* (3rd ed., pp. 221–262). New York: Macmillan.

Shepard, L. A. (1984). Setting performance standards. In R. A. Berk (Ed.), *A guide to criterion-referenced test construction* (pp. 169–198). Baltimore: Johns Hopkins University Press.

Thorndike, R. L. (1982). *Applied psychometrics.* Boston: Houghton Mifflin.

Thorndike, R. M. (1999). IRT and intelligence testing: Past, present, and future. In S. E. Embretson and S. L. Hershberger (Eds.), *The new rules of measurement: What every psychologist and educator should know* (pp. 17–35). Mahwah, NJ: Erlbaum.

Wainer, H. (1990). *Computer adaptive testing: A primer.* Mahwah, NJ: Erlbaum.

Yen, W. M. (1986). The choice of scale for educational measurement: An IRT perspective. *Journal of Educational Measurement, 23,* 299–325.

CHAPTER 4

Qualities Desired in Any Measurement Procedure: Reliability

Introduction
Reliability as Consistency
    Sources of Inconsistency
Two Ways to Express Reliability
    Standard Error of Measurement
    Reliability Coefficient
Ways to Assess Reliability
    Retesting with the Same Test
    Testing with Parallel Forms
    Single-Administration Methods
    Comparison of Methods
Interpretation of Reliability Data
    Standard Error of Measurement
    Reliability Coefficient

Factors Affecting Reliability
    Variability of the Group
    Level of the Group on the Trait
    Length of the Test
    Operations Used for Estimating Reliability
    Practical versus Theoretical Reliability
Minimum Level of Reliability
Reliability of Difference Scores
Effects of Unreliability on Correlation Between Variables
Reliability of Criterion-Referenced Tests
Reliability of Computer Adaptive Tests
Summary
Questions and Exercises
Suggested Readings

INTRODUCTION

Whenever we would like to use a test or other measurement procedure to provide information to help in some decision, we face the problem of which test or procedure to use or whether there is any instrument that will really help in the decision. There are usually several tests that have been designed to help or that seem at least to have the possibility of helping with the decision. We would like to know whether any of the available tests will indeed provide useful information. And if any will, which is the best one to use? (For simplicity, we use the term *test* throughout this chapter and the next, but the issues we present apply to all forms of measurement and all sources of information. Where special concerns arise, they will be addressed in the chapter dealing with that type of assessment procedure.)

Many specific factors enter into the evaluation of a test, but we will consider them under two main headings: **reliability** and **validity.** *Reliability refers to the accuracy or precision of a measurement*

109

procedure. Indices of reliability give an indication of the extent to which the scores produced by a particular measurement procedure are consistent and reproducible. *Validity has to do with the degree to which test scores provide information that is relevant to the inferences that are to be made from them.* Thus, a judgment of validity is always in relation to a specific decision or use, and evidence that test scores are appropriate for one purpose does not necessarily mean that the scores are appropriate for another. A third consideration, practicality, is concerned with a wide range of factors of economy, convenience, and interpretability that determine whether a test is realistically employable for our purpose. Issues of practicality are presented in Chapter 6.

Reliability and validity are both required of any test that we would choose, regardless of how practical it is to use. Validity of test scores for their intended use is the absolutely essential quality for a test to have, but in a sense, reliability is a necessary precondition for validity. Test scores must be at least moderately reliable before they can have any validity, but a reliable test may be devoid of validity for the application we have in mind. Although the true bottom line in selecting a test is the test's validity for our proposed use, we discuss reliability first as a necessary condition for validity to exist. Validity is discussed in Chapter 5.

RELIABILITY AS CONSISTENCY

When we ask about a test's reliability, we are asking not what the test measures but, instead, how accurately it measures whatever it does measure. What is the precision of the resulting score? How consistently will the score be reproduced if we measure the individual again?

Some degree of inconsistency is present in all measurement procedures. Consider the experience of your author who bought a new, digital electronic bathroom scale because he did not trust the old spring-operated one he had been using for 20 years. When I took the new scale home and tried it out, the first reading seemed reasonable. Then, just to show myself that the new scale was an improvement, I tried it again. The reading was 7 lbs lower! Not believing that a diet could work that fast, I took a third reading and then a fourth. After 10 minutes of testing the scale, I decided to return it because the readings had spread over a range of 15 lbs.

This little experience illustrates the central issue in reliability. My actual weight was, for all practical purposes, constant throughout the series of measurements, but my scores differed from one testing to the next. If we call my real, constant weight my **true score** (T), then each **observed score** or measurement (X) includes this true score plus some **error of measurement** (e). That is,

$$X = T + e \qquad (4.1)$$

Any difference between an observed score and the true score is an error of measurement. Therefore,

$$e = X - T$$

On the bathroom scale, and indeed in all measurements, many errors of measurement appear to be random; sometimes they are positive, making the score too high, and sometimes they are negative, making the score too low. Most of them are fairly small, but some can be quite large. Their distribution often looks like the normal distribution that was discussed in Chapter 2.

There are other errors of measurement that remain constant from one measurement to another. The scale could have read 10 lbs too high on every repetition. Errors of this kind cannot be detected just by repeating the measurement; the instrument must be compared to another one in which the error is not present. However, constant errors do not lead to inconsistency, so they do not affect the reliability of the measuring instrument.

The bathroom scale offers a unique opportunity to observe random errors of measurement in action, because we can make repeated independent measurements in a situation where we know the true score is constant. Therefore, all variations in scale readings are due to errors of measurement. However, that situation is far removed from the environment in which educational or psychological measurements are made. Measurements of human behavior are particularly susceptible to inconsistency but seldom can be repeated to reveal the inconsistency directly.

Let us consider a second example that is also somewhat artificial but more nearly approximates a testing context. Suppose we were to test all the girls in a class one day and again the next day to see how far each could throw a football. We might mark a starting line on the field, give each girl one of the old footballs that the physical education department has for team practice, send an assistant out to mark where the ball hit, and tell each girl to throw the ball as far as she could. With a steel tape, we would measure the distance from the starting line to where the assistant marked the fall of the ball. On each day, we would have each girl make one throw, with each attempt giving us one measurement of that girl's ability to throw a football.

In comparing the two scores for an individual, we would find that they are seldom exactly the same. In these tests, most of the differences will be fairly small, but some will be moderately large. The differences show that one throw is not perfectly reliable as a measure of a person's throwing ability. Results are, to some degree, inconsistent from one day's throw to the next.

Sources of Inconsistency

We can identify three classes of reasons for inconsistency between a throw one day and a throw the next day, or two repetitions of any other form of measurement.

1. *The person may actually have changed from one testing to the next.* On one day, a girl may have been more rested than she was on the other. On one day, she could have been motivated to try harder on the task, or she could even have gotten some special coaching from a parent between the two testings. If the interval between the two tests happened to be months rather than days, there could have been real physical growth, differing from girl to girl, that affected the two testings. This example has involved changes affecting physical performance, but it is easy to think of similar categories of change that would apply to a test of mental ability or to a self-report inventory dealing with mood or with interests.

2. *The task could have been different for the two measurements.* For example, the ball Betty used one day could have been tightly inflated, whereas the one she had on the next day could have been a squashy one that permitted a somewhat different grip. Or, one day the examiner may have permitted the girls to take a run up to the release line, whereas on the second day the examiner may have allowed only one or two steps. Environmental factors such as the presence of a head wind could also have been present on one day and not on another. Any of these variations could have helped some girls more than others. In paper-and-pencil tests we often use one form of the test on one occasion and a second, parallel form on the second occasion. The specific items are different, and some pupils may happen to be better able to handle one sample of tasks, while others are better at the other sample.

3. *The limited sample of behavior could have resulted in an unstable and undependable score.* Even if we had each girl make two throws with the same ball and the same instructions, with only a

5-minute rest in between, the two distances would rarely come out the same. A single throw, like a single test item, is a meager sample of behavior. That sample and the evaluation of it are subject to all sorts of chance influences. Maybe Betty's finger slipped. Maybe she got mixed up in the coordination of her legs and her arm. Or maybe the ball was held a little too far forward or a little too far back, the scorer was looking the other way when the ball landed, or there was a gust of wind just as Betty threw. Maybe any of a hundred things occurred—some favorable, some unfavorable. The effect of such unknown random influences on an observed performance is that a small sample of behavior does not provide a stable and dependable characterization of an individual— whether the sample is of footballs thrown for distance or of sentences read for understanding. The average of 100 throws of the football would provide a much more stable index of this ability than would the result of a single throw, and performance on 100 reading comprehension items would likewise provide a more stable assessment of that ability than a single item.

TWO WAYS TO EXPRESS RELIABILITY

Standard Error of Measurement

There are two ways to express the reliability, or precision, of a set of measurements or, from the reverse point of view, the error of measurement within the set. One approach directly addresses the amount of variation to be expected within a set of repeated measurements of a single individual. If we were to take 200 readings of my weight on the bathroom scale or if it were possible to have Betty throw the football 200 times (assuming for the present that this could be done without introducing effects of practice or fatigue), we could produce a frequency distribution of my weights or of her distances thrown. The frequency distribution has an average value that we can think of as my "true" weight or the "true" distance that Betty can throw a football. The distribution also has a standard deviation describing the spread, or scatter, of the measurements around their mean. Because the scatter results from errors of measurement, we will call this *standard deviation of the variations in our measurements* the **standard error of measurement.** It is the standard deviation of the distribution of "errors" of measuring football-throwing ability or my weight. Looking back at Eq. (4.1), we can see that if T is constant, then any variation from one measurement to the next must be due to errors in the measures, and the distribution of scores is a distribution of errors around the true score.

With psychological or educational data, we usually cannot make a whole series of measurements on each individual because of practice and fatigue effects, as well as time constraints: Time does not permit giving 200 reading tests or 200 interest inventories. Often, we are fortunate if we can get two scores for each individual. But, if we have a pair of measurements for each individual, we can make an estimate (see *Interpretation of Reliability Data* section later in this chapter) of what the scattering of scores would have been for the average person if we had made the measurements again and again.

Reliability Coefficient

Reliable measurement also implies that each individual stays in about the same place in the group on each testing. The girl who scores highest on the football throwing test the first time should also be one of the highest the next time, and each person in the group should stay in *about* the same relative position on successive occasions. The correlation coefficient provides a statistical index of the extent to which two measurements tend to agree or to place each person in the same relative position, high with high and low with low. If the two things we are correlating happen to be two applications of the same measure, the resulting correlation provides an indicator of reliability. We can designate it a **reliability coefficient.** We have already seen the characteristics of the correlation coefficient in Chapter 2. But the relationship now before us is that of two measurements with the same or an equivalent measuring instrument. The more nearly individuals are ranked in the same order the second time as the first, the higher the correlation and the more reliable the test.

The reliability coefficient and the standard error of measurement are intimately related. Consider the components of an observed score as we described them in Eq. (4.1). Observed score is a combination of true score and error of measurement. If we have given a test to a group of people, the variance of their observed scores, SD_X^2, shows how much spread there is in the group. But each observed score is a combination of true score and error. Therefore, assuming that the members of our group do not all have the same true score, and that the errors are independent and random, it can be shown that the variance in observed scores is made up of variance in true scores (true differences between people) plus the variance in the errors of measurement. That is,

$$SD_X^2 = SD_T^2 + SD_e^2 \qquad (4.2)$$

where SD_X^2 is the variance of observed test scores,

SD_T^2 is the variance of true scores, and

SD_e^2 is the variance of the errors of measurement.

Note that SD_e^2 is the square of the standard error of measurement. It can also be shown (see Lord & Novick, 1968, or Feldt & Brennan, 1989) that the correlation between two measures of the same trait, the reliability coefficient, is

$$r_{tt} = \frac{SD_T^2}{SD_X^2} \qquad (4.3)$$

That is, *the reliability coefficient is equal to the proportion of variance in the observed scores that is due to true differences between people.*

We can also show that the standard error of measurement is a function of the standard deviation of observed scores and the reliability coefficient:

$$SD_e = SD_X \sqrt{(1 - r_{tt})} \qquad (4.4)$$

From Eq. (4.4) it is clear that within a group of given variability, as the reliability coefficient goes up, the standard error of measurement goes down. Individual differences in scores on a highly reliable test are primarily composed of true differences between the people being measured.

WAYS TO ASSESS RELIABILITY

A measure is reliable, then, to the extent that an individual's score or position in a group remains nearly the same on repeated measurements—that is, nearly the same, as represented by a low standard error of measurement (low variation in the person's performance over repeated measurements) or by a high reliability coefficient (consistent ranking of individuals within the group from one measurement to another). But what exact type of data do we need to get an appropriate estimate of this degree of stability or precision of measurement? We will consider three distinct possibilities, noting their similarities and differences and evaluating the advantages and disadvantages of each:

1. Repeating the same test or measure (test-retest)
2. Administering a second "equivalent" form of the test (also called parallel or alternate test forms)
3. Subdividing the test into two or more equivalent fractions from a single administration (single-administration methods).

Retesting with the Same Test

If we wish to find out how reliably we can evaluate an individual's football throw, we can test the person twice. It may be a reasonable precaution to have the two measures taken independently by two testers. We do not want the examiner's recollection of the first score to affect perception of the second. It may be desirable to have the two testings done on different days, depending on what we are interested in. If we want to know how accurately a single throw (or possibly a single set of throws) characterizes a person *at a specific point in time,* the two measurements should be carried out one immediately after the other. Then, we know that the *person* has stayed the same and that the only source of variation or "error" is in the measuring operation. If we want to know how precisely a given measurement characterizes a person from day to day—how closely we can predict an individual's score next week from what he or she does today—it would be appropriate to measure the person on two separate occasions. In this second case, we are interested in *variation of the individual from time to time,* as well as *variation due to the operation of measurement.* Because there are now two possible sources of variation, we would expect this second procedure to show larger errors of measurement.

Sometimes we are interested in variation in the individual from day to day; sometimes we are not. We may ask "How accurately does our measurement characterize Sam at this moment?" Or we may ask "How accurately does our measurement of Sam describe him as he will be tomorrow, or next week, or next month?" Each is a sensible question. But the questions are not the same. The data we must collect to answer one are different from the data we need to answer the other.

Repetition of the measurement is a straightforward and satisfactory operation for studying the reliability of measurement of such a physical characteristic as the weight or height of a person. The reading of a bathroom scale on one occasion is not affected by the reading it gave on a previous weighing. Use of simple repetition of the measurement also seems satisfactory and applicable with some simple aspects of behavior, such as speed of reaction or the type of motor skill exemplified by the football throw. Suppose, however, that we are interested in the reliability of a measure of reading comprehension. Let us assume that the test is made up of six reading passages with five questions on each. We administer the test once and then immediately administer it again. What happens? Certainly the people taking the test are not going to have to reread all of the material that they have just read. They may do so in part, but to a considerable extent, their answers the second time will involve merely remembering what answers they had chosen the first time and marking them again. Those who had not been able to finish the first time will now be able to work ahead and spend most of their time on new material. These same effects hold true to some degree even over longer periods of time. Clearly, a test like this one given a second time does not present the same task that it did the first time because the examinees are now familiar with the test items.

A second consideration enters into the repetition of a test such as a reading comprehension test. Suppose that one of the six passages in the test was about baseball and that a particular girl was an expert on baseball. The passage would then be especially easy for her, and she would, in effect, get a bonus of several points. This portion of the test would overestimate her general level of reading ability. But note that it would do so consistently on both testings if the material remained the same. The error of measurement for this individual would be a **constant error** in the two testings. Because the error would affect both her scores in the same way, it would make the test look reliable rather than unreliable.

In an area of ability such as reading, we must recognize the possibility that an individual does not perform uniformly well throughout the whole area. Specific interests, experiences, and backgrounds give individuals different strengths and weaknesses. A particular test is *one sample* from the whole domain of behavior. How well an individual does on the test, relative to other people, is likely to depend to some degree on the particular sample of tasks chosen to represent the particular domain of ability or personality we are trying to appraise. If the sample remains the same for both measurements, the person's behavior will stay more nearly the same than if the sample of tasks is varied between measurements.

So far we have identified three main sources of performance variation that will tend to reduce the consistency, or stability, of a particular score as a description of an individual:

1. Variation from trial to trial in the individual's response to the task at a particular moment
2. Variation in the individual from one time to another
3. Variation arising out of the particular sample of tasks chosen to represent a domain of behavior.

Retesting the individual with an identical test can reflect the first two sources of "error," but this procedure cannot evaluate the effects of the third type. In addition, memory or practice effects such as those referred to above may come into play.

Testing with Parallel Forms

Concern about variation resulting from the particular sample of tasks chosen to represent a domain of behavior leads us to another set of procedures for evaluating reliability. If the sampling of items may be a significant source of "error" and if, as is usually the case, we want to know with what accuracy we can generalize from the specific score based on one sample of tasks to the broader domain that the sample is supposed to represent, we must develop some procedures that take into account the variation resulting from the sample of tasks. We may do this by correlating scores from two alternate, parallel or equivalent forms of a test.

Alternate forms of a test should be thought of as forms built according to the same specifications but composed of separate samples from the defined behavior domain. Thus, two parallel reading tests should contain reading passages and questions of the same difficulty. The same sorts of questions should be asked; for example, there should be a balance of specific-fact and general-idea questions. The same types of passages should be represented, such as expository, argumentative, and aesthetic. But the specific passage topics and questions should be different.

If we have two forms of a test, we may give each examinee first one form and then the other. The tests may follow each other immediately if we are not interested in stability over time, or they may be separated by an interval if we are interested in stability. The correlation between the two forms will provide an appropriate reliability coefficient. If a time interval has been allowed between the testings, all three sources of variation will have a chance to get in their effects—variation arising from the measurement itself, variation in the individual over time, and variation resulting from the sample of tasks.

To ask that a test yield consistent results under the conditions of parallel tests separated by a time interval is the most rigorous standard we can set for it, because all three sources of variation can affect the scores. And, if we want to use test results to generalize about what Jennifer will do on other tasks of this general sort next week or next month, then this standard is the appropriate one by which to evaluate a test. For most educational situations, this procedure is the way we want to use test results, so evidence based on equivalent test forms with a time interval between administrations should usually be given the most weight in evaluating the reliability of a test.

The use of two parallel test forms does provide a sound basis for estimating the precision of a psychological or educational test. This procedure, however, also raises some practical problems. It demands that two parallel forms of the test be available and that time be allowed for testing each person twice. Often, no second form of the test exists or could reasonably be constructed, or no time can be found for a second testing. Administration of a second test is often likely to represent a somewhat burdensome demand on available resources. These practical considerations of convenience and expediency have made test makers receptive to procedures that extract an estimate of reliability from one administration of one form of a test. However, such procedures are a compromise at best. The correlation between two parallel forms, usually administered after a lapse of several days or weeks, in most applications represents the preferred procedure for estimating reliability.

Single-Administration Methods

Subdivided Tests

A procedure that has been widely used in the past for obtaining a reliability estimate from a single administration of a test divides the test into two presumably equivalent halves. The half-tests may be assembled on the basis of a careful examination of the content and difficulty of each item, making a systematic effort to balance the content and difficulty level of the two halves. In essence, this is the same as constructing two, short, parallel tests and then combining them for a single administration. After testing, the two forms are separated for scoring. The correlation between the two separate half-length tests is used to estimate the reliability of the whole test. This approach must be used when tests that measure more than one trait are being developed because items measuring each trait must be present in each half-test. With this procedure it is also possible to separate the administration of the two halves by hours, days, or weeks to simulate parallel forms, but this has seldom been done.

A simpler procedure, often relied on to give equivalent halves, is to put alternate items into the two half-tests, that is, to put the odd-numbered items into one half-test and the even-numbered items in the other half. This procedure is usually a sensible one because items of similar form, content, or difficulty are likely to be grouped together in the test. For a reasonably long test, 60 items or more, splitting the test in this way will tend to balance out factors of item form, content covered, and difficulty level. The two half-tests will have a good probability of being "equivalent" tests.

These procedures divide the test in half only for scoring, not for administration. That is, a single test is given with a single time limit at a single sitting. However, two separate scores are derived—one by scoring one half, or the odd-numbered items, and one by scoring the other half, or the even-numbered items. The correlation between these two scores, called an odd–even reliability coefficient or, more generally, a **split-half reliability,** provides a measure of the accuracy with which the test is measuring the individual at this point in time. Split-half reliability coefficients provide an estimate of what the correlation would be between two equivalent tests given at the same time.

Note, however, that the computed correlation is between two half-length tests. This value is not directly applicable to the full-length test, which is the actual instrument prepared for use. In general, the larger the sample of a person's behavior we have, the more reliable the measure will be. That is, the more behavior we record, the less our measure will depend on chance elements in the behavior of the individual or in the particular sampling of tasks. Single, lucky answers or momentary lapses in attention will be more nearly evened out.

Where the halves of the test that gave the scores actually correlated are equivalent, we can get an unbiased estimate of the total-test reliability from the correlation between the two half-tests. The estimate is given by the following equation:

$$\hat{r}_{tt} = \frac{2r_{AB}}{1 + r_{AB}} \tag{4.5}$$

where $\hat{r}_{tt}$ is the estimated reliability of the full-length test and

r_{AB} is the actual correlation between the two half-tests.

Thus, if the correlation between the halves of a test is 0.60, Eq. (4.5) would give

$$\hat{r}_{tt} = \frac{2(.60)}{1 + .60} = \frac{1.20}{1.60} = .75$$

as our best estimate of the reliability of scores on the total test. This equation, referred to generally as the **Spearman-Brown prophecy formula** from its function and the names of its originators, makes it possible to compute an estimate of reliability of measurement from a single administration of a single test. It has the advantage over the internal consistency methods (discussed below) that it does not assume homogeneous content across all items, only between the two halves, but it is still a single-administration method.

However, the split-half method is sensitive to the equivalence of the two halves. If the split does not produce equivalent tests, the correlation between them will underestimate the reliability of the full-length test. The use of any particular split of the test is somewhat arbitrary, and different splits will produce different estimates of the test's reliability. Internal consistency methods were developed in part to overcome this problem.

Internal Consistency Reliability

Practical considerations often dictate that a reliability estimate be obtained from a single administration of the test. The split-half method, developed almost 100 years ago, has largely been replaced by methods based on the idea that each item in a test can be considered to be a one-item test. The total test of n items is then seen as a set of n parallel, but very short, tests. (Here, n is the number of test items.) An estimate of the reliability of the total test is developed from an analysis of the statistics of the individual items.

The procedure for estimating the reliability of a test from a single administration of a single form depends on the consistency of each individual's performance from item to item and is based on the variance of the test scores and the variances of the separate items. In its most general form, this procedure is called **coefficient alpha** and is given by the following equation:

$$\alpha = \left(\frac{n}{n-1}\right)\left(\frac{SD_X^2 - \sum SD_i^2}{SD_X^2}\right) \tag{4.6}$$

where α is the estimate of reliability,

n is the number of items in the test,

SD_X^2 is the variance of the test scores,

$\sum$ means "take the sum of" and covers the n items, and

SD_i^2 is the variance of the scores from a group of individuals on an item. There are n values of SD_i^2 which are summed to give the second term in the numerator.

The value given by coefficient alpha is the average of all possible Spearman-Brown-corrected split-half correlations, so it evens out the possible effects of an inappropriate split of the test into halves.

Let's take a small example to see how Eq. (4.6) works. Suppose we have given a test with three short essay items to a group of five examinees. Each item is worth five points, so scores on the test can range from 0 (every item completely wrong) to 15 (a perfect score on each item). Our five examinees gave us the following scores:

Examinee	Item 1	Item 2	Item 3	Test Score
1	2	3	1	6
2	3	3	3	9
3	4	5	4	13
4	3	4	5	12
5	5	4	5	14
$\sum X$	17	19	18	54
$\sum X^2$	63	75	76	626
Variance	1.04	.56	2.24	8.56

Putting these values into Eq. (4.6), we get

$$\alpha = \left(\frac{3}{2}\right)\left(\frac{8.56 - 3.84}{8.56}\right) = (1.5)(.551) = .827$$

This short test shows a very high level of reliability, which means that the items all tend to place the examinees in about the same order.

When each item is scored as either 1 or 0, that is, as either passed or failed, the item variance becomes

$$SD_i^2 = p_i q_i$$

where p_i is the proportion of examinees passing the item and

q_i is the proportion failing the item.

Equation (4.6) then becomes

$$r_{tt} = \left(\frac{n}{n-1}\right)\left(\frac{SD_X^2 - \sum p_i q_i}{SD_X^2}\right)$$

(4.7)

where r_{tt} is the estimated reliability of the full-length test. This equation, called **Kuder-Richardson Formula 20** (KR-20) after its originators and the equation numbering in their original article, is a special form of coefficient alpha that applies when the items are scored right or wrong. Both coefficient alpha and KR-20 provide an estimate of what is called the **internal consistency** of a test, that is, the degree to which all of the items measure a common characteristic of the person and are free from measurement error. When the test is homogeneous, in the sense that every item measures the same general trait of ability or personality as every other item, coefficient alpha and KR-20 estimates can reasonably be interpreted as reflecting the reliability of the test.

A formula involving simpler calculations and based on an assumption that all items are of the same difficulty is called **Kuder-Richardson Formula 21** (KR-21). This formula substitutes $M_t(1 - M_t/n)$, where M_t is the mean score on the test, for $\sum p_i q_i$ in Eq. (4.7) and yields a close, but conservative, approximation to KR-20. KR-21 can be useful for teachers who would like a quick estimate of the reliability of a test they use in their classes, because it can be easily calculated from the mean and standard deviation of the distribution of test scores. However, the assumption that all items are of equal difficulty is quite restrictive and seldom true in practice. This fact, coupled with the availability of computers to do the extra work required by the KR-20 and coefficient alpha formulas, suggests that KR-21 should seldom be used. It is a relatively easy matter to set up an Excel spreadsheet to compute α. With rows representing examinees and columns representing items, pasting the appropriate variance function at the bottom of each column will produce the $\sum SD_i^2$ values. The variance of the row sums produces SD_X^2, and putting Eq. (4.6) in an open cell of the spreadsheet with the appropriate cell references will complete the task.

The appealing convenience of the internal consistency procedures has led to their wide use. Many test manuals will be found to report this type of reliability coefficient and no other. Unfortunately, KR-20, KR-21, and coefficient alpha have several types of limitations.

First, because all of the item responses have occurred during a single testing, they all necessarily represent the individual as he or she is at a single moment in time. Even events lasting only a few minutes will affect several items about equally. In other words, variation in the individual from day to day cannot be reflected in this type of reliability coefficient. It can only give evidence on the precision with which we can appraise the person at a specific moment.

A second factor will sometimes make item sets more alike than would be true of separate parallel forms. If the test includes groups of items based on common reference material, such as reading items based on a single passage or science items all referring to a single described experiment, performance on all of these items will depend to some extent on the common act of comprehending the reference materials. Thus, the examinee who succeeds on one item of the set is more likely to succeed on the others than would be the case for truly independent items.

For some situations, the assumption that all items on a particular test measure a single trait may be too restrictive. An achievement test in general science might include items on biology, chemistry, and geology. To the extent that there is a single trait of general science knowledge, the items should show consistent performance, but if there are separate, only moderately correlated, traits of biology knowledge, chemistry knowledge, and geology knowledge, we should find three clusters of items, each cluster showing high internal consistency. It would be inappropriate for a test like this to show high internal consistency across the whole test. A split-half reliability coefficient in which an effort has been made to create parallel forms would be more appropriate in this situation.

Finally, all single-administration reliability coefficients become meaningless when a test is highly speeded. Suppose we had a test of simple arithmetic made up of 100 problems like $3 + 5 =$ ___?___ , and that the test was being used with adults, with a 2-minute time limit. People would differ widely in scores on such a test, but the differences would be primarily differences in speed. Computation errors would be a minor factor. The person who got a score of 50 would very probably have attempted just 50 items. The position of an item in the test then determines almost completely whether an individual attempts the item. Because almost everyone who attempts an item gets the item correct, the values of p and q for the item are determined by its placement in the test, and this fact will greatly inflate the apparent consistency of performance.

Few tests depend as completely on speed as does the one chosen to illustrate this point; however, many tests involve some degree of speeding. This speed factor tends to inflate estimates of reliability based on internal consistency procedures. The amount of overestimation depends on the degree to which the test is speeded, being greater for those tests in which speed plays a greater role. But speed enters in sufficiently general a manner that internal consistency estimates of reliability should usually be discounted somewhat for tests of ability.

The split-half procedure does offer an alternative that is appropriate for use with speeded tests. The two halves of the test can be administered separately as two independent short tests. The correlation between the independently administered half tests, corrected using Eq. (4.5), gives a useable value for the reliability of measurement in such situations.

MAKING THE COMPUTER DO IT

Coefficient Alpha

Any of the reliability indices that involve correlating two scores can, of course, be calculated in either SPSS or EXCEL by the methods we described in Chapter 2 for computing correlation coefficients. If you wish to compute coefficient alpha, the easiest way to do it with SPSS is to use the Reliability Analysis subprogram within the Scale option on the Analysis menu. The program asks you to list the variables to be included in the analysis. This means listing the items as variables. If you have 20 items and they are listed together in the data file with names such as item1, item2, . . . , item20, just move the item names into the analysis window. The "statistics" option allows you to obtain a number of useful statistics that are beyond our concern as well as item descriptive statistics. One particularly interesting option is to have the program calculate what coefficient alpha would be with each item individually removed from the instrument. If removing an item would improve alpha, the item probably should be modified. To compute coefficient alpha using EXCEL, you must have the program compute the individual item variances and the total test variance, then use these quantities in Eq. (4.6) as described earlier.

Comparison of Methods

A summary comparison of the different procedures for estimating reliability is given in Table 4–1. The table shows the four factors (sources of variation) we have discussed that may make a single test score an inaccurate picture of the individual's usual performance and which sources of error are reflected in score variation in each of the procedures for estimating reliability. In general, the different procedures are not equivalent; the more Xs there are in a column, the more conservative (i.e., lower) the estimate of a test's reliability. Only administration of parallel test forms with a time interval between testings permits all sources of instability to have their effects. Each of the other methods masks some source of variation that may be significant in the actual use of the test. Retesting with an identical test neglects variation arising out of the sampling of items. Whenever all testing is done at one time, day-to-day variation in the individual is omitted. When the testing is done as a single unit with a single time limit, variation in speed of responding is neglected. The facts brought out in this table should be borne in mind when evaluating reliability data found in a test manual or in the report of a research study. Test users should demand that commercial publishers provide estimates based on parallel forms of the test and on retesting after a delay, whenever possible, so that a reasonable estimate of the effects of the sources of unreliability can be assessed. Because it is convenient, coefficient alpha is the most commonly reported index of reliability in research studies.

Table 4–1
Sources of Variation Represented in Different Procedures for Estimating Reliability

Sources of Variation	Experimental Procedure for Estimating Reliability				
	Immediate Retest, Same Test	Retest After Interval, Same Test	Parallel Test Form Without Interval	Parallel Test Form with Interval	Single-Administration Methods[a]
Variation arising within the measurement procedure itself	X	X	X	X	X
Changes in the person from day to day		X		X	
Changes in the specific sample of tasks			X	X	X
Changes in the individual's speed of work	X	X	X	X	

Note: X indicates that this source of variation can affect reliability from this method of testing.
[a] The single-administration methods are Kuder-Richardson Formulas 20 and 21, coefficient alpha, and split-half.

INTERPRETATION OF RELIABILITY DATA

Suppose that analysis of data obtained from an elementary school test of academic aptitude has yielded a reliability coefficient of .90. How should we interpret this result? What does it mean concerning the precision of an individual's score? Should we be pleased or dissatisfied to get a coefficient of this size?

Standard Error of Measurement

One interpretation of test reliability is found in the relationship between the reliability coefficient and the standard error of measurement. Remember that *the standard error of measurement is the standard deviation that would be obtained for a series of measurements of the same individual.* (It is assumed that the individual is not changed by being measured.) We saw in Eq. (4.4) that the standard error of measurement can be estimated from the reliability coefficient by the following equation:

$$SD_e = SD_X \sqrt{(1 - r_{tt})}$$

Suppose that the test with a reliability of 0.90 has a standard deviation of 15 points. Then, we have

$$SD_e = 15 \sqrt{(1 - .90)} = 15 \sqrt{.10} = 15(0.316) = 4.7$$

In this instance, a set of repeated measures of some one person (such as that obtained for my weight) would be expected to have a standard deviation (i.e., a standard error of measurement) of 4.7 points. Remember that in a normal distribution a fairly uniform proportion of observations falls within any given number of standard deviation units of the mean; about 32% of cases, or about one in three, differ from the mean by more than 1 standard deviation; 4.6%, by more than 2 standard deviations. This situation is illustrated for the present example in Figure 4–1.

Applying this to a case in which the standard deviation is 4.7 points, one could say that there is about one chance in three that an individual's observed score differs from his or her "true" score

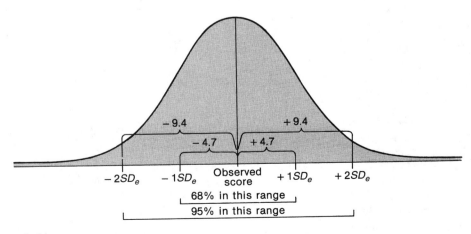

Figure 4–1
The standard error of measurement (SD_e) can be used to determine a range for estimating an individual's true score.

(falls outside the 68% band in Figure 4–1) by as much as 4.7 points in either direction. There is about 1 chance in 20 that it differs by as much as 9.4 points (2 standard errors of measurement). A little less than one-third of the scores from such a measurement are likely to be in error by about 5 points or more, while about 1 in 25 will be in error by 10 or more points.

Another way to view the standard error of measurement is as an indication of how much a person's score might change on retesting. Each person's score on the first testing includes some amount of error. Most of the errors will be fairly small, but some will be quite large. About half of the errors will be positive (make the observed score too high) and about half will be negative (make the observed score too low). But we see only the observed score and have no way of knowing how large the error of measurement is for any individual—or in what direction.

The numerical values of .90 for the reliability and 15 for the standard deviation are fairly representative of what might be found for standard scores from one of the commercially distributed academic aptitude tests for children in the upper elementary grades. Note that even with this relatively high reliability coefficient, appreciable errors of measurement are possible in at least a minority of cases. With a standard deviation of 15, shifts of 5 or 10 points from one testing to another can be expected fairly frequently, just because of errors of measurement. Anyone who is impressed by— and tries to interpret—a score difference of 5 points between two people or between two testings of the same person on a test such as this has been fooled into thinking that the test has a precision that it simply does not possess. Further testing could reverse the result. Any interpretation of test scores must be made with acute awareness of the standard error of measurement.

The manner in which the standard error of measurement is related to the reliability coefficient is shown in Table 4–2. Column 1 contains selected values for the reliability, column 2 gives the value of the expression $SD_X \sqrt{1 - r_{tt}}$, and columns 3 and 4 give the value of SD_e when SD_X is 15 or 100, respectively. Note that the magnitude of errors decreases as the reliability coefficient increases, but also that errors of appreciable size can still be found with reliability coefficients of .90 or .95. *It is the standard error of measurement that we must keep in mind when interpreting the score of an individual.* A range extending from 2 standard errors of

Table 4–2
Standard Error of Measurement for Different Values of the Reliability Coefficient

Reliability Coefficient	Standard Error of Measurement		
	General Expression[a]	When $SD_x = 15$	When $SD_x = 100$
.50	.71 SD_X	10.6	71
.60	.63 SD_X	9.5	63
.70	.55 SD_X	8.2	55
.80	.45 SD_X	6.7	45
.85	.39 SD_X	5.8	39
.90	.32 SD_X	4.7	32
.95	.22 SD_X	3.4	22
.98	.14 SD_X	2.1	14

Note: SD_X signifies the standard deviation of the test.
[a]$(SD_X) \sqrt{1 - r_{tt}}$.

measurement above the obtained score to 2 SD_e below will produce a band that we can be reasonably sure (19 chances in 20) includes the individual's true score. Thus, in the case of the aptitude test described in this section, we can think of a test standard score of 90 as meaning rather surely a true score lying between about 80 and 100. If we think in these terms, we will be much more aware of the imprecision of our tests and more discreet when interpreting and using test results.

Reliability Coefficient

When interpreting the test score of an individual, it is desirable to think in terms of the standard error of measurement and a band of uncertainty, and to be somewhat humble and tentative in drawing conclusions from that test score. But for making comparisons between tests and for a number of types of test analyses, the reliability coefficient will be more useful. Where measures are expressed in different units, such as height in inches and weight in pounds, the reliability coefficient provides the only possible basis for comparing precision of measurement. Because the competing tests in a given field, such as reading comprehension, are likely to use types of scores that are not directly comparable, the reliability coefficient will usually represent the only satisfactory basis for test comparison. *Other things being equal,* the test with the higher reliability coefficient, that is, the test that provides a more consistent ranking of the individuals within their group, should be preferred.

The other things that may not be equal are primarily considerations of validity and practicality. Validity, insofar as we can appraise it, is the crucial requirement for a measurement procedure. Reliability is important only as a necessary condition for a measure to have validity. The ceiling for the possible validity of a test is set by its reliability. A test must measure *something* before it can measure what we want to measure. A measuring device with a reliability of zero is reflecting nothing but chance factors. It does not correlate with itself and cannot correlate with anything else.

Assuming that reliability has been computed using either the test–retest or the parallel forms method, the theoretical ceiling for the correlation between any two measures is the square root of the product of their reliabilities:

$$r_{12} = \sqrt{r_{11}r_{22}}$$

Thus, if a selection test has a reliability of .80 and a set of supervisory ratings has a reliability of .50, the theoretical maximum for the correlation between the two is

$$\sqrt{(.80)(.50)} = \sqrt{.40} = .63$$

Often there is not too much we can do about the reliability of the outcome variable we are trying to predict except to get information about it, but we can take steps to assure reasonable reliability in our predictor tests.

The converse of the relationship we have just presented does not follow. A test may measure with the greatest precision and still have no validity for our purposes. For example, we can measure head size with a good deal of accuracy, but this measure is still practically useless as an indicator of intelligence. Validity is something beyond mere accuracy of measurement.

Considerations of cost, convenience, and so on may also sometimes lead to a decision to use a less reliable test. We may accept a less reliable, 40-minute test in preference to a more reliable, 3-hour one, because 3 hours of testing time is too much of a burden in view of the purpose that the test is designed to serve.

FACTORS AFFECTING RELIABILITY

Within the limitations discussed in the preceding paragraphs, we prefer the more reliable test. Several factors must be taken into account, however, before we can fairly compare the reliability coefficients of two or more different tests:

1. Variability of the group on the trait the test measures
2. Level of the group on the trait the test measures
3. Length of the test
4. Operations used for estimating the reliability.

Variability of the Group

The reliability coefficient indicates how consistently a test places each individual relative to others in the group. When there is little shifting from test to retest or from Form A to Form B, the reliability coefficient is high. But the extent to which individuals will switch places depends on how similar they are. It does not take very accurate testing to differentiate the reading ability of a second grader from that of a seventh grader. But to place each second grader accurately within a second-grade class is much more demanding.

If the scores of children from several different grades are pooled, we may expect a much higher reliability coefficient. For example, the manual for the Otis Quick-Scoring Mental Ability Test–Beta once reported alternate-form reliabilities for single grade groups that ranged from .65 to .87, with an average value of .78. But for a pooling of the complete range of grades (grades 4–9), the reliability coefficient was reported as .96. These data are all for the same testing with the same test. They are the same set of scores, just grouped differently. They reflect the same precision of measurement. Yet the coefficient for the combined groups is strikingly higher simply as a function of the greater range of individual differences in the combined group. The standard error of measurement characterizes the accuracy with which a single individual is measured by a test. Because this value cannot depend on the group in which the individual is embedded, Eq. (4.4) shows us that as the variability of the group goes up, the reliability coefficient of the test must also rise.

In evaluating the reported reliability coefficient, we must take into account the range of ability of the group tested. A reliability coefficient based on a combination of age or grade groups must usually be discounted. But, even in less extreme cases, we must still take into account variability of the group on the trait. Reliability coefficients for age groups will tend to be somewhat higher than for grade groups, because a group of children of the same age will usually contain a greater spread of talent than will the students in a single grade. A sample made up of children from a wide range of socioeconomic levels will tend to yield higher reliability coefficients than a very homogeneous sample. In comparing different tests, we must take account of the type of sample on which the reliability data were based, insofar as this can be determined from the author's report, and judge more critically the test whose estimated reliability is based on data from a more heterogeneous group.

Level of the Group on the Trait

Precision of measurement of a test may be related to the ability level of the people being measured; however, no simple rule can be formulated for stating the nature of this relationship. The nature of the relationship depends on the way the test was built. For those people for whom the test is very hard, such that they are doing a large amount of guessing, accuracy is likely to be low. At the other extreme, if the test is very easy for the group, such that all of the examinees can do most of the items very easily, that test also may be expected to be ineffective in discriminating among the group members. When most of the items are easy for the group being tested, it is as if the test were shortened, because all differentiation is based on just those few harder items that some can do and some cannot. Item response theory (IRT) tells us that we only get information about an examinee's position on the trait when there is some uncertainty whether he or she will pass the item. The factor of most of the examinees getting extreme scores is a particular concern in mastery testing, which is given special consideration later in this chapter in the *Reliability of Criterion-Referenced Tests* section.

Also, the test may vary in accuracy at different intermediate difficulty levels. The meticulous test constructor will report the standard error of measurement for the test at different score levels. When separate values of the standard error of measurement are reported in the manual, they provide a basis for evaluating the precision of the test for different types of groups and permit a more appropriate estimate of the accuracy of a particular individual's score. Each individual's score can be interpreted in relation to the standard error of measurement for scores of that level. For example, the Iowa Tests of Basic Skills–Form G/H, which reports scores in grade equivalents, reported the standard error of measurement at different score intervals for the vocabulary test shown in Table 4–3.

This test measures somewhat more accurately those pupils who score near the center of the distribution than those who succeed with only a few items or with almost all. The test authors produced this result intentionally by including many items of moderate difficulty, which discriminate degrees of ability in the middle range, and relatively few very hard or very easy items.

Table 4–3
Iowa Tests of Basic Skills Standard Error of Measurement for the Vocabulary Test

Grade Equivalent Interval	Standard Error of Measurement in Grade-Equivalent Units		
	Grade 4	Grade 6	Grade 8
20–29	5.4		
30–39	3.8		
40–49	3.1	9.0	
50–59	3.6	6.3	10.1
60–69	4.0	4.5	8.1
70–79	4.9	3.8	6.8
80–89		5.3	5.9
90–99		7.6	5.5
100–109			5.3
110–119			5.7
120–129			6.1
Total distribution	4.5	5.5	6.6

In effect, a longer test is operating for pupils in the middle range rather than at the extremes, and the result is a more accurate measurement of this large, middle group.

Length of the Test

As we saw earlier in discussing the split-half reliability coefficient, test reliability depends on the length of the test. If we can assume that the quality of the test items, the traits measured by those items, and the nature of the examinees remain the same, then the relationship of reliability to test length can be expressed by the following equation:

$$\hat{r}_{kk} = \frac{kr_{tt}}{1 + (k - 1)r_{tt}} \qquad (4.8)$$

where $\hat{r}_{kk}$ is the estimated reliability of a test k times as long as the original test,

r_{tt} is the reliability of the original test, and

k is the factor by which the length of the test is changed.

This is a more general form of Eq. (4.5).

Suppose we have a spelling test made up of 20 items that has a reliability of .50. We want to know how reliable the test will be if it is lengthened to contain 100 items comparable to the original 20. The answer is

$$\hat{r}_{kk} = \frac{5(.50)}{1 + 4(.50)} = \frac{2.5}{3.0} = .83$$

As the length of the test is increased, the chance errors of measurement more or less cancel out, the score comes to depend more and more completely on the characteristics of the person being measured, and a more accurate appraisal of the individual is obtained.

Of course, how much we can lengthen a test is limited by a number of practical considerations. It is limited by the amount of time available for testing, by factors of fatigue and boredom on the part of examinees, and sometimes by our inability to construct more equally good test items. But within these limits, reliability can be increased as needed by lengthening the test, subject only to the constraint that each item measures with some reliability greater than zero.

We should note, however, that there is a point of diminishing returns in lengthening a test. When the reliability is already moderately high, it takes a considerable increase in test length to accomplish a modest increase in reliability. Quintupling the length of our 20-item spelling test would yield a substantial increase in its reliability (from .50 to .83). But, doubling the length again to 200 items would produce only a modest increase, from .83 to .91. Adding 200 more items would bring the reliability to .95, a rise that is hardly worth the increase in testing time.

One special type of lengthening is represented by increasing the number of raters who rate a person or a product the person has produced. To the extent that the unreliability of an assessment results from the inconsistency with which a sample of behavior is judged, this source of unreliability can usually be reduced by increasing the number of judges, or raters. If several raters are available who have equal competence with the materials to be rated, or equal familiarity with the ratees if the ratings are of persons, then a pooling of their ratings will produce a composite that is more reliable; the increase to be expected is described approximately by Eq. (4.8). For example, if a typical pair of judges evaluating samples of writing show a correlation of .40, then the pooled ratings of three judges could be expected to correlate with three others, as follows:

$$\frac{3(.40)}{1 + 2(.40)} = \frac{1.2}{1.8} = .67$$

It is also possible to estimate the loss in reliability that would occur if a measurement procedure is shortened. Suppose we have a 100-item spelling test that has a reliability of .90, and we wish to estimate the reliability of a 40-item test made up of a sample of items from the longer test. The length of the new test is 40/100 = .40 times the length of the original one, so our estimate of the reliability of the shorter test is

$$\hat{r}_{kk} = \frac{.40(.90)}{1 + (.40 - 1.00)(.90)} = \frac{.36}{1 + (-.60)(.90)} = \frac{.36}{.46} = .78$$

This procedure is quite useful for judging whether the shortened test would have sufficient reliability for our purposes.

Operations Used for Estimating Reliability

How high a value will be obtained for the reliability coefficient depends also on which of the several sets of experimental operations is used to estimate the reliability. We saw in Table 4–1 that the different procedures treat different sources of variation in different ways and that it is only the use of parallel forms of a test with a period intervening that includes all four possible sources of instability as "error." That is, this procedure of estimating reliability represents a more exacting definition of the test's ability to reproduce the same score. The individual must then show consistency both from one sample of tasks to another and from one day to another. In Table 4–4, we have gathered a few examples that show reliability coefficients for the same test when the coefficients have been computed by different procedures and with different time intervals.

The procedures compared in Table 4–4 are test–retest correlations with an interval of 8, 24, or 48 months, correlations between equivalent forms with a very short interval, and KR-20 internal consistency reliabilities. Note that the test–retest correlation is as low as, or lower than, the other coefficients in every case and is lower for longer intervals than for shorter ones. The differences between the procedures vary, but in every case, it is necessary to discount the internal consistency estimate. Had alternate forms of these tests been administered with an interval of 8 months, we would expect the correlations between different forms of the test on different occasions to be lower than the test–retest coefficients.

Practical versus Theoretical Reliability

The AERA/APA standards (American Educational Research Association, American Psychological Association, & National Council on Measurement in Education, 1999) require test publishers to report reliability and standard error of measurement information for tests offered for public use. Because the potential users of tests will examine the reliability evidence presented by the publisher closely, it is to the publisher's advantage to report the highest values possible. We have reviewed several factors that can influence the apparent reliability of a test, the most potent of which in most cases will be group variability and test length. An additional source of error variance, and hence unreliability, in test scores is examiner/scorer inconsistency. For machine-scored

Table 4–4

Comparison of Reliability Coefficients Obtained from Test–Retest and Kuder-Richardson Formula 20 (KR-20) and Equivalent Forms

Test	Test–Retest (Months)			KR-20	Equivalent Forms[b]
	8	24[a]	48[a]		
Cognitive Abilities Test, Level C					
Verbal	.91	.85	.83	.93	
Quantitative	.87	.82	.79	.91	
Nonverbal	.86	.75	.73	.93	
Iowa Tests of Basic Skills, Grade 5					
Mathematics composite	.85	.84	.64	.94	.88
Language composite	.88	.89	.75	.96	.91
Gates-MacGintie Reading Test, Survey D					
Vocabulary, Grade 4	.87			.91	.89
Comprehension, Grade 4	.82			.91	.82

[a]24- and 48-month retests were not available for the Gates-MacGintie Reading Test.
[b]Equivalent forms correlations were not available for the Cognitive Abilities Test.

tests this source is limited to errors in test administration and should be essentially zero, but for essay tests, product ratings, and many of the assessments made in clinical and educational practice, the potential for errors from this source is very real.

The reliability of a test score depends on the context in which the particular measurement was made. If the conditions that obtain in test use are different from those during standardization, the reliability of the scores is likely to be different. For example, a test publisher may base estimates of the reliability of a test on test protocols that have been scored by two or more carefully trained raters who are also monitored for the consistency of their scoring, thus eliminating most scorer variability. This was the case for the scoring of the Wechsler Intelligence Scale for Children, Third Edition, standardization data (WISC-III; Wechsler, 1991a). Reliability estimates obtained under these conditions approximate the maximum or *theoretical reliability* of the test. When the test is used in practice, the real or *practical reliability* of the scores will be lower than that estimated during standardization to an unknown degree, because practitioners may not be as highly trained and certainly are not subject to the same level of scoring verification. Kaufman (1990), for example, documents the high number of scoring errors made, even by experienced clinicians, in administering and scoring the Wechsler scales. Belk, LoBello, Ray, and Zachar (2002) reported that *all* test protocols administered by a sample of graduate student trainees contained administrative or scoring errors. The number of errors ranged from 3 to 116 with a mean of 45.2!! Consequently, the standard error of measurement will be higher when a test like the WISC-III is used "in the field." No single value represents the correct reliability of a test. The most appropriate estimate depends on how the scores will be obtained and used. When estimating the reliability of a test, the design for data collection should allow for all sources of error variation that are likely to occur in the application of the test to be present in the reliability study. Only then can the test user know how much confidence to place in the test scores.

MINIMUM LEVEL OF RELIABILITY

Obviously, other things being equal, the more reliable a measuring procedure, the more satisfied we are with it. A question that is often raised is "What is the minimum reliability that is acceptable?" If we must make some decision or take some course of action with respect to an individual, we will do so in terms of the best information we have—however unreliable it may be—provided only that the reliability is better than zero, in which case we have no information. (Of course here, as always, the crucial consideration is the validity of the measure.) The appraisal of any new procedure must always be in terms of other procedures with which it is in competition. Thus, a high school mathematics test with a reliability coefficient of .80 would look relatively unattractive if tests with reliabilities of .85 or .90 were readily available at similar cost. On the other hand, a procedure for judging "leadership" that had a reliability of no more than .60 might look very attractive if the alternative was a set of ratings having a reliability of .45 or .50.

Although we cannot set an absolute minimum for the reliability of a measurement procedure, we can indicate the level of reliability that is required to enable us to achieve specified levels of accuracy in describing an individual or a group. Suppose that we have given a test to two individuals and that Individual A fell at the 75th percentile of the group while Individual B fell at the 50th percentile. What is the probability that Individual B would surpass Individual A if they were tested again with the same test? In Table 4–5, the probability of such a reversal is shown for different values of the reliability of the test. Thus, where the reliability is zero, there is exactly a 50–50 chance that the order of the two individuals will be reversed because both measurements represent completely random error.

Table 4–5
Percentage of Times Direction of Difference Will Be Reversed in Subsequent Testing for Scores Falling at 75th and 50th Percentiles

Reliability Coefficient	Percentage of Reversals with Repeated Testings		
	Scores of Single Individuals	Means of Groups of 25	Means of Groups of 100
.00	50.0	50.0	50.0
.40	40.3	10.9	.7
.50	36.8	4.6	.04
.60	32.5	1.2	
.70	27.1	.1	
.80	19.7		
.90	8.7		
.95	2.2		
.98	.05		

When the reliability is .50, the probability of a reversal still is more than 1 in 3. For a correlation of .90, there remains 1 chance in 12 that we will get a reversal on repetition of the testing. To have 4 chances in 5 that our difference will stay in the same direction, we must have a reliability of .80.

Table 4–5 also shows the percentage of expected reversals of two groups—groups of 25 and of 100. For example, if in Class A of 25 pupils, the average fell at the 75th percentile of some larger reference group and in Class B, also of 25 pupils, the average fell at the 50th percentile, what is the probability that we would get a reversal if the testing were repeated? Here, we still have a 50–50 chance in the extreme case in which the reliability coefficient is zero. However, the security of our conclusion increases much more rapidly with groups than with individuals as the reliability of the test becomes greater. With a reliability of .50, the probability of a reversal is already down to 1 in 20 for groups of 25, to 1 in 2,500 for groups of 100. With a correlation of .70, the probability of a reversal is only 1 in 1,000 for groups of 25 and is vanishingly small for groups of 100. Thus, a test with relatively low reliability will permit us to make useful studies of and draw dependable conclusions about groups, especially groups of substantial size, but quite high reliability is required if we are to speak with confidence about individuals.

RELIABILITY OF DIFFERENCE SCORES

Sometimes we are less interested in single scores than we are in the relationship between scores taken in pairs. We may be concerned with the differences between scholastic aptitude and reading achievement in a group of pupils, or we may wish to study gains in reading from an initial test given in October to a later test given the following May. In these illustrations, the significant fact for each individual is the difference between two scores. We must inquire how reliable our estimates of these differences are, knowing the characteristics of the two component tests.

It is unfortunately true that the appraisal of the difference between two test scores usually has substantially lower reliability than the reliabilities of the two tests taken separately. This lower reliability is due to two factors: (1) The errors of measurement in both separate tests accumulate in the difference score, and (2) whatever is common to the two tests is canceled out in the difference score. We can illustrate the situation by a diagram such as that in Figure 4–2.

Each bar in Figure 4–2 represents performance (more precisely, variance in performance) on a test, broken up into a number of parts to represent the factors producing this performance. The first bar represents a reading test, and the second, a scholastic aptitude test. Notice that we have divided reading performance into three parts. One part, labeled "Common factors," is a complex of general intellectual abilities and test-taking skills that operate in both the reading and the scholastic aptitude tests. We may view this component as what causes the correlation between the two tests. Another part, labeled "Specific reading factors," includes abilities that appear only in the reading test. These are reliable individual differences, but due to factors not shared with the scholastic aptitude test. The third part, labeled "Error," is the chance error of measurement that is represented by the standard error of measurement for the reading test. Three similar parts are indicated for the aptitude test. The reliability of each test reflects the combination of its common and specific factors.

Now examine the third bar (and the fourth, which shows the third with blank space removed). This bar represent the difference score—that is, the reading score expressed in some type of standard score units minus the aptitude test score expressed in those same units. In this bar, the common factors have disappeared. They appeared with a positive sign in the reading test and a negative sign

Figure 4–2
Nature of a difference score.

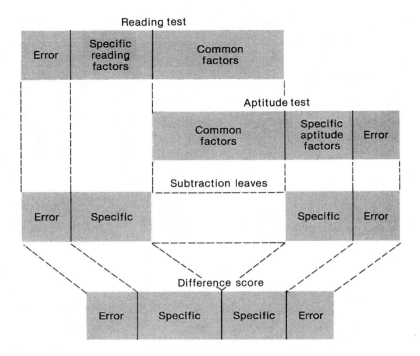

(due to the subtraction) in the aptitude test and thus canceled out. Only the specific factors and errors of measurement remain. The specific factors are the factors that determine the difference score. The errors of measurement make up a much larger proportion of the fourth bar, showing that the reliability of the difference scores will be lower than that of either of the original tests. For example, if error made up 25% of each test, and specific factors made up another 25% of each test, the difference score would contain 50% error and 50% specific factors. Thus, the difference score would be much less reliable than either of the original tests. If the two tests measured exactly the same abilities so that there were only common and error factors, only the errors of measurement would remain in the difference scores, and these scores would have exactly zero reliability. This problem is particularly acute in attempts to assess educational gains by retesting with the same or a parallel test, because in such a case the common factors are at a maximum.

The reliability of the difference between two measures expressed in standard scores can be obtained by the following fairly simple equation:

$$r_{diff} = \frac{\frac{1}{2}(r_{AA} + r_{BB}) - r_{AB}}{1 - r_{AB}}$$

where r_{diff} is the reliability of the difference score,

r_{AA} is the reliability of Test A,

r_{BB} is the reliability of Test B, and

r_{AB} is the correlation between the two tests.

Table 4–6
Reliability of a Difference Score

Correlation Between Two Tests (r_{AB})	Average of Reliability of Two Tests $[\frac{1}{2}(r_{AA} + r_{BB})]$					
	.50	.60	.70	.80	.90	.95
.00	.50	.60	.70	.80	.90	.95
.40	.17	.33	.50	.67	.83	.92
.50	.00	.20	.40	.60	.80	.90
.60		.00	.25	.50	.75	.88
.70			.00	.33	.67	.83
.80				.00	.50	.75
.90					.00	.50
.95						.00

Thus, if the reliability of Test A is 0.80, the reliability of Test B is 0.90, and the correlation between Tests A and B is 0.60, for the reliability of the difference score, we get

$$r_{diff} = \frac{\frac{1}{2}(.80 + .90) - .60}{1 - .60} = \frac{.25}{.40} = .62$$

In Table 4–6, the value of r_{diff} is shown for various combinations of values of $\frac{1}{2}(r_{AA} + r_{BB})$ and r_{AB}. If the average of the two reliabilities is 0.80, the reliability of the difference score is 0.80 when the two tests are exactly uncorrelated and is zero when the correlation is 0.80. It is clear that as soon as the correlation between the two tests begins to approach the average of their separate reliabilities, the reliability of the difference score drops very rapidly.

The low reliability that tends to characterize difference scores is something to which the psychologist and educator must always be sensitive. Lower reliability becomes a problem whenever we wish to use test patterns for diagnosis. Thus, the judgment that Herbert's reading lags behind his scholastic aptitude is a judgment that must be made a good deal more tentatively than a judgment about either his scholastic aptitude or his reading taken separately. The conclusion that Mary has improved in reading more than Jane must be a more tentative judgment than that Mary is now a better (or poorer) reader than Jane. Any score difference needs to be interpreted in the light of the standard error of measurement *of that difference,* which will be about 1.4 times as large as the average of the standard errors of measurement of the two tests. This caveat applies with particular force to the practice of assigning grades to students based on an assessment of their improvement or growth.

Many differences will be found to be quite small relative to their standard errors and, consequently, are quite undependable. This caution especially applies for the interpretation of profiles and of gain scores. (Recent work on patterns of growth suggests that some of the problems with measures of change may be overcome by using measurements at more than two points in time. However, the problems with interpreting differences between scores in a profile remain. See Willett, 1988, for a review. Also, Kaufman, 1990, shows how the distribution of difference scores in a standardization sample can be used to improve the interpretation of profiles.)

EFFECTS OF UNRELIABILITY ON CORRELATION BETWEEN VARIABLES

One further consequence of measurement error merits brief attention here because it affects our interpretation of the correlations between different measures. Let us think of a measure of reading comprehension and one of mathematical reasoning. In each of these tests, the individual differences in score result in part from true differences in ability and in part from chance errors of measurement. But, if the errors of measurement are really chance events, the reading test errors and the mathematical reasoning test errors are uncorrelated. These uncorrelated errors are part of the total or observed score for each individual and therefore of the total variance of each test, which means that they must dilute any correlation that exists between the true scores on reading and the true scores on mathematical reasoning. That is, because the observed scores are a combination of true scores and errors of measurement, the correlation between observed scores is a compromise between the correlation that exists between the underlying true scores and the zero correlation between the errors of measurement on the two tests.

The effects of measurement error on the correlation between two tests is illustrated in Figure 4–3, where a test of reading (first bar) and a test of mathematical reasoning (second bar) are shown.

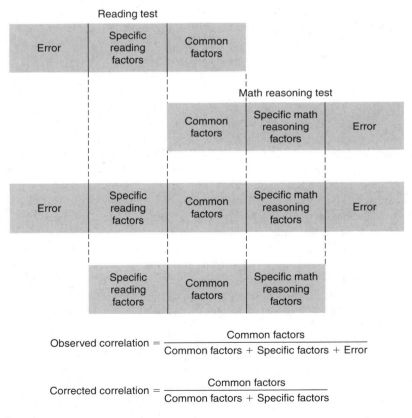

$$\text{Observed correlation} = \frac{\text{Common factors}}{\text{Common factors} + \text{Specific factors} + \text{Error}}$$

$$\text{Corrected correlation} = \frac{\text{Common factors}}{\text{Common factors} + \text{Specific factors}}$$

Figure 4–3
Why the correlation between true scores will be higher than the correlation between observed scores.

As in Figure 4–2, each test is composed of some common components (which causes the correlation between them), some components specific to the test, and some error. By definition, both the specific and error components are uncorrelated across tests. The third bar shows the correlation between the observed variables. The correlation is represented by the proportion of the bar that is due to common factors. You can see that in the fourth bar, reflecting the relationship between error-free true scores, the common components make up a larger proportion of the bar, revealing a higher correlation.

We would often like to extract an estimate of the correlation between the underlying true scores from our obtained data to understand better how much the functions involved have in common. Fortunately, we can do this quite simply. The process is called **correcting for attenuation due to unreliability.** The estimate is provided by the following equation:

$$\hat{r}_{T_1 T_2} = \frac{r_{12}}{\sqrt{r_{11} r_{22}}}$$

where $\hat{r}_{T_1 T_2}$ is the estimated correlation of the underlying true scores,
r_{12} is the correlation of the observed scores, and
r_{11} and r_{22} are the reliabilities of the two measures.

If, for example, the correlation between the reading test and the mathematical reasoning test was found to be .56 and the reliabilities of the two tests were .71 and .90, respectively, we would have

$$\hat{r}_{T_1 T_2} = \frac{.56}{\sqrt{(.71)(.90)}} = \frac{.56}{.799} = .70$$

Our estimate of the correlation between error-free measures of mathematics and reading would be .70. In thinking of these two *functions,* it would be appropriate to think in terms of the correlation as .70 rather than .56, though the *tests* correlate only .56.

RELIABILITY OF CRITERION-REFERENCED TESTS

Our discussion of reliability up to this point has assumed that our tests are continuous variables that have no upper limit, or "ceiling," which is usually the case for tests that are developed for use within a normative frame of reference. We have excluded the idea that a large number of examinees would achieve perfect or near-perfect scores. However, criterion-referenced tests are generally designed to be sharply focused on a limited range of behavior that is being taught in a program of instruction. For tests of this type, it is reasonable to expect that a substantial proportion of the examinees may get perfect or near-perfect scores on the test. Traditional measures of reliability do not work well for tests of this type because there is little variability in the set of scores and, as we saw earlier, this lack of variability tends to yield a low reliability coefficient.

Criterion-referenced test scores are interpreted in three basic ways. The first of these is mastery/nonmastery of the particular skill or body of knowledge being tested. Individuals are classified as masters (as having achieved the requisite level of performance with this material) if their test scores surpass a preset cutoff, and as nonmasters if their scores fail to reach this level. There is no middle ground, and all masters are considered equal.

Second, criterion-referenced test scores are interpreted as reflecting the degree of mastery. In this approach, each person's score is again compared to a preset standard, but people whose scores greatly exceed the cutoff are considered to be more complete masters than are those who just barely surpass the cutoff. Likewise, people whose scores fall far short of the cutoff are considered farther from mastery than are those who just missed the cutoff.

The third interpretation of criterion-referenced tests is based on the idea that the test items sample a domain of content. The examinee's score on the test is seen as an estimate of the **domain score,** the score he or she would have gotten on a test that included every item in the domain. The question becomes one of how accurately the domain score is estimated.

Considerable progress has been made in the estimation of reliability for criterion-referenced tests. Although somewhat different approaches are required for each interpretation of a criterion-referenced test, all approaches share the notion of consistency of information. We next examine in detail the issue of consistency as it applies to mastery/nonmastery decisions and then mention briefly some of the issues for the other interpretations. Systematic reviews of the available methods for all three interpretations are provided by Berk (1984), Brennan (1984), and Subkoviak (1984).

The mastery/nonmastery approach requires that examinees be classified into one of two categories. Reliability for this interpretation is assessed by evaluating the consistency with which classifications are made either by the same test administered on two occasions or by alternate forms of the test. (There are also single-test methods analogous to KR-20.) As an example, consider a test that was designed for use with foreign students studying English to assess their mastery of certain specific English constructions. In one such test, Blatchford (1970) assessed mastery of each of 10 English constructions, using four items for each construction. Two forms of the test were developed and administered to groups of students with an interval of about 1 week between testings. Students were required to choose the construction that was correct English usage. Multiple-choice items illustrating two of the constructions are shown in Figure 4–4. Each item is followed by a table showing the percentage of students getting zero, one, two, three, or four items correct on each of the testings. For example, the entry in the top row and first column for Set 6 shows that 2% of the group got zero correct on Form A and four correct on Form B.

Let us look first at Set 6 in Figure 4–4. Note that 36% of the students got perfect scores of four on *both* testings and 21% got zero scores on *both* testings. For this 57% of the group, the little four-item test gave perfectly consistent and unequivocal information. One group appeared to have completely mastered the correct usage, and the other group appeared to be completely in the dark or to possess misinformation. The other 43% showed some inconsistency within a test or between the two tests. How shall we express this degree of inconsistency or unreliability?

The important thing to remember is that a test such as this is being used to decide whether each student has mastery of a specific skill. We might set a severe standard and accept only a perfect performance—four correct out of four—as indicating mastery. Or we might be willing to accept a more relaxed standard of three out of four as satisfactory performance, recognizing that lowered vigilance or some extraneous factor might have been responsible for a single error. Whichever standard is adopted, the question we ask is "How often would the decision have been reversed on the other testing?" Or "How often would we have switched from 'pass' to 'fail' or the reverse?"

Set 6. The use of "but" after an "although" clause.
(1) Because he was late, he still attended the meeting.
*(2) Although he was late, he still attended the meeting.
(3) Although he was late, but he still attended the meeting.
(4) Because he was late, but he still attended the meeting.

Number Correct—Form B	Number Correct—Form A					Total
	0	1	2	3	4	
4	2	1	2	6	36	47
3	1	1	1	4	7	14
2	1	1	1	1	1	5
1	3	1	1	1	1	7
0	21	3	1	1	1	27
Total	28	7	6	13	46	

Set 10. The use of "most" with plural nouns.
(1) The most of the students must study three hours every night.
*(2) Most students must study three hours every night.
(3) Most student must study three hours every night.
(4) Most of student must study three hours every night.

Number Correct—Form B	Number Correct—Form A					Total
	0	1	2	3	4	
4	1	3	4	12	18	38
3	1	2	3	5	5	16
2	2	2	1	3	2	10
1	4	4	1	1	1	11
0	15	5	1	3	1	25
Total	23	16	10	24	27	

Figure 4–4
Two samples from a mastery test of English constructions. Asterisk indicates the correct answer. (Numbers in the table are percents.)

The results from Set 6 are shown here for the two standards:

	Severe Standard (All Four Correct) Form A			Lenient Standard (Three Out of Four Correct) Form A	
Form B	Fail	Pass	Form B	Fail	Pass
Pass	11	36	Pass	8	53
Fail	43	10	Fail	33	6

Using the severe standard, we would reach the same decision for both forms for 79% of students and opposite decisions for 21%. With the more relaxed standard, the corresponding percentages are 86% and 14%.

The decisions for Set 10 can be expressed in the same way:

Form B	Severe Standard (All Four Correct) Form A		Form B	Lenient Standard (Three Out of Four Correct) Form A	
	Fail	Pass		Fail	Pass
Pass	20	18	Pass	14	40
Fail	53	9	Fail	35	11

Clearly, the percentage of reversals is greater for Set 10 than for Set 6. There are 29% and 25% reversals by the severe and lenient standards, respectively. This set provides a less reliable basis for the central question: "Has the student mastered the skill?"

For a test that is being used for the single "go no go" decision of mastery versus nonmastery, the percentage of consistent decisions seems to be a reasonable index of reliability. Unfortunately, this index is a function of the characteristics of the group as well as of the test. If many students are close to the threshold of mastery—having learned a certain skill, but just barely having learned it—there are likely to be numerous reversals from one testing to another. If, on the other hand, there are many who have considerably overlearned the skill or many who have never learned it at all, reversals will be relatively infrequent. Also, if the consistency of the decisions is assessed during a period of active instruction in the skill, students may be changing from non-masters to masters in the interval between administrations, giving the appearance of unreliable assessment. It will be important, therefore, to evaluate the reliability of a test that is intended for mastery decisions by using groups of students who have reached just about the same degree of assurance in their mastery of the skill as those with whom the test will eventually be used. It is also important to conduct the reliability study when active instruction is not taking place.

We now need some way to decide what percentage of consistent decisions represents a satisfactory test. At one extreme, with two choices (i.e., master or nonmaster), pure chance would produce agreement 50% of the time. If the test yields no more consistent results than flipping a coin, it is obviously worthless. At the other extreme, if there were 100% agreement between the two forms in the decision to which they led, the reliability of that decision is clearly perfect. It is the intermediate percentages, which almost always occur, that require evaluation. Are the agreements of 79%, 86%, 71%, and 75% that were found for the two four-item tests by two standards of mastery good, just tolerable, or unsatisfactory?

It is hard to give a general answer to the above question. The answer depends on the length of the test on the one hand, and on the seriousness and irreversibility of the decision on the other. The shorter the test, the more reversals we can expect. The less crucial the decision, the more reversals we can tolerate. Considering that the tests that we have analyzed were composed of only four items, consistencies ranging from 70% to 85% are probably as good as can be expected. If the test results were to be used merely to guide review and remedial instruction, this level of consistency might be quite tolerable because errors in the initial decision would usually be corrected in later testing.

The illustration that we have discussed used data from alternate test forms given about 1 week apart. Of course, it would be possible to subdivide a test and get two scores from a single testing. These scores could be tabulated to determine the frequency of reversals of the decision of mastery. However, it seems likely that with students who are just on the threshold of mastery, changes from one testing to another will be much more common than those from one subscore to another at a single point in time. Blatchford (1970) found median reliability coefficients for a four-item test at a single time to be .80, whereas the median correlation between forms given 1 week apart was only .61. Such a result suggests that two very short tests given on different days may provide a good deal more conservative, and probably sounder, basis for a decision on mastery than a longer test at one time if the students are still in a period of instruction on the skill.

Methods for estimating the reliability of degree of mastery measurements, as well as methods for assessing the accuracy of estimates of domain scores, require a more complex statistical methodology than we can cover thoroughly in this book. Detailed reviews of available methods are given by Berk (1984) and Brennan (1984). We will, however, describe the logical processes that underlie these methods.

The basic feature of methods for estimating reliability in these cases is the use of **variance components.** As we noted in Chapter 2, variances are squares of standard deviations. (More accurately, they are what you have before you take the square root to get the standard deviation.) The size of the variance of any set of scores depends on how many sources of variability go into the scores. For example, the scores of a group of White, middle-class, 10-year-old girls from a farming community in Kansas could be expected to show a much smaller variance on a test measuring knowledge of the geography of the American Great Plains than would the scores from a group of the same size drawn at random from the general American population on a test of general American geography. The reason for the difference is that the scores on the test in the latter case might be affected by variation in racial or ethnic background (race, socioeconomic status, and geographic factors), gender, age, and the greater diversity of the test items themselves.

It is possible to estimate the effect of each of these factors (and many others that might be of interest) on the variance in a set of test scores by systematically controlling the other sources of variability. For example, the difference in reliability using the test–retest procedure and that obtained from a procedure with parallel forms provides a simple estimate of the variance that can be attributed to the sampling of items, because in the first case the items remain constant, and in the second they vary. The impact of gender, age, and many other variables can be estimated by comparing the variances of scores when these characteristics are held constant with the variances from groups where they vary.

The procedures for assessing the reliability of estimates of domain scores and of degree of mastery measures require variance components that reflect both the variability among all examinees across all items in the test and the inconsistency of each person's performance from item to item across the test. Different variance components are used, depending on which type of consistency is being assessed. The resulting ratios indicate the proportion of variance in test scores that can be attributed to different sources, some of which represent reliable aspects of performance. A detailed discussion of this issue and other advanced issues in reliability estimation is provided by Feldt and Brennan (1989).

RELIABILITY OF COMPUTER ADAPTIVE TESTS

Computer adaptive tests focus on the standard error of measurement to assess the reliability of measurement. That is, they are concerned with the uncertainty that remains about a person's true score after the person has been measured (SD_e) rather than the consistency with which the test ranks the individuals in a group (r_{XX}). The reason they must take this approach is that different examinees take different tests. Effectively, each person–test combination is unique. Therefore, one person's score on the test, expressed as number of items answered correctly, cannot be directly compared with another person's score. To be compared, the test scores must be converted into the scale of the latent trait. However, we can get a standard error of measurement for each examinee based on the items they have answered by treating each item as a short test.

If we know nothing about a person, our best guess of his or her score on a test is the mean of the test's norm group because the mean is the point on the score scale for which the average of squared errors is smallest. That is, for any given group of observations on test X, M_X is our best guess for the score of any member of the group. For almost everyone, this guess will be in error by some amount, and the distance of a person's score from the mean is the error in our guess. The standard deviation is a measure of how large the errors are, on average. Therefore, before we test Joshua with a test such as the Wechsler Intelligence Scale for Children, our best guess of his true score is 100 (the mean of the norm group), and the standard deviation of errors in our guesses would be 15 (the standard deviation of the norm group). After giving him the test, our best guess of his true score is his observed score, and the standard error of measurement is the standard deviation of the errors we would make if we repeated the process many times. (See Feldt and Brennan, 1989, p. 121, for a detailed discussion of estimates of true scores.)

When we use computer adaptive testing, each item functions as a mini-test. We administer one item, and Joshua's response gives us a new estimate of his true score. If he passes the item, we raise our estimate; if he fails the item, we reduce the estimate. We ask successively more difficult questions until we reach one he cannot answer or successively easier ones until we reach an item he can answer. Each item improves our estimate of his ability and reduces our uncertainty about his true score. The question is "How do we express our uncertainty?"

Recall from our discussion of computer adaptive testing (CAT) in Chapter 3 that each item has an item characteristic curve or trace line that describes the relationship between the ability level of an examinee and the probability that the person will answer the item correctly. For produce-response items such as fill-in-the-blank items, the probability of a correct response goes from zero for very low ability persons to 1.00 for very high ability persons. When the items are of the select-response variety, low-ability examinees have a probability of selecting the correct response equal to 1 divided by the number of alternatives provided. For example, on multiple-choice items with five alternatives, the probability of getting the item correct by chance (the c parameter in IRT vernacular) is 1/5 or .2. We will use produce-response items to illustrate the necessary principles so we do not have to consider the issue of guessing. For a description of how to estimate SD_e for select-response tests, see Thissen (1990).

We observed in Chapter 3 that the only items that give us any information about the ability level of an examinee are those where we do not know *a priori* whether he or she will answer correctly. The amount of information that the item provides, called the **item information,** is a function of the *change in probability of a correct response,* which is itself a function of the slope of the trace line at that point. The more rapid the change in probability of a correct response (a steeper slope), the greater the information provided by the item. This feature is illustrated in Figure 4–5. The symbol used in IRT vernacular for a person's ability level is the Greek letter theta (θ). For people in the range of ability from θ_1 to θ_2 in Figure 4–5 there is no change in the probability of a correct response; it is zero throughout the range. Therefore, the item tells us nothing about the differences between people at this level of ability, and the item information is zero at this range of θ-levels. In the somewhat higher

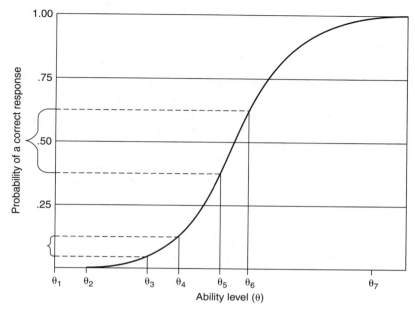

Figure 4–5
Item trace line showing how the change in the probability of a correct response is different at several levels on the ability continuum.

ability range bounded by θ_3 and θ_4, the probability of a correct response is higher for people at the top of the range (about .12) than for people at the bottom (about .05). The item information for people in this range of θ-levels is greater than zero, but not very high.

Consider next the situation for people in the range between θ_5 and θ_6, which are the same distance apart as the previous two pairs of θs. Here, the rate of change in probability is at its maximum for this item (the slope equals the item slope parameter, a). The change in probability of a correct response across this range is from about .35 to about .65. It is at this level that the item information is greatest. This is the range where the ability level of the examinees (θ) matches the difficulty level of the item (the b parameter). Information is at a maximum when $\theta = b$. As ability levels increase above this range, the item information decreases, returning to zero at an ability level of about θ_7. Above this ability level, all examinees get the item correct.

IRT test developers often plot a curve, called the **item information function,** to describe the change in item information at different levels of θ. Figure 4–6 shows two typical item information functions. They start at zero, rise to a maximum at $\theta = b$, and drop back to zero for levels of θ well above b. The units along the baseline are differences between θ and b. The closer the item is to the ability level of the individual, the more information the item gives about that person. The same test item may give no information about some people and a great deal of information about others. (See Wainer and Mislevy, 1990, for a description of how item parameters and item information are calculated.)

The two information function curves in Figure 4–6 are for two items that are of equal difficulty but differ in their discriminations. The curve for Item A is narrower and rises to a

Figure 4–6
Two item information curves. The more discriminating item functions over a narrower range of the ability scale.

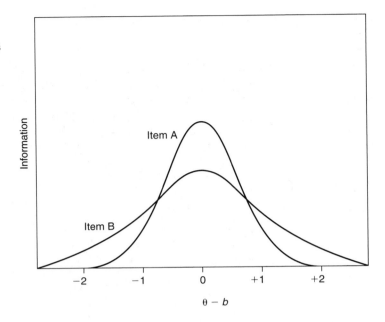

higher peak than the curve for Item B. The curves show that Item A has a higher discrimination (the slope of its trace line is steeper and it yields more information in the range near $\theta - b = 0$) than does Item B. However, Item B provides *some* information over a wider range on the trait.

For any given person (more precisely, for people at ability level θ_i, the ability level of this person), the information we obtain about them is an additive combination of the item information values *for all the items they have taken*. Therefore, we can think of the *particular* test that Joshua has taken as providing information from each of the items he attempted and the total information that his test provides about him (the *test information*) is the sum of those individual item information contributions. We can convert the test information into a metric equivalent to the standard error of measurement using the following relationship

$$SD_e = \sqrt{\frac{1}{Test\ Information}}$$

That is, the measure of our uncertainty about an individual's true score derived from a computer adaptive test is equal to the square root of the reciprocal of the test information. This value is interpreted in exactly the same way as the traditional standard error of measurement.

One of the advantages of CAT is that, given an adequate pool of items, test information and SD_e can be calculated after each item is given, so testing can continue until any desired level of precision is reached. With traditional tests, SD_e tends to be smallest for those who score in the middle of the test's range and larger for those at the extremes because more items are providing information about examinees in the middle of the range. By using item information, the test administrator can continue testing just long enough to reach a desired level of precision that can depend on the use to which the test scores will be put.

SUMMARY

Reliability, or consistency, is a necessary property for any measurement procedure to have. The differences in individuals revealed by the measuring instrument should represent, to the greatest extent possible, real differences on the characteristic of interest. Because any measurement is made with some error, reliability may be viewed as the instrument's relative freedom from error.

No one, single value is the correct reliability for any instrument. The observed reliability is a function of the properties of the underlying trait, the test itself, the group being tested, and the situation in which the information about reliability is obtained. All of these factors must be considered when evaluating the reliability of a test.

How reliable a test must be depends on the purpose of the testing. If the decisions to be made from the test scores are relatively unmodifiable, we would want to be quite certain of the accuracy of our information and would require the highest possible reliability. If, on the other hand, the instrument is being used for short-range decisions that are easily changed, a considerably lower level of reliability may

be satisfactory. Also, the intended use of the scores affects the type of reliability needed. If we are concerned with assessing current levels of performance, a reliability coefficient that reflects the internal consistency of the test or its short-term stability will yield the necessary information. By contrast, if the use for the scores involves forecasting future levels of achievement, a reliability index that shows the stability of those scores over an equivalent time span is needed. In either case, when we are concerned with describing the performance of individuals, the standard error of measurement derived from the appropriate design is the best index of the consistency we can expect for individual scores. The better test publishers provide several types of reliability information for their products so the user can make an informed decision.

The reliability of computer adaptive tests is expressed as the standard error of estimate of the test, which is a function of the information provided about the examinee by each item. Testing using CAT methods can continue until any desired level of precision is reached.

QUESTIONS AND EXERCISES

1. Look at the evidence presented on reliability in the manuals of two or three tests. How adequate is the evidence? What are its shortcomings? For what types of test use is it appropriate? What sources of variability does each type of evidence permit?

2. List two situations in which the standard error of measurement would be needed as an index of stability of performance.

3. The publishers of Test X suggest that it can be used to assess current levels of achievement in reading and to predict reading achievement after an additional year of instruction. What evidence of reliability should you expect the publisher to provide to support each test use?

4. The manual for Test T presents reliability data based on (1) retesting with the same test form 2 weeks later, (2) alpha coefficients, and (3) correlating Form A with Form B, the two forms having been taken 2 weeks apart. Which procedure would you expect to yield the lowest coefficient? Why? Which one should yield the most useful estimate of reliability? What additional information do you need to give an answer?

5. For each of the following situations, indicate whether the change would raise or lower the reliability:
   a. Reliability is determined for scores from all elementary grades combined, rather than within each grade.

b. A test with 25 items is used in place of a 100-item test.

c. The ratings of four judges are averaged, instead of using a single judge.

d. Reliability is determined using Kuder-Richardson Formula 20 rather than correlating scores on equivalent forms.

6. A student has been given a Wechsler Intelligence Scale for Children test four times during her school career, and her cumulative record shows the following global intelligence quotients: 98, 107, 101, and 95. What significance should be attached to these fluctuations in scores?

7. A school plans to give Form R of a reading test in September and Form S in May to study individual differences in improvement during the year. The reliability of each form of the test is known to be about .85 for a grade group. The correlation between the two forms on the two occasions turned out to be .80. How much confidence can be placed in individual differences in amount gained? What factors other than real differences in learning can account for individual differences in gain?

SUGGESTED READINGS

American Educational Research Association, American Psychological Association, & National Council on Measurement in Education. (1999). *Standards for educational and psychological testing*. Washington, DC: American Psychological Association.

Belk, M. S., LoBello, S. G., Ray, G. E., & Zachar, P. (2002). WISC-III administration, clerical, and scoring errors made by student examiners. *Journal of Psychoeducational Assessment, 20,* 290–300.

Blixt, S. L., & Shama, D. B. (1986). An empirical investigation of the standard error of measurement at different ability levels. *Educational and Psychological Measurement, 45,* 545–550.

Brennan, R. L. (1984). Estimating the dependability of the scores. In R. A. Berk (Ed.), *A guide to criterion-referenced test construction* (pp. 292–334). Baltimore: Johns Hopkins University Press.

Feldt, L. S., & Brennan, R. L. (1989). Reliability. In R. L. Linn (Ed.), *Educational measurement* (3rd ed., pp. 105–146). New York: Macmillan.

Jarjoura, D. (1985). Tolerance intervals for true scores. *Journal of Educational Measurement, 10,* 1–17.

Kane, M. T., & Wilson, J. (1984). Errors of measurement and standard setting in mastery testing. *Applied Psychological Measurement, 4,* 107–115.

Kaufman, A. S. (1990). *Assessing adolescent and adult intelligence*. Boston: Allyn & Bacon.

Lord, F. M. (1984). Standard errors of measurement at different score levels. *Journal of Educational Measurement, 21,* 239–243.

Lord, F. M., & Novick, M. R. (1968). *Statistical theories of mental test scores*. Reading, MA: Addison-Wesley.

Rogosa, D. R., & Willett, J. B. (1983). Demonstrating the reliability of the difference score in the measurement of change. *Journal of Educational Measurement, 20,* 335–343.

Thissen, D. (1990). Reliability and measurement precision. In H. Wainer (Ed.) *Computer adaptive testing: A primer* (pp. 161–186). Mahwah, NJ: Erlbaum.

Thorndike, R. L., & Thorndike, R. M. (1994). Reliability in educational and psychological measurement. In T. Husen & N. Postlethwaite (Eds.), *International encyclopedia of education* (2nd ed., pp. 4981–4995). New York: Pergamon Press.

Thorndike, R. M. (2001). Reliability. In B. Bolton (Ed.), *Handbook of measurement and evaluation in rehabilitation* (3rd ed., pp. 29–48). Gaithersburg, MD: Aspen.

Wainer, H., & Mislevy, R. J. (1990). Item response theory, item calibration and proficiency estimation. In H. Wainer (Ed.) *Computer adaptive testing: A primer* (pp. 65–102). Mahwah, NJ: Erlbaum.

CHAPTER 5

Qualities Desired in Any Measurement Procedure: Validity

Introduction
Content-Related Evidence of Validity
    Preparing a Test Blueprint
    Content Validity for Measures of Aptitude and
        Typical Performance
Criterion-Related Evidence of Validity
    Face Validity
    Empirical Validity
Construct-Related Evidence of Validity
    Predictions About Correlations
    Predictions About Group Differences
    Predictions About Responses to Experimental
        Treatments or Interventions

The Unified View of Validity
    Validation as a Scientific Enterprise
    Construct Validity as the Whole of Validity
    Messick's Unified Theory of Validity
    Beyond Messick: Refinements and Shifts in Focus
Validity Theory and Test Bias
Overlap of Reliability and Validity
Validity for Criterion-Referenced Tests
Meta-Analysis and Validity Generalization
Summary
Questions and Exercises
Suggested Readings

INTRODUCTION

Although reliability is a necessary feature that a test must have to be useful for decision making, it is not the most important characteristic. A test may be highly reliable and still bear no relationship to the property we wish to assess. Who, for example, would suggest that head circumference, which can be measured quite reliably, provides a measure of reading achievement? In education and psychology, as elsewhere, the foremost question to be asked with respect to any measurement procedure is "How *valid* is it?" When we ask this question, we are inquiring whether the test measures what we want to measure, all of what we want to measure, and nothing but what we want to measure. In words from the *Standards for Educational and Psychological Testing*, "Validity refers to the degree to which evidence and theory support the interpretations of test scores entailed by proposed uses of tests" (American Educational Research Association, American Psychological Association, & National Council on Measurement in Education, 1999, p. 9). Thus, a test does not have validity in any absolute sense. Rather, the scores produced by a test are valid for some uses and not valid for others.

When we place a tape measure on the top of a desk to determine its length, we have no doubt that the tape does in fact measure the length of the desk. It will give information directly related to our intended use, which may be to decide whether we can put the desk between two windows in a room. Long-time experience with this type of measuring instrument has confirmed beyond a shadow of a doubt its validity as a tool for measuring length. But we would surely question the validity of this instrument if the intended use was to measure head circumference to make a college admissions decision. Note that if we measured head circumference to determine what size hat to buy, the measurement would be valid *for this use*.

Now suppose we give a test of reading achievement to a group of children. This test requires the children to select certain answers to a series of questions based on reading passages and to make pencil marks on an answer sheet to indicate their choices. We count the number of pencil marks made in the predetermined correct places and give the children as scores the number of correct answers each one marked. We call these scores measures of their reading comprehension. But a score by itself is not the comprehension. It is the *record* of a *sample of behavior* taken at a particular point in time. Any judgment regarding reading comprehension is an inference from this number of correct answers. The validity of the score interpretation is not self-evident but is something we must establish on the basis of adequate evidence.

Consider also the typical personality inventory that endeavors to provide an appraisal of "emotional adjustment." In this type of inventory, the respondents mark a series of statements about feelings or behaviors as being characteristic of or not characteristic of themselves. On the basis of this type of procedure, certain responses are keyed as indicative of emotional maladjustment. A score is obtained by seeing how many of these responses an individual selects. But making certain marks on a piece of paper is a good many steps removed from actually exhibiting emotional disturbance. We must find some way of establishing the extent to which the performance on the test actually corresponds to the quality of the behavior in which we are directly interested. Our problem is to determine the validity of such a measurement procedure.

These three instances of measurement, the tape, the reading comprehension test, and the personality inventory, all require evidence that the numbers they produce are useful for their intended purpose. The measurements differ from each other in two important respects: the length of the chain of inference between the measuring act and the interpretation of the resulting number, and the social consequences that may follow from the measurement. With the tape the chain of inference is short and the social consequences generally are negligible (although not so if the tape is being used to lay out a site for a toxic waste dump). With the psychological measurements, both issues are more problematic. The relationship between reading comprehension test items and an inference about a person's level on the trait requires a careful consideration of the content of the behavior domain, but this analysis is reasonably direct. Likewise, the use that will be made of the test score usually will relate fairly directly and in a socially positive way to the education of the examinee. But if the test is used inappropriately, for example, with a child for whom English is a second language, then the score, although accurately representing the child's reading comprehension *in English,* may result in a decision that has adverse consequences for the child. The consequences of the decision are part of the use that is made of the test score and, therefore, are inextricably bound up with the issue of validity. Examples of this type of test misuse are becoming more rare, but test users must always be aware of the consequences that decisions will have. Of course, with the personality inventory the chain of inference is longer and the consequences for the test taker can also be adverse.

A test may be thought of as corresponding to some aspect of human behavior in any one of three senses. The terms that have been adopted to designate these senses are (1) *content-related validity,* (2) *criterion-related validity,* and (3) *construct-related validity.* We will examine each of these senses so that we may understand clearly what is involved in each case and for what kinds of tests and testing situations each is relevant. At the end of the chapter we will present the unified view of validity that has developed in the last decade.

CONTENT-RELATED EVIDENCE OF VALIDITY

Consider a test that has been designed to measure competence in using the English language. How can we tell whether the test does in fact measure that achievement? First, we must reach some agreement as to the skills and knowledge that comprise correct and effective use of English. If the test is to be used to appraise the effects of classroom instruction, we must specify the subset of skills and knowledge that have been the objectives of that instruction. Then we must examine the test to see what skills, knowledge, and understanding it calls for. Finally, we must match the analysis of *test content* with the analysis of *course content* and *instructional objectives* to see how well the former represents the latter. To the extent that our objectives, which we have accepted as goals for our course, are represented in the test, the test appears valid for use in our school. A similar process is involved in developing assessments for industrial and military training programs as well as for licensing and certification exams such as tests for drivers' licenses.

Because the analysis is essentially a rational and judgmental one, this process has sometimes been spoken of as *rational* or *logical validity.* The term *content validity* has also been used widely because the analysis is largely in terms of test content. However, we should not think of content too narrowly because we may be interested in cognitive processes as much as in simple factual content. In the field of English expression, for example, we might be concerned on the one hand with such content elements as the rules and principles for capitalization, use of commas, or spelling words with *ei* and *ie* combinations. But we might also be interested in such process skills as arranging ideas in a logical order, writing sentences that present a single unified thought, or picking the most appropriate word to convey the desired meaning. In a sense, *content* is what the examinees work with; *process* is what they do with the content. The term **content-related validity** refers to an assessment of whether a test contains appropriate content and requires that appropriate processes be applied to that content.

To either assess the content validity of an existing test or to construct a test that measures a particular set of contents and processes requires that we specify the contents and processes to be measured explicitly. This explicit statement of what a test is intended to measure is called a *test blueprint.* The correspondence between the test blueprint and the definition of the trait to be measured *is* the content validity of the test.

Preparing a Test Blueprint

A **test blueprint** (also called a **table of specifications** for the test) is an explicit plan that guides test construction. The basic components of a test blueprint are the specifications of cognitive processes and the description of content to be covered by the test. These two dimensions need to be matched to show which process relates to each segment of content and to provide a framework for the development of the test. It is useful for the test constructor, in planning the evaluation of a unit, to make a test blueprint that includes not only the cognitive processes and the content but also the method or methods to be used in evaluating student progress toward achieving each objective. The illustrations we use in this section are couched in terms of guidelines that an individual teacher or test constructor would use to produce a good achievement test for local use. Standardized achievement test construction applies the same procedures, but to more broadly specified curricula. When evaluating a test for content validity, you would use the same steps of domain definition, but the validity question would relate to whether the test matches your domain rather than to serve as a guide for item writing. In Chapter 15 we cover the principles of item writing and analysis that experts use to produce content-valid measures of educational achievement.

A blueprint for an examination in health for an eighth-grade class is provided in Table 5–1. The test will use a short-answer, or objective, format and contain 60 items. This test is the type for which a formal blueprint is most useful, but the kind of thinking that goes into formulating a blueprint is useful even in constructing an essay test with five or six items. The issues that are involved in the decision about the type of test item to use are considered later.

The cognitive processes to be assessed by the test are listed in the left-hand column of the table. The titles of each of three content units have been entered as column headings. Each box, or cell, under the unit headings contains content entries that relate to the cognitive process on the same line with the cell. The complete blueprint specifies the content deemed important and how it will be measured. Most standardized achievement tests would cover a broader array of content than is shown here, but content definition and test construction would proceed in the same way.

In some states, test blueprints for most subject matter and courses are prepared centrally. These serve as guides for commercial test producers. Preparing a two-dimensional outline for a test is an exacting and time-consuming task, but once such a complete blueprint has been prepared, it can be used until the curriculum or teaching emphasis is changed.

An examination of the blueprint should make it clear to you that tests are just samples of student behavior for four reasons:

1. Only those objectives suitable for appraisal with a paper-and-pencil test are included in the blueprint. (Procedures for assessing other objectives are discussed briefly in Chapter 10.)
2. The entries in the cells under each area of content are examples that illustrate, but do not exhaust, the total content.
3. There are an unlimited number of items that could be written for the material that is included in the blueprint.
4. The time available for testing is limited, and, therefore, the test can include only a small sample from the domain of all possible items.

If a test is to reflect local goals, you must carefully choose the items to include on your tests or select carefully a test that measures those goals. The following four issues should guide your construction or evaluation of the test:

1. What emphasis should each of the content areas and cognitive processes receive on the test? In other words, what proportion of all the items on the test should be written for each content area and for each cognitive process within each content area?
2. What type or types of items should be included on the test?

3. How long should the test be? How many questions or items should the total test contain? How many items should be written for each cell of the blueprint?
4. How difficult should the items be?

Relative Emphasis of Content Areas and Process Objectives

The proportion of test items allocated to each content area and to each cognitive process should correspond to the instructional emphasis and importance of the topic. The decision-making process involved is subjective, but the test user should ensure that the test has maintained an appropriate balance in emphasis for both content and mental processes. Allocating a different number of items to each topic and cognitive process is the most obvious way of weighting topics and processes on the test.

The initial weighting of the content areas and cognitive processes requires the assignment of percentages to each content area and cognitive process such that the total for both is 100%. In the blueprint shown in Table 5–1, the test maker decided that Topic A, nutrition, should receive a weight of 40%; Topic B, communicable diseases, should also receive a weight of 40%; and Topic C, noncommunicable diseases, should receive a weight of 20%. If the curriculum guide calls for 5 weeks of instructional time to be spent on Topic A and also on Topic B, and only 2 weeks on Topic C, the allocation of weights corresponds roughly to teaching time.

For the cognitive processes in Table 5–1, the test maker decided that 20% of all the items should be allocated to Process 1, 30% each to Processes 2 and 3, and 10% each to Processes 4 and 5. These allocations imply that the curriculum has emphasized remembering or recalling terms, specific facts, principles, concepts, and generalizations. In other words, the course was primarily focused on increasing the students' fund of knowledge, with less attention given to improving their ability to use the information in novel situations. If the allocation of items to the cognitive processes truly reflects the emphasis in the curriculum, then the allocation is appropriate. We might take issue with the emphasis, but, given that emphasis, we cannot say that the allocation of test items is inappropriate.

Types of Items to Be Used

The types of items that can be used on a test can be classified into two categories: (1) those for which examinees produce their own answers, which are sometimes labeled **supply-response, produce-response** or **constructed-response items,** and (2) those for which students select their answers from several choices, which are labeled **select-response items.** Examples of supply-response items are the essay item requiring an extended answer from the student, the short-answer item requiring no more than one or two sentences for an answer, and the completion item requiring only a word or a phrase for an answer. Examples of select-response items are true–false, multiple-choice, and matching items. The decision about which type of item to use will depend on the cognitive process to be measured, the strengths and weaknesses of each item type for the process and content to be measured, and the way the test will be used and scored.

Total Number of Items for the Test

If the decision is made to use an essay type of test, there will be time for only a few questions. The more elaborate the answers required, the fewer the number of questions that can be included. For example, a 40-minute test in high school might have three or four essay questions requiring extended answers of a page each. Select-response and short-answer tests can involve a much larger number of items.

Table 5–1
Blueprint for Final Examination in Health in Eighth Grade

Process Objectives	Content Areas
	A. Nutrition, 40%
1. Recognizes terms and vocabulary 20%	Nutrients Incomplete protein Vitamins Complete protein Enzymes Amino acids Metabolism Glycogen Oxidation Carbohydrates 4 or 5 items
2. Identifies specific facts 30%	Nutrients essential to health Good sources of food nutrients Parts of digestive system Process of digestion of each nutrient Sources of information about foods and nutrition 7 or 8 items
3. Identifies principles, concepts, and generalizations 30%	Bases of well-balanced diet Enzyme reactions Transfer of materials between cells Cell metabolism Functions of nutrients in body 7 or 8 items
4. Evaluates health information and advertisements 10%	Analyzes food and diet advertisements Interprets labels on foods Identifies good sources of information about foods and diets 2 or 3 items
5. Applies principles and generalizations to novel situations 10%	Identifies well-balanced diet Computes calories needed for weight-gaining or weight-losing diet Predicts consequences of changes in enzymes on digestive system Identifies services and protection provided by the Federal Food and Drug Act 2 or 3 items
No. of items	24
Total time for test—90 minutes	

Content Areas		No. of Items
B. Communicable Diseases, 40%	C. Noncommunicable Diseases, 20%	
Immunity Epidemic Virus Pathogenic Carrier Endemic Antibodies Protozoa Incubation period 4 or 5 items	Goiter Deficiency diseases Diabetes Cardiovascular diseases Caries 2 or 3 items	12

Common communicable diseases
Incidence of various diseases
Methods of spreading disease
Types of immunization
Symptoms of common
    communicable diseases
 	
7 or 8 items
	Specific diseases caused by lack of
	    vitamins
	Specific disorders resulting from
	    imbalance in hormones
	Incidence of noncommunicable diseases
	Common noncommunicable diseases of
	    adolescents and young adults
	
	3 or 4 items
		18

Basic principles underlying control of disease Actions of antibiotics Body defenses against disease Immune reactions in body 7 or 8 items	Pressure within cardiovascular system Control of diabetes Inheritance of abnormal conditions Abnormal growth of cells 3 or 4 items	18

Distinguishes between adequate and
    inadequate evidence for medicines
Identifies misleading advertisements
    for medications
2 or 3 items
	Identifies errors or misleading information
	    in health material
	Identifies appropriate source of
	    information for health problems
	1 or 2 items
		6

Recognizes conditions likely to result
    in increase of communicable
    disease
Identifies appropriate methods for
    sterilizing objects
Gives appropriate reasons for regu-
    lations, processes, or treatments
2 or 3 items
	Predicts consequences of changes in
	    secretion of certain hormones
	
	Predicts probability of inheriting
	    abnormal conditions
	
	1 or 2 items
		6

24	12	60
	Total number of items—60	

The total number of items included in a test should be large enough to provide an adequate sample of student performance across content areas and across cognitive processes. The greater the number of content areas and cognitive processes to be measured by a test, the longer the test needs to be.

The time available for testing is also a factor that limits the number of items on a test. Most achievement tests should be *power tests,* not *speed tests,* meaning that there should be enough time for at least 80% of the students to attempt to answer every item. There are few subject areas in which speed of answering is a relevant aspect of achievement. The number of test items that can be asked in a given amount of time depends on the following factors:

1. *The type of item used on the test.* A short-answer item for which a student has to write his or her answer is likely to require more time than a true–false or multiple-choice item for which a student is only required to choose an answer from among several choices. Of course, items that call for more extended written responses will take even more time.

2. *The age and educational level of the examinees.* Students in the primary grades whose reading and writing skills are just beginning to develop require more time per test item than older students do. Young children cannot attend to the same task for a long period of time. Testing time for them must be shorter, further reducing the number of items. With younger children, achievement testing is often distributed in short blocks over several days. For college students and adults, we can expect faster performance and more sustained attention, except for those for whom testing is a novel experience.

3. *The ability level of students.* Compared to lower ability students, high-ability students have better developed reading and writing skills. They also have a better command of the subject matter and better problem-solving skills. As a rule, high-ability students can answer more questions per unit of testing time than low-ability students of the same age and grade can. Thus, a test for an advanced class could be longer, and a test for a slower learning class should be shorter than a test for students of average ability.

4. *The length and complexity of the items.* If test items are based on reading passages, tabular materials, maps, or graphs, time must be provided for reading and examining the stimulus material. The more stimulus material of this type that is used on a test, the fewer the number of items that can be included on it.

5. *The type of process objective being tested.* Items that require only the recall of knowledge can be answered more quickly than those that require the application of knowledge to a new situation. Thus, tests intended to assess higher cognitive processes should include fewer items for a given amount of testing time.

6. *The amount of computation or quantitative thinking required by the item.* Most individuals work more slowly when dealing with quantitative materials than when dealing with verbal materials; therefore, if the items require mathematical computations, the time allotted per item must be longer than that for purely verbal items.

Conclusions on Total Number of Test Items

It is impossible to give hard-and-fast rules about the number of items to be included in a test for a given amount of testing time. As a rule, the typical adult will require from 30 to 45 seconds to read and answer a simple, factual-type multiple-choice or true–false item and from 75 to 100 seconds to read and answer a fairly complex, multiple-choice item requiring problem solving.

Keep in mind that a great deal of variation exists among examinees regarding the number of items that each one can complete in a given amount of time and that this variation is not always related to reading ability or knowledge of the content being assessed. This characteristic is also related to individual learning styles. The total amount of time required for a number of items sufficient to provide adequate coverage of the blueprint may, in some cases, be more than is available in a single testing session. The most satisfactory solution to this problem is to divide the test into two or more separate subtests that can be given on successive days. As we will see in Chapter 9, this is the usual procedure for standardized achievement test batteries.

Determining Item Distribution

For the examination in eighth-grade health (see Table 5–1), the test maker decided to have 60 items. The blueprint is used to determine how many items to write for each cell. The first step is to determine the total number of items for each content area and cognitive process. The blueprint in Table 5–1 specifies that 40% of the items, or 24 items (0.40 × 60), should be on Topic A; 24 items (0.40 × 60) on Topic B, and 12 items (0.20 × 60) on Topic C. These numbers are entered in the row labeled "No. of items." The percentage assigned to each cognitive process is likewise multiplied by the total number of items to determine the number of items that should be written to measure each process. When this is done, we get the numbers entered in the extreme right-hand column of the blueprint.

To determine the number of items in each cell of the blueprint, we multiply the total number of items in a content area by the percentage assigned to the cognitive process in each row. For example, to determine the number of items for the first cell under Topic A, recognizing nutrition terms and vocabulary, we multiply 24 by 0.2 (20%), which gives 4.8 items. Because the number 4.8 is between 4 and 5, we can note that we should have either 4 or 5 items covering this content and this process. The other cells in the blueprint are filled in in the same way. It must be recognized that some process outcomes are related primarily to certain aspects of content. For instance, on a social studies examination, a process objective related to map reading might be testable primarily in a content unit on natural resources rather than in one on human resources. Cell entries may need to be modified to make the content and process congruent. Furthermore, it is probably desirable to indicate a range of items for each cell, as our example does, to provide flexibility.

Appropriate Level of Difficulty of the Items

Difficulty implies something different for an essay than it does for a short-answer or objective test item. An item that is of appropriate difficulty for an essay test is one for which each member of the class can produce a credible answer and which elicits responses varying in completeness, thoughtfulness, and quality of organization of ideas.

For objective items, difficulty can be thought of in terms of individual items or of the whole test. The difficulty of an item is determined by dividing the number of students getting the item correct by the total number of students attempting the item. (Usually we assume that all students have the opportunity to attempt all items.) The difficulty of the entire test is determined by dividing the mean of the test by the total number of items on the test, and it can be thought of as the average difficulty for all of the items on the test. For example, if a particular item on a test is answered correctly by 40% of all students who take the test, we say the item has a 40% or .40 difficulty. An item that 75% of the students get correct would have a difficulty of .75. (This system can be confusing because the larger the difficulty index the easier the item. The value used could more logically be called the "easiness" of a test.) The difficulty of the whole test is the average of the individual item difficulties.

The appropriate average difficulty and spread of item difficulties differs for norm- and criterion-referenced tests. In general, criterion-referenced tests are constructed to be easier (in the sense of average item difficulty) than norm-referenced tests. On a diagnostic test intended to locate isolated individuals who are having special difficulty, it is reasonable to expect a large number of perfect or near-perfect scores and very few relatively low scores. On the other hand, if we administer a test to find out how much students already know before beginning instruction on a new topic, we should not be surprised to get a large number of near-zero scores, because the material has not yet been taught.

On criterion-referenced tests, diagnostic tests, or pretests administered prior to instruction, we are not concerned about maximizing variability. Even if everyone gets a perfect score or if everyone gets a zero score, we are obtaining the information that we were seeking. On the other hand, when the purpose of the test is to discriminate levels of achievement among different members of the class or group, then we want the test to yield a spread of scores. We want to be able to separate the really high achiever from the next highest achiever and the really low achiever from the next lowest achiever. Ideally, we would like to have every student get a different score on the test because that would increase variability and facilitate ranking. It is undesirable for anyone (or more than one person) to get a perfect score on such a test because that would decrease variability and make ranking more difficult. It would also mean that the test lacked sufficient ceiling to allow the really able students to demonstrate the limits of their knowledge. On the other hand, we would not want to get a zero or chance-level score, indicating that the student could not successfully answer any items, because then we would not have gotten down to his or her level. On such a test, we would not want an item that everyone got correct or an item that everyone got incorrect, simply because neither of these items contributes to making discriminations among students according to their levels of achievement. (In IRT vernacular, we would like the range of b parameters for the items to exceed the range of θ values for the examinees.)

As a rough rule of thumb, the difficulty of a test should be about halfway between the number of items a student could get correct by guessing and 100%. Because the effect of guessing adds chance variability to test scores, it is generally better to have the test be slightly easier than this guideline would suggest rather than more difficult. For a multiple-choice test with four options, the preferred level of difficulty would be about .65 to .70; for a true–false test, the optimum difficulty level would be about .75 to .80. Because the probability of getting an item right by chance is 1 divided by the number of answer choices, this rule leads to the conclusion that the average difficulty for items with five alternatives should be about .60 to .65. (Chance variability is 20%, and halfway between chance variability and a perfect score is .60.)

Continuing with our example in Table 5–1, suppose the 60 items on the health test were all completion items and that the purpose of the test is to rank students on their knowledge. We would want the average score for the class to be about 30 items correct (.50 × 60) because the probability of guessing the correct answer to a supply-response item is assumed to be zero. If the 60 items had been five-alternative multiple-choice items, we would have wanted the average score to be about 36 items correct (.60 × 60).

Difficulties as low as this sometimes bother teachers and students who are accustomed to thinking of "passing" or "failing" scores in terms of the percentage of the items that a student gets correct on a test. The above suggestions have nothing to do with passing or failing; a decision based on any assessment device, including assigning marks or grades to students, is an entirely different problem that should be kept separate from the proportion of items correctly answered. The percentages that are suggested here will tend to yield a set of scores that will be maximally useful to test users who want to discriminate levels of achievement among examinees. It is for this reason that people who construct standardized achievement tests tend to use items with the properties outlined here.

In the process of achieving the desired average level of difficulty, the teacher is likely to produce some difficult items that are passed by as few as 30% or 40% of the students (assuming a four-choice multiple-choice item) and some easy ones that are passed by 80% to 90% of the students. We would hope that many of the items would approach the desired average level of about 65%, and they should be written with that goal in mind. However, achieving optimum difficulty levels is less important than ensuring that the items provide a good coverage of content and that each one is answered correctly more often by able than by less able students. Ensuring proper content establishes content validity.

The problem of appraising content-related validity is closely parallel to the problem of preparing the blueprint for a test and then building a test to match the blueprint. A teacher's own test has content validity to the extent that a wise and thoughtful analysis of course objectives has been made in the blueprint and that care, skill, and ingenuity have been exercised in building test items to match the blueprint. A standardized test may be shown to have validity for a particular school or a particular curriculum insofar as the content of that test corresponds to and represents the objectives accepted in that school or that curriculum.

It should be clear that rational or content validity evidence is of primary importance for measures of achievement. In particular, validity of a formative test concerned with mastery of one or more specific educational objectives, the type of test that has been called content or criterion referenced, will be judged on how well the test tasks represent the defined objectives. But for the summative, norm-referenced achievement test (such as a standardized, end-of-course test) as well, the primary concern will be with how well the test represents what the best and most expert judgment would consider to be important knowledge and skill for the academic environment. If the correspondence is good, the test will be judged to have high validity for this application; if poor, the validity must be deemed low.

Responsible makers of tests for publication and widespread use go to considerable pains to determine the widely accepted goals of instruction in the fields in which their tests are to be developed and used. Test constructors may, and often do, resort to many sources, including the following:

1. The more widely used textbooks in the field
2. Recent courses of study for the large school units, such as state, county, and city school systems
3. Reports of special study groups that often appear in yearbooks of one or another of the educational societies
4. Groups of teachers who give instruction on the topic
5. Specialists in university, city, and state departments concerned with the training or supervision of teachers in the field.

Gathering information from these sources, the test maker develops a blueprint for the test, and the test items are prepared in terms of this blueprint. Because of variations from community to community, no test published for national distribution can be made to exactly fit the content or objectives of every local course of study. In this sense, a test developed on a national basis is always less valid than an equally well-developed test tailored specifically to the local objectives. However, the well-made commercial test can take the common components that appear repeatedly in different textbooks and courses of study and build a test around these components. Such a test represents the common core that is central to the different specific local patterns. In addition, commercial tests are prepared by people who are testing specialists. The items are written by experienced and well-trained item writers and the tests are subjected to a thorough review both for style and for possible bias in either phrasing or content. Thus, the items are likely to be of high quality, which may be a reasonable trade-off for the poorer fit to local instructional objectives.

It should be clear from the previous paragraphs that the relationship between teaching and testing is typically intimate. Test content is drawn from what has been taught or what is proposed to be taught. An instructional program is the original source of achievement test materials. Sometimes the specification of test content may precede the curricular objectives underlying a local course of study, as when specialists have been brought together to design a test corresponding to some emerging trend in education. Sometimes the test may lag behind, as when the test is based on the relatively conventional objectives emphasized in established textbooks. But usually, test content and classroom instruction are closely related to each other, and the test may be appraised by how faithfully it corresponds to the significant goals of instruction.

For appraising the validity of test scores as representing the degree of achievement of curricular objectives, there is no substitute for a careful and detailed examination of the actual test tasks. A test may be labeled "mathematical concepts," but call for nothing except knowledge of definitions of terms. A test of "reading comprehension" may only call for answers to questions concerning specific details that appear in the passages. It is the tasks presented by the items that really define *what* the test is measuring, and one who would judge a test's content validity for a specific curriculum must take a hard look at the individual items.

Content Validity for Measures of Aptitude and Typical Performance

The need for content validity and how to evaluate it is fairly straightforward with achievement tests, but it is also an issue for measures of aptitudes and for instruments designed to measure personality or interests. In both of these latter cases, however, the definition of the domain is rather more complicated and indirect. Suppose we wish to construct a test that measures a person's general level of cognitive functioning, what we typically call a general intelligence, or IQ, test. How shall we decide what is the appropriate domain of content? The answer to this question is inextricably bound up with what we consider general intelligence to be, and that implies a theory about the nature of intelligence. Our theory defines both what intelligence is for us and what behaviors can be used as indicators of it. Our theory comes to occupy the place of the curriculum plan for an achievement test. Once we have specified our theory, we can proceed to construct and evaluate test items to measure the content and cognitive processes specified by the theory. We cover several major current theories of intelligence and the tests designed to fit those theories in Chapter 8.

Content validity can also be an issue for measures of typical performance, but here the relationship is seldom direct because the behaviors associated with personality constructs can seldom be listed exhaustively. Thus, one may be able to judge whether a given test item is an exemplar of the trait "sociability," but it would be impossible to list all of the contexts in which sociable behavior might occur and all the forms it might take. For this reason, and because little general agreement exists about which personality or interest constructs are most useful, the assessment of content validity for these instruments is much more an individual matter of whether the items included in the scale conform to the theory espoused by the test user. As we shall see later in this chapter, the fit of test items to a theory about behavior is an integral part of what has come to be called construct validity.

CRITERION-RELATED EVIDENCE OF VALIDITY

Frequently, we are interested in using a test in connection with a decision that implies predicting some specific future outcome. We give a scholastic aptitude test to predict how likely a high school student is to be successful in College X, where success is represented at least approximately by grade-point average. We give an employment test to select machine operators who are likely to be successful employees, as represented by some criterion such as high production with low spoilage and low personnel turnover. For this purpose, we care very little what a test looks like. We are interested almost entirely in the degree to which it correlates with some chosen criterion measure of job or academic success. Some other measure (often, but not necessarily, one that becomes available later) is taken as the criterion of "success," and we judge a test in terms of its relationship to that criterion measure. The higher the correlation, the better the test.

Face Validity

The statement that we do not care what a test looks like is not entirely true. What a test "looks like" may be of importance in determining its acceptability and reasonableness to those who will be tested. A group of would-be pilots may be more ready to accept a mathematics test dealing with wind drift and fuel consumption than they would be to accept a test with the same essential problems phrased in terms of costs of crops or recipes for baking cakes. This appearance of reasonableness is often called **face validity,** and although it is never a sufficient condition for the use of a test, it can be considered a necessary condition whenever the voluntary cooperation of the examinees is important. Unless the test looks like it could be used for the purpose the examinees have been told it will be used for, they may give less than their maximum effort or may not provide sincere responses. As Sackett, Schmitt, Ellingson, and Kabin (2001) note, "When a test looks appropriate for the performance situation in which examinees will be expected to perform, they tend to react positively. . . . Equally important, perhaps, may be the perception that one is fairly treated" (pp. 315–316).

Empirical Validity

Evaluation of a test *as a predictor* is primarily an empirical and statistical evaluation, and the collection of evidence bearing on this aspect of validity has sometimes been spoken of as **empirical** or **statistical validity.** The basic procedure is to give the test to a group that is entering some job or training program, to follow them up later, to get for each one a specified measure of success on the job or in the training program, known as the **criterion,** and then to compute the correlation between the test scores and the criterion measures of success. The higher the correlation, the more effective the test is as a predictor and the higher is its **criterion-related validity.**

There are really two broad classes of criterion-related validity, with the differentiation depending on the time relationship between collecting the test information and the criterion information. If the test information is to be used to forecast future criterion performance, as is the case in all selection decisions, then we speak of **predictive validity.** On the other hand, in some cases we would like to be able to substitute a test for another more complex or expensive procedure. This might be the case when we use a group test of intelligence in place of an individually administered one. The question then is whether the two different sources of information have a strong enough relationship that the less expensive one can be used in place of the more expensive one. If this is our concern, we would want to know that scores on one test correlate highly with scores obtained concurrently on the other. When scores on the test and the criterion are obtained at essentially the same time, we speak of **concurrent validity.** The two labels, *predictive* and *concurrent,* have more to do with the purpose of the study than with the time relationship between the assessments, but these are the terms that have evolved. Because predictive validity is the more widespread concern, we will use that term in the discussion to follow, but the procedures and issues are the same for both types of empirical validity.

We can picture the relationship between a predictor and a criterion in various ways. For example, the bar chart in Figure 5–1 shows the percentage of candidates passing air force pilot training at each of nine score levels on a test battery designed to assess aptitude for flight training. The chart shows a steady increase in the percentage passing as we go from low to high scores, so successful completion of training is related to aptitude level. A similar chart could be produced to show the relationship between scores on a college admissions test and subsequent grades in college or between clerical aptitude test scores and success in clerical training. The relationship pictured in the chart corresponds to a correlation coefficient of .49. A higher correlation would result in a greater difference in success rates for increasing levels of aptitude score.

The Problem of the Criterion

We have said that empirical validity can be estimated by determining the correlation between test scores and a suitable criterion measure of success on the job or in the classroom. The joker here is the phrase "suitable criterion measure." One of the most difficult problems that the investigator of selection tests faces is that of locating or creating a satisfactory measure of success to be used

Figure 5–1

Percent of cadets completing pilot training at each aptitude level. The correlation coefficient is .49.

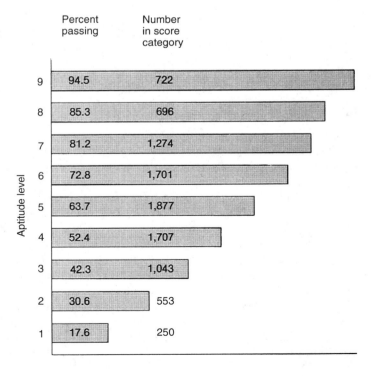

Aptitude level	Percent passing	Number in score category
9	94.5	722
8	85.3	696
7	81.2	1,274
6	72.8	1,701
5	63.7	1,877
4	52.4	1,707
3	42.3	1,043
2	30.6	553
1	17.6	250

as a criterion measure for test validation. This problem is most serious in employment settings but is also quite troublesome in the academic environment. It might appear that it should be a simple matter to decide on some measure of rate of production or some type of rating by superiors to serve as a criterion measure. It might also seem that this measure, once decided on, should be obtainable in a simple and straightforward fashion. Unfortunately, identifying a satisfactory criterion measure is not so easy. Finding or developing acceptable criterion measures usually involves the tests-and-measurements research worker in a host of problems.

Each possible type of criterion measure presents its own problems. A record of actual performance has a good deal of appeal—number of widgets made, freedom from errors as a cashier, or amount of insurance sold, for example. But many jobs or positions, such as physician, teacher, secretary, or receptionist, yield no objective record of the most important elements of performance or production. And, when such records do exist, the production is often influenced by an array of factors that are outside the individual's control. The production record of a lathe operator may depend not only on personal skill in setting up and adjusting the lathe, but also on the condition of the equipment, the adequacy of the lighting in the work environment, or the quality of the material being machined. The sales of an insurance agent are a function not only of individual effectiveness as a seller, but also of the territory to be covered and the supervision and assistance the agent receives.

Because of the absence or the shortcomings of performance records, the personnel psychologist has often depended on some type of rating by a supervisor as a criterion measure. Such ratings may exist as a routine part of the personnel procedures in a company, as when each employee receives a semiannual efficiency report, or the ratings may have to be gathered especially for the selection study. In either event, the ratings will typically be found to depend as much on the person giving them as on the person being rated. Ratings tend to be erratic and influenced by many factors other than performance. The problems involved with using rating procedures to describe and evaluate people are discussed in Chapter 12.

There are always many criterion measures that might be obtained and used for validating a selection test. In addition to using quantitative performance records and subjective ratings, we might also use later tests of proficiency. This type of procedure is involved when a college entrance mathematics test is validated in terms of its ability to predict later performance on a comprehensive examination on college mathematics. Here, the comprehensive examination serves as the criterion measure. Another common type of criterion measure is the average of grades in some type of educational or training program. Tests for the selection of engineers, for example, may be validated against course grades in engineering school.

All criterion measures are partial in the sense that they measure only a part of success on the job or only the preliminaries to actual job or academic performance. This last point is true of the engineering school grades just mentioned, which represent a relatively immediate—but partial—criterion of success as an engineer. The ultimate criterion would be some appraisal of lifetime success in a profession. In the very nature of things, such an ultimate criterion is inaccessible, and the investigator must be satisfied with substitutes for it. These substitutes are never completely satisfactory. The problem is always to choose the most satisfactory measure or combination of measures from among those that it appears feasible to obtain. The investigator is then faced with the problem of deciding which of the criterion measures is most satisfactory. How is that decided?

Qualities Desired in a Criterion Measure

Four qualities are desired in a criterion measure. In order of their importance, they are (1) relevance, (2) freedom from bias, (3) reliability, and (4) availability.

We judge a criterion measure to be *relevant* to the extent that standing on the criterion measure corresponds to, or exemplifies, level or status on the trait we are trying to predict. In appraising the relevance of a criterion, we must revert to rational considerations. No empirical evidence is available to tell us how relevant freshman grade-point average is, for example, as an indicator of someone having achieved the objectives of Supercolossal University. For achievement tests, therefore, it is necessary to rely on the best available professional judgment to determine whether the content of a test accurately represents our educational objectives. In the same way, with respect to a criterion measure, it is necessary to rely on professional judgment to provide an appraisal of the degree to which some available criterion measure can serve as an indicator of what we would really like to predict. We could even say that relevance corresponds to the content validity of the criterion measure. A relevant criterion corresponds closely to the behaviors of ultimate interest.

The second most important factor in the criterion measure is *freedom from bias*. By this, we mean that the measure should be one on which each person has the same opportunity to make a good score or, more specifically, one on which each equally capable person obtains the same score (except for errors of measurement), regardless of the group to which he or she belongs. Examples of biasing factors are such things as variation in wealth from one district to another for our previous example of the insurance agent, variation in the quality of equipment and conditions of work for a factory worker, variation in "generosity" of the bosses who are rating private secretaries, or variation in the quality of teaching received by students in different classes. To the extent that the criterion score depends on factors in the conditions of work, in the evaluation of work, or in the personal characteristics of the individual, rather than on status on the trait of interest, there is no real meaning to the correlation between test results and a criterion score. A criterion measure that contains substantial bias cannot at the same time reveal relevant differences among people on the trait of interest. We discuss bias in measuring instruments in more detail later in this chapter.

The third factor is *reliability* as it applies to criterion scores. A measure of success on the job must be stable or reproducible if it is to be predicted by any type of test device. If the criterion score is one that jumps around in an unpredictable way from day to day, so that the person who shows high job performance one week may show low job performance the next, or the person who receives a high rating from one supervisor gets a low rating from another, there is no possibility of finding a test that will predict that score. A measure that is completely unstable itself cannot be predicted by anything else.

Finally, in choosing a criterion measure, we always encounter practical problems of *convenience and availability*. How long will we have to wait to get a criterion score for each individual? How much is it going to cost—in dollars or in disruption of normal activities? Though a personnel research program can often afford to spend a substantial part of its effort getting good criterion data, there is always a practical limit. Any choice of a criterion measure must take this practical limit into account.

Making Predictions

We have seen in Chapter 2 that the correlation coefficient tells us the degree of association between two variables and the direction of that relationship. We can use this information, along with the means and standard deviations of the predictor and criterion variables, to make the best possible prediction about criterion performance for each person, based on his or her score on the predictor. To do this we use what is called a **regression equation.** The regression equation tells us what our best guess of a person's score on the criterion would be, given the person's score on the predictor.

To see how the regression equation works, let us look at the scatterplot of the relationship between scores on the reading test and scores on the spelling test for Mr. Cordero's and Ms. Johnson's

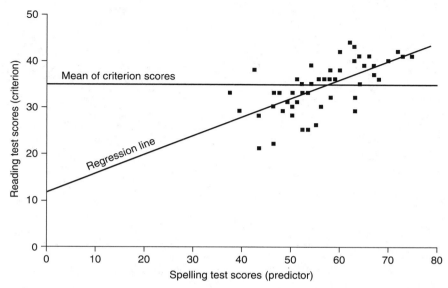

Figure 5–2
Scatterplot of scores from the reading and spelling tests given by Mr. Codero and Ms. Johnson showing the overall mean of criterion scores and the regression line.

sixth-grade classes from Chapter 2. Suppose we wish to use the spelling test to predict what level of reading proficiency we might expect from Heloise Abelard, a student who is being considered for transfer into this school. The scatterplot for the combined classes is shown in Figure 5–2. We have drawn two lines through the scatterplot. One is a horizontal line that shows the mean reading test score for all students for whom we have test scores. This is our best guess about Heloise's likely reading level *if we know nothing else about her.* In general, the mean of the criterion scores will always be our best guess about a person's score if we don't have any additional information. The regression equation is designed to allow us to make optimal use of any additional information we may have. What the regression equation does is describe the other line through the scatter plot, called the **regression line.** This line results in the most accurate predictions we can make *using the information from our predictor.*

We can use the regression line in either of two ways. The first is visual and is illustrated in Figure 5–3. Suppose Heloise earned a score of 50 on the spelling test. If we draw a line from the spelling test score of 50 directly up to the regression line, and then horizontally over to the scale for the reading test, the value on the reading test scale will be the best prediction we can get of reading performance *for people with this spelling test score.* For Heloise, her predicted reading test score appears to be about 31.

If we had data on a very large number of people for which the relationship resembled that in Figure 5–2, many people would have spelling test scores of 50. The value on the reading test scale for the point on the regression line that corresponds to the spelling score of 50 would be the mean reading score for all people with that spelling score. This feature of the scatterplot is shown in Figure 5–4. Here a vertical slice is drawn through the scatterplot at a score of 50 and the normal distribution is the distribution of scores for all people who would have earned a score of 50 in the very large group. In this way, the regression line allows us to make predictions for new individuals. Our

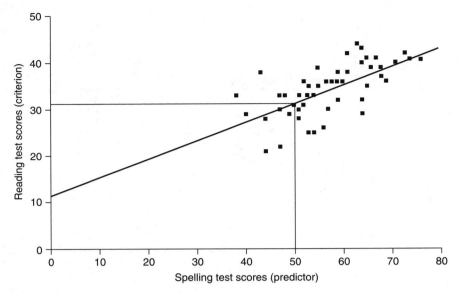

Figure 5–3
Using the regression line visually to make the best prediction of reading test score for Heloise.

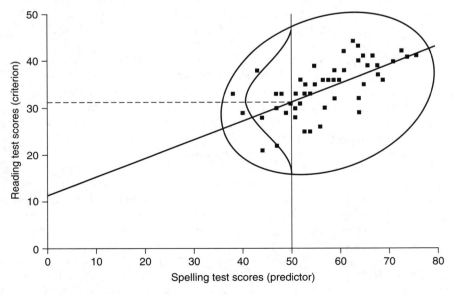

Figure 5–4
Scatterplot of reading and spelling test scores for a large group showing the distribution of reading test scores for all people who earned spelling scores of 50. The standard deviation of this distribution is the standard error of estimate.

prediction is the mean of the theoretical group whose predictor score is 50, which is a point on the regression line, and the uncertainty of our prediction is shown by the spread of the distribution around the regression line.

The second way we can use the regression line is for direct computation of a predicted score. Any straight line can be described by a simple equation, and the **regression equation** is the equation that describes the regression line. The equation for a line has the general form

$$\hat{Y} = B_{YX}X + A \tag{5.1}$$

where $\hat{Y}$ is the predicted score on the criterion,

B_{YX} is the *slope of the regression line* for predicting Y from X (the slope is the number of units that the line rises in the scale of the criterion variable for every unit of increase we have in the predictor),

X is the person's score on the predictor, and

A is the *intercept*. The intercept is the value where the regression line crosses the criterion scale axis. It is the value of the criterion we would predict for someone with a predictor score of zero.

Using relationships we will describe shortly, the slope and intercept for predicting reading score from spelling score are $B = .393$ and $A = 11.8$, respectively. Therefore, the predicted reading score for Heloise is

$$\hat{Y}_{Heloise} = .393(50) + 11.8 = 31.45$$

This is very close to the predicted score of 31 we got from examining the regression line in the scatterplot.

Finding the Regression Line. An intimate relationship exists between the coefficients that define the regression line and the correlation coefficient. In fact, if we prepare a scatterplot of standard scores (Z-scores or scores in any other metric where *both variables have the same standard deviation*), the slope of the regression line is the correlation coefficient. That is, when $SD_Y = SD_X$,

$$B_{YX} = r_{YX}$$

However, when the two standard deviations are not equal, B is related to r by the ratio of the SDs. Specifically, when we are predicting Y from X, the relationship is

$$B_{YX} = \left(\frac{SD_Y}{SD_X}\right) r_{YX} \tag{5.2}$$

To see how Eq. (5.2) works, let's take the data for our two sixth-grade classes from Chapter 2 and compute the slope coefficient for our regression equation. The standard deviations for the two variables are $SD_{Spelling} = 9.04$ and $SD_{Reading} = 5.55$. The correlation between the two variables is $r_{YX} = .64$, so Eq. (5.2) produces

$$B_{YX} = \left(\frac{5.55}{9.04}\right)(.64) = (.61)(.64) = .393$$

The value of A, the intercept, depends on the value of B and the means of the two variables. Recalling that the intercept is the point on the criterion variable (Y) axis when X is zero (or the value of Y on the regression line where the regression line crosses the Y axis), we can see that to get from the point where X is zero to the point where $X = M_X$ we must increase the value of X by the amount M_X. But if we increase X by M_X, the regression line is going to change by $B(M_X)$. Since the only point we know for certain in the Y distribution is the mean of $Y(M_Y)$, we can find A by the relationship

$$A = M_Y - B_{YX}M_X \tag{5.3}$$

In words, we can say that the intercept is the mean of the criterion variable minus (B times the mean of the predictor variable). For the two variables in our example we have $M_{Reading} = 34.44$ and $M_{Spelling} = 57.54$. Equation (5.3) therefore produces a value of

$$A = 34.44 - [(.393)(57.54)] = 11.8$$

Interpretation of Validity Coefficients

Suppose that we have gathered test and criterion scores for a group of individuals and computed the correlation between them. Perhaps the predictor is a scholastic aptitude test, and the criterion is an average of college freshman grades. How will we decide whether the test is a good predictor?

Obviously, other things being equal, the higher the correlation, the better. In one sense, our basis for evaluating any one predictor is in relation to other possible prediction procedures. Does Peter's Perfect Personnel Predictor yield a higher or lower validity coefficient than other tests that are available? Does it yield a higher or lower validity coefficient than other types of information, such as high school grades or ratings by the school principal? We will look with favor on any measure whose validity for a particular criterion is higher than that of measures previously available, even though the measure may fall far short of perfection.

A few representative validity coefficients are exhibited in Table 5–2. These give some picture of the size of correlation that has been obtained in previous work of different kinds. The investigator

Table 5–2
Validity of Selected Tests as Predictors of Certain Educational and Vocational Criteria

Predictor Test[a]	Criterion Variable[b]	Validity Coefficient
CogAT	TAP reading (Grade 12)	.79
Verbal	TAP social studies (Grade 12)	.78
Quantitative	TAP mathematics (Grade 12)	.79
ITED composite (Grade 9)	Cumulative high school GPA	.49
	College freshman GPA	.41
	SAT total	.84
ITBS composite (Grade 6)	Final college GPA	.44
Seashore Tonal Memory Test	Performance test on stringed instrument	.28
Short Employment Test		
Word knowledge score	Production index—bookkeeping machine operators	.10
Arithmetic score	Production index—Bookkeeping machine operators	.26

[a]CogAT = Cognitive Abilities Test; ITED = Iowa Tests of Educational Development; ITBS = Iowa Tests of Basic Skills.
[b]TAP = Tests of Achievement and Proficiency; GPA = grade-point average; SAT = Scholastic Aptitude Test.

MAKING THE COMPUTER DO IT

Regression

It is quite simple to get the regression equation from either SPSS or Excel. Both have a program called Regression that will compute the necessary values. In SPSS the Regression program is under the Analysis menu. The program offers several types of regression, but the one we want is called "Linear." When you see the following screen, simply place the criterion variable in the Dependent box and the predictor in the Independent box. You can use the Statistics button to request additional output such as the means and standard deviations (under Descriptives). Click OK and you will get the regression slope and intercept. The value for the intercept is in the row labeled Constant, and the value for the predictor will be in the row with its label. The program can handle many predictors simultaneously.

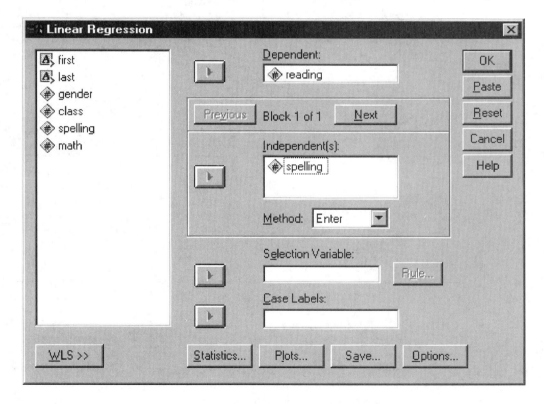

Excel has a regression program under the Data Analysis option on the Tools menu. When you select this option, you will be prompted to "Input Y range" and "Input X range." *Y* is the criterion and you specify the cells in which the *Y* scores are located. Do the same for *X*. If you wish the results to be displayed in the same spreadsheet as the data, select Output Range and specify a cell in which the output should start, usually a cell to the right of the data. For our example, the screen should look like this:

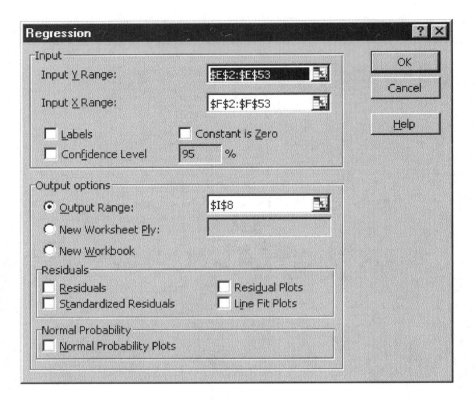

If you use either program to replicate the analysis we have described in this section, you will get slightly different values than we did when these were calculated by hand. Both programs output values of $B = .394$ and $A = 11.76$. The reason for the difference is that the programs keep more decimal places in their intermediate calculations. It will often be the case that hand calculations will differ slightly from the computer for this reason.

concerned with a particular course of study or a particular job will, of course, need to become familiar with the validities that the tests being considered have been found to have for the criterion measure to be used.

The usefulness of a test as a predictor depends not only on how well it correlates with a criterion measure but also on how much *new* information it gives. For example, the social studies subtest of the Tests of Achievement and Proficiency (TAP) was found to correlate on the average .51 with ninth-grade social studies grades, and the reading comprehension subtest to correlate .51 with the same grades. But, the two tests have an intercorrelation of .77. They overlap and, in part at least, the information either test provides is the same as that provided by the other test. The net result is that pooling information from the two tests can give a validity coefficient of no more than .53. If the two tests had been uncorrelated, each giving evidence completely independent of the other, the combination of the two would have provided a validity coefficient of .70. Statistical procedures have been developed that enable us to determine the best weighting to give to two or more predictors and to calculate the regression equation and correlation that result from this combination. (The procedures for computing the weights for the predictor tests [regression weights] and the correlation [multiple correlation] resulting from the combination are specialized topics in statistics. A complete presentation of these methods can be found in intermediate statistics texts such as those of Cohen & Cohen, 1983; Darlington, 1990; and McClendon, 1994.)

Clearly, the higher the correlation between a test or other predictor and a criterion measure, the better. But, in addition to this relative standard, we should like some absolute one. How high must the validity coefficient be for the test to be useful? What is a "satisfactory" validity? This last question is a little like asking "How high is up?" However, we can try to give some sort of answer.

To an organization using a test as a basis for deciding whether to hire a particular job applicant or to admit a particular student, the significant question is "How much more often will we make the right decision on whom to hire or to admit if we use this test than if we operate on a purely chance basis or on the basis of some already available but less valid measure?" The answer to this question depends in considerable measure on the proportion of individuals who must (or can) be accepted, called the **selection ratio,** and the prevalence of "success" in the population, called the **base rate.** A selection procedure can do much more for us if we can accept only the individual who appears to be the best 1 in every 10 applicants than if we must accept 9 out of 10. However, to provide a specific example, let us assume that we will accept half of the applicants. Let us examine Table 5–3.

Table 5–3 is set up to show 200 people in all, 100 in each half on the test and 100 in each half on the job. If there were absolutely no relationship between the test and job performance, there would be 50 people in each of the four cells of the table. Defining "success" as being in the top half on the job (a base rate of .50), the success rate would be 50 in 100 for those accepted and also for those rejected. There would be no difference between the two, and the correlation between the selection test and job performance would be zero.

Table 5–4 shows, for correlations of different sizes and a selection ratio of .50, the percentage of correct choices (i.e., "successes") among the 50% we accept. A similar percentage of correct rejections occurs in the 50% who are not accepted. The improvement in our "batting average" as the correlation goes up is shown in the table. Thus, for a correlation of .40, we will make correct decisions 63.1% of the time and be in error 36.9% of the time; with a correlation of .80 the percentage of correct decisions will be 79.5, and so forth.

Table 5–3
Two-by-Two Table of Test and Job Success

| | | Performance on the Job | | |
		Bottom Half—"Failures"	Top Half—"Successes"	Total
Score on Selection Test	Top half (accepted)			100
	Bottom half (rejected)			100
	Total	100	100	200

Table 5–4
Percentage of Correct Assignments When 50%
of Group Must Be Selected

Validity Coefficient	Percentage of Correct Choices
.00	50.0
.20	56.4
.40	63.1
.50	66.7
.60	70.5
.70	74.7
.80	79.5
.90	85.6

Table 5–4 shows not only the accuracy for any given correlation but also the gain in accuracy if we improve the validity of the predictor. If we were able to replace a predictor with a validity of .40 by one with a validity of .60, we would increase the percentage of correct decisions from 63.1 to 70.5. The percentages in this table refer, of course, to the ground rules set above; that is, that we are selecting the top 50% of the group on the prediction test and that 50% of the complete group of 200 candidates would be successful. However, Table 5–4 gives a fairly representative basis for understanding the effects of a selection program from the point of view of the employing or certifying agency.

In many selection situations, the gain from greater validity can be crudely translated into dollars-and-cents savings. If it costs a company $500 to employ and train a new employee to the point of useful productivity, a selection procedure that raises the percentage of successes from 56.4 to 63.1 would yield a savings in wasted training expenses alone of $3,350 per 100 new employees. This computation of benefits takes no account of the possibility that the test-selected workers might also be *better* workers after they had completed their training. The dollar savings would have to be balanced, of course, against any increase in cost in applying the new selection procedure. A selection procedure that costs $5,000 per candidate to administer would hardly be worthwhile for such modest savings.

Another way of appraising the practical significance of a correlation coefficient—and one that is perhaps more meaningful from the point of view of the person being tested—is shown in Table 5–5. The rows in the tabulations represent the fourths of a group of applicants, potential students or employees, with respect to a predictor test. The columns indicate the number of cases falling in each quarter on the criterion measure. Look at the tabulation in Table 5–5 corresponding to a validity coefficient of .50. Note that of those who fall in the lowest quarter on the predictor, 480 out of 1,000 (48.0%) fall in the lowest quarter in terms of the criterion score, 27.9% in the next lowest quarter, 16.8% in the next to highest quarter, and 7.3% in the highest quarter. Another way to view this relationship is in terms of our previous example, which defined successful performance as being in the top half on the criterion. Only about one person in four who scored in the lowest quarter on the predictor test (168 + 73 = 241 out of 1,000) would prove to be a "successful" employee. The diagonal entries in boldface print represent cases that

Table 5–5
Accuracy of Prediction for Different Values of the Correlation Coefficient (r).

$r = .00$						$r = .60$				
Quarter on Predictor	Quarter on Criterion					Quarter on Predictor	Quarter on Criterion			
	4th	3rd	2nd	1st			4th	3rd	2nd	1st
1st	250	250	250	**250**		1st	45	141	277	**537**
2nd	250	250	**250**	250		2nd	141	264	**318**	277
3rd	250	**250**	250	250		3rd	277	**318**	264	141
4th	**250**	250	250	250		4th	**537**	277	141	45

$r = .40$						$r = .70$				
Quarter on Predictor	Quarter on Criterion					Quarter on Predictor	Quarter on Criterion			
	4th	3rd	2nd	1st			4th	3rd	2nd	1st
1st	104	191	277	**428**		1st	22	107	270	**601**
2nd	191	255	**277**	277		2nd	107	270	**353**	270
3rd	277	**277**	255	191		3rd	270	**353**	270	107
4th	**428**	277	191	104		4th	**601**	270	107	22

$r = .50$						$r = .80$				
Quarter on Predictor	Quarter on Criterion					Quarter on Predictor	Quarter on Criterion			
	4th	3rd	2nd	1st			4th	3rd	2nd	1st
1st	73	168	279	**480**		1st	6	66	253	**675**
2nd	168	258	**295**	279		2nd	66	271	**410**	253
3rd	279	**295**	258	168		3rd	253	**410**	271	66
4th	**480**	279	168	73		4th	**675**	253	66	6

Note: There are 1,000 cases in each row and column.

fall in the same fourth on both the predictor and the criterion. The farther we get from the diagonal, the greater the discrepancy between prediction and performance. Cases on or near the diagonal represent cases where the predictor has been accurate; cases falling far from the diagonal represent cases in which the predictor has been decidedly wrong.

As an empirical example of the spread of criterion performance that one may find for people with the same predictor score, consider Table 5–6. This table shows the distribution of scores on the SAT earned by 260 11th-grade students with different levels of performance on the reading comprehension test of the Tests of Achievement and Proficiency (TAP). It is clear from the table that as TAP scores go up, SAT scores also tend to go up, but it is equally clear that some students with TAP scores of 200 earn higher SAT scores than do some of the students with TAP scores of 250.

Table 5–6
Probabilities of Scoring Within Specified Ranges on the Verbal Test of the Scholastic Aptitude Test (SAT), Given Scores on the Reading Comprehension Test of the Tests of Achievement and Proficiency (TAP)

TAP Standard Score Range	SAT Verbal Score Range					
	200–250	251–350	351–450	451–550	551–650	651+
251+			10	40	40	10
241–250		6	19	44	25	6
231–240		4	11	53	28	4
221–230			20	44	28	8
211–220			31	48	21	
201–210		11	36	40	3	
191–200	3	14	43	40		
181–190	3	20	56	21		
171–180	11	22	61	3	3	
Below 171	23	54	19		4	

Note: The data in this table represent a correlation of 0.61 between the reading comprehension test of TAP and the verbal test of the SAT.

Tables 5–5 and 5–6 emphasize not so much the gain from using the predictor as they do the variation in criterion performance still remaining for those who are similar in predictor scores. From the point of view of schools or employers, the important thing is to improve the percentage of correct decisions (see Table 5–4). In dealing with large numbers, they can count on gaining from any predictor that is more valid than the procedure currently in use. From the point of view of the single individual, the occasional marked discrepancies between predicted and actual success shown in Tables 5–5 and 5–6 may seem at least as important. Applicants who have done poorly on the test may be less impressed by the fact that the *probability* is that they will be below average on the job or in the training program than by the fact that they *may* still do very well. Each individual may be the exception.

Base Rates and Prediction
We noted in introducing Table 5–3 that a selection procedure is most helpful if we need to accept only a small number of candidates. Although this principle is true, the facts in Tables 5–5 and 5–6 reveal that we would miss many potentially successful candidates if we took only those in the top 10% to 20% on the predictor. The overall value of a selection procedure depends on several factors, including (1) how we define success, (2) the selection rule that we use, (3) the "value" of a correctly identified success, (4) the "cost" of accepting someone who subsequently fails, and (5) the "cost" of missing a candidate who would have succeeded.

We called the proportion of a group of applicants who would have succeeded if all were admitted the base rate for success. If being in the top half on the criterion is considered success, then the base rate is 50%. The selection rule used with the predictor is known as the **cutting score.** The cutting score is the lowest predictor score that leads to a decision to accept the applicant.

When we use any particular cutting score, some of our decisions will be correct and some will not. At one extreme, if we admit all candidates, we will correctly identify all potentially successful individuals, but at the cost of admitting the 50% who will be failures. At the other extreme, if we reject all candidates, we will admit no failures, but at the cost of missing all of the potentially successful candidates. The proportion of correct decisions that result from our selection strategy—the proportion of correctly identified successes plus the proportion of correctly rejected failures—is known as the **hit rate** for the cutting score. Each cutting score has a hit rate that depends on the base rate of success in the population and the correlation between the predictor and the criterion. The values in Table 5–4 show the hit rates for a base rate of 50% and a cutting score that admits the top half of the applicants on the predictor variable.

As the base rate departs from 50% (either higher or lower), the hit rate for the selection procedure diminishes. If we define success as being in the top 25% on the criterion (i.e., the base rate is 0.25) and consider the results of using a predictor that has a correlation of 0.60 with this criterion, the results from using four cutting scores are as follows:

Cutting Score	Hit Rate
Admit all	.25
Admit top 75%	.37
Admit top 50%	.66
Admit top 25%	.77

The hit rate of 0.66 for a cutting score that admits the top 50% on the basis of the predictor test is slightly lower than the value of 70.5% in Table 5–4 (where the base rate was 50%), and the drop results from the change in base rate. The decrease in overall gain from using the predictor becomes much more marked in situations with more extreme base rates. The greatest total gains from using a selection procedure occur in those situations where the rate of successful criterion performance in the population is close to 50%.

Standard Error of Estimate

We have seen that when the relationship between a predictor and a criterion is less than perfect, there will be some variability in criterion performance for people who all have the same predictor score. Not all people who fall in a given quarter of the predictor test distribution will fall in the same quarter of the criterion distribution. More generally, as we saw in Figure 5–4, there will be a distribution of actual criterion performances around the predicted criterion score for people with any given score on the predictor. There will be an average criterion performance for people with a particular predictor score, and there will be variation around that average. Regression procedures are used to find the mean criterion performance for all people scoring at the same level on the predictor. The spread of actual criterion performances around that mean is reflected by the **standard error of estimate.** The standard error of estimate is the standard deviation of the distribution of actual criterion performances around predicted performance. Another way to say the same thing is to say that *the standard error of estimate is the standard deviation of criterion scores for people who all got the same score on the predictor variable.*

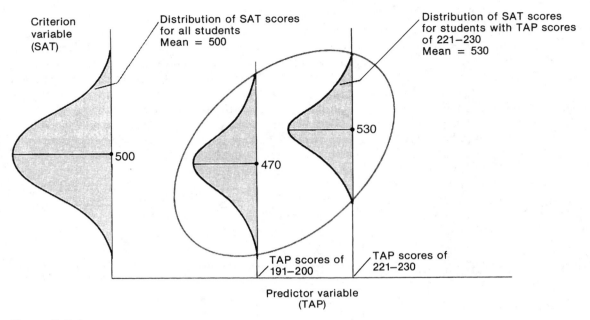

Figure 5–5
Predicted score on the criterion variable (SAT) is the mean of criterion scores earned by those at a chosen level of predictor (TAP). Standard error of estimate is the standard deviation of observed scores around that mean.

This principle is illustrated schematically in Figure 5–5 for the data in Table 5–6. The large normal distribution on the left in the figure is the distribution of *all* SAT scores. It has a mean of 500 and a standard deviation of 100. The ellipse is the scatterplot of SAT and TAP scores, and the two smaller normal distributions to the right are the distributions of SAT scores for those individuals who earned TAP scores between 191 and 200 and 221 and 230, respectively. The mean of the first distribution is 470, and this mean is the SAT score that we would predict for this group of individuals. The mean of the second distribution, 530, is the SAT score we would predict for individuals with TAP scores of 221 to 230. The standard deviations of these distributions are the standard errors of estimate for predicting SAT scores from TAP scores.

Two things are important to note in the figure. First, because there is a moderate positive correlation ($r = .61$) between the two variables, the predicted score is higher in the right-hand group than in the one to the left. People with higher TAP scores are predicted to earn higher SAT scores. Second, the predictions are in error by some small amount for most people and by a considerable amount for some. The standard deviation of observed scores around the predicted score is the standard error of estimate. An overall value for the standard error of estimate can be obtained from the following equation:

$$SD_{Y \cdot X} = SD_Y \sqrt{1 - r_{YX}^2} \qquad (5.4)$$

where $SD_{Y \cdot X}$ is the standard error of estimate (the subscript $Y \cdot X$ is read "Y given X"),

SD_Y is the standard deviation of the entire distribution of criterion scores, and

r_{YX}^2 is the squared validity coefficient of the predictor test for predicting this criterion.

Notice that this formula looks quite similar to Eq. (4.5) (Chapter 4) for the standard error of measurement. The standard error of measurement is an index of instability of performances on a single test. It uses the test reliability to provide a way of estimating how much an individual's score might change from one testing to another. The standard error of estimate is an index of the error that may be made in forecasting performance on one measure from performance on another. It uses the correlation between the predictor test and some criterion to provide an estimate of how much a predicted score might be in error as an estimate of a person's actual performance on the criterion. Both the standard error of measurement and the standard error of estimate are important, but for criterion-related validity, the standard error of measurement is a property that can be determined by the test publisher as characterizing the predictor test, while the standard error of estimate is unique to each criterion measure and must therefore be determined locally.

Let us look again at predicting SAT performance from scores on the TAP. We found (in Table 5–6) a correlation of .61 between the test and the criterion measure, and the standard deviation of SAT scores is 100. Using Eq. (5.2), we find

$$SD_{Y \cdot X} = 100\sqrt{1 - .61^2} = 100\sqrt{.63} = 79$$

The standard error of estimate for predicting SAT scores from TAP scores is 79.

We may use standard error of estimate to place a band of uncertainty or a **prediction interval** around our predicted score for a person in the same way that we used standard error of measurement to produce a band of uncertainty for the person's true score. If we assume that the errors of prediction have a normal distribution, about two out of three students will earn SAT scores within 1 standard of error of estimate of the score that was predicted for them and 95% will get SAT scores within the 2 standard-errors-of-estimate band. In the example shown in Figure 5–6, 68% of the students for whom a prediction of 530 was made will actually earn SAT scores between 450 and 610 (SAT scores are reported only in multiples of 10), while about 95% will have criterion performances between 370 and 690.

The standard error of estimate is a sobering index because it illustrates clearly the limitations we face in predicting human behavior. *Even with the best measures available, predictions in psychology and education are approximate.* The regression techniques that are used to make predictions yield point estimates such as the predicted SAT score of 530 in Figure 5–6. By considering the standard error of estimate, teachers, counselors, and personnel workers get an appropriately pessimistic view

Figure 5–6

Two people out of three will have criterion scores within 1 standard error of estimate $(SD_{Y \cdot X})$ of their predicted scores on the SAT. Nineteen in 20 will be within $2\ SD_{Y \cdot X}$.

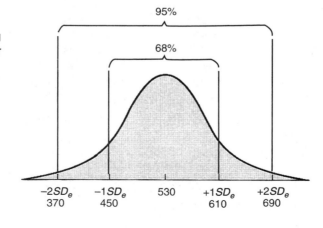

of our present ability to predict human performance. This is not to say that we should stop trying to predict or that tests are often seriously wrong. On the contrary, predictions made from test scores are, *on the average,* correct. But, healthy skepticism is required to keep from overinterpreting test scores, particularly when, as is usually the case, we are making predictions about individuals.

Two other factors tend to distort validity coefficients and complicate their interpretation. The first is unreliability of the predictor and of the criterion that is being predicted. This attenuation effect was discussed in Chapter 4. The second is restriction in the range of ability in the group by some type of preselection, often based on the predictor itself. Low reliability on the one hand or preselection on the other will tend to lower the values that are obtained for validity coefficients, so that "true validities" are typically higher than the values obtained in validation studies.

As an example of the effect that restricting the range in the predictor can have on the apparent validity of a predictor, consider the recent experience at a public university that experienced dramatic growth in its pool of applicants. With over three times as many applicants as could be accommodated, the school changed from what had been a first-come, first-served admissions policy to one in which students were admitted on the basis of a combination of high school grades and aptitude test scores. The correlation of college grades with high school grades in the last class admitted under the old rules was 0.61. When the new admissions criteria were applied and only those students who would have been admitted under the new rules were included, the correlation dropped to 0.47. This change in the apparent validity of high school grades as a predictor of college grades occurred solely as a result of the smaller range of talent among the selected students.

Let us emphasize one additional point. Validity is fairly specific to a particular curriculum or a particular job. Although the concept of validity generalization, discussed below, indicates that certain tests may be valid across a range of jobs, when an author or publisher claims that a test is valid, it is always appropriate to ask "Valid for what?" For example, an achievement test in social studies that accurately represents the content and objectives of one program of instruction may be quite inappropriate for the program in a different community. An achievement test must always be evaluated against the objectives of a specific program of instruction. An aptitude test battery that is quite valid for picking department store sales clerks who will be pleasant to customers, informed about their stock, and accurate in financial transactions may be entirely useless in identifying insurance agents who will be effective in going out and finding or creating new business. Validity must always be evaluated in relation to a situation as similar as possible to the one in which the measure is to be used.

Criterion-related validity is most important for a test that is to be used to predict outcomes that are represented by clear-cut criterion measures. There are two key elements in this statement: *prediction* and *clear-cut criterion measures.* The main limitation to using criterion-related validity within the prediction context usually lies in the limited adequacy of the available criterion measures. The more readily we can identify a performance criterion that unquestionably represents the results that we are interested in, the more we will be prepared to rely on the evidence from correlations between a test and measures of that criterion to guide our decision on whether to use the test scores.

CONSTRUCT-RELATED EVIDENCE OF VALIDITY

Sometimes, with respect to an educational or psychological test, we ask neither "How well does this test predict future performance?" nor "How well does this test represent our curriculum?" Instead, we ask "What do scores on this test *mean* or *signify*?" What does the score tell us about an individual? Does it correspond to some meaningful trait or construct that will help us to understand the person? For this last question, the term **construct validity** has been used. (The term *construct* is used in psychology to refer to something that is not observable but is literally *constructed* by the investigator to summarize or account for the regularities or relationships in observed behavior. Thus, most names of traits refer to constructs. We speak of a person's "sociability" as a way of summarizing observed consistency in past behavior in relation to people and of organizing a prediction of how the individual will act on future occasions. The construct is derived from observations, but constructs may actually predict what we would observe in new situations. Such is the case in the research program described next.)

Let us examine a classic case of one specific testing procedure and see how its validity as a measure of a useful psychological quality or construct was studied. McClelland, Atkinson, Clark, and Lowell (1953) developed a testing procedure to appraise an individual's need or motivation to achieve—to succeed and do well. The test used pictures of people in various ambiguous situations. Examinees were called on to make up stories about each picture, telling what was happening and how it turned out. A scoring system was developed for these stories, based on counting the frequency with which themes of accomplishment, mastery, success, and achievement appeared in the story material. In this way, each individual received a score representing the strength of his motivation to achieve (all subjects were male). The question posed by construct validity is whether this measure has validity in the sense of truthfully describing a meaningful aspect of the individual's makeup. Does the test measure the need to achieve? McClelland and his coworkers proceeded as described next.

In essence, the investigators began by asking "To what should a measure of achievement motivation, as we have conceived of it, be related?" They made a series of predictions, some of which were as follows:

1. Those students scoring high on achievement motivation should do well in college in relation to their scholastic aptitude. That is, their college grades should be higher than would be predicted from their SAT scores.
2. Achievement motivation should be higher for students just after they have taken tests described to them as measuring their intelligence.
3. Those students scoring high on achievement motivation should complete more items on a speeded test where the students are motivated to perform well.
4. Achievement motivation should be higher for children of families emphasizing early independence.

Each of these predictions was based on a "theory of human behavior." For example, academic achievement is seen as a combination of ability and effort. Presumably, those with higher motivation to achieve will exert more effort and therefore will, ability being equal, achieve higher grades. A similar chain of reasoning lies behind each prediction.

In general, McClelland et al. (1953) found that most of their predictions were supported by the experimental results. The fact that the test scores were related to a number of other events in the way that had been predicted from a rational analysis of the trait that the test was presumably measuring lent support to the validity of the test procedure as measuring a meaningful trait or construct. The essential characteristics of the trait are fairly well summarized by the label "achievement motivation." When a series of studies supports the construct validity of a measure, the validity of the theory that gave rise to the construct is also supported.

A great many psychological tests and, to a lesser extent, some educational tests are intended to measure general traits or qualities of the individual. General intelligence, verbal reasoning, spatial visualization, sociability, introversion, and mechanical interest are all designations of traits or constructs. Tests of these functions have construct validity insofar as the scores they yield behave in the way that such a trait should reasonably be expected to behave in light of the theory that gave rise to the construct. A theory about a trait will lead to predictions of the following types, all of which can be tested to see if they hold up.

Predictions About Correlations

The nature of the trait, and therefore of valid measures of it, will indicate that it should be positively related to certain other measures and, perhaps, unrelated or negatively related to still others. These other measures might be already accepted measures of the function in question. Many subsequent group intelligence tests, for example, have been validated in part by their correlations with earlier tests, especially the Stanford-Binet. Also, the other measures may be ones with which the trait should logically be related. Thus, intelligence tests have been validated, in part, through their correlation with success in school and measures of mechanical aptitude by their correlation with rated proficiency in mechanical jobs.

One way of studying the constructs or traits that a test measures is to study jointly the intercorrelations of this test and a number of others. The patterning of these correlations makes it possible to see which tests are measuring some common dimension or factor. An examination of the tests clustering in a single factor may clarify the nature and meaning of the factor and of the tests that measure it. This means of studying the constructs that underly performance on a test is known as **factor analysis.** However, this internal structural or "factorial" validity still needs evidence of a relationship to life events outside the tests themselves if the factors are to have much substance, vitality, and scientific or educational utility.

It may also be appropriate to predict that the measure of Construct X will show low or zero correlations with measures of certain other attributes; that is, that the construct is different from what the other tests measure. A test designed to measure mechanical comprehension should show only a modest correlation with a test of verbal ability. A measure of sociability should not show too high a correlation with a measure of assertiveness, if the two assess genuinely different constructs. High correlations between measures of supposedly unrelated constructs are evidence against either the validity of the instruments as measures of the constructs, the validity of the constructs as separate dimensions of human functioning, or both.

Multitrait, Multimethod Analysis

An explicit method for studying the patterns of high and low correlations among a set of measures was suggested by Campbell and Fiske (1959). Their procedure, which they called the analysis of a multitrait, multimethod matrix of correlations, requires that several different methods be used to measure each of several different traits. Figure 5–7 provides an illustration of a multitrait, multimethod (MTMM for short) correlation matrix. The entries in the matrix in Figure 5–7 are given as letters, although the results of an actual study would produce numerical values.

As is shown in Figure 5–7, we might measure each of three traits, ascendance, sociability, and trustworthiness, in each of three ways, self-report, ratings by friends, and observations in a controlled setting. Thus, we have nine scores for each person (three traits each measured in three ways), and the MTMM matrix contains the correlations among these nine variables. The essence

		Self Rating			Friend Rating			Observation		
		A	S	T	A	S	T	A	S	T
Self	Ascendance	a								
	Sociability	b	a							
	Trustworthiness	b	b	a						
Friend	Ascendance	c	d	d	a					
	Sociability	d	c	d	b	a				
	Trustworthiness	d	d	c	b	b	a			
Observe	Ascendance	c	d	d	c	d	d	a		
	Sociability	d	c	d	d	c	d	b	a	
	Trustworthiness	d	d	c	d	d	c	b	b	a

A = Ascendance

S = Sociability

T = Trustworthiness

Figure 5–7
The multitrait, multimethod (MTMM) matrix.

of the MTMM method for assessing construct validity is that *scores resulting from different ways of measuring of the same trait should correlate more highly with each other than they do with scores for other traits measured by the same method.*

The cells of the matrix that contain the letter *a* are known as **reliability diagonals.** They represent the correlation between two assessments of the same trait using the same measurement method (remember that we characterized reliability as being the correlation of a test with itself). We would want these values to be as high as possible, and they should be the highest values in the matrix. In the parlance of MTMM analyses, these are *monotrait, monomethod correlations.*

The values in the cells labeled *b* are the correlations between different traits assessed by the same measurement method (*heterotrait, monomethod correlations*). These correlations represent similarities due to both the natural relationships between the constructs and the fact that they have been measured by the same method. They should be substantially smaller than the reliabilities.

As far as construct validity is concerned, interest usually focuses on the values in the *c* cells (called **validity diagonals**). These are the correlations between different ways of assessing the same trait (*monotrait, heteromethod correlations*). If we have two or three good ways of measuring ascendance, then they should agree with each other, even though they use different measurement methods. In a sense, this is a little like the question of parallel forms reliability: Do different selections of items produce the same measurement. For well-defined measures of a well-defined construct, the answer should be yes. To the extent that different ways of measuring the same trait yield high correlations, the construct and its measures are said to demonstrate **convergent validity.** The different methods of measurement converge on the trait.

Finally, we come to the *d* cells. These are the correlations between different traits measured by different methods (*heterotrait, heteromethod correlations*). They represent the purest index of the association between the different traits, and they should be the smallest values in the matrix because they include only trait correlations.

To the extent that the values in the *b* cells are larger than those in the *d* cells, we say that **method covariance** is present. That is, there are consistent individual differences in scores that result not only from status on the trait but also from the way the trait was assessed. The presence of method variance reduces the construct validity of the measure because scores on the instrument include something else in addition to the person's status on the trait of interest. The extent to which measurements are free of method variance and are pure measures of discrete traits is called **discriminant validity.** Note, however, that the traits need not have near-zero correlations to demonstrate evidence of convergent and discriminant validity. A test of reading comprehension and one of general cognitive ability should be quite highly correlated because the traits seem to be highly correlated in the natural world, but the cross-trait correlations should be consistently lower than the within-trait correlations. The main issue is whether the different kinds of correlations show the pattern predicted by MTMM methodology.

Predictions About Group Differences

A theory will often suggest that certain kinds of groups should possess an especially high or low amount of a trait and, consequently, should score exceptionally high or low on a test of that trait. It seems reasonable that a group of successful salespeople should be high on a measure of ascendance, or assertiveness, and that a group of librarians should be low. We would probably predict that children of professional and business parents would be more ascendant than those whose parents were in clerical or semiskilled occupations. For any given trait, our general knowledge of our society and the groups within it will suggest an array of group differences that seem to make sense. Applying a test to these groups, the investigator finds out how consistently the predictions are borne out. Of course, the predictions could fail because, on the one hand, the test is not a valid measure of the characteristic or, on the other, because the world is not consistent with the theory that gave rise to the predictions. Failure of our predictions does not tell us which of these conditions exists (or is correct).

Predictions About Responses to Experimental Treatments or Interventions

A theory may imply that the expression of a human characteristic will be modified as a result of certain experimental conditions or treatments. For example, one could reasonably predict that anxiety would increase just before a person was to undergo a minor operation. Rate of flicker fusion has been proposed as an indicator of anxiety level. (The rate of flicker fusion is the rate at which alternation of black-and-white stimulation fuses into a steady gray.) In one study (Buhler, 1953), it was found that, as predicted, the flicker fusion threshold was lower before the operation than after it, when anxiety had presumably relaxed. Other studies using anxiety-arousing stimuli such as dental chairs have found similar results, lending credence to the construct of anxiety and to certain measures of it.

For any test that presumes to measure a trait or quality, we can formulate a network of theory, leading to definite predictions that can be tested. Insofar as the predictions are borne out, the validity of the test as a measure of the trait or construct is supported. Insofar as the predictions fail to be verified, we are led to doubt either the validity of the test, our theorizing, or both.

THE UNIFIED VIEW OF VALIDITY

Beginning about 1980, a new unified view of validity gradually has emerged. We have alluded to some aspects of this new conceptualization already, but we now explore it in detail. According to this view, test validity (or even test validation) is something of a misnomer since what is validated are *interpretations* of test scores and the *uses* of those scores for particular applied purposes, not the test itself (Cronbach, 1988; Messick, 1989; Shepard, 1993). If we construct a test but never administer it, validation is not an issue. If we give our test to a group of examinees and collect some test scores but then lock those scores away in a vault, validation is still not an issue. But, once we take the scores from the vault and use them for a purpose—any purpose—we must ask about the appropriateness of the scores for that use. The inferences in need of validation are of two main types, interpretive or action. An **interpretive inference** is a statement of what test scores mean—that is, our interpretation of them. An **action inference** is a claim regarding the appropriateness and utility of test scores as the basis for some specific action such as applied decision making.

"Test validation" may be viewed as the *process* of gathering evidence in support of these score-based inferences. Validation of interpretive inferences involves bringing together multiple lines of evidence in support of certain interpretations of test scores while, at the same time, demonstrating that other interpretations are less plausible. Validation of action inferences requires both evidence of score meaning and evidence of the appropriateness and usefulness of the test scores for particular applied purposes. The goal of test validation is, therefore, to build the best possible case we can for the inferences we would like to make.

Thus far, our discussion of test validation has focused primarily on the compiling of evidence to support action inferences. Messick (1989) has expanded the boundaries of validity beyond score meaning to include the value implications of score interpretation and the utility, relevance, and social consequences associated with test use. He argued that validation must go beyond evidence related to test score meaning to include the consequences of score interpretation and test use—both actual and potential.

Assigning meaning to test scores carries with it certain value implications. Values impact score meaning at multiple levels—from the construct labels themselves to theory in which the construct is imbedded, and to the larger ideology that gave rise to the theory. Because no interpretation is value free, value implications of score meaning should be included in any discussion of validity. In addition, each decision involving test scores has consequences, some of which may be unintended. Judging whether or not a test does what we want it to do—that is, whether it functions acceptably in an applied setting—requires evidence of the relevance and utility of test scores for the proposed use and consideration of both intended and unintended social consequences of such use. Any time we use test scores to make decisions about people, some type of social impact results. The appropriateness of a particular test use must be justified in light of all possible outcomes. Such justification requires not only that the test serve its intended purpose but also that the value of doing so outweighs the impact of any adverse social consequences.

Validation as a Scientific Enterprise

According to Angoff (1988), Messick (1980, 1988, 1989), and others, the processes we use to collect, organize, and summarize evidence to support particular score-based inferences are, for all intents and purposes, the methods of science. What separates science from nonscience is the willingness to expose our ideas about the nature of a phenomenon under study to threat of refutation.

To the extent that the testing community adheres to scientific methods, measurement may be considered a science and validation a form of scientific inquiry. In 1980, Messick stated that validation involves the "testing of rational hypotheses about theoretically relevant relationships" (p. 1015). A decade later he declared that score-based "inferences are hypotheses and the validation of inferences is hypothesis testing" (Messick, 1989, p. 14).

Hypothesis testing, in general, involves making assertions about the nature of some phenomenon of interest and then checking to see if one's ideas are in reasonably good accord with the evidence. Optimally, specific predictions are derived from a relevant theoretical framework that gives meaning to the predictions themselves as well as to the data against which the predictions will be tested. If the observations are not as expected—if the data are not consistent with predictions—the plausibility of one's assertions has been refuted. If observed outcomes are as forecast, the hypothesis remains tenable and a thread of support for one's ideas about the phenomenon under study has been gained. The important point is that hypotheses are stated in such a way that they *can* be refuted. Confirmation is not enough. We must seek evidence to the contrary in order to challenge our ideas.

The first step in the validation process, as with hypothesis testing more generally, is to state exactly what sorts of inferences are desired—that is, what interpretations and uses of test scores we would like to make. The next step is to determine the kinds of evidence we would accept as confirming or refuting the plausibility of those inferences. Finally, a determination is made regarding the reasonableness of the desired inferences in light of any accumulated evidence.

Multiple explanations can be advanced for just about any phenomenon. To justify desired score-based inferences, it is critical that we explore—and rule out—competing explanations. We can demonstrate the tenability of our hypothesis by exposing it to threat of refutation, but doing so does nothing to discredit any number of rival hypotheses. Therefore, in addition to testing our hypothesis directly, we can gain powerful evidence to confirm its plausibility by demonstrating that competing explanations are less well supported.

To the extent that our score-based inferences gain their meaning and import from substantive theory, validation is also theory testing. If a theory entails that a particular outcome should occur and it does not, this evidence reflects poorly on the theory. There is continual interaction between scores produced by a test and the theoretical framework within which the test was developed. Data and theory test and modify each other. In addition, identification and testing of counter-hypotheses is an efficient way of exposing any vulnerabilities in our construct theory. As with hypothesis testing, support of a theory involves both the confirmation of expected outcomes in addition to the refutation of plausible rival explanations.

The validation of inferences regarding the *use* of test scores as a basis for action almost always occurs in a social and political context full of conflicting (and sometimes implicit) agendas. Any scientific enterprise that occurs in a political setting is, by definition, an *applied* science. Consequently, the testing of hypotheses (and theories) related to use—those inferences about test score relevance, utility, and social impact—constitute scientific inquiry in the applied sense.

Although science was once thought to be apolitical and value neutral, it has generally become accepted within the scientific community that this is not now, nor ever was, the case. As recent philosophers of science—as well as test theorists—have pointed out, our data bear the mark of our theories and our theories reflect our values (Messick, 1989; Shepard, 1993). Given the value-laden, political reality of contemporary test use, it seems constructive to note the potentially positive impact of such contentiousness. Cronbach (1988) points out that the presence of conflicting points of view often forces us to articulate and carefully consider the values underlying the intended uses of test scores. Messick (1989) weighs in with his observation that acknowledgment of multiple perspectives can help offset the "preemptiveness of [our own] value commitments" (p. 87). In addition, recognizing and taking into account the factors that have helped shape our positions may actually strengthen the case we are trying to make in support of a particular inference.

Construct Validity as the Whole of Validity

According to Messick (1989), construct validity encompasses all of the "evidence and rationales supporting the trustworthiness of score interpretations in terms of explanatory concepts that account for both test performance and relationships with other variables" (p. 34). A critical feature of construct validation efforts is that there be some organizing theoretical or conceptual framework (Messick's "explanatory concepts") to serve as a guide to score interpretation.

Evidence to Support the Construct Validity of Score-Based Inferences

Validity is not an all ("valid") or nothing ("invalid") proposition; rather it is a matter of degree. One may have a lot of evidence, or very little, with which to build a case in support of certain interpretations or uses of test scores. Further, different kinds of evidence may be brought to bear on the validation of score-based inferences. An effective argument for the construct validity of any score-based inference should include both rational and empirical evidence (Shepard, 1993); neither is adequate on its own. When inferences about the appropriateness and adequacy of score interpretations or the usefulness of test scores for certain applied purposes are supported both by strong empirical evidence and a compelling theoretical rationale, the case for those inferences is more persuasive than when less (or weaker) evidence is provided. If, at the same time, one can demonstrate that alternative hypotheses are less well supported, the case in support of one's desired inferences becomes especially strong.

Sufficient justification of inferences requires both reasoning in light of a conceptual framework of the phenomenon in question and the presence of relevant data. Our assertions must be tested against reality. Data have no meaning unless interpreted within some theoretical context—they do not "speak for themselves." In addition, although relevant behavioral theory is optimally the source of our inferences, it can have little bearing on the validation of those inferences unless grounded in the measurement of pertinent theoretical constructs. The process of construct validation—of building a case that test scores do indeed tap into the desired underlying construct or that scores are relevant and useful for an applied use—is both a rational and empirical enterprise.

Validation is a never-ending process of collecting and evaluating evidence to determine the plausibility of score-based inferences. Since we never have "all the evidence," validation is always incomplete. Future findings may strengthen or undermine existing validity evidence. Validation, then, may be thought of as an ongoing process of making the most reasonable case we can for currently relevant interpretive or action inferences with the evidence that is presently available.

Threats to Construct Validity

Test scores are imperfect measures of constructs. This is due, in part, to the imprecision that results from random errors of measurement but also because test scores are inherently inadequate measures of the constructs they are supposed to assess. Test scores are described as "tapping into" constructs or as being "indicators of" constructs, but not usually as direct "measures" of them (Borsboom & Mellenbergh, 2002). This careful semantic choice acknowledges the limitations of test scores as exemplars of constructs.

Test scores fail to adequately represent the constructs they purport to measure in two basic ways: Tests can leave something out that theoretically should be included or they can include something that is theoretically irrelevant and, therefore, should be left out. These two threats to construct validation are labeled **construct underrepresentation** and **construct-irrelevant test variance,** respectively (Messick, 1989). Construct underrepresentation occurs when the scope of the test is too narrow and it fails to include important aspects of the construct. Construct-irrelevant test variance refers to the presence of reliable variance that is extraneous to the construct being quantified. Note that these two concepts are similar to the issues we raised under the heading of content validity.

The two main types of construct-irrelevant test variance are (1) construct-irrelevant test difficulty and (2) construct-irrelevant test easiness. The former refers to the presence of factors unrelated to the construct being assessed that make the test more difficult for some individuals or groups. A high degree of test anxiety, for instance, has been shown to negatively impact test scores when compared with other indicators of knowledge and skill such as written papers or homework. In this case, the test scores of anxious examinees would be invalidly low relative to their actual standing on the construct. Construct-irrelevant test easiness, on the other hand, occurs when something about the test provides cues that permit certain individuals to respond correctly in ways that are unrelated to the construct. The phenomenon of *testwiseness* in academic settings—that is, when familiarity with item types, effective time management strategies, recognition of patterns among correct answers, and so on contribute to improved test scores for some individuals—is a prime example of construct-irrelevant test easiness. Test scores are invalidly high for examinees who benefit from this type of score contamination.

Both construct underrepresentation and construct-irrelevant test variance are sources of construct invalidity. Each undermines the tenability of interpretative inferences through the misrepresentation of the construct invoked as a basis for score interpretation. Care taken at the time of test construction to ensure that the breadth of content coverage on the test matches the breadth of the construct can help minimize content underrepresentation. Because it is easier both to underrepresent a construct and to include contaminating irrelevant variance when using only a single indicator, it is recommended that multiple indicators of each construct be obtained as part of a construct validation effort. Cook and Campbell (1979) refer to the potentially misleading effects of using a single indicator as *mono-operation bias.*

Relationship Between the Centralized View of Construct Validity and Traditional Types of Validation Evidence

If construct validity is the "whole of validity," where does that leave the other two traditional types of validation evidence? What traditionally has been labeled *construct evidence* has always contributed to the construct validity of score-based inferences—albeit in a narrower sense of the term—but how is it that content and criterion-related evidence are now also thought to be part of construct validity? The answer lies in the centrality of score meaning in all validation efforts. Construct validity is currently viewed as a unitary, though multifaceted, concept involving the justification of particular interpretations of scores. Therefore, any information—whether about test content, relationships between test scores and criteria, or evidence that we have tapped into the underlying construct we sought to measure—that impacts our understanding of score meaning may be considered construct evidence.

Recall that the process of construct validation involves the integration of all available lines of evidence in support of score meaning. The meaning of a measure, captured in construct validation, must be invoked anytime we attempt to substantiate a particular interpretation of a test score or to justify the use of test scores for any applied purpose (Messick, 1988, 1989). Content evidence impacts score meaning by indicating what sorts of characteristics or behaviors are being sampled by the test. At the same time, construct theory helps us to judge the relevance and representativeness of test content to the desired interpretive or action inferences. Empirical test-criterion relationships provide evidence for the construct validity of inferences regarding theoretical relationships between traits or behavioral domains those measures are presumed to reflect. Construct theory provides a rational explanation for any observed test-criterion relationships, which, in turn, helps to justify test use. Test scores and criterion measures may be viewed as indicators of underlying traits *or* behavioral domains. The traditional—narrower—view of construct validity involves providing evidence to support assertions that test scores or criterion measures actually tap into the underlying constructs they claim to represent.

Currently each type of evidence—the traditional content, construct, and criterion-related forms—is viewed as "necessary but not sufficient" for adequate justification of score-based inferences. Together they build a stronger case for the validity of interpretative or action inferences.

The central feature of any validation effort is the justification of score-based inferences through the statement and testing of hypotheses. This process should always be guided by an organizing network of constructs and their interrelationships that serves both as a source of hypotheses and as a basis for explaining observations. A combination of empirical and rational analysis should be used in all validation inquiries.

In addition to this key characteristic, several other important issues need to be emphasized. First, any evidence—regardless of its source—that bears on the meaning of test scores contributes to the validity of an inference. Second, a thorough examination of construct validity should address both the internal structure of the test and the relationships between test scores and other, external variables (Embretson, 1983; Messick, 1989; Shepard, 1993) as dictated by construct theory. Finally, compelling support of score-based inferences requires both corroborating evidence and the ruling out of plausible rival hypotheses.

Internal and External Components

Each construct is embedded in a theory (or network of theories) that describes our understanding of a phenomenon of interest. This conceptual framework includes both an internal model of the interconnected facets or dimensions of a construct and an external model detailing the relationships between that construct and other constructs. Construct validation of score-based inferences traditionally has incorporated both components.

The internal model of a construct consists of all elements of a theory that are necessary to define the construct. This includes features such as a construct's dimensionality and organization as well as a description of the processes thought to underlie performance on a test tapping into that construct. Specific, theoretically derived construct characteristics then may be translated into testable hypotheses that are, in turn, open to empirical confirmation or refutation.

Methods for evaluating a construct's internal structure are becoming increasingly complex. The internal component of construct validation goes beyond traditional psychometric concerns about a test's internal structure—interitem correlations and so on. Conceptual issues such as appropriate weighting of different aspects for multidimensional (and perhaps hierarchically arranged) constructs or the suitability of different item formats relative to the underlying processes to be tested are addressed in this expanded notion of internal structure. These issues cannot be tested very easily with simple correlation coefficients. Test theorists currently rely on the sophisticated mathematical models of item response theory as a way of evaluating theoretically specified internal relationships.

The external model of a construct details its expected relationships with other constructs. The conceptual framework in which a construct is embedded includes other constructs as well as the relationships among them. Construct theory specifies the direction and magnitude of links between certain pairs of constructs and, in some cases, the absence of relationship between others. The specifications of the external model can be stated formally as hypotheses to be tested. Evaluation of a construct's external model involves collection of both convergent and discriminant evidence. Scores on a test reflecting a given construct should correlate more highly with other indicators of the same construct than they do with measures of different constructs.

In the case of the construct validity of inferences pertaining to test use, Shepard (1993) argues for a more encompassing notion of the external portion of a construct's conceptual network. As we saw when discussing criterion-related evidence, predictor-criterion relationships contribute to test score meaning and are, therefore, part of construct validity. Shepard advocates including in the external model not only the traditional components of convergent and discriminant evidence for the referenced construct but also theoretical conceptualizations of relevant domain performance for multiple criterion measures and the relationships among relevant construct and performance-domain theories. Messick (1989) concurs, pointing out that we must be able to link our predictor and criterion measures conceptually (rather than just empirically) in order to justify a particular test use.

Plausible Rival Hypotheses

What separates science from non-science is the willingness of practitioners to expose their ideas to the threat of refutation. Scientific inquiry requires more than confirmatory evidence of one's desired interpretations. If we seek evidence that is consistent with our views, we will probably find it. However, such an approach merely shows that our preferred explanation is consistent with our observations, not that it is the only—or even the best—explanation that could be advanced. To demonstrate that a favored interpretation is "better" than other plausible alternatives, we must design studies to evaluate the rival explanations. This is true for hypothesis testing generally and for construct validation in particular.

Much of the current validity research in this vein started as a response to concerns about bias in testing. When groups perform differently on a test, the initial question is "Why?" Typically one of the first explanations advanced has to do with the "fairness" of the test to groups who test poorly. Test critics rightly want to see evidence that differences in test performance can be traced to differences in the underlying construct or performance domain and not to factors that are construct irrelevant. If, for example, we notice that females tend to outperform males on an English placement test, we could advance a number of explanations. Initially we might speculate that, on average, females simply have superior language skills (as assessed by the test). When we note that the placement test is in an essay format, we might conjecture that females have an advantage on variables such as writing ability, composition quality, neatness, or clarity of handwriting that account for some (or all) of the observed gender differences. Still other factors—interest level for instance—could be responsible. In terms of evaluating bias, we need to determine whether or not the reasons for observed differences are construct relevant or irrelevant. In terms of building a good case for the construct validity of a desired score-based inference, we need to keep in mind that there are always possible counter-explanations and that those rival hypotheses need to be explored.

Messick's Unified Theory of Validity

Samuel Messick's (1989) chapter in the third edition of *Educational Measurement* is currently the most authoritative, widely cited reference on the topic of validity. Messick's chapter has done two main things for the measurement community. First, it clearly established construct validity as the single, centralized conceptualization of validity. The idea was not new; in fact, as Shepard (1993) points out, the notion had been advanced decades earlier, but Messick's chapter formally codified a growing consensus in the measurement community. The second major contribution of Messick's work was that it expanded the concept of validity beyond issues of score meaning to include evidence of the relevance and utility of test scores as well as consideration of the consequences of test interpretation and use. While the rational or empirical analysis of *consequences as part of construct validation* has yet to be embraced wholeheartedly by all members of the testing community, it is still a major milestone in the evolution of validity theory. Messick's model is a unified, yet multi-faceted, conceptualization of validity.

Messick (1989) presented his validity framework in a fourfold table shown in Table 5–7 (Table 2.1 in his original text).

> A unified validity framework . . . may be constructed by distinguishing two interconnected facets of the unitary validity concept. One facet is the source of justification of the testing, being based on appraisal of either evidence of consequence. The other facet is the function or outcome of testing, being either interpretation or use. If the facet for source of justification (that is, either an evidential basis or a consequential basis) is crossed with the facet of function or outcome (that is, either test interpretation or test use), we obtain a four-fold classification as in Table 2.1 (Messick, 1980).
>
> As indicated in Table 2.1, the evidential basis of test interpretation is construct validity. The evidential basis of test use is also construct validity, but as buttressed by evidence for the relevance of the test to the specific applied purpose and for utility of the test in the applied setting. The consequential basis of test interpretation is the appraisal of the value implications of the construct label, of the theory underlying test interpretation, and of the ideologies in which the theory is embedded. A central issue is whether or not the theoretical implications and the value implications of the test interpretation are commensurate, because value implications are not ancillary but, rather, integral to score meaning. Finally, the consequential basis of test use is the appraisal of both potential and actual social consequences of applied testing. (p. 20)

We have already discussed the fundamental issues related to the evidential basis of test interpretation and test use, labeled "Construct validity" and "Construct validity + relevance/utility" in Table 5–7. We turn now to Messick's thoughts on the consequential basis of test interpretation and test use: value implications and social consequences, respectively.

Table 5–7
Facets of Validity

	Test Interpretation	Test Use
Evidential Basis	Construct validity	Construct validity + relevance utility
Consequential Basis	Value implications	Social consequences

Source: Reprinted with permission from Messick, S. (1989). Validity. In R. L. Linn (Ed.), *Educational measurement* (3rd ed., pp. 13–103). New York: Macmillan.

Consequential Basis of Test Interpretation: Value Implications

There is no longer any debate about *whether* values should be involved in science—they clearly are. Scientific judgments *are* value judgments. For instance, rather than relying on the strictly empirical orientation to validation that dominated prior to the 1950s, we now invoke constructs as a basis for testing our hypotheses. Doing so is a choice based on what currently is deemed valuable and important. Furthermore, that we use hypothesis testing at all is, itself, a choice. So the question is not *if* values should have a role in science, but *how* we can take values into account in scientific enterprises.

Messick's (1989) inclusion of the consequences of score interpretation in his conceptualization of validity requires that, as part of our validation efforts, we explicitly deal with the value implications associated with the constructs we invoke. He argues that values are intrinsic to validity considerations because they impact score meaning through the construct interpretation of test scores. Interpretation of any event or behavior involves matching it to some larger schema to which value is already attached. Any individual event or behavior is viewed as an exemplar of the broader category to which it belongs and is thereby suffused with the values associated with that categorization. Each of these broader categories is, in turn, a subclass of some even more general conceptualization with yet another layer of value affixed. In the context of validation, values are thought to impact score meaning at three levels: through (1) the labels we give to constructs, (2) the theories that give constructs their meaning, and (3) the ideologies reflected in those theories.

In the case of value assumptions associated with construct labels, consider the difference in the interpretive meaning of scores if the end points on a scale are called "flexibility versus rigidity" as opposed to "confusion versus consistency" (Messick, 1989). What value assumptions underlie the label "personal crisis"? What if the concept was relabeled "opportunity for personal growth"? If we presume something to be a "good" or "bad" thing, that value connotation often finds its way into the construct label and steers score interpretation in the direction consistent with our assumption. We need to be careful that construct labels accurately reflect the entire range of value connotations implied by the theoretical conceptualization of the construct and its empirical referents.

A theory is a broader category than a construct and has its own values and assumptions attached. A construct gains meaning from its place within a broader theoretical framework. We might find, therefore, different interpretations of the same scores depending on the theoretical perspective through which the construct and its indicator are being viewed. This effect can be most easily seen in the case of competing theories of the same phenomenon. Consider the different interpretations of the same aptitude test score if, from one theoretical perspective, the construct tapped by the test is seen as relatively fixed but, in light of the other theory, the construct is viewed as infinitely improvable through effort (Ames & Archer, 1988). In light of the first perspective, an examinee's score would be interpreted as indicative of a trait that is beyond the individual's control. From the second perspective, however, examinees' scores are perceived as indicators of a construct that is malleable and individuals might be held personally responsible (at least in part) for their current standings or any improvement that might occur. It doesn't take much of a stretch to see that such differences in interpretation can have a dramatic effect on the justification of various uses of the test in an applied setting.

Finally, the third major source of value implications is the ideology in which theories are embedded. Ideology refers to a "complex configuration of shared values, affects, and beliefs that provides . . . an existential framework for interpreting the world" (Messick, 1989, p. 62). Rubin (1988) refers to ideology as one's "implicit model of reality" (p. 243). In any scientific inquiry, including validation, ideology impacts the questions we ask, the answers we seek, and the meaning we attach to whatever we observe in response to our inquiries. Take, for example, differing beliefs about the universality versus individuality of just about any human phenomenon. Some theorists believe that, in the ways that really matter, human beings are more similar than different. Their theories reflect this belief by focusing on characteristics or experiences that are universal. Variance attributable to individual differences cannot be interpreted within such a framework and generally is considered uninterpretable "error." On the other hand, other theorists believe that each of us is, most importantly, a unique individual and that understanding how and why we are different from one another is of greater import than looking at the ways in which we are all alike. These theorists develop theories about the roles of context, culture, individual experience, and the like in an attempt to understand our differences. Because ideology is a fundamental way of looking at and interpreting the world, those with differing ideologies may be thought of as experiencing functionally different worlds. While this makes it difficult, if not impossible, to see things from another ideological point of view, confronting other perspectives creates fertile ground for debate over both how to frame the issues themselves and about the values attached to those issues. The difficulty in dealing explicitly with values that stem from ideology is that these value assumptions are often tacit; we must first uncover them before we can consider their impact on score interpretations.

Consequential Basis of Test Use: Social Consequences

Examination of the impact of test use informs our judgments about the functional worth of test scores for a particular applied purpose in a specific applied setting. According to Messick (1989), consideration of both the actual and potential social consequences of testing is rightly part of construct validation. First of all, rational prediction of potential outcomes must be based in construct theory. The construct meaning of scores plays an essential role in the reasonable anticipation of results—both desired and unintended—of the proposed test use just as it did when hypothesizing about relationships between test scores and criteria. Furthermore, actual outcomes provide empirical evidence that contributes directly to score meaning through the confirmation or refutation of expectations. All of the previously discussed facets of construct validity—score interpretation, the relevance and utility of scores for a particular applied purpose, and the value implications associated with score meaning—converge in this last cell of Messick's table.

Historically the central question in test use has been "Does the test do what it was employed to do, does it serve its intended purpose?" Messick (1989) argues that the *intended* outcomes of testing do not, in and of themselves, provide sufficient justification for a particular test use. To assess the functional worth of testing in a certain context, we must consider *all* of its effects—intended and unintended, positive and negative—to determine whether or not a proposed test use is justified. This is especially true if adverse consequences have a basis in test invalidity.

Evaluation of the source(s) of adverse, as well as desirable, social consequences is an important part of the validation of score-based inferences regarding test use. If two groups have different score distributions on a test and that test is used as a selection device, the higher scoring group will be selected disproportionately, and the lower scoring group will experience adverse impact. If the differences in test scores do *not* correspond to equivalent differences in the underlying construct, the valid use of this test for selection purposes is jeopardized. Recall that the two main threats to the construct validity of a score-based inference are construct underrepresentation and construct-irrelevant test variance. Whenever test scores or criterion measures are influenced by either of these factors, especially when they impact groups differentially, the validity of inferences based on those scores is called into question. Therefore, *it is not the existence of adverse impact that makes a proposed test use invalid; invalidity occurs when our scores misrepresent the construct being referenced.* On the other hand, if these sources of invalidity can be ruled out, then any group differences on the test may be presumed to reflect actual differences in the implied construct. In this case, the proposed use of the test is valid and the presence of group differences actually contributes to score meaning. In cases where adverse consequences cannot be traced to sources of test invalidity, a judgment about whether to go ahead with the proposed test use in spite of the undesirable outcomes for some individuals or groups is one of political and social policy, not validity.

Adverse consequences and side effects of test use impact more than just individuals and groups; they also impact institutions and society at large. Most states have implemented mandatory competency testing in schools. The desired outcome of such testing is to ensure that all students graduating from high school meet certain performance standards—that they are competent to take their places in society. The unintended side effects of this type of testing are beginning to be seen. To ensure that all students pass, teachers are spending instructional time teaching to the specific characteristics of these tests in terms of both test-taking strategies and content. If tests use a multiple-choice format, emphasis is placed on memorization and details rather than thinking skills. The side effects of such "high-stakes testing" are explored further in Chapter 14.

Messick (1989) notes that appraisal of consequences is important for another reason: Judgments of the functional worth of test scores for a proposed test use often serve as a basis for social action. For instance, decisions about the allocation of limited resources (such as jobs or slots in competitive academic programs) must be made according to some sorting principle or decision rule. Questions of fairness or unfairness of those procedures typically are raised by those who have been excluded from a desired job or program. All of the validation concerns already discussed bear on issues of fairness. However, it is not just the use of a test that must be justified, but the whole selection process. A central issue in consideration of fairness is this: If a different decision rule is applied—informed by a different set of test scores or even no scores at all—is allocation actually fairer or has the perceived unfairness simply been shifted to another group?

In practice, it is often the latter of these options. The determination of who should get something that is in short supply is a matter of one's perspective and is, in essence, a value judgment. For example, the typical practice of basing selection on predicted criterion performance implies that efficiency and economy (in terms of high hit rates) for the institution are the primary social values to be served. As ubiquitous as this value is in our decision making, it is not the only value that might be invoked. While efficiency and economy are definitely important—sometimes the most important—values to consider, it is vital to keep in mind that no value perspective automatically has primacy. Whatever the basis for selection, there will be perceived injustice to those disadvantaged by the decisions, as well as to those simply favoring another value basis.

In many instances, differing value positions are conflicting and there is simply no way to serve multiple perspectives simultaneously. Consider four of the most common value bases for academic decisions: selection according to ability, effort, accomplishment, or need. In practice we cannot serve all of these values simultaneously because the "needy may not be the most able [and] those who work the hardest may not accomplish the most" (Deutsch, 1975, p. 140). We have to make a judgment about which of any number of competing value perspectives is the most important in a given applied context. Messick (1989) and Cronbach (1988) recommend that multiple value perspectives be examined and that the consequences associated with the use of each in decision making being fully explored before determining which value basis is most the appropriate for a particular situation.

Beyond Messick: Refinements and Shifts in Focus

Validity conceptualizations continue to evolve. While Messick's model represents a dramatic shift in our conceptualization of validity and remains central to current testing theory, other theorists have weighed in with their own perspectives. In 1993, Shepard offered a refinement of Messick's model. While she does not dispute that Messick's model accurately portrays the current state of validity theory and has no quibble with the substance of his arguments, Shepard's main concern revolves around how these issues should be communicated. Messick's chapter is extremely complicated and nearly 100 dense pages long. Shepard believes that it is simply too difficult to wade through to be of practical use. She notes that Messick's attempts to deconstruct his extraordinarily complex model into a fourfold table—followed by four separate sections in the text—may serve to reinforce the long-standing habit in the testing community of segregating validation activities into different types. While Shepard acknowledges that this was certainly not Messick's intent, she points out that such an interpretation of his model could potentially undermine a truly unified view of validity. Shepard worries that any appearance of segregation of validation activities once again may prompt test users to focus on only a few aspects of validity (evidence) while neglecting others (consequences). The consensus that construct validation is a never-ending process (Cronbach, 1971, 1988; Messick, 1988, 1989) only adds to her concern about the discrepancy between validity theory and the actual practices of test publishers and users. If our evidence, analyses, and arguments for construct validity are always incomplete, some may be inclined to proceed with score interpretations and uses even when those inferences are supported by precious little evidence or lack any comprehensive evaluation of consequences.

Shepard (1993) cites Cronbach's (1988) conceptualization of the process of construct validation as one that closely resembles her own. Cronbach emphasizes different aspects of the issues formalized in Messick's chapter and views the process of validation as an exercise in evaluative argumentation. Consistent with Messick's model, Cronbach states that comprehensive validation arguments must link "concepts, evidence, social and personal consequences, and values" (p. 4). Cronbach, like Messick and Shepard, stresses the importance of a truly integrated approach to validation. However, unlike many people's misinterpretations of Messick's work, Cronbach's proposal clearly models a validation process that addresses these issues simultaneously.

Cronbach (1988) notes that validation now occurs in a very public arena, with the lay public interested in and concerned about—even skeptical of—all aspects of applied testing. Test use in applied decision making—especially high-stakes testing in employment, credentialing, and higher education—is currently a matter of heated public debate (Sackett, Schmitt, Ellingson, & Kabin, 2001). According to Cronbach, the validity of any score-based inference should be open to debate and those involved in the interpretation or use of test scores should be prepared to justify their positions. He recommends that validators—whether test publishers or users—work on their validity arguments in the same way debaters about any other topic do. A good debater will begin by carefully examining all sides of an issue and, after having done so, ideally argue just as effectively from any point of view. As with any topic under debate, arguments in support of particular score interpretations or proposed uses will be strengthened through consideration—and possible neutralization—of counterarguments.

Given the value-laden, political nature of testing, Cronbach (1988) emphasizes the importance of taking multiple perspectives into account in order to build a truly persuasive argument for the score-based inferences we would like to make. Public acceptance or rejection of a proposed test use happens when a community is persuaded by an argument. This judgment is influenced, to a large extent, by the degree to which the proposed practice is consistent with the prevailing belief system. To complicate things further, ideologies often differ dramatically for different constituencies. Testing professionals need to take these beliefs into account in preparing validation arguments and must adequately communicate their rationale to the public in light of these multiple points of view. If professionals do not guide them, nonprofessionals certainly will evaluate—and develop their own arguments in regard to—proposed score interpretations and uses themselves.

VALIDITY THEORY AND TEST BIAS

Bias in testing has been a recurring theme in educational and psychological measurement since the 1920s. In the decades since, considerable attention has been paid to the detection and elimination of bias both in the items that make up the tests and in the uses of test scores in applied decision-making (Cole & Moss, 1989). The issues surrounding test bias are complex and their resolution has been difficult due, in no small part, to the diversity of perspectives held by those concerned with these matters. Different people hold various beliefs about the appropriate values to invoke when making decisions, whether or not those decisions are based on test scores. We have stressed repeatedly that all uses of test scores carry value connotations and any applied test use is attended by concerns about fairness and adverse impact. A particular test score interpretation or use might be "unbiased" in the psychometric sense, but be labeled "biased" by those who dislike the value implications associated with a certain score meaning or the consequences resulting from a specific use.

In point of fact, the term *test bias* has been defined in numerous ways. In this section, we use the technical, psychometric definition—the one associated with validity theory. As with validity more generally, what is evaluated as being "biased" or "unbiased" is an *inference* based on a test score, not the test (or an item) itself. As we have already discussed at length, an inference is judged to be valid when there is sufficient rational and empirical evidence supporting it. An inference is considered *biased* when it is *differentially valid* for different groups. If test scores fail to reflect the intended construct the same way across groups or situations (or appear to tap into different constructs for different groups), then score interpretations are biased. When test scores differentially predict criterion performance for different groups, the use of those scores in decision making is biased.

The terms *bias* and *fairness* are often used in the same context but represent quite different concepts in measurement (Murphy & Davidshofer, 2001). Bias is typically demonstrated through empirical evidence—such as when test scores overpredict criterion performance for one group but not another—and is, therefore, primarily a statistical concept. As such, the existence of bias can be revealed using scientific methods. At the item level, bias can be detected by examining item responses for group $\times$ item interactions, that is, patterns of differential performance on items. In the case of prediction, the presence of bias can be detected by examining the regression equations of the groups in question. Differences in slopes or intercepts are indicative of differential validity.

Fairness, on the other hand, is a value judgment about the appropriateness of decisions or actions based on test scores. It is a philosophical or political concept, not an empirical one; there are no statistics that reveal the presence or absence of fairness in a decision. Judgments of fairness are based on comparison of what actions have been taken versus those that "should have been" taken. Individuals tend to find decisions that are consistent with their beliefs and values to be "fair," whereas those that are based on a different ideology are seen to be "unfair" regardless of desirable or adverse personal consequences. It is entirely possible, therefore, for an inference to be universally valid and, thus, unbiased, yet be judged by some to be unfair.

OVERLAP OF RELIABILITY AND VALIDITY

One way of thinking about the usefulness of a test is to ask to what extent one might safely generalize from a test score. If two forms of the test are given on the same day, the correlation between them tells us with what degree of confidence we can generalize from one set of test tasks to another set built to the same specifications and, by implication, with what degree of confidence we can generalize from the score to the whole domain of tasks sampled by the test. If the testing is conducted on different days, we gather evidence over a domain of occasions. And, if the testing on different days is also with different test forms, we gather evidence on the degree of generalizability over both tasks and occasions. If two different but similar tests are given, each intended by its author to measure the same trait or construct, we get evidence of generalizability from test to test. We are now considering a still broader domain that includes not merely samples of tasks chosen according to a common blueprint or design but also a range of blueprints or designs prepared by different authors. We are moving beyond what is ordinarily thought of as reliability into the realm of validity. And, of course, it is possible to consider generalizability from a test to other indicators of the same attribute, such as self-description or ratings by peers, supervisors, or teachers. Do the test scores allow us to draw inferences about what those ratings would be?

The notion of generalizability encompasses both reliability and validity, indicating that the two concepts differ only in the breadth of the domain to which generalization is undertaken. The concept of generalizability may eventually come to replace the several types of reliability and validity that we have discussed in this and the preceding chapter. Figure 5–8 provides an illustration of the notion of generalizability. We can view the situation as resembling the layers of an

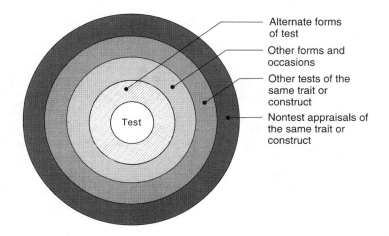

Figure 5–8
Layers of generalization from a test score.

Alternate forms of test

Other forms and occasions

Other tests of the same trait or construct

Nontest appraisals of the same trait or construct

Test

onion and can ask concerning any test how well it enables us to generalize our conclusions to situations at successive levels of remoteness from the central core.

VALIDITY FOR CRITERION-REFERENCED TESTS

Criterion-referenced tests are concerned with the measurement of particular, narrowly defined instructional objectives. For this reason, the critical concern in assessing the validity of criterion-referenced tests is *content validity*. An instructional objective includes two elements: the information content of the domain and what the student should be able to do with that content. Both of these elements must be present in the item in the form called for by the objective if the item is to be considered a valid indicator of achievement of that objective.

An often overlooked part of the content of a test is the conditions under which the examinees exhibit their performance. If the time allowed for testing is too short to enable most of the examinees to attempt all of the items, then speed of performance becomes a part of the content of the test. If the administration conditions are poor, these conditions become part of the test content *for these examinees*. To the extent that factors such as these vary from one group of examinees to another, the content of the test also varies. Content validity relates to the test score and all of the factors that affect it, including clarity of directions and adequacy of scoring procedures. When the content is critical to the use of the test scores, careful attention must be paid to all factors that make up the test's content.

Content validity, as we have seen, is primarily a matter of professional judgment on the part of teachers and subject-matter experts. There is, however, a useful type of empirical or statistical evidence that can be used to appraise the validity of criterion-referenced tests. This type of procedure is based on the point, made by Berk (1980), that a criterion-referenced test should maximize differences between groups that have achieved mastery of the objectives and those that have not achieved mastery, while it should minimize differences within the groups. That is, the ideal mastery-oriented test should divide the examinees into two homogeneous groups of individuals: those who have achieved mastery and those who have not.

The problem, of course, is how to define *mastery*. One commonly used approach is to have teachers identify those pupils who they are certain have mastered the objective and those who they are certain have not mastered it. This method can yield two widely separated groups, but the middle pupils must be omitted. A second approach is to compare those who have received instruction on the objective with those who have not yet had such instruction. Still another approach is to compare the performance of students before instruction with their performance following a period of instruction. Each of these approaches has certain limitations, and all are affected by the problem of the unreliability of difference, or change, scores. But any one of the approaches provides some evidence of the joint validity of the instructional activities aimed at the objectives, and the test as a measure of mastery of those objectives.

The validation procedure is similar to the item analysis methods discussed in Chapter 15. The examinees are divided into two groups: masters versus nonmasters or instructed versus uninstructed. The proportion in each group who answered each item correctly is then determined. The valid items are those for which the success rate in the master or instructed group is substantially higher than the success rate in the nonmaster or uninstructed group. In the extreme case, the success rate on each item for masters should be 100%, while the nonmasters should experience a chance rate of success. The total test should divide the examinees into masters, all of whom achieve perfect or near-perfect scores, and nonmasters, all of whom score at about the chance level. In the ideal test, there should be no misclassifications.

Mastery of an instructional objective is seldom an all-or-none thing. In any class, there will be varying degrees of mastery. In fact, one problem with the mastery concept in testing is deciding on an acceptable definition of mastery. The advantage of the criterion-referenced mastery philosophy of evaluation is that we know, in theory, what the students who have gained mastery can do, that is, what classes of problems or tasks they can solve. This type of knowledge is an essential part of formative evaluation. But, there are many situations, both in the school setting and elsewhere, in which the question asked is one of relative position. Summative evaluations often call for norm-referenced tests that focus explicitly on relative performance.

META-ANALYSIS AND VALIDITY GENERALIZATION

In psychology and education, studies are often carried out with rather small samples, and, partly as a consequence of this fact, different studies have often given quite inconsistent results. In the past two decades, researchers have sought better ways of distilling an essence of truth from a mass of seemingly contradictory results. The term **meta-analysis** was coined (Glass, 1977) to apply to the systematic pooling and integration of results from many different studies of the same phenomenon.

A specific example of meta-analysis is the integration of test validity data for different groups and from different sources. As soon as ability tests became available, researchers started to collect data on the validity of those tests for both educational and vocational criteria. For any given test or type of test, validity coefficients were found to vary rather substantially for the same school subject or for what appeared to be the same job. For example, the predictive validity coefficient for English grades predicted from the verbal reasoning subtest of the Differential Aptitude Tests (DAT) ranged, in different groups, from .07 to .76.

People came to accept the doctrine, especially in relation to vocational prediction, that validity must be established in each specific situation. However, more recently, Schmidt and his associates (Schmidt, 1988a, 1988b; Schmidt & Hunter, 1981; Schmidt, Hunter, Pearlman, & Hirsh, 1985) have demonstrated that much of the variation in results from one study to another can be attributed to a variety of statistical artifacts: sampling errors in small samples, criterion unreliability, or differing degrees of restriction in the range of ability in the sample studied. They propose that meta-analysis be applied to the accumulated data, thus pooling results from separate studies and arriving at an average value that may be taken as a more stable and generally applicable estimate of test validity, one that is closer to the true value than the value obtained from a local sample, usually of quite modest size. Thus, unless the English program in School System X is *radically* different from the program in most schools, the median validity coefficient of .49, based on pooling the results from many schools, will probably be a more appropriate value for School System X to use in thinking about the validity of the verbal reasoning test of DAT for predicting English grades than will be whatever value might be obtained from a limited local study. Schmidt and Hunter have attached the name **validity generalization** to this application of meta-analysis.

The procedures for meta-analysis and validity generalization are still controversial, but the methods are being applied to an increasingly wide variety of topics in education and occupational psychology. We may anticipate that the next 10 or 20 years will see a more systematic synthesis of the validation research that has accumulated during the past 50 years, leading to stable, generalized estimates of test-criterion relationships. We may hope that these relationships will be accepted by the Equal Employment Opportunity Commission, other government agencies, and the courts as superior replacements for local studies on necessarily small samples and that objective testing procedures will again become a practical procedure for appraising job applicants.

SUMMARY

The most important characteristic for a test to have is validity. But, validity is the responsibility of both the test constructor and the test user because validity refers to the use or interpretation that is made of a test score. In one context, one interpretation of a test score may be appropriate, but in a different context or for a different purpose, the same interpretation might well be invalid.

Three general types of evidence bear on the question of whether a particular test use is a valid use. First, content-related evidence reveals the relationship between the test content and the proposed interpretation. If the correspondence, which is largely a matter of expert judgment, is good, the proposed use is supported. Second, empirical or criterion-related evidence is obtained from the relationships of test scores with other variables of interest, particularly occupational and educational outcomes. Substantial correlations between test scores and measures of performance in the outcome task support the use of the test for prediction, selection, or placement decisions. Finally, construct-related evidence comes from the correspondence of the test scores to deductions from theory. Content- and criterion-related evidence help to determine fit to predictions from theory, but response to experimental interventions and agreement with predicted patterns of relationship with other variables are also important.

QUESTIONS AND EXERCISES

1. If the American College Testing Program were to develop a general survey test in science for high school seniors, what steps might the developers take to establish evidence of the validity of the test?

2. What type of validity evidence is indicated by each of the following statements that might have appeared in a test manual?
   a. Scores on the Attitudes Toward School Inventory correlated +0.43 with teachers' ratings of adjustment.
   b. The objectives to be assessed by XYZ Reading Test were rated for importance by 150 classroom teachers.
   c. Scores on the Wunderkind Programming Aptitude Test correlated +0.57 with supervisors' ratings after 6 months on the job.
   d. The Factors of Brilliance Intelligence Test yields scores that correlate +0.69 with scores on the Wechsler Adult Intelligence Scale.
   e. The Accurate Achievement Battery is based on an analysis of 50 widely used texts and 100 courses of study from all parts of the country.

3. Comment on the following statement: The classroom teacher is the only person who can judge the validity of a standardized achievement test for his or her class.

4. Examine the manuals for two or three tests of different types. What evidence for validity is presented in each? How adequate is the evidence for each test?

5. Using Table 5–5, determine what percentage of those selected would be above average on the job if a selection procedure with a validity of .50 were used and only the top quarter of applicants were accepted for the job. What percentage

would be above average if the top three-quarters were selected? What would the two percentages be if the validity were only 0.40? What does a comparison of the four percentages indicate?

6. If personnel psychologists for the navy were doing research on tests for the selection of helicopter maintenance trainees, what might they use as a criterion of success in such a specialty? What are the advantages and disadvantages of each possible measure?

7. What are the advantages of using freshman grade-point average as a criterion measure for validating a college admissions test? What are the disadvantages?

8. A test manual contains the following statement: The validity of Test Q is shown by the fact that it correlates .80 with the Stanford-Binet. What additional evidence is needed to evaluate this assertion?

9. You are considering three reading tests for use in your school. As far as you can judge, all three are equally valid, and each reports a reliability of .90. What else would you need to know to make a choice between the tests?

10. Examine several tests of aptitude or of achievement that would be appropriate for a class you might teach. Write up an evaluation of one of these tests, using the guidelines given in the last section of this chapter.

11. Consider the test you examined in Question 10 from the unified validity theory approach. What are some of the theoretical constructs underlying the test? What are some of the possible positive and negative consequences of using this test? How might this test be used for purposes other than those intended by the test's author, and what would the consequences of such misuse be?

SUGGESTED READINGS

American Educational Research Association, American Psychological Association, & National Council on Measurement in Education. (1999). *Standards for educational and psychological testing.* Washington, DC: American Educational Research Association.

Ames, C., & Archer, J. (1988). Achievement goals in the classroom: Students' learning strategies and motivation processes. *Journal of Educational Psychology, 80,* 260–267.

Anastasi, A. (1986). Evolving concepts of test validation. *Annual Review of Psychology, 37,* 1–15.

Angoff, W. H. (1988). Validity: An evolving concept. In H. Wainer & H. Braun (Eds.), *Test validity* (pp. 19–32). Mahwah, NJ: Erlbaum.

Borsboom, D., & Mellenbergh, G. H. (2002). True scores, latent variables and constructs: A comment on Schmidt and Hunter. *Intelligence, 30,* 505–514.

Cook, T. D., & Campbell, D. T. (1979). *Quasi-experimentation: Design and analysis issues for field settings.* Chicago: Rand McNally.

Cronbach, L. J. (1971). Test validation. In R. L. Thorndike (Ed.), *Educational measurement* (2nd ed., pp. 443–507). Washington, DC: American Council on Education.

Cronbach, L. J. (1988). Five perspectives on validation argument. In H. Wainer & H. Braun (Eds.), *Test validity* (pp. 3–17). Mahwah, NJ: Erlbaum.

Deutsch, M. (1975). Equity, equality and need: What determines which value will be used as the basis of distributive justice. *Journal of Social Issues, 31,* 137–149.

Ebel, R. L. (1983). The practical validation of tests of ability. *Educational Measurement: Issues and Practices, 2*(2), 7–10.

Embretson (Whitely), S. (1983). Construct validity: Construct representation versus nomothetic span. *Psychological Bulletin, 93,* 179–197.

Fredericksen, N. (1986). Construct validity and construct similarity: Methods for use in test development and test validation. *Multivariate Behavioral Research, 21,* 3–28.

Gardner, E. F. (1983). Intrinsic rational validity: Necessary but not sufficient. *Educational Measurement: Issues and Practices, 2*(2), 13.

Haertel, E. (1985). Construct validity and criterion-referenced testing. *Review of Educational Research, 55,* 23–46.

Hambleton, R. K. (1984). Validating the test scores. In R. A. Berk (Ed.), *A guide to criterion-referenced test construction* (pp. 199–230). Baltimore: Johns Hopkins University Press.

Messick, S. (1980). Test validity and the ethics of assessment. *American Psychologist, 35,* 1012–1027.

Messick, S. (1988). The once and future issues of validity: Assessing the meaning and consequences of measurement. In H. Wainer & H. Braun (Eds.), *Test Validity* (pp. 33–45). Mahwah, NJ: Erlbaum.

Messick, S. (1989). Validity. In R. L. Linn (Ed.), *Educational measurement* (3rd ed., pp. 13–103). New York: Macmillan.

Rubin, D. B. (1988). Discussion. In H. Wainer & H. Braun (Eds.), *Test Validity* (pp. 241–256). Mahwah, NJ: Erlbaum.

Sackett, P. R., Schmitt, N., Ellingson, J. E., and Kabin, M. B. (2001). High-stakes testing in employment, credentialing, and higher education. *American Psychologist, 56,* 302–318.

Schmidt, F. L. (1988). Validity generalization and the future of criterion-related validity. In H. Wainer & H. Braun (Eds.), *Test validity* (pp. 173–189). Mahwah, NJ: Erlbaum.

Schmidt, F. L., Hunter, J. E., Pearlman, K., & Hirsh, H. R. (1985). Forty questions about validity generalization and meta-analysis. *Personnel Psychology, 32,* 697–798.

Shepard, L. A. (1993). Evaluating test validity. In L. Darling-Hammond (Ed.), *Review of research in education* (Vol. 19, pp. 405–450). Washington, DC: American Educational Research Association.

CHAPTER 6

Practical Issues Related to Testing

Factors Making for Practicality in Routine Test Use
    Economy
    Features Facilitating Test Administration
    Features Facilitating Interpretation and Use
        of Scores
    E-Testing
Guide for Evaluating a Test
    General Identifying Information
    Information About the Test
    Aids to Interpreting Test Results
    Validity

    Reliability
    Administration and Scoring
    Scales and Norms
Getting Information About Specific Tests
    What Tests Exist?
    Exactly What Is Test X Like?
    What Do Critics Think of Test X?
    What Research Has Been Conducted on Test X?
Summary
Questions and Exercises
Sources of Test Information

FACTORS MAKING FOR PRACTICALITY IN ROUTINE TEST USE

Although validity and reliability may be all-important for measures in psychology and education, when a test is to be used in classrooms throughout a school or school system or in any large or ongoing testing application, a number of down-to-earth, practical considerations must also be taken into account. It is easy for the administrator to pay too much attention to small financial savings or to economies of time that make it possible to fit a test into a standard class period with no shifting of schedules; nevertheless, these factors of economy and convenience are real considerations. Furthermore, other factors relating to the readiness with which the tests may be given, scored, and interpreted bear importantly on the use that will be made of the tests and the soundness of the conclusions that will be drawn from them.

Economy

The practical significance of dollar savings need not be emphasized in the current environment of tight educational and corporate budgets. Dollars are of real significance for any educational or industrial enterprise, and research users must also watch expenses. Economy in the case of tests depends in part on the cost of test materials and scoring services per examinee and in part on the possibility of reusing the test materials. For example, in the upper elementary grades and beyond, tests can be administered that have separate test booklets and answer sheets, so that the test booklets can be used for a number of testings. Also, if a test is used in successive years or if testing can be scheduled so that different classes or schools can be tested on different days, an important economy can be effected. Publishers sell test booklets and answer sheets separately for just this reason.

A second aspect of economy is time savings in test administration; however, this economy is often a false one. We saw in Chapter 4 that the reliability of a test depends largely on its length. As far as testing time is concerned, we get about what we give. Some tests may be designed a little more efficiently so that they give a little more reliable measurement per minute of testing time, but, by and large, any reduction in testing time will be accomplished at the price of loss in precision or breadth of our appraisal, unless it is possible to use a computer adaptive test.

A third, and quite significant, aspect of economy is the ease of scoring. The clerical work of scoring a battery of tests by hand can become either burdensome if it is done by the already busy teacher or psychologist or expensive if it is carried out by clerical help hired especially for the purpose. As a result, test users rely heavily on mechanized scoring, and test publishers are producing tests that can be processed by the increasingly sophisticated equipment being developed. A number of commercially published tests, such as the SAT and the Strong Interest Inventory, can be scored only by the publisher or at special centers licensed by the publisher. Other tests, such as the individually administered Stanford-Binet and Wechsler scales, are scored only by hand. But, for many published tests, test users have the option of hand scoring their own tests, of setting up their own mechanized scoring units, or of sending tests to one of the test scoring services that specialize in test processing.

Computer Scoring

Several test-scoring services, many run by the test publishers themselves, provide efficient test scoring and reporting, often giving 24-hour turnaround; that is, they will score the tests and put the results in return mail within 24 hours of their receipt of the completed answer sheets. Also, test scoring equipment is becoming so inexpensive and readily available that many schools, school districts, or personnel offices maintain their own scoring services. The basic equipment consists of a photoelectric document reader combined with a computer. The document reader responds to marks on an answer sheet or in the test booklet. (At least three companies sell the scanning part of a test scoring system for under $5,000, a cost that is within the means of many school districts and modest-sized companies.)

Using a separate answer sheet is familiar to most American college students, but separate answer sheets are not satisfactory for young children. The complications of finding an answer in the test booklet, keeping the code letter or number of the chosen answer in mind while locating the proper place on the answer sheet, and then marking the proper spot on the answer sheet are too much for children in the primary grades. However, current equipment makes it possible to use a booklet at the primary level. Students mark their answers directly in the test booklet. For scoring, the test can be designed so that either one slices the bound edge off the test booklet and runs the separate pages through the scanner or the test is printed in a fanfold booklet that can be unfolded and run through the scanner as a unit. Modern scanning equipment can handle 50 or more different answer sheet patterns in a single run.

The information from the optical scanner is fed into the computer where it is compared with a key that has been recorded in the computer's memory. One or more scores are determined and stored in a file for later analysis or printing out on a record form. The computer can also produce various statistics, such as means and standard deviations, as well as local percentiles, for classes, schools, or school systems. Thus, the scoring service, whether it is a commercial agency or a district or local office, can generally provide not only test scores for individuals, but also the complete range of statistical information about the test results that might be of interest to the local teacher or school system. Some of the scoring services will also accumulate results over a period of years, providing a longitudinal picture of the local test results. One advantage to the local school of having its own scoring and computing equipment is that it is then much easier to carry out item analyses (see Chapter 15) on locally constructed tests, as well as to accumulate local norms and longitudinal results.

Perhaps one of the least expected developments in test processing software has been the development of programs that score essay tests (Page, 1994) using scoring rubrics and model answers. A **rubric** is a set of directions for how to compare an answer with the model answer and how to evaluate elements such as grammar and spelling. Page and his associates report that their program produces results that are as reliable as the average of up to six human judges. Of course, the quality of the output depends critically on the adequacy of the scoring rubric, but as more experience is accumulated with computerized scoring of produce-response tasks, we may see a move toward increased use of items of this type in standardized tests.

A test deemed economical for use in large-scale testing programs will be available in a format for scoring by different types of scanning and scoring equipment. Almost any type of answer sheet can be hand scored relatively efficiently by using an overlay stencil. Some test publishers supply plastic overlay stencils for this purpose. Others use a special type of answer sheet made up of two sheets fastened together, the back of one being carbon covered or pressure sensitive. The key is printed on the back of the first sheet, and as the examinee marks the front, the carbon-covered or pressure-sensitive material transfers the marks to the back of the sheet, where the number of marks falling in the printed key spaces can be counted.

Potential test purchasers will want to determine what types of answer forms and what scoring services are available for any test under consideration. If scoring is to be done locally, they should know of any restrictions imposed by the available scanner. Test publishers who allow local scoring of their tests will generally have answer sheets that can be scored by the common types of scanners. Several of the popular tests also have software packages available that will produce score profiles and the various types of reports described in Chapter 3.

Computerized Test Interpretation

Test authors and publishers have increasingly relied on computers to generate narrative reports of test results that interpret the numerical scores for the user. A catalog of statements is stored in computer memory, and the computer is programmed so that a score falling in a given range, a particular combination of two or more scores, or even a combination of responses to specific questions triggers the production of one or more of these statements. The elements in the narrative may be as simple and as directly related to a particular score as "Henry is somewhat below the average in arithmetic problem solving" or as extended as the interpretive personality picture provided in Chapter 11. The report may focus solely and very specifically on one examinee's scores, or it may include an extended general discussion of the conceptual basis for the instrument. For example, National Computer Systems produces a report for the Strong Interest Inventory that is 20 pages long and provides, as a basis for interpreting the examinee's scores, a full exposition of the general nature of the instrument and of the rationale for the different types of scores that it produces, together with suggested sources for further information about occupations that appear congruent with the examinee's pattern of interests. As we saw in Chapter 3, scoring services can also produce computer-generated summary reports for classes and districts.

Narrative computer printouts can be no better than the wisdom and clinical experience on which they are based. However, they do permit the distillation of that experience as it has accumulated in the professional literature and in the pooled background of a number of experts. Computer-generated printouts protect the examinee from possible bias or inexperience of a local practitioner, while also expediting what can be a time-consuming and tedious chore of report writing. Their use guarantees that aspects of the record dealt with by the narrative will not be inadvertently overlooked by a current interpreter and also ensures uniformity and consistency in interpretation. The narrative *does* need to be evaluated by a counselor or clinician who knows other facts about the client, but it can serve as a useful foundation for such an evaluation.

Features Facilitating Test Administration

In evaluating the practical usability of a test, one factor to be taken into account is the ease of administration. A test that can be handled adequately by the regular classroom teacher with no more than a session or so of special briefing fits much more readily into a testing program than a test requiring specially trained administrators and large blocks of time for testing. Several factors contribute to the ease of giving and taking a test:

1. *A test is easy to give if it has clear, full instructions.* The instructions for test administration should be written out completely, so that all the examiner must do is read and follow them. Everything the examiner should say to the examinees should be included, *verbatim,* in the instructions, preferably in contrasting color or boldface type. Instructions for the examinee should also be complete and should provide appropriate practice exercises. The amount of practice that should be provided depends on how novel the test task is likely to be for those being tested. When it is a familiar type of task or a simple and straightforward instruction, no more than a single example may be needed; however, for an unusual item format or a complex test task, more practice will be desirable. The better test publishers make practice tests available so students can gain experience with the types of items included on the test.

Familiarity with the types of tasks the test requires is also a possible source of irrelevant differences between examinees. Many underprivileged children are not as familiar with testing situations as are children from more advantaged homes. A plentiful supply of practice items can help reduce the negative effect of task unfamiliarity and yield a more accurate picture of the abilities of disadvantaged children. With the prevalence of tests in society, instruction in how to take tests (through administering a number of practice tests) may even be a reasonable educational activity in the earlier grades because it would reduce "testwiseness" as one irrelevant source of individual differences in scores.

2. *A test is easy to give if there are few separately timed units and if close timing is not crucial.* Timing a number of brief subtests to a fraction of a minute is a bothersome undertaking, and the timing is likely to be inaccurate unless a stopwatch is available for each tester. Some tests have as many as 8 or 10 parts, each taking only 2 or 3 minutes. A test made up of 3 or 4 parts, with time limits of 5, 10, or more minutes for each, will be easier to use. Errors in timing, which can produce inaccurate test scores, are also less likely with fewer and longer parts.

3. *The layout of the test items on the page has a good deal to do with the ease of taking the test.* Items in which the response options all run together on the same line or those with small or illegible pictures or diagrams or which are crowded together or run over from one page to the next all create difficulty for the examinee. Item difficulty should come from the content and the cognitive processes required to determine the right answer, not from the test format. Print and pictures should be large and clear. Response options should be well separated from one another. All parts of an item and all items referring to a single figure, problem, or reading passage should appear on the same page or a double-page spread. Also, to the extent that the physical layout of the test is difficult for examinees to follow, scores may be lower than they should be, a fact that would adversely affect the validity of the test and be particularly detrimental for a criterion-referenced test.

Features Facilitating Interpretation and Use of Scores

Although the point is sometimes overlooked, it seems axiomatic that a test is given so that the results can be used. If the score is to be used, it must be interpreted and given meaning. The author and publisher of the test have the responsibility of providing users with information that permits them to make sound appraisals of the test in relation to their needs and to give appropriate meaning to the score of each individual. The authors and publishers do this primarily through the test manual and other collateral materials prepared to accompany the test. What may the test user reasonably expect to find in the manual for a test, together with its supporting materials? We have outlined below the aids that the user should expect.

1. *A statement of the functions the test was designed to measure and of the general procedures by which it was developed.* In this statement, the author tells what he or she considers to be the appropriate uses of test scores and provides the evidence that proper steps have been taken to ensure that recommended interpretations are supported. Particularly for achievement tests, in which the primary concern is that the test measures specific content areas and cognitive processes, the manual should describe the procedures by which the choice of content was made or how the analysis of the functions being measured was carried out. If the author is unwilling to expose his or her thinking to our critical scrutiny, we may perhaps be skeptical of the thoroughness or profundity of that thinking.

Procedures to be reported include not only the rational procedures by which the range of content or types of objectives were selected but also the empirical procedures by which the items were reviewed, tried out, and screened for final inclusion in the test. The validity of the test—the interpretations it supports, caveats regarding these interpretations, and the uses to which the scores may properly be put—is its most important property. The author's plan and procedures for construction are vital steps in achieving validity and should be explicitly stated so that potential users can judge the quality of these activities.

2. *Detailed instructions for administering the test.* Earlier in this section we discussed the need for this aid to uniform and easy administration by teachers or others who will have to use the test. Of course, proper administration is also vital to achieving scores that are valid for the user's purpose.

3. *Scoring keys and specific instructions for scoring the test.* The problems of scoring have also been discussed. If the test can or must be scored locally, the manual and supporting materials should provide detailed instructions on how each score is to be computed, how errors are to be

treated, and how part scores are to be combined into a total score. Scoring keys and stencils should be planned to facilitate, as much as possible, the onerous task of hand scoring when scoring is to be done by the local user, and instructions should also be given for electronic scoring.

4. *Norms for appropriate reference groups.* These norms, together with information on how the norms were obtained and with instructions for their use, should be included in the test manual or a separate publication devoted to normative information. A full consideration of types of test norms and their uses was presented in Chapter 3. It is therefore sufficient at this time to point out the responsibility of the test producer to develop suitable norms for the groups with which the test is to be used. General norms are a necessity, and norms suitable for special types of communities, special occupational groups, and other more limited subgroups will add to the usefulness of the test in many cases.

5. *Evidence of the reliability of the test.* This evidence should indicate not only the simple reliability statistics but also the operations used to obtain the reliability estimates and the descriptive and statistical characteristics of each group on which reliability data are based. If a test is available in more than one form, it is highly desirable for the producers to report the correlation between the two forms, in addition to any data that were derived from a single testing. If the test yields part scores, and especially if it is proposed that any use be made of these part scores, reliability data should be reported for the separate part scores. It is good procedure for the author to report standard errors of measurement, as well as reliability coefficients. An author who indicates what the standard error of measurement is at each of a number of score levels should particularly be commended because this information shows the range of scores over which the test retains its accuracy.

6. *Evidence on the intercorrelations of subscores.* If the test provides several subscores, the manual should provide information on the intercorrelations of the subscores. This information is important in guiding the interpretation of the subscores and particularly in judging how much confidence to place in the *differences* between the subscores. If the correlations among the subscores approach their reliabilities, indicating that they measure much the same things, the differences between them will be largely meaningless and uninterpretable. Information on the reliability of the subscores, coupled with knowledge of their correlations, permits an accurate evaluation of the degree to which difference scores add information to the original scores. Some test publishers also provide information on the frequency with which score differences of a particular magnitude occurred in the standardization sample. This is excellent practice when patterns of differences between scores are claimed to have particular interpretive meaning. Factor analyses of the correlations among subscores should be reported to confirm that any recommended combinations of subscores can reasonably be considered to measure a common dimension. Such analyses support claims of content and construct validity.

7. *Evidence on the relationship of the test to other variables.* Insofar as the test is to be used as a predictive device, correlations with criterion measures constitute the essential evidence on how well it does in fact predict. Full information should be provided on the nature of the criterion variables, the groups for which data are available, and the conditions under which the data were obtained. Only then can the potential test user fairly judge the validity of the test as a predictor.

It will often be desirable to report correlations with other measures of the same function as collateral evidence bearing on the construct validity of the test. For example, correlations with an individual intelligence test are relevant in the case of a group measure of intelligence.

Finally, indications of the relationship of test scores to age, gender, type of community, socioeconomic level, and similar facts about the individual or group are often helpful. They provide a basis for judging how sensitive the measure is to the background of the group members and to the circumstances of their lives and their education. Evidence of this kind is also useful for judging whether the norm groups used by the publisher are appropriate for the local population.

8. *Guides for using the test and for interpreting results obtained with it.* The developers of a test presumably know how it is reasonable for the test to be used and how the results from it should be evaluated. They are specialists in that test. For the test to be most useful to others, especially the teacher with limited specialized training, suggestions should be given of ways in which the test results may be used for diagnosing individual and group strengths and weaknesses, forming class groupings, organizing remedial instruction, counseling the individual, or whatever other activities may appropriately be based on results from that particular type of instrument. Computerized test interpretations can be particularly valuable here.

A final point to keep in mind is that the care that has gone into preparing the test manual is often itself a good indicator of the care that has been exercised in constructing the test. Test authors who do a careful, thorough job of describing how the test was constructed and how evidence of its reliability and validity was obtained probably cared enough to give their very best. They are likely to have carried out the steps for constructing the test in a thoughtful, professional manner as well.

E-Testing

A recent innovation that can make test use much easier but that has some potential pitfalls is test administration over the Internet. The Psychological Corporation has developed a Web site they call the Psychological Corporation Assessment Center (http://www.PsychCorpCenter.com) where qualified professionals in assessment can order a variety of instruments for their clients. Clients are notified by e-mail that an assessment instrument has been ordered for them and they can log onto the Web site and complete the assessment at their convenience. The instrument is then scored and an interpretive report generated by the company's software. The average time for the scoring process is claimed to be 3 minutes. The person who ordered the assessment is notified that the testing has been completed and can download the report. The potential time savings for both the examiner and the client could be substantial. At this writing, 32 instruments from the Psychological Corporation catalog are available in this format. Consulting Psychologists Press, another major test publisher, offers five instruments for e-testing, and we may expect other large test publishers to follow suit soon.

The Psychological Corporation reports having taken elaborate measures to ensure the security of the identity of the tester and examinee, the test responses, and the report generated from the e-test. This, of course, is essential for responsible test use and reduces the worry about test security. However, two additional caveats remain regarding Internet testing. The first, and less critical, potential problem is one of control of the testing environment and applicability of test norms. Norms for tests are developed in particular environments in which efforts are made to ensure that examinees are taking the testing seriously and responding in a conscientious and truthful manner. Until research has shown that responses obtained over the Internet correspond to those obtained using more traditional methods, we must treat with caution interpretations of Internet test scores based on norms obtained in other ways.

The second and more serious problem is that we have no way of knowing who is actually providing responses to the test if the testing is taking place in the privacy on one's home. Psychological Corporation attempts to control this problem by requiring the examinee to log on with identifiers provided by the person who ordered the test, but this cannot guarantee the identity of the person who actually fills out the test. Some of the tests included in the PsychCorpCenter list are ability measures that a company might use for employee selection. Examinees motivated by a desire to obtain employment could fill out the test with the help of friends, or could even have friends take the test in their place. The only sure solution to this difficulty seems to be to have examinees take their tests using computers supplied by the testers at locations that can be monitored, but this eliminates much of the convenience that Internet test administration might offer. (In a related development, Petrill, Rempell, Oliver, and Plomin, 2002, have shown that it is possible to administer cognitive ability measures over the telephone. In this case, however, the examinees were children and a parent helped with test administration.)

GUIDE FOR EVALUATING A TEST

As an aid to the potential user, we end this section with a guide for evaluating a test. This guide consists of a series of questions, based in large part on the *Standards for Educational and Psychological Testing* (American Education Research Association, American Psychological Association, & National Council on Measurement in Education, 1999). Careful study of the complete *Standards* will reward the person who would become a more sophisticated test user. (The most recent editions of the *Standards* differ from their predecessors in that they place more emphasis on the proper interpretation and use of test results. The validity of test scores depends heavily, some would say entirely, on the context of their use, and *it is the responsibility of the test user to guarantee that inferences and decisions based on test scores are supported by appropriate evidence.*)

You will note that many of the questions in this guide relate to the availability and adequacy of information reported about the test. There is an implied, although not explicitly stated, second question as a sequel to many of the sections of the guide, especially those relating to reliability and validity. That question is "Given that the information is provided, how satisfactory does the test appear to be, in comparison with others that are available, as well as by absolute standards, for the use I want to make of it?" A significant portion of the responsibility for valid testing rests with the test user. You must evaluate the evidence provided by the publisher, as well as what you know about the examinees and the intended uses of the test scores. In light of this information, you must decide whether the evidence justifies using this test for this purpose.

A number of questions in this guide also refer to the adequacy of norms and converted scores. You may wish to review Chapter 3 as you study this portion of the guide.

General Identifying Information

1. What is the name of the test?
2. Who are its authors—by name and position if that information is available? (It should be.)
3. Who publishes the test? And when was it published?
4. Is more than one form of the test available? If so, how many?

5. How much does the test cost?
6. How long does it take to administer the test?

Information About the Test

1. Is there a test manual (or some other similar source of information, such as an article in a journal) that is designed to provide the information a potential user needs to administer the test and interpret the results properly?
2. How recently have there been revisions in the test, the manual, and the norms? (For major commercial tests it is reasonable to expect that both the test and its manual will be revised at least every 10 years and that new norms will accompany the revisions.)

Aids to Interpreting Test Results

1. Does the manual provide a clear statement of the purposes and applications for which the test is intended?
2. Does the manual provide a clear statement of the qualifications needed to administer the test and interpret its results properly?
3. Do the test, manual, record forms, and accompanying materials guide users toward sound and correct interpretation of the test results?
4. Are the manual's statements expressing relationships presented in quantitative terms so that the reader can tell how much confidence to attach to them? (For example, it is much more informative to say that the correlation with Variable X is .55 than to say that the test correlates substantially with Variable X.)

Validity

1. Does the manual report evidence on the validity of the test for each type of inference for which the test is recommended?
2. Does the manual *avoid* referring to correlations between items and total test score as evidence of validity?
3. If the test is designed to be a sample of a specified domain of behaviors (e.g., an achievement test), does the manual define the domain clearly and indicate the procedures used for sampling from that domain?
4. When criterion-related validity is involved, does the manual describe the criterion variables clearly, comment on their adequacy, and indicate what aspects of the criterion performance are *not* adequately reflected in these criterion measures?
5. Are the samples used for estimating criterion-related validity adequately described? And are they appropriate to the purpose? One way spuriously to inflate apparent validity is to use samples that are much more heterogeneous than those that can be expected in actual use. Are such tricks avoided?
6. Are statistical analyses for criterion-related validity presented in a form that permits the reader to judge the degree of confidence that can be placed in inferences about individuals?
7. If the test is designed to measure a theoretical construct (e.g., trait of ability, temperament, or attitude), is the proposed interpretation clearly stated and

differentiated from alternate theoretical interpretations? Is the evidence to support this interpretation clearly stated and fully presented?

8. Are potential threats to valid use of the test scores, such as language handicaps and learning disabilities, identified and appropriate cautions noted? Does the manual consider possible unintended outcomes of using the test?

In summary, to what extent does the available validity evidence justify the uses of the test suggested in the manual or the use that you would want to make of the test results? Remember that *if you intend to use the test for some purpose other than that contemplated by the test developer, the responsibility for demonstrating the validity of the test for that use rests with you.*

Reliability

1. Does the manual present data adequate to permit the reader to judge whether scores are sufficiently dependable for the recommended uses (or for your contemplated uses, if these are different from the recommended ones)?

2. Are the samples on which reliability data were obtained sufficiently well described that the user can judge whether the data apply to his or her situation? As with validity, one way spuriously to inflate apparent reliability is to use samples that are much more heterogeneous than those that can be expected in actual use. Are such tricks avoided?

3. Are the reliability data presented in the conventional statistical form of product-moment correlation coefficients and standard errors of measurement? Are standard errors presented for different levels of performance?

4. If more than one form of the test was produced, are data provided to establish comparability of the forms?

5. If the test purports to measure a generalized homogeneous trait, is evidence reported on the internal consistency (interitem or interpart correlations) of the parts that make up the test?

6. Does the test manual provide data on the stability of test performance over time?

In summary, to what extent do the reliability data provided in the manual justify the uses for the test results suggested by the authors or the uses that you want to make of the test results?

Administration and Scoring

1. Are the directions for administration sufficiently clear and fully stated so that the administrator will be able to duplicate the conditions under which the norms were established and the reliability and validity data were obtained?

2. If the test is administered by computer or provides computer-assisted administration, are the programs written to run on the equipment you have available? Is adequate documentation and technical support provided?

3. If the test can be scored locally, are the procedures for scoring set forth clearly and in detail, in a way that will maximize scoring efficiency and minimize the likelihood of scoring error? Are the directions for determining subscores clear? If scoring software is available, are adequate documentation and technical support provided?

4. If the test is to be scored by the publisher or a commercial scoring service, does the test scoring service provide for the accumulation of results over time to aid in preparing local norms and local validity evidence?

Scales and Norms

1. Are the scales used for reporting performance clearly and carefully described so that the test interpreter will fully understand them and be able to communicate the interpretation to an examinee?
2. Are norms reported in the manual in appropriate form—usually standard scores or percentile ranks in appropriate reference groups?
3. Are the populations to which the norms refer clearly defined and described? And are they populations with which you can appropriately compare your examinees?
4. If more than one form of the test is available, including revised forms, are tables provided showing equivalent scores on the different forms?
5. Does the manual discuss the possible value of local norms? Does it provide any help in preparing local norms?
6. Is a computer program available to assist with test interpretation and report writing? If so, is the program appropriately interactive; do the interpretations and reports it generates make suggestions about test results and avoid drawing definitive conclusions?

In summary, many factors should be considered when selecting a test, no one of which is conclusive. It will be your responsibility as a measurement professional to gather evidence related to using a particular test for a particular purpose. No test is perfect, and you will have to weigh the benefits of using each test against the possible costs and consequences. Only when you feel confident that the advantages outweigh the risks should you use the test.

GETTING INFORMATION ABOUT SPECIFIC TESTS

There were 2,780 published tests in English available for sale in 2002, a decrease of 229 from 8 years earlier. In addition, many more than this number are out of print, were produced locally, or were developed for specific research projects. Many of these are available from one source or another. A single text cannot even begin to list, much less describe, all the instruments developed that might interest you. A few of the best known and most widely used tests will be reviewed in later chapters as illustrations of different types of tests. For the rest, we try in the remainder of this chapter to provide you with some tools to find the tests you need and information about them. We have organized the sections around the questions that you are likely to ask, in the order that you would ordinarily ask them, and we try to give useful ways to find answers to these questions.

What Tests Exist?

What tests of reading comprehension are suitable for fourth graders? What tests of vocational interests exist for high school seniors? What measures of attitudes toward nuclear power are available? The first thing we need to know is what already exists. When we have a catalog of possibilities, we can begin to pick and choose. Or, if nothing satisfactory is available, we can undertake to construct something from scratch. Where should we go to assemble a catalog of possibilities?

The first source to turn to is *Tests in Print VI* (Murphy, Plake, Impara, & Spies, 2002). This catalog (also known as *TIP-VI*) is revised about every 5 years and provides an alphabetical listing of the 2,780 instruments that were confirmed as being available from commercial test publishers at the time of its release, with information on when each was published and by whom. A subject-matter index is provided to help the reader locate the tests in a given category. There is also a list of tests that have gone out of print since 1983 and an index of test publishers and test acronyms. *Tests in Print* is a companion volume to the *Mental Measurements Yearbook* series (hereafter referred to as *MMY*), which is described in a later section. *Tests in Print* includes references to entries in the *MMY*s dealing with the test in question, as well as updates of the bibliography of references relating to that test. Each edition of *Tests in Print* replaces the previous one, deleting entries for tests no longer available and adding references to new ones.

Two companion sources to *Tests in Print* are *Tests: A Comprehensive Reference for Assessments in Psychology, Education and Business* (hereafter referred to as *Tests*) (Maddox, 1997) and the *Dictionary of Behavioral Assessment Techniques (Dictionary)* (Hersen & Bellack, 1988). The entries in these volumes are alphabetically arranged within topic areas and have an advantage over *Tests in Print* in that they provide a brief description of each entry, as well as information about the publisher and price. The descriptions are not evaluative; they closely follow the author's or publisher's statement of what the test measures. The information in *Tests* is somewhat sketchy, in that it does not identify the author, give the date of publication of an instrument, or give any statistical information about it. *Tests* contains about 2,500 entries for current tests and an index of out-of-print tests and their publishers. The *Dictionary* lists 288 clinical rating scales and questionnaires and does give the names and addresses of sources for the instruments.

Tests in Print, the *Dictionary,* and *Tests* are useful for finding tests, but they fall short in two respects. They do not give information on the most recent tests, and, except for some entries in the *Dictionary* and the out-of-print list in *TIP-VI,* they do not give information about unpublished instruments. (By unpublished instruments, we mean tests that are not offered for sale. An attitude scale that is given in full in a book or article is, for our purposes, unpublished unless its author offers it for sale.)

To find the most recently published tests, you need to obtain copies of test publishers' current catalogs. They describe the tests and services that the publisher is currently promoting and even some expected to be available in the near future. A large number of publishers produce an occasional test, but relatively few are regular and substantial producers of testing instruments. A complete listing of test publishers can be found in *Tests in Print VI.* A file of current test catalogs may sometimes be available through the measurement facility of your university or through the testing center in your local school system. If such a resource is not available, write to those publishers who have produced tests like the one you seek and request a copy of their current catalog. Some professional journals carry ads from test publishers, as do *The Monitor,* the newsletter of the American Psychological Association, and similar publications from other professional associations. Most publishers also maintain Web sites that contain information about their products.

Locating unpublished instruments that have been locally developed or that have been used only in research studies can be a bit tricky. However, several source books and directories have been prepared that provide assistance in such an undertaking. Probably the most useful of these sources is the test collection *Tests in Microfiche,* developed by Educational Testing Service (ETS). Beginning in 1975, ETS started distributing not only an index of unpublished tests but also copies of the tests on microfiche. At the end of 2002 the collection included more than 10,000 instruments. Internet access to this collection is now maintained by the Educational Resources Information Center Clearinghouse on Assessment and Evaluation (ERIC/AE) housed at the University of Maryland (http://ericae.net). The ERIC/AE site gives a description of each instrument and an address where a copy may be obtained, but does not contain copies of the instruments themselves.

The ETS collection *Tests in Microfiche* is a service to which many university libraries subscribe. However, the subscription contains the following restriction (printed in the *Annotated Index*):

> The materials included in the microfiche may be reproduced by the purchaser for his or her own use. Permission to use these materials in any other manner must be obtained directly from the author. This includes modifying or adapting the materials or selling or distributing them to others. (p. iii)

A number of other sources also provide references to unpublished tests. The *Directory of Unpublished Experimental Mental Measures* (Goldman & Busch, 1978, 1982; Goldman & Mitchell, 1990; Goldman & Osborne, 1985; Goldman & Sanders, 1974) includes more than 3,000 entries describing such instruments, while *Tests and Measurements in Child Development: Handbook II* (Johnson, 1976) and *Tests and Measurements in Child Development: A Handbook* (Johnson & Bommarito, 1971) are other sources of unpublished instruments for use with young children. The *Handbook of Tests and Measurement in Education and the Social Sciences* (Lester & Bishop, 1997) lists about 80 relatively obscure instruments primarily related to education.

Several volumes cover the field of attitude measurement and reproduce the actual scales used (Robinson, Athanasion, & Head, 1969; Robinson, Rusk, & Head, 1968; Robinson & Shaver, 1973; Shaw & Wright, 1967). More recently, O'Brien (1988) has published a bibliography of selected references on testing, which includes 2,759 sources categorized by the topic or subject covered in the article, and ETS has published a six-volume *Test Collection Catalog* listing (1) achievement tests, (2) vocational tests, (3) tests for special populations, (4) cognitive, aptitude, and intelligence tests, (5) attitude tests, and (6) affective measures and personality tests. In addition to the sources already mentioned, the *Sources of Test Information* list at the end of this chapter presents some references that cover more limited areas.

A new resource that describes a variety of instruments for use with family counseling and research is the three-volume set of *Handbook of Family Measurement Techniques*. Volume 1 (Touliatos, Perlmutter, & Straus, 2001) and Volume 2 (Touliatos, Perlmutter, & Holden, 2001) contain abstracts of research reports using 168 instruments. Volume 3 (Perlmutter, Touliatos, & Holden, 2001) contains copies of the instruments, scoring instructions, and references to the source articles in which the instruments were first presented. If you need tests for use in a family environment, this resource may prove useful.

An additional resource that may be useful in certain circumstances is the *Directory of Selected National Testing Programs* (Educational Testing Service, Test Collection, 1987). This three-volume series gives the names, publishers or producers, addresses, and general descriptions of a wide range of national testing programs. Volume 1 covers selection and admission programs for secondary and postsecondary institutions, government service, graduate and professional schools, and health-related programs. Volume 2 lists academic-credit and advanced-placement testing programs, and Volume 3 gives the testing programs for certification and licensing. The tests covered in this series generally are not available for public review.

Exactly What Is Test X Like?

Once you have identified a promising reading test, interest inventory, or attitude measure (called, say, Test X), you will want to find out more about it. Where should you turn?

A certain amount of descriptive information about the test will appear in some of the sources listing tests and in evaluations that appear in the *MMY*s. However, there is really no substitute for examining the test firsthand. So, the first thing to do, if possible, is to obtain a copy of the test and look at it. A **specimen set,** which usually includes a copy of the test, an answer sheet, and the manual for the test, may be available through your university, in either the library, counseling center, or measurement-area files for published tests. Or the testing office of your school system may be able to provide one. A new resource for locating copies of tests is the *Directory of Test Collections in Academic, Professional, and Research Libraries* (Fehrmann & O'Brien, 2001). This volume lists 77 libraries that allow outside professionals to use their facilities and have collections of at least 100 tests. If you cannot examine the test of your choice in one of these ways, you may have to order a specimen set from the publisher; the catalog will indicate the price.

A publisher is likely to require some credentials to show that you are an appropriate person to have access to the testing materials. A letter from your instructor or from a supervisor in the company or school system where you work may suffice. However, some types of instruments, such as personality inventories and individually administered cognitive ability tests, that call for special training or skills will have further restrictions on their distribution, and you may have to complete a form to verify that you have the required qualifications. In a few cases, it may be necessary to have a person with the required professional credentials order the test for you and supervise your examination of it.

Many of the unpublished instruments are reproduced in full in some of the compendia listed in the *Sources of Test Information* section at the end of this chapter, particularly in the *Tests in Microfiche* collection. Others are reproduced in full in articles reporting their development and use. If an unpublished test you wish to examine is not available from one of these sources, you may have to try to get a copy from its author.

Once you have a copy of the test or inventory, what information should you try to get from it? The answer depends on the type of test. If it is a test of school achievement, you should examine the items and ask yourself if the content covered and the processes called for match the objectives you have set for your teaching or that are contained in the school or district curriculum guide. For all kinds of tests, you should ask whether the items are clearly stated, the answer choices plausible, the directions clear, and the page layouts attractive and legible. Of course, for unpublished tests, the quality of the test materials may ultimately be up to you because you are likely to have to produce your own copies of the test.

Of equal importance to the test itself are the supporting materials that describe the test's psychometric properties, the form in which test results are to be reported, and the aids provided for test use and interpretation. For tests available from commercial publishers, this information should appear in one or more test manuals, possibly in a manual for test administrators or one for counselors or supervisors, and in a technical manual that gives, in considerable detail, the psychometric properties of the test. These manuals should be examined thoroughly.

For unpublished tests, the primary sources of technical material about the tests will be in articles or books reporting studies in which the tests were used. The quality of this information is likely to be much lower than that which you will find in the manual for a good commercial test. For relatively new tests or tests that have not been widely used, it is often necessary to contact the author. It is not uncommon to encounter a measuring instrument developed for use in a research study, for which there is no information about reliability or validity except for the findings from that one study. In some cases there may be no evidence at all of instrument quality. When this happens, the test should not be used other than for research purposes, and then only with caution.

Most commercially published tests provide accompanying scoring and reporting services. The services range from simply scoring the test answer sheets and reporting raw scores and percentiles or standard scores to providing extended narrative interpretations of each individual's test results. Examples of some of these reports were given in Chapter 3. The specimen set should describe, and perhaps illustrate, the types of reports that are available, and you should determine how adequately these will serve your needs.

The evidence on reliability and validity should be scrutinized with a particularly critical eye. Remember that the specimen set is primarily a promotional piece. You can expect the publisher to accentuate the positive, so try to cut through the puffery and get down to the basic evidence; be suspicious if evidence is incompletely or vaguely reported. Chapters 4 and 5 and the guide for test evaluation provided earlier in this chapter indicate what evidence you can reasonably expect to find.

What Do Critics Think of Test X?

Because materials from the test publisher focus on selling the test (some do so blatantly; some, subtly), it is highly desirable to get an evaluation by a competent and unbiased reviewer. The one source to automatically consult for such critical reviews is the series of *Mental Measurements Year-books*. This series was initiated by the late Oscar Buros in 1936 and published by him until 1978. Preparation of subsequent volumes in the series is in the hands of the Buros Institute of Mental Measurements at the University of Nebraska. At this writing, the *Fifteenth Mental Measurements Yearbook* (Plake, Impara, & Spies, 2003) has recently been published. The *MMY*s provide reviews, by presumably competent and disinterested people, of each published test of any significance. In recent *MMY*s, the publishers have obtained at least two independent reviews of each new test. (See Thorndike, 1999b, for a thorough description and review of the *Twelfth MMY*.)

The volumes of this series are cumulative. That is, a test is reviewed when it first comes out, and it is generally not reviewed again unless there has been a significant change in the test or the material supporting it, or unless it is a test of unusually widespread and continuing use. *Tests in Print VI* provides an index giving the volume and page numbers for reviews of tests still in print in the first 14 *MMY* volumes.

In 1988, the Buros Institute of Mental Measurements began a new schedule for producing the *MMY*s. That year saw the publication of a *Supplement to the Ninth Mental Measurements Yearbook* (Conoley, Kramer, & Mitchell, 1988), which gave full *MMY* treatment to 89 new tests that had been published since 1985. The *Tenth Mental Measurements Yearbook* was published in 1989, and its supplement appeared in 1990. The staff of the Buros Institute announced plans to publish a complete volume in alternate years thereafter, with supplements in the intervening years, but the *Eleventh Mental Measurements Yearbook* arrived in 1992, followed by its supplement in 1994. The *twelfth MMY* was published in 1995; the *Thirteenth MMY* appeared in 1998, followed by a *Supplement to the Thirteenth MMY* in 1999; the *Fourteenth MMY* became available in 2001; and the *Fifteenth MMY* appeared in 2003, so the Buros Institute may have achieved its goal. Beginning with the *Eleventh MMY,* the yearbooks have been available on CD-ROM. This format has the advantage of permitting automated searches, but it is more difficult to flip back and forth between two or more instruments to compare them directly unless you print the reviews in which you are interested.

The Buros Institute also maintains a Web site at http://www.unl.edu/buros/. This site has links to other testing-related Web sites, including the ERIC/AE test locator and the American Psychological Association (APA) site. It also has the ability to search for reviews of tests published in either the *MMY*s or *Tests*. A classified subject index lists all entries after 1985 (*Ninth MMY*) where all reviewed tests are listed under one of 19 subject headings. The site does not contain copies of the reviews, but you can determine whether a test has been reviewed and where to find the review.

Each of the 15 *MMYs* and the supplements include tests of all types. The *MMYs* and *Tests in Print* should be available at the reference desk of any good university library, at many larger public libraries, and at the testing bureau in many school systems. The Buros Institute Web site has a link to the SilverPlatter Information database where one can obtain copies of reviews for a fee, and one can order fax copies of individual reviews directly from the Buros Institute as well, also for a fee. The *MMYs* provide the most important source for evaluative reviews of tests. They also include reviews of books and monographs on testing, a listing of test publishers, and nearly complete bibliographies of published material on each of the tests.

Another source of critical reviews of tests is the 10-volume series *Test Critiques* (Keyser & Sweetland, 1984). Each volume in the series contains a single review of each of several hundred tests. The reviews are often somewhat longer and more detailed than those in the *MMYs*, but lack the contrasting opinions that multiple reviews provide. Each of the last eight volumes contains a subject index to all preceding ones, but within a single volume, the tests are arranged alphabetically by title without regard to topic. This system may cause difficulty in finding a specific test.

Brief reviews of some American tests and a large number of tests published in Great Britain may be found in *Tests in Education: A Book of Critical Reviews* (Levy & Goldstein, 1984). The tests are organized into six general categories: early development, language, mathematics, achievement batteries, general abilities, and personality and counseling.

Reviews of new and important tests will occasionally be found, along with book reviews, in some psychological and educational journals such as the *Journal of Psychoeducational Assessment*. However, they appear sporadically and include the opinions of only one reviewer. There does not seem to be any journal that has a policy of systematically and regularly reviewing new published tests. At this time, the best source of evaluative information seems to be the *MMYs* and their supplements, particularly now that they are updated more regularly in print and on the computer database.

A different approach to test evaluation has been taken by Hammill, Brown, and Bryant (1992) in their *A Consumer's Guide to Tests in Print*. This volume contains ratings of seven technical aspects of the quality of a number of published instruments and observations about several nontechnical features of these instruments, as well as an overall rating of quality. The ratings are provided for each subscale of multiscore tests, like the Wechsler scales and the Stanford-Binet, and are presented as: A, highly recommended; B, recommended; and F, not recommended. The tabular form is compact, but the organization of the scales by the function measured results in splitting up the subscales of the multiscore instruments so that one must consult several pages to get an overall impression of a particular test.

What Research Has Been Conducted on Test X?

What studies have been made of the test's reliability? Of validity as a predictor of *Z*? Of influence of coaching on its scores? Of relation to measures of *Y*?

For the major, commercially produced instruments, of course, some material will appear in the technical manual for the test. Manuals vary widely in the amount of statistical and research information that they report. Some of the better ones become almost a full-length book and report a wide range of analyses of the test's reliability, correlations with other instruments, and predictive validity for academic or job criteria. The manual will also often include a bibliography, providing references to specific research studies. But, for widely used tests, the manual can hardly provide complete information; for example, in the course of its 90-year history, the Stanford-Binet Intelligence Scale has been used in more than 6,000 studies, and in only 65 years, even more have been carried out with the Minnesota Multiphasic Personality Inventory and the various Wechsler scales. It is also difficult for a manual to be up to date with recent studies. In fact, it is rare for a test publisher to bring out a revision of a test manual that does not correspond to a revision of the test itself, so even the manuals for the best commercially produced tests may be 5 to 10 years old.

As already noted, for published tests, very comprehensive bibliographies appear in the *MMYs* and *Tests in Print.* As is the case with the reviews of the tests themselves, these reference sources include only references to articles and books published since their last editions. Even so, for a number of the popular and widely used tests, the bibliography is so extensive, running to hundreds of entries, that it becomes almost unusable. However, these bibliographies permit you to scan through titles with the hope of identifying the ones that deal with the specific problem of interest.

The other main avenue for locating research on tests and testing is through the index and abstract services, which appear as monthly journals and are then combined into annual volumes. The ones most likely to be useful for a person interested in testing are *Dissertation Abstracts International,* the *Education Index,* and *Psychological Abstracts.* Another resource is the *Index to Tests Used in Educational Dissertations* (Fabiano, 1989). *Dissertation Abstracts International* has had an online computer search service since 1980, which has recently been extended to cover American dissertations back to 1861! This reference categorizes more than 50,000 tests alphabetically by title. The entries for each test include the type of examinees, the volume and page number of the abstract, and the author's name.

Two more general databases that include many references to tests and testing topics are the ERIC/AE and PsychLit collections. ERIC/AE includes information about articles in education and related areas, while PsychLit provides a computerized version of much of the material in Psychological Abstracts. Both services are available at many university libraries and contain the complete citation for each article, a set of keywords, and an abstract of the study. They have the advantage that they can search the entire content of each entry for any desired word or phrase. Thus, if you search for a test title, the program will produce a list of all entries that include the name of that test in the title, abstract, or keywords. Searches can also be carried out by author or subject. The half hour or so that it takes to become familiar with these facilities will be time well spent.

Finally, there is the burgeoning world of the Internet. There is no way to tell what will be available in a year or two, but it is clear that web pages and databases in addition to the ERIC/AE, APA, and Buros Institute sites will be available for searching, as will the holdings of many major libraries. Most psychology and education journals have web pages, as do all of the major professional organizations. Notices of Web page addresses are published frequently in the journals and newsletters of the professional organizations.

In using any database, the secret of a successful search is a shrewd selection of keywords that serve to guide the search engine in identifying relevant entries. In some instances, preparers of the database provide a glossary of terms that the computer will recognize. It is the responsibility of the user to generate—or to select from the glossary—the entries most likely to elicit relevant items from the database. Although test titles are unlikely to appear as keywords and may not appear in the abstract, the general traits measured by the instrument may well give access to publications in which the test is referenced.

Generally, a person who wishes to search one of the databases will find it desirable, and perhaps necessary, to work through the reference division of a university or public library. The library is likely to have a computer terminal with direct access to the data files in question. If not, the reference librarian should be able to help arrange such access. There may be a charge for the search, and you will want to get an estimate of any costs before starting this undertaking.

SUMMARY

In addition to yielding information that is valid for the proposed use, the test must be practical to use. Practicality relates to matters of expense, ease of administration and scoring, and ease with which appropriate inferences can be derived from the test scores, including the adequacy and availability of norm- or criterion-referenced interpretations.

When reviewing a test, it is important to examine all the factors that make for a quality instrument. The test manual or other sources should provide information about the purpose of the test, its reliability and validity, what scales the test provides and what norms are available, and how the test should be administered and scored. When considering which of several tests to use, you will also want to obtain information about what aids are available to assist in score interpretation.

There are several published sources of information about specific tests, including *Tests in Print VI*, *Tests* and the *Dictionary of Behavioral Assessment Techniques.* Copies of unpublished tests can be obtained from *Tests in Microfiche,* the *Dictionary of Unpublished Experimental Mental Measures,* and several other more specialized sources. Critical reviews of tests can be found in the *Mental Measurements Yearbooks* and *Test Critiques* as well as in various professional journals and newsletters.

QUESTIONS AND EXERCISES

1. Using the resources listed in the text, prepare as complete a list as you can of currently available standardized tests for a specific purpose (e.g., tests in first-year French, tests of reading achievement, inventories to measure adjustment to college life).

2. For some characteristic that interests you (e.g., self-concept, attitude toward pollution, creativity), determine what research tests are available in the literature, using the compilations and bibliographic sources referred to in this chapter.

3. Using the volumes of *Mental Measurements Yearbooks,* find out what reviewers think of a particular test that interests you. Do the reviewers agree with each other?

4. To what sources would you go to try to answer each of the following questions? To which would you go first? What would you expect to get from each?
   a. What test should you use to study the progress of two classes in beginning Spanish?
   b. What kinds of norms are available for the Metropolitan Achievement Tests?
   c. Is the Rorschach test of any value as a predictor of academic success in college?
   d. What is the most recent version of the Wechsler Intelligence Scale for Children?
   e. What measures of verbal ability have been published for use with the blind?

   f. What are the significant differences between the Iowa Tests of Basic Skills and the Metropolitan Achievement Tests?

   g. How much does the Cognitive Abilities Test cost?

   h. What do testing people think of the Career Occupational Preference System?

5. Look at two or three publishers' catalogs. Compare the announcements of tests of the same type. How adequate is the information provided? How objective is the presentation of the tests' values and limitations?

SOURCES OF TEST INFORMATION

Of General Interest

Buros, O. K. (Ed.). (1978). *The eighth mental measurements yearbook.* Highland Park, NJ: The Gryphon Press. (This volume is now handled by the Buros Institute of Mental Measurements at the University of Nebraska, Lincoln, NE.)

Conoley, J. C., & Impara, J. C. (Eds.). (1994). *Supplement to the eleventh mental measurements yearbook.* Lincoln, NE: Buros Institute of Mental Measurements.

Conoley, J. C., & Impara, J. C. (Eds.). (1995). *The twelfth mental measurements yearbook.* Lincoln, NE: Buros Institute of Mental Measurements.

Conoley, J. C., & Kramer, J. J. (Eds.). (1989). *The tenth mental measurements yearbook.* Lincoln, NE: Buros Institute of Mental Measurements.

Conoley, J. C., Kramer, J. J., & Mitchell, J. V., Jr. (Eds.). (1988). *Supplement to the ninth mental measurements yearbook.* Lincoln, NE: Buros Institute of Mental Measurements.

Fabiano, E. (1989). *Index to tests used in educational dissertations.* Phoenix, AZ: Oryx Press.

Fehrmann, P. G., & O'Brien, N. P. (2001). *Directory of test collections in academic, professional, and research libraries.* Chicago: Association of College and Research Libraries.

Goldman, B. A., & Busch, J. C. (1978). *Directory of unpublished experimental mental measures: Vol. 2.* New York: Human Sciences Press.

Goldman, B. A., & Busch, J. C. (1982). *Directory of unpublished experimental mental measures: Vol. 3.* New York: Human Sciences Press.

Goldman, B. A., & Mitchell, D. F. (1990). *Directory of unpublished experimental mental measures: Vol. 5.* Dubuque, IA: Wm. C. Brown.

Goldman, B. A., & Osborne, W. L. (1985). *Directory of unpublished experimental mental measures: Vol. 4.* New York: Human Sciences Press.

Goldman, B. A., & Sanders, J. L. (1974). *Directory of unpublished experimental mental measures: Vol. 1.* New York: Behavioral Publications.

Hammill, D. D., Brown, L., & Bryant, B. R. (1992). *A consumer's guide to tests in print* (2nd ed.). Austin, TX: PRO-ED.

Hepner, J. C. (1988). *ETS test collection cumulative index to tests in microfiche, 1975–1987.* Princeton, NJ: Educational Testing Service.

Hersen, M., & Bellack, A. S. (Eds.). (1988). *Dictionary of behavioral assessment techniques.* New York: Pergamon.

Impara, J. C., & Plake, B. S. (1998). *The thirteenth mental measurements yearbook.* Lincoln, NE: Buros Institute of Mental Measurements.

Johnson, O. G. (1976). *Tests and measurements in child development: Handbook II.* San Francisco: Jossey-Bass.

Johnson, O. G., & Bommarito, J. W. (1971). *Tests and measurements in child development: A handbook.* San Francisco: Jossey-Bass.

Keyser, D. J., & Sweetland, R. C. (1984). *Test critiques.* Kansas City, MO: Test Corporation of America.

Kramer, J. J., & Conoley, J. C. (Eds.). (1992). *The eleventh mental measurements yearbook.* Lincoln, NE: Buros Institute of Mental Measurements.

Krug, S. E. (Ed.). (1988). *Psychware sourcebook* (3rd ed.). Kansas City, MO: Test Corporation of America.

Lake, D. G., Miles, M. B., & Earle, R. B. (1973). *Measuring human behavior: Tools for the assessment of social functioning.* New York: Teachers College Press.

Lester, P. A., & Bishop, L. K. (1997). *Handbook of tests and measurement in education and the social sciences.* Lancaster, PA: Technomic Publishing Company.

Levy, P., & Goldstein, H. (1984). *Tests in education: A book of critical reviews.* London: Academic Press.

Mauser, A. J. (1977). *Assessing the learning disabled: Selected instruments* (2nd ed.). Novato, CA: Academic Therapy Publications.

Miller, D. C. (1983). *Handbook of research design and social measurements* (4th ed.). New York: Longman.

Mitchell, J. V., Jr. (Ed.). (1985). *The ninth mental measurements yearbook.* Lincoln, NE: Buros Institute of Mental Measurements.

Murphy, L. L., Plake, B. S., Impara, J. C., & Spies, R. A. (2002). *Tests in print* (6th ed.). Lincoln, NE: Buros Institute of Mental Measurements.

O'Brien, N. P. (1988). *Test construction: A bibliography of selected resources.* New York: Greenwood.

Perlmutter, B. F., Touliatos, J., & Holden, G. W. (Eds.). (2001). *Handbook of family measurement techniques: Vol. 3, Instruments & index.* Thousand Oaks, CA: Sage.

Plake, B. S., & Impara, J. C. (1999). *Supplement to the thirteenth mental measurements yearbook.* Lincoln, NE: Buros Institute of Mental Measurements.

Plake, B. S., & Impara, J. C. (2001). *The fourteenth mental measurements yearbook.* Lincoln, NE: Buros Institute of Mental Measurements.

Plake, B. S., Impara, J. C., & Spies, R. A. (2003). *The fifteenth mental measurements yearbook.* Lincoln, NE: Buros Institute of Mental Measurements.

Robinson, J. P., Athanasion, R., & Head, K. B. (1969). *Measures of occupational attitudes and occupational characteristics.* Ann Arbor: University of Michigan.

Robinson, J. P., Rusk, J. G., & Head, K. B. (1968). *Measures of political attitudes.* Ann Arbor: University of Michigan.

Robinson, J. P., & Shaver, P. R. (1973). *Measures of social psychological attitudes* (rev. ed.). Ann Arbor: University of Michigan.

Shaw, M. E., & Wright, J. W. (1967). *Scales for the measurement of attitudes.* New York: McGraw-Hill.

Sweetland, R. C., & Keyser, D. J. (Eds.). (1986). *Tests: A comprehensive reference for assessments in psychology, education and business* (2nd ed.). Kansas City, MO: Test Corporation of America.

Touliatos, J., Perlmutter, B. F., & Holden, G. W. (Eds.). (2001). *Handbook of family measurement techniques: Vol. 2, Abstracts.* Thousand Oaks, CA: Sage.

Touliatos, J., Perlmutter, B. F., & Straus, M. A. (Eds.). (2001). *Handbook of family measurement techniques: Vol. 1, Abstracts.* Thousand Oaks, CA: Sage.

Publications and Collections Available from the Educational Testing Service. For information regarding the Test Collection Data Base, Tests in Microfiche, the Tests in Microfiche Annotated Index, and the Test Collection Bibliographies, consult the ERIC/AE Web site at http://www.ericae.net.

Other Publications Related to the Test Collection

Educational Testing Service Test Collection. (1986). *The ETS test collection catalog* (6 vols.). Phoenix, AZ: Oryx Press.

Educational Testing Service Test Collection. (1987). *Directory of selected national testing programs.* Phoenix, AZ: Oryx Press.

In Specific Subject Areas

Beere, C. A. (1990). *Gender roles: A handbook of tests and measures.* Westport, CT: Greenwood.

Beere, C. A. (1990). *Sex and gender issues: A handbook of tests and measures.* Westport, CT: Greenwood.

Braswell, J. S. (compiler). (1981). *Mathematics tests available in the United States and Canada.* Reston, VA: National Council of Teachers of Mathematics.

Grommon, A. H. (Ed.). (1976). *Reviews of selected published tests in English.* Urbana, IL: National Council of Teachers of English.

Johnson, T. F., & Hess, R. J. (1970). *Tests in the arts.* St. Ann, MO: Central Midwestern Regional Education Laboratory.

Mangen, D. J., & Peterson, W. A. (Eds.). (1982). *Research instruments in social gerontology.* Minneapolis, MN: University of Minnesota Press.

Northwest Regional Educational Laboratory, Center for Bilingual Education. (1978). *Assessment instruments in bilingual education: A descriptive catalog of 342 oral and written tests.* Los Angeles: National Dissemination and Assessment Center.

Ostrow, A. C. (1990). *Directory of psychological tests in the sport and exercise sciences.* Morgantown, WV: Fitness Information Technology.

Savard, J.-G. (1969). *Analytical bibliography of language tests.* Quebec: International Center for Research on Bilingualism.

Scholl, G., & Schnur, R. (1976). *Measures of psychological, vocational and educational functioning in the blind and visually handicapped.* New York: American Foundation for the Blind.

Valette, R. M. (1977). *Modern language testing* (2nd ed.). New York: Harcourt Brace Jovanovich.

Wall, J. (1981). *Compendium of standardized science tests.* Washington, DC: National Science Teachers Association.

Part Two

Testing and Measurement Devices

CHAPTER 7

Assessment and Educational Decisions

Introduction
Values and Decisions
Placement Decisions
    Issues Related to Mainstreaming
    How Placement Decisions Are Made
Classroom Instructional Decisions
    The Use of Objectives
    Types of Assessment Instruments
Day-by-Day Instructional Decisions
Reporting Academic Progress
    Performance in Relation to Perfection

Performance in Relation to Par
Performance in Relation to Potential
    Assigning Grades
    Importance of Grades
Planning Educational Futures
    Selection Decisions
    Curricular Decisions
    Public and Political Decisions
Summary
Questions and Exercises
Suggested Readings

INTRODUCTION

You are probably aware by now that a major theme of this book is the relationship between measurement and decision making. In the educational arena, educators, students, and parents are required to make a dizzying number of decisions that impact students' educational experiences. Teachers, for example, must decide not only how to evaluate student progress but also how to best tailor the curriculum to meet the needs of individual students. Students, as they achieve higher levels of education, need to make decisions about their own futures, including selection of courses and vocational planning. Parents, acting in partnership with their child and the schools, also contribute to the decisions that shape a student's educational path.

To make good decisions, every decision maker needs information. More specifically, decision makers must know what information is needed to understand and analyze a problem, where that information can be obtained, how to weigh it, and how to use it effectively to arrive at a course of action. In many instances such information can be obtained, at least in part, through educational testing and measurement.

VALUES AND DECISIONS

Decision making involves values. In education, a decision maker must determine not only what information is relevant to a particular decision, but also which educational goals are most important and what are the most desirable or expedient methods of achieving those goals. Typically, there is no objective way to answer these questions; they are issues of values. Values, both personal and societal, are difficult to quantify. Although it may be possible to measure the degree to which an individual holds a certain value, there is no available assessment procedure that can tell us what values an individual, school, or agency *should* have or which are most important to consider in making a particular decision. Values may differ markedly across subgroups within a community, and there is often considerable variation in opinion among individuals and agencies regarding which values should take precedence. Many of the controversies surrounding the use of tests and evaluation procedures in decision making, particularly for selection and placement decisions, stem from differences in value systems. In some instances, these conflicts have been resolved by the state and federal courts, which have mandated certain actions designed to promote societal goals for education. In other instances, state curricular bodies, local school boards, or school faculties have reached a consensus on what values should be considered in making decisions. In most cases, however, conflicts about values remain.

PLACEMENT DECISIONS

Classroom teachers frequently divide classes, particularly at the elementary school level, into smaller, within-class groups for instruction. The primary purpose of such grouping is to make instruction more effective by forming small clusters of students who have similar instructional needs. The decision to assign a student to a relatively homogeneous, within-class group is an example of a placement decision that usually is made solely by the teacher. Such decisions typically are based on information about each student's progress in mastering educational objectives.

Sometimes placement decisions must be made for students whose instructional needs differ so markedly from those of other students in the class that the teacher is unable to make the necessary adjustments within the classroom. Typically, these students are of two kinds. At one extreme are gifted students whose level of achievement and speed of learning greatly exceed those of other students in the class, and at the other are students who are having great difficulty mastering basic educational skills such as reading, are unable to adapt to classroom demands, or are so disruptive that they interfere with the learning of other students in the classroom. A teacher may decide to refer these kinds of students to a school psychologist or counselor for assessment and possible alternative placement. Issues related to the use of tests with exceptional students are discussed in Chapter 13.

The primary focus of a placement decision is—or should be—on the individual being placed and on the benefits that would accrue to him or her from a particular placement. However, some placement decisions also benefit the classroom teacher or other students in the class. For example, the decision to remove a particularly disruptive student from the regular classroom and to place him or her in a small class with a teacher trained to handle such students can benefit not only the disruptive student but also others in the regular classroom.

A great deal of controversy exists surrounding placement decisions in educational settings. However, because of the existence of individual differences in achievement among students and the tendency for these differences to become larger, not smaller, as students progress through school, it is likely that such decisions will always be necessary. Students differ markedly in how much they have learned from previous instruction, their motivation to learn, the instructional conditions under which they learn best, their rate of learning, and their ability to apply previous experience to new learning situations. Furthermore, an instructional program that facilitates learning and growth for one student may hinder it for others. Classroom teachers and other educators have long recognized the need to adapt teaching methods, learning materials, and curricula to meet individual differences among students and to place students in the kind of learning environment that will optimize their educational opportunities.

Issues Related to Mainstreaming

In 1975, the passage of the Education for All Handicapped Children Act, otherwise known as Public Law (PL) 94-142 (see Chapter 13), guaranteed students with disabilities the right to be educated with their nondisabled peers. This law requires that public schools educate children with disabilities in the least restrictive environment conducive to their development. The requirement that a child be educated in the least restrictive environment has been more commonly referred to as **mainstreaming.**

Prior to the passage of PL 94-142, comparisons between regular and special education classrooms yielded a dismal picture. Well-controlled studies comparing the academic achievement of special education students with equivalent students who remained in the regular education classroom found an overall negative effect of being in the special class. Furthermore, in examining special education classrooms, it was found that the teachers were not better trained, that the curricula generally were watered-down versions of regular programs, and that the classes were overpopulated with minority children. These findings precipitated the legislation mandating a change in our approach to educating exceptional students.

Currently, approaches to the education of exceptional learners range from full inclusion, in which students spend all day in regular classrooms, to full exclusion where learners spend all of their time outside of regular class. Full exclusion, once the norm, is now a relatively uncommon option reserved only for students with very severe disabilities. Most children with identified disabilities spend at least part of their school day in the regular education classroom and are thus at least partially mainstreamed. The special services typically required by these students may be delivered by regular teachers or by special education personnel, depending on the preference of the school system, the severity of the student's disability, and the facilities and resources available in the district.

Each child identified for special services under PL 94-142 must also have an individualized education program (IEP) that provides a detailed description of the kinds of services and educational experiences he or she will receive and how the effectiveness of those services will be evaluated. A student's IEP, which must be revised annually, should also include individualized goals and objectives, with timelines, and a description of the child's current level of functioning with respect to these objectives.

Students directly impacted by PL 94-142, typically classified as either mentally retarded, emotionally disturbed, or learning disabled, are an extremely heterogeneous group. Placing each student in the most appropriate category is necessary not only for purposes of funding and allocation of educational services in schools, but also for creating the best match between a student's needs and the type of resources that he or she receives. Research has shown that particular qualities of instruction, rather than the classroom setting per se, are more important in predicting academic as well as social outcomes for students with disabilities (Shepard, 1989).

Mainstreaming clearly presents some challenges for regular education teachers, many of whom are not adequately trained to meet the needs of exceptional students. Because educational funding is limited, political and value questions remain about how financial resources should be allocated within the schools. PL 94-142 reflects the relative importance society has placed on the value of normalizing the educational experiences of students with disabilities. Unfortunately, relatively little attention usually is given to the needs of students at the other end of the educational spectrum. Because exceptionally able students succeed and often excel without special facilities or attention, they are not given the opportunity to optimize their achievement.

How Placement Decisions Are Made

When considering what sort of placement is best for a particular student, recall that the primary goal is to find the best match between the student's instructional needs and the educational experiences to which he or she is exposed. Assignment to Placement A (a particular course, section of the class, or type of special service) rather than to Placement B might seem advantageous either because the two placement options differ, in whole or in part, in the goals toward which they are directed or because they differ in the means used (or route taken) to reach common goals. Thus, the prime goal of a remedial college English section might be to teach correctness and clarity in writing a simple essay, whereas the prime goal of a creative writing class might be to encourage originality and dramatic effectiveness in writing narrative prose or poetry. Different goals are seen as appropriate for the two groups. On the other hand, the goals of both a regular and an advanced placement mathematics section in a high school might be to progress toward and master a domain designated as "mathematical analysis," but with the expectation that the advanced placement group would pursue topics in greater depth and at a faster rate. In the latter case, a common assessment procedure would indicate how far the members of each group had progressed toward their common goals.

The use of testing to aid with placement decisions is widespread. For decisions about course selection or entry points for instruction, assessment usually involves some test of initial achievement. These tests are most likely to permit constructive placement decisions when (1) they assess specific entry-level knowledge and skills for a particular subject area and (2) when the alternative instructional treatments differ substantially in method, content, or tempo.

Testing for the purpose of securing special services for a student is somewhat different. Whenever a student is identified for special services under PL 94-142, documentation, in the form of test scores, is legally required. The type of test evidence needed to support different classifications varies by state and by classification. For example, assessment of mental retardation typically involves administration of an individual intelligence test such as the Stanford-Binet or the age-appropriate Wechsler scale. Because limited intelligence is considered the central feature of mental retardation, comparison of a student's test score to national norms of children of the same age is the primary means of identifying this disability.

A classification of **learning disability** involves more extensive testing. An intelligence test generally is administered to establish that a student's intellectual functioning is normal, not retarded. Standardized achievement tests are also administered to substantiate teacher reports of classroom failure in particular skill areas and to more clearly identify specific deficits. A discrepancy between intellectual capacity, as measured by the intelligence test, and level of academic performance, both in the classroom and on standardized achievement tests, is the key feature of the learning disability construct.

The third major category of disability, **emotional disturbance,** is also assessed through testing. The most common source of evidence for this classification is behavioral assessment. This entails the systematic gathering of behavioral data from numerous sources, including parents, teachers, school psychologists, classmates, and the child in question. In some cases, personality measures may also be used to assess emotional disorders. Those interpreting test data for classification of emotional disturbance should also consider age-appropriate norms and the context of the child's behavior. Because substantial variation is expected among children on any social or maturation dimension, a child generally would only be considered disturbed if he or she consistently scored in the first or second percentile among age-mates.

CLASSROOM INSTRUCTIONAL DECISIONS

One of the most important tasks for classroom teachers is to ensure that students achieve instructional objectives. Teachers must monitor the progress of both the class and of the individual students in order to make good decisions about where to begin teaching, when to move on to the next unit of instruction, whether to reteach the present unit, or whether a particular student or subgroup of students needs special help to master the learning task. The quality of these decisions can strongly influence the effectiveness of the classroom instructional program.

Effective teaching requires that student progress be monitored through a process of both formal and informal assessments. Informal assessments include such techniques as questioning, observing students while they work on tasks, and asking students to read aloud or to verbalize the working through of a mathematics problem. These assessments are useful in gauging student understanding of the material presented and thus in helping teachers to make better decisions in planning instruction. Specifically, teachers need to know whether further review is required or if the students are ready for the introduction of new material. Informal assessment procedures also give teachers immediate feedback about the effectiveness of the teaching methods being employed. If students are not learning as expected, the teacher must decide whether to alter the instructional methods. Assessment techniques that guide the course of instruction are referred to as **formative evaluation.**

"High-stakes" decisions about students—such as grades and changes in placement—are usually based on a more formal assessment called **summative evaluation.** Summative evaluation techniques, usually in the form of tests, are used after instruction is completed to summarize what students have learned. This category includes both the teacher-constructed and -administered tests, which are typically used to make decisions about grades, and standardized achievement tests, which are used to evaluate instruction and identify exceptionally high- or low-performing students. Results of these tests may prompt a teacher to refer a student to a school psychologist or counselor for a more in-depth diagnosis, including clarification of the areas in which the student is having particular success or difficulty and identification of possible reasons for any learning problems. Additional testing is routinely done to aid in placement decisions, including placement in special education or gifted classes.

Surveys of teacher behavior have shown that teachers prefer informal methods of assessment and use them more often than they use formal approaches. This pattern of use probably occurs because the informal assessments require less preparation and skill to construct. However, informal assessments should be used in concert with more formal approaches when making decisions about individual students. As test users, teachers must take care to ensure that all assessments used in decision making are reliable and valid for their intended use. When using informal assessments, teachers need to record the results carefully or they may have insufficient information about the performance of their students. Classroom teachers may be reluctant to keep such records because of the time and work involved. However, if this is the case, they should place more reliance on formal techniques, which lend themselves more easily to systematic record keeping. As a purely practical matter, teachers need to keep accurate records of their assessments to be able to communicate with parents and, perhaps, defend a decision they have made.

The Use of Objectives

Typically, classroom teachers employ a wide range of instructional objectives for a particular class. Cognitive objectives may include the building of a knowledge base or the development of cognitive skills, such as reading or writing. Affective objectives involve the development of attitudes, values, interests, and personal or social attributes. Depending on the area of instruction, assessing achievement of these objectives may focus on evaluation of products or performances as well as on acquired cognitive skills and information.

Different methods of assessment are often required to determine if different types of objectives have been achieved by students. However, it is critical, regardless of the approach to assessment, that the information collected be accurate and relevant. If the techniques used to collect information about the achievement of an objective do not yield high-quality information, decisions or actions based on those data are likely to be faulty.

Types of Assessment Instruments

Standardized Achievement Tests

At the beginning of the school year, when he or she is facing a new class, student scores on standardized achievement tests might help a teacher in planning instruction for that class. For example, knowledge of test scores may aid in the selection of reading materials that are suitable for the students' current level of achievement or in deciding where to start instruction in mathematics or language. However, once instruction has actually begun, the teacher needs information on student achievement of specific instructional objectives, and this information is needed promptly. Standardized achievement tests do not provide this kind of information. Because such tests must focus on objectives that are common to schools throughout the United States, they emphasize general skills and are unlikely to assess objectives related to the specific content emphasized in a particular classroom. Furthermore, they measure only cognitive objectives that can be appraised by paper-and-pencil tests. Affective, procedural, and other objectives requiring skill in oral communication or motor performance are not usually measured by these tests. Standardized tests also are quite expensive and require several hours for administration. Both of these factors make them impractical for frequent use and for certain purposes. In addition, teachers may have to wait a long time for test results, which means that the results might not be available when instructional decisions need to be made.

Assessment Material Packaged with Curricular Materials

Some classroom teachers, particularly in the lower grades, use tests accompanying published curricular materials instead of constructing assessments of their own. Most basal reading series and many textbooks include such tests. These instructional materials usually match the test items with the instructional objectives that guided the development of the parent material, and may also suggest a passing score to be used to classify students as masters or nonmasters of those objectives. Although such materials can reduce the burden of test construction, they should be examined carefully before they are used. In many instances, they are poorly constructed. In addition, the number of items appraising each objective is usually too small to permit judgments about mastery. Despite being labeled as criterion-referenced tests, the domain assessed is seldom defined adequately and the items may not be sufficiently representative for the tests to support this classification. Another important point is that these prepackaged tests are not standardized tests and, therefore, include no normative information to aid interpretation of test scores.

Teacher-Made Assessment Instruments

To obtain information for making day-to-day instructional decisions, classroom teachers usually must devise their own tests or assessment procedures. Five general methods are used for collecting data on the achievement of instructional objectives:

1. Paper-and-pencil tests
2. Oral tests
3. Product evaluations
4. Performance tests
5. Affective measures.

Each of these methods has advantages and disadvantages, and each is appropriate for appraising the achievement of only certain types of objectives.

1. *Paper-and-pencil tests.* Objectives that call for knowledge about a particular subject area, the capacity to use that knowledge to solve problems, or a general educational skill such as reading can be most reliably and validly appraised by teacher-made **paper-and-pencil tests.** Unfortunately, most teacher-made tests are poor measuring instruments. There are typically two problems with these kinds of tests. First, the items on the tests often do not match the stated goals of the class, and second, the tests tend to have poor psychometric qualities because the items are not well written. Surveys of teachers suggest that they seldom use even minimal data-analysis procedures, such as determining the central tendency or variability on their test results. As a result of these weaknesses, the information obtained from such tests may be of questionable value in making instructional decisions. Some guidelines for writing and improving test items are provided in Chapter 15.

2. *Oral tests.* Although **oral tests** are more time consuming for the teacher, they can be used to assess many of the same types of objectives assessed by paper-and-pencil tests. There are also other objectives, particularly in language classes, where oral assessment may be the best or only way to appraise achievement of course objectives. Oral tests have the additional advantage of providing an opportunity to assess the integration of ideas, while removing the effect of level of skill in written expression. The major disadvantage to the use of this method is that the evaluation of performance tends to be more subjective.

Another use for individually administered oral tests is the identification of learning problems. For example, a teacher could give a student a series of two-digit addition problems and ask the student to solve them aloud, that is, to talk through the procedures being used to arrive at an answer. These verbalizations can provide clues about the misconceptions that underlie not only errors but also sometimes even correct responses. Oral tests provide fewer clues about a student's underlying difficulty in reading, although the tests might help a teacher identify missing subskills required in the complex process of reading. For students with sensory or motor impairments, oral assessment may provide more accurate information than can be obtained by other methods.

3. *Product evaluations.* Some instructional objectives, such as those related to penmanship, to constructing a birdhouse in wood shop class, or to typing a business letter, require a student to produce a product that meets certain standards of acceptability. These kinds of objectives cannot be assessed directly by paper-and-pencil tests; it is better to evaluate the product itself. This type of assessment is called **product evaluation.** The major problems with product evaluation stem from the task of identifying the aspects of the product that are relevant to its quality and of establishing standards to measure the aspects that will define different degrees of adequacy or excellence in the product. Product evaluation is discussed in more detail in Chapter 10.

4. *Performance tests.* Some instructional objectives require a student to carry out a procedure such as giving an oral report, playing a musical instrument, or using a spreadsheet on a computer. As a rule, these kinds of performances do not leave a tangible product that can be judged, or if they do, the actual procedures used by the student to produce the product are as important as the final product. These kinds of objectives can be appraised only by assigning an appropriate task to the student, such as giving an oral report to the class, and then observing and rating the performance as it occurs. This type of evaluation is called **performance assessment.** The major problems with performance assessment are (1) identifying the critical, or salient, aspects of the performance that should be observed and (2) identifying and applying the appropriate criteria for discriminating different degrees of competency in the performance. Methods for improving performance assessments are presented in Chapter 10.

5. *Affective measures.* Almost all instructional programs, particularly at the elementary and secondary school levels, have affective as well as cognitive objectives. Affective objectives deal with personal and social attributes that educators want students to develop, such as values, interests, self-concept, and cooperation with others. Assessing objectives such as these can be quite difficult because they involve the inner feelings or motivations of students, which cannot be measured directly. Currently, the best that we can do is to observe behavior, and from this observation, try to infer what lies behind the behavior, have peers or teachers rate students, or ask students to provide self-reports of their own feelings or motivations. Methods for eliciting these reports are discussed in Chapters 11 and 12. None of these **affective assessment measures** is entirely satisfactory. However, if teachers and schools are serious about affective objectives, they need to monitor students' achievement of affective objectives so that adjustments in instruction or in classroom or school organization can be made if the level of achievement is not satisfactory, even if the measures are not wholly satisfactory.

DAY-BY-DAY INSTRUCTIONAL DECISIONS

One important role of achievement assessments is to help the classroom teacher make decisions about what is to be taught, studied, and/or practiced by students in the class. The weekly spelling test is a venerable classroom tradition, and quizzes in grammar and mathematics have been prepared and used by teachers for many years to help them make decisions about the next day's lesson or to evaluate a child's progress.

Interest in test use for guiding instructional decisions is on the increase, as is interest in the development of procedures that can provide information about whether a student has mastered a topic or skill. The knowledge provided by such assessments can help the teacher or the student decide whether there is a need for further instruction before the student moves to the next unit. This kind of information is especially relevant for subjects that have a hierarchical structure—that is, when progress on Topic B depends on an adequate understanding of Topic A. While mathematics is the prime example of such a subject, other topic areas show a similar structure. For example, children must know the alphabet and be able to recognize letters before they can learn to spell.

A test used to measure competence in a particular skill will usually be concrete and specific. In using such tests, teachers often set some criterion—usually an arbitrary one—to represent an adequate degree of competence. The use of a criterion has occasionally caused the tests to be incorrectly labeled as criterion-referenced tests. (The qualities that a test must have to be criterion referenced are listed in Chapter 3.) What these tests do have in common with criterion-referenced tests is the presentation of a representative sample of tasks from a narrowly defined domain. Because the domain is relatively narrow, all test items tend to require the same skill, and it is reasonable to expect that a person will either correctly answer all or almost all of the items or perform not much better than at a chance level.

By way of illustration, Figure 7–1 presents two teacher-made tests. The first assesses the students in a fifth-grade class on their knowledge of prime numbers. (For those who have forgotten or may never have known, a prime number is one that cannot be divided evenly by any number

---

Test of Prime Numbers

Directions: Do you know what a prime number is? Look at the numbers below. Six of them are prime numbers. For each one, see if it is a prime number. If it is, draw a circle around it. If it is not, leave it unmarked.

31	47	143
33	49	293
35	51	415
38	59	763
41	97	942

Test of Capitalization

Read the paragraph. The punctuation is correct, and the words that begin a sentence have been capitalized. No other words have been capitalized. Some need to be. Draw a line under each word that should begin with a capital letter.

We saw mary yesterday. She said she had gone to chicago, illinois, to see her aunt helen. Her aunt took her for a drive along the shore of lake michigan. On the way they passed the conrad hilton hotel where mary's uncle joseph works. Mary said that she had enjoyed the trip, but she was glad to be back home with her own friends.

Figure 7–1
Samples of teacher-made tests.

other than itself or 1 [unity]. Examples are 2, 3, 5, and 7, but not 9.) The second test, which also appeared in Chapter 3, assesses skill in capitalization of proper names and is designed to identify students who are having trouble with this skill.

You can see that each little test is quite short; there are 15 numbers from which to choose 6 prime numbers in the first, and 13 words that should be underlined in the second. Setting a criterion level of 90% correct on each test as constituting adequate competence permits the examinee to miss one item on each test, but assumes that more frequent mistakes imply inadequate mastery of the concept or skill. These tests illustrate one extreme in specificity and are clearly related to judgments about what a pupil has learned. They sample from narrowly and explicitly defined domains of instruction that are relatively easy to specify.

In much of education, the domain represented by a unit of instruction is much fuzzier, and, consequently, the stock of appropriate problems or items is much less clearly defined. Consider, for example, a unit of instruction on the Bill of Rights. We could test an individual's ability to identify or to recall each of the first 10 amendments to the Constitution. But, if we were concerned with the meaning, the significance, and the application of these same 10 amendments to the problems of contemporary America, how could we meaningfully define and sample from that domain? In this instance, the notion of "mastery" slips through our fingers.

When we cannot define the boundaries of a domain, it becomes impossible to determine what constitutes a representative sample of exercises to assess degree of mastery of that domain. Different test makers may produce dissimilar sorts of test exercises to measure what is nominally the same domain. Specifying a criterion level of performance that represents a defined level of "mastery" becomes almost impossible with subject matter that cannot be concretely defined. Therefore, a teacher-made test of knowledge about abstract material may still provide some useful information to guide decisions about further teaching, but the information will not be as concrete as that provided by tests such as those in Figure 7–1.

REPORTING ACADEMIC PROGRESS

It is important to ensure that the student, the parents, and the school know whether a particular student is making satisfactory progress in schoolwork. To the student, evidence of progress and accomplishment is a substantial motivating force, and evidence of specific difficulties should be a signal indicating a need to seek help to overcome the difficulties. Focused tests of the sort found in Figure 7–1 provide an important form of feedback to guide students, as well as teachers, in identifying gaps in knowledge or skills that call for further study or practice.

Most parents are vitally concerned with the progress of their children in school. Of course, families differ in the depth of this concern and differ even more in the resources they provide for coaching in school skills and for supporting their child's efforts to learn. But all parents must be considered partners with the school, and, if they are to be effective partners, they must know how their child is progressing. Parents specifically need to know the level at which their child is functioning in each school subject and be warned promptly of any potential difficulties. All kinds of test results provide a concrete basis for communication from school to parent and for interpretation of the child's progress and difficulties.

As described in Chapter 3, the teacher or school may provide a criterion-referenced interpretation of student progress, which would include a list of competencies that the child has recently developed to a satisfactory level of mastery or of the specific skills with which the child is currently having difficulty. More conventionally, a norm-referenced interpretation is provided that compares the child's general level of performance in a subject area with that of his or her class, other students in the school, or a broader regional or national reference group.

It is necessary, in reporting a child's academic progress to parents, to compare the performance to something. Three commonly used approaches to defining the merit of a child's performance are to define

1. Performance in relation to perfection
2. Performance in relation to par (some expected or average level of accomplishment)
3. Performance in relation to potential.

Performance in Relation to Perfection

When judging performance in relation to perfection we ask "How close did the student come to exhibiting a perfect score on the quiz?" We are likely to interpret a perfect score as "complete mastery," but this interpretation is dangerous even in the case of a narrowly focused test and is completely inappropriate for a test that covers a broad domain. In the latter case, there are always more difficult tasks that could have been set for the examinee, and we never can say that he or she knows everything there is to know about a subject. Even with tasks as specific as identifying prime numbers, some numbers turn out to be a good deal more difficult than others. So "perfection" is displayed only on the specific sample of tasks that is used to represent the domain. Interpreting "80% correct" on the usual teacher-made test as "knows 80% of the subject" is completely absurd, and at most, the interpretation might be "knows 80% of the answers that the teacher thinks a student should be expected to know." On the other hand, this standard of what the teacher expects is a very real one and can be important to both pupil and parent.

Performance in Relation to Par

By performance in relation to par, we mean the typical, norm-referenced interpretation of a test score; adequacy of performance is defined by the performance of others. For a teacher-made test, it may be the student's standing relative to others in the class. For a published test, it is a student's standing in relation to a broader reference group, such as all children at this same age or grade level.

In Chapter 3, we discussed various sorts of converted scores, using different scales and reference frames for reporting the score of an individual. We expressed a preference for percentile ranks or standard scores to represent a student's performance in relation to other members of a group to which he or she logically belongs. Of these two types of converted scores, the one that probably conveys the most immediate meaning to a parent or other person not particularly sophisticated about measurement issues is the score reported in terms of relative position—at the 15th percentile, in the second 10th, or in the bottom quarter.

Two aspects of such a report are troubling. One problematic feature of these scales is that it is possible (although perhaps not likely) within a specific class that the differences in performance are so small that the distinction between the top and bottom quarters is of no practical importance. That is, one may be forcing distinctions where no real differences exist. The other troubling aspect is that in using the group as a standard, there must always be 50% of the total group "below the average" and 25% "in the bottom quarter," with the implication that they have somehow "failed" (but see the discussion of the "Lake Wobegon effect" in Chapter 9). We face a basic problem in our use of language: To the statistician, *average* means "middle of the group," but to most people, it has come to mean "minimally acceptable," so that anything below the average carries the connotation of "unacceptable." Somehow, the two interpretations of "average" must be separated in our thinking, so that the student who falls at the 20th or 30th percentile of the group on some measure is not viewed as having failed.

With a standardized test, the normative data supplied by the publisher permit "par" to refer to some national or regional group, or the school system may develop system-wide norms. The use of national norms may ease the pressure on some fortunately situated schools that draw primarily from an advantaged community in which most children approach or exceed the national average. However, if this par is used, it accentuates the sense of failure in schools from districts or communities that are at the low end of the scale in economic and cultural resources, where a very large proportion of the students will not reach the national or regional average. A blind application of national norms, whether to schools or individuals, is likely to lead to a sense of unreality and frustration.

The same type of problem can occur for individual students of average ability who happen to be in classes primarily composed of unusually talented students. The "normal" students might very well come in at the bottom of the class in every subject no matter how hard they try, with a resulting sense of frustration and failure, simply because the other students are exceptional. A nationally standardized test can provide a welcome reality check for such students by revealing their level of accomplishment relative to a broader sampling of society.

Performance in Relation to Potential

Recognition of the inequity of assessing performance in relation to a uniform and unvarying set of standards has led test users and educational evaluators to try to express performance in relation to potential. This orientation rejects the notion that all people are identical and interchangeable and that the same par is applicable to each person. Those reporting academic progress in terms of potential must establish a standard for each child, which asks, in light of all we know about this child, "What level of performance should we reasonably expect?"

This question is easy to phrase. When we start to explore it, however, we find that it becomes a tricky one to answer, with a wide range of technical and even ethical overtones. How do we determine the expected level of achievement for an individual? For example, we know that it is unreasonable to expect an 8-year-old to jump as far, run as fast, read as well, or do as wide a range of arithmetic problems as a 12-year-old can. Eight-year-old children also differ in size. Perhaps it is unreasonable to expect an undersized child of this age to jump as far as an oversized one. By the same token, children also differ in their performance on tests designed to measure general intellectual development. Perhaps it is unreasonable to expect the same level of reading or arithmetic performance from the child who obtains a low score on a scholastic aptitude test that we do from the child who obtains a high score.

Statistical analyses of the relationship between aptitude and achievement tests do yield high correlations. Children with low scores on measures of general intellectual functioning tend to get poor scores on measures of reading and mathematics achievement. In one sense, therefore, it might be correct to conclude that they have a lower potential for academic achievement. Because this relationship exists, we are tempted to modify our interpretations of test scores. Unfortunately, what at first seems to be a reasonable course of action turns out to be unworkable in practice. The approach does not work because the difference between the two types of tests is more a function of the way they are used and interpreted than of the underlying capacities assessed. The similarities between the two tests mean that students can be expected to perform the same on both. In the event that scores on the two tests are discrepant, we must first consider measurement error as the most likely cause of the difference. When this explanation has been ruled out, we may entertain a hypothesis of specific learning disability, or an emotional problem if "aptitude" exceeds "achievement."

In addition to the technical problems, social consequences may result from an application of different expectations and standards for different individuals. People tend to adjust their level of effort to the level of expectation that is set for them. Thus, low expectations may become a partial cause for low achievement. Higher expectations tend to raise achievement. On the other hand, more able students may question the equity of being required to meet a higher level of achievement to receive a particular grade. For this reason, some schools allow teachers to report effort and achievement separately.

Assigning Grades

Many teachers consider assigning grades one of the most unpleasant tasks required of them. It takes up a large amount of time, causes anxieties, and tends to leave a sour taste in their mouths. Few students enjoy being assigned grades, and for teachers, assigning grades is an activity that requires a great deal of time and effort. The payoff to teachers is too often a sizable number of dissatisfied students.

The evaluation of student performance is typically summarized in some condensed and highly abstract symbol. A survey by the National Education Association in 1967, supported by another study by Pinchak and Breland in 1974, found that a system of numerical or letter grades was used in about 80% of American school systems, except in the first grade, where the percentage was 73, and in kindergarten, where it was 17. Unfortunately, the study of grading has not received much attention in recent literature (Stiggins, Frisbie, & Griswold, 1989).

The use of highly condensed symbols to convey the teacher's evaluation has frequently been criticized for the reasons we consider next. The alternatives that have been offered to replace the conventional A, B, C, D, or F system have problems of their own, and no fully satisfactory replacement for this type of grade seems to be at hand.

Importance of Grades

Grades are deeply embedded in the educational culture. They have become the basis, in whole or in part, for a wide range of actions and decisions within educational institutions and between these institutions and the outside world. Eligibility for admission to certain programs or departments, for scholarship aid, for membership on athletic teams, and for continuing in school is often determined by academic standing. Admission to college or graduate school is usually based, at least in part, on grades received at the previous academic level. Thus, there are many points within the educational system where grades interact with the administrative and instructional process to affect the student's progress.

Most learning theorists, from behaviorists to cognitive psychologists, have emphasized the need for feedback in the facilitation of learning. We know that it is difficult for someone to improve unless they know how well they are doing. The process of growing and developing requires the testing of limits, and children need to know how they stand in relation to peers or to some goal. This process is interrupted when the feedback is inaccurate. The natural inclination of teachers is to be helpful and supportive, and they tend to dislike giving feedback that is not positive. Unjustified positive feedback should be avoided, however, because such approaches often backfire, resulting in decreased student motivation and stunted academic progress. If students are to improve, they need to know where improvement is needed, but it is also critical that the feedback be presented in such a way that it does not imply an evaluation of the students' worth as individuals.

Parents also need to know how their children are progressing in school. A number of possible means exist for fulfilling this need, including anecdotal records, teacher conferences, and/or lists of objectives mastered or not mastered. Experience has shown that parents know, understand, and respond best to the traditional methods of assigning grades. To institute an alternate system of providing feedback to parents and students would require a tremendous amount of parent education. To date, attempts to substitute alternate methods of reporting student progress have met with strong parental objections. Typical parents, faced with a list of objectives their child has mastered, will ask what grade this implies.

Furthermore, parents have a right to the accurate reporting of their children's progress in school, in terms that they understand. Avoiding the anguish of assigning grades by only giving high grades is a dereliction of duty. Nothing is more damaging to parent-school rapport than to have parents erroneously believe that their child has no academic problems. The school does no one a favor by shielding a child in this manner. In fact, successful lawsuits have recently been filed against schools for awarding students high school diplomas when they could not do sixth-grade work.

The school also has a responsibility to certify that students have mastered the assigned curriculum, at least at some minimal level, in the courses they have taken. If a student receives a satisfactory grade in a course, it is reasonable for a prospective employer or school to assume that the grade represents a meaningful mastery of subject matter. Clearly, certification is not a school's only responsibility, or even its first responsibility, but it is a responsibility nevertheless, and accurate reporting of student achievement in the form of grades is the form that employers and others outside the education establishment have come to expect. The traditional grading system has been durable and resistant to change both for the reasons discussed and because no alternative system has been found that better meets the needs of the wide array of consumers of this information.

PLANNING EDUCATIONAL FUTURES

As children progress through the school system, they gradually take on more responsibility for decisions concerning their future educational plans. Past achievement is one type of information that should influence their decisions. Present measured achievement is the best predictor we have of future achievement. General level of achievement may therefore affect the child's future educational decisions, and performance in a particular course may influence his or her decisions about educational specialization.

Grades obtained in school provide one indicator of achievement, but the variability of standards from teacher to teacher within a school and from school to school limits their value as guides to planning academic futures. Grades are personal and local in their significance. For this reason, standardized tests, with broadly representative norms that are comparable from one content area to another, provide a more uniform and universal basis for appraising overall level of achievement, as well as specific strengths and weaknesses.

Two mistakes must be avoided in using test results for planning purposes. One mistake is premature decision making. Individuals change, and present performance predicts the future imperfectly. Counselors should avoid closing out options—such as going to college—prematurely. The other mistake is making a predominantly negative use of test results. Test scores are more constructive if they are used to open doors rather than to close them. It is as important for test results to identify talent and encourage its further development as it is for them to redirect individuals for whom the typical college education seems an unrealistic goal. One of the consequences of the widespread use of standardized tests for college admissions—coupled with more extensive financial aid programs—is that educational opportunity based on ability to learn rather than ability to pay has become a realistic expectation for most of America's youth.

Selection Decisions

Selection decisions represent attempts to choose the individuals who are likely to make the greatest contribution to a particular organization or institution. That is, selection decisions emphasize the welfare of the organization or the society over the welfare of the individual. This type of decision can be contrasted with placement decisions, which are intended to benefit the individual who is being placed in a particular educational setting. Thus, value for an employer hiring a keyboard operator might be expressed (crudely) as number of error-free lines of text entered in an average working day, whereas value for a college might be expressed (perhaps even more crudely and incompletely) as freshman grade-point average (GPA). In the simplest terms, the purpose of a system for selection decisions is to hire or admit those individuals who will maximize the total value to the institution, that is, usually those who will have the greatest probability of success.

The notion of value is both fuzzy and complex. Any simple indicator, such as text lines entered or GPA, is at best a rough, pragmatic approximation of a person's true contribution to an organization, be it an employer or an educational institution.

Both past achievements and present performance often have a good deal of validity as predictors of future value. Thus, high school grades consistently have been found to be among the best predictors of future college grades, with correlations typically in the .50s and .60s, and job skills at the time of hiring provide some of the best indicators of how well those same skills will be performed on the job.

The rationale for using an objective test of achievement in one or more academic subjects to replace or supplement high school grades as a predictor of college success is that such a test would provide a uniform set of tasks for all applicants and, thus, a way of compensating for the differences in grading standards, students' socioeconomic status, and specific content foci of secondary schools. For this reason, the widely used college admission tests, the Scholastic Assessment Test (SAT) and the American College Testing Program (ACT Assessment), have been based on rather general reading, verbal, and quantitative skills.

In the world of work, academic achievement tests appear to be an inappropriate selection device for most jobs. Mental ability tests work reasonably well in situations where the focus is on potential for learning new skills or performing intellectually demanding tasks, but in most situations, proficiency tests that measure specific job skills seem to be the best option. Examples of occupations for which such tests might be appropriate are carpenters, machinists, and electricians, as well as office jobs such as keyboard operator, bookkeeper, or computer programmer. Tests for job skills need to be employed with caution. Although it is possible to measure with some degree of accuracy the most obvious skills related to each job, in most cases the most important characteristics are personal, such as getting along with others and not using drugs, characteristics that are quite difficult to measure.

Whenever using test results to aid in selection decisions, the decision-making institution or organization must be able to document the validity of the test for each particular use. (Some of the legal requirements and court decisions relating to the use of tests for selection are reviewed in Chapter 14.) Consider that when a student submits his or her SAT or ACT scores as part of an application to college, these scores, in addition to their being used in the admissions decision, are also often used to award scholarships, to help counsel the student in course and program choices, and to identify the need for remedial classes or tutoring. For each of these additional uses of test data, validity must be demonstrated in order for use of the data to be appropriate. Just because a test is a good predictor of freshman GPA (and therefore valid for use in the admissions decision), one should not assume that the test scores can also validly be used for other types of decisions.

Curricular Decisions

One function for which measures of achievement are needed is the evaluation of alternative curricular materials or instructional designs. In education, there is a steady flow of proposals for change—change in curricular emphasis, change in instructional materials, and change in instructional procedures. If innovations are to be introduced rationally rather than capriciously and if education is to show any cumulative progress in effectiveness rather than oscillating from one fad to another, systematic evaluation of the outcomes from any change is imperative. Carrying out adequate studies to evaluate any proposed change is admittedly difficult. But without evaluative research studies, decisions to change are made blindly, supported only by the eloquence of their proponents.

A first requirement for any evaluative research is clear specification of what a proposed innovation is designed to achieve. That is, we need a comprehensive statement of the objectives of the program, covering the full range of outcomes sought for both the proposed new program and the program it is designed to replace. If a revised mathematics program is designed to produce improved understanding of the number system, and the program it is replacing is one that has emphasized computational skills, it is important in evaluating the outcomes that the two programs be compared both in terms of furthering understanding of the number system and in terms of computational skills. Are losses in computational skills offset by improved understanding of the number system? The identification of the better of the two systems can only rationally be made if we know how well each program achieves not only its own objectives but also other relevant objectives. The choice also depends on the value we place on each outcome. This information puts us in a position to judge the importance of different aspects of achievement in terms of a specified system of values and comes up with a composite decision about which set of outcomes is preferred.

Once the objectives of an instructional program have been stated with enough detail and explicitness to guide instruction and evaluation, we may ask whether some or all of the objectives can be assessed appropriately using existing published tests. There are, of course, economies of time and effort associated with use of existing tests, as well as some gain in the availability of normative data. The design of most published tests involves a thorough analysis of both the content and objectives of the field that they are meant to cover. For existing tests, these analyses may have been done some years before publication, and will have been done in terms of a curriculum that contains elements common to all school districts. In the case of basic skills such as those encompassed in reading and mathematics curricula, this presents no particular problem because there is considerable agreement among school districts regarding what should be taught. Although this agreement will not always be found in other curricular areas, most of the content of education changes slowly and therefore even programs that differ in form and in specific content may have much in common in terms of their underlying educational objectives. For this reason, advantages result from examining existing tests before attempting to invest the resources of time, skill, and money to produce a new test specifically for the local evaluation project.

One feature of carrying out curricular evaluations, or any analysis that leads to a decision applied to a whole class, school, or school system, is that it is not necessary that every pupil be assessed with every test exercise. Suppose, for example, so many items are needed to assess a set of objectives adequately that it would take 4 hours for a student to complete a test made up of these items. If only 30 minutes of testing time were available, it might be possible to divide the material into eight test forms to correspond to the eight 30-minute testing segments needed to accommodate 4 hours of testing material and to have each student take one of the test forms. If a school has, for example, 120 sixth-grade students, approximately 15 children will take each of the eight forms. It would then be possible to determine average level of test performance for the school as a whole, on the complete test, because all of the items would have been used and all of the pupils would have served as examinees. When a large pool of examinees is available, this procedure, which is called **item sampling,** provides a practical way to assess a wide range of curricular objectives, with each examinee spending only a relatively short time being tested. One drawback of item sampling is that it requires the assembly of tests specifically for the current occasion, either through local efforts or from the item files of commercial publishers. Note that with item sampling, we do not get a meaningful or useful score for any single student. The College Basic Academic Skills Examination, a college-level achievement test described in Chapter 9, is an example of a commercially available standardized test that uses the item sampling approach.

Public and Political Decisions

Every community is interested in and concerned about its school system. Expenditures for education represent a major budget item of every community and every state, and citizens want to know whether they are getting good value for their money. Citizens are also interested in how their schools compare with other schools in the state and throughout the country, and how well the children in their community are learning the things that they, as parents and citizens, deem important. Citizens do not make decisions about schools very often, but when they do, the decisions frequently are negative. They may vote down a school budget, school bond issue, or school board member, or they may organize a protest against a person, program, or policy. Conversely, of course, they may decide to support the school with money, time, or approbation. The action that they select will depend on how they feel about their schools, and this feeling, in turn, will depend in part on what they know about their schools.

Knowing about schools is, in part, a matter of knowing what is going on in them: available activities, resources for learning, and new ideas. Of greatest importance to most citizens is information about how much children are learning. Thus, in its relationship with the public, each school system faces the problem of presenting to that public some picture of student progress.

One approach to reporting school progress is to report in terms of very specific competencies. Thus, the school might report that 78% of pupils at the end of grade 3 were able to identify the number of thousands, hundreds, tens, and units in a number such as 7,562. But such a report conveys little meaning to even an informed citizen. The likely response might be "So is that good or bad? What percentage should be expected to do this? How does this compare with last year? How does this compare with the Centerville school system next door?" If specific accomplishments are reported, there are likely to be so many of them that teachers and citizens alike would be overwhelmed by the details.

Some type of summary, then, seems necessary in reporting to the public. By its nature, the summary will involve comparison—comparison with last year's performance, national norms, or some group of similar schools or communities. It is possible for a school system to develop its own set of assessment instruments, to use these in successive years, and to make limited types of comparisons, but locally constructed tests with local norms might not satisfy the public. In most cases, we need a way to make comparisons with other communities, states, and the nation as a whole. These comparisons can only be supplied by a test for which normative data are available. In addition, the development of good tests is difficult, expensive, and time consuming. One significant role for standardized achievement tests is to provide the basis for making comparisons with other communities.

The test that forms the most appropriate basis for presenting a school's results to the public is the test that best represents the school's educational objectives. Thus, there are no new or different criteria for selecting a test that is to provide public information; it will be the same test that is most useful for appraising the achievement level of individual students.

Once the test has been administered and scored, it is necessary to assemble the data and present them in a form that will fairly and clearly communicate the results to the public. "Fairly" relates to the proper comparison group; "clearly" relates to the form of presentation. Some of the problems and pitfalls of presenting achievement test results to the public are discussed in Chapter 9.

SUMMARY

A major theme of this book is the examination of the relationship between measurement and decision making. Information gained from tests and other assessment procedures is used to aid many kinds of educational decisions. Whether testing is used to guide decisions about student placement, instruction, or student progress, decision making is an inherently value-laden process.

The nature of the decisions to be made, and hence the type of information needed, determines which approaches to assessment are most appropriate. Whether a teacher chooses achievement tests, the assessment material packaged with instructional materials, oral tests, product evaluations, performance tests, or affective measures is determined by the types of decisions he or she must make. Tests are also used to make placement and selection decisions, to guide day-by-day instructional choices and curriculum evaluation, and to report academic progress to parents and the public.

QUESTIONS AND EXERCISES

1. What role do values play in decision making?

2. What is PL 94-142? Discuss the potential implications of this law for schools, students, and teachers.

3. How is testing used to aid in placement decisions? What kind of evidence is necessary to support this use of tests? Why?

4. For a fifth-grade class, give an example of the type of objective that would be assessed by each of the following methods: a paper-and-pencil test, an oral test, a product evaluation, a performance test, and an assessment of affective characteristics.

5. Why might a test that is suitable as a measure of past achievement have limited value for a placement decision?

6. What procedures might a community college use to place entering freshmen into sections for a required English course? What would be the objectives of such sectioning? What gains might be expected? What losses?

7. In April of the sixth grade, Helen has a reading grade equivalent of 6.2 (second month of sixth grade) on the Iowa Tests of Basic Skills. How should this be interpreted if her nonverbal standard age score on the Cognitive Abilities Test is 85? If it is 115? If it is 135?

8. How does your answer to Question 7 change as you shift from performance in relation to potential to performance in relation to par?

9. What would be involved in preparing a proficiency test for television repairmen? What form might the test take?

10. In what ways might a testing program to evaluate a proposed modified mathematics curriculum differ from a program designed to place students in the appropriate mathematics section?

11. It has been proposed that, although the A, B, C, D, F system of grading is relative, a percentage system represents an absolute appraisal. What are the arguments for and against this point of view? Are any systems of appraisal based on an absolute standard? Identify one, and give the evidence to support your position.

12. In what way(s) is the grading system in a school similar to a rating procedure? In what way(s) does it differ? What factors that limit the effectiveness of ratings also limit the effectiveness of a grading system?

13. What should the role of a student's self-appraisal be in evaluating his or her educational progress? What are the limits of such an appraisal?

14. College Y has 10 sections of freshman English. What steps could be taken to ensure uniform grading standards, so that a student would not be penalized by being in a particular section?

15. It has been proposed that schools should abandon grades and report only pass or fail for students. What would be gained from such a procedure? What would be lost? How would the functions now served (admittedly imperfectly) by grades be discharged? How adequate would these alternative procedures be?

16. A school principal remarked to his board of education: "We have higher standards than Mason High. Our passing grade is 70, and theirs is only 65." What assumptions is he making in this statement? How defensible are these assumptions?

SUGGESTED READINGS

Bloom, B. S., Hastings, J. T., & Madaus, C. F. (1971). *Handbook on formative and summative evaluation of student learning.* New York: McGraw-Hill.

Gullickson, A. R., & Hopkins, K. D. (1987). The context of educational measurement instruction for preservice teachers: Professor perspectives. *Issues and Practices, 6*(3), 12–16.

Linn, R. L., & Gronlund, N. E. (2000). *Measurement and assessment in teaching.* (8th ed). Upper Saddle River, NJ: Merrill Prentice Hall.

Popham, W. J. (1990). *Modern educational measurement: A practitioner's perspective.* Upper Saddle River, NJ: Prentice Hall.

Slavin, R. E. (1987). Mastery learning reconsidered. *Review of Educational Research, 57,* 175–213.

Slavin, R. E. (1988). *Educational psychology: Theory into practice.* Upper Saddle River, NJ: Prentice Hall.

Stiggins, R. J., & Bridgeford, N. J. (1985). The ecology of classroom assessment. *Journal of Educational Measurement, 22,* 271–286.

Stiggins, R. J., Frisbie, D. A., & Griswold, P. A. (1989). Inside high school grading practices: Building a research agenda. *Educational Measurement: Issues and Practices, 8*(2), 5–14.

Terwilliger, J. S. (1989). Classroom standard setting and grading practices. *Educational Measurement: Issues and Practices, 8*(2), 15–19.

CHAPTER 8

Aptitude Tests

Introduction
Theories of Cognitive Abilities
    Binet's Theory
    Spearman's g
    Thurstone's Primary Mental Abilities
    Theories of Jensen and Wechsler
    Cattell-Horn Gf-Gc Theory
    Carroll's Three-Stratum Theory
    Sternberg's Triarchic Theory
    Das-Naglieri PASS Model
    Gardner's Proposal
Individual General-Ability Tests
    Stanford-Binet Intelligence Scale, Fourth Edition
    Stanford-Binet Intelligence Scale, Fifth Edition

Wechsler Scales
Woodcock-Johnson Psycho-Educational
    Battery–Third Edition
Das-Naglieri Cognitive Assessment System
Nonverbal Measures of Cognitive Ability
Abbreviated Individual Tests
Group General-Ability Tests
Tests of Multiple Abilities
    Differential Aptitude Test Battery
    General Aptitude Test Battery
Role of General Cognitive Ability: The Bell Curve
Summary
Questions and Exercises
Suggested Readings

INTRODUCTION

An **aptitude test** measures a person's present performance on selected tasks *to provide information that can be used to estimate how the person will perform at some time in the future or in a somewhat different situation.* The situation for which we wish to make a prediction may be school performance, job performance, or some more general adaptation to life's demands. An aptitude test differs somewhat from an achievement test in the tasks that it presents, but the differences are often small and technical. For example, measures of reading comprehension or of arithmetic problem solving may be found in both aptitude and achievement measures. Generally, aptitude measures depend *more* on general life experiences and *less* on specific instruction than do achievement tests, but the differences in content and process being measured are frequently of degree and not of kind. The one respect in which the two classes of tests *do* clearly differ is in the function that they are designed to serve. An achievement test is typically given to find out how much a student has profited from past instruction or what level of knowledge or skill a person possesses; an aptitude test is given to estimate how the examinee is likely to perform in the future. The key difference is one of purpose and function more than content.

The first aptitude tests were designed to assess broad, general cognitive ability, and much of aptitude testing still is, and probably always will be, conducted with the purpose of appraising general ability to carry out cognitive tasks. Subsequently, emphasis shifted somewhat, and a number of tests of more specialized abilities were developed to identify more specific strengths (and weaknesses) in the examinee.

In this chapter, we first examine several of the major theories that have been put forward about the nature of cognitive abilities and then devote our attention to tests that focus on general cognitive ability, those often familiarly labeled "IQ tests." Within the field of general-ability tests, we look first at those that are designed to be given on a one-on-one basis by a trained examiner and then at those designed for group administration. In the next chapter, we will turn our attention to some tests of more specialized abilities, in particular those that are the subject of instruction.

THEORIES OF COGNITIVE ABILITIES

For many centuries, people have recognized individual differences in human cognitive abilities. In *The Republic* Plato recommended that people be assigned places in society based on their cognitive abilities, as well as other characteristics. By the late 19th century Herbert Spencer, a British philosopher, was arguing that general cognitive ability, which he called *intelligence,* was the most important human characteristic and a basis for natural selection. As the 20th century dawned, practitioners of the new science of psychology were being called on to apply their methods to problems of social significance related to the schools and to mental deficiency. As we saw in the first chapter, Alfred Binet was one of the first to provide a practical measurement device. (See R. M. Thorndike, 1990a, or Rogers, 1995, for a description of this period.)

Binet's Theory

The international movement toward universal compulsory education had created in the minds of many educators a need to be able to identify two groups of children: those who *could not* learn because of low ability and those who *would not* learn because of poor motivation or other causes. The first widely acknowledged instrument intended to accomplish this separation was produced in France in 1905 by Alfred Binet and Theodore Simon.

Binet did not really have a theory of mental ability. Rather, he reasoned that cognitive ability developed with age, just as physical abilities did. Also, he felt that intelligence was expressed in the performance of complex mental acts. Therefore, the scale he and Simon devised was composed of a series of mental "puzzles" organized by the sequence in which children could successfully answer them. In the second edition of his instrument in 1908, the tasks he included were grouped into age levels, depending on when the "average" child could accomplish them. The puzzles or tasks at any age level were of several kinds, including two or three short-term memory items (repeats three numbers), some information items (names familiar objects), and some items that required reasoning (arranges scrambled words into a meaningful sentence). Quite different item types might be used at successive ages.

The objective of the Binet-Simon scale was to identify a child's "mental level," or, in modern terminology, *age equivalent.* Binet, however, was not interested in normative comparisons but in what each child actually could do. Thus, he stuck firmly to his concept of mental level, resisting attempts to change it to "mental age."

Although he is considered the founder of modern intelligence measurement, Binet did not offer a theory of cognitive ability. His work was entirely empirical and did not arise out of any theory. He believed that intelligence was a pervasive aspect of the person's functioning, but he did not speculate on how it was structured or operated.

Binet died at a relatively young age in 1911, the year in which the third edition of his test was published. That same year Wilhelm Stern, a German psychologist, introduced the term **intelligence quotient** to represent a child's standing, relative to his or her age-mates. Binet certainly would not have approved, but the deed was done. From then on "IQ" increasingly became part of 20th-century vernacular. As we saw in our discussion of norms in Chapter 3, the term *IQ* no longer has any meaning as a description of how the index should be interpreted. For this reason, and because the term has acquired so much surplus meaning over the years, it should be dropped. The term *intelligence,* however, still has useful meaning, so we will talk about intelligence tests, but not IQ tests. The latter do not exist.

Spearman's *g*

One of the earliest theories of intelligence was proposed by Charles Spearman, a British psychologist and statistician, in 1904. Spearman noted that all of the correlations between measures of cognitive abilities and academic achievements were positive, and this led him to the conclusion that there was a single global mental ability. He called this ability *general intelligence* and argued that its presence in various measures was the cause of the positive correlations between them. In a fully developed version of his **two-factor theory,** published in 1927, Spearman asserted that all measures of mental abilities were composed of two factors, general intelligence, which he called simply *g,* and a factor or ability specific to the particular test, which he called *s.* Thus, the reliable individual differences in a set of test scores could be explained, according to the theory, by the presence of individual differences in *g* and *s.* The remainder was measurement error. Spearman characterized *g* as being like a mental engine; it was the energizer of intelligent behavior. As we shall see, the theory still has many adherents, most notably Arthur Jensen (1998).

Thurstone's Primary Mental Abilities

In the United States Spearman's theory was viewed as too simplistic. Several psychologists, led by E. L. Thorndike and, later, L. L. Thurstone, argued that there were many different and largely independent dimensions of human intelligence. By the 1930s Thurstone was using a statistical technique he had developed, called **common factor analysis,** to identify these dimensions. This line of research culminated in 1938 in his monograph describing the **primary mental abilities,** of which Thurstone claimed there were at least 11 (Thurstone, 1938).

Factor analysis is a procedure that identifies groups of tests that correlate in such a way that they seem to share a common dimension. For example, tests requiring verbal ability tend to correlate more highly with each other than they do with tests of quantitative ability. Likewise, the quantitative ability tests show higher correlations among themselves than they do with tests of verbal or spatial skills. If we include several verbal tests, several quantitative tests, and several spatial tests in a study and examine their correlations using factor analysis, we will find, as we would expect, a dimension corresponding to each of the three types of tests. Factor analysis provides a precise quantitative way of describing these dimensions.

Thurstone argued that these common dimensions or factors were causal properties of behavior in the same sense that Spearman thought of *g* as a mental engine that energized behavior. Thus, although Thurstone was willing to talk about intelligence, he saw it as multidimensional. A person could be high on one dimension, or ability, and intermediate or low on others. However, Thurstone noted that the factors themselves seemed to be positively correlated, and toward the end of his life he came to accept a hierarchical view of intelligence: Something akin to *g* was the cause of the primary factors being correlated, and the primary factors were the cause of the correlations between the tests.

Spearman and Thurstone defined the basic dichotomy for theories of intelligence; was it one thing or many? Their theories and many that were to follow were derived from an examination of test relations and test content and have been called **psychometric** or **structural theories.** If a set of tests all correlated positively, there must be a common underlying cause. The nature of the cause was to be found in examining how the tests were similar in their content or process. For example, if we find positive correlations among a set of tests, all of which require rapid performance of relatively simple tasks, we might conclude that there is an ability (a dimension of intelligence) reflected in speed of performance.

One of the problems with approaching the definition of intelligence in this way is that the selection of tests controls the domain of study. This was made clear in the original Spearman/Thorndike debates from before 1920. If the battery being studied includes one test from each of a wide variety of performance domains (Spearman's approach), a single general factor of ability usually will be found. If, on the other hand, several measures from each domain are included (Thorndike's approach), a factor representing each domain will appear. Thus, the early theories based largely on an analysis of test content have not been very fruitful or satisfying.

Theories of Jensen and Wechsler

Two major contemporary theories of intelligence derive more or less directly from the Spearman and Thorndike/Thurstone traditions. One, epitomized in the work of Arthur Jensen, is based on studies of reaction time required to perform acts of varying complexity and the relationship of such measures to the first general factor found in a battery of diverse tests. It is centered in laboratory research and in studies of the predictive validity of intelligence tests. The other, originating in the work of David Wechsler, derives from a clinical tradition and has focused on the use of patterns of test scores for diagnosis of cognitive difficulties.

Jensen's Theory

In the 1880s Sir Francis Galton argued that reaction time in performing simple acts should measure a person's intelligence. The fact that such measures did not correlate with school grades and other intelligent behaviors shifted attention to the kinds of test tasks Binet was developing. However, beginning in the 1970s a series of studies by Jensen (1982), Hunt (1987), and others showed that stable *negative* correlations existed between various measures of reaction time and scores on complex cognitive tasks.

Computerized timing devices allowed researchers to record different aspects of the time a subject required to react to a stimulus. A typical study might have the subject seated at a console with a series of reaction buttons arranged in an arc around a "home" button. The subject would keep his or her finger on the home button until a light came on, at which time the subject was to move as quickly as possible to one of the other buttons. The simplest task, involving pure reaction with no decision other than that a stimulus had occurred, would be merely to go from Button A to Button B when the light came on. A more complex task would require the subject to go to different buttons, depending on the color of the light. In this case the subject must not only react but also decide which of several reactions to make. The difference between the time it takes to make the first kind of response and the time it takes to make the second is the time required for the cognitive processing of the decision task. The general trend of results from studies like this has been that people who process information faster (i.e., have shorter reaction times) also tend to earn somewhat higher scores on standard tests of intelligence.

What makes results like these interesting, relative to a theory about the nature of intelligence, is the finding Jensen has reported that reaction time measures primarily correlate with what he interprets as Spearman's g in the intelligence tests. That is, in his studies Jensen has found that it is the part of a series of intelligence tests that is common to all of them, which he uses as an approximation to g, that accounts for the correlation between the tests and reaction time. This has led Jensen to conclude that there is a biological basis for individual differences in intelligence that is very general in nature and can be described as differences in the efficiency of the brain for processing information (Jensen, 1991, 1993). Jensen (1998) has recently presented a thorough discussion of the history of g and research supporting its importance in a book titled *The g Factor*.

Further evidence for the presence of a broad cognitive ability that influences performance in a wide variety of areas comes from research on the predictive validity of ability tests. Several authors have reported that almost all of the predictive power of cognitive ability tests for most jobs and training applications is included in the first, or most general, factor of the battery (Gottfredson, 1997; Herrnstein and Murray, 1994; Ree and Earles, 1992; Schmidt and Hunter, 1992).

This theory is still at the level of basic research and has not resulted in any new practical measures of intelligence. However, it, and reactions to it, have created much public debate about the nature of intelligence and the proper use of intelligence tests. We consider some of these effects in our discussion of the book *The Bell Curve* later in this chapter.

Wechsler's Theory

In 1939 David Wechsler, then working as a clinical psychologist at Bellevue Hospital in New York, published a test called the Wechsler-Bellevue to measure the intelligence of adult patients. The test was really a collection of subtests, most of which had been used as group tests of the Alpha and Beta batteries in the military testing program during World War I. Wechsler adapted them for individual administration and divided them into two scales, one composed of the Form Alpha tests that had required the use of language, the other including the language-free tests from Form Beta. The tests from Form Alpha produced a Verbal Scale whose score reflected verbal intelligence (VIQ). The Form Beta tests yielded a score for performance intelligence (PIQ), and the sum of the two subscales gave full-scale intelligence (FSIQ), which Wechsler saw as roughly equivalent to g. Boake (2002) has traced the evolution of the Wechsler-Bellevue from its precursors in tests in use before World War I and shown that Wechsler's contribution was to combine already-existing instruments into a battery rather than to develop new ways to assess cognitive ability.

Spearman would have argued that the Wechsler-Bellevue FSIQ did not measure general intelligence, but rather what he called intelligence-in-general. He defined g as that which is common to diverse cognitive measures. But this is not the same as the sum of scores on the same diverse set of tests. This latter score combines g with all of the specific factors and errors of measurement into a conglomerate with no clear meaning. General intelligence, Spearman argued, can only be assessed by extracting the factor common to all the tests and discarding the specifics and error. For the same reason, he rejected Binet's approach as measuring general intelligence.

Wechsler (1944) defined intelligence as "the aggregate or global capacity of the individual to act purposefully, to think rationally and to deal effectively with his environment" (p. 3). But, his theory was driven by clinical practice. Therefore, patterns in the scores were believed to have clinical significance and could be used to diagnose disorders. The meanings of test scores and patterns of scores evolved over the years to such a degree that the practical theory implied by *test use* is complex and very applied. Wechsler's theory, which is embodied in the use of the three individual intelligence tests that bear his name, is perhaps the most influential current view on the subject and has given rise to thousands of research studies. It is, however, a clinical theory, a guide to the best or most informative use of test scores, rather than a theory about the scientific nature of intelligence. Kaufman (1990) devotes most of 700 pages of densely packed information to a discussion of the applications of the adult form of the Wechsler tests and has given a similar treatment to the children's version (Kaufman, 1994). Sattler (2001) devotes six of his nine chapters on intelligence tests to the Wechsler scales.

Cattell-Horn G_f-G_c Theory

In 1943 Raymond Cattell first proposed the division of cognitive processes into two broad classes based on their interaction with experience. The theory slept for over 20 years while Cattell focused his attention on the study of personality. Then, in 1966, he was joined by John Horn, and his study of intelligence was resumed. The 1966 Horn/Cattell statement identified **fluid intelligence** as a problem-solving and information-processing ability that is largely independent of experience. This ability can be invested in various cognitive activities and leads to the development of knowledge and skills. These latter abilities, which result from the application of fluid intelligence to life experiences, Cattell and Horn called **crystallized intelligence.** Because both of these abilities are broad based and general in nature, they were given the symbols G_f (general fluid ability) and G_c (general crystallized ability). Capital letters were used to distinguish them from Spearman's g.

Over the years, Horn and his colleagues have expanded to nine the number of abilities associated with the theory. Most of these dimensions have been identified by factor analyses of batteries of tests, but they cover a wider variety of tasks and seem more closely attached to biological processes than have previous factorial theories. The nine factors are as follows:

G_f—fluid intelligence—ability to reason in novel situations
G_c—crystallized intelligence—breadth and depth of general knowledge
G_q—quantitative ability—ability to comprehend and manipulate numerical symbols and concepts
G_v—visualization processing—ability to see spatial relationships and patterns
G_a—auditory processing—ability to discriminate sounds and detect sound patterns and relationships
G_s—processing speed—ability to reach quick correct decisions and maintain attention
G_{sm}—short-term memory—ability to hold and use a block of information over a short time span
G_{lr}—long-term retrieval—ability to transfer material to permanent storage and retrieve it later
CDS—correct decision speed—ability to reach correct judgments quickly.

The **Cattell-Horn theory** provides the theoretical basis for two of the most popular tests of cognitive abilities, the Stanford-Binet Fourth Edition and the Woodcock-Johnson Tests of Cognitive

Ability, which are discussed later in this chapter. Increasingly, this theory is influencing development of the Wechsler scales, and it has had a major impact on the structure of the latest version of the Stanford-Binet, the Fifth Edition.

Carroll's Three-Stratum Theory

In a statistical tour de force, John Carroll (1993) undertook to reanalyze the data from more than 400 factor analytic studies of abilities in an effort to find common themes. One of the difficulties in drawing conclusions from studies performed by different investigators was that there has been no common agreement on the appropriate way to conduct a factor analysis. Also, studies seldom shared enough variables to allow reasonable comparisons. Carroll attempted to overcome these problems by going back to the original data and applying a common methodology across all studies and, where possible, matching variables. The result was a hierarchical model similar to Thurstone's, with broad cognitive ability, general intelligence or g, at the top (Stratum III), a small number of general-ability factors similar to those of the Cattell-Horn model at a second level (Stratum II), and a large number of relatively specific factors describing the abilities required for performance on narrower test classifications at the lowest stratum (Stratum I). Recently, Carroll and Horn have emphasized the similarity of G_f-G_c theory and **three-stratum theory** and are calling the combined theory the Cattell-Horn-Carroll (CHC) theory.

Sternberg's Triarchic Theory

Beginning in the 1970s, Robert Sternberg conducted a series of studies that led him to propose a theory that attempts to place intelligence in a unified social, physiological, and psychometric context. He calls his theory a **triarchic theory** because it is composed of three subtheories (Sternberg, 1985).

The first subtheory is a *contextual subtheory,* which proposes that different behaviors will be considered intelligent in different environments. Traditional views of intelligence, Sternberg argues, have all been developed within an academic environment that values a large fund of information and the ability to reason abstractly and symbolically. However, the behaviors and abilities that are valued in nonacademic environments and in other cultures may be quite different. Sternberg has conducted studies of what he calls "street smarts" or "practical intelligence" and other nonacademic adaptive behaviors and has found them to be largely independent of scores on conventional measures of intelligence. This line of argument was anticipated by E. L. Thorndike in 1919. (A small problem with several of these studies is that they have often used college students, a group who are relatively homogeneous in intelligence. This would reduce the apparent relationship between Sternberg's tests and conventional measures of intelligence.)

The second subtheory in Sternberg's system is an *experiential subtheory*. Sternberg argues that a major aspect of intelligence is the ability to automate or routinize behaviors. When a novel situation is encountered, cognitive resources are applied to solve the problems posed by the novelty. The more intelligent person solves these problems more quickly, converting the novel into the familiar and freeing the intellect to deal with other problems. For example, a person visiting a new city for the first time initially has to invest considerable mental capacity in the problems of finding his or her way around. According to Sternberg, the more intelligent person will develop a cognitive map of the area and be able to navigate like a native more quickly than the less intelligent person, thus freeing attention and problem-solving abilities for new experiences.

The third subtheory is called the *componential subtheory*. This theory is similar to the issues considered by Jensen and Hunt in that it attempts to explain how problems are solved and information is processed.

The componential subtheory itself has three classes of components. The first of these are *performance components,* which are involved in attending to stimuli, holding information in working memory, retrieving data from long-term storage, and manipulating information. *Knowledge-acquisition components* function to acquire and store new information by selectively applying the performance components to stimuli. *Metacomponents* serve the managerial function of monitoring the application of performance and knowledge-acquisition components to the solution of a problem.

The triarchic theory holds promise as a model to explain how the human mind functions. At this time, however, no practical intelligence assessment procedures have been developed from the theory. Various tests have been developed for research studies to test elements of the theory, but until such instruments become available in a commercial form, the model will have little clinical or diagnostic application. Brody (2003) has reviewed the available evidence for the tests Sternberg has produced to date and found them lacking. See Sternberg (2003) for a response. In the same journal, Gottfredson (2003) has questioned many of the claims made for the practical implications of the triarchic theory.

Das-Naglieri PASS Model

Another theory that attempts to integrate physiology and information processing is the **PASS theory** of J. P. Das and Jack Naglieri (Das, Naglieri, & Kirby, 1994). Starting from a neurophysiological model of the brain proposed by A. R. Luria, these authors have divided intellectual performance into four basic processes: *Planning, Attention, Simultaneous processing,* and *Successive processing.* The model attempts to relate the four processes to specific neurological structures or areas which Luria called *functional systems* (Das & Naglieri, 2001).

The most basic function is attention. One must be attending to a stimulus in order to process the information it contains or solve the problem it poses. An inability to focus attention is seen as one reason for poor intellectual performance.

Once attention has been directed to a stimulus, the information it contains may require either simultaneous processing or successive processing. Information that is subject to simultaneous processing "is said to be surveyable because the elements are interrelated and accessible to inspection" either directly or from being held in memory (Das et al., 1994, p. 15). Simultaneous processing is involved in language comprehension and other tasks that require perception of the whole problem at once. Successive processing is required whenever the elements of the task must be performed in a particular order. Tasks such as performing skilled movements and serial recall of stimuli are examples of the application of successive processing.

The planning portion of the model is similar to Sternberg's metacomponents in that it is involved in deciding where to focus attention and which type of processing the task requires. The planning process also monitors the success of problem solving and modifies the approach as needed until a solution is achieved. The four processes operate within an existing knowledge base. "This fund of accumulated knowledge can be thought of as the cumulative result of a person's experiences that have been stored in memory. Because all processes operate within the context of knowledge, this base of information influences all cognitive processes and motor programs" (Das et al., 1994, p. 19).

Gardner's Proposal

In 1983 Howard Gardner published a proposal concerning the organization of human abilities which he labeled the **theory of multiple intelligences.** Gardner (1983) identified seven broad areas of human accomplishment in which one could observe individual differences and labeled them all different forms of "intelligences":

1. Linguistic—facility with words
2. Logical-mathematical—abstract reasoning with visual or quantitative material
3. Musical—fluency with tones and auditory material
4. Spatial—ability to see and manipulate spatial relationships
5. Bodily-kinesthetic—gross and fine-motor coordination
6. Interpersonal—ability to deal with others and work effectively in social situations
7. Intrapersonal—self-knowledge.

We mention Gardner's proposal here because it has become widely popular and influential, particularly in education circles, but there are at least two problems with it. First, it is clear that these are all areas of human behavior in which we may observe individual differences, and they are all more or less important and valued competencies. E. L. Thorndike proposed abstract, mechanical, and social intelligences in 1920, but interest has remained focused on the abstract abilities because of their social value. To use the word *intelligence,* as Gardner has, to refer to competencies as diverse and varied in social value as these is to use the term so broadly that it ceases to have any meaning. Gardner is not talking about intelligence in the sense that we are using the term, as cognitive ability. On the other hand, who would be interested in a theory of multiple competencies?

A second problem with Gardner's proposal is that it does not generate testable hypotheses about the organization of these competencies or their relative importance. Gardner does identify different occupations or activities where one or more of these competencies might be of particular value, but that is little more than stating the obvious. To date, there is little substantive research showing that these competencies have more than circular meaning (that is, athletes will be high in bodily-kinesthetic, musicians in musical, and so on).

From the practical point of view, Gardner's proposal also shares with triarchic theory the lack of usable measurement tools with which to assess individuals. Unlike triarchic theory, for which a substantial research base has been developed, the theory of multiple intelligences remains an abstract model. Until a research base and assessment tools are available and shown to have social value, the proposal will remain largely devoid of scientific content or utility.

INDIVIDUAL GENERAL-ABILITY TESTS

As we noted earlier, relatively few of the currently popular intelligence tests have been developed from a particular theory. However, most have been influenced by one theory or another. In this section we describe four widely used measures of cognitive ability and mention briefly a few others. All of these instruments are designed for individual administration by a trained examiner, and in many cases the clinical observations of the examiner during testing form an important part of the assessment report. Our review is far from complete. Sattler (2001) gives much more detail about most of these instruments and covers many more.

Stanford-Binet Intelligence Scale, Fourth Edition

Early Binet-Type Scales

At the time of Binet and Simon's work, Charles Spearman proposed a theory of intelligence that has had a directing influence on the development of all tests of ability. Spearman suggested that there is a single global intellectual function, which he called general intelligence, or *g*, underlying each individual's performance on all tests of ability. Many of the early tests were constructed either with this idea as their theoretical base or in an attempt to refute the theory of general intelligence. The scales that Binet created, and those developed in his intellectual tradition, were generally consistent with the theory of general intelligence, although, as mentioned earlier, Spearman would have called these instruments measures of intelligence-in-general.

Several adaptations of the Binet-Simon scales were published in the United States before 1920, but the version that has survived is the one developed by Lewis Terman in 1916 and known as the Stanford Revision of the Binet-Simon Scales. It has since come to be called the **Stanford-Binet Intelligence Scale,** the Stanford-Binet, or simply the Binet. The Stanford-Binet was extensively revised in the 1930s; two forms of the test, Forms L and M, were produced. In 1960, a third edition, Form LM, was released, which included the best items from the 1937 version. New norms were prepared in 1972, but the test itself was not changed. The first real revision of the test in almost 50 years was published in 1986, the Stanford-Binet Intelligence Scale, Fourth Edition (R. L. Thorndike, Hagen, & Sattler, 1986a, 1986b). A fifth edition, discussed later, was released in 2003.

As originally developed by Terman, and revised by Terman and Maud Merrill, the Stanford-Binet was organized by age levels and consisted of six quite different tests at each age level. Test content also varied from level to level, but collectively the levels included, among others, tasks involving picture and oral vocabulary; memory for objects, sentences, digits, and visual sequences in the form of bead strings; comprehension of what to do in practical situations; analogies; picture and verbal absurdities; similarities and differences; arithmetical problem solving; and sentence completion. In the fourth edition of the Stanford-Binet, the items are grouped by type so that the examinee attempts vocabulary items as one set of tasks, comprehension items as a second, separate set of tasks, and so forth. Most of the original item types were retained, and some new ones were added.

With the first three versions of the Stanford-Binet, the examiner usually started with tests a year or so below the examinee's current age. If all tests at this level were passed, the examiner continued up to the next age level, and so on, until a "ceiling" was reached—an age level at which all the tasks were failed. If one or more tests were failed at the initial entry level, the examiner dropped back until a "basal" age, the highest age at which all the tasks were passed, was found. The examiner then proceeded with testing to determine the child's ceiling. The result was a single score expressing the general ability of the examinee.

A mental age (MA) was determined by taking the basal age and adding to it months of mental age credit for each test passed beyond the basal level. For tests at the 5-year level and below, each test was worth 1 month because the tests were arranged in half-year increments. From Levels 6 through 14, 2 months were awarded for each success. Above that level, the tests received greater weight "in order to make IQs for the upper levels comparable to IQs for the lower age levels" (Terman & Merrill, 1960, p. 62). To illustrate, suppose a child passed all tests at the 6-year level, three at 7 years, one at 8 years, and none beyond that point. Then the mental age would be determined as follows:

Test Performance	Mental Age Credit
Basal age	6 years 0 months
Passed three out of six 7-year tests	6 months
Passed one out of six 8-year tests	2 months
Passed zero out of six 9-year tests	0 months
MA =	6 years 8 months

A normative index of cognitive ability was obtained by relating mental age to chronological age (CA) to yield an intelligence quotient, or IQ. Originally, the procedure was one of division, in which mental age was divided by chronological age. An IQ was obtained using the formula

$$IQ = (MA/CA)100$$

Because the tests were placed so that at each chronological age the average MA was equal to CA, this ratio yielded values with a mean of 100 (hence the origin of the idea that an intelligence quotient of 100 is average) and a standard deviation of about 16 (actual SD values ranged from about 12 to 20 points, depending on age). This **ratio IQ** was used with the first two editions of the instrument. However, since the 1960 revision, the Stanford-Binet has reported results as standard scores, adjusted to yield the same population mean (100) and standard deviation (16) that characterized the old ratio IQ. The use of standard scores equated the meaning of the index at all ages. (The values of 100 and 16 were chosen for continuity with earlier practice.) These standard scores produced nearly the same numerical scale as the original ratio IQs and had the advantage of uniformity for all ages. They also avoided the problem that we pointed out in Chapter 3, namely, that age equivalents become meaningless when the rate of development changes significantly.

The 1986 Stanford-Binet largely avoided the terms *intelligence quotient* and *IQ*, substituting the phrase *standard age score* (SAS) instead. This term is more descriptive of what the index really is, and it is possible that the change in terminology will eventually eliminate some of the connotations that have grown over the years around the term *IQ*. However, the SAS and IQ numerical scales are essentially identical (mean of 100 and standard deviation of 16). The relationship between the SAS of the Stanford-Binet and the percentile rank within the individual's age group is approximately as follows:

Stanford-Binet SAS	Percentile Rank
130	97
120	89
110	73
100	50
90	27
80	11
70	3

Subtests of the Stanford-Binet

The 1986 revision of the Stanford-Binet is composed of many of the same item types as the earlier editions, but as already noted, the items are grouped by type into 15 subtests. The items are graded in difficulty from extremely simple items appropriate for below-average 2-year-olds up to items of a high level of difficulty. There are two items at each level of difficulty. The 15 types of items included in the current form of the Stanford-Binet are listed and briefly described here. They may be combined to yield four ability scales or an overall measure of cognitive ability. Not all subtests are administered at all ages.

Verbal Reasoning Tests

1. *Vocabulary* (23 levels—test given at all ages). At the seven lowest levels, items are pictures that the examinee is required to name. In the 16 higher levels, words are presented, and the examinee must tell what each word means.

2. *Comprehension* (21 levels—test given at all ages). The three lowest levels require the examinee to point to named parts of a picture of a unisex, ethnically ambiguous child. The higher levels ask the examinee the why of things, starting with why people use umbrellas and going up to why it is advantageous to be able to amend a constitution.

3. *Absurdities* (16 levels—test given from age 2 years to about age 14 years). Each item consists of a picture that definitely has something wrong with it (e.g., a bicycle with square wheels or a person with two right hands). The examinee must tell what is wrong—what is "silly" in the picture.

4. *Verbal Relations* (9 levels—test begun at about age 11 years). This test calls for identification of the basis on which three terms are alike but are different from a fourth term. An easy item might read

cat fox horse but *not* pigeon

Abstract/Visual Reasoning Tests

5. *Pattern Analysis* (21 levels—test given at all ages). The lowest levels of this test use a three-hole form board that looks like this one:

The subject must replace the pieces in the holes. Difficulty is increased by rotating the board and by dividing the three pieces into halves.

Higher levels of analysis are based on an adaptation of the classic Kohs Blocks test. Each block is a black and white cube with a different design on each face. The six faces are displayed here:

Starting with the task of the examinee matching the face of the block shown by the examiner, the test progresses to assembling from two to nine blocks to produce a design, such as those shown here:

6. *Copying* (14 levels—test given from age 2 years to about age 8 years). The lowest levels require matching the arrangements of two or three blocks presented by the examiner. The higher levels call on the child to copy a simple figure, such as the ones displayed here:

7. *Matrices* (13 levels—test begun at about age 6 years). The examinee is presented with an incomplete matrix and is required to select the correct entry to complete the matrix. A relatively simple item might look like this:

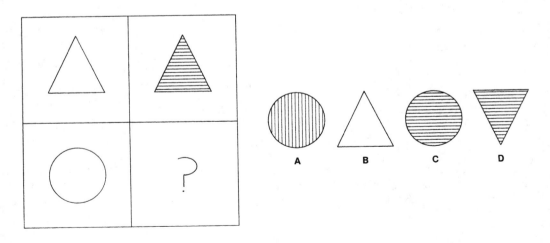

8. *Paper Folding and Cutting* (9 levels—test begun at about age 11 years). The examinee is presented with a demonstration of how a rectangle of paper has been folded and one or more pieces cut out of it. The examinee must indicate how the paper will look when unfolded. A relatively simple item is illustrated here:

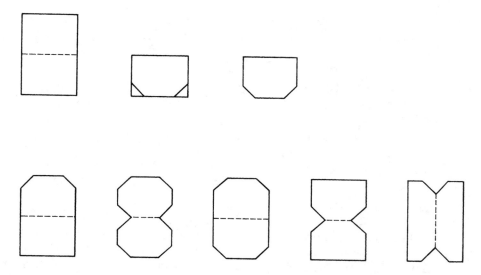

Quantitative Reasoning

9. *Quantitative* (20 levels—test given at all ages). The easiest items involve counting and adding or subtracting the spots on what are essentially dice. From this task, the test goes to a series of pictures, each involving a quantitative question, graded in difficulty. An early item might read, "These are Mary's six marbles. If she gave three to Jane, how many would be left?"

10. *Number Series* (13 levels—test begun at about age 6 years). Sequences of numbers are presented, and the examinee is required to state the two numbers that should come next. A very easy and a more difficult item are shown here.

3 4 5 6 7	_____ _____	(answer 8, 9)
4 6 5 8 6 10	_____ _____	(answer 7, 12)

11. *Equation Building* (9 levels—test begun at about age 11 years). This test presents the examinee with a set of numerals and operational signs. The examinee is required to rearrange the elements to produce a true number sentence, or equation. Again, a very easy item and a more difficult one are illustrated here.

2 2 4 − =	(answer $4 - 2 = 2$)
$\frac{1}{2}$ 1 5 7 − × ( ) =	(answer $(7 - 5) \times \frac{1}{2} = 1$)

For the more complex items in this test there may be more than one correct answer. The examiner's guide gives some, but not necessarily all of the correct alternatives.

Short-Term Memory Tests

12. *Memory for Sentences* (21 levels—test given at all ages). The examiner reads a sentence to the examinee, who is instructed to repeat it exactly as it was read. The test starts with two-word sentences, at the lowest level, and progresses to top-level sentences of more than 20 words.

13. *Bead Memory* (21 levels—test given at all ages). The test involves a stack of beads of four shapes and three colors. At the lowest levels, the examinee is shown a bead for 2 seconds and then

must find it on a card showing beads with all the shapes and colors. For most of the test, the examinee has 5 seconds to look at the picture of a stalk with a sequence of beads on it and then must, from memory, correctly reproduce the sequence on his or her own stalk.

14. *Memory for Digits* (7 levels forward, 6 levels reversed—test begun at about age 6 years). The examiner reads a sequence of digits at a rate of approximately one per second. In the first section of the test, the examinee must repeat the digits in the order that they are read. In the second section, the examinee must recite them in reverse order.

15. *Memory for Objects* (7 levels—test begun at about age 6 years). A sequence of pictures of objects is shown to the examinee, one at a time. Then a picture is shown that includes all the objects that were shown in the series, plus several others. The examinee must point to all objects that had been shown to him or her in the order that they were shown.

Organization of the Stanford-Binet

The fourth edition of the Stanford-Binet represents a marked shift from the theoretical position held by Binet and Terman. Until 1986, the Stanford-Binet yielded only a single global score for general intelligence. The fourth edition is grounded in the much more recent G_f–G_c theory of Cattell and Horn. The tests of this Stanford-Binet are organized to yield scores in four areas, or broad dimensions, of ability. The vocabulary, comprehension, absurdities, and verbal relations tests are combined to yield an area score for *verbal reasoning*. Pattern analysis, copying, matrices, and paper folding and cutting are summed to give an *abstract/visual reasoning* area score. A *quantitative reasoning* area score is derived from the combination of the quantitative, number series, and equation-building tests. Finally, the four memory tests yield an area score for *short-term memory*. The verbal-reasoning and quantitative-reasoning scales are intended to represent the crystallized abilities of the Cattell-Horn theory and may be combined to give a score for such abilities, while abstract/visual reasoning is seen as a fluid ability. The short-term memory area score is an indicator of G_{sm}. When all four area scores are combined, the resulting composite score is essentially equivalent to the general intellective dimension measured by earlier forms of the Stanford-Binet.

Administration of the Stanford-Binet IV (SB-IV) is somewhat more complex than its predecessors. Testing starts with the vocabulary test, and the examiner begins with the items at or just below the examinee's chronological age. (A basal level is defined as the point where the child passes both items at two successive ages.) Then, more difficult items are given until the point is reached where three out of four or all four items at two successive ages are failed, which yields a ceiling. The raw score is determined by giving credit for all items below the basal level and one additional point for each item attempted and passed. The vocabulary score and the child's age are then used to determine a starting point for each of the remaining tests. A basal level and a ceiling are found for each test in the same manner as that used for vocabulary. (See Sattler, 2001, for a detailed description of how to administer the later tests.)

A raw score is assigned in each subtest administered, giving the examinee credit for having passed all the easier items below the basal level. Raw scores on each of the subtests are then converted to normalized standard scores for that age level, using tables in the examiner's manual. The individual subtest standard scores have a mean of 50 and a standard deviation of 8. These can be combined to yield the four area scores and a composite of all of the subtests. The scores for areas and for the total are expressed as SASs—normalized standard scores for that age level—with a mean of 100 and a standard deviation of 16.

The composite standard age score has many of the same properties as the mental age and IQ of the earlier versions of the Stanford-Binet. However, it is also possible to work with the four area scores: verbal reasoning, abstract/visual reasoning, quantitative reasoning, and short-term memory. These area scores are all related to one another and contribute to the overall measure, but they are sufficiently distinct so that each describes a somewhat different aspect of a person's cognitive functioning.

In the fourth edition of the Stanford-Binet, a major effort was made to adapt the testing to the ability level of the person being tested, so that the tasks presented are closely matched to his or her ability level. This adaptation is accomplished by using the vocabulary **routing test** to determine, in combination with chronological age, the level at which the examinee is likely to succeed. Thus, the intent is to bracket the examinee's ability level as efficiently as possible to minimize time wasted on items that are too easy for the examinee and frustration on items that are too hard.

Even though the individual tests of the Stanford-Binet are quite short, they are reasonably reliable. Median KR-20 reliabilities computed within age groups for the individual tests run from 0.73 to 0.94, with all but memory for objects—which has fewer levels than any other subtest—exceeding 0.83. Within-age-group reliabilities for the area scores are higher, and the composite score based on four area scores generally yields a KR-20 reliability in excess of 0.95.

The individual tests show moderate to high correlations with each other. Median within-age-group correlations in the standardization data range from .29 between paper folding and cutting and memory for objects, to .73 between vocabulary and comprehension, with most of the correlations in the 30s, 40s, and 50s. In general, the tests within an area correlate more highly with other tests in the same area than they do with tests in other areas. The area scores all correlate in the 60s and 70s with each other, indicating that they measure somewhat discrete concepts that share a common core. These correlations are consistent with the theory that guided the development of the instrument. Independent analyses of the standardization data for the Stanford-Binet (Boyle, 1989; R. M. Thorndike, 1990b) have confirmed that the individual tests generally relate to each other in the manner predicted by the theory used in test development.

Stanford-Binet Intelligence Scale, Fifth Edition

In February 2003, the fifth edition of the Stanford-Binet Intelligence Scale (SB5) (Roid, 2003) was released. There is a clear filial relationship between the SB5 and the SB-IV, but there are also significant changes. The instrument yields scores for five factors rather than four, each based on one verbal test and one nonverbal test. Four additional scores can be obtained, a verbal IQ, a nonverbal IQ, a full scale IQ, and an abbreviated scale IQ. The arrangement of tests and the scores they yield are listed in Table 8–1.

Like the SB-IV, the SB5 uses a routing test procedure to fine tune where testing should start on subsequent subtests for an examinee. The nonverbal fluid reasoning test and the vocabulary test, which also make up the short form of the instrument, comprise the routing test. Each of the other tests is divided into five or six levels, and testing of examinees begins at the level indicated by their score on the routing tests.

A major difference between the SB5 and its immediate predecessor is that when the full battery is given after the routing tests, all nonverbal tests are administered, then all verbal tests are administered. The SB-IV mixed subtest types. An even bigger difference, and a return to the style of earlier Binets, is that at each level of testing all four types of nonverbal items are given before moving to the next level. For example, if testing is to start at level 3, the nonverbal knowledge, quantitative reasoning, visual-spatial processing and working memory tests for level 3 are

Table 8–1
Full Scale IQ[a]

Nonverbal IQ[b]	Factor Indices[c]	Verbal IQ[b]

Fluid reasoning (36 items)[d]
    Object series/matrices
	Fluid reasoning	Fluid reasoning (5 levels)
		    Early reasoning (2–3)
		    Verbal absurdities (4)
		    Verbal analogies (5–6)

Knowledge (5 levels)
    Procedural knowledge (2–3)
    Picture absurdities (4–6)
	Knowledge	Vocabulary (44 items)[d]
		    Items 15–44 worth 1 or 2 points
		    depending on quality of answer

Quantitative reasoning (5 levels)
    Various item types at each level
	Quantitative reasoning	Quantitative reasoning (5 levels)
		    Various item types at each level

Visual-spatial processing (6 levels)
    Form board (levels 1–2)
    Pattern analysis (levels 3–6)
	Visual-spatial processing	Visual-spatial processing (5 levels)
		    Relative position (levels 2–3)
		    Directions (levels 4–6)

Working memory
    Spatial and numerical sequences
    (levels 2–6)
	Working memory	Working memory
		    Word/sentence memory
		    (levels 2–3) Last word memory
		    (levels 4–6)

[a]Full scale IQ is computed from the sum of scaled scores for verbal IQ and nonverbal IQ.
[b]Nonverbal and verbal IQs are computed from the sum of scaled scores on the five subtests in their columns.
[c]The five factor indices are computed from the sum of the two scaled scores in their rows.
[d]The two routing tests are not structured into levels.

administered before any level 4 tests are given. After all of the nonverbal tests have been completed, the verbal tests are given in the same manner. In our example, the verbal fluid reasoning, quantitative reasoning, visual-spatial processing, and working memory items at level 3 would be administered before moving to level 4 of the verbal tests. In the SB-IV, each subtest was completed before another item type was introduced.

Another change from traditional Binet practice is the use of differential scoring for some items. The last 30 vocabulary items and various items on other subtests can be scored 0 (wrong), 1 (OK but not perfect) or 2 (exactly right or showing a higher level of abstraction). The Wechsler scales (see below) have used differential scoring throughout their history, but it is a new practice for the Binet. The publisher's reliability estimates (factor scores and IQs in the 90s and subtests in the 80s) suggest that allowing examiners to judge the quality of responses has not hurt the tests' accuracy, but this may be due, in part to the high level of training of the examiners in the standardization studies. Reliability may be lower in field use.

The new Binet is also appropriate for a wider age range than previously. Norms are provided for children as young as 24 months and go up to age 90. There were 4,800 people in the nationally representative norming sample. Norms tables are provided for 2-month intervals up to age 5,

4-month intervals from ages 5 through 16, and coarser intervals, but never more than 5 years, thereafter. This is a significant improvement over past practice, where a norms table might cover half a year or more.

The publisher's studies indicate that the cognitive ability constructs measured by the SB5 are similar to the cognitive abilities measured by earlier editions of the Binet and by the various Wechsler scales. Full-scale IQ correlations are in the .80s and appropriate subscale correlations with the SB-IV are .64 or higher. Correlations with homologous Wechsler IQs are all .66 or higher.

An exciting change in the new Binet is the availability of "change-sensitive scores." At a conference in 1997 I issued a call for test publishers to abandon the IQ scale in favor of a scale based on IRT methods (R. M. Thorndike, 1999a). E. L. Thorndike had produced a prototype of such a test in 1926, but the idea did not catch on due to computational difficulties and opposition by entrenched testing interests. It appears that the publishers of the Binet have gone halfway to my goal by introducing IRT-based score metrics for the nine scores one can obtain from the test. However, they also abandoned the "standard age score" of the SB-IV and returned to the *IQ* label for the scales. This is unfortunate because, as we saw in Chapter 3, the term *IQ* either has no meaning or has surplus meaning.

There is one other reservation that we must note in considering the SB5. The test manual (Roid, 2003) reports "confirmatory" factor analyses of the 10 scales that were able to produce the five factor indices the test claims to measure. The publisher cites these findings as evidence of the construct validity of the factor index scores. When I replicated the publisher's analysis method exactly, I was able to replicate their result. However, when I used less restrictive factor methods, such as those employed by Carroll (1993), in an attempt to recover the same five dimensions of performance, I was only able to find factors corresponding to the verbal dimension and the non-verbal dimension (Thorndike, 2003). The fact that the hypothesized 5-dimensional structure can only be replicated using very specific (and powerful) procedures causes me to question the validity of the five factor index scores. Until there is independent confirmation of this claimed structure and interpretation, I cannot recommend use of the factor index scores for applied work.

Wechsler Scales

The other senior series of individually administered tests of general ability is the Wechsler series, the first of which, the Wechsler-Bellevue, was published in 1939. Periodically, the tests have been extended and revised. The series currently is composed of three test levels: the **Wechsler Preschool and Primary Scale of Intelligence–Third Edition** (WPPSI-III) (Wechsler,* 2002), the **Wechsler Intelligence Scale for Children–Third Edition** (WISC-III) (Wechsler, 1991a), and the **Wechsler Adult Intelligence Scale–Third Edition** (WAIS-III) (Wechsler, 1997). These are intended for ages 2-6 (2 years, 6 months) to 7-3, 6-0 to 16-11, and 16-0 and above, respectively. The scales were developed from the start as sets of subtests, each containing items graded in difficulty. They were also designed from the beginning to produce two subscores (verbal IQ and performance IQ), as well as an overall ability score (full-scale IQ). (The Wechsler literature still uses the term *IQ,* so we will use it also in our discussion of these instruments.) The titles of the subtests from the WISC-III (Wechsler, 1991a), together with their subscale arrangement and an illustrative item (similar to those included in the actual test) are

---

*All of the Wechsler tests are produced by the staff of the Psychological Corporation. David Wechsler died in 1981. Some of the tests that bear his name were not even developed until years after his death.

shown here. In an actual testing situation more detailed instructions would be given. (A fourth edition of the WISC has recently been released. Changes from the WISC-III are described below.)

Verbal Scale

1. *General Information.* What day of the year is Independence Day?
2. *Similarities.* In what way are wool and cotton alike?
3. *Arithmetic Reasoning.* If eggs cost 60 cents a dozen, what does 1 egg cost?
4. *Vocabulary.* What does *corrupt* mean?
5. *Comprehension.* Why do people buy fire insurance?
6. *Digit Span.* I am going to say some numbers. Listen carefully, and when I am through, say the numbers right after me.

7   3   4   1   8   6

Now, I am going to say some more numbers, but this time when I stop, I want you to say them backward.

3   8   4   1   6

Digit span is an optional subtest on the Verbal Scale.

Performance Scale

7. *Picture Completion.* I am going to show you some pictures. In each there is an important part missing. Tell me what is missing.

					2003	
S	**M**	**T**	**W**	**T**	**F**	**S**
		1	2	3	4	5
6	7	8	9	10	11	12
13	14	15	16	17	18	19
20	21	22	23	24	25	26
27	28	29	30	31		

8. *Picture Arrangement.* The pictures below tell a story. Put them in the right order to tell the story.

9. *Block Design.* Using the four blocks that I have given you, make a design just like this one.

10. *Object Assembly.* If these pieces are put together correctly, they will make something. Go ahead and put them together as quickly as you can.

11. *Coding.* In the top row, each figure is shown with a number. Fill in the number that goes with each figure in the second row.

Code

△	○	▱	✕	8
1	2	3	4	5

Test

△	8	✕	○	△	▱	8	✕	△	8	etc.

12. *Symbol Search.* See this shape (on the left). Now look at these shapes (on the right). Are any of these shapes the same as this one? If any of them are the same, mark *yes,* if none of them are the same as this shape, mark *no.*

13. *Mazes.* This subtest includes pencil mazes like those found in newspapers.

Symbol Search and Mazes are optional subtests in the Performance Scale.

Each subtest of a scale yields a separate score, which is then converted into a normalized standard score with a mean of 10 and a standard deviation of 3 for that subtest, based on a sample of individuals of the same age as the examinee. The subtest standard scores are combined in three different groupings to yield total scores for verbal, performance, and overall abilities, and from these total scores, three different types of IQ may be read from norm tables. The three IQs are (1) a verbal IQ (VIQ) from subtests 1 through 6, (2) a performance IQ (PIQ) from subtests 7 through 13, and (3) a total IQ (full-scale IQ, or FSIQ) from the combined VIQ and PIQ.

In addition to the three basic scales, the manuals for the WISC-III and WAIS-III (but, as of this writing, not the WPPSI-III) allow for computing four index scores derived from factor analyses of the subtests. For the WISC-III these are a *Verbal Comprehension* (VC) score based on Information, Similarities, Vocabulary and Comprehension; a *Perceptual Organization* (PO) score obtained from Picture Completion, Picture Arrangement, Block Design, and Object Assembly; a *Freedom from Distractability* (FD) score from Arithmetic and Digit Span; and a *Processing Speed* (PS) score composed of Coding and Symbol Search. On the WAIS-III a *Working Memory* index is substituted for FD. The separate verbal and performance scores may have diagnostic significance in the case of certain individuals with verbal, academic, or cultural handicaps; however, such interpretations should be made only by individuals with extensive clinical training. (See Hildebrand and Ledbetter, 2001, for a discussion of these issues.) Studies of the value of such diagnoses have yielded conflicting results. The value of the four index scores is a topic of debate in the professional community. The verbal, performance, and overall IQ scores on the WPPSI-III and WAIS-III are also transformed standard scores. The scale on all the Wechsler instruments is set to make the mean of the normative sample 100 and the standard deviation 15.

The Wechsler scales report internal consistency reliabilities generally in the 90s for the individual subtests. Test–retest reliabilities are somewhat lower, but generally in the 80s. Correlations of the verbal and performance Wechsler IQs with the area standard age scores of the Stanford-Binet IV are all above .60 except for correlations of the WPPSI scales with abstract/visual reasoning. Wechsler full-scale IQs correlate from .80 to .91 with the Stanford-Binet IV composite (R. L. Thorndike, Hagen, & Sattler, 1986a). Thus, although the two instruments were independently developed, they yield a consistent assessment of general intellectual ability.

WISC-IV

The WISC-IV has dropped the Mazes and Picture Arrangement subtests and abandoned the Verbal and Performance IQs in favor of the four factor index scores described for the WISC-III. Full-scale IQ has been retained. Five subtests have been added to the instrument to better measure the four factors. These are Word Reasoning (the child is required to identify an underlying concept from verbal cues), Matrix Reasoning (similar to the matrix items on the SB-IV), Picture Concepts (the child identifies objects that share some property), Letter-Number Sequencing (a working memory test that requires the child to reorganize letters and numbers and repeat them back to the examiner), and Cancellation (the child must mark animal objects that have a particular property). Other aspects of the test remain the same.

Woodcock-Johnson Psycho-Educational Battery–Third Edition

A battery of tests that attempts to measure both intelligence and achievement is the **Woodcock-Johnson Psycho-Educational Battery–Third Edition** (WJ-III) (Woodcock, McGrew, & Mather, 2001). This instrument is derived directly from the Cattell-Horn-Carroll model and purports to measure eight of the nine factors listed for that theory (Correct Decision Speed is omitted). Like the Stanford-Binet, the WJ-III provides a single instrument for use at all ages. The cognitive portion of the battery (WJ-III COG) contains 20 subtests measuring seven CHC factors, with varying numbers of tests being given at different ages. Quantitative ability is measured by tests from the achievement part of the battery (WJ-III ACH). There are 22 achievement tests measuring skills in oral language, reading, mathematics, written language, and general knowledge. The subtests and broad ability factors they measure are listed in Table 8–2. Note that tests intended to measure G_c are included in both portions of the battery.

One of the basic objectives of the WJ-III is to provide a combined set of aptitude and achievement tests normed on a single sample so that discrepancies between aptitude and achievement can be used for diagnosis of educational problems. The tests are normed on large samples, ranging in age from 2 years to over 90 (a total of more than 8,800 cases). This is clearly one of the most ambitious efforts at wide-range norms ever undertaken for an individually administered test.

Reliability estimates for the WJ-III are quite satisfactory. Individual subtest internal consistency reliabilities range from .76 to .97 with a median of .87. Reliabilities for the seven scales of the CHC model run from .81 to .95, and the reliability reported for the General Intellectual Ability (GIA) index is .97 for the standard battery (.98 for the extended battery). The GIA correlates in the 60s and 70s with other measures of general intelligence.

Das-Naglieri Cognitive Assessment System

One of the newest members of the growing family of individually administered intelligence tests is the Das-Naglieri Cognitive Assessment System (CAS), which attempts to operationalize the PASS model of cognitive functioning. The instrument includes three subtests to measure each of the four elements in the model (12 tests in all). Two subtests for each function are included in the Basic Battery, and the Standard Battery adds one more. The tests and their arrangement are as follows (the first two tests for each function are included in the Basic Battery).

Planning

Matching Numbers—Examinees underline the two numbers in each row that are the same.
Planned Codes—Similar to the Coding subtest of the WISC-III.
Planned Connections—Examinees connect numbers or numbers and letters in a specified order.

Attention

Expressive Attention—Examinees identify words or pictures when there is interference (such as the word *red* printed in blue).
Number Detection—Examinees must circle numbers that have a special feature (e.g., boldface print) and not circle numbers that do not have this feature.
Receptive Attention—Examinees must circle pairs of letters that share a common feature (either physical identity [KK but not KP] or lexical identity [Aa but not Ab]).

Table 8–2
Distribution of the Woodcock-Johnson Subtests to Ability and Achievement Factors

General Function	Cognitive Battery			Achievement Battery		
	Broad Factor	Standard Battery Test	Extended Battery Test	Broad Factor	Standard Battery Test	Extended Battery Test
Verbal Ability	Verbal Comprehension/ Knowledge (G_c)	Verbal Comprehension	General Information	Oral Language (G_c)	Story Recall (R)	Picture Vocabulary
					Understanding Directions (R)	Oral Comprehension (R)
				Knowledge (G_c)		Academic Knowledge
Thinking Abilities	Long-Term Retrieval (G_{lr})	Visual-Auditory Learning	Retrieval Fluency (T)		Story Recall-Delayed (S)	
		Visual-Auditory Learning-Delayed (S)				
	Visual-Spatial Thinking (G_v)	Spatial Relations	Picture Recognition			
	Auditory Processing (G_a)	Sound Blending (R)	Auditory Attention (R)			Spelling of Sounds (R) (S)
		Incomplete Words (R) (S)				Sound Awareness (R) (S)
	Fluid Reasoning (G_f)	Concept Formation	Analysis-Synthesis Planning (S)			
Cognitive Efficiency	Processing Speed (G_s)	Visual Matching (T)	Decision Speed (T)			
			Rapid Picture Naming (T) (S)			
			Pair Cancellation (T) (S)			
	Short-Term Memory (G_{sm})	Numbers Reversed (R)	Memory for Words (R)			
		Auditory Working Memory (R) (S)				

Domain	Cluster	Test	Test
Reading (G_{rw})	Basic Reading Skills	Letter-Word Identification	Word Attack
	Reading Fluency	Reading Fluency (T)	
	Reading Comprehension	Passage Comprehension	Reading Vocabulary
Written Language (G_{rw})	Basic Writing Skills	Spelling	Editing
	Writing Fluency	Writing Fluency (T)	Punctuation & Capitalization (S)
	Written Expression	Writing Sample	
Mathematics (G_q)	Math Calculation Skills	Calculation	
	Math Fluency	Math Fluency (T)	
	Math Reasoning	Applied Problems	Quantitative Concepts

Note: (R) = recorded, (S) = supplemental test, (T) = timed.

Simultaneous Processing

Nonverbal Matrices—Similar to the Raven's Progressive Matrices (see below).
Verbal-Spatial Relations—Examinees match a verbal description with the picture it describes.
Figure Memory—After seeing a geometric figure, examinees must trace the figure within a more complex geometric design.

Successive Processing

Word Series—Similar to the Memory for Digits subtest of the Stanford-Binet, but using single syllable words instead of numbers.
Sentence Repetition—Examiner reads sentences in which color words are substituted for parts of speech (e.g., "Black is bluing the green"). Examinees must repeat the sentence exactly.
Sentence Questions—Examinees must answer questions based on sentences like the ones in Sentence Repetition (e.g., "Who is being blued?" Answer: Green). With examinees under the age of 8, a speech rate test is used here. Examinees must repeat a three-word sentence 10 times.

Six of the subtests require precise timing, either for stimulus presentation or for speed of response. For several tests, the score is number of seconds to complete the task.

Scaled scores based on a norm sample of 1,100 boys and 1,100 girls between the ages of 5 and 17 have a mean of 10 and standard deviation of 3 for the individual subtests. Full-scale scores have a mean of 100 and standard deviation of 15. The test authors report internal consistency reliabilities for the 12 subtests ranging from .75 to .89 with a median of .82. Reliabilities for the four scales range from .88 to .93, and the reliability of the full scale is about .96. Test–retest reliabilities over a period of about 21 days averaged .73 for the subtests and .82 for the full-scale scores. Das and Naglieri (2001) give an example of how the CAS can be used in diagnosis of learning disabilities.

Nonverbal Measures of Cognitive Ability

The importance of language in the measurement of intelligence has been a concern ever since the earliest efforts to develop measures. Before World War I, Porteus had developed a series of visual mazes to test cognitive ability without the use of language, and during the war, psychologists working for the U.S. army formulated a battery of nonverbal tests designed to be used with recruits who could not read or had limited proficiency in English. Wechsler included subtests in his scales that were based on these army tests. In this section we describe two tests that have been designed to measure cognitive abilities without the use of language, one a tried and true veteran and the other of very recent origin.

Raven's Progressive Matrices

The original version of this test was published by J. C. Raven in 1938 to measure the higher level abilities implied by Spearman's theory of intelligence. That is, this test is intended as a measure of g. Jensen (1998) considers Raven's test to be an almost pure measure of g, so much so that it is used as a marker for g in factor analyses of batteries of tests. Because it is untimed (examinees can work as long as they wish) it is considered a *power test* to assess the highest level an individual can reach rather than a *speed test* to see how fast one can solve problems. All items are in what is called a **matrix format,** and the test is progressive in the sense that the items get harder as one proceeds through the test. Examinees select their responses from a set of up to eight alternatives.

At the simplest level, items in the test require pattern recognition. A stimulus page is shown with a section cut out and the examinee's task is to select the alternative that fits. An example might look like this:

Raven's Progressive Matrices
Sample 1

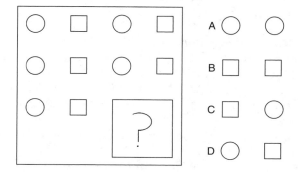

The general form of a matrix item is that stimuli are arranged in two dimensions and features of the stimuli change in two or more regular patterns. A simple item in which two stimulus features change, one by rows and the other by columns, is shown for the Matrices subtest of the Stanford-Binet on page 250. A more complex item would have anywhere from three to five features of the stimulus changing by rows, columns, diagonals, or in a circular pattern. An item might look like this:

Raven's Progressive Matrices
Sample 2

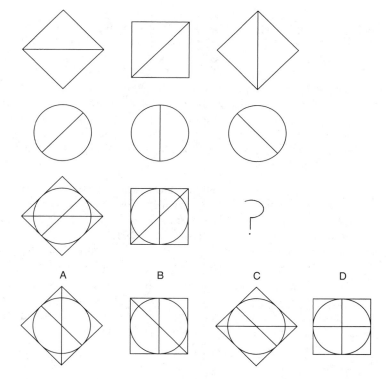

Norms for the Raven's Progressive Matrices test have not been systematically developed for a representative sample of the American population, and since the test yields only a global cognitive ability score, it is most useful for general screening and research applications rather than clinical diagnosis. Reliability estimates generally are in the .80s, but depend on the variability of the group being tested.

Universal Nonverbal Intelligence Test

In 1998 Bruce Bracken and Steve McCallum introduced the Universal Nonverbal Intelligence Test (UNIT) "to measure fairly the general intelligence and cognitive abilities of children and adolescents from ages 5 through 17 years who may be disadvantaged by traditional verbal and language-loaded measures" (p. 1). The test has six subtests, three of which are described as tests utilizing memory processes and three as reasoning processes. The subtests are additionally classified as being symbolic or nonsymbolic in content. The six tests are classified as follows:

	Reasoning Subtests	Memory Subtests
Symbolic Subtests	Analogic Reasoning	Symbolic Memory
		Object Memory
Nonsymbolic Subtests	Cube Design	Spatial Memory
	Mazes	

This two-way classification of the tests produces five possible scores, which, unfortunately, the authors refer to as quotients; a memory quotient (which is essentially the G_{sm} factor in the Cattell-Horn-Carroll model), a reasoning quotient, a symbolic quotient, a nonsymbolic quotient, and a full-scale intelligence quotient. The authors recommend the test for a wide variety of clinical applications, including individuals with hearing impairments, persons from other than the majority culture, and individuals with limited English proficiency. All instructions for the test are given in pantomime and responses are made by pointing or by manipulating objects. Because the test stimuli and, indeed, the testing process, are assumed to be unfamiliar to examinees, practice items are provided for each subtest. The general item forms of the various subtests are as follows.

1. *Symbolic Memory.* The examinee is given 10 tiles. Each tile has the international symbol for a man, woman, male child, female child, or baby on it in either black or green. The examinee is then shown a card with one or more (up to six) figures in a particular order for 5 seconds. As soon as the stimulus card is removed, the examinee is instructed by hand signals to use the tiles to reproduce the sequence. This test is similar to the Bead Memory test from the Stanford-Binet, but with fewer variables (five shapes, two colors).

2. *Cube Design.* The examinee is given up to nine cubes with two white faces, two green faces, and two diagonally white and green faces. A stimulus picture is presented and the examinee is instructed to replicate the design. The difference between this test and Block Design from the WISC-III is that the designs may be three dimensional.

3. *Spatial Memory.* The examinee is given 16 chips, 8 black and 8 green, and a response grid that is either 3×3 (items 1–11) or 4×4 (items 12–27). A stimulus card is presented for 5 seconds

and then removed. As soon as the card is removed the examinee is instructed to place chips of the correct color in the correct squares of the grid to replicate the pattern on the card.

4. *Analogic Reasoning.* This test consists of matrix items similar to those in the Raven's Progressive Matrices test or the Matrices subtest of the Stanford-Binet. There are 31 items.

5. *Object Memory.* Similar to the Stanford-Binet Memory for Objects subtest. The examinee is shown a picture containing from one to seven objects for 5 seconds. The picture is removed and a second picture with the same objects plus some others is presented. The examinee places chips on the pictures of the objects that were in the first stimulus array.

6. *Mazes.* Similar to the Mazes subtest of the WISC-III. The examinee is shown a picture of a mouse in a maze with one or more pieces of cheese outside the maze. The task is to trace a path from the mouse to the correct piece of cheese, the one that can be reached without crossing one of the lines in the maze.

The UNIT was normed on a nationally representative sample of 2,100 children and adolescents between the ages of 5 years 0 months and 17 years 11 months 30 days. Norms are presented for an Abbreviated Battery composed of the Symbolic Memory and Cube Design subtests that is appropriate for screening (yields only a full-scale IQ); a Standard Battery, which adds Spatial Memory and Analogic Reasoning and provides scores on all five test dimensions; and an Extended Battery of all six tests. Average within-age reliabilities as reported in the test manual range from .64 (mazes) to .91 (cube design) for the subtests, .91 for full-scale IQ from the Abbreviated Battery, from .87 (symbolic IQ) to .94 (full-scale IQ) for the Standard Battery, and from .88 (reasoning IQ) to .93 (full-scale IQ) for the Extended Battery. Reliabilities reported for clinical samples are higher. In general, the UNIT scales show appropriate correlations with various scores derived from the WISC-III, including a correlation of .88 between full-scale IQ on the two instruments.

Abbreviated Individual Tests

A major problem in using individually administered tests of aptitude is that they are very costly. A trained examiner must spend at least an hour with each examinee. This costliness has led to three responses: the development of group-administered tests such as those described in the next section, the use of short forms of standard tests in which only some of the tests are given (note that the SB5, CAS, and WJ-III have basic and extended testing options), and the preparation of some short individual tests.

Various short forms of the Wechsler scales have been proposed. Sattler (2001) provides tables listing the various subsets of subtests that have been used for special situations and a discussion of appropriate testing and interpretive procedures. For the shorter batteries, scores should only be interpreted as indicating FSIQ.

Based on the median correlations of the individual subtests with the full composite score as reported in the technical manual (R. L. Thorndike et al., 1986a), the best two tests from the Stanford-Binet to use to represent the full test are vocabulary (correlation coefficient $r = .81$) and quantitative ($r = .82$). An optimum four-test composite sampling all four areas would be Vocabulary, Quantitative, Pattern Analysis ($r = .74$), and Bead Memory ($r = .72$) (R. L. Thorndike et al., 1986b). Each of these tests is used at all age levels. The authors suggest adding Memory for Sentences and Comprehension to these four to give "a reasonably accurate estimate of overall cognitive level and pattern of cognitive abilities" (p. 35). These are the six core tests that are administered at all ages. These reduced batteries should not be used to estimate scores for the four cognitive areas.

The consistent finding that verbal tests show high correlations with broader measures of intellectual ability has led to the development of various short tests based entirely on verbal material. A particularly popular type, because of its inherent interest to children, is the picture vocabulary test, of which the Peabody Picture Vocabulary Test–Third Edition (PPVT-III) (Dunn & Dunn, 1997) is probably the best known. Each of the two forms of the test has 204 plates (12 items at each of 17 levels). Each plate contains four pictures. The examiner gives a word, and the examinee indicates the picture that relates to the word. The test takes about 10 to 15 minutes and provides an indication of general verbal ability. For brief discussions of many others, see Sattler (2001).

Kaufman and Kaufman (2001) have raised serious objections to the use of abbreviated versions of full-length tests, preferring instead any of three recently published brief tests, the Kaufman Brief Intelligence Test (K-BIT), the Wechsler Abbreviated Scale of Intelligence (WASI), and the Wide Range Intelligence Test (WRIT). The primary problem with short forms of existing tests, according to Kaufman and Kaufman, is inadequate or inappropriate norms. In most cases, short forms extract subtests from larger batteries and apply the norms developed for the complete battery. When the tests have been examined in isolation, not embedded in their normal place in the battery, the difficulty of the material is reduced, giving spuriously high estimates of cognitive ability. The brief tests reviewed by Kaufman and Kaufman were all normed as complete brief tests, so their norms are not distorted. All three instruments are normed for childhood (about age 5) through maturity (about age 85).

Kaufman and Kaufman's (2001) criticism of short forms probably does not apply to the abbreviated version of the SB5 because the two tests that make up the scale are always administered first in a testing session as routing tests. Therefore, the brief form is always given, and the rest of the instrument is appended to it, obviating the criticism that the short-form tests have been isolated from their usual context. Norms for the brief form are based on the same testing sessions that were used to norm the entire test.

The K-BIT (Kaufman & Kaufman, 1990) uses two subtests, a vocabulary test to measure the verbal aspects of intelligence and a matrices test to measure nonverbal ability. The test takes 15 to 30 minutes to administer. The WASI (The Psychological Corporation, 1999) has two versions. The short version includes vocabulary and matrix reasoning to measure verbal and nonverbal abilities and takes about 15 minutes to administer. The longer version adds subtests for similarities (verbal) and block design (nonverbal) and takes about 30 minutes. The four subtests are similar to subtests of the full Wechsler batteries. The WRIT (Glutting, Adams, & Sheslow, 2000) can be administered in about 30 minutes and has four subtests: two nonverbal (matrices and block design) and two verbal (vocabulary and analogies). All three tests yield a global cognitive ability measure with reliability exceeding .90, and all are recommended for quick screening and research applications but not for comprehensive cognitive diagnosis.

GROUP GENERAL-ABILITY TESTS

There are certain advantages to having a test administered to a person one-on-one with a trained examiner. No reading need be required on the part of the examinee, so it is possible to test young children and people of limited literacy. And an empathic and perceptive examiner can maintain a continuing high level of motivation on the part of the examinee. Furthermore, the examiner can observe aspects of the examinee's behavior in the testing session that are not reflected in the numerical score but that would assist in diagnosis. There are also disadvantages, however. Examiners may vary in their presentation of tasks and their evaluation of responses, thus introducing measurement error. Some examinees may be self-conscious in a face-to-face situation and block out responses that they really know. But the most critical point is that individual testing is expensive—prohibitively so if information is desired on each child in a school or on each applicant for admission to an educational institution or a training program. Primarily because of cost considerations, most ability testing has become group testing, using paper-and-pencil or computer-administered testing instruments that can be scored objectively. (A test can be administered by computer even if it is not computer adaptive.)

A number of series of group tests are available for use in educational settings. Three relatively widely used series are the Test of Cognitive Skills produced by the California Test Bureau (CTB) and McGraw-Hill, the Otis-Lennon School Ability Test published by the Psychological Corporation, and the School and College Ability Tests prepared by the Educational Testing Service and CTB/McGraw-Hill. However, we will illustrate this category of test with the series with which we are most intimately acquainted—the Cognitive Abilities Test, or CogAT. Like many other group-administered tests of general ability, these are multiscore tests providing one score for verbal ability, one for quantitative ability, and one for nonverbal ability. In addition, an overall ability score, called a standard age score (SAS), is reported. The most recent edition (R. L. Thorndike & Hagen, 1993) of these tests is composed of nine subtests. Sample items like those in each of the subtests are shown in Figures 8–1, 8–2, and 8–3.

The tests are organized in a multilevel format and printed in a single booklet that covers the range from grade 3 to grade 12. (There are also primary level tests for kindergarten through grade 3, and the publisher, at a user's request, will provide booklets containing only a single level of the tests.) The multilevel booklet is arranged so that testing can be carried out at any one of eight levels of difficulty, depending on where an examinee is started and stopped. The pattern

Figure 8–1
Sample verbal test items like those used in the Cognitive Abilities Test.

Vocabulary
Impolite:
    A. unhappy   B. angry   C. faithless
        D. <u>rude</u>   E. talkative

Sentence Completion
Mark was very fond of his science teacher, but he did not _____his mathematics teacher.
A. obey   B. discuss   C. regard   D. desire   E. <u>like</u>

Verbal Classification
Dove   Hawk   Wren   Sparrow
A. moth   B. bat   C. <u>gull</u>   D. bee   E. squirrel

Verbal Analogy
Pea is to **bean** as **peach** is to
A. pit   B. tree   C. eat   D. skin   E. <u>apple</u>

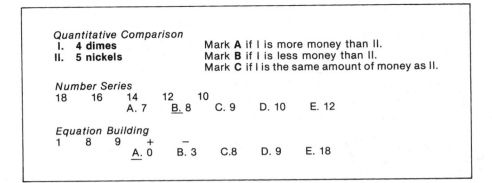

Figure 8–2
Sample quantitative test items like those in the Cognitive Abilities Test.

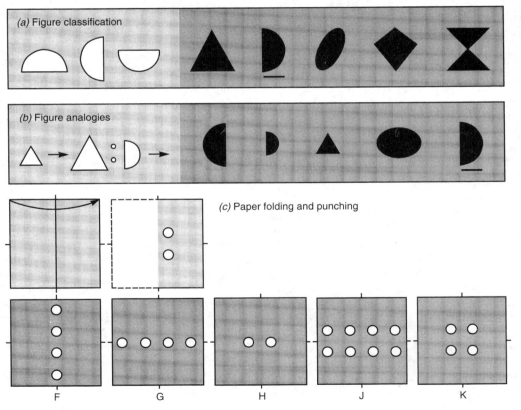

Figure 8–3
Sample nonverbal items like those in the Cognitive Abilities Test.

illustrated here is for the Sentence Completion subtest, and a similar pattern is used for each of the other subtests.

	Pattern of Item Ranges for the Sentence Completion Subtest of the CogAT		
Level	Start at Item	End at Item	Usual Grade Level
A	1	25	3
B	6	30	4
C	11	35	5
D	16	40	6
E	21	45	7
F	26	50	8–9
G	31	55	10–11
H	36	60	12+

Responses are marked on a separate answer sheet, and a different answer sheet is provided for each level, with spaces for only the items that are to be answered at that level. The test exercises get progressively more difficult, so the format permits a good deal of flexibility in selecting a test level that is appropriate in difficulty for a given class, or even a particular individual. Thus, for a school located in a disadvantaged community, more accurate information about pupils would be likely to result if an easier level of the test were used, so that sixth graders, for example, might be tested with Level C rather than with Level D. More accurate information is obtained from testing when the difficulty of the test tasks closely matches the ability level of the people being tested.

Nonreading group tests can be prepared, as evidenced by the types of tasks represented in Figure 8–3. For very young children, it is, of course, necessary to avoid requiring them to read. It is also desirable to monitor rather closely the progress of children to be sure that they continue to work on the tasks—and to work on the proper tasks. The use of group testing is more questionable with young children, but it is possible after they have been in school for a while and have gotten used to following directions.

Two levels of a primary test have been prepared for the CogAT, to extend the range of the multilevel version downward. These levels are intended for use from late kindergarten to grade 3. In most instances, directions for each item are read aloud by the examiner, who proceeds at a pace that permits each child to respond by marking the test booklet. At these levels, a separate answer sheet is not used, and the tests are composed of only two verbal, two quantitative, and two nonverbal subtests. Illustrations of some of the types of items are provided in Figure 8–4.

The CogAT provides three separate scores: verbal, quantitative, and nonverbal. As was the case with all of the individually administered tests, although these scores represent distinguishable dimensions of individual differences, they are not unrelated. In fact, the correlations among the three scores are quite high, averaging about .70. Thus, although what each measures is somewhat different from what the others measure, all three scores have a good deal in common; this commonality can be thought of as the general cognitive ability factor.

Verbal

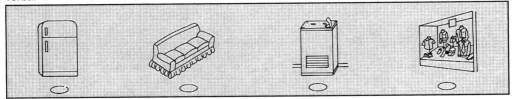

Fill the oval under the <u>refrigerator.</u>

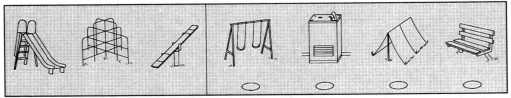

See the slide, the jungle gym and the teeter-totter. Which one belongs with them?

Quantitative

Mark the oval under the <u>biggest</u> piece of pie.

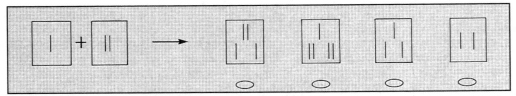

Which one on the right equals the <u>sum</u> of the two boxes on the left?

Figure 8–4
Items like those in the Cognitive Abilities Test—Primary Levels.

This point can be brought out more clearly by looking at the results from a factor analysis of the nine subtests that compose the CogAT. The results are shown in Table 8–3. A factor loading can be interpreted as the correlation of a test with an underlying dimension. In Table 8–3, to simplify the picture, values less than .10 have been omitted because such values can be considered negligible.

The pattern that emerges in this factor analysis is quite clear. For *each one* of the subtests, the predominant loading is on the general factor shared by all of them. In addition, a verbal factor of moderate size appears in all the subtests of the verbal scale and a somewhat smaller figural

Nonverbal

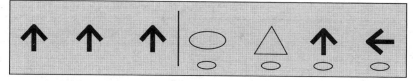

Which one on the right belongs with the three on the left?

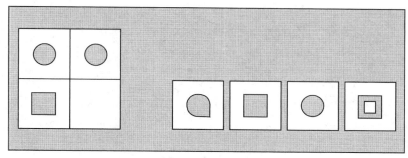

Which one on the right belongs in the empty box on the left?

Figure 8–4
(Continued)

visualization factor is found in the subtests of the nonverbal scale. The quantitative subtests are not very successful in defining a quantitative factor; they tend to load almost solely on the general-ability factor. In addition, each of the nine subtests involves some elements of ability that are unique to that subtest (specific factors), the nature of which is not made clear by a factor analysis.

The question that you might raise next is "How much of whatever validity is found for the CogAT is to be attributed to the common general ability factor and how much to the less

Table 8–3
Median Factor Loadings of the Multilevel Battery of the Cognitive Abilities Test

Subtest	General	Verbal	Quantitative	Nonverbal
Verbal classification	.71	.48		
Sentence completion	.72	.48		
Verbal analogies	.76	.42		
Quantitative relations	.82		.14	
Number series	.81		.16	
Equation building	.71		.18	
Figure classification	.72			.30
Figure analogies	.77			.34
Figure analysis	.62			.36

Table 8–4

Correlations of the Cognitive Abilities Test (CogAT) Scores in Grades 5, 7, and 9 with Class Marks in Grade 9

CogAT Score	Grade 9 Courses				
	English	Social Studies	Mathematics	Science	Overall
Grade 5 V	.46	.49	.34	.46	.51
Q	.45	.49	.39	.50	.54
NV	.38	.39	.34	.42	.45
Total	.48	.52	.40	.52	.56
Grade 7 V	.49	.53	.36	.49	.55
Q	.51	.54	.45	.56	.61
NV	.41	.43	.38	.46	.49
Total	.53	.56	.45	.57	.62
Grade 9 V	.52	.56	.39	.52	.58
Q	.52	.57	.48	.59	.63
NV	.42	.45	.41	.48	.52
Total	.55	.59	.48	.60	.65

Note: V = verbal; Q = quantitative; NV = nonverbal.

extensive factors, that is, verbal and spatial?" A partial answer to this question can be obtained by looking at a set of data available from one large, suburban school district. The CogAT had been given in grades 5, 7, and 9 of this school system, and it was possible to compare the results with teachers' grades in specific courses and with grade-point averages in grade 9. Selected results based on about 4,300 cases are shown in Table 8–4. In this table, the higher correlations are generally those for the verbal and quantitative scores, with nonverbal scores tending to be a rather poor third. Such a result might be expected because education relies heavily on the symbol systems of words and numbers. But you should note that the highest correlation is almost universally that for the simple sum of the three scores. Such a simple sum accentuates and is a reliable measure of the general factor that is shared by all three tests, although, as we pointed out earlier, it confounds the general, specific, and error components of Spearman's theory.

You might also ask what validity there would be for a *difference* score that brings out what is distinctive to one or another of the three scores. The answer for these data is the following: Across the group as a whole, almost none; the validity of a difference score for predicting relative academic performance in particular subjects is never as much as .05. So, in the pure prediction of academic performance, it is almost exclusively the common general-ability factor that forecasts performance.

The value of the three separate scores is primarily in the attention they call to a certain (usually small) number of children who display an uneven pattern of scores on the three tests. For *most* children, SASs on the three tests will be similar, differing by not more than about 10 points, as is indicated by the relatively high correlations among the scores. Differences of this magnitude generally have little predictive or descriptive value. However, a few individuals will be found who show differences of 20 or even 30 points. Thus, a child may be encountered who has a verbal SAS of 80 but a nonverbal score of 105. One might be moved to ask what produced this dramatic difference. Was English not the language of the home? Some groups of Hispanic students have been found to exhibit this pattern. By contrast, some groups of Asian children have shown much higher performance on the quantitative scale than on the verbal or nonverbal scales. Was a child dyslexic? Or had there been some failure in early teaching of reading skills? And what can be done to help the child's school progress? Would remediating the verbal deficit or exploiting the nonverbal capabilities accomplish the desired goal? One can raise similar questions about other patterns of high and low scores. The key is to use marked discrepancies in scores as a warning light that there may be a nonstandard situation and that developing the best educational program for the child may require further exploration, often in the form of an individually administered test. (For a more thorough discussion of testing children with nonstandard ability profiles, see Chapter 13.)

One way to judge whether the difference between two scores is large enough to attract attention is to consider the standard errors of measurement of the two scales. The standard error of measurement, you will remember from Chapter 4, is an index of the random variation expected in a person's score when that person is retested several times with equivalent tests. Unless the difference between two scores is substantially larger than the standard error of measurement, it should probably be ignored as resulting from random fluctuations in test performance. A reasonable standard to apply is that the difference should be at least three times as large as the larger of the two standard errors. Thus, if the standard errors of measurement for verbal and nonverbal scores are 4.3 and 5.7, respectively, we should probably not interpret a score difference of less than about 18 points as important. The score difference of 20 to 30 points mentioned earlier exceeds this criterion and may therefore indicate an important inconsistency. However, we should not treat large score differences in a mechanical manner. The presence of an unusually large difference between two scores should be viewed as a signal that there may be something going on that merits closer scrutiny through an individually administered test, a supplementary set of assessment devices, or careful observation.

TESTS OF MULTIPLE ABILITIES

During the past 60 years, a number of test batteries have been developed that are designed to provide differential predictions of success in specific jobs or training programs. These grew out of job analyses suggesting that different jobs called for quite different abilities. Thus, each of the armed forces developed a classification battery to be used in helping to assign each recruit to a military occupational specialty in which he or she could perform effectively. Because of the large samples that accumulate in military training programs, studies based on these batteries provide some of the most substantial bodies of data that have ever been available on tests as predictors of training success and, to a lesser extent, of job success. We refer to some of these data in the sections that follow. However, of more practical interest to people in civilian settings are batteries that have been developed for civilian use. We describe and illustrate two of these: the Differential Aptitude Test, designed primarily for use in high school guidance programs and the U.S. Employment Service General Aptitude Test Battery, designed for vocational counseling services and job placement.

Differential Aptitude Test Battery

The Differential Aptitude Test (DAT) battery was originally published by the Psychological Corporation in 1947 as a guidance battery for use at the secondary school level, and revised and streamlined forms were produced in 1963, 1972, 1982, and 1990. In the design of the battery, some attention was paid to having separate tests with low intercorrelations, but the main focus was on getting measures that would be meaningful to high school counselors. As a result, with the exception of the test of clerical speed and accuracy, intercorrelations are about .50. However, because the reliabilities of the parts are about .90, it is clear that more than one ability is being measured. The eight subtests are briefly described and illustrated here. A ninth score, Scholastic Aptitude, may be obtained from the sum of Verbal Reasoning and Numerical Reasoning.*

1. *Verbal Reasoning* (25 minutes). Items are of the double-analogy type, that is,

_____ is to A as B is to _____.

Five pairs of words are provided to complete the analogy.

_____ is to night as breakfast is to _____.

    A. supper—corner
    B. gentle—morning
    C. door—corner
    D. flow—enjoy
    E. supper—morning

2. *Numerical Reasoning* (30 minutes). This subtest consists of numerical problems emphasizing comprehension rather than simple computational facility.

$$3 = \underline{\qquad} \% \text{ of } 15$$

    A. 5
    B. 10
    C. 20
    D. 30
    E. none of these

3. *Abstract Reasoning* (20 minutes). A series of problem figures establishes a relationship or sequence, and the examinee must pick the choice that continues the series.

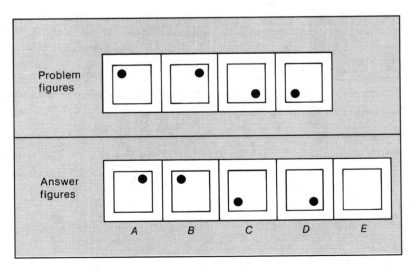

4. *Spatial Relations* (25 minutes). A diagram of a flat figure is shown. The examinee must visualize and indicate which solid figure could be produced by folding the flat figure, as shown in the example here:

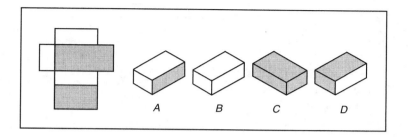

5. *Mechanical Reasoning* (25 minutes). A diagram of a mechanical device or situation is shown, and the examinee must indicate which choice is correct for the situation.

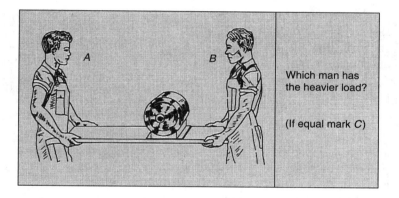

6. *Perceptual Speed and Accuracy* (6 minutes). Each item is made up of a number of combinations of symbols, one of which is underlined. The examinee must mark the same combination on his or her answer sheet.

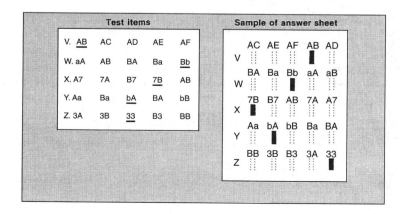

7. *Spelling* (10 minutes). A list of words is given, some of which are misspelled. The examinee must indicate whether each word is spelled correctly or incorrectly.

	Right	Wrong
gurl	‖	‖

8. *Language Usage* (15 minutes). A sentence is given, divided by marks into four subsections. The examinee must indicate either which section—A, B, C, or D—contains an error or, if there is no error, mark E.

A	B	C	D	A	B	C	D	E
Ain't we / going to / the office / next week?				‖	‖	‖	‖	‖

The tests of the DAT are essentially power tests, with the exception of the Perceptual Speed and Accuracy test, and time limits in most cases are 20 to 30 minutes. Total testing time for the battery is about 3 hours (2.5 hours working time plus 30 minutes for administrative matters and directions). Percentile ranks, stanines, and scaled scores are available for each grade from grades 7 through 12. Norms are provided for each of the subtests and also for the sum of verbal reasoning and numerical ability, which is offered as a general appraisal of scholastic aptitude.

General Aptitude Test Battery

The General Aptitude Test Battery (GATB) was produced by the Bureau of Employment Security of the U.S. Department of Labor in the early 1940s. It was based on previous work in which experimental test batteries had been prepared for each of a number of different jobs. Analysis of more than 50 different tests prepared for specific jobs indicated that there was a great deal of overlap in some of them and that only about 10 different ability factors were measured by the complete set of tests. The GATB was developed to provide measures of these different factors. In its most recent form, the GATB includes 12 tests and gives scores for nine different factors. One is a factor of general mental ability resulting from scores on three tests (Vocabulary, Arithmetic Reasoning, and Three-Dimensional Space) that are also scored for more specialized factors. The other factors and the tests that contribute to each are described here. Each factor is scaled to yield scores with a mean of 100 and a standard deviation of 20.

1. *Verbal Aptitude.* The score is based on one test, Number 4—Vocabulary. This test requires the examinee to identify the pair of words in a set of four that are either synonyms or antonyms. For example,

      a. cautious   b. friendly   c. hostile   d. remote

      a. hasten   b. deprive   c. expedite   d. disprove

2. *Numerical Ability.* The appraisal of this aptitude is based on two tests. The first of these, Number 2—Computation, involves speed and accuracy in simple, whole-number computation. For example,

$$\text{Subtract } (-) \quad \underline{\begin{array}{r} 256 \\ 83 \end{array}} \qquad \text{Multiply } (\times) \quad \underline{\begin{array}{r} 37 \\ 8 \end{array}}$$

The second test comprising the numerical ability score, Number 6—Arithmetic Reasoning, involves verbally stated quantitative problems, such as

John works for $5.20 an hour. How much is his pay for a 35-hour week?

3. *Spatial Aptitude.* One test, Number 3—Three-Dimensional Space, enters into appraisal of this aptitude. The examinee must indicate which of four three-dimensional figures can be produced by folding a flat sheet of a specified shape, with creases at indicated points.

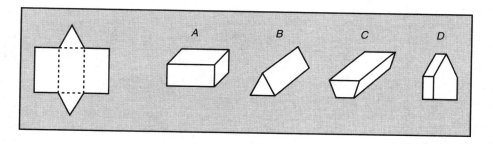

4. *Form Perception.* This aptitude involves rapid and accurate perception of visual forms and patterns. It is appraised in the GATB by two tests, (1) Number 5—Tool Matching and (2) Number 7—Form Matching, which differ in the type of visual stimulus provided. Each requires the examinee to find from among a set of answer choices the one that is identical with the stimulus form.

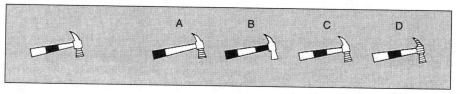

TOOL MATCHING

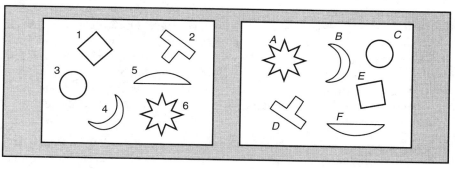

FORM MATCHING

5. *Clerical Perception*. This aptitude also involves rapid and accurate perception, but in this case, the stimulus material is linguistic instead of purely figural. The test, Number 1—Name Comparison, presents pairs of names and requires the examinee to indicate whether the two members of the pair are identical or whether they differ in some detail.

John Goldstein & Co.—John Goldston & Co.
Pewee Mfg. Co.—Pewee Mfg. Co.

6. *Motor Coordination*. This factor has to do with speed of simple, but fairly precise motor response. It is evaluated by one test, Number 8—Mark Making. The task of the examinee is to make three pencil marks, arranged as shown here, as quickly as possible within each of a series of boxes on the answer sheet.

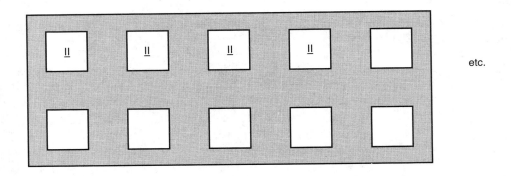

The score is the number of boxes correctly filled in a 60-second test period.

7. *Manual Dexterity*. This factor involves speed and accuracy of fairly gross hand movements. It is evaluated by two pegboard tests: (1) Number 9—Place and (2) Number 10—Turn. In the first of these tests, examinees use both hands to move a series of pegs from one set of holes in a pegboard to another. In the second test, examinees use their preferred hand to pick a peg up from the board, rotate it 180°, and reinsert the other end of the peg in the hole. Each task has a short enough time limit that few examinees are able to move or turn all of the pegs. Three trials are given for each of these tests, and the score is the total number of pegs moved or turned.

8. *Finger Dexterity*. This factor represents a finer type of dexterity than that covered by the previous factor, calling for more precise finger manipulation. Two tests, Number 11—Assemble and Number 12—Disassemble, use the same pieces of equipment, a board with 50 holes in each of two sections. Each hole in one section is occupied by a small rivet. A stack of washers is piled on a spindle. During *assemble,* the examinee picks up a rivet with one hand and a washer with the other, puts the washer on the rivet, and places the assembly in the corresponding hole in the unoccupied part of the board. The task is to assemble as many rivets and washers as possible in 90 seconds. During *disassemble,* the examinee removes the assembly and returns the washer to its stack and the rivet to its original place. The score is the number of items assembled or disassembled, as the case may be.

The apparatus tests (non–paper-and-pencil tests)—Motor Coordination, Manual Dexterity, and Finger Dexterity—are all arranged so that at the completion of testing, the equipment has been returned to its original condition and is ready for the testing of another person.

Table 8–5

Intercorrelations of Aptitude Scores (from the GATB) for 100 High School Seniors

	G	V	N	S	P	Q	K	F	M
G—Intelligence	—								
V—Verbal	.73	—							
N—Numerical	.74	.42	—						
S—Spatial	.70	.40	.34	—					
P—Form Perception	.43	.34	.42	.48	—				
Q—Clerical Perception	.35	.29	.42	.26	.66	—			
K—Motor Coordination	−.04	.13	.06	−.03	.29	.29	—		
F—Finger Dexterity	−.05	−.03	−.03	.01	.27	.20	.37	—	
M—Manual Dexterity	−.06	.06	.01	-.03	.23	.17	.49	.46	—

A comparison of the GATB and the DAT reveals that the DAT includes tests of mechanical comprehension and language that the GATB lacks, while the GATB includes form perception and several types of motor tests that are missing in the DAT. Thus, the GATB is more work oriented and less school oriented in its total coverage. Inclusion of the motor tests results in somewhat lower correlations, on the average, among the GATB scales, although the "intellectual" tests correlate about as highly as those of the DAT. The correlations between the different aptitude scores of the GATB for a group of 100 high school seniors are shown in Table 8–5. Excluding the correlations of the verbal, numerical, and spatial scores with the score for the general intelligence scale (G) (which is composed of verbal, numerical, and spatial scores), the correlations range from −.06 to .66. The three motor tests show fairly marked correlations, but they are only moderately related to the perception tests and are practically unrelated to the tests that make up the general intelligence scale. The perceptual and intellectual scores also relate closely to each other, and there is a strong relationship between the two types of perceptual ability.

Quite substantial correlations exist between the corresponding factors of the DAT and the GATB. Representative values from one study (U.S. Employment Service, 1967) are as follows:

Scale	Correlation
Verbal	.74
Numerical	.61
Spatial	.65
Clerical	.57

However, the correlations are low enough that it is clear that the tests cannot be considered identical. One important difference in the two tests is the fact that the DAT tests are in most cases purely power tests, while the GATB tests are quite highly speeded.

ROLE OF GENERAL COGNITIVE ABILITY: THE BELL CURVE

Every few years a book or monograph is published that attracts wide public attention to various aspects of the data regarding human mental abilities. Such a book, *The Bell Curve,* was published in 1994 (Herrnstein & Murray, 1994). The basic premise advocated by the authors is that human cognitive ability is extremely important in all aspects of life in a complex society and that differences in this ability are related to a wide variety of both cognitive and social outcomes. The authors point to the use of cognitive ability tests such as the SAT and the Graduate Record Examination (GRE) by highly selective educational institutions as creating an intellectual elite whose members occupy a disproportionate number of positions of political and economic power. The fact that the children of highly educated parents tend themselves to become highly educated and that the children of economically and socially disadvantaged parents tend to suffer their parents' fate leads the authors to argue that American society in particular, and perhaps other diverse societies in general, may be developing such an extreme social stratification based on cognitive ability that a permanent underclass will result. While the authors make their basic argument without reference to racial or ethnic groups (their data indicate that their conclusions are independent of race and the authors maintain that they are steadfastly "agnostic" about racial factors), the fact that racial groups differ in the proportion of their members who are found in the different social strata makes their argument seem racist because it implies that there are racial differences in ability.

The Bell Curve has been attacked from just about every possible direction, sometimes with justification, other times on largely frivolous grounds. Some authors have suggested that the book addresses questions about race and intelligence that should not even be asked, while others have questioned details of the statistical methodology. Although the social-policy implications and recommendations that Herrnstein and Murray have offered may be highly questionable (critics would say totally unjustified), we may reasonably ask what the data have to say about the value of general cognitive ability and more specific abilities as predictors of academic and job performance. How useful are batteries such as the DAT and the GATB, and how much do they enable us to improve the prediction of educational and occupational success over what is possible from a general measure of cognitive ability? Because of the sample sizes involved, the wide variety of occupational specialties, and the quality of the outcome measures, some of the best studies of these relationships have been conducted by military psychologists.

There have been hundreds, probably thousands, of studies in which ability test scores have been related to some criterion measure of success on a job. For many years results were found to vary from study to study and from job to job. As a consequence, personnel psychologists tended to emphasize the specificity of jobs in the abilities that they required and the need to carry out local job analyses and specific validation studies, not only for each category of job but even for each local setting in which the job appeared. This call for specific validation studies, given the force of law in the guidelines of the federal Equal Employment Opportunity Commission, becomes a counsel of despair for using tests in vocational selection, placement, and counseling decisions, because relatively few employment situations provide a flow of new employees sufficient in number to generate stable validity data. But more recently, this doctrine of validity specificity has been seriously questioned.

It was pointed out by Schmidt and Hunter (1981) that much of the variation in results from one study to another can be attributed to a combination of (1) small sample size, (2) differences in degree of curtailment or preselection in the group studied, and (3) differences in the nature and reliability of the criterion measures. Schmidt, Hunter, and their associates (Schmidt & Hunter, 1992; Schmidt et al., 1985) have carried out a number of **meta-analyses** of existing data.

Meta-analyses are reanalyses that pool data from the large number of existing studies to correct for the deficiencies just mentioned and to extract the findings that transcend the individual studies. Jensen (1998, Chapt. 9) has reviewed much of the recent evidence, and a good summary is also provided by Gottfredson (1997). The following general conclusions emerge from this work:

1. General cognitive ability has significant validity for practically all jobs. The level of validity is related to the complexity of the job, being higher for more complex jobs and lower for simpler jobs.
2. The true validity of general cognitive ability for job performance is quite high, after allowance for the depressing effects of preselection in those studies and for the unreliability of criterion measures.
3. General psychomotor ability also has some validity, its validity tending to be greater for the simpler jobs (such as machine tending or packing and wrapping) in which the demand for cognitive ability is lowest.
4. Measurement of mechanical or technical understanding adds to validity for a range of occupations in which one works with machines or repairs mechanical, electrical, or electronic devices.
5. Beyond the conclusions just listed, there is little evidence for the validity of other and more specific abilities.

These basic findings have been borne out in studies of other contexts by other investigators. A study by Nyborg and Jensen (2001) found a substantial relationship between g and both income and job prestige in both Black and White samples. Perhaps the best evidence, because of the relatively high quality of the criterion measures and the large sample sizes, has been summarized by Ree and Earles (1992). Using the Armed Services Vocational Aptitude Battery (ASVAB) and samples with thousands of subjects in both training and job situations, the authors found a single general cognitive ability composite to be the most effective predictor of performance. In fact, for many of the military jobs these studies investigated, the general cognitive ability factor was the *only* useful predictor.

The term that Schmidt and Hunter (1981) apply to their meta-analytic approach is **validity generalization.** Although they have been criticized for overstating both the uniformity of validity patterns across a range of jobs and the size of "true" test validity, their work provides a healthy corrective influence to the job specificity doctrine that was prevalent in the period from 1950 to 1980. And one thing that becomes abundantly clear from their work and that of Ree and Earles (1992) is that if data on the distinctive validity patterns for specific educational programs or specific jobs are to be demonstrated at an acceptable level of confidence, groups used in validation studies must be *much* larger than those that have appeared in validation studies in the past.

Schmidt and Hunter (1981) have examined the correlational evidence for ability tests as predictors of educational and vocational success. There is another way to look at the relationship between test scores and occupations; we can ask how and to what extent people in different occupations differ in their test scores. We can designate this a *taxonomic,* as contrasted with a *predictive,* view of test validity. That is, if we give a test to individuals employed in different occupations, will we find that their patterns of abilities differ? Let us look first at the level of general cognitive ability. Though a number of data sets provide such information, U.S. Employment Service data on the GATB have certain advantages in terms of the number and variety of occupations covered, so we will focus on those data. Among the more than 400 different occupations that have been studied with the GATB, there were clearly substantial differences in average score on the *G* scale. These ranged from a high of 143 for mathematicians to a low of 55 for tomato peelers. But, before

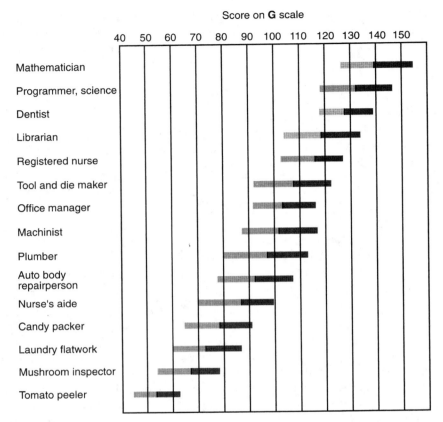

Figure 8–5
Mean general intelligence scores (*G* scores) on the General Aptitude Test Battery for selected occupations. Bar around mean shows ±1 standard deviation range.

we look at the differences, let us ask how consistent they were from one sample to another in the same job. Among the jobs studied by the U.S. Employment Service, for 48 jobs there were two or more independent samples of 50 or more cases. And across these jobs, the correlation between Sample A and Sample B was .93. Clearly, average *G* score was a very reliable, very stable characteristic of people in a given occupation.

At the same time that we find these quite stable differences *between* occupations, we also find quite a wide range of scores *within* a given occupation. Figure 8–5 shows the average *G* score for a selection of occupations and also the ±1 standard deviation range, the range that includes about two-thirds of all the persons in that occupation. Although the differences in average score are quite dependable, the overlap is considerable for all but the extreme groups. It is also true that among the occupations studied by the U.S. Employment Service, most fall within a fairly narrow range in average *G* scores. This fact is shown in Table 8–6, where 246 out of the 442 jobs have average *G* scores falling between 90 and 109, or within half a standard deviation of the overall population mean of 100. A minority of occupations are highly restrictive in the level of *G* score required to enter the particular occupation and then to survive in it. Thus, only 30 of the

Table 8–6

Frequency Distribution of Average General Intelligence (*G*) Scores
in Different Occupations

Score Level	Frequency
140+	1
130–139	6
120–129	23
110–119	57
100–109	107
90–99	139
80–89	89
70–79	18
60–69	1
Below 60	1

occupations were characterized by average *G* scores of 120 or more. A person of near-average ability can fit into a wide range of occupational niches.

We may ask to what extent occupations display distinct and stable *patterns* of abilities. To what extent do we find occupations in which the members are especially high (or low) in verbal ability? In quantitative ability? In motor coordination or finger dexterity? The GATB data also help to answer these questions. We have taken the 48 jobs with at least duplicate samples and for each job have computed the correlations between the paired samples across the eight primary scores of the GATB (excluding *G*). The 48 correlations ranged from −.02 to +.97; their distribution is shown in Table 8–7, where the median value is .72. Figure 8–6 shows the pattern of scores for

Table 8–7

Profile Correlations for Pairs of Jobs

Correlation	Frequency
.90–.99	11
.80–.89	9
.70–.79	7
.60–.69	6
.50–.59	6
.40–.49	1
.30–.39	3
.20–.29	1
.10–.19	1
.00–.09	2
Negative	1

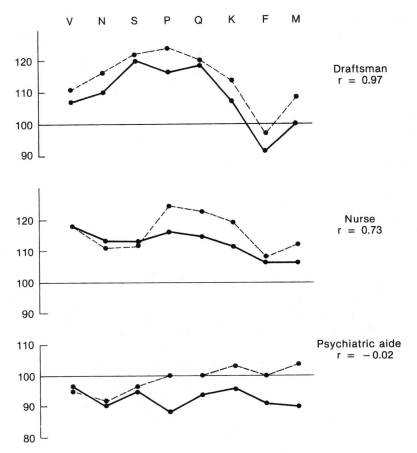

Figure 8–6
Profiles of mean scores for pairs of job samples from the General Aptitude Test Battery. Dashed lines are for Sample 1; solid lines are for Sample 2.

duplicate samples for three jobs, one highly consistent, one of average consistency, and one completely lacking in consistency. The conclusion that may be drawn is that questions about consistency of patterning can only be answered on a job-by-job basis. Some jobs do show consistency, but others do not.

SUMMARY

Individual tests of aptitude were first developed near the turn of the century in response to educational problems. The Stanford-Binet soon became the leading test in the United States. The demands of World War I led to the development of group aptitude tests. The Wechsler series of tests was produced first to measure adults and, later, people of all ages. Currently, the WPPSI-III, the WISC-III, and the WAIS-III are the most widely used individually administered aptitude tests. Many group tests have descended in one way or another from those of World War I, of which the CogAT is a good example.

Test batteries were introduced in the early 1940s to give better differential prediction of occupational and training potential. Two of the major current batteries are the DAT, which is designed for school counseling, and the GATB, which is used primarily in employment situations. The two batteries are similar, but the GATB places more emphasis on speed and on perceptual and clerical abilities. Recent evidence suggests that it is primarily the general ability measured by each of these batteries that is responsible for their ability to predict scholastic and occupational success.

QUESTIONS AND EXERCISES

1. It has been proposed that all intelligence tests be called scholastic aptitude tests. What are the merits and limitations of this proposal?

2. In what respects is it preferable to rely on a good aptitude test for an estimate of a student's intelligence rather than on ratings by teachers? Are there situations where teacher ratings would be preferable?

3. In each of the following situations, would you elect to use a group intelligence test or an individual intelligence test? Why?
   a. You are studying a boy with a serious speech impediment.
   b. You are selecting students for admission to a nursing program.
   c. You are preparing to counsel a high school senior on educational and vocational plans.
   d. You are studying the academic progress of Hispanic children in a school system in Texas.
   e. You are working with a group of boys, in a state institution, who have been convicted of criminal offenses.
   f. You are trying to identify the sources of difficulty for a child who is a nonreader.

4. Are the usual group intelligence tests more useful for those students who are considering professional occupations or for those considering occupations in the skilled trades? Why?

5. A newspaper article reported that a young woman who had been placed in a mental hospital with an IQ score of 62 had raised her IQ score to 118 during the 3 years she spent there. What is misleading about this statement? What factors could account for the difference between the two IQ scores?

6. In what respects are intelligence tests better than high school grades as predictors of college success? In what respects are they not as good?

7. Why do intelligence tests show higher correlations with standardized achievement tests than they do with school grades?

8. You are a fourth-grade teacher, and you have just received the results for your class from a citywide administration of the Cognitive Abilities Test in all fourth-grade classes. What use might you make of the results? What additional information would you need?

9. An eighth-grade student received the following standard age scores on the Cognitive Abilities Test: Verbal, Grade 4—98; Grade 6—116; Grade 8—104. What would be the best figure to represent the child's true scholastic ability level?

10. During the first 2 weeks of school, a school in a well-to-do community gave the Stanford-Binet Fourth Edition to all entering kindergarteners and all first graders who had not been tested in kindergarten. How desirable and useful is this procedure? Why?

11. A school system wanted to set up procedures for identifying students to receive remedial instruction in reading. Students whose reading achievement was seriously behind their potential for learning to read were the target group. What would be a sound procedure for accomplishing this goal?

12. A number of aptitude test batteries have been developed for use at the secondary school level and with adults but few for use at the elementary school level. Why? Is this a reasonable state of affairs?

13. What are the advantages of using a battery such as the Differential Aptitude Tests instead of tests selected from a number of different sources? What are the limitations?

14. A vocational high school offers programs to train bookkeepers, cosmetologists, dental assistants, and office managers. Studies with the General Aptitude Test Battery have yielded data on the mean (*M*), standard deviation (*SD*), and correlation (*r*), with supervisory ratings shown here for these four occupations. As a counselor in the school, how would you use this information in helping students to choose among the four programs?

15. How sound is the statement "The best measure of aptitude in any field is a measure of achievement in that field to date?" What are the statement's limitations?

16. What are the differences between a reading readiness test and an intelligence test? What are the advantages of using the readiness test rather than the intelligence test for first-grade students?

17. In what ways could a follow-up study of graduates of a high school help in improving the school guidance program?

Occupation	Verbal			Numerical			Spatial			Manual Dexterity		
	M	*SD*	*r*	*M*	*SD*	*r*	*M*	*SD*	*r*	*M*	*SD*	*r*
Bookkeeper	106	16	.51	112	15	.37	103	20	.38	105	21	.36
Cosmetologist	96	15	.24	92	13	.31	100	16	.25	98	17	.07
Dental assistant	106	13	.26	102	14	.34	107	16	.30	115	19	.36
Office manager	105	12	.21	105	14	.24	106	16	.06	103	21	.09

SUGGESTED READINGS

Belk, M. S., LoBello, S. G., Ray, G. E., & Zachar, P. (2002). WISC-III administration, clerical, and scoring errors made by student examiners. *Journal of Psychoeducational Assessment, 20,* 290–300.

Boake, C. (2002). From the Binet-Simon to the Wechsler-Bellevue: Tracing the history of intelligence testing. *Journal of Clinical and Experimental Neuropsychology, 24,* 383–405.

Bond, L. (1989). The effects of special preparation on measures of scholastic ability. In R. L. Linn (Ed.), *Educational measurement* (3rd ed., pp. 429–444). New York: Macmillan.

Bracken, B. A., & McCallum, R. S. (1998). *The Universal Nonverbal Intelligence Test.* Itasca, IL: Riverside.

Brody, N. (2003). Construct validation of the Sternberg Triarchic Abilities Test: Comment and reanalysis. *Intelligence, 31,* 319–329.

Carroll, J. B. (1993). *Human cognitive abilities: A survey of factor-analytic studies.* Cambridge, MA: Cambridge University Press.

Das, J. P., & Naglieri, J. A. (2001). The Das-Naglieri Cognitive Assessment System in theory and practice. In J. J. C., Andrews, D. H. Saklofske, & H. L. Janzen (Eds.), *Handbook of psychoeducational assessment* (pp. 33–63). San Diego, CA: Academic Press.

Das, J. P., Naglieri, J. A., & Kirby, J. R. (1994). *Assessment of cognitive processes: The PASS theory of intelligence.* Boston: Allyn & Bacon.

Eysenck, H. J. (1986). Inspection time and intelligence: A historical perspective. *Personality and Individual Differences, 7,* 603–607.

Eysenck, H. J. (1988). The concept of "intelligence": Useful or useless? *Intelligence, 12,* 1–16.

Garber, H. L. (1988). *The Milwaukee Project: Preventing mental retardation in children at risk*. Washington, DC: American Association on Mental Retardation.

Glutting, J., Adams, W., & Sheslow, D. (2000). *WRIT: Wide Range Intelligence Test manual*. Wilmington, DE: Wide Range.

Gottfredson, L. S. (1997). Why g matters: The complexity of everyday life. *Intelligence, 24,* 79–132.

Gottfredson, L. S. (2003). Dissecting practical intelligence theory: Its claims and evidence. *Intelligence, 31,* 343–397.

Gregory, R. J. (1987). *Adult intellectual assessment*. Boston: Allyn & Bacon.

Guilford, J. P. (1985). The structure-of-intellect model. In B. B. Wolman (Ed.), *Handbook of intelligence* (pp. 225–266). New York: Wiley.

Herrnstein, R. J., & Murray, C. (1994). *The bell curve: Intelligence and class structure in American life*. New York: The Free Press.

Hildebrand, D. K., & Ledbetter, M. F. (2001). Assessing children's intelligence and memory: The Wechsler Intelligence Scale for Children–Third Edition and the Children's Memory Scale. In J. J. C. Andrews, D. H. Saklofske, & H. L. Janzen (Eds.), *Handbook of psychoeducational assessment* (pp. 13–32). San Diego, CA: Academic Press.

Horn, J. L. (1985). Remodeling old models of intelligence. In B. B. Wolman (Ed.), *Handbook of intelligence* (pp. 267–300). New York: Wiley.

Jensen, A. R. (1991). General mental ability: From psychometrics to biology. *Diagnostique, 16,* 134–144.

Jensen, A. R. (1993). Spearman's hypothesis tested with chronometric information-processing tasks. *Intelligence, 17,* 47–77.

Jensen, A. R. (1998). *The g factor*. Westport, CT: Praeger.

Kaufman, A. S., & Kaufman, N. L. (1990). *Kaufman Brief Intelligence Test*. Circle Pines, MN: American Guidance Service.

Kaufman, J. C., & Kaufman, A. S. (2001). Time for the changing of the guard: A farewell to short forms of intelligence tests. *Journal of Psychoeducational Assessment, 19,* 245–267.

Mather, N., & Gregg, N. (2001). Assessment with the Woodcock-Johnson–III. In J. J. C. Andrews, D. H. Saklofske, & H. L. Janzen (Eds.), *Handbook of psychoeducational assessment* (pp. 133–165). San Diego, CA: Academic Press.

Newmark, C. S. (Ed.). (1996). *Major psychological assessment instruments* (2nd ed.). Boston: Allyn & Bacon.

Nyborg, H., & Jensen, A. R. (2001). Occupation and income related to psychometric g. *Intelligence, 29,* 45–56.

The Psychological Corporation. (1999). *Wechsler Abbreviated Scale of Intelligence (WASI)*. San Antonio, TX: Author.

Ree, M. J., & Earles, J. A. (1992). Intelligence is the best predictor of job performance. *Current Directions in Psychological Science, 1,* 86–89.

Roid, G. H. (2003). *Stanford-Binet Intelligence Scales, Fifth edition*. Itasca, IL: Riverside Publishing.

Sattler, J. M. (2001). *Assessment of children: Cognitive applications* (4th ed.). San Diego, CA: Author.

Schmidt, F. L., & Hunter, J. E. (1992). Development of a causal model of processes determining job performance. *Current Directions in Psychological Science, 1,* 89–92.

Snow, R. E., & Lohman, D. F. (1989). Implications of cognitive psychology for educational measurement. In R. L. Linn (Ed.), *Educational measurement* (3rd ed., pp. 263–331). New York: Macmillan.

Sternberg, R. J. (1985). *Beyond IQ: A triarchic theory of intelligence*. Cambridge, MA: Cambridge University Press.

Sternberg, R. J. (2003). Issues in the theory and measurement of successful intelligence: A reply to Brody. *Intelligence, 31,* 331–337.

Thorndike, R. L., & Hagen, E. P. (1993). *Cognitive Abilities Test*. Chicago: Riverside.

Thorndike, R. L., Hagen, E. P., & Sattler, J. M. (1986). *The Stanford-Binet Intelligence Scale: Fourth edition. Technical manual*. Chicago: Riverside.

Thurstone, L. L. (1938). *Primary mental abilities*. Psychometric Monographs, No. 1.

Woodcock, R. W., McGrew, K. S., & Mather, N. (2001). *Woodcock-Johnson III*. Itasca, IL: Riverside.

CHAPTER 9

Standardized Achievement Tests

Introduction
Distinctive Features of Standardized
   Achievement Tests
Uses of Standardized Achievement Tests
Types of Standardized Achievement Tests
Group Standardized Achievement Tests
Individually Administered Achievement Tests
Secondary-School and College-Level Achievement Tests
Problems with Statewide Administration of Achievement
   Test Batteries: The "Lake Wobegon Effect"

Interpreting Standardized Achievement Test Batteries
Diagnostic Achievement Tests
Criterion-Referenced Standardized Achievement Tests
   Examples of Criterion-Referenced Standardized
     Achievement Tests
   Problems with Criterion-Referenced Standardized
     Achievement Tests
Summary
Questions and Exercises
Suggested Readings

INTRODUCTION

In Chapter 8 we distinguished between aptitude tests and achievement tests largely on the basis of the inferences that were to be drawn from the scores and the degree to which content validity was a central issue in test design. We described a number of tests of aptitude or general cognitive ability where the cognitive process being assessed was the prime concern. This chapter examines the other side of the coin: tests designed to measure how much individuals have learned, or what their store of information is. Here we focus on centrally produced tests, that is, standardized achievement tests, published commercially or by a state or national testing agency for use in a large number of schools and across school districts. The processes are similar to those an individual teacher might follow in preparing a classroom achievement test; however, important differences exist between locally prepared achievement tests and those intended for wider distribution.

DISTINCTIVE FEATURES OF STANDARDIZED ACHIEVEMENT TESTS

In anticipation that their tests will achieve widespread acceptance and use over a period of several years, commercial test publishers have shown a willingness to invest substantial amounts of time and money in developing achievement tests and test batteries that will appeal to a broad spectrum of users. State testing agencies must also develop their instruments to cover material common to all school districts that will use the test. The development of such broad-spectrum tests requires that a number of processes be carried out. These include reviewing current curricula for the region where the test is to be used, preparing detailed blueprints of content and skill, writing test exercises, reviewing items to eliminate ambiguous or potentially biased items, completing item analyses to provide objective verification of item quality, and assembling the surviving items into the resulting test. We discussed issues and procedures related to test blueprints and test bias in Chapter 5 under the heading of *Content-Related Evidence of Validity*. The general processes of item writing, analysis, and selection are covered in Chapter 15. Here we consider the features unique to achievement tests intended for widespread use, as well as the properties of some example instruments.

Breadth of Objectives. Because centrally produced tests are designed to be as widely marketable as possible—across districts, states, and the nation as a whole—standardized achievement tests can include only material that every student at the level for which the test is intended would reasonably have had the opportunity to learn. Test authors must examine the objectives for all potential school districts and select only those objectives common to all. As a result, standardized achievement tests do not emphasize the recall of facts, as is commonly believed, because this sort of content is not likely to be similar across curricula. Rather, they tend to include tasks that require information-acquiring skills such as reading comprehension and graph interpretation.

Inclusion of Norms. The most distinctive feature of centrally produced tests—in contrast to locally produced tests—is the availability of norms. The term **standardized test** implies the availability of normative data (although the term really refers to the use of uniform administration procedures), and publishers of these tests provide a range of normative information to help give meaning to test scores. The types of normative information typically provided with these instruments was described in detail in Chapter 3.

Normative data provide meaning through comparisons with other students at the same grade level. They permit statements about how Amanda is doing in mathematics or social studies in relation to other students of the same age or grade or from the same type of school system. Because all of the tests in a battery are usually normed on the same student sample, the norms also permit statements about how Amanda is doing in mathematics relative to her performance in reading, or how Jason's reading achievement compares with his performance on tests of scholastic aptitude. They may also be used to tell how a particular school compares with schools all over the country, with schools of a particular type, or with schools in a particular type of community, but, as we pointed out in Chapter 3, comparisons of this kind must be made with caution.

The quality of the norm sample is largely a function of how much the publisher is willing to spend; because norm samples may include hundreds of thousands of students, they can be expensive. When reading the manual for a standardized achievement test, a reviewer may be easily impressed by the effort and expense that has gone into ensuring a large representative sample. It is, of course, impossible to obtain a truly random sample because test publishers must conduct pilot and standardization testing in those school districts where they can obtain permission to do so. These pilot school districts often turn out to be the districts that already use a particular publisher's tests. However, all of the major test publishers go to great effort to ensure that the norm samples for their standardized achievement tests are representative of the population of likely test users in terms of important demographic variables, such as community type and geographic region. It is commercial suicide not to do so.

USES OF STANDARDIZED ACHIEVEMENT TESTS

In considering both the characteristics of standardized achievement tests just mentioned and the information from Chapter 7 on the types of decisions for which achievement test results may be helpful, we come to the following conclusions about the types of decisions for which standardized achievement tests are likely to provide the most useful information:

1. Day-to-day instructional decisions should depend primarily on locally constructed rather than standardized tests.
2. Grading decisions should be based primarily on locally constructed tests covering what has been taught in a given unit or course.
3. Diagnostic and remedial decisions can be based on information both from commercially produced diagnostic tests and from locally produced tests.
4. Placement decisions require a broad appraisal of achievement, and standardized tests with a uniform score scale can be useful in identifying an individual's entry-level performance.
5. Guidance and counseling decisions are usually based on the type of normative comparisons made possible with standardized tests.
6. Selection decisions generally imply comparison with others, and for these comparisons, adequate normative information is often important, which implies the use of standardized tests.
7. Curricular decisions between alternative programs imply a broadly based comparison in which standardized measures can play a role, often supplemented by measures developed locally for distinctive special objectives.
8. Like curricular decisions, public policy decisions require a comprehensive view of how well a school is doing. For this the broad survey and comparison features that standardized tests permit have significant value.

TYPES OF STANDARDIZED ACHIEVEMENT TESTS

The early objective achievement tests generally measured performance in individual subjects. A school district that wanted to measure the achievement of students in several subjects such as reading, mathematics, and social studies had to administer a different test for each use. The use of so many different tests was expensive and time consuming, and it required that teachers be familiar with the norming and administrative procedures for a number of different instruments. During the last several decades these separate, uncoordinated tests have gradually been replaced by test batteries that can be administered together using a single test booklet.

These coordinated batteries have several important advantages. Planning is comprehensive, and the test components are designed to provide integrated coverage of the major academic skills and curricular areas. Each part is planned with an awareness of the other parts so that duplication can be minimized and joint coverage of important material, guaranteed.

More important than these advantages is the fact that all of the subtests of such batteries have been normed on the same sample of students. Comparisons within and between individuals and comparisons within and between groups are more straightforward when norms for all parts of a battery are based on the same group of students; the batteries become much more "iffy" when the reference group changes from test to test. Of course, there are possible drawbacks to the use of achievement test batteries. Comparing different batteries, we may prefer a mathematics test from one, a language test from another, and a reading test from still another on the basis of the correspondence of each to our local curriculum and objectives. But, for the types of comparisons for which standardized tests are most appropriately used, the gains from unified norms (and test design) seem to outweigh any losses from having to accept a package in which one or two elements are judged to be less than ideal.

GROUP STANDARDIZED ACHIEVEMENT TESTS

There are five major, large-scale achievement test batteries: the California Achievement Test (CAT), published by McGraw-Hill; the Comprehensive Test of Basic Skills (CTBS), also published by McGraw-Hill; the Iowa Tests of Basic Skills (ITBS), published by the Riverside Publishing Company; the Metropolitan Achievement Tests (MAT), published by the Psychological Corporation; and the Stanford Achievement Test (SAT) series, also published by the Psychological Corporation. All of these instruments cover more or less the same skills, but each breaks the pie up into a different number and arrangement of slices, and some begin coverage of a given topic at earlier ages than others. The general content areas covered include reading, language skills, mathematics, science, social studies, study/research skills, and a composite achievement score. The grade ranges for each of the batteries are given in Table 9–1.

All of these batteries have been around for many years and have undergone several revisions. In most cases, at least two editions of the tests are available at any one time. The tests are similar in terms of the time and effort that have gone into their development and the time it takes to administer them. Their overall quality is high, and they cover the same range of students and have similar content areas, although the number of separate scores that can be obtained from the different tests varies from as few as 5 to more than 20. The test development and norming procedures, generally, are exemplary. The tests differ in terms of specific items, subscales, and techniques of test development, as well as

Table 9–1
Grade Ranges Covered by the Major Standardized Achievement Tests

Level[a]	CAT	CTBS	ITBS	MAT	SAT
1	K.0–K.9	K.0–K.9	K.1–1.5	K.0–K.5	1.5–2.5
2	K.6–2.2	K.6–1.6	K.8–1.9	K.5–1.5	2.5–3.5
3	1.6–3.2	1.0–2.2	1.7–2.6	1.5–2.5	3.5–4.5
4	2.6–4.2	1.6–3.2	2.5–3.5	2.5–3.5	4.5–5.5
5	3.6–5.2	2.6–4.2	3	3.5–4.5	5.5–6.5
6	4.6–6.2	3.6–5.2	4	4.5–5.5	7.5–8.5
7	5.6–7.2	4.6–6.2	5	5.5–6.5	8.5–9.9
8	6.6–8.2	5.6–7.2	6	6.5–7.5	9.0–9.9
9	7.6–9.2	6.6–9.2	7	7.5–8.5	10.0–10.9
10	8.6–11.2	8.6–11.2	8[b]	8.5–9.5	11.0–13.0
11	10.6–12.9	10.6–12.9	9[b]	9	
12			10[b]	10	
13			11–12[b]	11–12	

[a]Different publishers use different labels for the various levels of their tests. The values given here do not correspond to those of any particular publisher.
[b]Coverage provided by the Iowa Tests of Educational Development and the Tests of Academic Proficiency.

the factor of greatest importance, the specific objectives assessed by each. Anyone involved in making decisions concerning which test to use needs to compare tests carefully to determine which objectives and score reports are most appropriate for the local situation.

To illustrate how the form and content of a test changes from the elementary to advanced levels, Figure 9–1 contains sample items similar to those used in the reading subtest of the

ITBS Level 6 (K.8–1.9) Early Primary Battery
Reading: Words (13 items) 10 minutes

Teacher reads "Fill in the circle under the word *tell.*"

Take   Tell   Talk   Yell
O   O   O   O

Reading: Pictures (13 items) 8 minutes

Teacher reads "Fill in the circle for the word that best tells what is in the picture."

Boy   Coat   Boat   Bat
O   O   O   O

Reading: Sentences (13 items) 10 minutes

Child is instructed to choose the word that goes best in the blank.

Billy walked his _____ .

Dog   Cat   Mother   Duck
O   O   O   O

Reading: Word Attack (7 items) 5 minutes

Child is instructed to fill in the circle under the picture that tells what the last word in the sentence is.

The cat sits in the window.

O   O   O

Reading: Picture Stories (3 pictures, 13 items) 12 minutes

A picture shows two people interacting in some way. The child answers 4 or 5 yes-no questions about what is going on in the picture.

Figure 9–1
Items similar to those used to assess reading on the Iowa Tests of Basic Skills (ITBS)/Iowa Tests of Educational Development (ITED).

ITBS Level 7 (1.7–2.6) Primary Battery
Reading: Pictures (6 pictures, 23 items) 12 minutes

> Same as at Level 6, except three of the pictures have yes-no items (14 items) and the other three have multiple-choice answers.

Reading: Sentences (14 yes-no items) 7 minutes

> If your father always cooks dinner, does your mother ever cook it?

Reading: Stories (5 stories, 19 items) 15 minutes

> The child reads a four- or five-sentence story and answers three or four multiple-choice items about it. The last story is much longer than the first four.

ITBS Level 8 (2.5–3.5) Primary Battery
Reading: Pictures (6 pictures, 23 questions) 12 minutes

> Same as at Level 7. All questions are multiple choice.

Reading: Sentences (14 yes-no questions) 7 minutes

> Same as at Level 7.

Reading: Stories (3 stories, 24 items) 15 minutes

> Same as at Level 7, but stories are more complex.

ITBS Multilevel Battery (Grades 3–9)
The test booklet contains twenty-four reading passages of increasing complexity and length, including selections of poetry. Questions become increasingly complex and require greater abstraction and interpretation. Tests are arranged so that students at different levels start at different places in the test booklet. For example, students at Level 9 start with the first item and stop at item 44, while students at Level 10 start at item 19 and work through item 68. The groups share items 19–44. The overlapping format makes it possible to test students from different grades as a single group.

Level	Start Item	Stop Item
9	1	44
10	19	68
11	30	83
12	45	100
13	68	124
14	84	141

ITED Reading Comprehension (Grades 9–12)
The reading score is based on 118 comprehension items distributed throughout the Social Studies, Natural Sciences, and Literary Interpretation sections of the Battery.

Figure 9–1
(continued)

ITBS/ITED. As the examinees get older and become more capable of working independently, the presentation shifts from a teacher-paced, oral format to a student-paced, entirely written format. Pictures are used frequently at the lower levels, at the point where basic decoding skills are still being established. Also, emphasis is placed on word analysis and decoding skills at the lower levels, while at the higher levels, more emphasis is on knowledge of word meanings and the reading of continuous text, followed by answering questions that assess reading comprehension.

Two aspects of these changes in the test focus over age ranges are particularly notable. First, to match the capabilities of the maturing students, there is a progressive shift in the nature of what is tested. Second, at the higher levels, the test provides a broad survey of complex skills rather than a specific analysis of sharply defined competencies.

INDIVIDUALLY ADMINISTERED ACHIEVEMENT TESTS

In the last several years, there has been increasing interest in using individually administered tests of academic achievement either as a supplement to measures of cognitive ability or, in some cases, to replace the other measures. This interest springs mainly from a need to diagnose various learning disabilities. One of the primary indicators that a learning disability is present is a larger-than-expected discrepancy between cognitive ability scores and achievement test scores. The discrepancy often is first noticed in examining the results from group testing.

When a learning disability is suspected, based on group testing results, the normal procedure usually involves obtaining more precise estimates of the child's cognitive abilities and academic achievement. This means administering an individual cognitive ability test, such as one of those described in Chapter 8, and, increasingly, an individual measure of achievement. Several such measures have recently been developed, and more are on the way.

One of the first individual achievement tests was the Peabody Individual Achievement Test (PIAT), published by American Guidance Service. Originally released in 1970, the test was revised in 1989. The PIAT-R can be used with students from kindergarten through grade 12 and takes about 60 minutes to administer. Scores can be obtained for General Information, Reading Recognition, Reading Comprehension, Total Reading, Mathematics, Spelling, Test Total, Written Expression, and Written Language. Not all scores are available at all ages.

In 1985 the Kaufman Test of Educational Achievement (K-TEA) was published, also by American Guidance Service. This test is available in two versions. The Brief version, which takes about 30 minutes to administer, provides scores for Reading, Mathematics, Spelling, and Battery Composite. The Full version, requiring 60 to 75 minutes, subdivides Reading Achievement into Reading Decoding, Reading Comprehension, and Reading Composite. Likewise, the mathematics test produces scores for Mathematics Applications, Mathematics Computation, and Mathematics Composite. Spelling and Battery Composite scores are also given. Either form can be used for students in grades 1–12.

The PIAT-R and the K-TEA have been available in their present editions for longer than is usual for standardized tests. However, both instruments were administered to a new norm group in 1998. The sample of more than 3,000 individuals was stratified on region of the country, sex, age, grade, race/ethnicity, and parental education. Each examinee took not only the PIAT-R and the K-TEA but also two individually administered diagnostic achievement tests, Key-Math and the Woodcock Reading Mastery Tests. Having all four of these tests co-normed on the same sample provides the counselor with a broad range of options for individual assessment.

A third entry in the field of individually administered achievement tests is the Woodcock-Johnson–III Tests of Achievement (WJ-III), published by Riverside Publishing Company. This test is unique in that it is a companion to the individual cognitive ability test by the same name (see Chapter 8) and was normed on the same sample. The common norm sample makes achievement-ability comparisons more direct than is possible with other instruments. In addition, the norm sample included people ranging from 2 to 90 years of age, allowing the test to be used appropriately with individuals both below and above normal school age. The Standard Battery takes about 50 to 60 minutes to administer and has 11 subtests. The subtests are combined in various ways to yield six general academic cluster scores: Broad Reading (Letter–Word Identification, Reading Fluency, and Passage Comprehension subtests), Oral Language (Story Recall and Understanding Directions subtests), Broad Math (Calculation, Math Fluency, and Applied Problems subtests), Math Calculation (Calculation and Math Fluency), Broad Written Language (Spelling, Writing Fluency, and Writing Samples), and Written Expression (Writing Fluency and Writing Samples). Four special-purpose cluster scores can also be calculated from these subtests: Academic Skills (Letter–Word Identification, Calculation, and Spelling), Academic Fluency (Reading Fluency, Math Fluency, and Writing Fluency), Academic Applications (Passage Comprehension, Applied Problems, and Writing Samples), and Total Achievement (all subtests except the ones for oral language). The extended battery adds eight subtests and nine clusters. As we noted in Chapter 8, the quantitative subtests of this battery provide the quantitative ability score for the WJ-III Cognitive battery. The WJ-III Achievement battery is the most comprehensive of the individually administered achievement batteries, and its co-norming with the WJ-III Cognitive battery provides a highly flexible assessment system.

SECONDARY-SCHOOL AND COLLEGE-LEVEL ACHIEVEMENT TESTS

At the elementary school level, standardized tests tend to focus on the basic skills of operating with words and numbers. At the secondary school and college levels, the emphasis shifts to the substance of particular curricular areas and even to particular courses. Because the curriculum becomes more differentiated, with a core that is common to all students representing a smaller fraction of the total, there is less need for a uniform comprehensive assessment. However, in some situations a standardized achievement test battery can appropriately be used.

At the end of World War II, there was a need to evaluate and give credit for educational experiences obtained in the armed forces, so the Iowa Tests of Educational Development were developed. Like all general-ability tests, the ITED battery, which now provides the upper end to the Iowa Tests of Basic Skills for the series of achievement tests produced by Riverside Publishing Company, was designed to be appropriate for individuals who come from varied backgrounds. The tests, therefore, tends to emphasize general knowledge and the ability to read and understand material from various fields of knowledge. The present version, the ninth edition of the ITED (Forsyth, Ainsley, Feldt, & Alnot, 2001), has several parallel forms (Forms K, L, M, and most recently A) and three levels (Level 15 for grade 9, Level 16 for grade 10, and Level 17/18 for grades 11 and 12). Form A contains the subtests and items listed in Table 9–2. In addition, it provides a composite reading test score. The emphasis on getting, using, and interpreting material of various types and from various sources is apparent in the test titles. Almost all of the subtests make a substantial demand on reading skills, and most of the subtests are highly correlated with each other. As a result, although the entire test provides a good prediction of later academic

Table 9–2
Time Limits and Number of Items for the Subtests of the ITED Form A

Test	Working Time	Test Level Grade	Number of Items 15 9	16 10	17/18 11–12
Core Battery					
Vocabulary	15		40	40	40
Reading Comprehension	40		44	44	44
Language: Revising Written Materials	40		56	56	56
Spelling	10		30	30	30
Mathematics: Concepts and Problem Solving	40		40	40	40
Computation	15		30	30	30
Core Total	160		240	240	240
Supplementary Tests					
Analysis of Social Studies Materials	40		50	50	50
Analysis of Science Materials	40		408	48	48
Sources of Information	20		40	40	40
Complete Total	260		378	378	378

performance, the subtests are not effective diagnostic tools. They also do not correspond closely enough to what is taught in any specific course to have value in indicating how effective a total school program has been.

More conventional and more representative of other high school batteries is the Tests of Achievement and Proficiency Forms K, L, and M (Scannell, Haugh, Loyd, & Risinger, 1993, 1996). There are eight subtests in the basic battery:

1. Reading Comprehension
2. Vocabulary
3. Written Expression
4. Information Processing
5. Mathematics Concepts and Problem Solving
6. Social Studies
7. Science
8. Math Computation (optional).

The complete battery provides a Reading Total score, which combines Vocabulary and Reading Comprehension; a Core Total score, which combines Written Expression and Mathematics Concepts with Reading Total; and a Complete Battery score, which combines all subtest scores. As you can see from the titles, the battery is a mixture of basic skills (reading, writing, and mathematics) and of content (social studies, science, and literature). However, even in the content areas, a fair amount of emphasis is placed on functional knowledge, for example, interpretation of data and of experimental designs in science. Such adaptations bring the tests closer to the common core of secondary education and make them more useful for comparing different schools and curricula and for making guidance decisions relating to a particular student. However, the emphasis on functional knowledge renders the tests less useful as measures of what has been taught in any specific course. A writing assessment can be added to either the ITED or the TAP. Both the ITED and the TAP were co-normed with the Iowa Tests of Basic Skills and the Cognitive Abilities Test (Chapter 8) to provide a complete assessment package across the entire K–12 grade range.

In addition to batteries such as those just described, there are series of tests whose titles correspond rather closely to the names of specific courses. One extensive series was developed by the Cooperative Test Division of the Educational Testing Service (ETS). The nature of the tests is suggested by the types of tests in mathematics: structure of the number system; arithmetic; algebra I, II, and III; geometry; trigonometry; analytic geometry; and calculus. Typically, the tests in this series are designed for students who have completed some specific course, such as beginning algebra, biology, or world history. Norms usually are based on samples of students who have completed such a course. Therefore, individual factors that influence a student's decision to enroll in a course may affect the integrity of the norming procedures. Little attempt has been made to maintain comparability of the score scale from one field to another, so comparisons across fields are rather questionable. Test content may in some cases match course content well enough that the test can play a role in the end-of-year evaluation of each student, but such a step should be taken with care to ensure that the course objectives correspond to those covered by the test. Alternatively, the standardized test can be used to assess achievement of those objectives it does cover, and locally constructed measures can be used for the rest. Such an approach requires that all of the objectives covered by the test also be objectives for the course.

One role suggested for tests designed to match specific courses is that of exempting particular students from individual course requirements. In part because many young adults have received various kinds of training in the armed forces and in part in recognition of the fact that some individuals may have been educated through media other than formal schooling—for example, through reading, radio and television, or work experience—it seems desirable to some educators to provide a channel for accreditation of such experience through examinations. The College Level Examination Program (CLEP) of the Educational Testing Service is such a channel.

The CLEP was established to provide a uniform nationwide procedure for evaluating experience claimed as the equivalent of specific college courses. Examinations have been prepared for 35 areas ranging from accounting and African American history to tests and measurements, trigonometry, and Western civilization. Normative data have been obtained from college students who have completed the designated course, as well as from those who have taken the equivalency test. Scores are presented as standard scores that range from 200 to 800, with 500 representing the average score for the basic reference population (the same metric that ETS uses for its Scholastic Assessment Test). The way that the results from such a test will be used is determined by the college to which the student is applying and from which he or she wishes to receive equivalency credit. As with any accrediting or licensing examination, the decision on what constitutes a minimum acceptable level is quite arbitrary. Although general normative data may be available for those who have taken the course for which the examination is a substitute, it is likely that no data will be available specifically for the college to which an individual is applying.

The score at which the balance shifts in favor of the gain in time saved, yet away from the risk of misclassifying a student as having mastered a course must be determined intuitively. The use of examinations for licensure and certification of competence is widespread in our society. States use tests for everything from granting driving privileges to deciding who can offer psychological and counseling services, but the system for setting cutoff scores for certification generally falls far short of being rational.

PROBLEMS WITH STATEWIDE ADMINISTRATION OF ACHIEVEMENT TEST BATTERIES: THE "LAKE WOBEGON EFFECT"

Several years ago, John Cannell (1988), a physician in West Virginia, became concerned when the results of the administration of the CTBS in his state were announced. It seemed that his state was above the national average in all grade levels tested. These results were reported in the face of convincing evidence that West Virginia had serious educational problems. The state had the highest percentage of adults without college degrees, the second lowest per capita income, and the third lowest scores on the tests of the American College Testing (ACT) Program. When Cannell began to check the results of standardized achievement test administrations around the country, what he found was even more disconcerting. He discovered that none of the 50 states were below average at the elementary level. This phenomenon was quickly labeled the "Lake Wobegon effect" after Garrison Keillor's description of his fictional hometown on the syndicated public radio program, A Prairie Home Companion, as a place "where all the women are strong, all the men are good-looking, and all the children are above average."

The discovery that all states are above average should cause the same alarm as the sound of a clock striking 13. There is certainly something wrong; basic rules of statistics dictate that it is impossible for every child or every state to be above average. Test publishers and the school districts that used these tests were quick to defend themselves against charges that they were guilty of any wrongdoing.

The most often heard explanation for these high scores is that the achievement of students has increased since the tests were standardized. With a 7- to 8-year turnaround between revisions, there is a sizable gap between standardization and use. The available evidence, however, fails to support this explanation. ACT and SAT scores have declined (although they have shown some recovery in recent years); National Assessment of Educational Progress scores show little increase nor do Armed Services Vocational Aptitude Battery scores. The hypothesis that overall achievement has increased since the tests were most recently normed would be supported if test results were much lower the first year the test was introduced. The MAT Form 6, the CAT Form E, and the ITBS Forms G and H were all introduced during the 1985–1986 school year, and for each, states that immediately administered the test reported scores that were quite high. The high scores were not the result of teachers teaching to the test because the teachers had not seen the test before the test date. The high scores also could not have resulted from improvement since the last norming because not enough time had passed since that norming.

A second explanation for the high proportion of students who score above average on standardized achievement tests is that the students taking these tests differ from the norm sample. Although the test publishers spend enormous sums norming their tests, including samples that typically exceed 200,000, there is no way to ensure that the sample is truly representative because, as mentioned previously, the administration of the test for norming purposes can take place only where permission can be obtained. For this reason, these samples may be different in important ways from the students that are assessed when the tests are administered "for real." This problem is exacerbated by the tendency of many school districts to exclude from testing students who might be expected to obtain low scores, such as special education and other special program students. Norming studies usually require that these students be included so that the norms will represent the actual population of students rather than a selected subset. Some school districts or specific teachers within a district might exclude, or at least not encourage, the participation of students who are not expected to do well. When low-performing students are excluded, classroom teachers or districts that engage in such practices can expect their performance to be high, relative to the norming population.

A third explanation for the high proportion of students who score above average relates to changes in the curriculum that are the direct result of the testing process. As more importance is placed on test results, the likelihood that curricula will be altered to fit what is being tested will increase. Some such alterations may be considered legitimate—to the extent that they do not involve teaching to the test. But, even in its most legitimate forms, altering the curriculum to increase the match with test objectives will violate the sampling assumptions of the test, and the resulting standard scores will lose their meaning. To some extent, test publishers may be contributing to the problem by including detailed reports of student and class performance on an item-by-item basis, as described in Chapter 3. There is educational value for the teacher and students in knowing where errors occur most frequently, but to the extent that this knowledge narrows the focus of instruction, the practice may backfire by gradually invalidating the normative data.

If a teacher realizes that a class is consistently failing to answer correctly an item from the test that requires the capitalization of the name of the state of Arizona, it would obviously be inappropriate for the teacher to tell his or her students to always capitalize the word *Arizona*. On the other hand, it seems acceptable for a teacher to alter the lesson plan to emphasize the need to capitalize the names of all states. But such a practice can change the meanings of scores derived from norms, because standardized achievement tests are intended to sample student behavior, which permits generalizations about a wide range of behaviors. If the teachers do not know what is included on a test, they have to make sure that they cover everything that could be included. On the other hand, if a teacher knows the general categories included on the test and teaches only these categories, the content sampling of the test will be compromised. Students taking the test under these circumstances will be taught and assessed only over the narrow range of content covered on the test. This narrowing of the curriculum focus occurs, for example, when a teacher, knowing that items assess this knowledge on the test, emphasizes the capitalization of states but fails to teach the students to capitalize the names of countries, because this type of item is not assessed by the test.

Another possible explanation for the high proportion of above-average students is that teachers could actually be teaching the items from the test or administering the test in a nonstandard way that causes scores to be inflated. For instance, a teacher could provide inappropriate assistance when the test is administered or give students too much time to complete sections of the test that they have trouble completing in the allotted time. At the elementary level, common practice is for teachers to administer the tests in their own classrooms, with no supervision. When undue importance is placed on student performance and there is an absence of supervision of the test administration, the likelihood that cheating will take place increases.

Two public policy factors contribute to this problem. First, teachers are under pressure to ensure their students do well on tests, because the teachers may be evaluated on the basis of the test results. A teacher whose class shows below-average performance on a state- or district-wide test may have his or her own competence questioned. Second, all the way up the chain of command, those who are responsible for seeing that proper test administration procedures are maintained have a second, and perhaps more important, interest in seeing the scores rise: because they are often evaluated on the basis of these scores. In many states standardized test results are viewed by the public, the media, and the legislature as a report card for the educational system. As a result, the individuals in charge at all levels of the testing program may face a serious conflict of interest and be tempted to overlook inappropriate practices that could lead to inflated scores.

Obviously, a teacher who is giving students too much time to complete a section of a test or actually helping students answer questions is guilty of cheating. Likewise, a teacher who drills students on actual items from a test is involved in a practice that is generally perceived to be inappropriate. On the other hand, a teacher who, because of concern about her students' performance on an achievement test, worked extremely hard to get her students to learn more or who encouraged students to work hard on the test is not engaged in cheating. In fact, such behaviors would probably be viewed as exemplary. But gray areas, such as the following, cause problems: teachers using items similar to those that appear on a test to be administered, or focusing instruction on those topics that are known to appear on the test. Such practices are generally considered unethical but, unfortunately, are common.

Some school districts have even implemented system-wide programs that involve a curricular emphasis on the specific content of the achievement tests that they use. Test publishers also make available instructional materials that can have a similar impact on student performance. Of course, the relationship between curriculum guides and test content can be a two-way street. If test publishers take their content from an examination of popular curriculum guides, it is equally possible for the tests to influence the curriculum writers.

INTERPRETING STANDARDIZED ACHIEVEMENT TEST BATTERIES

The standardized achievement test is designed to yield a reliable score for each of the skill areas covered. (Reliability coefficients in the high 80s or low 90s would be fairly typical.) Interest tends to focus on the subtest scores and the student's, class's, school's, or district's profile of strengths and weaknesses. We not only want to know how Peter's achievement in mathematics compares with national norms, but how it compares with his achievement in other areas covered by the battery. We may want to know how Ms. Albertson's class is progressing in mastery of mathematics concepts in comparison with their computational skills. We also may want to know in what respect schools of the Peterboro district appear better than average and in what respects they show deficiencies. There may be a further interest in knowing whether these differences reflect the desired curricular emphasis; if school administrators, teachers, parents, and the public should be concerned; and if remediation efforts should be initiated.

When it comes to classroom instructional decisions, the subtest scores on a survey achievement battery are of limited value. If Peter's achievement is a full grade below his current grade placement in capitalization skills, what is to be done about it? If Ms. Albertson's class shows an average grade equivalent a half grade lower in mathematics concepts than in mathematics computation, what steps should Ms. Albertson take? What should she teach or reteach? One way to answer these questions is to look at the individual items on the capitalization test that Peter answered incorrectly or the specific mathematics concepts that many of the children in Ms. Albertson's class did not know. This information about individual and collective student performance can be provided by the scoring services made available by test publishers.

Because large-scale testing programs are scored and interpreted by computer, only fairly simple modifications in the scoring program are required to permit more detailed information about the responses of individual children and classes. Report forms can be provided that will indicate which items Peter answered incorrectly on the capitalization subtest. The items can even be grouped by the capitalization rule that they exemplify. Information about the types of mathematics skills with which the class as a whole is experiencing difficulty also can be identified. From this information, Ms. Albertson can determine whether Peter made errors in capitalizing at the beginning of a sentence, at the beginning of a quotation, for names of persons, for names of places, and so forth. She can also see the frequency of errors in various concept and computational mathematical-skill areas for the entire class. This analysis of the test results has the potential for identifying specific difficulties and giving clues for instruction. Through these reports, the test author can assist teachers in what they have always been urged to do, that is, dig beneath the normative test score to identify the specific test exercises with which individuals and the class as a whole are encountering difficulty.

Detailed analysis of successes and failures on specific items can be quite useful for the teacher. However, there are some important cautions about such an approach. First, these tests do not contain enough items to assess each specific skill adequately. Because there may be only one or two items per skill, a child might answer these items correctly and thereby "pass an objective" by making a lucky guess, or answer items incorrectly because of some distraction or reason not relevant to the basic skill the item is testing. One or two items are insufficient to permit a reliable mastery/nonmastery decision about a child, though failure to answer an item correctly can alert the teacher to the need to more fully test the skill being measured, perhaps with a short, teacher-made test focusing specifically on the skill covered by the item answered incorrectly. Similarly, failure on an item by a substantial percentage of students in a class suggests the need to test that skill more thoroughly to determine whether some part of the class lacks mastery of the skill involved in that item.

There is a still more serious problem with the practice of assessing objectives with one or two items. If teachers are familiar with the specific items students are missing and are under pressure to have their students improve their scores, they may be tempted to teach the specific items or at least the specific types of items, a practice that leads to inflated test scores and the Lake Wobegon effect.

If the analysis of test results is to be helpful to a teacher, it should be in the teacher's hands as soon after testing as possible. Because modern, computer-based test scoring usually must be done centrally, there inevitably will be a lag between testing and the teacher's receipt of the test-result report. Each added week of delay makes the results less timely for instructional decisions concerning specific children or the whole class. New learning has taken place, previously learned material may have been forgotten, and the details of the descriptive picture will be less accurate. For these reasons, it is important to expedite completion of a testing program, assembly of answer sheets from the participating schools, and shipment of the materials to the processing agency. From that point on, teachers are at the mercy of the U.S. Postal Service and the agency conducting the scoring and report preparation.

Most test scoring services take very seriously the problem of lag between testing and results and, hence, they provide a 24-hour turnaround option. With many services it is also possible to transmit test results electronically, so the test papers never leave the school or district.

This procedure requires that the necessary scanning and computer equipment be available, but this is now the case in all but the smallest districts. The problem of turnaround time is likely to be particularly serious in statewide testing programs if there is a requirement that returns from all school systems be received before test analysis can be conducted and results provided. In some cases, processing problems resulting from technical or political issues have delayed reporting beyond the year in which the test results were obtained. By the time these results are in the hands of the teachers, it is too late to use them for instructional planning for specific students.

DIAGNOSTIC ACHIEVEMENT TESTS

Diagnosis relates primarily to the single individual. Why does Sarah get a low score on a survey test of reading comprehension? Why does Peter get a low score on the mathematics subtest of the achievement battery? What are the sources of difficulty? Much, probably most, diagnostic testing is conducted with single students after it has been determined from a survey test or from the observations of the teacher that a student is not making satisfactory progress in reading, mathematics, or some other segment of the school program. Although most testing of this kind is done individually, perhaps using one of the individually administered achievement tests described earlier, some standardized tests are available that serve a diagnostic function and can be administered to a group. We will describe one of these, indicating what it undertakes to do and the problems that arise in its use and interpretation.

The Stanford Diagnostic Mathematics Test, Fourth Edition, is designed for use in grades 1.5 through 13. Levels are designated by colors: The red level is for students at the middle of 1st grade through the middle of 2nd grade and low-performing students in 3rd grade. The orange level is for middle 2nd grade through middle 3rd grade. The green level is for 3rd–4th and low-performing 5th-grade students. Purple is for mid-4th through mid-6th grade and low-performing 7th graders. The brown level is for 6th-, 7th-, and 8th-grade students. The blue level is for the 8th- through 13th-grade levels. All six levels assess mathematical competence in (1) concepts and applications and (2) computation.

Norm-referenced scores include scaled scores, grade equivalents, percentile ranks, normal curve equivalents, and stanines for each subtest. Information is also provided on the performance of students on each separate skill measured within each of the subtests, given in the form of raw scores, and indicating whether the child was above or below a cutoff score.

The test has been normed for both fall and spring administration, but for maximum value it is recommended that the test be administered in the fall so that diagnosis and remediation can be undertaken immediately. In selecting which level to administer, both the grade and the level of functioning of the student should be considered. Little diagnostic information can be derived from a test that is either too easy or too difficult. The test is structured so that either one or two tests can be administered on the same day. If two tests are administered on the same day, a 10-minute rest period between tests is recommended.

Analysis of subtest scores is only the initial step in diagnosis. Performance on the specific skills subsumed within the subtests must also be examined. But even these analyses may not be sufficient. If Peter's scores are compared with the norms for his grade group and it is found that his lowest score is in multiplication of whole numbers, we still do not know what aspect of multiplication is giving him trouble. We have some guidance on where we should focus further scrutiny, but we still need to analyze Peter's errors in multiplication problems to see if we can determine whether his problem is errors in conception or procedure, or a deficit in the mastery of number facts. Upon tentatively identifying an area of weakness, we need to observe the process of Peter's functioning in that area to determine exactly what he does incorrectly and to generate hypotheses on why he does it. A thorough diagnostic study typically requires observation of the process, as well as the product, of student performance.

If a weakness on a particular subtest identifies an individual student in a class, we first look for deficits in that student's acquisition of knowledge. If the class as a whole performs poorly on some subtest, we should ask whether the quality of instruction was as it should have been or whether the introduction of certain topics was delayed in the local curriculum. A discrepancy between local performance and national norms signifies a problem only to the degree that the local curriculum agrees with the assumptions made by the publisher regarding when topics should be introduced. If a topic (such as fractions) has not been taught to a particular class at the time of testing, obviously there is no reason to be concerned if the topic has not been mastered. The group's past instructional history and instructional emphasis must influence interpretation of class-average profiles on such a diagnostic battery.

Because the subtests in a battery provide meaningful diagnostic clues only when the material covered by a subtest has been taught to the students, we may question whether the material on fractions and decimals provides useful diagnostic information for fourth- and fifth-grade groups. We cannot identify deficient performance on a subtest if the average performance is very close to a chance score, which is what we should expect if the students have not received instruction in the skills being measured. In general, the better adapted a test is for displaying a serious deficiency, the poorer it will be for identifying levels of achievement. There is an essential incompatibility between the functions of diagnosing deficiency and assessing all degrees of excellence. The test that is good for one of these purposes is unlikely to be good for the other. Usually, a diagnostic test should be designed more like a criterion-referenced, or mastery, test, so that the expected score for the average examinee is close to a perfect score and so that there is a wide range of possible below-par scores to express degrees of deficiency.

A parallel set of tests, the Stanford Diagnostic Reading Test, is available to assess students' performance in reading. The test has the same six levels (with the same color codes) and the same types of normative score scales. Vocabulary and reading comprehension are assessed at all six levels. The first three levels also have a phonics analysis subtest, and the three higher levels have a scanning subtest. Both of these diagnostic achievement tests were co-normed with the ninth edition of the Stanford Achievement Test Series.

CRITERION-REFERENCED STANDARDIZED ACHIEVEMENT TESTS

The enthusiasm that surrounded the introduction of criterion-referenced approaches to classroom tests generated a parallel interest in the application of this methodology to standardized achievement tests. A criterion-referenced standardized achievement test can be constructed in one of two ways: (1) Objectives can be associated with items from existing norm-referenced achievement tests to give them the appearance of a criterion-referenced test, or (2) achievement tests can be constructed from the ground up as criterion-referenced tests. The first approach is widely employed; however, for criterion-referenced tests of the second type, availability is more limited.

Examples of Criterion-Referenced Standardized Achievement Tests

The Psychological Corporation has two reading achievement subtests that are part of the Metropolitan Achievement Test (MAT) series: (1) the reading survey tests and (2) the reading diagnostic tests. The first subtest is a survey battery similar to other norm-referenced survey achievement batteries, and the second is a criterion-referenced test covering basic reading skills. Houghton Mifflin, in its School Curriculum Objective-Referenced Evaluation, provides 5,000 items that can be put together in various combinations for constructing criterion-referenced tests to meet the specific needs of teacher and classroom settings.

Steven Osterlind at the University of Missouri has attempted to construct a test to measure achievement of basic academic subjects and skills for the college level. His instrument, the College Basic Academic Subjects Examination (College BASE) can be used for individual or institutional assessment. The test measures student achievement in English, mathematics, science, and social studies. Scores are reported for these four subjects, as well as overall achievement, nine achievement clusters, and 23 specific skills. Scores can also be provided for three reasoning competencies: interpretive, strategic, and adaptive. Individual assessment requires about 3 hours, but institutional assessment for program review, where results are averaged across students, can be accomplished in about 45 minutes, because each student takes only one-fourth of the battery. A writing sample can be added to the subject matter tests to assess writing competence. The test is available from the University of Missouri.

Problems with Criterion-Referenced Standardized Achievement Tests

In general, it is not possible for a single test to serve the purposes of both a norm-referenced and a criterion-referenced assessment because criterion-referenced tests need to be tied closely to the specific instructional objectives of the classroom or school district. The publishers of nationally distributed achievement tests must avoid any objectives that are not found in the curricula of most school districts. This need to focus on common objectives works better in the early grades and in reading and mathematics, where school districts have the greatest consensus concerning which objectives should be emphasized. The demand for criterion-referenced achievement tests has led some test publishers to associate instructional objectives with existing items and to claim that these new tests have the properties of, or can be used as, criterion-referenced tests. Such tests are better described as objective-referenced tests and are considered to be poor forms of assessment. Criterion-referenced assessment is attractive because it seems to avoid some of the negative associations that surround testing by avoiding the labeling of students as failures. It is seen as more constructive because it provides specific information about student performance.

Although criterion-referenced tests have important advantages, such as those just cited, the use of criterion-referenced techniques with standardized achievement tests is fraught with logistic problems. It is necessary to administer many items to reliably assess a large number of objectives. For instance, the Metropolitan Reading Diagnostic Test includes more than 200 items at most grade levels but assesses some objectives with only three items. The MAT, on the other hand, uses only 60 items to obtain an overall reading score. To measure something, whether it is a skill such as reading comprehension or an objective such as *can add two-digit numbers,* an adequate number of items is required; that is, a test reporting performance on a large number of objectives must be much longer than one reporting seven subtest scores.

SUMMARY

Most standardized testing involves the use of survey test batteries selected from a small number of similar tests. Testing is also conducted using diagnostic and criterion-referenced tests. Survey tests are useful primarily in connection with selection, placement, guidance, curricular, and public policy decisions. Diagnostic tests are used to determine a student's strengths and weaknesses. Diagnostic testing is difficult and time consuming to implement.

At the secondary and college levels, centrally produced achievement tests provide evidence both of outstanding competence—to serve as a basis for advanced placement—and of minimal competence. An important controversy in statewide achievement testing is the existence of the "Lake Wobegon effect," which, because it inflates scores, makes the interpretation of the results of such tests difficult. Another problem is the tendency by educators to vacillate between attempts to make objective-referenced interpretations of achievement in local schools and attempts to make global appraisals of the effectiveness of different schools and school systems at the state level.

QUESTIONS AND EXERCISES

1. For which of the following purposes would a standardized test be useful? For which purposes should teachers expect to make their own tests? Why?
   a. To determine which students have mastered the addition and subtraction of fractions
   b. To determine which students are below the expected skill level in mathematics computation
   c. To determine the subjects in which each student is strongest and weakest
   d. To determine for a class which punctuation and capitalization skills need to be taught further
   e. To form subgroups in a class for the teaching of reading

2. Obtain a curriculum guide covering the content and objectives of a subject that you are teaching, plan to teach, or someday might want to teach. Examine a standardized achievement test for that subject. Which of the objectives in the curriculum guide are adequately measured by the test? Which ones are not? How adequately is the content covered by the test?

3. Make a critical comparison of two achievement test batteries for the same grade. How do they differ? What are the advantages of each, from your point of view?

4. The manual for a test states that it can be used for diagnostic purposes. What criteria could you use to determine whether it has any real value as a diagnostic tool?

5. Why should we be concerned about the reliability of the scores resulting from a set of diagnostic tests? What implications does the reliability have for using and interpreting such tests?

6. A senior high school that draws from three feeder junior highs has a special accelerated program in mathematics. What are the advantages and disadvantages of selecting students for this program based on scores of a standardized achievement test in mathematics given at the end of the ninth grade (the last year in junior high)?

7. In October you gave a standardized achievement battery to your fourth-grade class. How might you, as a teacher, use the results?

8. A school using a centralized scoring service buys item analysis data that show the percentage of students answering each item correctly for each grade and each classroom in the school. How could the school as a whole use

these results? How could individual teachers use them?

9. Miss Carson, a sixth-grade teacher, says, "I am not as much interested in a student's level of performance as I am in the growth that he or she shows while in my class." In terms of measurement, what problems does this point of view raise?

10. The school system of Centerville is proposing to introduce a revised mathematics curriculum on an experimental basis in selected elementary schools. It wishes to evaluate the effectiveness of the program before introducing it throughout the system. How adequate would a standardized achievement test in elementary school mathematics be for this

type of evaluation? What problems are likely to arise? How might these problems be dealt with?

11. A state legislature has passed a law requiring all students to show adequate competency in skills needed for everyday living before they are awarded a high school diploma. What is the first problem that needs to be solved to implement the legislation? What would be the advantages and disadvantages of using the following types of tests to determine adequate competency?
   a. Centrally produced tests by the state education department
   b. Locally constructed tests by each school
   c. A nationally published achievement test

SUGGESTED READINGS

Cannell, J. J. (1988). Nationally normed elementary achievement testing in America's public schools: How all 50 states are above the national average. *Educational Measurement: Issues and Practice,* 7(2), 5–9.

Hall, B. W. (1985). Survey of the technical characteristics of published educational achievement tests.

Educational Measurement: Issues and Practice, 4(1), 6–14.

Mehrens, W. A. (1987). *Using standardized tests in education.* New York: Longman.

CHAPTER 10

Performance and Product Evaluation

Introduction
Artificiality of Conventional Cognitive Tests
Conventional Cognitive Tests
Assessing Products
Applying Performance and Product Evaluation to
  Cognitive Tasks
    Scoring Performance Tests
Assessing Processes
    Using Checklists
    Using Rating Scales

Assessing Products and Performances
    Advantages of Multiple Observers
    Reliability or Agreement for Multiple Observers
Systematic Observation
    Conducting the Systematic Observation
    Advantages and Disadvantages of Systematic
      Observation
Summary
Questions and Exercises
Suggested Readings

INTRODUCTION

To most people, in and out of education, the word *testing* means the sort of paper-and-pencil instruments that are customarily used to assess cognitive objectives. Such tests often employ select-response item formats in which the examinee chooses an answer from among a set of available alternatives. Experience has shown that clever teachers and test writers can construct cognitive tests for assessing *almost* any learning outcome, and for many instructional objectives, this is appropriate. However, for some types of objectives, a paper-and-pencil assessment is too far removed from the instructional objective that it is intended to measure to be useful. Outside the academic world there are also many tasks and behaviors for which conventional tests may be inappropriate.

ARTIFICIALITY OF CONVENTIONAL COGNITIVE TESTS

Almost all testing is to some degree artificial because we seldom directly measure instructional goals or job performance. Test standardization exacerbates this problem by increasing the need to use select-response type items to facilitate machine scoring and computer analysis. Even with cognitive material, such as reading comprehension, that we think of as most appropriate to be assessed with an objective test format, problems can arise in matching the assessment task to the instructional goal. Reading comprehension is usually measured by assessing a student's ability to answer multiple-choice items about the meaning of short paragraphs. This method of assessing reading comprehension contrasts with the conventional definition for comprehension, which is based on the capacity of students to understand what they have read, to relate new information to previously learned material, and to critically evaluate long passages of reading. Artificiality also occurs with objective spelling tests that require a student to select the correctly spelled word from among three or four misspelled words, or English usage tests that require the student to distinguish between grammatically correct and grammatically incorrect sentences. The usual process of spelling requires one to generate a correctly spelled word rather than to recognize the correct spelling. Likewise, our interest in assessing knowledge of correct English usage most often calls for the production of a correctly worded sentence. Instruction in English composition classes generally is intended to bring students to the point where they can combine these skills to write grammatically correct paragraphs with a minimum of misspelled words. Achievement of this objective is most directly assessed by evaluating paragraphs that students have written. The mere identification of grammatical errors or misspelled words is not an equivalent form of cognitive functioning. However, despite the indirectness of objective paper-and-pencil tests, educators are usually willing to accept the artificiality in exchange for objectivity and ease of administration.

CONVENTIONAL COGNITIVE TESTS

There are, however, important instructional objectives and cognitive functions that cannot be appropriately assessed, even to an approximation, by paper-and-pencil tests. These include behaviors associated with subject matter that calls for a product or a process—for example, the performances required in a music, physical education, speech, or drama class or the projects required in art, industrial arts, and home economics classes.

Evaluating performance in such situations can be quite difficult; as a result, teachers of such courses may avoid assessment altogether. This tendency to de-emphasize assessment often is exacerbated by a perception that processes and products are not academic and are therefore less important, an attitude that is sometimes used as a justification for a lack of emphasis on assigning grades in these settings.

The reluctance of teachers to evaluate educational products in the same critical manner that they evaluate more academic activities may partially stem from the belief that performances in areas such as music, art, and physical education are strongly influenced by prior ability. It is widely believed that the quality of the products and the performance of students is to a great degree a function of skills and abilities that the student possessed prior to entering a class and not necessarily the result of instruction. There are art students, for instance, who can produce the best painting in their class on the first day and others who can never paint anything acceptable no matter how much instruction they receive. Of course, this phenomenon might also apply to English composition or the solving of calculus problems, but there is a reluctance to believe that success in these areas is also the result of ability and not just effort. A poor singing voice, therefore, is more likely to be attributed to factors outside of the control of the student than is an inability to solve arithmetic problems.

ASSESSING PRODUCTS

In the past, it was useful to distinguish between assessment situations involving a concrete product, such as a sculpture made in art class, and those performances that left no permanent record, such as a speech or an interpretive dance. The former could be assessed at leisure, while evaluation of the latter had to take place at the time of performance or be based on a potentially faulty memory. However, with the widespread availability of video cameras the distinction no longer applies; performances can be transformed into concrete products.

In most cases, it is the product rather than the process by which it was produced that is the focus of assessment. For example, a teacher is usually more interested in the poem a student has written than the process of its composition. In addition, it is usually easier to evaluate a product than a process. With a product, there is a single object (or performance) that can be compared to others. A process is made up of many parts, each of which probably is transitory even if it is recorded, and performance of the parts must be weighted to obtain a summary evaluation. Standards also must be established for each step in the process. However, sometimes the process and the product are not easily distinguishable, such as for a speech or a dance. There are also situations for which the process itself is as important if not more important than the product: (1) when safety is a primary concern, (2) when the student's product itself can be considered transitory, and (3) when it is particularly difficult to evaluate a product. Even in each of these cases, however, modern recording procedures can produce a permanent record of the performance for later evaluation.

Safety. When the process can be dangerous, emphasis is necessarily placed on ensuring that it is carried out correctly. Examples include the procedures used in a chemical experiment, a gymnastic performance, or the use of power tools in a woodworking or machine shop. We may be interested not only in whether the person knows the correct procedural steps or safety measures, but also whether these are carefully followed. Our evaluation of a person in these situations would be influenced to a considerable degree by the person's adherence to the specified procedures.

Transitory Product. In some circumstances the particular product or performance is secondary to the process, because the product is just a step in the direction of better products and performances. An example of this would be a tennis serve. A good athlete might be able to serve more effectively than anyone else in his or her class, despite a lack of correct form. Even if such a serve wins points, a tennis instructor would not give it high marks. A good serve cannot be evaluated in terms of its success alone because *improvement* cannot occur without the use of correct form. Most tennis instructors would be happier with a serve that was going into the net but was based on correct form than with a serve that, while winning points, was the product of incorrect form. Computer programming is another area where there may be a need to emphasize proper procedures. Just because a computer program is capable of performing a designated task does not necessarily mean that the program is acceptable. Appropriate procedures and efficiency of programming might also be considered important.

Difficult-to-Evaluate Products. When the evaluation of a product is subjective, it may be more practical to evaluate the components of the process rather than the product. For example, it is easier to evaluate the process of teaching than to evaluate its products because no satisfactory system of evaluating the effectiveness of teaching has yet been devised. However, there are systems for evaluating the process of teaching—for example, systems based on the results of process-product research. Counseling is another activity for which the process is more easily evaluated than the product, as is management style.

APPLYING PERFORMANCE AND PRODUCT EVALUATION TO COGNITIVE TASKS

Although in the past, cognitive skills typically were not evaluated using performance and product evaluation techniques, there is increasing interest in using these techniques in this context. Some recent calls for educational reform are based on developments in the role of cognitive psychology in education. These developments have led to an increased interest in assessing the products and processes of cognitive functioning. The interest in cognitive psychology also stems from criticisms of current educational practice, which relies heavily on objective, paper-and-pencil tests as the sole criterion for measuring educational effectiveness (Nickerson, 1989). As discussed above, select-response tests are considered artificial because they do not allow students to demonstrate directly their attainment of educational objectives. In addition, the increasing interest in implementing principles of cognitive psychology in the classroom has resulted in a desire to encourage the development of higher order processing and critical-thinking skills. There is a general belief that these must be evaluated with performance- and product-assessment techniques. Although it may be technically feasible to assess the processes used in meeting educational goals, most of the emphasis in evaluation of cognitive objectives currently involves the assessment of products. The terms **performance test** and **performance assessment** are commonly associated with this practice.

In most cases, evaluation of cognitive objectives by means of performance tests involves the use of constructed-response items. Constructed-response items require that students generate answers in response to questions or prompts rather than choose from a set of available alternatives. Depending on the educational objective being assessed, students might be asked to write an essay, solve a problem, or in some other way perform a skill. The fundamental characteristic of performance test items is that they simulate actual situations, so that the examinee has the opportunity to demonstrate his or her proficiency at an exemplary task.

Scoring Performance Tests

Scoring of performance test items typically takes one of two forms: keyed response or variable response. Keyed-response formats are quite straightforward in that they involve items with one or more keyed correct responses. A student's response is considered correct if his or her answer matches one of the keyed responses. Variable-response scoring is much more complex than keyed-response scoring. For variable-response items, there is no one correct answer or small set of correct answers. Instead, scores are grounded in a set of scoring criteria called **rubrics.** In most cases, rubrics describe a hierarchy of potential responses and identify the qualities of knowledge or skill one would expect at different points along the scale. A sample performance test item in eighth-grade mathematics and its accompanying scoring rubrics are presented in Figure 10–1.

It is essential in using rubrics for scoring that there be explicit criteria for indicating proficiency in the skills specified in the educational objectives and that scorers have adequate training in applying those criteria. In addition, it is desirable to provide scorers with samples of examinees' responses that are exemplary of different points along the scoring rubric. If either poorly trained scorers or vague scoring criteria are used, scores from performance tests will be substantially less objective and less reliable than their multiple-choice counterparts. However, as Fredericksen and Collins (1989) point out in their discussion of the increasing use of statewide writing assessment, through use of trained scorers and carefully delineated standards, variable-response scoring using rubrics can produce accurate and dependable results. Recent advances in computerized scoring of essay responses have also made constructed-response assessment much more feasible. Resources at the web site http://www.ets.org/research/erater.html will help you gain access to this rapidly developing technology.

EXERCISE C

Mr. Ramirez helped four other students make key holders. He gave Rhonda, Sam, Tony, and Uta a board and told them to share it equally.

Rhonda measured and cut one fourth of the board.

Next Sam measured and cut one third of the remaining board.

Then Tony measured and cut one half of the remaining board.

Uta used the piece that was left.

10. Did the four students share the board equally? Draw a picture and explain your answer. Use the Review Check List below to help you write so that your ideas will be understood.

_____
_____
_____
_____
_____
_____
_____

Review Check List
☐ This picture and explanation clearly describe how the students shared the board.
☐ The ideas in this explanation follow a logical order.
☐ This explanation contains correct spelling, capitalization, and punctuation. It is neatly written.

Figure 10–1
Example of a performance assessment exercise in mathematics, with scoring rubrics.
(Adapted from F. L. Finch (Ed.), (1991), *Educational performance assessment.* Chicago: Riverside.)

(*continued*)

Scoring Rubrics

Note: Accept synonymous phrases when appropriate. Evaluation should be on content and evidence of understanding.

Question 4, page 3
If the students continued to measure and cut off one fourth of the length of the remaining board, what would happen? Explain your answer fully. (2 points possible)

Award 2 points to a response explaining that if the students continued to measure and cut off one fourth the length of the remaining board, each succeeding piece would be smaller than the previous one and, theoretically the students would never come to the end of the board, or actually the students would eventually be cutting sawdust.

Award 1 point to a response explaining that the board would eventually be used up but offering no recognition of a pattern.

Question 5, page 3
The students did not clearly understand Mr. Ramirez's directions for cutting the board. What could Mr. Ramirez have said to make his directions clearer? (1 point possible)

He could have told the students each to measure and cut off 16 inches or one fourth of the total length of the 64-inch board. (See note.)

Question 10, page 5
Did the four students share the board equally? Make a drawing and explain your answer. (4 points possible)

Assign score points to student responses that most closely match the characteristics listed. (See note.)

A 4 response
    -contains *both* a picture and an explanation that indicate a clear understanding of the pattern
    -contains a picture showing a whole divided into four equal parts
    -contains an explanation which enhances the picture by comparing the size of each piece using either sentences or computations, or a combination of both

A 3 response
    -contains a picture that indicates a clear understanding of the pattern but only an attempt at an explanation
    -contains an explanation that indicates a clear understanding of the pattern but only an attempt at a picture
    -has limited detail in the picture or the explanation

A 2 response
    -offers an adequate picture only
    -offers an adequate explanation only
    -contains an explanation that does not enhance the picture
    -may be difficult to understand due to errors in language and grammar

A 1 response
    -makes some attempt at a picture *or* an explanation
    -is unclear

A 0 response fails to attempt the question.

An N/S (nonscorable) response is illegible or unreadable.

Figure 10–1   *Continued*

ASSESSING PROCESSES

A process is always made up of a number of parts or steps and, therefore, is typically assessed with an emphasis on evaluating each of the steps in the process. Checklists and rating scales are the primary instruments used to assess these steps.

Using Checklists

It is customary when evaluating whether a student has used the appropriate process to use either a checklist or rating scale. In general, the checklist is preferred to the rating scale. With a checklist, the observer is required only to observe the performance and to mark on the observation form whether the desired behavior was present or absent. In contrast, the observer using a rating scale must make decisions about how often the behavior occurs or the quality of the behavior. Also, with a rating scale, judging may be time consuming, which can severely limit the number of behavior classes that are rated.

The person constructing a checklist should follow several steps:

1. Designate the appropriate performance or product.
2. List the important behaviors and characteristics.
3. Include common errors that the individual being evaluated might make.
4. Put the list into an appropriate format.

Designate an Appropriate Performance or Product.   The construction of a checklist should always begin with the designation of what the end product is expected to be. In most cases when the focus is on a checklist to evaluate a process, it may not be possible to precisely define the product itself, but it is necessary to specify it in general terms. The purpose of this step is to provide a focus for delineating the important behaviors and characteristics.

List the Important Behaviors and Characteristics.   Developing a list of behaviors and characteristics that describe a successful performance or product is the critical part of constructing a checklist. A good checklist will include all of the important and relevant behaviors and characteristics necessary to achieve the final product or performance. Behaviors and characteristics that are exhibited by all persons (for example, heart continues to beat) and those that cannot be assessed for any student (such as "has positive cognitive experience") should be excluded because they contribute no useful information and they clutter the checklist. The statements designating the behaviors should be worded to minimize the need for interpretations by the observers. The list should be as inclusive as possible without being so lengthy and detailed that the process of judging becomes unwieldy. Following is an example of a partial list of behaviors that an individual who is able to play tennis well should exhibit:

1. Use the correct grip.
2. Have his or her feet in the correct position when hitting the ball.
3. Keep the elbow straight.
4. Hit a forehand to the opposite court.
5. Hit a backhand to the opposite court.
6. Serve the ball to the correct part of the opponent's court.
7. Volley effectively.
8. Hit overheads.

Of course, each of these behaviors could be broken down even further. Numerous steps are associated with, for example, serving correctly or hitting an overhead. How specific the behaviors in the checklist are depends on how specific or global the behavior being observed is.

Associated with any such list of behaviors and characteristics, either implicitly or explicitly, are standards. These standards can be as formal as the distance in fractions of an inch that a student's grip can deviate from the ideal grip on a tennis racket or as informal as a consensus among judges about what would be considered a correct grip. The intent of standards is to increase the probability that all judgments have the same basis for determining whether the behavior is present or absent. For example, the judges at a figure skating competition collaborate and compare judgments on the performance of some of the early, lower rated skaters to calibrate their personal standards and reduce the variability of ratings for the skaters who are serious candidates for the championship.

Include Common Errors that the Individual Being Evaluated Might Make. It is not sufficient to determine that a student is performing all of the requisite steps in a procedure; it is also important to note the presence of specific behaviors that are considered inappropriate as well. For instance, in observing a teacher, it might be found that he or she exhibits most of the behaviors associated with good teaching but, in addition, responds to student misbehavior with sarcasm. It is important to note such negative behaviors along with all of the positive ones.

Put the List into an Appropriate Format. Once the list of desirable and undesirable behaviors and characteristics has been formulated, it should be organized into the sequence that observers are most likely to encounter. The list should be placed on the observation form in such a way that it is easily readable. Also, space should be provided for the observer to mark a check if the behavior is present. For repeated behaviors such as disruptions, the response form should be organized by time periods. Then the observer can merely place a check mark if the behavior occurred during a designated period of time. Alternative methods can require the observer to indicate the number of times the behavior occurred or to estimate the amount of time that a given activity took. Appropriate space should be provided for the specific type of response.

Once the checklist has been completed, the results must be interpreted. As long as the results are to be used to provide feedback to students about their performance or to help teachers improve their teaching, the components (behaviors and characteristics) can be interpreted separately. If the results of the checklist are to be used to make summative evaluations, the components must be summarized into a total score. This summarizing can be accomplished by summing the items, taking into account, of course, those that refer to behaviors to be avoided. It might also be desirable to weight the items according to their importance.

Using Rating Scales

Rating scales can be used to evaluate a set of behaviors and characteristics in much the same way that checklists are used. Rating scales differ from checklists by having the observer provide a number, or rating, for each behavior to indicate either its quality or how often the behavior occurred. For purposes of evaluating processes that are ongoing, checklists are usually preferred because of the additional time required to respond to a rating scale. Additional information about how to construct rating scales is included in Chapter 12.

The simplest rating scale would consist of a set of behaviors and characteristics with instructions to the observers to respond to each by selecting a number within a designated range to indicate some quality of the behavior. But, more often the scale is presented in a graphic form, with anchors at either end and numbers or words designating the points on the scale. Scales can take many forms, including approaches as simple as the following ones:

Uses proper safety procedures in the chemistry laboratory

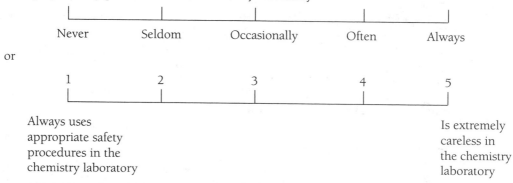

or

Another option is to have the observers imagine an individual who was the best possible exemplar of a particular behavior or characteristic and put him or her on one end of the scale and then to imagine the worst possible exemplar and put that individual on the other end. The observer then has the task of indicating where along the continuum the individual being observed should be placed. An example of this approach follows:

Rate the quality of the student's introduction to his or her speech relative to the two examples given.

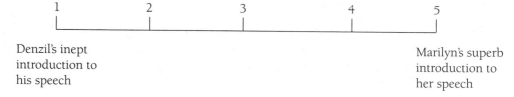

ASSESSING PRODUCTS AND PERFORMANCES

In a product or performance evaluation, it is preferable to compare a student's work to a predetermined performance standard rather than to the performance of the student's peers. In Chapter 3 we made the distinction between these two approaches to assessment: using a predetermined standard, referred to as *criterion-referenced evaluation,* and having peers provide the standard, called *norm-referenced assessment.* As defined by Nitko (1984), criterion-referenced tests are those "deliberately constructed to yield measurements that are directly interpretable in terms of specified performance standards" (p. 12). We have seen that a major goal of product and performance assessment is to obtain an indication of a student's mastery of specific educational objectives. Norm-referenced evaluation indicates a student's relative level of performance compared to peers but tells us nothing about mastery of objectives.

In addition to their being inconsistent with the basic philosophy of performance testing, normative comparisons pose certain problems in evaluating products and performances. In many cases, the products of students are different along many dimensions, which creates difficulties in making legitimate comparisons between the products. Any two products can be different in numerous ways, and each may be superior in some aspects and inferior in others. For instance, in a science project, the teacher or judge must consider originality, scientific contribution, neatness, sturdiness, creativity, extensiveness and quality of narrative explanations, the use of references, and so forth. How do you weigh these qualities in making normative comparisons? How do you compare a bold and unusual, yet somewhat awkwardly presented, project with a more conventional, less creative one that is neat, carefully constructed, and meticulously documented? Under these circumstances, it obviously is difficult to compare two such different products. Determining which dimensions are important aspects of the educational objectives being assessed and explicitly delineating mastery criteria make evaluation of such products much more straightforward.

Advantages of Multiple Observers

A teacher who creates a performance test or checklist will usually be the only person to administer it. However, distinct advantages accrue from using multiple observers in research and clinical settings. First, comparisons can be made among the judges to obtain information about the reliability of the assessment. If the responses are the same, the indication is that the judgments are reliable. When two observers are in disagreement, the suggestion is that there is something wrong with the directions for making the observations, the scoring of observations, or the abilities of the observers. The particular items for which there is disagreement can be examined to decide whether the items or their scoring rubrics need to be defined more clearly. Also, inadequate training of observers is often responsible for lower levels of interrater reliability.

　　Using more than one observer has other advantages. For example, it is possible to obtain a more accurate score by pooling the responses of several observers than could be obtained from a single observer because the errors of each observer tend to compensate for the errors of others. In fact, pooling ratings can be thought of as having the same effect on reliability of measurement that lengthening a test does.

Reliability or Agreement for Multiple Observers

Several methods are available for evaluating the reliability of rate of agreement among behavioral observers. The most generally applicable and satisfactory approach is based on an application of generalizability theory (which was mentioned briefly in Chapter 4). The statistical aspects of the method are beyond what we can cover (see R. L. Thorndike and R. M. Thorndike, 1994, for a discussion and example), but the basic logic is fairly straightforward. If each of several persons (N of them) is observed by each of several judges or observers (J of them) on each of several behaviors (B of them), them the total variability in the $N \times J \times B$ observations can be broken down into several sources. There will be one source for real differences between the N people observed, one for differences in the characteristics of the J observers, and one for differences in the characteristics of the B behaviors. In addition, whenever judges are inconsistent across behaviors for one person (called a judge by behavior or $J \times B$ interaction), or persons are inconsistent across behaviors for a judge (a persons by behaviors or $N \times B$ interaction), or judges are inconsistent across persons for a behavior (a persons by judges or $N \times J$ interaction) these sources will contribute additional variability among the observations. The inconsistency of judges across persons can be viewed as unreliability in the assessment of persons on the behavior in question. That is, if the assessment is perfectly reliable, each judge should assign the same rating to person 1 on the behavior of interest. There should also be perfect agreement among the judges in the rating of person 2 on the behavior, and so forth. The ratings given to different people will differ, but the judges will be in agreement for each individual. Therefore, as the variation associated with the judge by person interaction becomes greater than zero, we can say that the ratings lack perfect reliability.

When we wish to assess the reliability of dichotomous judgments, such as the presence or absence of a particular behavior, for a pair of judges, a much simpler statistic is available. It is called *kappa,* and it can be interpreted as the proportion of agreements, corrected for the probability of agreement by chance. The statistic is computed from a fourfold table like this one:

		First Judge	
		Present	Absent
Second Judge	Present	a	b
	Absent	c	d

where each letter has the following meaning:

a = both judges report the behavior as present (agreement)

b = first judge says the behavior is absent, second judge reports behavior present (disagreement)

c = first judge says the behavior is present, second judge reports the behavior absent (disagreement)

d = both judges report the behavior as absent (agreement)

and N is the total number of observations ($N = a + b + c + d$). The proportion of agreements is

$$A = \frac{a + d}{N}$$

and the proportion of agreement expected by chance can be shown to be

$$C = \left[\left(\frac{a + b}{N}\right) \times \left(\frac{a + c}{N}\right)\right] + \left[\left(\frac{c + d}{N}\right) \times \left(\frac{b + d}{N}\right)\right]$$

The kappa statistic is defined as

$$kappa = \frac{A - C}{1 - C}$$

Suppose two judges rate the presence of aggressive behavior in 100 observation segments with the following results

	First Judge	
Second Judge	Present	Absent
Present	50	13
Absent	16	21

Then the rate of agreement expected by chance is

$$C = \left[\left(\frac{50+13}{100}\right) \times \left(\frac{50+16}{100}\right)\right] + \left[\left(\frac{16+21}{100}\right) \times \left(\frac{13+21}{100}\right)\right]$$
$$= .4158 + .1258 = .5416,$$

the total rate of agreement is

$$A = \frac{50+21}{100} = .71$$

and the value of kappa is

$$kappa = \frac{.71 - .5416}{1 - .5416} = \frac{.17}{.46} = .37$$

For these judges the rate of agreement does not substantially exceed what would be expected by chance, indicating that more training may be called for.

The kappa statistic can also be used to assess the reliability of mastery judgments. In this case, the decision is master/nonmaster rather than behavior occurred/did not occur. The two judgments can result from either two separate tests or from split halves of a single test.

SYSTEMATIC OBSERVATION

Some instructional objectives and clinical interventions require neither cognitive behaviors nor a product but instead focus on changes in personality traits and attitudes. One way to obtain information about personality traits and attitudes is by using systematic observations in natural settings. Other procedures are discussed in Chapter 11.

Observing behavior in the naturally occurring settings of daily life offers important advantages, although these situations are often not uniform from person to person. Avoiding the need to stage special events just for testing purposes makes observation of real-life situations appealing and may yield more accurate reflections of behavior.

Of course, as part of our normal lives we observe the people with whom we associate every day, noticing what they do and reacting to their behavior. Our impressions of people are continuously formed and modified by our observations. But these observations are casual, unsystematic, and undirected. If asked to document with specific instances our judgment that Helen is a leader in the group or that Henry is undependable, most of us would find it difficult to provide more than one or two concrete observations of actual behavior to back up our general impressions. In fact, people tend to categorize each other based on a small number of salient observations and apply the general impression to all traits. This is known as the **halo effect.** Observations must be organized, directed, and systematic if they are to yield dependable information about individuals and avoid halo.

It is appropriate at this point to note a distinction between the observational procedures that we are currently discussing and the rating procedures described in Chapter 12. In collecting systematic observations, the observer is required to function as an objective and mechanical recording instrument, whereas in the use of ratings, the rater must synthesize and integrate the evidence presented. With systematic observations, the function of the observer is strictly that of providing an accurate record of the number of social contacts, suggestions, aggressive acts, or whatever the behavioral category of interest is. The observer serves as a camera or recording device with enhanced flexibility and versatility. In ratings, however, the human instrument must judge, weigh, and interpret the information.

Systematic observational procedures have been most fully developed in connection with studies of young children. They seem particularly appropriate in this setting. Young children have not learned to camouflage or conceal their feelings as completely as have older individuals, so there is more to be learned from observing them. They also may be less able to tell us about themselves in words because they have not developed the self-knowledge or the verbal skills required. For these reasons, observational procedures have had their fullest development in the study of infants and young children.

Conducting the Systematic Observation

Extracting a meaningful, dependable, and relatively objective appraisal of some aspect of an individual's personality by observing a sample of behavior is far from easy. First, behavior flows continuously without any clear breaks. A preschooler is at the sand table making a "cake" at one moment, moves on to listen to the teacher talking to a group, and again moves on to build a house with the giant blocks. On the way, the child sits down for a short rest, takes a playful poke at some other child, and shouts to the teacher (or the world in general), "See me! See what I've made." But, this report is only partial. No verbal description can capture the full details of even 5 minutes of the life of an active child. What should be observed? What behaviors represent a personality attribute? When and for how long should observations be made? How should observers be trained? How should the observations be organized? We now turn our attention to these practical questions.

What Should Be Observed? If anything meaningful is to emerge from observing the complex flow of behavior, the observations must have some focus. We must be looking at something or for something—for indications of leadership, insecurity, sociability, emotional strain, energy level, aggressiveness, dependency, or indicators of several such personal attributes—and we may have to look for all of them at the same time. The particular research or practical problem specifies what aspect or aspects of behavior should be observed, and the plan for observing follows from a definition of the aspects of behavior that will be relevant to the problem.

What Behaviors Represent a Personality Attribute? Even after we have selected an attribute to study, a decision as to what behaviors will be acceptable indicators of that attribute still must be made. Consider the following behaviors:

> Sitting alone
> Kicking another child
> Holding onto a teacher's hand or apparel

Calling attention to a mess on the floor
Tattling on another child
Volunteering information in a discussion

Which of these behaviors should be tallied as indicators of *dependency* in a kindergartener? What behaviors should be added? This type of decision must be made with knowledge of typical childhood behavior and the dynamics underlying it if the observational data are to have real meaning.

When and For How Long Should Observations Be Made? When a program of systematic observations is begun, decisions about where, when, and for how long each person is to be observed must be made. These decisions will reflect a compromise between the cost of extended observations and the need for a representative and reliable picture of the person. Because people and situations vary from day to day, it is generally preferable to have a number of relatively brief periods of observation on different days than to have only one or two long periods of observation. Under these conditions, the sample of the person's behavior will be more representative and the score we obtain will be more reliable. We must be careful not to make the observation too brief a sample of behavior, or it may be difficult to judge what a particular action signifies. Practical considerations such as travel time and the administrative tasks associated with the observation process also may limit the number of observations that we can make on a particular child or group.

To make the decision process more manageable, it might even be useful to break daily, 5-minute observation sessions into still shorter segments of, say, no more than 1 minute or even 30 seconds. The observation made can then consist of an indication of whether the behavior occurred. For instance, each child might be observed for ten 5-minute periods occurring on different days, each 5-minute period might be further subdivided into ten 30-second periods, in which observers would record whether the particular child did or did not exhibit any of a set of defined aggressive behaviors. Assuming that the observers decide to count only the number of observation periods in which children engaged in the target behavior, each child would receive a score, with a possible range from zero to 100, indicating the number of periods in which he or she engaged in aggressive acts. A somewhat different score would result if the number of aggressive acts were recorded in each period. In either case, such scores, based on an adequate number of short samples of observed behavior, have been found to show satisfactory reliability.

The interpretation of the reliability of behavioral observations can be somewhat misleading. Under these circumstances, reliability is often defined in terms of the agreement between two observers, and the size of the coefficient depends on the method used to determine the degree of agreement. The percentage of agreement, which reflects the percentage of times that two observers agree, tends to be inflated when the rate of the behavior is either very high or very low. When a behavior occurs often, it is likely that two observers will both record it and therefore will agree. Likewise, when a behavior hardly ever occurs, it is likely that both observers will seldom report it and, again, will agree. Therefore, with a very high or low behavior rate, the reliability will always be high. The kappa statistic, discussed earlier, corrects for these chance associations. Naturally, it is desirable to plan to make observations in settings where the target behavior is likely to occur. Observations of aggressive acts, for example, are better made during a period devoted to free play than during one devoted to listening to stories or watching television.

How Should Observers Be Trained? Disagreements among observers can occur even when the behaviors have been carefully defined. In one extreme case, a researcher reported the rate of interobserver agreement on the gender of the teacher in classrooms where the observations were taking place to be 95%. To some extent, discrepancies are unavoidable because of fluctuations in attention or legitimate differences of opinion about whether a behavior occurred. Reliability can be increased, however, through training. Training sessions in which two or more observers make records based on the same sample of behavior, compare notes, discuss discrepancies, and reconcile differences provide a good means of increasing uniformity of observations. It can also be useful to have previously trained observers sit in on these sessions to offer suggestions. Such procedures can enhance both the uniformity of interpretation and observation and the placement of behavior samples into correct observation categories.

How Should Observations Be Organized? It is of primary importance that the observations be recorded immediately after they are made. Recent research (Hyman & Kleinknecht, 1998) on the observations of witnesses recounting events that they have observed has shown that the errors and selectivity of memory can bias the reporting of even outstanding and unusual events. For the rather ordinary and highly repetitive events that are observed in watching a child in preschool, for example, an adequate account of what occurred is possible only if the behaviors are recorded immediately. There is so much to see, and one event is so much like others that relying on memory to provide an accurate after-the-fact account of a child's behavior is likely to lead to serious omissions and distortions of what really happened.

Any program of systematic observation must, therefore, provide a method for immediate and efficient recording of observed events. Many possibilities exist for facilitating recording of behavioral observations. One that has been widely used is a systematic code for the behavioral categories of interest. For example, preliminary observations might be made to define the range of aggressive acts that can be expected from 3- and 4-year-old children. Part of the code might be set up as follows:

h = hits
p = pushes
g = grabs materials from others
c = calls a nasty name

and so forth. A blank observation form can be prepared and divided to represent the time segments of the observations, and code entries can be made quickly while the child is observed almost without interruption.

If it is important for observers to record *who* did *what* to *whom,* a two- or three-part code—with the first symbol designating the actor, the second, the action, and the third, the person acted upon—can represent the information in detail. Obviously, with a recording scheme as complicated as this, it would be essential to train the observers well. Observers skilled in shorthand, of course, could take fuller notes of the observations. (Space would have to be provided on the form for such notes.) These notes would then be coded or scored later.

Another effective approach is to videotape the scene being observed or make audiotape recordings of the observer's observations. These procedures provide a permanent record of the behaviors in a relatively complete form. The tapes can be analyzed at a later date, and ambiguous behavior can be examined repeatedly to obtain accurate observations.

Laptop or handheld computers also have promise for easier, more accurate recording of behavior. They can be programmed to accept a set of codes, or information can be entered on templates. Such a procedure can not only ease the burden on the observer and increase accuracy of the observations, but subsequent data analysis by computer is made much easier and transcription errors are eliminated (although recording errors are not). The most important consideration in decisions about organization and formatting is to minimize the dependence on memory, to get a record that will preserve as much as possible of the significant detail in the original behavior, and to develop a recording procedure that will interfere as little as possible with the process of observing and the behavior being observed.

Advantages and Disadvantages of Systematic Observation

Systematic observations of behavior have a number of features that make them an attractive method for assessment of personality characteristics, but they have some significant limitations as well. We can summarize some of the advantages and disadvantages of direct observations as follows.

Advantages of Systematic Observation. The most salient advantages of systematic observations are (1) they provide a record of actual behavior, (2) they can be used in real-life situations, and (3) they can be used with young children.

1. *A record of actual behavior.* When we observe an individual, we obtain a record of what that person does rather than rationalizations and protestations. If observational procedures have been well planned and observers carefully trained, the scores obtained will to a large degree be free from the biases and idiosyncrasies of the observers. A record of the behavior of individuals is not a reflection of what they think they are, or of what others think they are; their actions speak directly. If, as is so often the case, the primary concern is with changes in behavior, observations are the most direct and, in most cases, the most useful way of obtaining information. Also, as has been found with attitudes, what we say about ourselves, our behavior, and our beliefs often bears little relationship to what we will do when faced with a real-life situation. Direct observation of behavior avoids this filter, this source of invalidity.

2. *Useful in real-life situations.* Observational techniques can be applied in the naturally occurring situations of life and are not restricted to laboratory settings. Observations can be carried out in the nursery school, in the classroom, in the cafeteria, on the playground, at camp, in the squadron day room, on the assembly line, or any place where individuals work or play. Practical difficulties and limitations are associated with observations, which we will discuss shortly, but in spite of some disadvantages, direct observation is a widely applicable approach to studying individual personalities in a natural environment.

3. *Useful with young children.* As we have already noted, observational methods can be used with small children, no matter how young, with the youngest being the easiest to observe. Infants are not self-conscious, which makes it easy for the observer to sit and watch what they do without needing special procedures or precautions. Because the presence of the observer may change the social situation with older children and adults, it is sometimes necessary to screen the observer from the person being observed, perhaps by using a one-way vision screen. Of course, using this type of physical arrangement seriously restricts the type of setting in which observations can take place. It may be simpler and more effective to have the observer function unobtrusively and be present long enough for those being observed to ignore him or her, accepting the observer as a natural part of the surroundings.

The value of direct observation is greatest where its application is most feasible—with young children. Young children are limited in their ability to communicate through language, they have little experience or facility in analyzing or reporting their feelings or the reasons for their actions, and they are often shy with strangers. For this group, systematic observation provides an important method of learning about personality.

Disadvantages of Systematic Observation.   In contrast to the positive aspects of observations as an information-gathering technique, a number of factors seriously limit the usefulness of observational methods. These limitations, or disadvantages, range from practical considerations, which we will consider first, to issues of theory.

1. *Cost of making the observations.* Observations are costly primarily because of the demands they make on the time of trained observers. In most applications, each individual must be observed for a number of periods, extending in some instances to several hours. When observations are made of a substantial number of individuals or a particular group, the hours rapidly add up. Therefore, systematic observations, as well as recordings of behavior, are usually limited to research projects in which the necessary time commitments can be made. In routine school operations, it is seldom possible for teachers or counselors to find the resources needed to make direct observations of very many students. However, direct observation can provide useful information about single individuals who may be candidates for special services or other exceptional programs.

The cost of direct observation goes beyond the expenditure of time needed to record information. Any need for special settings or recording devices requires additional funds. Furthermore, when the original record is a running diary account or a videotape of an individual's or a group's actions, analysis of the record is likely to be time consuming, and thus costly.

2. *Problems in fitting the observer into the setting.* There is always a concern about whether having an observer present who is watching and taking notes of what happens will actually change what happens. In many of the situations we wish to observe, it is not practical to have the observer hidden from view. We hope, with some justification, that after an initial period in which the presence of the observer is noticeably intrusive, the individuals being observed will gradually begin to ignore the presence of the observer. Getting subjects to ignore the observer may be easier in some situations than in others. When the group is small, when it is necessary for the observer to see the activities closely, or when the group meets for too short a time to get used to being observed, the members may not come to think of the observer as part of the normal environment.

3. *Difficulties in eliminating subjectivity and bias.* It is necessary with observational procedures to take precautions to keep the observer's interpretations and biases out of the observations. The observer should not know much about the study being conducted, the experimental treatment the individual being observed is receiving, or test scores or other facts about that individual, lest this knowledge affect the observer's perceptions. It is best for the observer to function as a neutral recording instrument that is sensitive to and makes a record of certain categories of behaviors. However, the observer is human. We can minimize subjectivity in the observations by careful training and by keeping the observer blind as to the purposes of the observations, but we cannot eliminate it. We must be aware of the role of the observer in the final result, especially when the phenomena being studied are complex or involve an element of interpretation.

4. *Difficulties in determining a meaningful and productive set of behavior categories.* Observations are always selective; only certain limited aspects of an individual's behavior can be observed and recorded. Furthermore, if observations are to be treated quantitatively, they must be classified, grouped, and counted. Any system of classification is a somewhat arbitrary framework imposed on the infinitely varied events of life. It is not always easy to set up a framework that well serves the intended purposes. There will never be complete agreement about the categories of behavior

used in a particular observation scheme or the types of activities included under a given heading. For one purpose, we might decide to classify aggressive acts in terms of overt behaviors like hitting, pushing, or grabbing. For other purposes, it might be better to note the precipitating event (if we can observe it): aggression in response to conflict over property, as a reaction to verbal disparagement, or after the thwarting of some activity in progress. In any event, scores based on observations of behavior can be no more significant and meaningful than the categories devised for recording and analyzing the behavior.

5. *Difficulties in determining the significance of isolated behavior.* To make the assessment reliable and objective, systematic observations usually focus on rather small and discrete acts or break the observations and analyses into small parts. There is a real danger here for the meaning of the behavior, the true significance of the action, to be lost. We observe a 3-year-old hugging another 3-year-old. Is this an act of aggression or affection? In isolation, we have no way of telling. Or, suppose that one child hits another. This behavior is obviously an aggressive act, but what does it signify in a child's life? Is it a healthy reaction to earlier domination by another child? Or is it a displaced aggression resulting from events occurring at home? Or does it signify something else? Or nothing? In such cases the meaning attached to the act must be considered tentative, to be confirmed or refuted by other information.

6. *The external character of observation.* Observations are external; that is, they focus only on what can be seen. Observations are not intended to inform us about internal states. The "outsideness" is exaggerated when little bits of behavior are analyzed out of context. But the outsideness is a fundamental feature of any observational approach to studying behavior. We always face the problem of determining the meaning of the behavior and must recognize that what we have before us is only what the individual does, not what it signifies.

SUMMARY

Although most instructional objectives and many behaviors of interest in psychological and educational research can be evaluated using conventional cognitive tests, in some circumstances other techniques must be used. Alternative methods are particularly important when performances, products, attitudes, or personality traits are assessed. When we have a choice, it is generally easier to assess products than to assess processes, but in certain circumstances the focus of assessment efforts must be on processes. Processes are usually evaluated either with checklists or with rating scales.

Checklists should include the following elements: (1) designation of the appropriate performance or product, (2) listing of the important behaviors and characteristics, (3) inclusion of common errors, and (4) placement of the list into an appropriate format. Rating scales are more effectively used with products than with processes because their use requires more time. With processes, we are usually faced with much to evaluate and little time in which to do it.

Behavior in naturally occurring situations can best be assessed by systematic observations. To make systematic observation more effective, the following questions must be answered: What should be observed? What behaviors represent the attribute of interest? When and for how long should observations be made? How should observers be trained? How should the observations be organized?

Systematic observation has the advantages of (1) representing actual behavior, (2) being applicable to real-life situations, and (3) being usable with young children and others with whom verbal communication is difficult. However, observational procedures present a number of problems and thus have the following disadvantages: (1) cost of making the observations, (2) problems in fitting the observer into the setting, (3) difficulties in eliminating subjectivity and bias, (4) difficulties in determining a meaningful and productive set of behavior categories, (5) difficulties in determining the significance of isolated behavior, and (6) the external character of observation.

QUESTIONS AND EXERCISES

1. Consider the following objectives from a general science class at a junior high school. Specify the most appropriate type of assessment: paper-and-pencil test, process evaluation, or product evaluation. Provide a justification for your selection. Each student will:
   a. prepare a project for the science fair.
   b. demonstrate a knowledge of the taxonomic classification of vertebrates.
   c. conduct a successful titration experiment.
   d. make a presentation on one local threat to the ecology.

2. Construct a checklist that would be appropriate for judging a science fair project.

3. Construct a rating scale that could be used to evaluate performance in a unit on softball in a physical education class.

4. Design a behavior test to measure a personality trait desired of students in music appreciation class.

5. How could a classroom discussion serve as the basis for systematic observation? Make a plan for recording these observations.

6. In a research study, you propose to use systematic observations of schoolchildren as a method of studying their social adjustment. What problems would you encounter? What precautions would you need to take in interpreting the results?

7. What advantages do systematic observations have over the observations of everyday life?

SUGGESTED READINGS

Barrios, B. A. (1988). On the changing nature of behavioral assessment. In A. S. Bellack & M. Hershon (Eds.), *Behavioral assessment: A practical handbook* (pp. 3–41). New York: Pergamon.

Berk, R. A. (Ed.). (1986). *Performance assessment: Methods and applications.* Baltimore: Johns Hopkins University Press.

Evertson, C. M. (1986). Observation as inquiry and method. In M. C. Witrock (Ed.), *Handbook of research on teaching* (pp. 162–213). New York: Macmillan.

Finch, F. L. (Ed.). (1991). *Educational performance assessment.* Chicago: Riverside.

Fitzpatrick, R., & Morrison E. J. (1971). Performance and product evaluation. In R. L. Thorndike (Ed.), *Educational measurement* (pp. 237–270). Washington, DC: American Council on Education.

Hyman, I. E., Jr., & Kleinknecht, E. (1998). False childhood memories: Research, theory, and applications. In L. M. Williams & V. L. Banyard (Eds.), *Trauma and memory* (pp. 175–188). Thousand Oaks, CA: Sage.

Kubiszyn, T., & Borich, G. (1987). *Educational testing and measurement.* Glenview, IL: Scott, Foresman.

Nitko, A. J. (1984). Defining "criterion-referenced test." In R. Berk (Ed.), *A guide to criterion-referenced test construction* (pp. 8–28). Baltimore: Johns Hopkins University Press.

CHAPTER 11

Interests, Personality, and Adjustment

Introduction
Interest Measurement
    Strong Interest Inventory
    Career Assessment Inventory
    Self-Directed Search
Personality and Adjustment Assessment
    Dynamic Approaches
    Trait Approaches
    Humanistic Approaches: Personality
      as Self-Perception
    Behavioral Approaches

Problems with Personality and
    Interest Measures
Computerized Scoring and Interpretation
    Advantages
    Disadvantages
Summary
Questions and Exercises
Suggested Readings

INTRODUCTION

We turn now to published instruments and procedures that assess interest, personality, and personal adjustment. Our focus shifts from what a person is capable of doing with best effort, to what that person is likely to do under the day-to-day circumstances of living. Most people are curious about personality and interest tests because they want to be able to better understand themselves or to make better decisions, and they believe that these tests may be helpful in this regard. Interest tests provide information that can be very valuable to those making career choices since knowledge about one's individual pattern of interests helps to identify career options and opportunities that are most compatible with individual lifestyles and goals.

Self-understanding is so important to most of us that it is easy to be uncritical of this type of test. The person who is very skeptical of tests of cognitive ability, including those instruments that have been developed in accordance with the highest standards of test construction, is often quite willing to accept the results of a personality test that might have been developed without consideration for these standards. We want to emphasize that while tests of interest and personality can be very useful for their intended purposes, this is only true when the tests have been carefully constructed, standardized, and used only within the limits prescribed by the test developer.

Interest tests provide information about a person's general pattern of likes and dislikes. People vary considerably in this regard. When two individuals are given choices about how to spend free time, one might choose to sit quietly and read, while the other would choose to be outside engaged in some type of physical activity. What would you choose? Do you prefer to work on projects as part of a team, or do you prefer to work independently? Would you rather visit a flower shop or an amusement park? Would you rather attend the opera or a rock concert? It is easy to see how preferences of this type might influence career satisfaction. After all, the more we are able to engage in tasks that we enjoy while at work, the greater will be our overall satisfaction with our work situation.

Personality tests are designed to assess the constellation of personal characteristics that are unique to each individual. In some cases these assessments are quite global and are intended to paint a broad picture of what an individual is like. Other personality tests are designed to measure more specific characteristics, such as the extent to which an individual may be characterized as introverted or extroverted. **Measures of adjustment** assess the extent to which an individual's personal characteristics may be considered adaptive in day-to-day life. Certain personality characteristics such as the ability to deal effectively with feelings of anger are associated with psychological health and good adjustment. Other characteristics, such as deeply imbedded feelings of mistrust or suspicion, are associated with psychological difficulties. In this chapter we will discuss three of the major interest tests, as well as several tests of personality and adjustment. We will then examine some of the special problems in the assessment of personality and interest. We will conclude by examining the uses of computerized scoring and interpretation for interest and personality tests.

Various measures of personality and interest are designed to serve different purposes and may be used in very different ways. Three general uses for these tests include research, self-exploration, and clinical decision making. Personality tests that are used primarily for research purposes are often designed to provide information on specific personality characteristics, either as a measure of change in response to some experimental manipulation or as a basis for comparison across groups of individuals. Furthermore, in research situations tests often stand alone and are not used in conjunction with other instruments or interviews. Personality tests that are used primarily for self-exploration usually provide information on global characteristics or interest patterns. While many of the tests used for self-exploration are designed in such a way that they can be scored and interpreted by the examinee alone, they are most effective when combined with an interview and feedback from a trained counselor who is skilled in the interpretation of the particular instrument(s) involved. Finally, personality tests play an important role in clinical decision making and may involve both diagnostic and treatment decisions. When chosen for this purpose, it is extremely important that the tests be utilized in conjunction with a thorough clinical interview and client history. The test then becomes part of the process of clinical assessment that begins with data collection and proceeds through to construction of a treatment plan.

INTEREST MEASUREMENT

Strong Interest Inventory

The Strong Interest Inventory (SII) is the current version of an instrument originally developed by E. K. Strong and first published in 1927 as the Strong Vocational Interest Blank (SVIB). A major revision of the SVIB was published in 1974 under the title Strong-Campbell Interest Inventory (SCII). With the next major revision in 1985, the name was changed to the Strong Interest

Inventory. This name was retained for the most recent revision completed in 1994. The significant revisions of the test over the years reflect the belief by the publishers that psychological instruments must be updated to retain their quality and usefulness. That point of view is certainly supported, for the Strong remains one of the most respected of all the available interest inventories.

The underlying principle that has guided the development of all of the Strong instruments is the idea that people who are satisfied within a given occupation share a pattern of interests that differentiates them from individuals in other occupations. Determining how closely an individual's interests match the distinctive pattern of persons in a specific occupation should be a predictor of how content a person would be in that occupation and even, to some extent, whether the person would actually enter and stay in the occupation.

The Strong Interest Inventory, closely following the design of the original SVIB, is made up of 377 items presented in three different formats. Most of the test utilizes a format that requires the examinee to respond to items by selecting *L* (Like), *I* (Indifferent), or *D* (Dislike). Items include occupations (florist, surgeon, editor), school subjects (chemistry, physical education), activities (repairing a clock, meeting and directing people), leisure activities (boxing, skiing, entertaining others), and types of people (ballet dancers, babies, prominent business leaders). In the second format, examinees identify their preferences between two general activities (taking a chance vs. playing it safe), and activities in the world of work (ideas vs. things). In the third format, examinees are asked to indicate whether or not they believe certain personal characteristics are typical of themselves (stimulate the ambitions of my associates; enjoy tinkering with small hand tools).

Considering that the Strong takes only about 40 to 50 minutes to complete, it provides a considerable amount of information for the examinee. Scores are reported in five main forms, including the Occupational Scales, General Occupational Themes, Basic Interest Scales, Personal Style Scales, and Administrative Indexes. The score report is organized to encourage the examinee to observe overall trends in personal interest and to note how these trends are related to the world of work.

Occupational Scales

The original type of score developed by Strong is the Occupational Scale (OS). This score has appeared in every version of the Strong and has been updated with each revision. This is the score that provides information about how closely the examinee's pattern of responses matches that of people in a specific occupation. The scoring key for an occupation such as chemist was developed by administering the inventory to several hundred employed chemists who met certain standards, including length of employment and stated satisfaction with and success in the occupation. For each item, the percentage of chemists who indicated liking (or disliking) the topic or activity was compared with the percentage of people making that choice from among a large group of *people in general* assembled from many different occupations. If the two percentages differed substantially, the item was scored in the key for chemist. A person's raw score on the chemist scale would be the number of items on which he or she responded the way typical chemists did. The raw score is then converted to a standard score in which the mean of the occupational group (chemist in this example) was set at 50 and the standard deviation at 10. For interpretation purposes, the standard scores are represented on the report form along a range of similarity. Scores of 40 or above indicate that the individual shares the likes and dislikes of persons within the occupation, scores of 30 to 39 indicate that the person shares *some* of the likes or dislikes of persons within the occupation, and scores of 29 or below indicate that the person shares *few* likes and dislikes with persons in the occupation. We would predict that persons with scores of 40 or above would enjoy the daily activities of the occupation in question, while those with scores below 29 would probably not enjoy the work of that occupation.

The 1994 Strong contains a total of 211 Occupational Scales. This includes 102 pairs of separate scales for men and women (204 scales). Separate scales for men and women are necessary because men and women within the same occupation do not necessarily display the same pattern of interests. An additional seven scales are included that have scores for only one gender. These scales represent occupations that are dominated by one gender or the other, such as child care worker (women) and plumber (men). For these occupations it is extremely difficult to obtain adequate samples for both genders. The *Applications and Technical Guide* for the Strong Interest Inventory (Harmon, Hansen, Borgen, & Hammer, 1994) provides detailed information about the nature of the sample for each occupational group.

The occupational scoring keys of the Strong are examples of a strictly empirical, atheoretical approach to interest assessment. The original pool of items was assembled with no clear rationale other than to include a wide range of stimuli that would be likely to elicit "liking" in some people and "disliking" in others. The scoring keys were developed solely on the basis of group differences, with no psychological constructs in mind as to what the specific occupations represented. This method of key development is referred to as **empirical scale construction.** The sample from each occupation was quite large, typically over 200, so that the scoring keys are unlikely to include many items that just happened to differentiate in that particular sample of cases. Each score tells how similar an individual's interest pattern is to that typical of individuals in a specific occupation. But it is not easy to tell what an individual is like by simply knowing that she received a 45 on the scale for chemist (female). What sorts of individuals' interests are similar to those of female chemists? What are female chemists like anyhow? Of course the Strong provides scores for numerous other occupations besides chemist. Quite early in the history of the SVIB, the author provided data on the correlation coefficients between the scales, finding that some of these coefficients were decidedly high. The correlation coefficients for one group of science-related scales are shown here:

Job Title	1	2	3	4	5	6
1 Psychologist		.77	.72	.40	.71	.74
2 Mathematician	.77		.91	.66	.80	.72
3 Physicist	.72	.91		.85	.93	.78
4 Engineer	.40	.66	.85		.88	.52
5 Chemist	.71	.80	.93	.88		.73
6 Physician	.74	.72	.78	.52	.73	

The finding that certain occupations are correlated with one another encouraged the test developers to group the scales into clusters and to pay attention to the scores of an individual for all the scales in a cluster rather than to those for single, isolated occupations. The cluster "physical scientist" carries more breadth of meaning than "chemist" considered by itself, especially since the scales in the "physical scientist" cluster all tend to show a negative correlation with scales in the "sales" cluster.

The pattern of an individual's high and low values on a scale in relation to the occupational clusters begins to generate a psychological as well as a vocational picture of that individual. However, the correlation coefficients between the scales of the Strong inventories are difficult to interpret for two reasons. First, scales in an occupational cluster are likely to include the same items, scored in the same direction. Likewise, scales in different clusters may well include some of the same items, but scored in opposite directions. This situation is quite a different matter from what we had in the case of a high correlation between two ability tests that included different items. The chemist and physicist scales are alike because, for some reason, the chemist and physicist reference groups responded in a similar way to the rather small set of statements that compose the Strong. The scales for other occupational groups show negative correlation coefficients because they include some of the same items, but the items are keyed in opposite directions because the members of one reference group marked "like" and the other marked "dislike."

A second confounding feature of correlations between scales on the Strong is that many people tend to mark "like" for roughly the same number of items. There is no profound meaning to be drawn from this, but it has the consequence, for purely statistical reasons, of making many of the correlation coefficients between scales negative. Thus, it would be unwise to attempt to draw substantive conclusions about the nature of interests as constructs from the fact that many of the scales for dissimilar occupations are negatively correlated.

The Occupational Scales are most useful for persons who are relatively close to making a career choice. Persons who are still at the career exploration stage would obtain more valuable information from the next two types of scores provided by the Strong, the General Occupational Themes and the Basic Interest Scales.

General Occupational Themes.   The second type of information contained in the Strong is found in the section known as the General Occupational Themes (GOT). The themes are a focused attempt to give psychological meaning to expressions of like and dislike for occupations and are directly derived from the work of John Holland (1985). Growing out of his experience with the SVIB and reviews of previous factor-analytic studies of interests, Holland concluded that there are six foci, or themes, of vocational interest that represent six different types of individuals and six types of work environments. He labeled them as realistic, investigative, artistic, social, enterprising, and conventional. Holland felt that the salience of one or more of these themes in an individual could be identified by the individual's expressed likes and dislikes for occupations. Starting with his *a priori* rational analysis, he assembled clusters of occupations to represent each focus. He refined the clusters by analyzing the correlations of single occupations with the cluster scores in their own and the other clusters until cluster scores were developed that showed reasonably high reliability, both internal consistency and stability over time, and that were largely unrelated to one another. The foci were visualized as the apexes of a hexagon, as shown in Figure 11–1. The numbers on the hexagon represent the correlations between the occupational themes for the 1994 Strong Interest Inventory. The correlation coefficients tend to confirm the hexagonal structure in that the larger correlation coefficients tend to be between adjacent foci. However, most of the correlation coefficients in the figure are quite low, indicating that each of the six scores provides distinct information about an examinee.

Holland viewed his six foci as a way to represent not merely groups of occupations, but also patterns of personality. Support for this view was gathered from an analysis of terms used to describe individuals high on each of the six foci. Some of the frequently mentioned descriptors are listed here:

Realistic	*Investigative*	*Artistic*
robust	task oriented	expressive
rugged	introspective	original
practical	analytical	intuitive
strong	curious	creative
athletic	independent	nonconforming
mechanical	reserved	introspective
direct	unconventional	independent
persistent	intellectual	aggressive

Social	Enterprising	Conventional
sociable	aggressive	conscientious
responsible	popular	efficient
humanistic	self-confident	obedient
group oriented	cheerful	calm
understanding	sociable	orderly
idealistic	energetic	practical
helpful	verbal	possession and status oriented
	power and status oriented	

Because the themes represent types of people, it is possible to describe individuals in general ways. *Realistic* individuals prefer to work outdoors and to build and/or repair things. Sample realistic occupations include auto mechanic, gardener, plumber, police officer, and rancher. Those who score high on the *investigative* theme enjoy forms of inquiry and like to analyze problems and do research. Sample occupations include college professor, physician, and psychologist. *Artistic* individuals enjoy creative activity including drama, music, writing, and art. Associated occupations include artist, lawyer, librarian, and reporter. Those with high scores on the *social* theme prefer activities that involve care giving and instruction. Occupations include

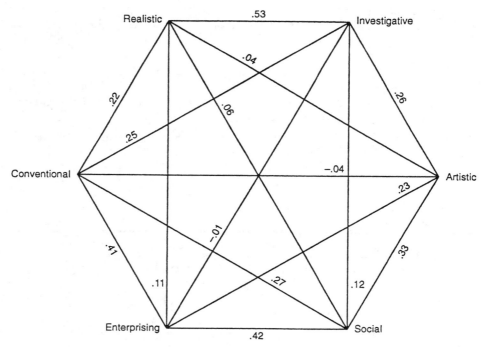

Figure 11–1
Holland occupational themes and correlation between themes for 1994 Strong.
Source: Modified and reproduced by special permission of the Publisher, CPP, Inc., Palo Alto, CA 94303 from the **Strong Interest Inventory®.** Copyright 1994, by the Board of Trustees of the Leland Stanford Junior University. All rights reserved. Further reproduction is prohibited without the Publisher's written consent. Strong Interest Inventory® is a registered trademark of the Stanford University Press.

child care provider and public health nurse. The *enterprising* theme is associated with the activities of selling, managing, and persuading. Enterprising occupations include realtor and traveling salesperson. The *conventional* theme incorporates the activities of data processing, accounting, and organizing. These individuals especially enjoy activities that require accuracy and attention to detail. Associated occupations include bookkeeper and clerical worker. While the six themes are meant to represent types of people, it is important to emphasize that few individuals represent pure types. That is, most people have interests that reflect two or more of the general themes, and this will be reflected in the score profile. For example, an individual might obtain relatively high scores on both the social and enterprising themes. Examples of associated occupations for the individual with such an interest pattern include high school counselor and parks and recreation coordinator.

Because of the overlap in item content between the older SVIB and subsequent instruments, it was quite easy to incorporate the Holland structure in the scoring and interpretation of the SCII. Scores for the six general occupational themes were first added to the Strong in 1974, supplementing the scores for the specific occupations. Moreover, in the report form provided to counselors and clients, separate occupations are grouped according to the theme or themes considered salient for the occupation. Thus, the user is provided with the empirically based occupation scores arranged according to the general themes, as well as the theme scores themselves.

Basic Interest Scales.   Scores of still a third type are also provided. The Basic Interest Scales (BIS) may be best understood as subdivisions of the General Occupational Themes. First introduced in the 1960s, the scales were significantly revised and updated for the 1994 revision of the Strong. There are 25 Basic Interest Scales, each composed of a set of homogeneous items. The items are homogeneous both in manifest content and in the statistical sense, since the items in a given scale all have substantial correlation with each of the other items in that scale. The BISs were derived directly from the items of the Strong, using only statistical criteria and without reference to any theory. They address more specific vocational themes than do the themes of Holland's model, but they are broader in content than the occupational scales and reflect the high correlation of some of those scales. Table 11–1 lists the Basic Interest Scales and shows the association for each to the General Occupational Themes.

Table 11–1
Basic Interest Scales and General Occupational Themes

Realistic	Investigative	Artistic	Social	Enterprising	Conventional
agriculture	science	music/dramatics	teaching	public speaking	data management
nature	mathematics	art	social service	law/politics	computer activities
military activities	medical science	applied arts	medical service	merchandising	office services
athletics		writing	religious activities	sales	
mechanical activities		culinary arts		organizational management	

Table 11–2
Brief Definitions of Poles for the Personal Style Scales

Personal Style Scale	Left Pole	Right Pole
Work Style	Work with ideas/data/things	Works with people
Learning Environment	Practical	Academic
Leadership Style	Leads by example	Directs others
Risk Taking/Adventure	Plays it safe	Takes chances

Personal Style Scales. The fourth type of information contained in the Strong score profile is the Personal Style Scales. There are four scales, each of which reflects preferences for broad styles of living and working. New to the Strong in 1994, the scales include Work Style, Learning Environment, Leadership Style, and Risk Taking/Adventure. Scores are reported on the profile form in a manner similar to the occupational themes and interest scales. However, they are constructed as bipolar scales and reported as a preference for both the left and right pole of the scale. Table 11–2 provides summary definitions for the right and left pole of each scale.

Administrative Indexes. The fifth type of information provided on the Strong profile sheet is the Administrative Indexes. Of most use to the counselor as an interpretive aid for the profile, these indexes provide statistical information about the examinee's responses, including the total number of responses, percentages of "like," "indifferent," and "dislike" responses, and the total number of infrequent responses. The indexes are most useful as a preliminary check on the validity of the individual test administration and scoring, but also have some interpretive value within the framework of the individual examinee's overall profile of scores.

When interpreting the Strong Interest Inventory, the counselor and the counselee are encouraged to proceed from the broad and theory-based occupational themes through the content-based homogeneous basic interest scores to the empirically determined scales for specific occupations. The instrument is now eclectic in the foundations on which its scoring systems have been based and comprehensive in the information that it provides.

The Strong Interest Inventory is now distributed and scored exclusively by CPP, Inc. (formerly Consulting Psychologists Press). A sample first page from the Strong profile form for college students is shown in Figure 11–2. The basic report is six pages long and contains several parts, beginning with a "snapshot" (Figure 11–2) that provides summary information on the General Occupational Themes and Basic Interest Scales and lists the 10 Occupational Scales on which the examinee obtained the highest scores. The check marks on the form highlight the examinee's performance. Increasing detail is provided on the remaining pages of the form, including more information about the General Occupational Themes and Basic Interest Scales. The complete profile also provides results for all Occupational Scales (sorted by occupational theme) and the Personal Style Scales. The report concludes with the Administrative Indexes and some guidelines to help the examinee interpret the test results.

CPP offers six other reports for the Strong, depending on the examinee's age and occupational experience. The interpretive report provides a 15-page written interpretation of a person's Strong profile. Samples of complete reports are available on the CPP web site at http://www.cpp-db.com/ products/reports.asp#strong. Counselors who wish to have their clients take the SII can have the

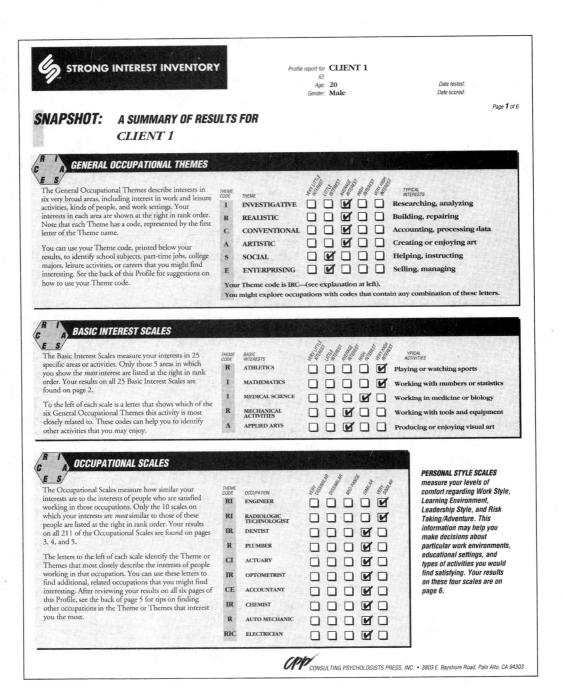

Figure 11–2

Sample profile form from the Strong Interest Inventory.

Source: Modified and reproduced by special permission of the Publisher, CPP, Inc., Palo Alto, CA 94303 from the **Strong Interest Inventory®.** Copyright 1994, by the Board of Trustees of the Leland Stanford Junior University. All rights reserved. Further reproduction is prohibited without the Publisher's written consent. Strong Interest Inventory® is a registered trademark of the Stanford University Press.

instrument administered and scored over the web using a link to CPP's scoring site, http://www. Skillsone.com.

We turn now to the reliability and validity of Strong Interest Inventory scores. The evidence reported on reliability consists primarily of test–retest correlations over various time intervals. The manual for the 1985 Strong reports average values as shown here for the three types of scores:

	Test–Retest Interval		
Scale	2 Weeks	30 Days	3 Years
GOT	.91	.86	.81
BIS	.91	.88	.82
OS	.91	.89	.87

All three types of scales show reasonable stability, although over the longer time period, the scales for specific occupations (OS) held up somewhat better than the other scales. Test–retest reliability information that is currently available for the 1994 Strong suggests that the instrument has retained its reliability and may have even been slightly improved for some scales. Studies of the original SVIB provide information on stability of the occupational scales over extended periods of time, as well as some indication of the relationship of stability to examinee age at the time of original testing. The data in Table 11–3 indicate that interests become increasingly stable during adolescence and early adulthood and that, as one might expect, shifts are more common over longer intervals, though there is still a substantial core of consistency over even the longest intervals.

It is not entirely clear what a prospective user should seek as evidence of the validity of an interest inventory. First, he or she can inquire into the meaningfulness of the constructs on which the inventory is based. For the occupational scales, the case has rested in large part on the effectiveness of the scales in differentiating members of a specific occupation from the broad reference group of people in general (concurrent validity). Although the situation varies somewhat from one occupation to another because some occupational groups are more distinctive than others, a rough but reasonably accurate overall summary would be that approximately 10% of people in

Table 11–3
Long-Term Stability of the Strong Interest Inventory

Age at First Testing	Test–Retest Interval					
	2 Weeks	1 Year	2–5 Years	6–10 Years	11–20 Years	20+ Years
17–18		.80	.70	.65	.64	
19–21	.91	.80	.73	.67	.67	.64
22–25			.78	.69	.75	.72
25+			.77	.81	.80	

Note: No data exist for time spaces where cells are blank.

general would be rated "high" or "very high" on an occupational scale, in comparison with 65% to 70% of those people actually in the occupation.

The meaning of the constructs implied by Holland's six general occupational themes lies in the manner in which each relates to a number of occupational scales, to item content areas expressed in the basic interest scales, and to characterizations of people rated high on each of the six themes. Of special interest in the appraisal of the validity of interest measures is the effectiveness of such measures as predictors of subsequent occupational histories (predictive validity). What percentage of individuals end up in occupations for which their inventory scores indicated high or very high interest? Serious problems arise in estimating congruence between actual occupation entered and interest scale scores because of the thousands of specific occupations and the limited number of scales on the SVIB and the SII. In spite of these problems, however, studies by different investigators are in reasonably good agreement that about 50% of individuals end up in occupations consistent with their interests expressed at about 20 years of age. This certainly represents a substantial relationship and, in view of the many other factors that can influence an individual's choice of occupation, can be considered evidence of good predictive validity for the instrument.

Career Assessment Inventory

An important limitation of the Strong Interest Inventory is its focus on primarily professional occupations, making it less useful for individuals who are interested in occupations that do not rely on completion of a college degree. The Career Assessment Inventory (CAI) was developed by Charles Johansson (1991) in order to fill this gap. Frankly modeled on the Strong, the Vocational Version of the CAI provides scores on Holland's six general occupational themes, 22 basic interest scales, and 91 occupational scales, varying widely in type and level (truck driver, school teacher, tool/die maker, nurse, etc.). An Enhanced Version is also available that provides information for 111 occupations with a wider distribution of educational requirements. A unique feature of the CAI is that scores are not reported separately for males and females. Only items valid for both genders were included in the scale construction in an effort to encourage freer access for both males and females into desired occupations and to allow for the broadest interpretation of test results. While this more gender-neutral perspective is valuable, many of the occupational samples on which the keys are based were relatively small. This is a matter of concern in assessing the validity of the instrument, particularly when judging it against the Strong and its larger sample sizes. However, the CAI (especially the vocational version) has been demonstrated to be a useful instrument for assessing vocational interest, particularly for non-college-bound high school students or adults who are seeking immediate job entry. Some additional information about the CAI can be obtained from the Pearson assessments web site at http://www.pearsonassessments.com/assessments/index.htm. From this page select the link to the instrument you wish to review.

Self-Directed Search

John Holland (1985, 1997) developed the Self-Directed Search (SDS) as a self-scoring tool that individuals could use to classify themselves according to the six personality types or occupational themes (realistic, artistic, investigative, conventional, social, and enterprising) and to assist them in career exploration and vocational choice. Most recently revised in 1994, the instrument itself consists of two booklets, the assessment booklet and the occupations finder, and can be completed in approximately 40 to 50 minutes (Holland, Powell, & Fritzsche, 1997). The assessment booklet gives the individual the opportunity to list occupational daydreams, to consider preferred activities and competencies, and to obtain scores on the six occupational themes. The scores on the three highest themes are used to develop a summary code. For example, an individual who scores highest on the social theme, followed by investigative and enterprising, would receive the summary code *SIE*. The person then refers to the occupations finder booklet for a list of occupations associated with that particular code. In the case of the *SIE* (*S*ocial, *I*nvestigative, *E*nterprising) summary code, the list includes medical records administrator, insurance claim examiner, school nurse, and physical therapist. The finder includes well over 1,000 occupations, each of which has been classified according to the Holland codes. The individual is encouraged to learn more about the occupations that are associated with the particular three-letter summary code. One important resource for obtaining information about various occupations is the *Dictionary of Occupational Titles* (1992), a U.S. Department of Labor publication that provides descriptions of over 12,000 occupations.

The unique feature of the SDS, as its name implies, is that it was designed to be used for career exploration without the aid of a career counselor. The booklets are self-explanatory and individuals can complete, score, and interpret the instrument on their own. While usually completed independently, the SDS can also be used in small groups. For example, a high school teacher or counselor might use the SDS with a class as part of a curriculum unit on career exploration. The instrument can also provide valuable information for a career counseling interview, and many career counselors incorporate it as part of the career counseling process. Counselor assistance in interpreting the scores is particularly important for adolescents, who often need to be encouraged to think more broadly about career choices and opportunities. In keeping with the current trend to make testing materials available on the Internet, the Self-Directed Search is also available online at http://www.self-directed-search.com. From this web site it is possible to take the test and receive a personalized report or to view a sample report and obtain general information about the test.

PERSONALITY AND ADJUSTMENT ASSESSMENT

Our lives would be so much easier if we could anticipate the feelings, thoughts, and actions of the people important to us. Psychologists and educators would also like to understand and anticipate their students and clients in order to do their jobs more effectively. If only we could know in advance how to motivate, teach, or intervene most effectively based on each student's personal characteristics. Unfortunately, professionals have only a slim advantage over the general public when forming impressions of other people (Garb, 1994). A number of personality and adjustment tests have been developed to compensate for the serious limitations inherent in subjective judgements. These tests have been refined and improved in recent decades. However, we have not progressed professionally or culturally to the point where we agree on the nature of human personality or what constitutes personal adjustment.

Four theoretical approaches dominate personality measurement. **Dynamic theories** describe components of personality, such as Freud's id, ego, and superego. Most dynamic assessments emphasize the importance of hidden or unconscious needs and conflicts that must be measured in ways that circumvent awareness. This approach relies heavily on the assessor's ability to understand and interpret the examinee's responses in order to conceptualize the entirety of the examinee's personality. **Trait theories** posit the existence of stable internal characteristics or tendencies that are usually measured with paper-and-pencil tests. An examinee may be asked to rate a series of statements as true or false. The presence or level of a trait is inferred from the examinee's responses to items (e.g., endorsing many items that suggest suspicion of others and their motives). Test scores are computed and interpreted by comparing them with established norms developed by testing a large number of people. **Humanistic theories** focus on how individuals conceive of and evaluate themselves. Early humanistic techniques asked examinees to act as their own assessors or analysts through self-observation and analysis. Contemporary humanistic assessments still focus on self-perceptions, but rely more on paper-and-pencil tests. Finally, **behavioral theories** challenge our basic assumptions by questioning the importance and even the existence of traditional personality constructs. Environmental or situational factors are seen as the primary determinates of behavior. Individual differences are attributed to the patterns of behavior that each individual learns as the result of past experiences. Behavioral assessments collect information about a person's pattern of actions and the situations associated with the actions of interest.

Dynamic Approaches

Dynamic approaches to personality assessment rely on the **projective hypothesis,** the assumption that our core concerns and conflicts color our every perception and action. Psychoanalysts developed projective techniques to facilitate this process. Ambiguous stimuli are used with the assumption that unconscious needs and conflicts, not the content of the stimulus itself, will determine the client's perceptions and reactions.

Rorschach Inkblot Test

The best known projective technique is Hermann Rorschach's inkblot test. Rorschach purportedly developed the test based on the common experience of looking at clouds and imagining them as objects, people, or whole scenes. He wondered if this childhood game might actually be an example of the projection of unconscious processes onto an ambiguous stimulus. Asking patients to look at clouds must not have seemed feasible. Instead, Rorschach created a set of 10 inkblots by placing ink on pieces of paper and folding them in half to form symmetrical patterns (see Figure 11–3).

Administration of the inkblots is done in two phases. In the **free association phase** the patient is shown the first card and asked to report what the blot might be or what it might represent. Each response is recorded. The process is repeated for the remaining nine cards. You may wish to try a little free association. Look at Figure 11–3. What do you see? Does the blot look like one object, or could it be seen in a number of different ways? The **inquiry phase** involves going over each card in order to determine the physical aspects of the card that prompted each response. The examiner notes the part of the card (all or a specific part of the card) and the characteristics of the card (shape, color, shading, etc.) that determined the patient's response. Look at Figure 11–3 again. Where on the card did you see an object? What aspects of the card suggested that object?

The administration of the test is fairly straightforward and may take as little as 10 minutes, although 45 minutes is more typical. However, the scoring and interpretation of the test is an arduous task that requires extensive training and considerable time. The contents, locations, and determinates of each response are carefully analyzed in order to compute a large number of scores and ratios between scores. The analysis and interpretation can be guided by comparing the scores and ratios to available norms, but a major factor in the final interpretation rests with the clinician.

Figure 11–3
An image like those used on the Rorschach.

Clinical lore is filled with tales of skilled examiners who diagnosed a brain lesion that had been missed by medical tests or who insightfully unraveled the secrets in a perplexing case. Unfortunately, clinicians are not able to live up to the lore. The Rorschach was a very popular test until the 1970s when evaluations of the Rorschach's reliability and validity produced such poor results that interest in the technique declined. Clinicians reviewing the same set of patient responses often arrived at inconsistent or even contradictory interpretations. John Exner and his colleagues (Exner & Exner, 1972) stimulated renewed interest in the test by trying to improve the test's psychometric properties. At least part of the problem was the many different systems for scoring and interpreting the test. Exner concluded that the scoring systems were so muddled clinicians usually simply interpreted the raw responses using their subjective impressions. He attempted to standardize the administration process and formalize the scoring system by integrating the best features from the existing systems. Exner began by culling through the confusion of existing scores and ratios and retaining only those that achieved an .85+ interrater reliability (Exner, 1974). The product was a new system that has been widely adopted by Rorschach users (Exner, 1993).

The Rorschach remains something of a psychometric nightmare despite Exner's work. There is no overall score to summarize the array of obtained scores and ratios. Some of the retained scores have acceptable interrater reliabilities (Acklin, McDowell, Verschell, & Chan, 2000). However, many scores with low interrater reliabilities are still being used and test–retest reliabilities for the various scores are either unknown or quite low (Lilienfeld, Wood, & Garb, 2000).

The validity of the Rorschach is even more problematic. The Rorschach has not demonstrated good predictive validity. For example, it is not a good indicator of prognosis or response to treatment (Groth-Marnat, 1999). The test has not even proven to be a good diagnostic tool to identify most types of psychological problems. The test may, however, be useful in identifying seriously disturbed psychiatric patients. Parker (1983) conducted a meta-analysis of available research and concluded that the Rorschach can be used to identify whether a set of responses was obtained from a normal or a seriously disturbed person. Seriously disturbed patients, especially individuals suffering from schizophrenia and other psychotic conditions, often provide very unusual responses to the Rorschach cards (Vincent & Harmon, 1991). However, their test responses are part of an overall pattern of bizarre behavior that may be obvious in even a brief interview. Therefore, the Rorschach test may be a good indicator of serious psychiatric conditions, but it may not be necessary to administer the test in order to diagnose the conditions. The psychometric evidence for the Rorschach is so weak that Lilienfield et al. (2000) called for strict limits on the use of the instrument, including the use of only well-validated scores and a de-emphasis of the test in clinical training programs.

Thematic Apperception Test

The Thematic Apperception Test (TAT) is another popular projective test. Henry Murray developed a psychodynamic theory of personality based on 28 needs including *affiliation, achievement, aggression, power,* and *sex.* He selected a set of black-and-white sketches and photographs to be used as stimulus cards to assess personality. Examinees are shown a series of the cards, one card at a time, and asked to make up a story that includes the present, a beginning, an end, and a description of thoughts and feelings that the characters in the story might experience. You may wish to make up a story to the TAT card reproduced in Figure 11–4 following these instructions.

Murray (1943) believed the stories people tell are filled with projections, such that the examinee "has said things about an invented character that apply to himself, things which he

Figure 11–4
Sample TAT card.
Reprinted by permission of the publishers from Henry A. Murray, THEMATIC APPERCEPTION TEST, Cambridge, Mass.: Harvard University Press, Copyright © 1943 by the President and Fellows of Harvard College, © 1971 by Henry A. Murray.

would have been reluctant to confess in response to a direct question. As a rule the subject leaves the test happily unaware that he has presented the psychologist with what amounts to an X-ray picture of his inner self" (p. 1). Does your story provide an X-ray of your personality? Perhaps Murray was overly enthusiastic about his technique. Nevertheless, people do tell very different stories to the same card and their stories often include themes and concerns from their own lives. Clinicians are often left with the impression that the stories do contain important information. The question is "Can the stories be interpreted in a way that provides valid information about the storyteller?"

Overall, psychometric evaluations of the TAT have been discouraging. Part of the problem is that the standardized procedures for administering the test are very cumbersome, requiring the administration of 20 cards in two sessions on successive days. The standard instructions also present the test as a task of imagination, a deception that many psychologists reject on ethical grounds. Examiners routinely streamline the administration by presenting fewer cards and completing the testing in a single session. The cards used for any particular administration vary based on examiner preference. Most examiners also modify the test instructions to avoid misleading clients about the purpose of the test. Inconsistencies in testing procedures are evident even in studies evaluating the test. Keiser and Prather (1990) found that published evaluations used very different administration procedures and usually administered only a few of the suggested 20 cards. Even small variations in instruction and procedure produce dramatic effects on the stories that are created (Lundy, 1988). An additional problem is that two psychologists may focus on different aspects of a story and provide very different interpretations from the same material. We may even think of story interpretation as a projective task in itself. How much does an interpretation reveal about the interpreter as opposed to the client?

Administering the test in a consistent manner and using well-defined criteria to obtain scores for a specific trait or characteristic can substantially improve estimates of test reliability and validity. Several systems have been developed to measure some of the needs originally delineated by Murray. For example, Spangler (1992) conducted a meta-analysis and concluded that a well-defined set of scoring criteria developed to measure the *need for achievement* produced high inter-rater reliabilities and adequate test–retest reliabilities. The *need for achievement* scores predicted "real-world" outcomes such as grades, income, occupational success, and leadership better than questionnaires designed for the same purpose. Promising results have been obtained using scoring systems to assess *affiliation* and *power* needs (Winter, John, Stewart, Klohnen, & Duncan, 1998), as well as the use of defense mechanisms (e.g., denial, projection, identification) and the maturity of interpersonal understanding and relating (Cramer, 1999). However, these scoring systems each address only a single facet of personality and do not individually or collectively provide a comprehensive picture of personality.

Trait Approaches

Trait approaches to describing personality evolved from the everyday characterizations we use to describe people. Gordon Allport (1937), a pioneer in the study of traits, believed that behind the deluge of everyday descriptors are a number of real neuropsychological structures or traits that account for consistency in behavior. Allport and Odbert (1936) used a dictionary to identify more than 18,000 words describing personality. They were able to reduce the list to approximately 4,500 descriptors by collapsing synonyms and retaining descriptors that implied consistent and stable modes of adjustment. Allport (1955) favored intensive, long-term individual case studies as the best method for investigating these structures. Despite his preferences, the study of personality traits quickly became a highly technical enterprise. Since the 1950s researchers have usually administered paper-and-pencil tests to large samples of people and analyzed the resulting mountains of data, using some of the most sophisticated statistical procedures available. These efforts have produced literally hundreds of different tests, each purporting to measure one or more traits.

Factor Analytic Explorations of Traits

Sixteen Personality Factor Questionnaire (16PF). Raymond Cattell (1950) did not believe that hundreds of different traits were needed to assess personality. He edited Allport and Odbert's list of 4,500 traits and selected 200 descriptors, which he referred to as *surface traits*. He selected a large sample of people and collected self-ratings, peer ratings, and behavioral assessments intended to measure the 200 surface traits. He then analyzed the relations between the 200 surface traits using factor analysis. **Factor analysis** provides a way to analyze the pattern of correlations between several measures in order to identify a smaller number of underlying components or factors (see Chapter 8). For example, a factor analysis of a wide variety of athletic activities (e.g., all the track and field events) might identify a list of relatively independent component athletic abilities (e.g., acceleration, upper body strength, endurance). A particular activity might rely primarily on a single component or factor (e.g., 100 dash: acceleration) or on a combination of factors (javelin toss: acceleration plus upper body strength). Cattell concluded that the 200 surface traits could be described as variants or combinations of 16 underlying factors or *source traits*, which he named Emotionally Stabile, Self-Assured, Relaxed, Trusting, Controlled, Conscientious, Outgoing, Group Dependent, Happy-Go-Lucky, Venturesome, Assertive, Artless, Radical, Imaginative, Tender Minded, and Intelligent.

Cattell developed the Sixteen Personality Factor Questionnaire (16PF) to measure the identified source traits. Each question on the test was designed to measure only one of the source traits, and each of the source traits should be relatively independent from the other source traits. Cattel successfully selected similar items to assess each source trait, but the source traits are not completely independent from one another. Does the overlap between source traits suggest the list could be further reduced without losing the ability to discriminate between people?

Many other researchers have also used the factor analytic approach. A large number of diverse test questions are given to a sample and the relationships between the various questions are statistically analyzed to identify underlying personality factors. Factor analytic studies of personality traits have been conducted using a wide variety of items and very diverse samples. These studies typically yield lists of 10 to 20 interrelated factors that are similar to Cattell's source traits. Researchers began to notice similarity in the content of the obtained factors, but also noted recurrent patterns in the interrelationships between the obtained factors. Further analyses designed to eliminate the overlap between the various factors suggest that the various lists of factors can be reduced to five higher order factors that have little overlap (Digman, 1990). These five factors, commonly referred to as the *Big Five,* are named Neuroticism, Extraversion, Openness, Agreeableness, and Conscientiousness.

Revised NEO Personality Inventory (NEO PI-R). Costa and McCrae (1992b) approached the task of test construction from the top, beginning with the five higher order factors, or *domains,* as they called them. Items were selected or written to measure each of the five higher order domains and administered to large numbers of people. Items that tapped one and only one domain were retained. The items for each domain were then factor analyzed in order to identify the subtraits or *facets* that make up the domain. The latest result of their efforts is the Revised NEO Personality Inventory (NEO PI-R). The *NEO* portion of the test name refers to the first three Big Five factors: Neuroticism, Extroversion, and Openness (*PI* = personality inventory). Earlier versions of the test measured only three of the five factors. The current version measures all five factors, but the original acronym has been retained.

The NEO PI-R is a 240-item test intended to measure normal adult personality. The test comes in two forms, one for self-report (Form S) and the other for observer ratings (Form R). Form R items are parallel to those on Form S but are stated in third person. The self and observer ratings can be plotted on the same profile sheet in order to provide a comparison of a person from two perspectives (see Figure 11–5).

The assumption of a hierarchical structure of personality traits is evident in the computed scores. The test yields a score for each of the five domains of Neuroticism, Extraversion, Openness, Agreeableness, and Conscientiousness. Each domain has six unique facets. Each domain score is calculated by summing the scores for its six facets. Each facet is measured by eight test items (5 domains × 6 facets/domain × 8 items/facet = 240 test items). See Table 11–4 for a list of domains and their respective facets.

NEO PI-R Form S (self-report) was developed using data from three different research projects including approximately 2,200 people. A norming sample of 1,000 (500 men and 500 women) was selected from the larger group. Selection was manipulated so that the age, gender, and race of the norming sample were congruent with demographic data from the latest census projections. However, the educational level of the sample is questionable in that almost all of the participants attained at least a high school education. The problem with educational level may actually have been compounded by the test authors' attempt to compensate for it. They eliminated individuals with high levels of education in order to keep the sample mean near the mean for the population. The NEO PI-R Form R (observer rating) was normed on a much smaller subsample, using spouse and peer ratings for 142 members of the Form S sample.

The psychometric properties of the NEO PI-R are quite impressive. Internal consistency analyses for the self-report domain scores produced coefficient alphas that varied from .86 for Agreeableness to .92 for Neuroticism. Observer ratings were even more consistent, with coefficient alphas ranging from .89 for Openness to .95 for Agreeableness. Self-report facet score reliabilities vary from .56 to .81, and those for observer ratings range from .60 to .90. Some of the facet reliabilities are particularly high, considering that each facet score is calculated from only eight items.

Good retest reliability should be obtained from tests purporting to measure stable personality traits. Unfortunately, most personality measures do not fare well when long-term temporal stability is assessed. A relative strength of the NEO PI-R self and observer ratings is their stability over extended retest intervals. For example, a 6-year interval study of self and observer ratings found temporal stability coefficients in the .68 to .83 range for the domain scores.

Costa and McCrae (1992b) have accumulated considerable evidence for some types of test validity. Factor analyses of the NEO PI-R consistently reproduce the hierarchical structure that the authors intended to create. The domain and facet scores also have been shown to have good convergent validity (correlate well with other tests purporting to measure the same traits and subtraits) and discriminant validity (low or near-zero correlation with measures of unrelated traits and subtraits). Correlation coefficients between self (Form S) and other (Form R) ratings demonstrate moderate to high levels of association between self-ratings and observer

NEO PI-R profile sheet.

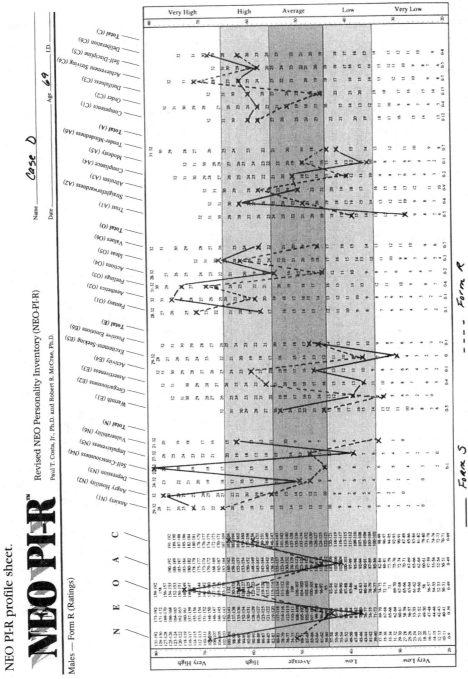

Figure 11–5

NEO PI-R profile sheet.

*Source:*Reproduced by special permission of the Publisher, Psychological Assessment Resources, Inc., 16204 North Florida Avenue, Lutz, Florida 33549, from the NEO Personality Inventory–Revised, by Paul Costa and Robert McCrae. Copyright 1978, 1985, 1989, 1992, by PAR, Inc. Further reproduction is prohibited without permission of PAR, Inc.

Table 11–4
Adjective Checklist Correlates

NEO PI-R Facet	Adjective Check List Items
Neuroticism facets	
N1: Anxiety	anxious, fearful, worrying, tense, nervous, −confident, −optimistic
N2: Angry Hostility	anxious, irritable, impatient, excitable, moody, −gentle, tense
N3: Depression	worrying, −contented, −confident, −self-confident, pessimistic, moody, anxious
N4: Self-Consciousness	shy, −self-confident, timid, −confident, defensive, inhibited, anxious
N5: Impulsiveness	moody, irritable, sarcastic, self-centered, loud, hasty, excitable
N6: Vulnerability	−clear-thinking, −self-confident, −confident, anxious, −efficient, −alert, careless
Extraversion facets	
E1: Warmth	friendly, warm, sociable, cheerful, −aloof, affectionate, outgoing
E2: Gregariousness	sociable, outgoing, pleasure-seeking, −aloof, talkative, spontaneous, −withdrawn
E3: Assertiveness	aggressive, −shy, assertive, self-confident, forceful, enthusiastic, confident
E4: Activity	energetic, hurried, quick, determined, enthusiastic, aggressive, active
E5: Excitement-Seeking	pleasure-seeking, daring, adventurous, charming, handsome, spunky, clever
E6: Positive Emotions	enthusiastic, humorous, praising, spontaneous, pleasure-seeking, optimistic, jolly
Openness facets	
O1: Fantasy	dreamy, imaginative, humorous, mischievous, idealistic, artistic, complicated
O2: Aesthetics	imaginative, artistic, original, enthusiastic, inventive, idealistic, versatile
O3: Feelings	excitable, spontaneous, insightful, imaginative, affectionate, talkative, outgoing
O4: Actions	interests wide, imaginative, adventurous, optimistic, −mild, talkative, versatile
O5: Ideas	idealistic, interests wide, inventive, curious, original, imaginative, insightful
O6: Values	−conservative, unconventional, −cautious, flirtatious
Agreeableness facets	
A1: Trust	forgiving, trusting, −suspicious, −wary, −pessimistic, peaceable, −hard-hearted
A2: Straightforwardness	−complicated, −demanding, −clever, −flirtatious, −charming, −shrewd, −autocratic
A3: Altruism	warm, soft-hearted, gentle, generous, kind, tolerant, −selfish
A4: Compliance	−stubborn, −demanding, −headstrong, −impatient, −intolerant, −outspoken, −hard-hearted
A5: Modesty	−show-off, −clever, −assertive, −argumentative, −self-confident, −aggressive, −idealistic
A6: Tender-Mindedness	friendly, warm, sympathetic, soft-hearted, gentle, −unstable, kind

(continued)

Table 11–4 *Continued*

NEO PI-R Facet	Adjective Check List Items
Conscientiousness facets	
C1: Competence	efficient, self-confident, thorough, resourceful, confident, −confused, intelligent
C2: Order	organized, thorough, efficient, precise, methodical, −absent-minded, −careless
C3: Dutifulness	−defensive, −distractible, −careless, −lazy, thorough, −absent-minded, −fault-finding
C4: Achievement Striving	thorough, ambitious, industrious, enterprising, determined, confident, persistent
C5: Self-Discipline	organized, −lazy, efficient, −absent-minded, energetic, thorough, industrious
C6: Deliberation	−hasty, −impulsive, −careless, −impatient, −immature, thorough, −moody

Source: Reproduced by special permission of the Publisher, Psychological Assessment Resources, Inc., 16204 North Florida, Avenue, Lutz, Florida 33549, from the NEO Personality Inventory–Revised, by Paul Costa, and Robert McCrae, Copyright 1978, 1985, 1989, 1992 by PAR, Inc. Further reproduction is prohibited without permission of PAR Inc.

Note: Correlates are given in descending order of absolute magnitude; all are significant at $p < .001$, $N = 305$. Minus signs before adjectives indicate negative correlations with the facet scale. Adapted from McCrae & Costa, 1992.

ratings for both the domains and the facets. The correlation coefficients between spouse and self-ratings are considerably higher than the correlation between peer and self-ratings, indicating that more knowledgeable and intimate judges provide ratings that are more consistent with self-perceptions.

McCrae and Costa (1997) argue that the five domains measured by the test are universal human characteristics evident across time and culture. Indeed, the test has been successfully translated into several different languages. Factor analyses of the translated versions of the test have usually yielded the five named factors across several cultures and age groups (DeFruyt, Mervielde, Hoekstra, Hans, & Rolland, 2000; Heuchert, Parker, Stumpf, & Myburgh, 2000; Piedmont & Chae, 1997). However, analysis of the NEO PI-R in conjunction with other measures developed within the indigenous culture suggests some culture-specific factors may be missed by the NEO PI-R and that the NEO PI-R factors may have somewhat different meanings within a specific culture (Cheung, Leung, Zhang, & Sun, 2001).

The main criticism that can be leveled against the NEO PI-R is that despite its psychometric elegance, it has not yet been shown to have wide practical application. Dimensions derived from factor analysis are statistical abstractions distilled from patterns of correlation. Names given to these abstractions such as "openness" or "neuroticism" are only verbal labels intended to symbolize the underlying statistical relationships. It is sometimes easier to compare statistically derived factors with other abstractions, such as scores or factors from other tests, than it is to apply them to real-world predictions and decision making. For example, Costa and McCrae (1992a) argue that the test may be useful in identifying people with personality disorders. However, Butcher and Rouse (1996) conclude that the NEO PI-R scores are too abstract and superficial to be useful in clinical assessment. While the NEO PI-R holds promise for practical applications, these applications have not yet been fully explored or confirmed. The weight of validity evidence still rests on correlations with other tests, many of which were used to develop the original five-factor model of personality.

A second concern is that the test, like all self-report measures, relies on the honesty and forthrightness of the person providing the ratings. Respondents are asked to report whether they have answered honestly, answered all of the questions, and marked answers in the correct spaces. The authors' faith in the forthrightness and competence of respondents in completing the test is based on a review of data from the test development samples. This faith may be severely tested in assessment situations where an examinee may have motivation to minimize or exaggerate personal difficulties (e.g., a disability evaluation or personnel screening). Several researchers have asked people to answer the test items in order to make either a positive or a negative impression. Participants seem to be quite capable of such a task and provide answers that are consistent with expectations (Caldwell-Andrews, Baer, & Berry, 2000; Topping & O'Gorman, 1997). Validity scales have been developed for the NEO PI-R. The validity scales appear to be useful in identifying people who are instructed to present either a positive or negative impression (Scandell, 2000; Schinka, Kinder, & Kremer, 1997), as well as psychotic patients who deny their condition (Yang, Bagby, & Ryder, 2000). However, the validity scales may not be necessary for more normal people in more normal situations (Piedmont, McCrae, Riemann, & Angleitner, 2000).

Earlier in this section, we asked whether Cattell's 16 factors could be reduced to an even smaller number of traits. Research by Gerbing and Tuley (1991) on the relationship between the 16PF and an earlier version of Costa and McCrae's test, the NEO PI, suggests that the NEO and 16PF scales measure essentially the same personality traits. Even though the names of the scales may be quite different, there is a strong correspondence between Cattell's 16 factors and corresponding facet scores on the NEO PI. In addition, Cattell's 16 factors can themselves be factor analyzed to produce a smaller number of higher order factors that correlate quite well with the domain scores on the NEO PI.

Identifying Traits Using Empirical Scale Construction

A number of personality and adjustment tests have been developed using **empirical scale construction** strategies, the same approach that was used in the development of the Strong Vocational Interest Blank/Strong Interest Inventory. In this procedure a large number of items are given to a selected group of people who are known to have a particular characteristic. The same items are also given to a sample that is representative of the general population. Items are selected based solely on their ability to differentiate between the selected and the representative groups.

Minnesota Multiphasic Personality Inventory (MMPI).   The MMPI was developed to provide objective scales that could be used to diagnose people with specific psychological disorders. The authors of the original version of the MMPI (Hathaway & McKinley, 1940) approached the assessment of pathology with an empirical scaling strategy. Existing tests, research, and texts addressing traits associated with pathology were used to construct a large pool of items that could be answered with a *yes* or *no* response. Hathaway and McKinley identified and tested small groups of individuals who were exemplars of particular psychological disorders. The test developers did not have *a priori* ideas about which characteristics would differentiate the normal and diagnosed groups. Instead, they administered the entire array of items and used statistical procedures to select the items that would be used to classify individuals. They began with a group of neurotic patients who presented somatic concerns for which physicians could find no organic basis. The test items were administered to the identified patients and to a comparison group of presumably normal individuals who were visitors at the hospital. Items that differentiated the two groups were retained and used to construct the Hypochondriasis scale of the MMPI. The scale was also administered to a second group of patients with hypochondriasis to ensure that it would also differentiate them from the "normal" group. The test developers proceeded in a like manner to develop **clinical scales** for nine additional groups.

One problem that has plagued the MMPI is the "normal" group that was used to develop the scales. There is good reason to believe that the hospital visitors did not represent the general population on either demographic or personality variables. Even if they did, the fact that they were visiting patients at a medical facility strongly suggests that many in the group were experiencing psychological duress at the time they completed the test items. Selection of good target and comparison groups is extremely important in empirical test construction because sampling errors will affect the items chosen for the scale.

Clinical Scales of the Minnesota Multiphasic Personality Inventory. The 10 basic scores established on an empirical basis carry the labels shown here. The labels are followed by a characterization of the group on which the scale was based.

1. *Hypochondriasis (Hs).* Worry excessively about health, report obscure pains and disorders, but with no organic basis for the symptoms (32 items).
2. *Depression (D).* Chronic depression, feelings of uselessness, and inability to face the future (57 items).
3. *Conversion Hysteria (Hy).* Reacts to personal problems by developing physical symptoms such as paralysis, cramps, gastric complaints, or cardiac symptoms. Denial of psychological problems (60 items).
4. *Psychopathic Deviate (Pd).* Irresponsibility, disregard for social norms or concern for others, and lack of deep emotional response (50 items).
5. *Masculinity-Femininity (Mf).* High scores suggest a tendency to diverge from culturally prescribed gender roles. Low scores suggest stereotypical sex-role perceptions (56 items).
6. *Paranoia (Pa).* Excessive suspicion of others and their motives, interpersonal sensitivity, and the belief that one is being persecuted (40 items).
7. *Psychasthenia (Pt).* Excessive fears (phobias) and compulsions to repeatedly perform certain acts, high moral standards, self-blame, and rigid impulse control (48 items).
8. *Schizophrenia (Sc).* Bizarre and unusual thoughts or behavior and subjective experiences out of step with reality (78 items).
9. *Hypomania (Ma).* Physical and mental overactivity, with rapid shifts in ideas or actions (46 items).
10. *Social Introversion (SI).* Tendency to keep to oneself and avoid social gatherings. Low scores indicate extroversion (69 items).

The MMPI scales include a somewhat unusual mixture of clearly pathological items and some items that seem neutral or innocent. The two types of statements are referred to as obvious and subtle items. The obvious and subtle items within the same scales are completely uncorrelated with one another. Cross-validation studies have shown that the obvious items, and not the subtle items, differentiate the pathological groups (Duff, 1965). Because the power of the scales lies in the obvious items, the MMPI is subject to distorted responding by individuals who have reason to exaggerate or minimize their difficulties. The test authors quickly recognized this problem because some patients who were exemplars of very severe disorders produced normal test scores.

They soon developed validity scales designed to identify and correct for respondent misrepresentations. Four validity scales are regularly used:

? The number of items that an individual does not mark. A large number of blank items is seen as an indication of defensiveness and withdrawal from the task.

L The number of obviously "good" but extremely improbable items endorsed (e.g., "I have *never* told a lie."). May indicate naive defensiveness or an attempt to portray virtuosity (15 items).

F The number of very rare and unusual items endorsed (e.g., "There is a worldwide plot to read my mind."). A high score may indicate that the respondent did not understand or follow the directions or that the respondent may be faking or exaggerating symptoms (60 items).

K The number of items endorsed by the examinee that were also frequently chosen by seriously disturbed individuals who obtained normal scores on the test (e.g., "I like *almost* everyone I meet."). High scores are seen as a sign of a sophisticated, defensive style and the tendency to describe oneself in a "socially desirable" manner (30 items).

The most interesting and controversial validity scale is the *K* scale. It is unclear how well this scale measures defensiveness as opposed to a genuine and legitimate positive self-image. Moderately elevated scores on the *K* scale are common among groups of successful individuals who appear to be getting on well in life, as well as among certain clinical populations. The *K* scale score is used to adjust 5 of the 10 clinical scales based on their relative susceptibility to this type of defensiveness.

Research on the MMPI during the first 50 years of its use produced volumes of data. In the 1980s, the body of research served as a basis for a revision of the instrument (Hathaway & McKinley, 1989), a revision that was intended to correct some of the deficiencies that had been noted in the original instrument. For example, new norms have been developed, based on a national sample of 1,138 males and 1,462 females. The sample now includes suitable representation of ethnic and minority group members. Unfortunately, the educational level attained by the new sample is much higher than the national average, raising questions about use of the test with less educated individuals. While the renorming was helpful in adjusting scores to fit current population characteristics, it did not rectify the original problem of using a nonrepresentative group for item selection. The original items were, nevertheless, culled and edited to correct items with outdated or offensive content, and 154 new items were tried out. The revised instrument (MMPI-2) contains 567 items, although the "basic scales are scored from the first 370 items" (Hathaway & McKinley, 1989, p. 15).

Like many other tests using empirical scale construction, the MMPI-2 has considerable item overlap among the various scales. A *yes* response on one item may add to the elevation of two scales and lower the elevation on a third. As a result the scales are not independent of one another. While this is a serious measurement concern, it also reflects a reality behind the construction of the test: People with two different psychological disorders may have some symptoms in common and exhibit other symptoms that are specific to their diagnoses. For example, intense feelings of inadequacy are common to many disorders including depression and eating disorders. However, each disorder also includes other symptoms that allow differential diagnosis.

The test authors originally envisioned a test that could diagnose clinical conditions based on single score elevations. Instead, interpretation of an MMPI-2 profile is based on the pattern formed by scores on several scales. In theory, depressed individuals should score highly only on the depression scale. In fact, depressed individuals often also obtain high scores on the Hs and Hy scales and low scores on the Ma scale because depressed mood is often accompanied by concern over physical symptoms and low levels of activity. Interpreting test results usually requires comparing the examinee's highest two or three scales with several hundred recognized clinical profiles (Hathaway & McKinley, 1989). Most of the recognized clinical profiles were developed using the original MMPI. The researchers who revamped the MMPI to create the MMPI-2 maintain that the conservative revision of the test allows the use of profiles developed from the MMPI to be used to interpret MMPI-2 profiles (Butcher & Williams, 1992a). However, direct comparisons between MMPI and MMPI-2 profiles obtained from the same examinees often reveal important differences that can alter interpretation and classification (Dahlstrom, 1992). The issue may be of less importance in clinical applications, because MMPI/MMPI-2 profile discrepancies occur primarily among normal examinees. Individuals with clinical conditions are more likely to produce consistent profiles across the two forms of the test (Butcher & Rouse, 1996).

Both test–retest and internal consistency reliability information are given for clinical scales of the MMPI-2. Retest reliabilities over an average interval of 1 week ranged from .67 to .92 for a sample of 82 males and from .58 to .91 for 111 females. Coefficient alpha reliabilities from .33 to .85 were reported for males, while the female sample yielded values from .36 to .87. Most of the item content of the MMPI-2 is essentially unchanged from its predecessor. Consequently, the validity evidence collected from a half century of research on the original MMPI, as well as some of the old reservations about its quality as a psychometric instrument, still apply.

The MMPI is alleged to be the most extensively used self-descriptive instrument in clinical practice and has been applied in a wide range of other settings. For example, the MMPI-2 is often used to diagnose and develop treatment plans for people suffering from psychological disorders. It is also frequently used in personnel selection for jobs that involve a high degree of responsibility or stress, such as police officer. The widespread use of the test in sensitive and even life-changing situations creates concern about its fairness. The original MMPI was developed and normed with little regard for cultural and ethnic diversity. The MMPI-2 norming sample was more diverse and representative of the national population. However, the use of an updated and more diverse norming sample does not diminish concern that the test content is biased since items were selected using only Caucasian samples. Indeed, African American samples do obtain higher average scores on several MMPI-2 scales. It is not clear whether these elevated scores reflect test bias or a higher level of some types of symptoms among African American groups (McNulty, Graham, Ben-Porath, & Stein, 1997).

In spite of its psychometric limitations, the MMPI has had wide acceptance and use, especially by clinical psychologists. In addition to use of the scores and overall profile, the clinician may look at the responses to specific questions or groups of questions as part of the search for insight about and understanding of a client. However, such use should be limited to individuals with extensive clinical training and should serve only as the starting point for diagnosis. The test authors propose that completion of graduate courses in testing and psychopathology should be the minimum educational standards for using the MMPI, but we would suggest higher standards unless you are working under the direct supervision of a trained clinician. You can get additional information about the MMPI-2, including the wide variety of specialized scales and reports that have been developed, from the publisher's web site at http://www.pearsonassessments.com/assessments/index.htm.

There is also a version of the MMPI for adolescents, the Minnesota Multiphasic Personality Inventory–Adolescent (MMPI-A) (Butcher & Williams, 1992b). The MMPI-A offers the same array of clinical and validity scales as the adult version. Scales were normed using an age-appropriate sample.

Humanistic Approaches: Personality as Self-Perception

Carl Rogers is most responsible for advancing the humanistic approach in psychology and making the term *self-concept* a part of popular culture. Rogers (1951) believed that humans have a basic drive toward self-improvement. He believed that we develop a sense of who and what we want to become and that we constantly strive to narrow the gap between this ideal and our current *self-concept* or self-appraisal. Rogers concluded that these self-evaluations are the core of personality. He proposed the novel idea that personality testing should simply be a formalized part of the self-evaluation process. The person, not the psychologist or analyst, should conduct the evaluation and interpret the results.

Rogers' earliest formal measure of self-concept was the *Q-sort*, a self-rating method that utilizes a set of cards with brief, self-descriptive statements. The examinee first ranks the cards from least descriptive to most descriptive of current self. The same cards are then ranked to describe the person's ideal self. The self-ratings provide a measure of self-concept and the difference between self and ideal ratings yields a measure of self-satisfaction. The humanistic psychologist acts as a consultant and coach, rather than as the outside evaluator in the interpretive process. Rogers encouraged examinees to interpret the test results and explore the meaning of the ratings for themselves.

Subsequent Measures of Self-Concept

A number of self-concept measures were soon developed by other authors. Paper-and-pencil formats displaced the Q-sort technique, and modern test technology was applied to the development and analysis of the tests that followed. The qualitative self-interpretation of the early instruments was replaced by normative comparisons of test scores. The format for contemporary self-concept measures has become almost indistinguishable from that of trait tests. The differentiating characteristic of self-concept tests is that they provide a measure of self-perception and/or self-satisfaction for the evaluation of individuals within the normal range of human behavior. The resulting scores, whether referred to as self-concept or self-esteem scores, tend to be highly intercorrelated measures of self-perceived adjustment (Bracken, 1991).

In recent years there has been a renewed interest in self-concept measurement, particularly regarding children and adolescents. Self-concept scores have been shown to correlate with a wide variety of indicators of development and social adjustment. The causal relationship between self-concept and adjustment is not clear. A positive view of oneself may, for example, be either the cause or the result of good adjustment. Nevertheless, many educators advocate teaching children to view themselves more positively, in the hope that better adjustment and higher achievement will follow.

Multidimensional Self-Concept Scale (MSCS).

The MSCS is a 150-item test developed by Bracken (1992) to assess self-concept among children and adolescents ages 9 to 19. Two decades of factor-analytic studies using a number of different self-concept measures indicated that self-concept is not unidimensional. Self-ratings vary depending on the aspect of ourselves that we rate and the social context in which we picture ourselves. For example, someone may have a positive image of himself in relationship to his family, yet be uncomfortable about himself in social situations. Another may see herself as a very competent person but be embarrassed about her body. The MSCS recognizes the complex nature of self-concept by providing a total score and six subscores for the domains of social, competence, affect, academic, family, and physical self-concepts as shown in Figure 11–6.

Bracken views these domains as highly interrelated subdivisions of the global self-concept. The test was normed on a school-age sample of 5th to 12th graders selected to be representative

Figure 11–6
Self-concept model—Bracken.
Source: B. A. Bracken,
*Multidimensional Self-Concept
Scale Manual.* Austin, TX:
PRO-ED, 1992, p. 5. Reprinted
by permission.

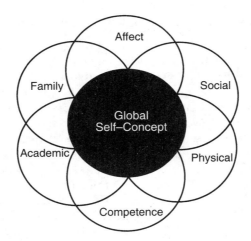

of the U.S. population within each age bracket. Rotatori (1994) points out that while the sample is representative for sex and race, some regions of the country are overrepresented, and data on socioeconomic status are not included. There is some evidence that the self-concept domains are consistent across several American ethnic minorities (Tansy & Miller, 1997; Wilson, 1998) and some of the domains can be assessed as early as the 3rd grade (Wilson, 1998).

The test has very good internal consistency, producing alpha coefficients in the high 90s for the total score at every age level. Domain scores are only slightly lower with alphas ranging from .85 for ninth graders on the Competence subscale, to .97 for several grade levels on the Family subscale. The test shows strong temporal stability, yielding a .90 test–retest coefficient for the total score over a 4-week test–retest interval. Temporal stability coefficients for the domain scores ranged from .73 for Affect to .81 for Academic and Physical subscales. The author argues for the test's content validity based on the match between the domains measured on the test and the self-concept factors identified by previous research.

Evidence for concurrent validity is found in the high correlation obtained when comparing MSCS scores with scores from other self-concept tests. The test manual also cites research indicating that the test was a good discriminator for identifying children who were rated as low in self-esteem or who obtained poor scores on a test of emotional disturbance.

Behavioral Approaches

Traditional behaviorism is the antithesis of conventional ideas about personality. John B. Watson and later B. F. Skinner adamantly opposed the use of constructs that could not be directly observed. Dynamic forces, traits, and self-conceptions are all examples of the class of constructs that traditional behaviorists wished to abolish. The advancement of cognitive psychology has had a profound effect on behaviorism. Of particular import is the work of theorists such as Albert Bandura, who came to realize that learning social behaviors involved both overt actions and "internal" behaviors such as representing events through images and words, making judgments, or experiencing emotion. The scope of behaviorism was greatly expanded once internal behaviors, particularly cognitions, were accepted as legitimate foci for study.

Traditional behaviorists do not believe that it is necessary to infer internal structures in order to explain consistency in behavior across time and situation. Rather, similar behavior in different contexts is explained as learned responses that are regulated by similarities in the different environments. Individual differences can be accounted for by one's previous learning history. People seek different situations or behave differently in the same situation because they have learned to associate different stimuli and behaviors with different consequences.

Initially, behavior patterns were assessed primarily by direct observation. An observer might record a specific behavior, the environmental stimuli that preceded the behavior, and the consequences that followed. Situational tests have also been used in which behavior patterns are assessed by placing a person in an actual situation in order to predict performance. For example, a job applicant's ability to manage work stressors could be evaluated by placing him or her in a stressful environment. The process was later abridged by the use of self-report forms that allowed respondents to recall or rate important stimuli, behavior patterns, and consequences. Eventually, paper-and-pencil self-report forms began to include accounts of cognitions, judgments, and emotions. Modern testing technology has also been applied to these self-report forms, such that the format is very similar to traditional trait inventories. Nevertheless, authors of these instruments assert that they are directly measuring behavior or behavior patterns and not internal structures (e.g., ego, trait, or self-concept) that control or direct behavior.

Millon Clinical Multiaxial Inventory–III (MCMI-III)

Theodore Millon (Millon, Millon, & Davis, 1994) has created a very innovative, behaviorally based test that has gained considerable popularity among clinicians. The test is a direct competitor with the MMPI-2 because it is also used to identify and classify people who have serious psychological problems. However, Millon used a theoretical approach to test development as opposed to the empirical scale construction used by Hathaway and McKinley. The MCMI-III is the latest revision of the test based on Millon's theory of personality and psychopathology (Millon, 1990). The 175-item test provides scores for 24 clinical scales, which are organized into four groups: clinical personality disorders (11 scales), severe personality disorders (3 scales), clinical syndromes (7 scales), and severe clinical syndromes (3 scales).

Clinical Personality Disorders Scales.   Millon believes that people with clinical personality disorders can be classified using two dimensions of behavior: pattern of reinforcement and style of coping behavior. He initially identified 10 clinical personality disorders based on five patterns of reinforcement and two styles of coping ($2 \times 5 = 10$). The 10 basic disorders, which are called *clinical personality patterns,* are listed in Table 11–5. The behavioral characteristics associated with

Table 11–5
Millon Clinical Personality Patterns

Reinforcement Pattern	Coping Style	
	Passive	Active
Detached	Schizoid	Avoidant
Dependent	Dependent	Histrionic
Independent	Narcissistic	Antisocial
Discordant	Self-Defeating	Aggressive
Ambivalent	Compulsive	Negativistic

Table 11–6
Millon Clinical Personality Disorders Behavioral Characteristics

Clinical Personality Disorder	Reinforcement Pattern	Coping Style
Schizoid	Detached: Few rewards for pleasures in life	Passive: Apathetic, resigned
Avoidant	Detached	Active: Actively avoid pain
Dependent	Dependent: Pleasure or pain derived from how others feel about them	Passive: Wait for others to direct or reach out of them
Histrionic	Dependent	Active: Manipulate in order to gain attention or favors
Narcissistic	Independent: Selfish gratification of own needs and wants	Passive: Bask in self-approval
Antisocial	Independent	Active: Exploit and use others
Self-Defeating	Discordant: Substitute pain for pleasure	Passive: Allow themselves to be used and abused
Aggressive	Discordant	Active: Seek pleasure through the abuse of others
Compulsive	Ambivalent: Conflict over seeking approval vs. expressing anger (independent vs. dependent)	Passive: Suppress resentment and are overconforming
Negativistic	Ambivalent	Active: Express resentment and feel guilt

each personality pattern are summarized in Table 11–6. An 11th personality scale, Depressive, was added to the basic 10 to account for people who cope by giving up. These individuals exhibit a loss of hope and a despair about the future. Thus, 11 clinical personality pattern scales are reported in the complete instrument.

Severe Personality Disorders Scales. The Severe Personality Disorders Scales assess personality disturbances that are marked by extremely dysfunctional coping styles and occasional loss of contact with reality. The three scales for these disorders are as follows:

Schizotypal: Detached, autistic, confused individuals who are perceived by others as being very strange. Their very dysfunctional coping style may include both active and passive features such as hypersensitivity and lack of emotional responding.

Borderline: Dependent individuals experiencing intense mood swings that are often triggered by perceived acceptance or rejection from another person. The dysfunctional coping style often includes suicidal behavior and/or self-mutilation in reaction to perceived rejection.

Paranoid: Independent individuals who engender anger and exasperation in others in reaction to their distrustful, deceptive, and defensive style, which projects blame onto other people. Vigorous resistance to input or direction from others marks their dysfunctional coping style.

Clinical Syndromes Scales. The Clinical Syndromes Scales describe relatively distinct patterns of symptoms that may develop as an extension of one's personality style. For example, compulsive types have a vulnerability to developing anxiety-related symptoms. The Clinical Syndromes Scales cover the following:

Anxiety: Symptoms of worry, apprehension, or fearfulness.

Somatoform: Symptoms related to health and bodily functions including aches, pains, health-related fears, fatigue, dizziness, and so on.

Bipolar-Manic: Periods of elation, inflated self-esteem, hyperactivity, distractibility, and unrealistic optimism.

Dysthymia: Extended periods of low to moderate levels of depression, periods that are not a core part of personality and that do not make one incapable of continued functioning.

Alcohol Dependence: Alcohol abuse that interferes with social adjustment and functioning.

Drug Dependence: Drug abuse that interferes with social adjustment and functioning.

Post-Traumatic Stress Disorder: Involuntary and intrusive memories or reexperiencing of a traumatic event, accompanied by hypersensitivity to and avoidance of reminders of the trauma.

Severe Clinical Syndromes Scales. The Severe Clinical Syndromes Scales describe symptom patterns that are extreme enough to cause severe disorientation and/or loss of the ability to function and cope. These include:

Thought Disorder: Psychotic thought patterns that include confused thinking, disorientation, hallucinations, delusions, or fragmented and peculiar ideas. Usually accompanied by bizarre behavior.

Major Depression: Depressive symptoms so severe that the person is not able to continue in a functional manner.

Delusional Disorder: Suspicions and delusions so extreme that the person loses contact with reality.

Each of the 24 clinical scales was developed to operationally measure personality types or syndromes described by Millon's theory (Millon et al., 1994). The scales were then compared to the diagnostic manual developed by the American Psychiatric Association, a list of the currently recognized mental disorders and their symptoms. Scale items were added or modified in an attempt to simultaneously satisfy the demands of both Millon's theory and the diagnostic manual. The resulting 325-item pool was administered to 600 psychiatric patients. Various combinations of scale items were statistically evaluated in order to select items that best described each diagnostic category while decreasing the number of items necessary to identify individuals with particular disorders. It is important to note that scale items were selected based on their ability to allow differentiation between different diagnostic groups, and not diagnostic versus normal groups, as with the MMPI scales. Another primary difference between the two tests is that the initial item selection for the MCMI-III was guided by theory and was subsequently checked using statistical methods. The MMPI scales were derived on a purely empirical basis.

In addition to the 24 clinical scales, Millon developed four scales that are similar to the MMPI validity scales. These include:

Validity: Items that describe extremely unlikely experiences.

Disclosure: Tendency to be open and revealing versus closed or secretive.

Desirability: Desire to present oneself as virtuous or socially attractive.

Debasement: Tendency to belittle or deprecate oneself.

The Disclosure, Desirability, and Debasement scales can be used to adjust clinical scale scores, as is done with the K scale of the MMPI.

Figure 11–7 is a sample profile summarizing the scores obtained from a hypothetical client. The Modifying Indices section of the profile contains information about the client's approach to the test. Scores for the Disclosure, Desirability, and Debasement scales are coded respectively as *X, Y,* and *Z.* The Clinical Personality Patterns section of the profile uses the codes of *1* to *8B* to report the scores for the Schizoid (1), Avoidant (2A), Depressive (2B), Dependent (3), Histrionic (4), Narcissistic (5), Antisocial (6A), Aggressive (6B), Compulsive (7), Passive-Aggressive (8A), and Self-Defeating (8B) clinical personality disorder scales. The Severe Personality section reports scores for the three severe personality disorders: Schizotypal (S), Borderline (C), and Paranoid (P). The Clinical Syndromes section reports scores for the scales of Anxiety Disorder (A), Somatoform Disorder (H), Bipolar-Manic Disorder (N), Dysthymic Disorder (D), Alcohol Dependence (B), Drug Dependence (T), and Post-Traumatic Stress Disorder (R). Finally, the Severe Syndromes section reports scores for the Thought Disorder (SS), Major Depression (CC), and Delusional Disorder (PP) scales.

An additional innovation in the MCMI-III is the manner in which the scores are reported. Millon decided that the use of normally distributed scores would be inappropriate, because scales intended to measure pathology should not produce a bell-shaped distribution. Instead, the test reports *base rate* (BR) scores, which are anchored to the prevalence of each disorder in the norming sample. The BR scores have a range of 0 to 115. A BR score of 75 to 85 indicates that characteristics of a particular disorder or syndrome are present, with a score of 85 or more indicating that the characteristics are very pronounced.

Internal consistency for the MCMI-III scales is adequate. Alpha coefficients range from .66 for Compulsive to .90 for Major Depression, with most coefficients falling in the .80 to .85 range. Test–retest coefficients for a 5- to 14-day interval range from .84 for Anxiety to .96 for Somatoform. Most coefficients are in the .89 to .93 range.

Millon investigated the concurrent validity of the MCMI-III by correlating scale scores with a wide variety of collateral instruments and with clinician ratings. The MCMI-III demonstrates moderate to strong convergent validity with a variety of instruments that purport to measure similar types of psychopathology. For example, the MMPI-2 Depression scale correlates with the MCMI-III Dysthymic (+.68), Major Depression (+.71), and Depressive (+.59) scales. Unfortunately, the MCMI-III scales do not always demonstrate good discriminant validity from other clinical measures. For example, the MMPI-2 Depression scale also correlates solidly with many other MCMI-III scales (Schizoid .46; Avoidant .46; Dependent .53; Histrionic .52; Narcissistic .52; Self-Defeating .49; Schizotypal .45; Borderline .47; Anxiety .52; Somatoform .65; Post-Traumatic Stress Disorder .50; and Thought Disorder .58). The situation is not surprising because the MCMI-III scales correlate highly with one another. The problem of scale overlap has been documented in independent clinical samples (Davis & Hays, 1997). The scale overlap decreases the test's diagnostic power because a person with one disorder may obtain high scores on scales intended to measure other disorders.

The manual does not report a factor analysis of the component scores, but inspection of the correlation matrix for the scales suggests that the scales are not as distinctive as the test developer intended. The high correlation between many of the scales (*r*'s in the .70+ range are very common) strongly suggests that the use of 24 different clinical scores may not be justified because of the overlap in scales. Despite the lack of scale purity, the test is fairly efficient in matching diagnoses assigned by clinicians. However, a part of the efficiency derives from using the same clinical ratings to both set and evaluate BR scores.

Figure 11–7
MCMI-III profile sheet.
Source: Used by permission of National Computer Systems, Minneapolis, MN.

357

The documented strength of the test appears to be in the evaluation of personality disorders. The test has been of keen interest in the criminal justice area, where the assessment of personality disorders is often crucial in determining competency to stand trial, criminal responsibility, sentencing, and prediction of future misconduct. While the MCMI-III appears to be useful in many phases of the judicial system, there is considerable debate over whether the test is sound enough to be used as evidence in criminal trial proceedings (Dyer & McCann, 2000; Rogers, Salekin, & Sewell, 1999; Schutte, 2000). Additional information, including reports and services available from the publisher are available at http://www.pearsonassessments.com/assessments/index.htm.

PROBLEMS WITH PERSONALITY AND INTEREST MEASURES

Paper-and-pencil interest and personality tests are subject to a number of problems and criticisms. One possible source of error is **response sets,** a tendency on the part of the examinee to approach the test in a manner that distorts the test results. For example, a person may have a tendency to *acquiesce,* or "yea-say." This response set is simply a propensity for accepting or agreeing to statements. In the context of the Strong Interest Inventory, a person with an acquiescent response set would mark too many of the items "like." The scores on a personality or adjustment test could be distorted by the examinee's willingness to conclude, "Yes, in some ways or at some times that might be true of me." Related response sets include favoring either midpoints or extremes when asked to respond on an item asking for degree of agreement/disagreement with a statement.

A second category of response sets involves approaching the test in a certain frame of mind or with the intent of creating a certain impression. For example, some examinees base their responses on **social desirability,** the tendency to choose responses that they believe are more socially approved of, or accepted. Interest statements are relatively neutral in value, so social desirability is not likely to become a serious problem with them. However, social desirability can become a problem in personality and adjustment measures where many items have high or low desirability or when examinees attempt to present themselves in a negative light. Care must be taken in interpreting test results when an examinee might gain from appearing troubled. Suppose you were claiming psychological damage in a lawsuit, taking a test as a part of a disability assessment that could result in support payments, or were claiming psychological impairment in relationship to a criminal charge. How might you approach the test differently than if you were taking the same test either in a research study or as a part of an employment screening?

Test results from self-report personality and adjustment measures can also be distorted by several other problems. The examinee may be unable or unwilling to read and understand an extensive list of items. Some people may not have the ability to stand back and view their own behavior and decide whether a particular statement applies. Others may be either too self-critical or too willing to admit to personal frailties. Validity indicators such as those on the MMPI-2 and the MCMI-III help to identify and adjust for these problems, but the validity scales are far from perfect. For example, it is often difficult to tell whether a person is truly confident or is trying to present him- or herself as such.

Of additional concern are ethical issues relating to testing situations that could involve the invasion of privacy, the requirement that individuals give information that may be against their own interests, or that certain "undesirable" personality or adjustment scores could limit one's opportunities. Consequently, personality and interest instruments should be used only when the results are to benefit the examinee and will be interpreted by a person with adequate clinical training and experience.

Interest and personality measures are notably different from cognitive ability measures. Scales on cognitive ability tests usually show substantial positive correlation with one another, allowing test results to be summarized with a single score. The result is that most of the ability to predict academic and job success is carried by the common general-ability factor. The simplicity of the factor structure makes the tests relatively easy to understand and interpret. Interest and personality measures are rather different. Several of the tests reviewed in this chapter include a number of different scores or scales that cannot be summarized in a single score. Thus, each score should provide new and distinct information about an individual's interests or personality. Factorially complex tests such as these make the assessment of validity and score interpretation very challenging, simply because of the multifaceted nature of the instrument. Tests such as the NEO PI-R, which come closer to achieving scale independence, present enough challenge. Others, such as the MMPI-2 and the MCMI-III contain scales that should be fairly independent but are actually highly correlated, a fact that further complicates the interpretation and validation of the test scores.

Perhaps the strongest as yet unanswered criticism of objective personality tests was outlined by Walter Mischel (1968). Mischel was familiar with a large body of research that had accumulated from studies in social psychology. The studies demonstrated that experimenters can create both laboratory and real-world situations that will largely determine behavior, irrespective of "personality differences." Social environments can be manipulated to almost completely determine whether people will act with honesty or dishonesty, altruism or apathy, conformity or independence, aggression or passivity, and so on. Mischel initially argued that the idea of personality is an illusion. People do not behave in a consistent manner over time and situations but instead are controlled by their social environments. He pointed out that personality tests are often consistent with themselves and with other tests, but that they do a very poor job of predicting actual behavior. His review of research concluded that personality tests almost always produce coefficients in the .20 to .30 range when correlated with external measures of behavior.

A number of researchers have criticized Mischel's conclusions on both logical and methodological grounds. They argued that a single behavior or situation is not an adequate measure of individual differences. Suppose you consider yourself to be a generous person. Are you generous all of the time in every situation? Would you consider one randomly selected incident on one randomly selected day to be a good indicator of your generosity? Critics argued that an adequate behavioral measure of a personality dimension should include ratings for a number of different behaviors associated with the characteristic, collected from several observers, in a variety of situations, across a reasonable time span. Epstein (1983) demonstrated that the correlations between personality measures and behavior do increase substantially when data from multiple observations are aggregated to provide a better behavior sample. Mischel (1993) has acknowledged limitations in his original conclusions due to the inadequacy of the behavioral samples. He now concedes that there is a stronger correspondence between tests and classes of behavior than he originally thought. However, he believes that individuals are not as consistent as we suppose. Mischel now believes that behavior is best understood as an interaction between individual characteristics and the social situation, with situational variables often having the greater influence.

COMPUTERIZED SCORING AND INTERPRETATION

Scoring and interpretation of interest and personality tests is often complicated and time consuming because of the complex nature of the various scales. For example, in some cases scoring requires differential weighting of the items, making hand scoring very laborious. Computer scoring for such instruments has been a boon to clinicians, as has the development of software that allows the instrument to be administered on a computer, making scoring almost instantaneous. Another important development has been the proliferation of organizations that produce computer-generated interpretive reports. A vast array of scoring services and computerized interpretive reports are available to the clinician, ranging from services that provide scores on specific scales to elaborate narrative reports that may even include predictive statements about performance or behavior (Herman & Samuels, 1985). Computer technology has certainly revolutionized the process of interest and personality testing; however, it is important to be aware that there are both advantages and disadvantages to the use of these automated systems.

Advantages

1. *Time savings and convenience.* Scoring and feedback can be provided in a much more timely manner, particularly when test administration is completed on the computer.
2. *Efficiency for clinician.* Use of computerized scoring systems frees the clinician to devote more time to the direct service of the client. Furthermore, the newer software systems for generating reports produce many alternative statements, allowing the clinician to pick and choose text that is most appropriate for the client and assessment question.
3. *Standardization.* The highly standardized nature of these reports helps to eliminate the variations and potential biases that follow from individual interpretations. The same scores will always generate the same narrative comments.
4. *Empirical predictions.* Computer-generated reports have the potential for being more directly tied to actuarial data because of the large database of case and client histories that can be built into the system.

Disadvantages

1. *Loss of individualization.* Reports generated by a computer may not be adequately individualized to capture the highly personal nature of the client's situation. Generic descriptions often produce statements that may apply to a number of people. They can also have a more mechanical tone and will miss subtlety and nuance in description.
2. *Documentation.* Scoring services do not necessarily provide documentation for the various narrative statements that are produced in the report, making it difficult to evaluate the quality of the report or the scoring service.
3. *Questions of validity.* While computer-generated reports may be based on a great many client cases, the number of clients who are similar to the particular client in question may actually be quite small. This can significantly affect the validity of predictions.

While the best scoring services are working to expand and strengthen the databases on which such predictions are made, this information is still not always available. Without adequate evidence of validity for any predictive statement, there is no reason to believe that a computer-generated prediction has any more validity than a prediction made by an experienced clinician.

SUMMARY

Tests designed to assess interests, personality, and adjustment are typically used for one of three purposes: research, self-understanding, or clinical assessment and diagnosis. While many of these tests are primarily of use to the clinician or academic psychologist, others do have much wider utility. Interest tests in particular have application to a variety of contexts. Because an individual's pattern of interests has considerable impact on career choice and work satisfaction, career counselors often make use of these instruments.

Furthermore, counselors may use interest tests and some personality inventories to help clients achieve greater self-understanding and to make better choices regarding work, relationships, and so forth. Educators are increasingly interested in the applications of self-concept scales to the study of various learning situations and the academic performance of children and adolescents. Tests of personality and adjustment provide useful information in the clinical diagnostic and treatment planning processes.

QUESTIONS AND EXERCISES

1. Consider the following interest inventories: (1) the Strong Interest Inventory, (2) the Career Assessment Inventory, and (3) the Self-Directed Search. Which one(s) would you recommend in each of the following situations? Give reasons for your choices.
   a. A college sophomore seeks counseling concerning his or her choice of major and occupation.
   b. A counseling program is being set up for students entering a vocational high school that has several different trade programs.
   c. An inventory is needed for a course for 10th graders exploring careers and the process of occupational choice.

2. How do you explain the lack of stability in the scores on interest inventories administered prior to adulthood?

3. Consider going to the career center on your campus and completing one or more interest inventories. Ask to have a counselor meet with you to discuss the instrument and its interpretation.

4. What is meant by the term *response set*? What are some potentially important response sets? How might they affect the results on an interest inventory, a personality inventory, and an adjustment inventory?

5. What conditions must be met if a self-report inventory is to be filled out accurately and give meaningful results?

6. What are the *Big Five* and how do they relate to personality measurement?

7. What important differences did you notice between the MMPI-2 and MCMI-III? What are the relative strengths and weaknesses of each test?

8. Why are personality, adjustment, and interest tests usually more difficult to understand and interpret than are tests of cognitive abilities?

9. What benefits are to be derived from computerized interpretations of personality inventories? What are the disadvantages of these automated systems?

SUGGESTED READINGS

Cramer, P. (1999). Future directions for the Thematic Apperception Test. *Journal of Personality Assessment, 72*, 74–92.

Exner, J. E. (1993). *The Rorschach: A comprehensive system, Vol. 1: Basic foundations* (3rd ed.). New York: Wiley.

Gottfredson, G. D., & Holland, J. L. (1996). *Dictionary of Holland occupational codes* (3rd ed). Odessa, FL: Psychological Assessment Resources.

Groth-Marnat, G. (1999). *Handbook of psychological assessment* (3rd ed.). New York: Wiley.

Harmon, L. W., Hansen, J. C., Borgen, F. H., & Hammer, A. L. (1994). *Strong Interest Inventory, applications and technical guide.* Stanford, CA: Stanford University Press.

Holland, J. L. (1997). *Making vocational choices.* Odessa, FL: Psychological Assessment Resources.

Lilienfeld, S. O., Wood, J. M., & Garb, H. N. (2000). The scientific status of projective techniques. *Psychological Science in the Public Interest, 1*(2), 1–66.

Millon, T. (1990). *Toward a new personology.* New York: Wiley.

Piedmont, R. L., McCrae, R. R., Riemann, R., & Angleitner, A. (2000). On the invalidity of validity scales: Evidence from self–reports and observer ratings in volunteer samples. *Journal of Personality and Social Psychology, 78*, 582–593.

U.S. Department of Labor. (1992). *Dictionary of occupational titles,* (4th Rev. Ed.) Washington, DC: U.S. Government Printing Office.

U.S. Department of Labor (2000–2001). *Occupational outlook handbook.* Washington, DC: U.S. Government Printing Office.

Wilson, P. L. (1998). Multidimensional Self-Concept Scale: An examination of grade, race and gender differences in third through sixth grade students' self-concepts. *Psychology in the Schools, 35,* 317–326.

CHAPTER 12

Attitudes and Rating Scales

Introduction
Learning About Personality from Others
    Letters of Recommendation
    Rating Scales
    Problems in Obtaining Sound Ratings
    Improving the Effectiveness of Ratings
    Improving the Accuracy of Ratings
    Rating Procedures for Special Situations

Measuring Attitudes
    Summative Attitude Scales
    Single-Item Scales
    Example of an Attitude Rating Scale
    Alternative Formats
Summary
Questions and Exercises
Suggested Readings

INTRODUCTION

As we discussed in Chapter 10, there are important educational decisions that require information that cannot be obtained with conventional cognitive tests. Some of these decisions involve objectives that refer to processes and products of instruction, and others require information about personality traits and attitudes. For example, the teacher of a music appreciation class may be concerned with the attitudes and feelings students have toward music, as well as their cognitive knowledge about the subject. Instructional objectives for social studies classes may emphasize both the development of good citizenship and positive attitudes toward peoples from different cultures, as well as knowledge of how government works. It is always more difficult to gain knowledge about personality traits and attitudes than about cognitive characteristics, because with cognitive tests we are measuring maximum performance, or how much the person can do. When assessing personality and attitudes, we are measuring typical performance, personal preferences, and dispositions. It is much easier to structure a test to elicit an accurate representation of maximum performance than one of typical performance.

We can learn about the characteristics of people in three main ways: (1) by observing for ourselves the behavior of the individual, using methods discussed in Chapter 10; (2) by obtaining information indirectly through another person, in the form of references and ratings; or (3) by gaining information directly from the individual; that is, with some form of self-report. Self-report measures of maximum performance (that is, cognitive tests) were covered in Chapters 8 and 9, and self-report assessments of personality characteristics and interests were discussed in Chapter 11.

This chapter introduces methods for soliciting information about a person through use of reports from other individuals. In addition, we cover ways to elicit self-report statements of attitudes or beliefs about persons or objects.

LEARNING ABOUT PERSONALITY FROM OTHERS

One important way in which an individual's personality is manifested is through the impression he or she makes on others. A second person can serve as a source of information about the personality of the first. We can ask teachers to provide information on the degree to which their students have learned to appreciate music or the degree of their opposition to drug use. Or, we could ask students to make this evaluation about each other. The first situation is an application of ratings by a superior or supervisor; the second illustrates ratings by peers.

These techniques for learning about the personality of others have proved useful in many situations. We might want answers to any of the following questions: How well does Person A like Person B? Does Person A consider Person B to be a pleasing individual to have around? An effective worker? A good job risk? Does Person A consider Person B to be conscientious? Trustworthy? Emotionally stable? Questions of this sort are regularly asked of teachers, supervisors, former employers, ministers, and even friends of individuals being rated.

Rating scales also can be used to learn about an individual's cognitive characteristics, abilities, and achievements. Usually such information is obtained directly with paper-and-pencil tests completed by the examinee, but rating scales can provide useful supplementary information about the impression a person's cognitive functioning makes. Under some circumstances, particularly for very young children or people who are unable to respond for themselves, rating scales may even replace paper-and-pencil tests. Of course, we need to be sure that these ratings provide accurate estimates if they are to be used to make important decisions.

Letters of Recommendation

One of the most commonly used ways to learn about other people in educational and occupational situations is through letters of recommendation provided by third parties. Information from letters of recommendation can be used for many different purposes, but letters are most commonly used to evaluate a candidate for something: for admission to a school, for awarding a scholarship or fellowship, or for a job, membership in a club, or a security clearance. How useful and how informative is the material that is included in free, unstructured communications describing a person? Actually, in spite of the vast number of such letters written every year (a review by Knouse, 1989, suggests that 90% of companies use such letters and virtually all graduate schools also use them), relatively little is known about the adequacy of letters of recommendation or their effectiveness. Opinions about their value vary widely, and factual studies are inconclusive as to the reliability and validity of information obtained from letters of recommendation or the extent to which such information influences actions taken with respect to the applicant.

A large portion of the research currently being done on letters of recommendation is specific to admission to graduate schools. In one early study of this kind, an analysis of 67 letters written for 33 psychology internship applicants (Siskind, 1966) found 958 statements distributed as follows:

Type of Statement	Number	Percentage
Positive statements	838	87
"Don't know" statements about a characteristic	17	2
Statements referring to natural shortcomings, the result of inexperience or youth	44	5
Other statements indicative of shortcomings	59	6

Reviewers do use such letters, and there is a moderate degree of consistency (reliability = .40) among letters written about a given person. One clue as to why this relationship occurs comes from a classic study of adjectives used in a series of letters written in support of applicants for engineering jobs (Peres & Garcia, 1962). Of 170 different adjectives extracted from the letters, almost all were positive in tone, but when the "best" employees were compared with the "worst" employees, the adjectives differed enormously in the degree to which they differentiated these groups. An applicant might be called "congenial," "helpful," and "open" or he or she might be called "ingenious," "informed," and "productive." The first three adjectives were applied about equally often to the best and to the poorest workers, while the last three adjectives were used only to describe the best workers. Apparently, the validity of the inferences drawn from a letter of recommendation depends to a considerable extent on the degree to which the reviewer has learned to "read between the lines" and to weigh the nice things that are said using an appropriate **discrimination factor** that identifies virtues mentioned as job relevant or tangential. Similar findings were obtained by Baxter, Brock, Hill, and Rozelle (1981) in a study of letters of recommendation for graduate school applicants, and Knouse (1989) reviews what is known about how to make letters particularly effective. Aamodt, Bryan, and Whitcomb (1993) found that if explicit scoring criteria were used, letters of recommendation were valid predictors of performance in graduate school.

In addition, writers of letters of recommendation are free to write whatever they choose, so there is no core of content common to letters about a single person or to the letters dealing with different people being considered for the same position. One letter may deal with a person's social charm; a second, integrity; and a third, originality. Furthermore, writers of recommendations differ profoundly in their propensity for using superlatives. Some employers and schools attempt to solve this problem by offering suggestions for specific traits that the letter writer should address.

An additional consideration is that the applicant usually is free to select the people who will write the letters. Certainly, we can expect all but the most naive applicants to select people who they believe will be supportive.

The extent to which a letter of recommendation provides a valid appraisal of an individual and the extent to which it is accurately diagnostic of outstanding points, strengths, or weaknesses are almost completely unknown. However, there is little reason for optimism in terms of their validity. The lack of a common frame of reference for such information makes interpretation particularly difficult and hazardous.

An article in the June 30, 2000, issue of the *Chronicle of Higher Education* provides anecdotal material about the way letters of recommendation function in the hiring practices of American colleges and universities (Schneider, 2000). The article cited the problems of ambiguity in language we have discussed, but an even more difficult barrier to ensuring honesty is lack of confidentiality. Writers of letters seldom can be sure who will read what they have written. The *Chronicle* article cites several cases where the person who was the object of a letter retaliated against the writer for what was written. However, with all their problems, it is likely that letters of recommendation will continue to be one of the main sources of information about candidates for positions in education and business.

Rating Scales

The extreme subjectivity of the unstructured statement, the lack of a common core of content or standard of reference from person to person, and the extraordinary difficulty in attempting to quantify unstructured materials gave impetus to the development of rating scales. Rating scales were developed to obtain appraisals on a common set of attributes for all raters and all individuals being rated and to have the attributes expressed on a common quantitative scale.

We have all had experience with ratings, either in the capacity of rating others or being rated ourselves. Rating scales appear on many report cards, particularly in sections reporting nonacademic performance. We often find a section phrased somewhat as follows:

Characteristic	First Period	Second Period	Third Period	Fourth Period
Effort	_____	_____	_____	_____
Conduct	_____	_____	_____	_____
Citizenship	_____	_____	_____	_____
Adjustment	_____	_____	_____	_____
H = superior S = satisfactory U = unsatisfactory				

Many civil service agencies and industrial firms send rating forms out to people listed as references by job applicants, asking for evaluations of the individual's "initiative," "originality," "enthusiasm," and "ability to get along with others." These same companies or agencies often require supervisors to give merit ratings of their employees, classifying them as "superior," "excellent," "very good," "good," "satisfactory," or "unsatisfactory" on a variety of traits or on overall performance. Colleges, medical schools, fellowship programs, and government agencies require ratings as a part of their selection procedures. Beyond these practical uses, ratings are used in many research projects; vast numbers of ratings are completed, often reluctantly, every day.

Most frequently ratings are retrospective, summarizing the impressions developed by the rater over an extended period of contact with the person being rated. Sometimes ratings are concurrent, arising out of an interview or a period of observation. Almost universally, a rating involves an evaluative summary of past or present experiences in which the "internal computer" of the rater processes the data in complex and unspecified ways to arrive at the final assessment.

The most common rating procedures involve presenting the rater with a set of traits and a range of numbers, adjectives, or descriptions that represent levels or degrees of the traits. The rater is asked to evaluate one or more people on the trait or traits by assigning a number, letter, adjective, or description to the trait. Figure 12–1 contains examples of two rating scales similar to ones that have been used by a company to evaluate middle-level managers. The first, which is one dimension from a set of eight addressed by the original instrument, assesses the trait of leadership; a general description of the trait is provided along with definitions of various levels of leadership. The second example requires an overall evaluation of how well an employee has carried out the responsibilities of a particular position. These are illustrations of the wide range of rating instrument formats. We shall turn shortly to some of the major variations in rating patterns, but now let us consider some of the problems that arise when one tries to get a group of judges to make such appraisals.

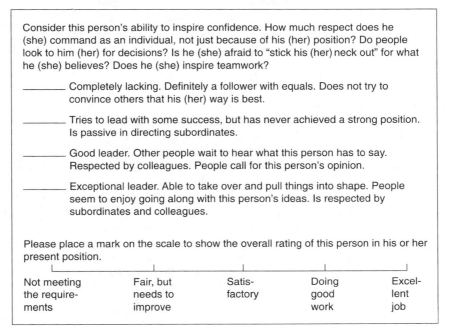

Consider this person's ability to inspire confidence. How much respect does he (she) command as an individual, not just because of his (her) position? Do people look to him (her) for decisions? Is he (she) afraid to "stick his (her) neck out" for what he (she) believes? Does he (she) inspire teamwork?

_____ Completely lacking. Definitely a follower with equals. Does not try to convince others that his (her) way is best.

_____ Tries to lead with some success, but has never achieved a strong position. Is passive in directing subordinates.

_____ Good leader. Other people wait to hear what this person has to say. Respected by colleagues. People call for this person's opinion.

_____ Exceptional leader. Able to take over and pull things into shape. People seem to enjoy going along with this person's ideas. Is respected by subordinates and colleagues.

Please place a mark on the scale to show the overall rating of this person in his or her present position.

| Not meeting the require-ments | Fair, but needs to improve | Satis-factory | Doing good work | Excel-lent job |

Figure 12–1
Two forms of rating scales.

Problems in Obtaining Sound Ratings

Two general classes of problems make it difficult to obtain accurate and valid ratings. First, there are factors that limit the rater's *willingness* to rate honestly and conscientiously, in accordance with the instructions for rating. Second, there are factors that limit a person's *ability* to rate consistently and correctly, even with the best of intentions. We consider each of these problem areas in turn.

Factors Affecting the Rater's Willingness to Rate Conscientiously

When ratings are collected, we commonly assume that each rater is trying to follow the instructions that have been given and that any shortcomings in the ratings are due entirely to chance and human fallibility. However, this is not necessarily true. There are at least two sets of circumstances that may impair the validity of a set of ratings: (1) The rater may be unwilling to take the time and trouble that is called for by the appraisal procedure and (2) the rater may have an emotional reaction to the person being rated to such an extent as to be unwilling to give a rating that will hurt (or benefit) the other person.

Unwillingness to Put Forth Sufficient Effort. Ratings are a nuisance under the best of circumstances. The careful and thoughtful rating of an individual requires considerable effort. In an attempt to provide a uniform frame of reference, the authors of some rating procedures have developed extensive lists of traits and elaborate descriptions of the behaviors that exemplify each trait. This practice can result in excellent ratings, but if the rating form is long and the number of individuals to be rated is large, the task may be so overwhelming that it seems not worth the effort. When ratings are carried out in a perfunctory manner, the rating process is less effective. Unless raters are really "sold" on the importance of the ratings, the judgments are likely to be hurried and superficial, with more emphasis on finishing the task than on making accurate analytical judgments.

Emotional Reaction to the Person Being Rated.   Ratings are often requested by distant administrators and impersonal agencies. The Civil Service Commission, the Military Personnel Division of a commanding general's headquarters, the personnel director of a large company, or the central administrative staff of a school system are all quite far removed from the first-line supervisor, the squadron commander, or the classroom teacher—the people who must do the ratings. The rater usually feels greater connection to the people being rated—the workers in the office, the enlisted personnel or junior officers in the outfit, or the pupils in the class—than to the agency requesting the ratings. One of the first principles of supervision or leadership is that "the good officer looks out for his/her people." The state of morale in an organization depends on the conviction that the leader of the organization takes care of its members. When ratings come along, "taking care of" becomes a matter of seeing to it that one's own people fare as well as—or even a little better than—those in competing groups.

As a result, in too many situations, the rater is more interested in ensuring that those with whom he or she works closely get high ratings than in providing accurate information. This situation is made even worse by the common policies of making the ratings public and requiring the rater to discuss with the person being rated any unfavorable material in the ratings. Administrative rulings that specify the minimum rating necessary for promotion or a pay increase aggravate the situation further. It should come as no surprise that ratings tend to climb or to pile up at a single scale point. There is a tendency for the typical rating, accounting for a very large proportion of all ratings given, to be "excellent." "Very good" almost becomes an expression of dissatisfaction, while a rating of "satisfactory" is reserved for the person the rater would like to get rid of at the earliest opportunity.

In some cases, the reverse effect can also occur. If a supervisor has recently had an unpleasant interaction with a subordinate, one way to retaliate is to give a rating that is lower than justified. When subordinates are rating their supervisor, as is the case when students rate the performance of their instructor, the opportunity for this form of payback is even greater, because the ratings generally are anonymous and may provide the only way for disgruntled subordinates to vent their hostile feelings.

It is important to be aware that a rater cannot always be depended on to work wholeheartedly at giving valid ratings for the benefit of the requesting agency, that making ratings is usually a nuisance to the rater, and that there is likely to be more of a commitment to the rater's own subordinates than to an outside agency. A rating program must be continuously "sold" and policed if it is to remain effective. However, there are limits to the extent to which even an active campaign can overcome a rater's natural inertia and interest in the group with which he or she identifies.

Factors Affecting the Rater's Ability to Rate Accurately

Even when raters are well motivated and try to do their best to provide valid judgments, a number of factors still operate to limit the validity of their judgments. These factors center on the lack of opportunity to observe the person to be rated, the covertness of the trait to be rated, ambiguity in the meaning of the dimension to be rated, lack of a uniform standard of reference, and specific rater biases and idiosyncrasies.

Lack of Opportunity to Observe.   Raters often have limited opportunities to observe the person being rated. For example, a high school teacher with five classes of 30 students each may be required to judge the "initiative" or "flexibility" of all 150 students. A college professor who has taught a particular class of 100 students may receive rating forms from an employment agency or from the college administration asking for similar judgments on some of the students. Under such circumstances, the amount of contact with individual students usually has been insufficient to provide an adequate basis for the judgments being requested. The person being rated may physically have been in the presence of the rater for many hours, possibly several hundred, but these were very busy hours in which the rater, as well as the person being rated, was concerned with more pressing matters than observing and forming judgments about the traits for which ratings have been requested.

In a civil service or industrial setting, the same problems arise. The primary concern is getting the job done. Even though, in theory, a supervisor may have a good deal of time to observe each worker, in practice, he or she is busy with other things. We may be able to "sell" supervisors on the idea of devoting more of their energy to observing and evaluating the people working for them, but there are very real limits on the amount of effort—thus time—that most supervisors can withdraw from their other functions and apply to this one.

The problem may not only be a lack of opportunity to observe but also a lack of opportunity to observe the particular characteristic in the person to be rated. Any person sees another only in certain limited contexts, and these contexts reveal only some aspects of behavior. The teacher sees a child primarily in the classroom, the foreman sees a worker primarily on the production line, and so forth. In a *conventional* classroom it is doubtful whether the teacher has seen a child under circumstances that might be expected to elicit much "initiative" or "originality." The college professor who teaches mainly through lectures is not well situated to rate a student's "presence" or "ability to work with individuals." The supervisor of a clerk doing routine work is not in a position to appraise "judgment." Whenever ratings are proposed, either for research purposes or as a basis for administrative actions, we should ask whether the rater has had an adequate opportunity to observe the people to be rated in enough situations for the ratings to be meaningful. If the answer is *no,* we would be well advised to abandon rating the trait in question.

Each rater sees a person in a different role and is therefore likely to focus on quite different aspects of the person. Students see a teacher from a different vantage point than does the principal. Classmates in officer candidate school have a different view of other potential officers than does their tactical officer. For those deciding who should be the rater, it is appropriate to ask who has had the best opportunity to see the relevant behavior displayed. Normally, that person should be the one from whom we request the ratings.

Covertness of the Trait.   If a trait is to be appraised by someone other than the person being rated, its existence must produce observable behavior. Such characteristics as appearing to be at ease at social gatherings, having a pleasant speaking voice, and participating actively in group projects are characteristics that are essentially social. They appear in interactions with other people and are directly observable. By contrast, attributes such as "feelings of insecurity," "self-sufficiency," "tension," or "loneliness" are inner personal qualities. They are private aspects of personality and can be inferred only crudely from what the person does. We refer to these as **covert characteristics.**

An attribute that is largely covert can be judged by an outsider only with great difficulty. Inner conflict, or tension, may not show on the surface, and when it does, it may reveal itself indirectly. Furthermore, it is unlikely to manifest itself in the same way for each person. For example, deep insecurity may express itself as aggression against other students in one child or as withdrawal into an inner world in another. Insecurity is not a simple dimension of overt behavior. It is instead an underlying trait that may be manifested in different ways by different people or in different ways by the same person at different times or in different circumstances. Only with a thorough knowledge of the person, combined with psychological insight, is it possible to infer from overt behavior the nature of a person's underlying covert dynamics.

For these reasons, rating procedures for covert aspects of personality are generally unsatisfactory except in special circumstances where highly trained observers are rating people they know very well. Qualities that depend both on a thorough understanding of a person and on the generation of inferences from behavior are measured with low reliability and poor validity in most common rating contexts. Ratings are more accurate for those qualities that show outwardly, that is, the overt ones, as a person interacts with other people. Experience has shown that these overt qualities can be rated more reliably and one feels confident that they are rated with more validity than are covert ones. The validity lies in part in the fact that these social aspects of behavior have their meaning and definition primarily in the effects one person has on others.

Ambiguity in the Meaning of the Dimension. Many rating forms require ratings of broad and abstract traits. For example, the rating scale presented earlier included "citizenship" and "adjustment." These are neither more nor less vague and general than the traits included in many rating forms. Agreement among raters regarding the meanings of these terms is unlikely. What do we mean by "citizenship" in an elementary school student? How is "good citizenship" shown? Does "good citizenship" mean not marking on the walls? Or not spitting on the floor? Or not pulling little girls' hair? Or does it mean bringing newspaper clippings to class? Or joining the Junior Red Cross? Or staying after school to help the teacher clean up the room? What does it mean? No two raters are likely to have exactly the same things in mind when they rate a group of students on "citizenship."

Or consider "initiative," "personality," "supervisory aptitude," "mental flexibility," "executive influence," or "adaptability." These are all examples drawn from rating scales in actual use. Although there is certainly some core of uniformity in the meaning that each of these terms will have for different raters, there is a great deal of variability in meaning from one rater to another. The more abstract a term, the more variable its meaning from person to person, and such qualities as those just listed are conspicuously abstract. The rating that a given child receives for citizenship will depend on what citizenship means to the rater. If to one teacher citizenship is indicated by a child conforming to school regulations, he or she will certainly rate high those children who conform. If to a different teacher citizenship is indicated by a child taking an active role in school projects, that teacher may give high ratings to quite different children. The first step in getting consistent ratings is to establish a minimal level of agreement among raters about the meanings of the qualities being rated. One way to accomplish this task is to provide the desired definition on the rating form. If a good citizen is defined as a "child who follows the school rules," then a common understanding of the term will be fostered if the definition is made explicit in the directions for the rating scale.

Lack of Uniform Standard of Reference. Many rating scales call for judgments of the people being rated in sets of categories such as the following:

Outstanding, above average, average, below average, unsatisfactory
Superior, good, fair, poor
Excellent, good, average, fair, poor
Outstanding, superior, better than satisfactory, satisfactory, unsatisfactory
Superior, excellent, very good, good, satisfactory, unsatisfactory

How good is "good"? Is a person who is "good" in "judgment" in the top 10% in judgment for the group with whom he or she is being compared? The top 25%? The top 50%? Or is this person just not one of the bottom 10%? And, what is the composition of the group with which this person is being compared? Are all members the same age? Are they all employees of the same company? Are they all persons in a particular job? Are all employees in the same job with the same length of service? If the latter, how is the rater supposed to know the level of judgment that is typical for people in a particular job with a given amount of experience?

The problem that all these questions bring up is the need for a standard against which to appraise the person being rated. Variations in interpretation of terms and labels, in definition of the reference population, and in experience with the members of that background population all contribute to rater-to-rater variability in the standards of rating. The phenomenon is familiar to those involved in academic grading. There are enormous variations among faculty members in the percentages of As, Bs, and Cs awarded in comparable courses. The same situation holds for any set of categories, numbers, letters, or adjectives that may be used. Standards are highly subjective interpretations, and they can therefore be expected to vary widely from one rater to another. (You can easily illustrate this problem for yourself. Take a set of words like *frequently, usually,* and *seldom,* and ask several of your friends what each word implies in terms of a percentage. In one group of 160 college freshmen I found the meaning inferred from the word *frequently* ranged from 50% up to 95%. Some people thought *usually* might mean as little as 50% of the time, while others thought *seldom* might imply as often as 65% of the time.)

Raters differ not only in the level of ratings that they assign but also in how much they spread out their ratings. Some raters are conservative and rarely rate anyone very high or very low; others tend to go to both extremes. Differences in variability in ratings reduce their comparability from one rater to another. These differences among raters appear not to be a chance matter but to be a reflection of the personal characteristics and value structures of individual raters.

One attempt to overcome the problem of a uniform frame of reference is to attach specific percentages to the verbal descriptions. For example, many college and graduate school reference forms will ask for ratings of "general academic ability," "knowledge of the discipline," and so forth on a scale such as

Outstanding,   Superior,   Above Average,   Average,   Below Average

and define "outstanding" as "being in the top 5% of the reference group." The other categories are given similar specific definitions, such as "top 10%," "top 25%," "top 50%," and "bottom half." The scale is given additional definition by asking the rater to specify the reference group, for example, "college seniors" or "first-year graduate students." Unfortunately, one sometimes finds that 25% of college seniors are in the top 5% of college seniors!

Specific Rater Biases and Idiosyncrasies.   Raters not only differ in general toughness or softness but may be characterized by other idiosyncrasies as well. Life experiences have provided each of us with likes and dislikes and an assortment of individualized interpretations of the characteristics of other people. You may distrust people who do not look at you when they are talking to you. Your teenage son may consider anyone who listens to classical music to be "not with it." Your boss may consider a firm handshake to be a guarantee of strong character. Your tennis partner may be convinced that people with small eyes are not trustworthy. The characteristics people believe indicate the presence of these traits are concrete, and the descriptions of these characteristics can be clearly verbalized by the person making judgments, regardless of the validity of the stereotype.

But there are myriad other more vague and less tangible biases that we each have and that can influence our ratings. These biases help to form our impressions of other people and influence all aspects of our reactions to them, and they can enter into our ratings too. In some cases, our rating of one or two traits may be affected. But often the bias is one of a general liking for or an aversion to the person, and this generalized reaction influences all of our ratings. Ratings, therefore, reflect not only the general subjective rating standard of the rater but also any biases about the characteristics of the person being rated.

A different type of idiosyncrasy that is likely to influence overall judgments of effectiveness on a job (or in an educational program) is individual differences in the types of behavior considered desirable. Supervisors of employees in closely similar jobs have been found to differ widely in the attributes they considered important. For example, some raters may consider "solving problems on one's own initiative" among the most important traits a subordinate could have, and others may consider it among the least important. To the extent that such differences in values prevail, it is inevitable that supervisors will fail to agree on who are their more effective subordinates.

The Outcome of Factors Limiting Rating Effectiveness

The effects of factors limiting rating effectiveness are manifested in systematic distortions of the ratings, in relatively low reliabilities, and in questionable validity of rating procedures. We summarize these problems under four headings: the generosity error, the halo effect, low reliability, and questionable validity.

The Generosity Error. We have already noted that raters often identify more with the people they are rating than with the agency for which ratings are being prepared. Over and above this, there also seems to be a widespread unwillingness, at least in the United States, to damn a fellow human with a low rating. The net result is that ratings tend generally to pile up at the high end of any scale. The unspoken philosophy of the rater seems to be that every person is as good as the next, if not better, so that the term *average* in practice is not the midpoint of a set of ratings but instead a point at the lower end of the group. It is a little like the commercial classification of olives, where the tiniest ones are called "medium," and the classification continues from there through "large" and "extra large" to "jumbo" and "colossal." I have occasionally quipped to my students that a good set of anchor points, guaranteed to move the center of the ratings toward the middle of the scale, for rating teacher effectiveness might be "poor," "average," "above average," "superior," and "godlike."

If the **generosity error** operated uniformly for all raters, it would not be particularly disturbing; we would merely have to remember that ratings cannot be interpreted in terms of their verbal labels and that "average" means "low" and "very good" means "average." Makers of rating scales have even countered this humane tendency with some success by having several extra steps on their scale on the positive side of average, so that there is room for differentiation without the rater having to be negative by labeling a person or trait as "average." The differences between raters in their degrees of "generosity error" are more troublesome than the fact that there is a generosity error. Corrections for such differences are difficult to implement.

The Halo Effect. Limitations in experience with the person being rated, lack of opportunity to observe the specific qualities that are called for in the rating instrument, and the influence of personal biases that affect general liking for the person all conspire to produce another type of error in ratings. This is the tendency of raters to evaluate in terms of an overall impression, without differentiating specific aspects of personality, to allow the total reaction to the person to color judgment of each specific trait. E. L. Thorndike in 1920 gave this type of rating error the name **halo effect.**

Of course, a positive relationship between desirable traits is to be expected. We find positive correlations between different abilities when these abilities are assessed by objective tests, and we do not speak of a halo effect that produces a spurious correlation between verbal and quantitative ability. Just how much of the relationship between the different qualities on which we get ratings is genuine and how much is a spurious consequence of halo is hard to determine, but when correlations between traits exceed the interrater agreement in ratings of the traits, there is cause for concern. Landy, Shankster, and Kohler (1994) note that a consensus seems to be emerging that, although the halo effect is a real phenomenon, its apparent presence is not a good index of the quality of a rating scale.

Low Reliability. The agreement between raters using conventional rating procedures has generally been found to be low. When two ratings are uncontaminated, which means the raters have not discussed the people being rated, and when the usual type of numerical or graphic rating scale is used, the resulting appraisals can be expected to have a low correlation, often in the 50s. However, evidence suggests that when great care is taken in structuring rating scales through a careful delineation of the end points, or anchors, on the scale, and when the raters are well trained and have had ample opportunity to observe those being rated, the reliability of ratings can be improved (Landy et al., 1994).

If it is possible to pool the ratings of a number of independent raters who know the people being rated about equally well, the reliability of the appraisal can be substantially increased. Pooling ratings has the same effect as lengthening a test, and the Spearman-Brown prophecy formula (discussed in Chapter 4) can legitimately be applied in estimating the reliability of pooled independent ratings. Thus, if the reliability of a single rater is represented by a correlation of .55, we have the following estimates for the reliability of pooled ratings:

.71 for 2 raters
.79 for 3 raters
.86 for 5 raters
.92 for 10 raters

Unfortunately, in many situations, obtaining additional equally qualified raters is impractical, if not impossible. An elementary school student has only one regular classroom teacher; a worker has only one immediate supervisor. Adding other raters who have more limited acquaintance with the person being rated may weaken rather than strengthen the ratings.

Questionable Validity. All the limiting and distorting factors that we have considered—in particular, rater biases and low reliability—tend to suppress the validity of rating instruments. However, it is seldom possible to empirically determine the validity of ratings. The very fact that we are using ratings suggests that no better measure of the characteristic in question is to be had. Usually there is nothing else available with which we can verify the accuracy of ratings.

In one sense, the validity of ratings is axiomatic. If we are interested in appraising how a person is perceived by other people, that is, whether a child is well liked by his classmates, or a foreman by her work crew, ratings *are* the reactions of these other people and are directly relevant to the trait or behavior in question.

When ratings are being studied as predictors, it is sometimes possible to obtain statistical data that can be used to quantify the accuracy of the prediction. This is something that must be determined in each setting and for each criterion that is being predicted. In some cases, ratings may be the most valid available predictors. One classic example comes from studies of the ratings of aptitude for military service that were given at the U.S. Military Academy at West Point (Adjutant General's Office, Personal Research Section, 1953). These ratings by tactical officers and fellow cadets were shown to correlate better with later ratings of combat effectiveness than any other aspect of the candidate's record at West Point. This criterion is again a rating, but it is probably as close to the real "payoff" as we are likely to get in this kind of situation. In other situations, of course, ratings may turn out to have no validity at all. Each case must be studied for its own sake.

Ratings usually are used as a criterion measure. When this is the case, everything possible should be done to ensure the accuracy and reliability of the ratings, because they represent the standard against which other procedures will be judged. It behooves us, therefore, to examine ways in which ratings can be improved.

Improving the Effectiveness of Ratings

Thus far we have painted a rather gloomy picture of rating techniques as measurement devices. It is certainly true that there are many hazards and pitfalls in rating procedures. But, in spite of all the limitations of ratings, they are and will continue to be the means of appraisal for a host of situations in which we have to rely on the judgments of people. The sincerity and integrity of a potential medical student, the social skills of a would-be salesperson, the maturity of a sixth grader, or the conscientiousness of a personal assistant can probably be evaluated only through the judgment that someone makes of these qualities in the people in question. On the positive side, Landy et al. (1994) note that when the best methods of scale construction are combined with adequate training procedures for the raters, the weight of evidence indicates that ratings can give accurate and valid appraisals of individual characteristics. What can be done, then, to mitigate the defects of rating procedures and achieve the conditions Landy et al. describe? We first consider the design of the rating instrument and then the planning and conduct of the ratings.

Refinements in the Rating Instrument

The usual rating instrument has two main components: (1) a set of **stimulus variables** (the qualities to be rated) and (2) a pattern of **response options** (the ratings that can be given). In the simplest and most conventional forms, the stimulus variables consist of trait names, and the response options consist of numerical or adjectival categories. Such a form was illustrated in the section on rating scales. This type of format appears to encourage most of the shortcomings discussed in the preceding section; consequently, many format variations and refinements have been tried in an attempt to overcome or at least to minimize these shortcomings. In the variations, the stimulus variables, the response options, or both have been manipulated. Some of the main variations are described next.

Refinements in Presenting the Stimulus Variables.
Simple trait names represent unsatisfactory stimuli, for two reasons. In the first place, the words mean different things to different people. The child who shows "initiative" to Ms. Johnson may show "insubordination" to Mr. Cordero, whereas Mr. Cordero's "good citizen" may seem to Ms. Johnson to be a "docile conformist." In the second place, trait names often are quite abstract and far removed from the realm of observable behavior. Consider "adjustment," for example. We cannot directly observe a child's adjustment. Instead, we can observe only the reactions of the child to situations and people. Some of these

reactions may be symptomatic of poor adjustment. But the judgment about the child's adjustment is an inference based on what we have a chance to observe.

Users of ratings have striven to obtain greater uniformity in the meaning of traits to be rated by basing the ratings more closely on observable behavior. These attempts have modified the stimulus aspect of rating instruments in three ways:

1. *Trait names can be explicitly defined.* "Social adjustment" is a rather nebulous label. It can be given somewhat more substance by elaborating on what the label is intended to mean, as in the following example.

> *Social adjustment.* Interest in and skills of interacting with both children and adults in work and play situations. Willingness both to give and to take in interpersonal situations. Conformity to basic social norms of behavior.

The elaboration attaches more substance to an intangible concept and should provide greater uniformity of meaning among different raters and between the raters and the designer of the rating form.

There is no question that an expanded definition of each attribute to be appraised is a desirable first step in improving rating procedures. However, it is doubtful that a brief verbal definition will do very much to overcome the raters' individual differences in the meanings that they attach to terms and, consequently, to the rating task.

2. *Trait names can be replaced by several more limited and concrete descriptive phrases.* For example, the abstract and inclusive term "social adjustment" might be broken down into several components, each relating to a more limited aspect of behavior. Thus, in place of the one term, we might have:

> Works in groups with other children.
> Plays with other children.
> Interacts with teacher and other adults.
> Obeys school rules.

A judgment would now be called for with respect to each of these more restricted and more tangible aspects of student behavior.

3. *Each trait can be replaced with a number of descriptions of specific behaviors.* This practice carries the move toward concreteness and specificity one step further. Thus, the general descriptor "works in groups with other children" might be elaborated with something like:

Works in groups with other children:

> Takes an active part in group enterprises.
> Makes and defends suggestions.
> Accepts majority decisions.
> Does his or her share of the work.
> Helps others with their work.

A similar subdivision would be carried out for each of the three other components listed in the previous step. The descriptions used to define "works in groups with other children" make the behavior still more tangible and specific. There should be much less ambiguity as to what it is that is to be observed and reported, but there is still an element of interpretation in deciding, for example, what level of involvement constitutes "takes an active part."

Replacing one general term with many specific behaviors gives promise of more uniformity in meaning from one rater to another. It may also bring the ratings in closer touch with actual observations the rater has had an opportunity to make of the behavior of the person being rated. If it is the case that the trait to be rated involves behaviors that the rater has had no opportunity to observe, replacing trait names with specific observable behaviors may make this fact painfully apparent and force the designer of the instrument to reexamine the problem of relating the instrument to observations the raters really have had an opportunity to make.

The gains that a list of specific behaviors achieves in uniformity of meaning and concreteness of behavior judged are not without cost. The cost lies in the greatly increased length and complexity of the rating instrument. There are limits to the number of different judgments that a rater can be asked to make. Furthermore, a lengthy, analytical report of behavior may be confusing to the person who tries to use and interpret it. The lengthy list of specific behaviors will probably prove most effective when (1) judgments are in very simple terms, such as "present" or "absent," and (2) provisions are in place for organizing and summarizing the specific judgments into one or more scores for broad areas.

Refinements in Response Categories.   Expressing judgments about a person being rated by selecting some one of a set of numbers, letters, or adjectives is still common on school report cards and in civil service and industrial merit rating systems; however, these procedures have little to commend them except simplicity. As we discussed earlier, often the categories are arbitrary and undefined. No two raters interpret them in exactly the same way. A rating of "superior" may be given to 5% of employees by one supervisor and to 25% by another. One teacher's A is another teacher's B. Subjective standards reign supreme.

Attempts to achieve a more meaningful scale or greater uniformity from rater to rater have included use of the following:

1. Percentages
2. Graphic scales
3. Behavioral statements
4. Present or absent scales
5. Frequency of occurrence or degree of resemblance judgments.

1. *Percentages.* In an attempt to produce greater uniformity from rater to rater and better discrimination among the ratings given by a particular rater, procedures sometimes call for raters to make judgments in terms of percentages of a particular defined group. Thus, a professor rating an applicant for a fellowship might be instructed to rate each candidate according to the following scale:

In the top 2% of students at this level of training
In top 10%, but not in top 2%
In top 25%, but not in top 10%
In top 50%, but not in top 25%
In lower 50% of students at this level of training

Presumably, the specified percentages of a defined group provide a uniform standard of quality for different raters and the asymmetric set of categories maximizes discrimination where it is most desired, among the top candidates. However, the stratagem is usually only partially successful. Individual differences in generosity are not that easily suppressed, and we may still find 25% of the people being rated placed in the top 10% category.

2. *Graphic scales.* Our second variation is more a matter of form than clarity of definition. Rating scales are often prepared so that judgments can be recorded by making a check mark at some

appropriate point on a line instead of choosing a number, letter, or adjective that approximates the level of the trait. These instruments are called **graphic scales** and have the following general form.

Responsibility for completing work

Very low   Average   Very high

The use of graphic scales results in an attractive page layout, can be compact and economical of space, and may seem somewhat less forbidding than a form that is all print. However, although the simplicity of graphic presentation may help newer raters to visualize the construct as being on a continuum, for sophisticated users, a graphic presentation seems to make little difference.

3. *Behavioral statements.* We have seen that the stimuli may be in the form of relatively specific **behavioral statements.** Statements of this sort may also be combined with the graphic layout to present the rating alternatives. Thus, we might have an item of the following type:

Participation in School Projects

| Volunteers to bring in materials. Suggests ideas. Often works overtime. | Works or brings materials as requested. Participates, but takes no initiative. | Does as little as possible. Resists efforts to get him/her to help. |

Here, three sets of statements describing behavior are listed on a graphic scale; they are used to define three points on the scale. The descriptions can be expected to make the task more concrete and the scale steps more uniform. However, the use of behavioral statements does not ensure that all raters will see things the same way, because raters must still make subjective decisions on how to interpret these behavioral statements.

A whimsical development of a rating form that provides a fairly clear illustration of behavioral statements is shown in Figure 12–2.

4. *Present or Absent Scales.* When a large number of specific behavioral statements are used as the stimuli, the response that is required could just be a series of checks to indicate which statements apply to the individual being rated. The rating scale then becomes a behavior checklist. An example of such a rating form, adapted from the Checklist of Adaptive Living Skills (Morreau & Bruininks, 1991), is shown in Figure 12–3.

If this type of appraisal procedure is to yield a score on a trait, rather than a long list of behaviors, the statements must be scaled or assigned score values in some way. The simplest way is to score each statement $+1$, -1, or 0, depending on whether it is favorable, unfavorable, or neutral, with respect to a particular attribute (e.g., perseverance, integrity, or reliability) or a particular criterion (such as, success in academic work, success on a job, or responsiveness to therapy). A person's score can then be the sum of the scores for the items checked. We shall consider checklists in more detail when we discuss adaptive behavior scales.

Area of Performance	Degree of Performance				
	Far exceeds job requirements	Exceeds job requirements	Meets job requirements	Needs improvement	Does not meet minimum requirements
Quality of Work	Leaps tall buildings in a single bound	Leaps tall buildings with a running start	Can leap short buildings with prodding	Climbs stairs effectively	Trips entering buildings
Promptness	Is faster than a speeding bullet	Is as fast as a speeding bullet	Would you believe a slow bullet?	Misfires frequently	Wounds self when handling guns
Adaptability	Walks on water	Swims well	Washes with water	Drinks water	Chronically waterlogged
Communication	Talks with God	Talks with the angels	Talks to others	Talks to self	Argues with self

Figure 12–2
Employee performance appraisal.

```
_____    1.5.23   Takes off boots with or without fasteners
_____    1.5.24   Buttons or snaps a shirt, blouse or coat
_____    1.5.25   Turns clothing right side out for dressing

_____    1.5.33   Ties own shoelaces
_____    1.5.34   Chooses clothes to wear that are clean, unwrinkled, and untorn
_____    1.5.44   Fastens and unfastens a safety pin on clothing
_____    1.5.50   Chooses clothes for a trip with attention to changes in climate
                     and activities
```
Numbers at left correspond to behavioral objectives in the Adaptive Living Skills
Curriculum.

Figure 12–3
Items from the *Checklist of Adaptive Living Skills*.
Source: Copyright © 1993 Riverside Publishing Company. Adapted from the *Checklist of Adaptive Living Skills* (Morreau & Bruinicks, 1991), by permission of the publisher, The Riverside Publishing Company.

5. *Frequency of Occurrence or Degree of Resemblance Judgments.* Instead of having to react in an all-or-none fashion to an item, as with checklists, the rater can be given choices such as "always," "usually," "sometimes," "seldom," or "never." (In formulating items to be responded to with these categories, you must take care that no term expressing frequency is included in the statement of the item. Otherwise, you might commit the syntactic atrocity of judging that Johnny "always" "usually accepts majority decisions.") Another approach is to have the person being rated characterized as "very much like," "a good deal like," "somewhat like," "slightly like," or "not at all like" the behavior described in the statement. The terms indicating frequency or resemblance may vary; the ones given here are only suggestive. Also, an individual's score could take account of both the significance and the frequency of the behavior in question. That is, an important attribute could receive more credit than a minor one, and a check that the behavior "always" occurred could be given more credit than "usually."

As we noted earlier, indefinite designations of frequency or degree of the sort suggested here will not be interpreted the same way by all raters, so the old problem of differences in rater biases and idiosyncrasies reappears. When asked to indicate what percentage of the time was implied by each of several terms, a class of introductory psychology students gave a wide range of answers. For some students *always* meant more than 80% of the time, while for others it meant *every* time. Words like *usually* and *frequently* were taken to mean somewhere between 50% and 95% of the time. Similar variation has been found for other frequency terms. Moreover, when the number of specific behaviors being checked is substantial, a simple checking of presence or absence correlates quite highly with the more elaborate form.

Improving the Accuracy of Ratings

The best designed instrument cannot give good results if it is used under unsatisfactory rating conditions. Raters cannot give information they do not have, and they cannot be made to give information they are unwilling to give. We must, therefore, try to select raters who have had close contact with the people being rated and ask them for judgments on attributes they have had an opportunity to observe. We also should give raters guidance and training in the type of judgment expected from them and, if possible, they should observe the people to be rated *after* they have been educated in the use of the rating form. When there are several people who know the individuals to be rated equally well, ratings should be gathered from each person and then pooled. Every effort should be made to motivate the raters to do an honest and conscientious job. Let us consider each of these issues in more detail.

Selecting Raters

For most purposes, the ideal rater is the person who has had the most extensive opportunity to observe the person being rated in those situations likely to elicit the qualities being rated. (Occasionally, it may be desirable to get a rating of the impression that a person makes on brief contact or in a limited experimental situation, but this is not the usual case.) It is also desirable that the rater maintain an impartial attitude toward the person being rated. The desirability of these two qualities, thorough acquaintance and impartiality, is generally recognized in the abstract. However, the goals may be only partially realized in practice, because knowing someone well and being impartial may be mutually exclusive.

Administrative considerations usually dictate that the rating and evaluation function be assigned to the teacher in a school setting and to the supervisor in a work setting. Since the relationship in each case is one of direct supervision, a continuing and fairly close personal relationship generally exists. But the relationship is a one-directional and partial one. The teacher or supervisor sees only one aspect of the student or worker, the side that is turned toward the boss.

Those qualities that the boss has a good chance to see, primarily qualities of work performance, can probably be rated adequately by a teacher or supervisor. We would expect ratings of job performance or subject-matter knowledge to correlate fairly highly across supervisors or teachers. However, those qualities that show themselves primarily in relationships with peers or subordinates probably would be evaluated more soundly by those peers or subordinates, and in such cases, they should be the ones to do the rating.

Deciding Who Should Choose the Raters

The selection of persons to rate applicants for a job or admission to a college requires consideration of another issue. The applicant usually is asked to supply a specific number of references or to submit evaluation forms filled out by a predetermined number of individuals. The choice of the raters is usually left up to the applicant, and we may anticipate that he or she will select people who will furnish favorable ratings. It might be more satisfactory if the applicant were asked to supply the names and addresses of people with whom there is a particular relationship and who could therefore be requested to supply relevant information, rather than leaving the applicant free to select the referees. A job applicant might be asked to give the names of immediate supervisors in recently held jobs; a fellowship applicant might be asked to list the names of major advisors and of any instructors from whom two or more courses have been taken. This action would shift the responsibility of determining who provides the ratings from the applicant to the agency using them. Such a shift should reduce the amount of positive bias for the applicant.

Providing Education for Raters

Good ratings do not just happen, even with motivated raters and good instruments for recording the ratings. Raters must be "sold" on the importance of making good ratings and taught how to use the rating instrument. However, this is often easier said than done. As indicated earlier, unwillingness to put forth the necessary effort, on the one hand, and identification with the person being rated, on the other, are powerful competing motives. These problems can only be overcome by education and indoctrination to convince the raters that their tasks are important, and the "selling job" must continue if raters are to maintain thoughtfulness and integrity in their appraisals over a period of time.

Raters should have practice with the specific rating instrument that they will use. A training session, in which the instrument is used under supervision, is often desirable. This enables raters to discuss meanings of the attributes, prepare sample rating sheets, and review the resulting ratings. Also, the prevailing generosity error can be noted, and raters can be cautioned to avoid it. Additional practice for raters may generate a more symmetrical distribution of ratings. Training sessions will not eliminate all the shortcomings of ratings, but they should reduce the more common distortions.

Selecting Qualities to Be Rated

Two principles appear to apply in determining the types of information to be sought through rating procedures. First, it is undesirable to use rating procedures to get information that can be provided by a more objective and reliable indicator. A score on a well-constructed aptitude test is a better indicator of cognitive ability than is a supervisor's rating of intellect. When accurate production records exist, they should be preferred over a supervisor's rating for productivity. We resort to ratings when we do not have better indicators available.

Second, we should limit ratings to relatively overt qualities—ones that can be expressed in terms of actual observable behavior. We cannot expect the rater to peer inside the person being rated and tell us what is going on. Furthermore, we must bear in mind the extent and nature of the contact between the rater and the person being rated. For example, a set of ratings to be used after a single interview should be limited to the qualities that can be observed in an interview. The interviewee's neatness, composure, manner of speech, and fluency in answering questions are qualities that should be observable in a single interview. Industry, integrity, initiative, and ingenuity are not directly observable in such a limited encounter, although these qualities might be appraised with some accuracy by a person who has worked with the interviewee for a time. Ratings should be of behavior observable in the setting in which the rater has known the person being rated.

Pooling Independent Ratings from Several Raters

One of the limitations of ratings is low reliability. If several people have had a reasonably good chance to observe the person being rated, reliability can be improved by pooling their independent ratings. Unfortunately, the number of persons well placed to observe a person in a particular setting—school, job, camp, and so forth—is usually limited. Often, only one person has been in close contact in a particular relationship with the person being rated. A student has had only one homeroom teacher; a worker, only one foreman; and a camper, only one tent counselor. Others have had some contact with the person, but the contact may have been so much more limited that pooling their judgments adds little to the information of the rater most intimately involved.

Note that we specified the pooling of *independent* ratings. If the ratings are independently made, the error components will be independent and will tend to cancel. If, however, the judgments are combined through some sort of conference procedure, we do not know what will happen. Errors may cancel, wisdom may win, or the prejudices of the most dogmatic and forceful rater may prevail. Pooling independent ratings is the only sure way to cancel individual errors.

Constructing Rating Scales Based on Input from Raters

A method that has become popular for developing instruments to evaluate performance is based on involving raters in developing the rating scales that they will eventually use. Development of such instruments proceeds in three stages:

1. A group of future raters agrees on the dimensions that can be distinguished as the important aspects of performance on a given job. For example, the following broad categories might be suggested as important qualities for first-line supervisors to have in a large company:

> Knowledge and judgment
> Conscientiousness
> Skill in human relations
> Organizational ability
> Objectivity
> Skill at observing situations.

2. The potential users then generate a pool of **critical incidents,** or examples of actually observed behavior, to illustrate superior, average, and inferior performance in each of the selected dimensions. (The term *critical incidents* comes from the idea that these behaviors should be critical to success or failure in the position.) Raters in a second independent group are then called on to assign each incident to the appropriate dimension. Only when the second group of raters agrees on the assignment of critical incidents to a dimension are these incidents retained in the final instrument.

3. Each person in the second group of raters indicates where on a scale of excellence each statement falls. The average level and the consistency of these judgments is scrutinized, and a subset of items is retained that shows good agreement among raters and for which the complete set shows a wide range of average scale values. The following items were taken from a scale entitled Interpersonal Relations with Students that has been used to evaluate college faculty (Harari & Zedeck, 1973). The scores on the scale range from 1 (low) to 7 (high).

Scale Value	Statement
6.8	When a class doesn't understand a certain concept or feels "lost," this professor could be expected to sense it and act to correct the situation.
3.9	During lectures, this professor could often be expected to tell students with questions to see him during his office hours.
1.3	This professor could be expected to embarrass or humiliate students who disagree with him.

To apply this methodology, the rater, having been provided with the set of statements for each dimension, indicates which statement comes closest to describing the person being rated. Users have reported that this procedure yielded less method variance, less halo error, and less leniency error than more conventional rating procedures (Campbell, Dunnette, Arvey, & Hellervik, 1973).

Focusing Raters on Behaviors Prior to Ratings

One objection to ratings is that they are usually made after the fact and are based on general, unanalyzed impressions about the person being rated. We can attempt to get away from a dependence on use of memory in ratings by introducing the rating program well in advance of the time at which the final ratings are to be made. Then, a record form can be developed in which critical areas of performance are identified, as described in the previous section, and a space provided for recording instances of desirable—as well as undesirable—actions of the person being rated.

The procedures for this type of scale development are quite time consuming, and the resulting instrument tends to be a little cumbersome. More experience is needed with developing rating scales using input from raters before we can judge whether gains from prior use of the scales are maintained in later use and whether the gains made are sufficient to justify the additional effort required in developing the scales. But an advantage of scales constructed in this way is that they result in specific behavioral descriptions, which often are more reliably rated and more valid than other methods (Landy et al., 1994).

Rating Procedures for Special Situations

Several rating procedures have been developed for special situations. In this section we discuss three of them: (1) adaptive behavior scales, (2) ranking procedures, and (3) the forced-choice format.

Adaptive Behavior Scales

Work with very young children and with individuals with severely limited abilities has led to the development of assessment procedures that combine some of the characteristics of rating procedures with those of ability tests. These instruments are designed to be completed by informants (parents, teachers, caregivers, and so forth) about the person being assessed. Examples of such instruments are the AAMR Adaptive Behavior Scales—Residential and Community, Second Edition (ABS-RC:2) of the American Association of Mental Retardation (AAMR) (Nihira, Leland, & Lambert, 1993), the AAMR Adaptive Behavior Scale—School Edition (ABS-S:2) (Lambert, Leland, & Nihira, 1993), the Checklist of Adaptive Living Skills (Morreau & Bruininks, 1991), and the Vineland Adaptive Behavior Scale (Sparrow, Balla, & Cicchetti, 1984a).

These instruments all have similar formats: a set of items that are based on either developmental tasks typical of children at different ages or skills needed for independent living. The informant is then asked to indicate whether the person can accomplish the task. The items can be scored either "yes/no" or rated along a range indicating how typical the behavior is. The responses are summed, and the total scores are compared to normative standards to indicate the child's developmental level or the person's level of impairment. The following items might be found on such a scale:

Uses toilet.
Uses knife and fork.
Throws ball.
Stacks three blocks.
Uses irregular verbs.
Makes friends.

Clearly, the number of potential items is enormous. The items can also be subdivided into categories such as motor, self-grooming, social, language, and school-related skills, with separate scores given for each area of functioning.

Adaptive behavior scales are most appropriately used when there is a need to obtain information about a person's level of functioning, either to supplement what can be learned from cognitive ability tests or to substitute for them. These instruments are most frequently used to assess children with learning problems, and they are particularly appropriate for trainable and young and educable children with mental retardation.

Concern about the disproportionate numbers of minority children enrolled in special education classes has increased interest in using adaptive behavior scales. There is concern that standardized intelligence tests may be unfairly labeling some minority children as mentally retarded. The unfairness stems from the ability of many of these students to function normally in nonschool settings. Adaptive behavior scales can be used to understand better the functioning of students in a wide range of settings and to help diagnostic teams make better decisions about placement.

Although the administration of one of these instruments can be a useful part of the overall diagnosis of a child with learning or developmental problems, the instruments share important limitations. A major deficiency of these instruments is their dependence on the ability or willingness of the informants to provide accurate information. Parents in particular are prone to see their children in the best possible light and to be hesitant to admit shortcomings in their offspring.

A related problem concerns the intrusive nature of some of the items and the appropriateness of asking informants to give the information to individuals who are, in many cases, strangers. The use of these adaptive behavior scales as substitutes for standardized measures of cognitive ability has not proved successful, because the scores from these instruments tend not to be strongly related to performance in school. They may, however, give valuable supplementary information about ability to function in nonacademic settings.

Ranking Procedures

When each rater knows a substantial number of the people being rated, raters may be asked to rank the ratees with respect to each attribute being assessed. Thus, a teacher might be asked to indicate the child who is most outstanding for contributing to class projects and activities "above and beyond the call of duty," the one who is second, and so on. Usually, the rater is instructed to start at the extremes and work toward the middle because the extreme cases are usually easier to discriminate than the large group of average ones in the middle. This feature is sometimes formalized as **alternation ranking,** that is, picking the highest and then the lowest, the next highest and then the next lowest, and so on. Tied ranks (where people being rated seem equal) may be permitted, to ease the task of the rater. If tied ranks are not permitted, the person doing the ranking may feel that the task is an unreasonable one, especially for a large group.

Ranking is an arduous task, but it does achieve two important objectives. First, it forces the person doing the evaluation to discriminate among those being evaluated. The rater is not permitted to place all or most of the people being rated in a single category, as may happen with other rating systems. Second, ranking washes out individual differences in generosity or leniency among raters. No matter how generous the rater is, someone must be last and no matter how demanding he or she is, someone must come first. Individual differences in standards of judgment are eliminated from the final score.

If scores based on rankings by different judges are to be combined, there is one assumption introduced in ranking that may be as troublesome as the individual judging-standard differences that have been removed. If we are to treat rankings by different judges as comparable scores, we must assume that the quality of the group ranked by each judge is the same. That is, we must assume that being second in a group of 20 represents the same level on the trait being appraised in all groups of 20. Usually, there is no direct way to compare the subgroups, so we have to assume that they are comparable. If the subgroups are fairly large (e.g., 30 people) and are chosen more or less at random from the same sort of population, this assumption may be reasonable. But, with small groups or groups selected in different ways, failure to meet the assumption of comparability may introduce substantial errors into scores based on ranking. Of course, when two raters rank the same people, this issue does not arise.

Ranks in their raw form do not provide a very useful type of score, because their meaning depends on the size of the group; being third in a group of three is quite different from being third in a group of 30. Furthermore, steps of rank do not represent equal units of a trait. As we saw in our discussion of percentile norms (Chapter 3), with a normal distribution, one or two places in rank at the extremes of a group represent much more of a difference than the same number of places in rank near the middle of the group. For this reason, it is common practice to convert ranks into normalized standard scores to obtain a type of score that has uniform meaning regardless of the size of the group, and has uniform units throughout the score range.

The Forced-Choice Format

All the variations considered so far operate on the same basic pattern. The rater considers one attribute at a time and assigns the person being rated to one of a set of categories or places him or her in a position relative to others on the particular attribute. Now, we will consider a major departure from that pattern. The essence of this procedure is that the rater must choose from a *set* of attributes and decide which one (or ones) most accurately represents the person being rated. For example, an instrument for evaluating instructors might include sets of items such as the following:

   a. Is patient with slow learners.
   b. Lectures with confidence.
   c. Keeps interest and attention of class.
   d. Acquaints classes with objectives for each lesson.

The rater's assignment would be to select the one or two items from the set that are *most descriptive* of the person being rated. Note that all of the statements in this set are positive; they are nice things to say about an instructor. They were selected to be about equally positive in their description of an instructor. They do differ, however, in the extent to which they distinguish between people who have been identified, on other evidence, as good or poor instructors. In this case, the most discriminating statement is Statement *a,* and the least discriminating one is Statement *b.* That is, good instructors were identified as being patient with slow learners and poor instructors were not. Both good and poor instructors were equally likely to be identified as lecturing with confidence. Good instructors were somewhat more likely to be judged as keeping the interest and attention of the class and acquainting the class with lesson objectives. Thus, a score value of 2 could be assigned to Statement *a,* 1 to Statements *c* and *d,* and zero to Statement *b.* An instructor's score for the set would be the sum of the scores for the two items marked as most descriptive of him or her. The score for the whole instrument would be the sum of the scores for 25 or 30 such blocks of four statements. Scores of this type have been found to have good split-half reliability (often .85 to .90), so this type of instrument can provide a reliable score, at least in the eyes of individual raters. Of course, this score does not tell us anything about the agreement or lack of agreement that might be found between different raters.

By casting the evaluation instrument into a forced-choice format, the scale maker hopes to accomplish three things:

1. *To eliminate variation in rater standards of generosity or kindness.* Because the items in a set include equally favorable statements about a person, those who prefer to be positive in their

evaluations of others will not be inclined to choose any particular statement over the others. Thus, a more accurate picture of the person being rated should emerge because the true nature of the ratee should determine which statements are selected.

2. *To minimize the possibility of a rater intentionally biasing the score.* With most rating scales, the raters control the process. They can rate a person high or low as they please. In a forced-choice instrument, the rater should be unable to easily identify positive and negative statements and should therefore be unable to raise or lower a score at will. The success of this approach will depend on the skill of the scale constructor in equating the attractiveness of the grouped items. Although there are some indications that a forced-choice format is less susceptible to intentional biasing than other rating scales are, it is still far from tamper proof in the hands of a determined rater.

3. *To produce a better spread of scores and a more nearly normal distribution of ratings.* Making all options equally attractive minimizes the effect of the generosity error, which results in a better spread of scores.

A variation on the forced-choice format is the **Q-sort.** This rating format provides the rater with a large number of statements that may be descriptive of the people to be rated. The rater places each item in one of several (often about seven) categories ranging from highly descriptive to not at all descriptive of the ratee. The unique feature of this approach, however, is that the rater is required to produce a particular distribution of placements. Consider this simple example: If there were 50 statements and five categories, the task would require that five statements be placed in the two most extreme categories, 10 statements be placed in the next two categories, and the remaining 20 statements would, by default, be assigned to the middle category. As with most of the forced-choice formats, the Q-sort has more often been used for personality description than for performance rating.

Disadvantages of the Forced-Choice Format. The most important disadvantage of the forced-choice format is that raters dislike using this approach, largely because it takes control away from them. They cannot easily rate an individual high or low depending on their overall feelings, which leads to frustration often manifested in an unwillingness to work diligently at the task of rating.

The forced-choice format also requires that the scale constructor exercise considerable skill in designing option choices that appear to be equally desirable but which differ in the extent to which they characterize more successful individuals. The method demands that the items go through extensive tryout prior to actual use, in order to determine which items differentiate between successful and unsuccessful people.

Forced-choice formats generated a good deal of interest, some research, and a certain amount of practical use during the period from 1945 to 1965, but the burden of preparing them and the negative reactions to them by raters have resulted in a gradual decline in interest in them in recent years. They continue to be used, however, in some personality and attitude scales and in some measures of vocational interests and preferences.

MEASURING ATTITUDES

In the previous sections, we discussed methods of learning about people—their abilities, as well as their personality traits and other attributes—by obtaining information from others who know them well in terms of the type of information sought. It is also possible to obtain this kind of information directly from the individuals being appraised.

The assessment of abilities and personality traits has been discussed in Chapters 8 through 11. In attitude measurement, we are interested in obtaining a reliable score that can represent the intensity of an individual's sentiments toward or against something. Like other self-report measures, attitude assessments are limited by what the individuals know and are willing to communicate about themselves.

Most people have similar perceptions about the social desirability of the items measuring personality traits, so there is a tendency for everyone to respond to items on such instruments in a similar fashion—generally, in a way that makes them look good; this tendency is a limitation inherent in such instruments. Because the social desirability of many attitudes differs from one person to another (that is, there is less agreement about what the "right" response is), these measures are less affected by this response bias. When we seek the overall attitude level of a group and do not need to know about the attitudes of individuals, it is possible to keep responses anonymous. This practice increases the probability that responses will represent a more genuine reflection of attitudes.

A major problem with attitude assessment instruments is the apparent ease with which they can be constructed. Just because items can be collected quickly and an instrument put together easily does not mean that the instrument will measure the constructs it is intended to measure in a reliable and valid manner. Unless attitude scales are created in a systematic fashion, using what is known about good scale construction, the results probably will be meaningless.

The construction of an attitude rating scale usually begins with a catalog of statements covering possible views on the target concept, drawn from readings, associates, and the recesses of the author's consciousness. The goal of this process is to select a broad range of statements that is representative of all the possible items that could be used to measure the attitude under investigation. These items should range from the most positive and favorable statements to the most negative and unfavorable and should cover all aspects of the attitude. Each statement should be clear and brief, present a single idea, and be focused on a feeling rather than on a fact, that is, an attitude rather than an item of information. The following list of suggestions for selecting statements to include in an attitude rating scale, adapted from Edwards' (1957) classic work, has been found to improve attitude scale construction:

1. Do not use statements that refer to the past rather than to the present.
2. Avoid statements that are factual or could be interpreted as factual.
3. Make sure no statement can be interpreted in more than one way.
4. Do not use filler statements that are irrelevant to the psychological construct being investigated.
5. Avoid statements that would be endorsed by almost anyone or by almost no one.
6. Be sure to include statements that cover the entire range of the construct of interest.
7. Keep the wording of the statements simple, clear, and direct.
8. Keep the statements short (rarely exceed 20 words).
9. Be sure each statement contains only one complete thought.
10. Avoid universals such as *all, always, none,* and *never* because they often introduce ambiguity (are they meant to be absolute?).
11. Words such as *only, just, merely,* and others of a similar evaluative nature should be used with care and moderation.
12. Statements should be written in simple sentences rather than compound or complex sentences unless this cannot be avoided.

13. Avoid using words that may not be understood by those who are to be given the completed scale. Make the reading level appropriate to the intended audience.
14. Do not use double negatives. (p. 14)

Summative Attitude Scales

Attitude scales usually require the subjects to respond to the statements by using a numerical indication of the strength of their feeling toward the object or position described in the statement. The responses are summed to estimate the strength of the attitude. The most frequently used technique for obtaining such a numerical indication is to have respondents indicate their level of feeling toward a number of statements, often in terms of the degree to which they agree or disagree with the statements. This technique is called a **summative rating,** because the person's attitude is then reflected by the sum of the responses to the individual statements. It is also called a **Likert scale** after Rensis Likert (pronounced "lick-urt"), who first introduced the technique in the 1930s. The following key is an example of the options that might be provided to an individual responding to the scale.

5—Strongly agree
4—Mildly agree
3—Don't know
2—Mildly disagree
1—Strongly disagree

If you wanted to measure the attitudes of teachers in a school toward grouping students by ability level, you might include statements such as the following:

1. Grouping students in classes by ability inhibits social development.
2. Students achieve more when they attend class with other students of similar ability.
3. Gifted students should be taught in classes made up of other gifted students.
4. Special education students should be assigned to regular classes.

Statements 1 and 4 express an attitude generally opposed to ability grouping, while Statements 2 and 3 are supportive of the practice. The teachers would respond by placing a number adjacent to each statement, indicating their degree of agreement with the statement. The scale should include statements that would be endorsed by people at both the positive and negative ends of the attitude continuum, to correct for the tendency of respondents to agree with most statements presented to them, a tendency called *acquiescence*. Those people who strongly agree with Statements 1 and 4 should disagree with Statements 2 and 3. If they do not, then we must question whether they are taking the task seriously. It is often extremely difficult to reverse statements without substantially changing the meaning, but it is essential to have both ends of the spectrum of sentiments represented.

In the process of summing across items to obtain an attitude score for each person, the scoring of negatively stated items is reversed, so that people who express disagreement with the negative statements receive a positive score. Strongly disagreeing with a negative statement is treated in the scoring like strongly agreeing with a positive one. This is accomplished by subtracting the subject's value assigned to an item from one point more than the highest value that can be assigned. For example, on the five-point scale described above, if the instrument is being scored so that high scores reflect a positive attitude toward ability grouping, a response of strongly agree (5) to Item 4 would be given a score of $6 - 5 = 1$. Thus, a person who strongly agreed with Statements 2 and 3 and strongly disagreed with Statements 1 and 4 would receive the maximum score of 20, while someone with exactly the reverse pattern would receive the minimum score of 4.

Number of Steps

The number of steps in the scale is important. The more steps, the greater the reliability of the scale, because the range available for expressing one's position increases (we saw the effect of restriction of range on reliability in Chapter 4). The increase is noticeable up to about seven steps. Items with more than seven steps are seldom used, because the increase in reliability resulting from the additional steps is slight, and it is often difficult to write meaningful anchors. It is easier to increase reliability by adding more items.

Types of Anchors

The five-point scale described earlier certainly is the most popular one to use for measuring attitudes. But even though the agree–disagree anchors are particularly flexible, other anchors should be used when they fit the meaning of the statements. For instance, anchors on a continuum such as "effective—ineffective," "important—unimportant," or "like me— not like me" have been used successfully when appropriate to the context.

An Odd or an Even Number of Steps

When constructing a scale you must also decide whether to use an odd or an even number of steps. Most respondents seem to prefer an odd number, so that they have an appropriate response option when they feel neutral toward a statement. With an even number of steps, they might feel as if they are being forced to take sides in an issue where they truly feel neutral. On the other hand, repeated selection of the neutral position can be an easy way out for the person unwilling to devote an appropriate amount of time to the task of responding to all items.

One drawback to using an even number of steps and denying the individual responding the opportunity to make a neutral response is a possible increase in the number of statements not responded to because some respondents may refuse to give any response if they cannot pick the midpoint. In general, there would seem to be more to be gained in goodwill with respondents by including a neutral point than would be lost by forcing them to choose sides. Where responses are made by checking or circling a number on a line, respondents may force a neutral point by marking the scale between the middle two categories.

Single-Item Scales

When interest is focused on the attitudes of a group of people rather than on single individuals, it is common practice to use a single questionnaire to assess attitudes toward each of several objects or points of view. Often, each issue under consideration is represented by a single statement. Although the response of a single individual lacks sufficient reliability to provide a useful assessment of the person's attitude, the trend in a group can be accurately determined in this way, because the response error tends to average out over the group and produce a reliable indication of the sentiments of the group. This is the basis for opinion polling.

Although single-item scales are common, they have some inherent problems. First, the single item prevents the assessment of internal consistency, so reliability is expressed as a margin of error in the proportion. This is the reason for the familiar statement in reports of opinion polls that the approval rating is "$X \pm 3\%$," or "the margin of error in the poll is $X\%$." The second problem is that if the one item is misunderstood by a respondent, the results of the assessment become invalid for that person. Third, there is also the danger that the single item may be written in a way that systematically biases the results. Consider the following two statements:

1. Parents should be forced to bus their children long distances for the purpose of achieving school desegregation.
2. The courts should use any reasonable means for achieving school desegregation.

It is likely that in the mind of the author both statements reflect a positive attitude toward the use of busing as a means of achieving school desegregation. But used as single items, the statements could be expected to yield quite different results. Even people who strongly support desegregation might respond negatively to the first statement. Instability of meaning due to subtle differences in the wording of single-item scales is often a problem in opinion polls and is the reason that proponents of two opposing positions can both claim that they enjoy the support of most of the public. This type of bias could occur to some degree with any attitude scale, but with use of a large number of items, the likelihood exists that the positive and negative items will cancel each other.

Example of an Attitude Rating Scale

The first task in developing an attitude scale on a topic such as equality for women in the workplace would be to gather a large number of items representing the full range of topics and views on the subject. For women's workplace opportunities, the topics would probably cover equal employment opportunities, child care, sexual freedom, personal independence, degree of role differentiation, and so forth. Each statement should be clear and brief, present a single idea, and focus on a feeling rather than on a fact, that is, on an attitude rather than information.

Item Selection

The total pool of items initially generated is usually much too large to use as a measuring instrument. Also, the ideal is to use only items that we can be confident measure the trait, so it is necessary to select the best subset of items. This subset is selected by having the items reviewed and rated by judges. The judges' function is not to indicate agreement or disagreement with any item but rather to assess where the statement falls on a "for to against" scale in relation to the target concept. Judges should also be asked to indicate any statements that seem irrelevant to the attitude dimension and to offer suggestions for aspects of the trait for which statements have not been provided. The scale points might range from nine, indicating a very strongly favorable statement, through five, or neutral, to one, indicating a very strongly negative or hostile statement.

The purpose of the judges' ratings is to find (1) where on the "for to against" dimension each statement falls and (2) how well a group of judges agree on the statement's meaning. The goal is eventually to select a set of statements that represent all degrees of favorableness and unfavorableness and have statements that convey nearly the same meaning to everyone.

The position of any item on the scale of "favorableness–unfavorableness" is indicated by the **median rating** that it receives from the judges, and its ambiguity by the spread of ratings as indicated by the **interquartile range.** Consider the following two statements where judges used a nine-point scale:

	Median	Interquartile Range
A wife's job and career are just as important as her husband's.	8.1	1.5
Feminine fashions are a device to hold women in an inferior role.	7.0	5.1

The first statement seems to be promising for inclusion in the final attitude scale. It is a strongly "pro" statement, and judges are in good agreement about where it falls on the attitude dimension. The second statement is a poor choice for the scale. Although on the average it is rated as implying a moderately favorable position toward equality for women in the workplace, there is great disagreement among judges on what the statement signifies. It was assigned by different judges to each scale position from one to nine. Furthermore, about 10% of the judges marked this statement as irrelevant to the dimension under study. Statements that elicit this level of disagreement should be eliminated from the scale.

Given the judges' ratings, we can select a reasonably brief set of statements that have clear meanings, that represent all degrees of intensity of views, and that cover the main facets of the domain being studied. The statements can usually best be presented to subjects in a format such as the one shown in Figure 12–4, on which the respondent indicates the degree of acceptance of each statement. Responses can be scored 4, 3, 2, 1, 0, with SA (strongly agree) getting a score of 4 and SD (strongly disagree), a 0. The item responses would all be entered into the computer in this way, and the nine negative items (3, 5, 8, 9, 14, 16, 17, 18, 19) would be reversed by the computer in obtaining total scores for the scale. The possible score for the 20 items would thus range from 80 (most strongly in favor of social equality for women) to 0 (most hostile). A score of 40 would be considered neutral.

Item Analysis

Once a set of statements is collected and assembled into an instrument, using the preceding suggestions, it should be administered to a pilot group. Ideally, responses should be made on a machine-scorable answer sheet, which facilitates entering the responses into a computer where they are accessible to the statistical analysis program being used. The responses should be summed, making sure that any negative items are reversed. (In SPSS the simplest way to accomplish this reversal is to use the "compute" statement on the Transformation menu to subtract the recorded response from one more than the number of options. In EXCEL you must create a new variable by placing the equation in the appropriate cell. For example, to reverse the scoring of the five-option variable in column Q and place the result in column P, type the statement "=6-Q? in each row of column P. In this case, the ? stands for the number of the row.) The responses to each item are then correlated with the total score, and the coefficient obtained indicates how much each item contributes to the overall reliability of the test. The higher the correlation, the better the item. The size of the correlation necessary for a good item depends on the subject matter and test length. A negative correlation may indicate an error in scoring or that the item needs to be revised. By deleting, replacing, or revising bad items, the reliability of the test can be greatly improved.

Read each statement. Then circle the symbol that best represents your reaction to the statement, according to the following scale:

SA — strongly agree with the statement.
A — tend to agree with the statement.
? — undecided. Neither agree nor disagree.
D — tend to disagree with the statement.
SD — strongly disagree with the statement.

SA A ? D SD   1. Men and women should receive the same pay for the same work.

SA A ? D SD   2. No woman should have to bear a child unless she chooses to.

SA A ? D SD   3. Most women are unsuited by temperament for supervisory or administrative jobs.

SA A ? D SD   4. There should be no clubs or public places that are restricted to a single sex.

SA A ? D SD   5. A woman's place is in the home.

SA A ? D SD   6. Standards for promotion should be the same for men and women.

7. A woman's job and career are just as important as her husband's.

SA A ? D SD   8. Men and women are basically different in their makeup and are suited to fill different roles.

SA A ? D SD   9. A woman who follows a career can seldom expect to have a satisfactory home life.

SA A ? D SD   10. There are no inborn psychological differences between men and women.

SA A ? D SD   11. Men should share equally in housework—getting meals, cleaning, etc.

SA A ? D SD   12. Every woman should have an independent career if she wants one.

SA A ? D SD   13. In matters of sex, there should be a single standard for men and for women.

SA A ? D SD   14. The workers for women's liberation are frustrated female failures.

SA A ? D SD   15. Except for physical strength, anything a man can do, women can do equally well.

SA A ? D SD   16. Women's liberation is of interest only to a few women on the lunatic fringe.

SA A ? D SD   17. It doesn't make sense to make a large investment in a woman's education, because she is likely to marry and not use her advanced training.

SA A ? D SD   18. By nature, women are submissive and men are dominant.

SA A ? D SD   19. The natural role for a woman is a secondary, supporting one.

SA A ? D SD   20. In all respects, men and women should receive the same treatment.

Figure 12–4
Sample of an attitude scale.

Reliability

It is important to determine the internal consistency reliability of attitude rating scales using coefficient alpha. As is true with other measures of reliability, the size of coefficient alpha is affected by the variability within the sample on the dimension being measured. Therefore, it is important for the scale to be administered to a sample that shows a reasonable amount of variability in the trait being measured. For instance, if you are assessing attitudes toward the value of higher education among a group of highly educated people, you are likely to find little variability and, consequently, low internal consistency reliability. Internal consistency is an indication that we can make discriminations in the sample and is also evidence that we are measuring a one-dimensional trait. If several traits are measured on a single scale and only one score is reported, the traits will tend to cancel each other and the scale will have low variability and low reliability. A factor analysis of the correlations among the items can indicate whether there is more than one dimension in the questionnaire.

Alternative Formats

Attitude measures sometimes use formats other than the summative one we have considered so far. One simple alternative is to present a set of statements such as those shown in Figure 12–4, being careful to include some neutral statements (neutral statements are not essential and often are not desirable in a summative scale), and to instruct the respondents to mark either (1) all statements that they agree with or (2) the statements—possibly a specified number—that *best* represent their views. With this format it is important to have accurately determined a scale value for each item because the score for an individual is the average of the scale values of the statements that person endorsed. This approach to attitude measurement was originally proposed by L. L. Thurstone in the 1920s and is known as **Thurstone scaling.**

A slightly different approach is to select a short set of statements (usually five or six) that are very homogeneous in content, differing only in degree of some specific attitude. An example relating to the acceptability of abortion might take the following form:

1. Abortion should be available to any woman who wishes one.
2. Abortion should be legal if a doctor recommends it.
3. Abortion should be legal whenever the pregnancy is the result of rape or incest.
4. Abortion should be legal whenever the health or well-being of the mother is endangered.
5. Abortion should be legal only when the life of the mother is endangered.

These five statements presumably represent a gradient of permissiveness. A person who agrees with Statement 1 would presumably agree with Statements 2 through 5 (if the statements are in correct order), a person who agrees with Statement 2 but not 1 would probably endorse Statements 3 through 5, and so forth. The person's position on the continuum is defined by the highest statement accepted. Scales of this type (called **Guttman scales,** after the psychologist who first proposed them) have some logical advantages but have proven very difficult to construct.

Semantic Differential

One other approach to attitude measurement has seen fairly wide use. This is the so-called **semantic differential,** which grew out of the work of Osgood and others on the structure of the domain of meaning represented by adjectives (Osgood, Suci, & Tannenbaum, 1957). Through factor analytic studies, these investigators found that most of the variations in meaning that are expressed by different adjectives can be represented by three main dimensions designated *evaluative, potency,* and *activity*. Adjective pairs that represent the extremes of each dimension are shown below.

Evaluative		Potency		Activity	
good	bad	strong	weak	energetic	lazy
nice	nasty	capable	helpless	busy	idle
fair	unfair	dominant	submissive	active	passive

A set of adjectives such as these can be used to get at a person's perception of any target. The target can be a general concept such as abortion, or it can be a specific person such as one's teacher or oneself. Usually the order of the adjective pairs is scrambled, and the positive and negative poles of some pairs are reversed on the page, to reduce thoughtless, stereotyped responding. A scale with five to nine steps is presented, and respondents are asked to indicate how the target concept or person appears to them by making a mark at the appropriate point between the two adjectives. For example, a respondent reacting to the concept of abortion as very good would make a check in the space nearest to "good"; someone perceiving abortion as neither good nor bad would check halfway between the two extremes, and so forth.

The semantic differential method provides a quick and easy way to collect impressions on one or several target objects or concepts. However, the set of adjective pairs can often seem inappropriate for the target, and it may stretch a person's imagination to respond. One suspects that in these circumstances the responses may be rather superficial and at a purely verbal level.

Implicit Attitudes

One limitation of all the attitude assessment procedures we have described so far is that they involve solely a verbal response. They communicate what people are willing to say they feel or believe, but the respondents may not be entirely open and forthright. More important, people's actions may not correspond to their verbally endorsed beliefs and feelings. A child who verbally subscribes to statements of goodwill toward members of another ethnic group may still avoid members of that group when picking playmates or friends to invite to a birthday party—or may not. The verbal statements of attitude must be recognized as just that. Although it may be of interest in its own right to learn that after a particular college course or television program students have changed in the verbally stated attitudes that they endorse, it must not be assumed automatically that other aspects of their behavior toward the target object or group will have changed.

The recent resurgence of interest in reaction time to measure intelligence (see Chapter 8) has led some investigators to apply similar methods to the measurement of unconscious beliefs and attitudes including stereotypes, which are beliefs about classes of people based on preconceptions more than evidence. The basic idea is that one will respond more slowly to pairs of concepts that one sees as incompatible, regardless of one's expressed attitudes toward the concepts. A number of methodologies have been developed to measure implicit attitudes and beliefs (Banaji, 2001, provides a review). One popular methodology, called the Implicit Association Test or IAT (Greenwald, McGhee, & Schwartz, 1998), can be illustrated using the concepts *male, female, mathematics,* and *arts* (see Greenwald & Nosek, 2001). If the assumptions underlying the IAT are true, a person who holds a sex stereotype that males are better at mathematics and females are better at the arts would respond more slowly to pairings of male–arts and female–mathematics stimuli than to pairings of male–mathematics and female–arts stimuli because the former two pairings are incompatible with the stereotype.

IAT testing proceeds through five stages. At each stage, the examinee is to press the right-hand key as quickly as possible if the word flashed on the screen is an example of one concept or pair of concepts and the left key if the word is an example of the other concept or pair of concepts. In the first stage, the examinee is to make a left-key response to male words such as *boy, his,* or *sir* and a right-key response to female words such as *woman, hers,* or *lady.* Art-related terms such as *poetry, music,* or *novel* are substituted for the male terms and mathematical words such as *equation, algebra,* or *multiply* are substituted for the female terms in the second stage of testing.

The third stage is the first "test" for the attitude. In this stage the examinee is instructed to press the left key if either a male word or an arts word (an incompatible pair if the stereotype is present) appears on the screen and to press the right key if the word is female or mathematical (also incompatible). The fourth stage switches the response keys for arts words (now right key) and mathematical words (now left key). Then, in the fifth stage, the examinee is to respond with the left key if the word presented is either male or mathematical (compatible with the stereotype) and with the right key if the word is female or arts (also compatible). The theory behind the IAT and similar procedures predicts that response times should be shorter when the same response is to be made to compatible pairs than to incompatible pairs. That is, response times should be shorter during stage 5 testing than during stage 3 testing if the person being tested holds the stereotype in question. The size of the difference between mean response times is considered a measure of the strength of the stereotype.

Many variations of the basic technique have been proposed to assess different attitudes. Much of this work has focused on attitudes toward people of different races. For example, a person who holds anti-Black attitudes would respond more quickly in the condition where pictures of Black faces and words with "negative" connotations share one response and White faces and "positive" words share the other response than when Black faces and "positive" words share one response and White faces and "negative" words share the other. The technique has been used with various racial comparisons (for example, Japanese and Koreans), but it is not limited to examples of prejudice or racial stereotypes.

The measurement of implicit attitudes has become a very active area for attitude research. Proponents claim that it gets at unconscious attitudes that are inaccessible with more conventional methods. Critics claim that measurement reliability and validity are low. A methodologically and statistically sophisticated study by Cunningham, Preacher, and Banaji (2001) lends support for the validity and reliability of the method, but it remains somewhat time consuming and cumbersome for large-scale use.

SUMMARY

To gain insight into the personality and attitudes of others, you can obtain information directly from individuals, observe their behavior, or obtain information from someone who is in a position to provide it. Personality and attitude assessments are usually accomplished either informally through letters of recommendation or formally, in a structured manner, using rating scales. Both methods have similar limitations centered on the raters' willingness and/or inability to provide accurate assessments. In spite of the limitations of ratings, assessments of an individual through ratings will undoubtedly continue to be widely used for administrative evaluations in schools, civil service, and industry, as well as in educational and psychological research. Every attempt should be made to minimize the limitations.

The limitations of rating procedures result from the following characteristics of the assessment technique:

1. Raters' unwillingness to make unfavorable judgments about others (generosity error), which is particularly pronounced when the raters identify with the person being rated.
2. Wide individual differences in "humaneness" among raters (differences in rater standards) or in leniency or severity of rating.
3. Raters' tendency to respond to another person as a whole in terms of general liking or aversion, and difficulty in differentiating among specific aspects of the individual personality (halo error).
4. Limited contact between the rater and person being rated—limited both in amount of time and in type of situation in which the person being rated is seen.
5. Ambiguity in meaning of the attributes to be appraised.
6. The covert and unobservable nature of many of the inner aspects of personality dynamics.
7. Instability and unreliability of human judgment.

In view of these limitations, the ratings will provide a more accurate picture of the person being rated when the following criteria are met:

1. Appraisal is limited to those qualities that appear overtly in interpersonal relations.
2. The qualities to be appraised are analyzed into concrete and relatively specific aspects of behavior, and judgments are made of these aspects of behavior.
3. The rating form forces the rater to discriminate, or it provides controls for rater differences in judging standards.
4. Raters selected are those who have had the greatest opportunity to observe the person being rated in situations in which the qualities to be rated are displayed.
5. Raters are "sold" on the value of the ratings and are trained in using the rating instrument.
6. Independent ratings of several raters are pooled when several people are qualified to conduct ratings.

Evaluation procedures in which the significance of the ratings is concealed to some extent from the rater also present an interesting possibility for civil service and industrial use, particularly when controls on rater bias are introduced through forced-choice techniques.

Attitude scales have been developed to score the intensity of favorable or unfavorable reactions to a group, institution, or issue. Although these reactions represent only verbal expressions of attitude and may be inconsistent with actual behavior, such expressions may presage behavioral changes. The Implicit Association Test and related methods offer some promise of overcoming these problems.

QUESTIONS AND EXERCISES

1. If you were writing to someone who had been given as a reference by an applicant for a job in your company or for admission to your school, what should you include in your letter, to obtain the most useful evaluation of the applicant?

2. Make a complete list of the different ratings used in the school that you are attending or the school in which you teach. What type of a rating scale or form is used in each case?

3. How effective are the ratings that you identified in Question 2? How adequate is the ratings spread obtained? How consistently is the scale employed by different users? What is your impression of the reliability of the ratings? What is your impression of their freedom from the halo effect and other errors?

4. What factors influence a rater's willingness to rate conscientiously? How serious is this issue? What can be done about it?

5. Why would three independent ratings from separate raters ordinarily be preferable to a rating prepared by the three raters working together as a committee?

6. In the personnel office of a large company, employment interviewers are required to rate job applicants at the end of the interview. Which of the following characteristics would you expect to be rated most reliably? Why?
   a. Initiative
   b. Appearance
   c. Work background
   d. Dependability
   e. Emotional balance

7. In a small survey of the report cards used in a number of communities, the following four traits were most frequently mentioned on the cards: (a) courteous, (b) cooperative, (c) good health habits, and (d) works with others. How might these traits be broken down or revised so that the classroom teacher could evaluate them better?

8. What advantages do ratings by peers have over ratings by superiors? What disadvantages?

9. What are the advantages of ranking, in comparison with rating scales? What are the disadvantages?

10. Suppose a forced-choice rating scale is developed to use in evaluating teacher effectiveness in a city school system. What advantages will this rating procedure have over other types of ratings? What problems will be likely to arise in using it?

11. Suppose you are placed in charge of a merit rating plan being introduced in your company. What steps will you take to try to get the best possible ratings?

12. What factors limit the usefulness of paper-and-pencil attitude scales? What other methods might a teacher use to evaluate attitudes?

13. Prepare a rough draft for a brief attitude scale to measure a teacher's attitudes toward objective tests.

SUGGESTED READINGS

Aamodt, M. G., Bryan, D. A., & Whitcomb, A. J. (1993). Predicting performance with letters of recommendation. *Public Personnel Management, 22,* 81–90.

Banaji, M. R. (2001). Implicit attitudes can be measured. In H. L. Roediger III & J. S. Nairne (Eds.), *The nature of remembering: Essays in honor of Robert G. Crowder* (pp. 117–150). Washington, DC: American Psychological Association.

Cunningham, W. A., Preacher, K. J., & Banaji, M. R. (2001). Implicit attitude measures: Consistency, stability, and convergent validity. *Psychological Science, 12,* 163–170.

Edwards, A. L. (1957). *Techniques of attitudes scale construction.* New York: Appleton-Century-Crofts.

Egan, O., & Archer, P. (1985). The accuracy of teachers' ratings of ability: A regression model. *American Educational Research Journal, 22,* 25–34.

Greenwald, A. G., McGhee, D. E., & Schwartz, J. L. K. (1998). Measuring individual differences in cognition: The Implicit Association Test. *Journal of Personality and Social Psychology, 74,* 1464–1480.

Greenwald, A. G., & Nosek, B. A. (2001). Health of the Implicit Association Test at age 3. *Zeitschrift fur Experimentelle Psychologie, 48,* 85–93.

Knouse, S. B. (1989). Impression management and the letter of recommendation. In R. C. Giacalone & P. Rosenfeld (Eds.), *Impression management in the organization.* Hillsdale, NJ: Erlbaum.

Lambert, N., Leland, H., & Nihira, K. (1993). AAMR Adaptive Behavior Scale—School Edition (2nd ed.). Austin, TX: PRO-ED.

Landy, F. J., Shankster, L. J., & Kohler, S. S. (1994). Personnel selection and placement. In L. W. Porter and M. R. Rosenzweig (Eds.), *Annual Review of Psychology, 45,* 261–296.

Morreau, L. E., & Bruininks, R. H. (1991). Checklist of adaptive living skills. Chicago: Riverside.

Morrison, R. L. (1988). Structured interviews and rating scales. In A. S. Bellack & M. Hershon (Eds.), *Behavioral assessment: A practical handbook* (pp. 252–278). New York: Pergamon.

Nihira, K., Leland, H., & Lambert, N. (1993). AAMR Adaptive Behavior Scales—Residential and Community (2nd ed.). Austin, TX: PRO-ED.

Saal, F. E., Downey, R. G., & Lahey, M. A. (1980). Rating the ratings: Assessing the psychometric quality of rating data. *Psychological Bulletin, 88,* 413–428.

Sparrow, S. S., Balla, D. A., & Cicchetti, D. V. (1984). Vineland Adaptive Behavior Scales. Circle Pines, MN: American Guidance Service.

Special Topics in Testing

CHAPTER 13

Assessment of Children with Disabilities

Introduction
Summary of Major Legislation and Litigation
    Influential Legislation
    Influential Litigation
Assessment Processes
    Referral to Placement Sequence
Major Domains of Involvement
    Intelligence and Cognitive Functioning
    Adaptive Behavior and Self-Help Skills
    Behavioral and Socioemotional Functioning
    Neuropsychological Functioning

Traditional Academic Functioning
    Reading, Math, and Written-Language
      Assessment
    Curriculum-Based Assessment
    Ecological Assessment
Current and Emerging Issues
    Minimum Competency Testing
    Outcomes-Based Assessment
Summary
Questions and Exercises
Suggested Readings

INTRODUCTION

The notion that test results may provide important information about individuals has been an accepted idea since the beginning of the testing movement. Although some aspects of testing and assessment remain controversial, there does appear to be relative agreement among professionals and laypersons alike as to the need for testing in certain situations and with certain populations. The assessment of children with disabilities is one such example. For most of these children, the route to special educational services generally begins with some component of standardized testing, the outcome of which will have a profound impact on the rest of the service delivery sequence.

Decisions to provide special services to certain groups of people are generally based on the priorities of the broader population. For children with disabilities, the basic assumption is that children have no control over the circumstances of their birth and very little control over the circumstances of their care (Safford & Safford, 1996). Prior to the 18th century, the general level of care for children with disabilities was very inconsistent and often inadequate. Archaeological evidence suggests that while some early societies were very accepting of persons with disabilities, many others were not. As an example, early Greek and Roman legal documents contained provisions for the abandonment, isolation, and extermination of infants and children with deformities (Boswell, 1988).

During the Middle Ages, the family or members of religious orders living in monasteries typically provided the care and treatment for persons with disabilities. The early role of monasteries is a historically important one for persons with disabilities in that the medieval abbeys offered physical protection in times of turmoil. They also offered information on educational, medical, and spiritual matters and were, in many locales, the organizational center of community life. Because the monasteries offered their inhabitants a broad-based level of care and nurturance, many parents who were unable to care for their children at home turned them over to the clergy. It was not long, however, before the notion of congregate care facilities gave rise to large-group living facilities for more secular, and often less humane, reasons. These asylums, as they came to be known, rose up throughout Europe to separate the most confused, disorganized, and violent members of society from the rest of the general population (Gallatin, 1982).

According to Safford and Safford (1996), pre-Revolutionary thought in France represented a watershed of new developments in the care and treatment of persons with disabilities. Inherent in the Renaissance-era principle of humanism was a heightened level of respect for the worth and dignity of the person and a new commitment to freedom of thought and spirit. Were it not for a few very active advocates who were willing to challenge the status quo and work to extend the precepts of humanism to the disenfranchised, the community integration movement of the late 20th century might never have occurred. Jean Etienne Esquirol's (1772–1840) work with people with epilepsy, Philippe Pinel's (1745–1826) work with those with mental illness, and Edouard Seguin's (1812–1880) work with people with mental retardation all serve as early examples of person-centered, practical approaches to early educational and psychological service delivery. In fact, Seguin's (1966) methods were considered by many educators to be so impressive that they served as early models for many teachers in special and regular education service settings.

In the post-Renaissance era, care evolved into diagnosis, treatment, and intervention. It became obvious that instructional methodology offered only a partial solution when it came to designing educational treatment strategies for persons with disabilities. The issue of the learner's ability level and specific pattern of strengths and weaknesses also had to be addressed. That information would come from the newly developing science of psychology. In the span of only a few decades, psychology moved from the psychophysical laboratory to the applied service delivery setting advocated by Lightner Witmer (1867–1956). While making many contributions to the discipline of psychology, one of Witmer's most important achievements was the founding in 1896 of America's first child guidance clinic at the University of Pennsylvania (Schultz & Schultz, 1996). A second major achievement was his role in the creation of two of psychology's core subspecialties, clinical psychology and school psychology. Most important, Witmer had demonstrated that science and service could be brought together to solve immediate, practical, and pressing problems of an applied nature. Through his many contributions and the contributions of those who came after, he was able to formally begin the process of offering psychoeducational services to one of America's most vulnerable populations, children with learning difficulties.

In this chapter we identify and explain important components of assessment as they relate to children with disabilities today. We begin with an overview of current legislation and litigation affecting testing practices with children. Following a discussion of the assessment process, an introduction to major domains of involvement, and an overview of traditional academic functioning, we turn our attention to current and emerging issues for children with disabilities.

Part Three

SUMMARY OF MAJOR LEGISLATION AND LITIGATION

Few activities conducted by educational and psychological service providers are as closely monitored by the legal system as those of standardized testing (Bersoff, 1981). The practice of psychoeducational assessment today stems from a number of different influences, many of which have emanated from judicial and legislative mandates to protect traditionally underserved segments of the population. Children and youth with disabilities are one such example. According to the most recent federal guidelines, children and youth with disabilities are students, preschool through 12th grade, who have mental retardation, hearing impairments including deafness, speech or language impairments, visual impairments including blindness, emotional or behavioral disabilities, orthopedic impairments, autism, traumatic brain injury, other health impairments, or specific learning disabilities; and who, by reason thereof, need special education and related services (Individuals with Disabilities Education Act Amendments [IDEA], PL 105-17).

Influential Legislation

Most educators in the public schools today have always worked within a system that requires that children with disabilities be provided with appropriate educational opportunities. Yet, this is really only a very recent phenomenon that began with the passage of the Education for All Handicapped Children Act of 1975 (PL 94-142). It was this piece of legislation that established the right to a free and appropriate public education for those with disabilities and established the initial parameters for providing that education, including the requirements that education be provided in the least restrictive environment possible and that the assessment process be nondiscriminatory. Prior to this legislative initiative, children with disabilities could be turned away from the public schools. Even in those cases where they were admitted, they did not necessarily receive educational experiences appropriate to their individual needs and were often separated from their nondisabled peers.

The Individuals with Disabilities Education Act of 1990 (PL 101-476) and the IDEA Amendments of 1997 (PL 105-17) updated PL 94-142 and brought it more in line with contemporary thought and social policy. Consistent with the original mandate of PL 94-142, IDEA continues to provide children and youth with the assurance of a free, appropriate, public education. It also provides assurances concerning the assessment process, emphasizing that the evaluation should include only meaningful tests and should provide information that can be used to guide instruction. Each child must have an Individualized Education Program (IEP) that identifies the child's current educational performance, specifies educational goals, and identifies appropriate special education services. Furthermore, those services must be provided in the least restrictive environment (LRE) possible—generally the regular classroom with special education aids and supports. Critical components of the IDEA amendments include a focus on connecting the IEP to the regular curriculum; including children with disabilities in school-wide assessments; mandating greater parental involvement in evaluation and placement decisions; and supporting mediation as an alternative to formal appeals (Dwyer, 1997).

Another major piece of legislation that has had a significant impact on the services provided to persons with disabilities is the Americans with Disabilities Act of 1990 (ADA; PL 101-336, 42 U.S.C. § 12101). This particular piece of legislation builds on other laws, including the Civil Rights Act of 1964, and offers specific protection for individuals with disabilities. While not directly tied to assessment-related practices, the ADA is important because it legally elevates people with disabilities to a status alongside other segments of the population who have previously been underserved and who are now offered special protections under the law. The Civil Rights Act of 1964 defined classes of individuals who are protected from discrimination on the basis of personal characteristics such as race, religion, or sex. The ADA adds persons with disabilities to the list of protected segments of the population.

The Family Educational Rights and Privacy Act of 1974 (FERPA) (PL 93-380) was the first major piece of legislation designed to protect the privacy of educational records. As such, it has had a significant impact on the way in which educational and psychological records are handled for all students. FERPA offers such guarantees as (1) the rights of parents or guardians to view all records pertaining to their children's education, (2) the rights of parents or guardians to challenge any information in the records, and (3) the securing of written consent prior to release of information from anyone's official records. Electronic data must be given the same care as information stored in more traditional paper form. In addition, educational and psychological service providers must not only protect the privacy of a person's records, but must also facilitate the person's understanding of their records. The components of IDEA that address assessment reinforce all of these guarantees specifically for people with disabilities.

Influential Litigation

Of all the major court cases presented in the name of public education, none stands out as more dramatic or foundational than *Brown v. Board of Education* (1954). This court case was built on the premise that all children are members of a broader *class* of citizenry (i.e., students) and, therefore, must all be treated equally when it comes to educational services and opportunities. While the U.S. Supreme Court's 1954 decision was initially designed to protect Black children against unfair discrimination in the provision of such services, the Court's decision has been used as a precedent for similar practices involving children with disabilities. As with children of color, children with disabilities may not be denied educational services on the basis of an enduring and unalterable trait that is beyond their control.

There have also been a number of well-documented court cases that have offered highly publicized decisions one way or the other on the issue of test bias. The first such case was *Hobson v. Hansen* (1967) and is noteworthy in two major respects. First, it called into question the notion of using a group test as the sole instrument for placing children into ability tracks, and second, the court condemned tests as racially biased when disproportionately high numbers of children who were poor and Black were found in lower ability tracks. In *Guadalupe Organization v. Tempe Elementary School District* (1972), it was determined that a child's primary language must be determined prior to assessment and that formal provisions to ensure accurate assessment must be made when the primary language is not English. Examples of provisions mentioned in this case include the administration of instruments by psychologists who are fluent in both the child's primary language and in English, the presence of an interpreter to assist with the assessment, the use of instruments that do not stress spoken language, and an assurance that the test results will be explained to parents or guardians in their primary language.

Finally, two historically important court cases have specifically targeted intelligence tests. *Larry P. et al. v. Wilson Riles et al.* (1979), is the court case known to most educational and psychological service providers as the case in which the validity of intelligence tests was called into question for Black children. In that decision, the presiding judge ruled in favor of the minority plaintiffs, finding that standardized, individually administered tests of intelligence were biased against children who were culturally different from those on whom the test was normed. Shortly thereafter, in a similar court case in Illinois, *Parents in Action on Special Education v. Hannon (PASE v. Hannon,* 1980), a very different decision was reached: that standardized measures of intelligence such as the WISC and Stanford-Binet, when taken in the context of a broader assessment system, were found not to be biased against children from culturally different backgrounds.

ASSESSMENT PROCESSES

Referral to Placement Sequence

Special education services form a system designed to provide extra care and attention to children most in need. Nevertheless, referring a child for special services is generally not done without a great deal of concern and anxiety on the part of those who care most for the child. Some parents or guardians are understandably hesitant about placing their children in such services, because they fear that placement will result in negative stereotyping and limited future options for the child. These concerns are usually allayed when they become aware of the procedural safeguards that are in place to protect children against unwarranted and invasive psychoeducational procedures. The following is a brief overview of the stages or steps typically associated with the process from referral for special education services to placement in one or more supportive educational settings.

Screening

Virtually all public school districts have a mechanism for identifying children 3 years of age or older who are at risk for school failure. Usually, the screening includes a brief health history and basic medical evaluation to detect such basic health impairments as difficulties with vision, hearing, or speech. School personnel then conduct additional evaluations using age-appropriate batteries to assess intellectual, social, and motor functioning. Screening evaluations are different from other, more in-depth evaluations in that they are generally conducted with all children in a grade, school, district, or community and are designed to identify children who are at high risk for learning difficulties. They are designed to be sensitive and therefore may mistakenly identify some children who will not need special services for school success. Such screening evaluations are important because children who are identified and offered services earliest show the greatest benefits from intervention.

Prereferral Intervention

Prereferral intervention teams consist of school personnel assembled to respond to the needs of children identified as being in the early stages of academic difficulty. The goal of a prereferral team is to work with the teachers of a child who is showing signs of difficulty in the regular classroom. About 10% of children are identified as needing this level of support. The prereferral team works on the assumption that many students can, with the aid of additional in-class supports and instruction, avoid placement in the special education program. After a period of prereferral intervention, evidence supplied by the traditional classroom teacher is then used to recommend one of three options: (1) termination of the in-class supports, (2) continued or altered in-class supports, or (3) referral for more in-depth psychoeducational evaluations.

Referral for Special Education Services

Referral for special education services can come from any person (parents, teachers, special services personnel, etc.) involved with a child experiencing academic, socioemotional, speech and language, or motor difficulties. In most cases the referral comes from either the parent or the classroom teacher, with input from the prereferral team. The referral is usually accompanied by a well-developed file of evidence compiled by school personnel, containing a record of the reasons for the referral and the outcomes of strategies utilized by the prereferral intervention team. Up to this point, the child is *not* part of the special education service delivery system. The child enters the special education system when he or she is assigned a case manager and the special education staff has requested parental permission for diagnostic testing.

If permission to evaluate is received, an interdisciplinary evaluation team composed of teachers, parents, parental advocates, and specialized personnel prepares a formal assessment plan covering the child's primary and related areas of difficulty. School support personnel such as school psychologists, counselors, physicians, social workers, physical and occupational therapists, and speech pathologists typically carry out the assessments. The rationale behind an interdisciplinary evaluation is twofold: First, it may take professionals from different disciplines to provide the broadest perspective on a given disability; and, second, a group of persons typically provides a better overall evaluation with more appropriate procedural safeguards than a single person could.

Eligibility Meeting

Once the assessment information has been gathered and synthesized by the child's case manager, an eligibility meeting is scheduled to determine if the child qualifies for special education. If the child qualifies, the interdisciplinary evaluation team prepares an IEP that outlines such things as the educational curriculum, learning objectives for the curriculum, criteria for achievement, length of time services are to be utilized, and the actual place of service delivery. Since IEPs are written annually, length of time is generally considered to be for the remainder of the school year unless otherwise specified.

Follow-Up Evaluations

One of the procedural safeguards provided by IDEA to children enrolled in special education programs and their families is the requirement that every child receiving special education services be reevaluated at least every 3 years. The IEP team makes the determination about what should be included in the reevaluation. With parental agreement the team may determine that no additional assessment data are necessary to conduct the reevaluation. The IEP evaluations and the 3-year reevaluations are routinely conducted to ensure parents and school personnel that the child still requires the extra attention and services necessary to perform adequately in school.

There is also a requirement that parents or legal guardians be notified of special education program meetings regarding their children. Foremost among the information that should be provided to parents is accurate, direct, informative feedback from diagnostic testing. Parents who have never been exposed to the assessment process can be very intimidated by all of the numbers and unfamiliar nomenclature. Support in understanding this information is critical in ensuring that the parent(s) will remain involved in the placement process. Simpson (1990) has identified a number of dimensions along which parents and family members may support the educational interventions of their children. Assistance in child and family advocacy, IEP planning, and home tutoring are some of the many areas in which parents can strengthen their involvement with their child's education.

MAJOR DOMAINS OF INVOLVEMENT

Intelligence and Cognitive Functioning

It is difficult to present any meaningful discussion of assessment concerning disabilities without giving attention, first and foremost, to the construct of intelligence. Whether interested in the more cognitive reasons for difficulty or the more practical side of assessment, those involved must consider the nature and impact of intelligence on academic performance and programming.

In almost all cases, state and local guidelines require that the assessment battery include a measure of intellectual functioning when a child is referred for special education services. The reason for this is fairly straightforward. Intelligence tests are typically the strongest, broadest, and most stable instruments used in the evaluation. The instruments are used as diagnostic tools to gather a wide range of information, from the simple recall of general information to the complex processing of new and nontraditional stimuli. Disorders and disabilities manifesting themselves through various psychomotor channels can also be identified with these tests. Furthermore, the purpose of the assessment is not only to determine eligibility for special education but also to identify the child's cognitive strengths and weaknesses in order to facilitate program planning. Tests of intelligence provide much valuable and specific information in this realm.

For children with speech and language disabilities—one of the largest groups of children receiving special education services today—intellectual assessment is less important than for the other high-frequency disability categories, learning disabilities and mental retardation. The main reason is that it is entirely possible for a child to have difficulty in expressive ability, either oral or written, without affecting other, higher order processing skills. However, for children in most other high-frequency categories, such as specific learning disabilities and mental retardation, basic psychological processes are implicated to such a level that multiple information processing pathways are undoubtedly involved and general tests of intellectual ability provide a great deal of useful information.

Children with low-frequency disabilities, such as visual, aural (hearing), or orthopedic problems, present a particular challenge in the assessment process, because most tests do not have provisions for children with these nontraditional types of disabilities. When intellectual assessments are conducted with children with such disabilities, the testing must be conducted using modified formats, due to the nature of the test items and the very real limitations of the child if he or she is not able to see, hear, or physically manipulate the test stimuli. The difficulty with individually derived adaptations to standardized instruments is that they are usually not the adaptations used during standardization and are often generated *on the spot* by examiners who mean well but do not see enough children with any particular disability to develop a familiarity with appropriate instruments.

In the measurement of intelligence, two major intelligence tests stand above the rest in both historical precedence and frequency of use: the Stanford-Binet Intelligence Scale, Fifth Edition (Roid, 2003), and the Wechsler intelligence scales. As noted in Chapter 8, the Wechsler scales are a set of related and highly similar test batteries that span the age range from early childhood

(Wechsler Preschool and Primary Scale of Intelligence–Third Edition; Wechsler, 2002), through childhood (Wechsler Intelligence Scale for Children–Third Edition; Wechsler, 1991a), to adulthood (Wechsler Adult Intelligence Scale–Third Edition; Wechsler, 1997). Within the scope of school-based assessments, a third instrument, the Kaufman Assessment Battery for Children (K-ABC; Kaufman & Kaufman, 1983), is also sometimes used. A number of other standardized instruments are available but are used to a lesser degree than either the Stanford-Binet or the Wechsler scales.

Adaptive Behavior and Self-Help Skills

The concept of adaptive behavior has undergone substantial revision in recent years. From its formal beginning as a component of social maturity to its status today as an independent, multifaceted construct, adaptive behavior has moved from a simple system of behavioral observations to one of relative psychometric complexity (McGrew, Ittenbach, Bruininks, & Hill, 1991). Until recently, adaptive behavior was considered to represent a person's ability to function effectively in his or her own environment. Since 1992, however, the American Association on Mental Retardation (1992) has attempted to redirect the focus and responsibility of adaptation away from the person with disabilities and onto the community, by way of identification of the supports needed for community living. Adaptive behavior is now considered to be a very important part of many assessment systems, but especially in evaluating children and youth with disabilities.

The construct of adaptive behavior has, until very recently, been atheoretical and has evolved in an inductive way based on the presence or absence of behaviors considered important for daily living. This has been a process whereby test items were developed from observation of specific behaviors (is able to tie own shoes) and from those items to scales (groupings of similar items) and, finally, from scales to instruments. It is from these instruments that theories describing the construct of adaptive behavior have been developed. One such theory is Greenspan and Granfield's (1992) **theory of general competence.** The theory postulates that general competence consists of two broad subdomains, **environmental competence** and **social competence,** which serve as third stratum factors. Both subdomains have intellectual and nonintellectual components that arise from more narrowly defined competencies (see Figure 13–1). Empirical validation for these dimensions has not been particularly supportive. While content analyses of published scales have suggested as many as 10 different content areas (Bruininks, Thurlow, & Gillman, 1987), factor analytic results have tended to indicate a single underlying factor.

Adaptive behavior assessment is most often associated with mental retardation. By law, a diagnosis of mental retardation cannot be made without a finding of significantly subaverage performance on a measure of intelligence and corresponding deficits in two or more adaptive skill areas. A definition such as this guards against a child being labeled as mentally retarded on the basis of scores on an intelligence test alone, and it is intended to preclude a classification of mental retardation for children who do poorly on standardized measures of intelligence but perform well in nonschool settings such as at home or in the community.

Adaptive behavior received its most important impetus from the court cases of the mid-1970s and early 1980s which forced examiners to rely less on single measures of intelligence and more on multiple measures of aptitude and ability prior to placement in special education programs. The reason for the decision then and its widespread appeal now is that adaptive behavior offers a much more practical perspective on what a child can do with the more immediate, pressing problems of everyday life than that offered by most intelligence tests. Four popular measures of

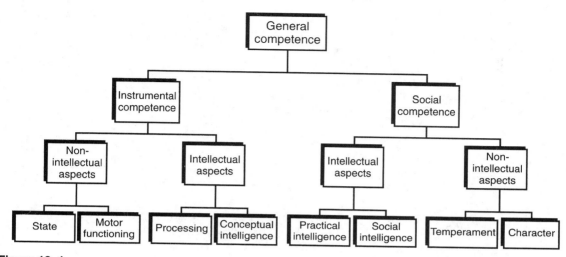

Figure 13–1
Comprehensive model of general competence.
Source: Reprinted with permission from Greenspan, S. R., & Granfield, J. M. (1992). Reconsidering the construct of mental retardation: Implications of a model of social competence. *American Journal of Mental Retardation, 96,* 447.

adaptive behavior are the AAMR Adaptive Behavior Scales (Residential and Community—Nihira, Leland, & Lambert, 1993; School—Lambert, Leland, & Nihira, 1993), the Scales of Independent Behavior–Revised (Bruininks, Woodcock, Weatherman, & Hill, 1996), and the Vineland Adaptive Behavior Scales (Sparrow, Balla, & Cicchetti, 1984a, 1984b, 1985).

Behavioral and Socioemotional Functioning

The problems associated with behavioral and socioemotional assessment are even more daunting than the problems encountered in intellectual and adaptive behavior assessment. As was discussed in Chapter 11, decisions about emotional and behavioral disorders are often based on clinical judgments, judgments that most often stem from the rather subjective nature of the construct itself. According to IDEA, children who have disabilities that are socially or emotionally based exhibit one or more of the following characteristics to a marked degree over an extended period of time:

- An inability to learn that cannot be explained by intellectual, sensory, or other health factors
- An inability to build or maintain satisfactory interpersonal relationships with peers and teachers
- Inappropriate types of behavior or feelings under normal circumstances
- A general pervasive mood of unhappiness or depression
- A tendency to develop physical symptoms or fears associated with personal or school problems.

Theories of personality and social functioning abound, with descriptions of various orientations ranging from the controversial psychodynamic models to the highly behavioral orientations. Such wide disparity in orientation leads to considerable problems with terminology. For example, a frequently used term is *emotionally disturbed*, but many behaviorists reject the emphasis on the unobservable psyche and, instead, prefer the term *behaviorally disordered*. To the average person, however, the terms mean essentially the same thing and are often used interchangeably. Furthermore, some in the field prefer to combine the two terms into the broader, seemingly less poignant classification of *behaviorally disturbed*. Whatever term is used, it is very important to be clear about the nature of the child's disruptive behavior, because children who simply misbehave are not eligible for special services in the school or community.

The term *emotionally disturbed* is reserved for those children whose behavioral response patterns are symptoms of deeper emotional problems. These children are eligible for special education services. The assessment of the disorder typically includes informal observations, systematic behavioral observations, interpretation of standardized test scores, and case studies. While there are examples in the professional literature of clinicians who make inferences about emotional disturbance based on the profiles of established cognitive ability tests such as the Stanford-Binet or the Wechsler scales, such an approach is not recommended. As Shepard (1989) asserts, when diagnoses of clinical syndromes are made on the basis of unusual or bizarre responses to aptitude test questions, it is highly likely that behavioral observations alone would be sufficient for identification. Consequently, she advocates diagnosing clinical syndromes on the basis of behavioral observations, a conclusion that many special education service providers also seem to be coming to in increasing numbers.

If a special education service provider is interested in the more social components of a child's functioning, it is likely that a behavioral instrument such as the Behavior Evaluation Scale II (McCarney & Leigh, 1990) or the Burks Behavioral Rating Scales (Burks, 1977) will be sufficient for gathering the needed information. However, if the concern pertains more to emotional functioning, with heightened concerns about deeper psychopathology, then it is good practice to include instruments such as the Child Behavior Checklist (Achenbach, 1991) or the Behavior Assessment for Children (BASC; Reynolds & Kamphaus, 1992). Both instruments include parent, teacher, and self-report rating forms.

Neuropsychological Functioning

Assessment of neuropsychological functioning represents a relatively new area of assessment for psychoeducational service providers. As a subdiscipline of psychology, neuropsychology builds on many of the new advances in clinical, cognitive, and school psychology, with shared contributions from medicine and neurology. Despite the equivocal results of early research in perceptual-motor abilities, much of the new research in neuropsychology continues to draw heavily on the perceptual-motor research of decades past.

The persistence and commitment of educational and psychological service providers to this all-important domain of human functioning is as much a testament to the importance of perceptual-motor and sensorimotor functioning as it is to the need for new developments in the psychodiagnostics of integrative functioning. According to Weeks and Ewer-Jones (1991), failure to perceive information correctly threatens one's ability to attach meaning to stimuli in a worthwhile manner. When meaning becomes distorted, responses to those meanings are often produced in unusual or atypical ways. This is the reason that basic avenues of sensory operations such as vision, hearing, and simple motor functioning are included in the first stage of assessment for children suspected of requiring special educational assistance.

Sometimes providing such simple devices as glasses or a hearing aid is all that is needed for problem resolution. Very frequently, though, assessment and intervention require much more than can be gleaned from a Snellin reading chart or a tone audiometer. Efforts to take perceptual-motor-skill development beyond simple sensory input have also met with mixed reviews. Whereas educational and psychological service providers formerly used tests of visual and auditory processing, integration, and discrimination, more contemporary assessments of brain-behavior relationships include everything from computerized tomography (CT) to magnetic resonance imaging (MRI) to positron emission tomography (PET). Consequently, the ability to diagnose and treat neuropsychological and sensorimotor disorders is much improved from that of even 20 years ago. In the field of reading for example, Feifer and DeFina (2000) suggest that the use of neuropsychological measures together with neuroimaging techniques can provide a clearer understanding of brain-behavior relationships in reading disorders. Similarly, Kennard, Stewart, Silver, and Emslie (2000) found that specific patterns of neuropsychological ability identified through assessment correlated with academic improvement in specific areas.

TRADITIONAL ACADEMIC FUNCTIONING

Reading, Math, and Written-Language Assessment

Any child can have difficulty in school. In fact, most children have difficulty at one time or another during their educational years. However, children who receive special education services typically experience a level of difficulty that requires intervention well beyond what the regular school curriculum can realistically provide. Measures of academic achievement such as those discussed in Chapter 9 are often used to estimate a child's level of content mastery in a given academic area. Measures of academic aptitude (such as those described in Chapter 8), on the other hand, are used to estimate how a child should be performing relative to same-age and same-grade peers. When taken together, standardized measures of academic achievement and aptitude can provide evaluators with a reasonably good picture of the disparity between actual and expected performances in traditional academic skill areas. For most children in special education, that disparity translates into deficits in the basics of reading, writing (written language), and/or arithmetic. For older children it can easily include other content areas such as science or social studies but will, in all likelihood, still involve the fundamental skills of reading, writing, or arithmetic.

More children are evaluated for reading disabilities than for any other single academic area (McLoughlin & Lewis, 2001). This is probably because reading pervades the general curriculum to a far greater degree than any other skill. A disability in reading will manifest itself across the curriculum because it interferes with the basic acquisition of written information. Mathematics ability represents the second most frequent area of referral for children with disabilities. Although mathematics is absolutely essential for quantitative thinking in a modern world, its contribution to the rest of the curriculum is more limited than that of reading and, as a result, is less often implicated. Written language constitutes the least frequently evaluated area of disability. Though sound writing ability is critical for successful functioning throughout life, it is an area in which the diagnostic and intervention research has lagged behind other areas, and school district personnel are hesitant to place children in special education solely on the basis of a disability in written language.

Assessment of basic academic skills has tended to take one of two paths. When a referral for evaluation is for general academic difficulty, that is, for trouble in more than one content area, a standardized measure of achievement that incorporates all three of the aforementioned areas is generally used. When a referral is for a single academic area such as reading, a specialized diagnostic instrument will be used. Although both types of instruments can provide an index of how a child compares with other children nationally, only in-depth, diagnostic instruments in specific content areas have the capacity to offer insight into the source or nuances of a specific disability.

A variety of measures are available that provide information about a child's general and relative levels of academic functioning. Group-administered tests include the Iowa Tests of Basic Skills (Riverside Publishing Company, 2001), the Stanford Achievement Test Series (Harcourt Brace, 1996) and the Metropolitan Achievement Tests (Harcourt Brace, 2000). In part because of regulations from IDEA, many school districts encourage or even require that children with disabilities take these exams. But not all children are able to take group-administered tests and many who do perform poorly. Individually administered tests of achievement provide a better option in these cases. The Kaufman Test of Educational Achievement (Kaufman & Kaufman, 1985, 1998), the Peabody Individual Achievement Test–Revised (Markwardt, 1989, 1997), and the Woodcock-Johnson Tests of Achievement (Woodcock, McGrew & Mather, 2001) are examples of the latter.

In addition to these test batteries, a number of individually administered batteries exist for diagnostic and program planning purposes. As one might expect, there are more reading instruments than anything else. The Gray Oral Reading Test–Third Edition (Wiederholt & Bryant, 1992), the Stanford Diagnostic Reading Test (The Psychological Corporation, 1995), and the Woodcock Reading Mastery Tests–Revised (Woodcock, 1998) are examples of such instruments. In the area of mathematics assessment, the Enright Diagnostic Inventory of Basic Arithmetic Skills (Enright, 1983), the Keymath–Revised (Connolly, 1988, 1997), and the Test of Mathematical Abilities–Second Edition (Brown, Cronin, & McEntire, 1994) tend to be used with greatest frequency. Finally, in the area of written-language assessment, the Test of Written Language–Third Edition (Hammill & Larsen, 1996) and the Woodcock Language Proficiency Battery–Revised (Woodcock, 1991) are the most commonly used instruments.

Curriculum-Based Assessment

Curriculum-based assessment (CBA) is an alternative assessment model that is receiving considerable attention within education today as greater emphasis is being placed on various performance models of assessment. The idea behind CBA is not new, however. Teachers in particular have long relied on a form of assessment based on direct observation of performance as it relates to specific areas of the curriculum. When students are asked to spell words taken directly from those studied in the spelling curriculum, the teacher is using curriculum-based assessment. Such informal measures provide valuable information about the performance of students in the local school or classroom that is quite different from what is learned when the students are given a standardized spelling test and compared to national norms. While the latter informs the teacher about the general performance of students when compared to similar students across the state or nation, the former can be used to gauge incremental improvement in the development of specified skills.

Curriculum-based measurement (CBM) is another important term in understanding current models of performance assessment. While sometimes used interchangeably with curriculum-based assessment, most school psychologists distinguish between the two terms. **Curriculum-based assessment** is the general term that applies to informal and customized testing conducted in the regular classroom for all students. **Curriculum-based measurement** is a form of performance assessment that uses materials from the regular curriculum to assess special education students, allowing the assessment specialist to determine how the individual student performs in relation to other students in specific areas of the local curriculum.

Curriculum-based measures represent an alternative assessment model for many psychologists practicing in educational settings. Most traditional training programs tend to emphasize the individually administered, norm-referenced tests of intelligence with some more recent attention given to measures of personality, adaptive behavior, and general development. In curriculum-based measurement, micro-level skills such as the ability to read, write, or spell words from a given list for a given week are the targets of choice. For children with specific learning disabilities, mental retardation, or even speech and language disabilities, the teacher is able to identify an objective for a day, test whether or not it was achieved, and then chart the child's progress in a way that the progress can be compared with the progress made on other days or weeks. The following are examples of curriculum-based measures adapted from Marston (1989):

- Count the number of words a student reads correctly from a word list, in a 1-minute interval.
- Count the number of words written during a 3-minute interval, given a story starter.
- Count the number of letter sequences spelled correctly during a 2-minute interval, given words dictated every 7 seconds.

The fact that CBA is an alternative assessment model for many educational and psychological service providers brings with it a number of assumptions for best practice. The first expectation is that the service providers are willing to learn new skills of assessment that may offer a quicker route to intervention. A second assumption lies in the direct, repeated nature of the evaluations. It is assumed that the child is evaluated on a constant and recurring basis so that actual trends in performance can be identified and used for further programming. A third assumption is that the teacher and psychological service provider will be responsible for determining the degree to which the local measures (e.g., weekly spelling tests or weekly math tests) are reliable and valid measures of the skills. It does little good for a teacher to design a series of tests that do not accurately reflect progress for a given semester (Marston, 1989).

An often-unintended by-product of such measurement practices lies in the generation of local norms. Educational and psychological service providers can gauge the progress a student is making relative to other children in the school or school district. Many CBM proponents will quickly state that the purpose of CBM lies more with the tests' representativeness for a given child's day-to-day skill development than with person–group comparisons. However, for the teacher or psychological service provider who is also interested in person–group comparisons, CBM allows for that possibility.

Ecological Assessment

Just as curriculum-based assessment represents an alternative model of assessment for educational and psychological service providers, so too does ecological assessment. In ecological assessment, the focus of assessment is shifted away from content and onto the entire psychoeducational service delivery system. The purpose of ecological assessment is to evaluate all factors influencing the learning process. Although the model works for children without disabilities just as well as it does for children with disabilities, many of the ecological models have emanated from use with special populations, since children with disabilities are usually exposed to a wider range of assessment activities (Browder, 2001).

As is often the case with new assessment models, the ecological models tend to be more casual than formal and are frequently based on the individual perspectives of the investigators. Most models, however, emphasize the importance of the interaction between the child and others in the environment and have, in part, stemmed from mental health models that have incorporated community- and socially based interventions. For children with disabilities, Witt, Elliott, Kramer, and Gresham (1994) contend that ecological assessment must also involve the classroom teacher. The assessment plan must include the teacher's expectations for the child, the physical environment of the classroom, and the learning tasks at hand. Furthermore, Browder (2001) stresses the importance of gathering data in a variety of settings.

The advantages of using an ecological model are both positive and complex. First, ecological assessment widens the scope of responsibility for ameliorating the disability to other forces in the environment, similar in many ways to the movement in adaptive behavior assessment. Second, it takes assessment beyond single entities such as the child, the family, or even academic expectations to include interactions between all parts of the environment. Third, it allows for new and innovative approaches to assessment to a greater extent than more traditional measures do. The model necessarily includes everything from traditional standardized measures to the most subjective, qualitatively based outcomes of day-to-day operations.

An obvious limitation to using ecological models in routine evaluations is the amount of time and energy it takes to gather the necessary information. There are very few instruments on the market today that are designed to handle, in any meaningful way, the broad-based interactions that are involved in the ecological models presented here and elsewhere. Those that tend to focus on one aspect of a child's learning environment often overlook other equally important components. Ysseldyke and Christenson (1993) have designed a fairly comprehensive ecological assessment instrument, The Instructional Environment System–II, that measures 17 key factors influencing a child's academic performance. Twelve factors are associated with the school setting and 5 factors are associated with home supports. Following is a listing of the 17 factors surveyed by the Instructional Environment System–II:

Instructional Environment Components

Instructional Match	Teacher Expectations
Classroom Environment	Instructional Presentation
Cognitive Emphasis	Motivational Strategies
Relevant Practice	Informed Feedback
Academic Engaged Time	Adaptive Instruction
Progressive Evaluation	Student Understanding

Home-Support-for-Learning Components

Expectations and Attributions	Discipline Orientation
Effective Home Environment	Parent Participation
Structure for Learning	

CURRENT AND EMERGING ISSUES

Minimum Competency Testing

An important aspect of the current educational reform movement is referred to as minimum competency testing—a process designed to determine if a child or adolescent has acquired the minimum level of academic skill considered necessary to certify completion of an educational program. Unacceptable performance on such measures may result in mandated remediation or retention and, at times, even denial of a diploma. These competency testing programs have three main purposes: (1) to identify students in need of remediation, (2) to ensure that graduates and/or those who are promoted to the next grade have reached some minimum level of competency, and (3) to provide additional motivation to students to increase their academic achievement. This approach has had great appeal to politicians and the general public because of its rather direct means of dealing with some of the perceived inadequacies of public instruction. Interest in minimum competency testing seems to have touched nearly every state, although there is considerable variability in how the process has been enacted. Many groups have designed minimum competency guidelines, and testing programs range from those centralized at the state level to those directed and implemented by local school districts. Some states have created their own tests, while others have contracted with outside agencies.

Questions as to the legality of minimum competency tests abound. The problem is not simply one of implementing the tests or even of establishing minimum guidelines for promotion or graduation. Instead the difficulty lies with the absolute nature of decisions regarding who will actually receive a diploma or the amount of time designated for remediation. While many legal issues have been resolved—generally in favor of minimum competency testing programs—more are sure to be introduced. Disparate racial impact and the higher failure rates of minority students are the areas of greatest concern. The courts have ruled that it is not necessary to prove discriminatory intent when the differential test scores were the result of past discriminatory policies of school segregation, corrected only a few years earlier.

Debra P. v. Turlington (1979) reaffirmed the mandate of fair warning and the requirement that minimum competency testing not carry forward the effects of racial segregation. The court of appeals also added one further condition, that the test had to have content validity. According to McClung (1979), content validity for minimum competency testing consists of two types: **curricular validity,** which refers to the match between the competency test and the curriculum, and **instructional validity,** which is the establishment of a match between what is assessed on the minimum competency test and what actually happens in the classroom. While this type of judgment represented a controversial decision for many school personnel in that it pertained to all types of tests, the courts have traditionally left such judgments in the hands of professional educators.

When minimum competency testing was first introduced, there was a widely held view that a successful legal challenge to this form of testing would come from critics who believed that such programs were unfair to special education students. However, the courts have consistently ruled that school systems can require special education students to take such a test and deny them a diploma if they do not pass. According to Jaeger (1989), the courts have also ruled that it is not necessary for those requiring such a test for students in special education programs to themselves establish curricular and instructional validity. These school systems also have not been required to defend the existence of disparate impact on special education students, which stands in sharp contrast to the judicial response to testing students from minority backgrounds.

Designing minimum competency tests presents no special problems once the assessment domain and level have been determined. Even so, such tests need to be different from typical achievement tests in that they should be designed in such a way as to be maximally sensitive at one specific ability level—the level chosen to represent minimum competence. The test items, then, should be targeted at a narrow band of difficulty and allow for differentiation between those falling just below and those just above the minimum passing score. It is impossible to determine this point with complete precision, and inevitably the test will differentiate over a fairly wide range of competence. The better job a minimum competency test does in allowing for differentiation of the minimally competent from those who fall just below this point, the less effective it will be in allowing differentiation among students across the full range of abilities.

Outcomes-Based Assessment

Outcomes-based assessment is a very important concept in contemporary thinking about evaluation and assessment in education. While competency-based assessment is focused on the establishment and measurement of minimum competencies or levels of performance, outcomes-based assessment is an approach with a much broader view. What should be the outcomes of education? This question is not just about minimums, but also about expectations. **Outcomes-based assessment** begins when professional educators, parents, students, and public policy makers identify the desired products of a public education and then redesign the educational system to develop those outcomes in all students. According to Salvia and Ysseldyke (2000), there are four main reasons why people have an interest in outcomes-based assessment: improvement of instructional programs, accountability, public information, and policy formulation.

The Individuals with Disabilities Education Act mandates that all state public education departments document the educational outcomes of children with disabilities. Evaluating the success of special education means much more than simply evaluating the progress of a child as she or he moves through the special education system (student accountability). It is also necessary to review the success of the entire service delivery system (system accountability). Just as state and local policy makers need information on the quality and productivity of their schools, teachers also need information on the progress of their respective students. As education continues to be a primary public policy and political issue, the principles of outcome-based assessment are likely to become more and more prominent. Furthermore, they show great promise as a new and rather innovative means of assessing student, school, and system-wide outcomes within the context of a single, unified framework.

SUMMARY

Testing, as it is currently practiced, bears little resemblance to its historical predecessors. Yet, the mission remains much the same: to identify and serve people in need, whether that means providing service delivery in the schools or in community mental health centers. In either case, children with disabilities are exposed to a wide range of assessment practices representing many different educational and psychological domains. While standardized measures of intelligence, personality, adaptive behavior, neuropsychological functioning, and achievement are essential to the assessment process, a new wave of assessment practices is flowing into special education service delivery. Curriculum-based assessment, ecological assessment, minimum competency testing, and outcomes-based assessment all represent new ways of conceptualizing the manner in which children with disabilities are evaluated and served by educational and psychological service providers.

QUESTIONS AND EXERCISES

1. How has the care and treatment of people with disabilities evolved through history to the present time?

2. Identify and briefly describe the three most important pieces of legislation affecting the lives of people with disabilities presented in this chapter. What are the main features of each?

3. Two very well known court cases constitute the center of the debate over the legality of standardized testing with cultural minorities, *Larry P. et al. v. Wilson Riles et al.* and *PASE v. Hannon*. What makes these two court cases so important and how were the outcomes different?

4. Briefly identify and explain the simple five-step referral to placement sequence used for serving children and youth with disabilities. Where does assessment fit into this sequence?

5. What role do standardized intelligence tests play in most multidimensional assessment systems? Identify the two intelligence tests most frequently used in the schools today.

6. For children who are referred for possible emotional disturbances, how might a multidimensional assessment battery differ from that traditionally used for academic difficulties only?

7. Identify and describe the three most frequently cited areas in which children encounter difficulty in academic achievement. Of the three discussed in this chapter, which single area accounts for more referrals than any other? Why do you believe this is the case?

8. What makes curriculum-based assessment plans different from other, more traditional assessment plans? How might curriculum-based assessment devices be used to complement the results of norm-referenced instruments?

SUGGESTED READINGS

Browder, D. M. (2001). *Curriculum and assessment for students with moderate and severe disabilities.* New York: Guilford.

Flanagan, D. P., Andrews, T. J., & Genshaft, J. L. (1997). The functional utility of intelligence tests with special education populations. In D. P. Flanagan, J. L. Genshaft, & P. L. Harrison (Eds.), *Contemporary intellectual assessment: Theories, tests, and issues.* New York: Guilford.

Merrell, K. W. (1999). *Behavioral, social, and emotional assessment of children and adolescents.* Mahwah, NJ: Erlbaum.

Safford, P. L., & Safford, E. J. (1996). *A history of childhood and disability.* New York: Columbia University, Teachers' College Press.

Salvia J., & Ysseldyke, J. E. (2000). *Assessment* (8th ed.). Boston, MA: Houghton Mifflin.

Sattler, J. M. (2001). *Assessment of children: Cognitive applications* (4th ed.). San Diego: Author.

Sattler, J. M. (2002). *Assessment of children: Behavioral and clinical applications* (4th ed.). San Diego: Author.

CHAPTER 14

Ethics and Issues in Assessment

Introduction
Professional Training and Competence
    Professional Training
    Professional Competence
    Validity of Clinical Opinion
Professional and Scientific Responsibility
    Standards for Educational and Psychological
       Testing
Respect for the Rights and Dignity of Others
    Privacy and Confidentiality
    Autonomy and Self-Determination
    Beneficence

Social Responsibility
    Distributive Justice
    Social Benefits of Testing
    Maximizing the Positive
Controversial Issues in Testing
    Test Bias
    Truth in Testing
    High-Stakes Testing
    Internet-Based Psychological Testing
Summary
Questions and Exercises
Suggested Readings

INTRODUCTION

According to one scholar writing in the area of legal and ethical issues, psychological tests represent one of the highest technical advancements in the field of psychology (Swenson, 1993). Others have placed intelligence tests among the 20 most important discoveries of the 20th century, right alongside other major discoveries such as atomic fission, the computer, Einstein's theory of relativity, and Watson and Crick's model of the double helix (Miller, 1984). Irrespective of testing's relative rank among other major advancements of our time, it is safe to assume that most people's lives have in some way been influenced by tests of one sort or another.

As an important part of our society and lives, the impact of testing cannot be overemphasized. For this reason, professional standards and ethics have been developed to promote responsible professional practice in psychological testing. Ethics can be viewed as a set of conduct rules that defines and synthesizes socially valued elements of right and wrong and that specifies guidelines for professional duties and moral obligations. Most professional organizations have published codes of ethics to assist their members with the more difficult decisions they face. The most important enforcement mode for ethical violations of members is typically group pressure applied by organization members. Although the ethics of testing are imprecisely defined and open to individual interpretation, there is general consensus among educational and psychological service providers that ethical guidelines are foundational components of effective service delivery.

The purpose of the present chapter is to identify and explain many of the ethical issues faced by educational and psychological service providers using some of education's and psychology's most valued tools—their tests. The discussion will be organized around several of the general ethical principles put forth by the American Counseling Association (ACA, 1995) and the American Psychological Association (APA, 2002). The five principal areas of focus are (1) professional training and competence, (2) professional and scientific responsibility, (3) respect for the rights and dignity of others, (4) social responsibility, and (5) controversial issues in testing.

PROFESSIONAL TRAINING AND COMPETENCE

Professional Training

To promote the welfare and best interests of clients in the development, publication, and utilization of educational and psychological assessment techniques, service providers must, out of necessity, develop skills in assessment and intervention. But one cannot become proficient at these tasks without first developing a depth of understanding in such areas of knowledge as cognition and learning, human growth and development, developmental abnormalities and psychopathology, and general human relations. In other words, assessment information obtained by a human service provider must stand in the context of other equally important information and must be interpreted within the context of the science of psychology. The notion that assessment as a viable skill can stand alone without the assessor having foundational skills in other related areas of human functioning and psychoeducational service delivery is a fallacy.

Proficiency in psychodiagnostic procedures depends in large part on how well the individual has been able to integrate the aforementioned areas and successfully blend that broad-based foundation of human functioning with principles of measurement and assessment. This is the major reason most licensure boards require that their applicants have graduated from a college or university having an accredited program with an integrated set of course work. Graduate training programs accredited by the American Psychological Association (for psychologists) and the Council on Accreditation of Counseling and Related Educational Programs (for counselors) both require courses and contact hours in assessment, diagnosis, and treatment intervention across a wide range of disorders and disabilities.

As with any profession, being well trained during graduate education is far different from staying abreast of new developments in a given field throughout one's career. Many, if not most, educational and psychological service providers leave school well trained and well prepared to offer assessment and intervention services. As time slips by and a professional routine sets in, however, a conscientious and dedicated service provider must work at staying on top of new developments in the field's theory and practice. The subfield of assessment is no different. The broader the provider's practice, the more difficult it is to stay on top of the many new tests published each year, let alone the research that serves as their conceptual foundation and documents their validity for the decisions for which they are used. Perhaps many service providers would be surprised to find out that staying current in one's field and with one's tools of inquiry means more than simply maintaining the standards learned in graduate school; constant retraining and professional growth are standards for best practice. According to Standard E.11 of the American

Counseling Association's Code of Ethics and Standards of Practice (1995), "counselors must not base their assessment or intervention decisions or recommendations on data or test results that are obsolete or outdated for the current purpose."

The problem with testing lies not so much with the characteristics of the tests, but, rather, with the ways in which they are often used (Moreland, Eyde, Robertson, Primoff, & Most, 1995). One way in which leaders within the disciplines of education and psychology responded to this phenomenon was through the creation in 1984 of a Joint Committee on Testing Practices (JCTP). A primary goal of this group was to develop "an empirical approach to test user qualification that would be helpful to those interested in improving how tests are used" (Moreland et al., 1995). The group identified a list of 12 minimum competencies for proper use of tests. A list of areas in which misuses are likely to occur is shown in Figure 14–1.

Misuse is likely to occur in a number of areas. Comprehensive assessment systems offer one such example. Any time an examiner is asked to record and integrate information from assessment batteries with clinical observations of behaviors that suggest serious psychological disturbance, the potential for error is great, particularly for those who do not keep up with new developments in their field. A second area of likely misuse is in the area of psychometric knowledge. Examiners who fail to understand such basics of psychometric theory as reliability and validity may overstate the accuracy of their information and instill in their examinees an

Item No.	Competency
1.	Avoiding errors in scoring and recording
2.	Refraining from labeling people with personally derogatory terms like *dishonest* on the basis of a test score that lacks perfect validity
3.	Keeping scoring keys and test materials secure
4.	Seeing that every examinee follows directions so that test scores are accurate
5.	Using settings for testing that allow for optimum performance by test takers (e.g., adequate room)
6.	Refraining from coaching or training individuals or groups on test items, which results in misrepresentation of the person's abilities and competencies
7.	Willingness to give interpretation and guidance to test takers in counseling situations
8.	Not making photocopies of copyrighted materials
9.	Refraining from using homemade answer sheets that do not align properly with scoring keys
10.	Establishing rapport with examinees to obtain accurate scores
11.	Refraining from answering questions from test takers in greater detail than the test manual permits
12.	Not assuming that a norm for one job applies to a different job (and not assuming that norms for one group automatically apply to other groups)

Figure 14–1
Twelve minimum competencies for proper use of tests.
Source: Moreland, K. L., Eyde, L. D., Robertson, G. J., Primoff, E. S., & Most, R. B. (1995). Assessment of test user qualifications: A research-based measurement procedure. *American Psychologist, 50,* 16.

inappropriately high level of confidence in their scores and profiles. A third example pertains to the appropriate use of norms. Testers who fail to examine the normative bases of their instruments may find that the tests they are using are not appropriate for all examinees. For example, asking an undergraduate student from Taiwan who reports difficulty adjusting to college and to the American culture to take a standardized measure of adjustment may result in very misleading information. (If no persons from Taiwan were included in the normative sample the test has not been shown to provide accurate information for such persons.) Simply stated, college students from Taiwan or any other non-Western culture may be completely unfamiliar with the culture and contexts in which the questions are presented. If life experiences relevant to an individual are not fairly represented on an instrument, then that instrument should not be used to make diagnostic evaluations of any importance (*cf.* Moreland et al., 1995).

Professional Competence

Professional training is only one of many broad areas of importance that bear directly on the ethics of testing and service delivery. Once a person leaves school and enters the world as a trained human service provider, it is assumed that the person is providing services that are in concert with sound ethical and legal standards, that the instruments used are based on sound scientific principles, and that the test-related decisions represent an integration of science, law, and ethics.

As you might imagine, there is a wide range of services available to people who are in need of educational and psychological assistance. Unfortunately, there is an equally wide range of competency levels among the professionals providing such services. People who are in need of educational and psychological services should not have to feel as if they must be vigilant or responsible for evaluating the services received, but such often seems to be the case in the highly competitive ways of the modern era. The notion of *caveat emptor,* "let the buyer beware," may now be as relevant for social science service delivery as it is in business and industry. Consequently, it is important for people to be protected from those who cannot perform the service competently. Because services are provided to the most vulnerable segments of the population (e.g., children, older adults, persons with disabilities), extra care and attention to the regulation of these services is absolutely essential.

The challenge to being a competent human service provider necessitates that the professional adhere to a number of broad-based expectations, but the tenets supporting the role of tester are relatively straightforward. For example, both the American Counseling Association (1995) and the American Psychological Association (2002) have devoted entire sections of their ethical standards manuals to evaluation and assessment. First and foremost among the two associations assessment standards is the issue of professional competence. More specifically, practicing professionals must respect the boundaries of their training and not administer or interpret tests for which they have not been trained (ACA Standard E.2[a], 1995; APA Standard 2.01[a], 2002). Further, it is understood that all assessments occur only within the context of a professionally defined relationship.

Second, service providers who conduct evaluations, and certainly those who design instruments that serve as the basis for those evaluations, are required to be sufficiently well grounded in the basics of psychometrics—from simple reliability and validity issues to more complex theories of measurement—that they can interpret test results in a competent, professional manner. Examiners who are unable to interpret the technical portions of the manuals for the tests they use are generally unable to differentiate good tests from bad tests. Additionally, those who overlook the research underpinnings of their instruments greatly devalue the scientific merits of both their efforts and the results of their evaluations.

Interpretation of assessment results represents a third important area of ethical emphasis. The competent evaluator is one who can readily blend the principles of psychometrics with other situational factors affecting the testing process. That is, competent professionals provide services "only within the boundaries of their competence, based on their education, training, supervised experience, consultation, study, or professional experience" (APA Standard 2.01[a], 2002). When the examinee's characteristics are such that the examiner's ability to interpret test results fairly and without reservation is compromised, then the examiner should withdraw from the evaluative process and refer the client to someone else for whom interpretation and service delivery is not compromised. There is a rapidly growing body of literature on diverse and cross-cultural strategies for assessment that professionals may consult if interested (Dana, 1990; Lonner, 1985).

A fourth issue very much related to assessment and evaluation lies within test scoring and interpretation services. Professionals sometimes contract with outside agencies to score their protocols, often the very test companies they bought the instruments from in the first place. Despite the fact that someone else, in this case, the test scoring service, is performing the scoring part of the evaluation, the test examiner remains responsible for the quality and efficacy of the entire testing operation, including the interpretation of the results (APA Standard 9.09[c], 2002). Examiners who defer to computer-generated recommendations of a test profile without verifying the appropriateness for their clients are clearly at odds with most organizations' codes of ethics, and even more important are at odds with best practices in the respective disciplines of education and psychology.

Validity of Clinical Opinion

The notion that validity is a function of a test, only, is dying slowly. With test publishers being more conscientious than ever about putting a wealth of validity information in their test manuals, it may indeed seem as if the validity of the testing process resides primarily in the instrument—but such is not the case. Increasingly, clinicians are being held accountable for their decisions, decisions that relate in part to the instrument but also in a very large part, to their own clinical acumen.

According to Matarazzo (1990), society now wants firmer evidence of the validity of opinions offered by psychologists. In support of this, he notes that "attorneys, juries, and judges are asking psychologists in the courtroom for considerably more evidence than our clinic or hospital colleagues have requested [in the past] to demonstrate that the instruments and techniques used, in part, in forming their clinical opinions are valid ones" (p. 1002). Despite the sobering and challenging tone of Matarazzo's position, he also provides evidence to suggest that the diagnostic consistency of clinicians' evaluations has increased substantially during the past several decades, from little to no interclinician reliability in the 1950s to the very high indices of the 1980s.

A major reason for the increase in estimated reliability over the years has to do with improvements in diagnosis and classification of disorders and disabilities. Brodsky (1991) contends that clinicians' ability to diagnose, classify, and treat a person in need of psychological services stems directly from their depth of understanding about the theoretical and scientific foundations of their opinions. In short, if they have a broader conceptual understanding of what they are doing they can answer the question "How do you know what you know?"

Is it possible that the science of psychology has advanced to the point that clinical opinions, if properly measured, are as accurate and useful as other, less subjective methods? Meehl (1986) and his colleagues (Dawes, Faust, & Meehl, 1989) don't believe so. For them, the subjectivity of clinical opinions causes them to fall far short of other, more data-based approaches. They provide several reasons for their conclusion:

- Overconfidence in one's clinical judgment
- Difficulty in separating valid from invalid variables of influence
- Tendency to overattend to factors that support one's hypothesis and to underattend to contradictory ones
- Influence of situational factors on the decision-making process (e.g., fatigue, experience, ordering of relevant variables).

In the opinion of Dawes et al. (1989) formula-based decision rules have proven to be far more reliable and valid than clinical opinions alone. Data-based equations for predicting human behaviors and outcomes not only have their place in psychological service delivery but can and should be used to improve the human condition. To do otherwise is unprofessional, unethical, and theoretically questionable (Meehl, 1986). Simply stated, clinicians should allow more science into the practice of the science of the mind, and this means, in part, more sophisticated use of the results of assessment devices.

Wood, Garb, Lilienfeld, and Nezworski (2002) recommend the use of structured interviews to aid in diagnostic decision making. When clinicians' diagnoses are compared with diagnoses based on structured interviews, it becomes clear that clinicians underdiagnose a range of mental disorders including mental retardation, major depressive disorder, personality disorders, substance abuse disorders, and anxiety disorders (obsessive-compulsive disorder and posttraumatic stress disorder). Paradoxically, in some circumstances clinicians tend to "overpathologize" clients, perceiving them as more psychopathological than they really are, and some popular psychological tests have a tendency to overpathologize clients, e.g., the Rorschach (Shaffer, Erdberg, & Haroian, 1999; Wood et al., 2002). When structured interviews are used, it is more likely that clinicians will adhere to diagnostic criteria, interrater reliability will be at least fair, and construct validity is at least fair to good for many structured interviews. Wood et al. recommend that psychologists increase their use of structured interviews in making diagnoses and that clinical graduate programs place greater emphasis on training students to use such interviews.

PROFESSIONAL AND SCIENTIFIC RESPONSIBILITY

Standards for Educational and Psychological Testing

Educational and psychological testing occurs in a variety of contexts and across a broad range of settings. Because of the great disparity in the origin, design, construction, and use of tests, three large governing bodies in education and psychology have jointly composed a set of standards to "promote the sound and ethical use of tests and to provide a basis for evaluating the quality of testing practices" (American Educational Research Association [AERA], APA, National Council on Measurement in Education [NCME], 1999, p. 1). This document, officially known as the *Standards for Educational and Psychological Testing,* which we will refer to as the *Standards* manual, represents the sixth in a series of publications that originated in 1954 to provide developers and users of tests with assistance in evaluating the technical adequacy of their instruments for educational and psychological assessment. The intent of the *Standards* manual is to promote the sound and ethical use of tests and to provide criteria for the evaluation of tests, testing practices, and the effects of test use. Unlike the 1985 standards, which designated each standard as "primary" (to be met by all tests before operational use), "secondary" (desirable, but not feasible in certain situations), or "conditional" (importance varies with application), the current *Standards* manual does not continue this practice of designating levels of importance. Instead, all standards are considered important in the context to which they apply.

This revision of the *Standards* manual is organized into three parts. Additionally, it contains more extensive introductory text material than its predecessor. We recommend that anyone who routinely engages in any form of testing—from test design and implementation to assessment and evaluation—obtain a copy of the *Standards* manual and become familiar with the guidelines.

Test Construction, Evaluation, and Documentation

This section of the *Standards* manual contains standards for validity; reliability and errors of measurement; test development and revision; scaling, norming, and score comparability; test administration, scoring, and reporting; and supporting documentation for tests. According to the *Standards* manual, "validity is the most fundamental consideration in developing and evaluating tests" (AERA et al., 1999, p. 9). The *Standards* manual addresses the different types of validity evidence needed to support test use. In addition, standards on reliability and errors of measurement address the issue of consistency of test scores. Although the *Standards* manual supports standardized procedures, it recognizes special situations that arise in which modifications of the procedures may be advisable or legally mandated, e.g., "persons of different backgrounds, ages, or familiarity with testing may need nonstandard modes of test administration or a more comprehensive orientation to the testing process" (AERA et al., 1999, p. 61). Standards for the development and revision of formal, published instruments, an often overlooked area of importance, describe criteria important for scale construction.

Fairness and Testing

This section of the *Standards* manual contains standards on fairness and bias; the rights and responsibilities of test takers; testing individuals of diverse linguistic backgrounds; and testing individuals with disabilities. It emphasizes the importance of fairness in all aspects of testing and assessment. "The fair treatment of test takers is not only a matter of equity, but also promotes validity and reliability of the inferences made from the test performance" (AERA et al., 1999, p. 85). Special attention to issues related to individuals of diverse linguistic backgrounds or with disabilities may be needed when developing, administering, scoring, interpreting, and making decisions based on test scores.

Testing Applications

This final section includes standards involving general responsibilities of test users; psychological testing and assessment; educational testing and assessment; testing in employment and credentialing; and testing in program evaluation and public policy. In addition to emphasizing the ethical obligations of test users, the *Standards* manual addresses specific issues related to psychological, educational, employment, program evaluation, and other specific applications of test results.

RESPECT FOR THE RIGHTS AND DIGNITY OF OTHERS

Privacy and Confidentiality

Client welfare should be the primary concern of all clinicians using psychological tests. Concerns about individual privacy have increased steadily during the past few years. The widespread and sometimes irresponsible use of databases, in which information about individuals can be stored and quickly accessed, has sensitized people to procedures that constitute unwarranted invasions into the private lives of others. Oftentimes, in order to receive psychological services through their employers' insurance companies, people waive the right of privacy of their medical or psychological records, including psychological test results.

It is important for educational and psychological service providers to distinguish between *privacy,* which refers to the degree of access others have to one's body or behavior, and *confidentiality,* which refers to the degree of access others have to information given voluntarily from one person to another (U.S. Department of Health and Human Services, 1993). From an evaluator's standpoint, when is it reasonable to demand such information? Additionally, under what circumstances may a societal need to know override individuals' rights to keep their own secrets, that is, their rights to privacy?

Presenting oneself for educational or psychological evaluation can be a most humbling experience, at times even intimidating. Answering questions about highly personal aspects of one's life is never done in a lighthearted or superficial manner. Consequently, highly personal questions should never be asked in anything other than an equally serious and humane way. It is well to ask under what circumstances and to whom such revelations should be made. While the personal exposure of information on an achievement test may be less revealing than that called for on a personality measure, both types of measures call for information that most people would probably rather not share with others. A number of questions are pertinent to any discussion of ethics in assessment.

Who Will Benefit from the Information Collected?

When assessment data are collected to provide specific help to an individual, objections will likely be minimal, particularly when the testing occurs at the request of the individual or parent. Examples of this arise when classroom tests are given and used to identify children in need of further academic assistance or when diagnostic tests are given as a prelude to program planning. The objective of the testing may be to provide instruction targeted at the level at which these children function, and in such a case, the children should benefit from a program that proceeds at their pace. But, children may also be identified as "second class" in some way if they do not make it into the top group. In such cases, the educational benefits for the children should be made clear to them and their parents before the testing is undertaken.

A second relevant example arises when a student goes to a counselor for help with personal or career concerns, and inventories are used to provide both the counselor and the client with information. In each of these cases the individual being evaluated is considered to be the direct beneficiary of the testing. At times, however, the benefits of the assessment flow indirectly back to the examinee, such as when the person being evaluated is a member of a class of persons on whom aggregate data are needed. The collection of achievement test data either to help guide school district personnel in the allocation of their resources or to help school personnel better understand their student body are examples of situations in which the examinees are the secondary beneficiaries of test data collected.

Licensure exams for practicing professionals (e.g., counselors, physicians, psychologists, teachers) constitute a third example. While information contained on most licensure exams does not benefit the test taker specifically, it is a gauge of general professional competence and a measure of likelihood for effective service delivery on the part of the service provider. Professionals taking such exams are direct beneficiaries only in the sense that they gain access to a professional practice; the primary beneficiary in this case is considered to be the people who request the professional's services and society in general.

How Will the Information Be Used?

Relevance of the information must be established prior to any formal assessment. Once relevance has been demonstrated, there must be compelling evidence that the test scores will provide information that will lead to correct decisions regarding service delivery. For example, to aid in determining client care (e.g., locus of treatment, type of treatment), ACA ethical guidelines state that "tests and other assessment techniques should be carefully selected and appropriately used" (ACA, Standard E.5[a], 1995). Even when the goal of assessment is worthwhile, there is little point to gathering evidence for which the likelihood for impact is questionable or small, with little hope for improvement in the decision-making process. Conversely, the more relevant the assessment information, the more justification there is in calling on the individual to provide it.

If a parent suspects the presence of attention-deficit disorder and takes the child to a counselor or school psychologist for evaluation, then the service provider gathers only the data needed to confirm or disconfirm this hypothesis. If secondary concerns emerge during the course of the evaluation, as may be the case for some children with emotional disorders or other learning disabilities, then additional evaluations may also be required. In either case, however, psychologists should gather only the information deemed "sufficient to substantiate findings" (APA, Standard 9.01[a], 2002). Gathering additional information to shed light on other unofficial hunches or because someone is already taking other tests should never occur.

A question very much related to proper use may be "What will happen to the assessment data once they are collected?" The issue here pertains to physical storage and handling of assessment-related information. If there is a risk of revealing confidential information to others, there is also a risk of having assessment information stored in such a way that others, whose interests are less direct or less noble, may also have access to it. An example from the contemporary press would be the disclosure of someone's personal medical history and records to insurance companies who, unknown to the person, disseminate the information to other organizations for managed-care decisions and cost–benefit analyses. The APA's Code of Conduct requires that when client information is included in databases that are available to others for whom recipient consent has not been given by the receiver of the psychological services, "coding or other techniques [should] be used to avoid the inclusion of personal identifiers" (APA, Standard 6.02[b], 2002). Within the areas of education and psychology, a similar case can be made for information that is archived for research purposes.

How Personal Is the Information Being Sought?

Some questions are perceived as much more invasive than others. In a study about privacy and personnel selection, Rosenbaum (1971) asked which items people felt were an invasion of their privacy. Five broad factors were identified from among a total item pool of 66 items: family background and influences, personal history, interests and values, financial management, and social adjustment. Two areas in particular, family background and influences and financial management, were viewed as the most invasive by 49% and 52% of the respondents, respectively.

As long as information is general and ambiguous, or when information is anonymous, as is the case many public surveys, people are not overly concerned about others' access to their information. However, when anonymity is not assured, for example, when personally identifiable information is available with written answers to certain questions, and particularly when the test or inventory contains highly sensitive information, people are justified in having concern about the confidentiality of their information. It is quite common for personality inventories to request information about attitudes, interests, and preferences in the areas of politics, religion, finances, and other personal matters. Consider the following questions:

- Do you have trouble making new friends?
- Did you ever want to run away from home?
- Do you sometimes have thoughts that are too bad to talk about?

These questions certainly ask the individual to make public—to whomever may have access to the responses—some quite personal aspects of his or her inner life. Although information on these topics can be very revealing, more dramatic examples are those questions pertaining to highly sensitive areas such as sexual behavior, illicit drug use, and matters of the law. Adequate provision for the security of this information is absolutely essential. Data should be available only to those who need it for legitimate decision-making purposes.

Some psychological tests can result in more than a feeling of invasion of privacy. Some tests used for diagnosis or treatment planning may assess psychological symptoms that may evoke an emotional or even physiological response from the test taker during or after taking the test. Psychological service providers need to be aware of possible reactions to the test-taking process and adequately prepare test takers prior to administering the test. Additionally, allowing time after the test to debrief and process the test taker's feelings is recommended.

Autonomy and Self-Determination

Respecting a person's right to autonomy and self-determination means respecting their right to self-governance and independent decision making. Additionally, it means respecting the person's right to deal effectively with the ambiguities of everyday living, particularly as it relates to actions on their own behalf. One way to minimize the offensiveness of any invasion of privacy is to conduct an assessment only after obtaining the **informed consent** of the person for whom an evaluation is needed.

Informed consent implies that the person to be tested has been told what information will be collected, why it is being collected, and how it will be used. It also implies that the consenter is competent to understand what information is being sought and that the person has the right to decide whether to participate or not. According to Porter (1995), informed consent is more of a process than a one-time occurrence. It is a means of keeping an examinee informed of what is going on throughout the entire evaluation and perhaps even after the evaluation has been completed. The whole notion of informed consent rests on three premises:

1. The information provided to the examinee is complete and allows for a fully informed decision.
2. The individual has the ability to comprehend the information presented.
3. The decision to participate is made voluntarily and without duress or undue influence.

All persons who present themselves for testing and psychodiagnostic evaluation should be presumed competent unless otherwise demonstrated. Meeting these conditions may be difficult when the consenter is of limited ability or is from a background different from that of the person soliciting the information. The term *informed consent* is generally reserved for those who are of legal age and have no mental disability that precludes them from understanding what is being requested and for giving truly informed consent. For persons who do not meet these criteria, such as children and adults with mental disabilities, consent is requested from a parent or legal guardian (ACA, Standard G.2[e], 1995, p. 17). Even in these cases, though, permission to evaluate should also be sought from the minor or person with disabilities—out of respect for the person and for the sheer practicality of trying to gather information from someone who has not consented. In this case, however, the term **assent** is used. APA ethical codes state that psychological service providers "inform persons with questionable capacity to consent about the nature and purpose of the proposed assessment services, using language that is reasonably understandable to the person being assessed" (APA, Standard 9.03[b], 2002). A third term, **coconsenter,** is used when a person has the legal right to consent to evaluation but for one reason or another the consent of another adult is deemed important to the decision-making process.

Informed consent raises problems for both the person seeking the information and for the person providing it. For the person being tested, the right to agree to formal evaluation must be made without undue influence. That is, unless there are extenuating circumstances requiring someone's participation, such as a court-ordered evaluation or an impending medical emergency, consent must be completely voluntary. College students who want to earn extra credit in a given course, job applicants who desperately want to be viewed positively on preemployment testing, and prisoners who believe that their privileges may depend on their willingness to cooperate are examples of three groups of people who may be under considerable pressure to consent to whatever evaluation procedures are requested and for whom true consent may actually be compromised.

Two problems with informed consent often emerge in educational and psychological testing. The first pertains to the need for informed consent within the context of **deception,** that is, the need to mask the true intent of an evaluation to get accurate results. Deception occurs when fully informed consent is likely to result in an alteration of behaviors or responses to questions during testing. In such cases, it is essential that the purpose of the assessment is fully justified and that the participants are informed of the true purpose, generally referred to as **debriefing,** as soon after participation as possible. In the case of a research study, review of the study design by other researchers is usually required, to verify the need for the deception. The second problem stems from the reality that requiring active, signed consent invites the possibility of **dissent,** a refusal that might never have been contemplated if acquiescence had been taken for granted. In projects where sample characteristics of experimentally accessible populations are so important (e.g., norming tests, surveying of abilities or attitudes), refusals and dropouts are a serious problem and often threaten the validity of the entire project.

A third concern, which is related to the prior two but retains a sense of importance all its own, is that of subjecting the person to physical or psychological risk. Testing in the social sciences does not usually pose much of a risk to test takers; however, formal testing does induce some level of anxiety in most persons. The greater the consequences, the greater the probability of anxiety. Personality inventories may pose another type of risk, that of requiring people to respond to questions that describe important yet highly revealing aspects of themselves. Individual reactions to the tests may very from minor anxiety to psychological or physiological distress.

Examiners must acknowledge that for test takers, taking tests and receiving their results may at times constitute hazards that go beyond those of everyday living. The problem for examiners is to judge the severity of the hazard and to balance it against the countervailing benefits to the person tested.

A somewhat different type of risk is that which may result from classifying individuals. In an effort to simplify the highly complex behaviors and personalities of others, many people resort to using labels. This labeling carries with it implications which may influence how people are viewed and treated in the educational and social service systems (e.g., mentally retarded, emotionally disturbed). When people are responded to as if they are representatives of a broader class, and particularly if the traits have little or no basis in reality, these labels deprive the person and other members of the class of their individuality and worth as individuals.

Beneficence

Treating people in an ethical, professional manner means more than simply protecting them from unnecessary risks; it means taking the necessary steps to secure their well-being (ACA, Standard A.1[a], 1995, p. 2). As indicated previously, the notion of educational and psychological service providers protecting the rights, dignity, and well-being of those in their charge is an ethical mandate; however, in today's world of automated assessments, profile analyses, and computer-generated reports, the well-being of the client sometimes seems to be less important than completion of the task on schedule.

According to The National Commission for the Protection of Human Subjects of Biomedical and Behavioral Research (1979), a commission established jointly by the National Institutes of Health, the Public Health Service, and the Department of Health and Human Services to specifically codify standards for the ethical treatment of human subjects involved in such research, the well-being of others extends far beyond common courtesy and thoughtfulness to that of a moral, ethical, and professional obligation. Built into this obligation is a twofold expression: Do no harm, and maximize the benefits while minimizing the risks. The difficulty for behavioral and biomedical scientists today lies in the need to expose people to some degree of risk to avoid a greater harm at a later date.

Not all persons needing educational and psychological services are capable of understanding the risks and benefits associated with an evaluation or an experimental treatment program. Of those who are capable of understanding the risks and benefits involved, not all are capable of acting on their own behalf. For these reasons, the government has identified several groups of people who are considered to be particularly vulnerable and for whom special protections are afforded: children, prisoners, pregnant women, persons with mental disabilities, and persons who are believed to be economically or educationally disadvantaged (Federal Policy for the Protection of Human Subjects, 1991). In work involving individuals in any of these categories, the benefits of the evaluations must be direct and the risks immediately justifiable in light of all possible alternatives.

SOCIAL RESPONSIBILITY

Test use takes place in a social context and has particular social consequences. As Cole and Moss (1989) and Messick (1989) point out, testing is also a matter of social policy. There is relatively little question that tests can improve efficiency and productivity in educational and occupational contexts, but at what cost and using which criteria? The formula for determining social worth varies from person to person and group to group, based on a number of complicated factors. Psychometric research alone cannot determine whether the cost in relation to one type of value is justified by the gain in another. That judgment must be made by society, its members, and the people responsible for establishing social policy. Irrespective of the approach or resolution, however, two questions remain to be answered in every social policy question pertaining to testing: "Is testing fair?" and "Is testing good for society?"

Distributive Justice

Let's first address the issue of fairness in regard to testing. Those who construct tests or teach about tests generally believe that the use of tests will permit, though certainly not guarantee, better, wiser, and more socially appropriate decisions. Despite the fact that testing is most often carried out to achieve positive outcomes both for the individual and for the larger society, it is sometimes difficult for members of the general public to appreciate how a system built on discrimination (i.e., discrimination between individuals of differing ability levels) can ensure egalitarian principles. In this section, we will consider those positive outcomes. In a later section we will present some of the more subtle factors influencing the sociopolitical context within which testing occurs.

The notion of distributive social justice, in this case, implies the principle of fairness in that the benefits of educational and psychological services to people, for people, and by people are distributed in an equitable and impartial way. As many members of our educational and social service delivery systems are so keenly aware, social injustices occur across a wide range of possibilities, from no or limited access to current service delivery systems to an undue burden imposed within the respective service delivery systems (The National Commission, 1979).

One commonly held view of how tests can advance egalitarian principles by using instruments known for their discriminative abilities is through objective standards of performance. People generally rise to meet the standards that are set for them. When standards such as minimum proficiency criteria are maintained for all students, those who are initially unable to reach the preestablished levels of proficiency soon raise their achievement levels to meet the standards for success, particularly if their efforts are supported by the larger society. One example is from the minimum competency testing movement in the state of Florida. When passing an objective test of academic skills became a requirement for graduation from a community college, the failure rate was initially much higher among minority students than among majority students. However, with instruction focused on the skills measured by the tests, the minority students soon raised their achievement levels to those required by the tests, improving the success rates dramatically (Gottfredson & Sharf, 1988).

Social Benefits of Testing

The second question, "Is testing good?" remains equally difficult to answer in a manner that would be applicable to all people and under all conditions. To those who construct the tests, the most immediate response is yes—but only in qualified hands and only for designated purposes. Consequently, there are a number of social problems at the individual, civic, and national levels for which testing can—and frequently does—play a constructive role. According to Messick (1993), and under the rubric of **unified validity,** the worthiness of a test cannot be separated from its use and the inferences that result; that is, the testing process and the people who direct it must offer their community appropriate, meaningful, and useful score-based inferences.

Medical training is an example of a scarce and heavily subsidized social resource that is helped by standardized testing. Providing the necessary faculty and laboratories for training medical students places a costly demand on society. It becomes important to society that those who are given the opportunity to receive this training be people who are likely to learn the skills and, thus, succeed in the specialty for which they are being trained. The field of medicine has seen some very interesting developments in examinations; these examinations involve assessing not only the individual's mastery of the content but also his or her ability to demonstrate mastery in diagnosing individual cases and in prescribing proper treatments. In one such examination, a computer is used to simulate a patient. The medical student taking the examination can ask initial questions, call for various tests, and ask more questions based on the results of answers to previous questions before diagnosing the case (Fredericksen, 1986). Obviously, no test can provide a perfect assessment of performance in a professional or occupational specialty, but a test can provide one important safeguard against the individual who is uninformed, incompetent, or inept. The health of society depends on it.

A markedly different example of the importance of efficient use of social resources lies in the production of durable goods. If a worker is ineffective in using expensive equipment for industrial production, this inefficiency represents a social cost, one that is perhaps less recognized as a general concern to society than is the allocation of positions in medical schools. However, over the years, improved efficiency in operating our whole production establishment has been one of the goals of personnel testing. The economic gains from applying selection procedures, even ones with modest validity, can be substantial; Schmidt (1988b) cites estimates that run into the tens of billions of dollars annually. Production losses of such a magnitude would seriously affect the prices and competitiveness of U.S. products in world markets.

Education is an expensive enterprise, and its productivity is not easy to assess. While performance on achievement measures provides an indication of the yield from an educational investment, this performance is a partial indication at best. Attention in recent years has been centered on educational standards and accountability, but good assessments of the educational system's more general output (e.g., socialization and critical thinking) are lacking. Thus, it becomes increasingly important to guide the educational enterprise so that it can be as effective as possible. Testing can assist with this function.

As indicated in Chapter 7, testing has a role in appraising the outcomes of education, particularly in evaluating curricular innovations at the individual, school, and district levels. For example, during the past few decades, much research has been directed toward the notion of learning styles, implying that information about a specific individual can help to provide an educational treatment that is appropriate and even beneficial for a specific child. To date, the amount of verifiable information on the relationship between learning styles and educational treatment is disappointingly limited. The basic premise does, however, remain attractive. With the increasing availability of microcomputers in classrooms and recent advances in computer-assisted evaluation and instruction, truly individualized learning programs may actually become possible.

One beneficial characteristic of tests is that they do not prejudge the abilities of any of their respondents; that is, they characterize the work of each person as an individual, not as a member of any particular group. The test has no preconceptions about who should do well or who should do poorly. Although total reliance on objective measures in most educational and psychological contexts is neither possible nor desirable, objective evidence can temper the natural human tendency to prefer members of one's own social or ethnic group and result in fairer treatment for all (see Ryanen, 1988). In this case, tests may actually be a liberating force that can help open up opportunities to talented individuals who, because of their group membership, might otherwise have been denied such possibilities.

Another benefit to which testing can contribute is the store of potentially useful knowledge about individuals. The sciences of psychology and education, inasmuch as education can be considered a science, depend on knowing how human beings develop and the factors that influence the critically important growth processes. If we wish to study the conditions that favor human growth and development, we must be able to measure the product of that development—often by some type of test. If we wish to map the factors that foster hostility of one group toward another group in society, we must also be able to measure that hostility—probably with some type of test or scale. With all of their shortcomings, tests of one sort or another will continue to play a central role in research on human growth, development, and learning.

Maximizing the Positive

We have tried to make it clear in the previous sections that although there are legitimate concerns about the uses of tests and test results, there are significant advantages to be gained from the practice of educational and psychological testing. Regrettably, not all of the decisions that emanate from evaluations will be the correct ones. Yet, choices have to be made and actions have to be taken based on the best available evidence. The decision to pursue one option generally implies a decision to disregard another, less appealing alternative. The best information available at the time should be weighed in light of all relevant factors. To do otherwise would diminish the importance of the testing process. We give here six maxims that subtly influence the decisions to use tests in a productive, beneficial way.

Examine and Be Clear About All Values Involved

Most decisions, whether they relate to one individual or to a whole class or category of individuals, involve a complex of interacting and competing values. The decision to place a student in a special class might mean more efficient learning for that child and a higher ultimate level of achievement, but the decision might also result, to a degree, in the student's social isolation from the mainstream of the school. The decision of a student to apply for admission to a particular law school might involve such satisfying consequences as personal prestige and future economic benefits, if admitted, but might result in such costs as the loss of self-esteem or missed opportunities at other institutions if the candidate is rejected or fails to meet the demands of the program. A personnel selection system may achieve benefits for the employer, such as money saved through shorter training programs, reduced personnel turnover, and higher worker productivity, but at a cost to the larger society in reduced employment opportunities for young persons from the inner city. Choices would exist for individuals and society whether tests had been invented or not, and the decision to ignore the possibility of alternatives is itself a decision. Only as the competing values are recognized and weighed can society decide how tests can contribute to better decisions.

Recognize That Test Scores Are Only Indicators or Signs

A score on a mathematics test is an indicator of mathematics ability, not the mathematics ability itself. A score on a scholastic aptitude test is one partial indicator of readiness to undertake school learning. The sign is at best an imperfect representation of reality, but the underlying reality is only accessible through the signs that it gives. We become aware that a person has a fever through a thermometer, or more crudely, through a hot and flushed face, but neither the thermometer nor the person's physical appearance is itself the fever. All measurement is more or less indirect, but when distorting physical, cultural, or social factors intervene, the significance of the indicator may become modified or blurred. Proper interpretation of the measurement requires a sensitivity to possible distortions.

Recognize Test Results As Only One Type of Descriptive Information

The key words in this statement are *one* and *descriptive*. In any type of decision, many other types of information are relevant, in addition to test scores. A score for the Stanford-Binet or the WISC-III may provide one item of information useful for prescribing a learning program for a poor reader, but an assessment of visual abilities, information about home circumstances, or knowledge about interests and hobbies may provide other equally relevant data. And, the ability test score can do no more than describe one aspect of the person's current functioning. Alone, it does not tell why the person performs in a particular way, nor does it reveal what causal relationships that performance has, for example, to the difficulties the person is having with reading. Test users must always guard against inferring more than is warranted from a test score.

Relate Test Results to Whatever Else Is Known About the Person or Group

Test scores do not exist in a vacuum. A score only gains maximum meaning when it is fitted into a complete and comprehensive constellation of information about the person. This constellation includes information about the cultural context of the individual, family background, personal history, physical and health status, and much, much more. Computers are being programmed to handle and summarize some portions of this information, but even so, there is a very real question of how fully and soundly the human mind can synthesize such a system of information about an individual case. The problem becomes more complex in dealing with substantial numbers of individuals, for example, as is the case with school and employment personnel. Yet, decisions must be made, and the wisest decisions will result when all the available evidence can be weighed, digested, and applied to the problem at hand.

Recognize the Possibilities of Error in All Types of Descriptive Information

We have discussed the measurement error in test scores. We have even pointed out the possibility of gross errors in test administration, scoring, or reporting. The users of test results need continuously to be aware of the approximate nature of any score and to bracket the score, at least mentally, with a band of uncertainty. But it is also true, although perhaps less explicitly recognized, that all the other kinds of information that we have about a person are also subject to error. The teacher's impression of how well Joyce reads, how popular she is with her classmates, or how interested her parents are in her school success are all rough and fallible judgments. The physician's appraisal of Joyce's health or the social worker's characterization of her home environment are both subjective, approximate, and fallible. We always arrive at decisions on the basis of partial and imperfect information, with test scores being imperfect along with everything else. They have the advantage, however, that they are usually more objective than other information and their fallibility has often been carefully studied and quantified.

Acknowledge the Limits of Human Wisdom and Maintain Tentativeness About the Basis for Decisions

We must make decisions, even though we have to make them on the basis of partial and fallible data. We make them as best we can with what wisdom is given to us. Some are tactical day-to-day decisions, such as those made while instructing or guiding a specific child, and the possibility exists of promptly changing direction, on the basis of new information from a continuous monitoring of progress. Other decisions are instrumental decisions that only partially commit one to the future, such as the decision to take mathematics courses because of a tentative commitment to enter an engineering program in college. The tentative nature of such decisions should be recognized; redirection can readily be undertaken in light of future evidence. With some decisions, though, redirection is more difficult than it is for a given student taking mathematics courses, and the decision may have permanent consequences. But for all decisions, no matter what role test results had in guiding them, we should always remember that a given decision might be wrong. The conscientious test user will always strive to minimize this possibility.

CONTROVERSIAL ISSUES IN TESTING

Test Bias

One of the most prevalent themes in popular discussions of testing is that tests are unfair to certain groups. The term used is **bias.** It is often asserted that standardized tests are used to deprive certain groups of access to educational and employment opportunities. To the extent that tests are used mechanically as selection and placement devices, and to the extent that some groups in our society have historically performed less well on tests, tests do become instruments through which access to education and employment is disproportionately barred to members of these groups. The question that must be addressed is whether individuals are unjustly barred and, more generally, what constitutes fair and equitable use of tests for the selection, placement, and classification of individuals.

The issue of bias in testing has probably been the most hotly debated topic relating to educational and psychological measurement during the past few decades. When Congress passed the Civil Rights Act of 1964 (PL 88-352), Title VII of the act expressly prohibited the use of tests for the purpose of employment discrimination based on race, creed, color, sex, or national origin. However, the framers of the act expressly permitted the use of tests for job-related decisions, when test scores could be shown to be related to an individual's level of job performance. Thus, the act required that the test be a valid predictor of job performance for all classes of individuals with whom it was to be used, and a test would be considered unbiased if it gave equally accurate predictions for members from any racial, ethnic, or gender group. Due to the random nature of errors present in any one individual's test scores and the fact that test validity for any particular decision is based on group data, the test score for any individual may be inaccurate, and hence the decision based on that score may be wrong. Assuming that decisions must be made, we may view a test as unbiased if it leads to the same average decision accuracy for the members of all groups with which it is used.

The situation changed dramatically for the use of tests in employment in 1971 when the U.S. Supreme Court, in the case of *Griggs v. Duke Power Company,* held that a test could be presumed to be biased if it gave differential predictions for various groups. This decision, subsequent amendments to the Civil Rights Act of 1964, and various federal administrative directives led to the development of the Uniform Guidelines for Employee Selection Procedures (Equal Employment Opportunity Commission, 1978), which hold that if the members of one group tend to score lower on a particular scale than members of another group, it becomes the responsibility of the employer to demonstrate that the test is a valid predictor of job performance. The principle developed by the Supreme Court in *Griggs* is called **adverse impact;** a demonstration of adverse impact by the plaintiff shifts the burden of proof to the employer to show that discrimination did not occur.

A 1976 suit in Illinois by the Golden Rule Insurance Company against the Educational Testing Service led to one solution to the test bias issue. Golden Rule alleged that differential passing rates for Blacks (52%) and Whites (77%) on the Illinois Insurance Licensure Examination was proof that the test was racially biased. In an out-of-court agreement in 1984, the parties agreed to a revised criterion for selecting items for the examination. The Educational Testing Service agreed to use items for which the success rate for Blacks and Whites differed by no more than 15%. The principle adopted in the Golden Rule case has been used in several other situations, in an effort to equate passing rates on various employment selection tests.

Simply barring the use of tests of aptitude or ability may have unintended consequences. W. B. Allen (1988), a California member of the U.S. Commission on Civil Rights, has described such a situation:

> In the case of Mary Amaya, a California mother, the state refuses to her son [sic] an IQ test on the grounds that it is *protecting* him from bias inherent in the test....
>
> Consider the irony: Mrs. Amaya's son has been recommended for assignment to remedial courses. She believes that he may not require them. In an earlier, less enlightened era, an older son of hers had a similar experience. In that case the IQ test refuted the psychologist's subjective evaluation and the lad was spared a potentially damaging assignment. Mrs. Amaya would like to have such an opportunity for her youngest son, as well. It has been denied.... Thus, a family of at best modest means is placed in a position of having to fight off the entire legal edifice of its state and federal courts in order to guarantee an opportunity for its son. (pp. 368–369)

Quoting the Superintendent of Public Instruction, Allen (1988) notes further that, in California:

> there is no fundamental civil right to be able to take an IQ test. Where such a test may be a means to establish one's eligibility for an opportunity, therefore, it may nevertheless be denied to a black child by the state. (p. 368)

Thus, protection can be a mixed blessing.

A number of other court cases have challenged the use of tests and other objective measures to aid in decision making in education and employment. The challenged procedures have included everything from aptitude and achievement tests to height and strength requirements. Until recently, the courts have tended to find in favor of the plaintiffs and against the tests and objective decision rules. Following is a summary of a 1988 U.S. Supreme Court decision that may indicate a change in direction (*Watson v. Fort Worth Bank and Trust*):

> Seven justices agreed that a statistical disparity is not always sufficient to make out a prima facie case [of discrimination].... In addition, a majority of the justices would require a plaintiff to identify the *specific* decision-making practice being challenged and then prove that this practice *caused* the exclusion of applicants for jobs or promotions because of their membership in a protected group [minority or female]. (Sharf, 1988, p. 242)

Challenges to the use of tests have had the beneficial effect of encouraging test developers to be much more careful in both the selection of test items and in the composition of norm groups. For example, in the preparation of the fourth edition of the Stanford-Binet, the authors used a panel of judges that included members of the larger minority groups to screen items for content that might be gender or race biased before the items were ever tried out. A second panel reviewed the items and item statistics from the initial tryouts to eliminate any items that were clearly biased. Other test developers use similar procedures. However, even with elaborate precautions taken to eliminate bias, differences often remain between the average test performances of different ethnic groups. Consequently, the question of test bias is inextricably bound to test validity. Remember that validity relates to the use that will be made of a test score. A test may be valid for one purpose and not for another. The notion of test bias is really a statement that a particular test is not appropriate for making certain decisions with a given group of individuals.

Truth in Testing

According to Rogers (1995), the criticisms of testing are greatest when information from tests constitutes the major driving force in the decision-making process. Where testing seems to have its greatest impact—and criticism is minimized—is when testing serves as an alternative to other forms of decision making; that is, when the testing process helps reduce the subjectivity of a decision-making process already in place. Instruments used at the beginning of a lengthy decision-making process and considered to be economical, nonintrusive, and yield a high probability of useful information are considered to be good candidates for public acceptance. One such example is the use of preschool screening instruments in community-based child-find programs. These evaluations are generally quick, performed free or at a minimal cost to parents, and usually yield important information about a child's level of development. Consequently, most parents are glad to avail themselves of the testing opportunity, and their use is typically not controversial.

Controversy usually enters when the costs are high and results are open to misinterpretation. In cases where the use of an instrument does not improve the decisions reached by other methods or, worse, when a test complicates the decision-making process, then it is time to reevaluate the rationale for testing in the first place. Consequently, professionals administering tests should be familiar with the basics of decision theory. In decision theory, the predictive accuracy of a decision-making process using a published instrument is formally analyzed on the basis of hits (correct decisions) and misses (incorrect decisions), with special attention given to the particular pattern of misses. Incorrect decisions can result in two ways:

1. **False positives.** People who perform sufficiently well on a test to give the impression that they have the necessary skills for a specific activity. In actuality, they do not have the necessary skills.
2. **False negatives.** People who perform sufficiently poorly on a test to give the impression that they do not have the skills necessary for a specific activity. In actuality, they do have the necessary skills.

Although Anastasi (1988) credits Wald (1950) with formally developing decision theory, and Cronbach and Gleser (1965) with its application to psychological tests, it was actually Taylor and Russell (1939) who laid out the basics of the theory well enough to be mathematically modeled by later researchers. Taylor and Russell were able to demonstrate the interrelationships between rates of selection without the instrument's information (**base rate**), ratio of people surpassing the cutoff score as compared with those who do not surpass the cutoff score (**selection ratio**), ratio of correct decisions to incorrect decisions (**hit rate**), and the instruments' validity coefficients.

Similar to the situation with validity of clinical opinion, generally only the largest and most progressive testing companies provide validity information from studies that use some aspect of decision theory.

In light of the less than perfect reliability of test scores, the occasional day when for irrelevant reasons an individual performs poorly, or the rare occurrence of errors in scoring, score conversion, or score handling, the possibility that a person may be condemned by an erroneous or flawed score is sufficiently real for the counselor or psychologist to wish to give the examinee (or a parent or guardian) an opportunity to see and respond to the score. The response might take the form of a description of mitigating circumstances, a request for a retest, or presentation of other compensating information. In any event, making results available to and perhaps discussing them with the concerned person avoids the impression of star chamber proceedings in which a person is forced to provide information that is otherwise secret or seems to be used in secretive ways—and may also avoid some decision errors that result from errors of measurement or errors in score processing.

Implementing these requirements, as specified in the Family Educational Rights and Privacy Act of 1974 (PL 93-380), has generated some practical problems for schools, yet it does provide a safeguard against the types of faulty test results just mentioned. Another reaction to the secrecy that has surrounded testing in education is the New York State law regarding truth in testing, which was enacted in 1979 in response to the aptitude testing programs of the Educational Testing Service. This law required companies that publish tests administered in the state of New York to do three things:

1. Disclose the results of all test validity studies.
2. Notify all students as to how their scores were calculated (any item weights used and the types of transformations applied) and what the scores mean (what norm groups were used).
3. Provide a copy of test questions, the answer key, and the participant's answers to an examinee who requests them.

One objective of this law was to enable people who felt that their test scores might be inaccurate to check one potential source of error and to rebut their test scores if errors were indeed found. This is a laudable purpose; however, in terms of the quality and economy of measurement, the law has had several adverse consequences. The New York law has resulted in an increase in test development costs; because examinees may have the tests, new items must be written each time a test is given. Hence, because they can be used only once, the validity of a particular set of items is less well established than was the case prior to enactment of the law. The cost of assessment for test users has increased accordingly. Further, it is much more difficult to equate the meaning of scores over a period of years because of the changing nature of the items and scales. It remains to be seen whether the law's potential benefits to individuals will offset the increased costs and losses to the educational system. To date, there have been very few requests for copies of the tests, suggesting that the law may have been unnecessary.

High-Stakes Testing

In the United States, accountability through **high-stakes testing** has become a major issue in the reform of school systems. High-stakes tests include all academic achievement tests that are used to make important decisions about the evaluation of K–12 students, including promotion, retention, and graduation (Paris, 2000). High-stakes tests are also used as an indicator of the educational impact of a school (Thorn & Mulvenon, 2002). A school whose students perform well on these tests may receive financial rewards and be publicly proclaimed a better quality or superior school. Some states rank schools from A to F based on overall achievement test scores with financial rewards contingent on the letter grade the school receives.

Difficult questions arise when tests are used as a sole determinant of a child's progress in school. What accommodations are provided for students who are visually handicapped or in special education classes? What special efforts are dedicated to helping students who fail to pass the tests? Will teachers simply "teach to the test" and focus on preparing students for the tests at the expense of other important educational objectives, such as encouraging creativity and the students' natural curiosity? The concern about high-stakes testing lies in the gap between testing principles and educational realities. The *Standards for Educational and Psychological Testing* present a number of principles that are designed to promote fairness in testing and avoid unintended consequences. They include the following:

- Any decision about a student's continued education, such as retention, tracking, or graduation, should not be based on the results of a single test, but should include other relevant and valid information.
- When test results substantially contribute to decisions made about student promotion or graduation, there should be evidence that the test addresses only the specific or generalized content and skills that students have had an opportunity to learn. For tests that will determine a student's eligibility for promotion to the next grade or for high school graduation, students should be granted, if needed, multiple opportunities to demonstrate mastery of materials through equivalent testing procedures.
- When a school district, state, or some other authority mandates a test, the ways in which the test results are intended to be used should be clearly described. It is also the responsibility of those who mandate the test to monitor its impact, particularly on racial and ethnic-minority students or students of lower socioeconomic status, and to identify and minimize potential negative consequences of such testing.
- Special accommodations for students with limited English proficiency may be necessary to obtain valid test scores. If students with limited English skills are to be tested in English, their test scores should be interpreted in light of their limited English skills.
- Special accommodations may be needed to ensure that test scores are valid for students with disabilities.

It is important to remember that no single test is valid for all purposes or for all students. School officials using such tests must ensure that students are tested on a curriculum that they have had a fair opportunity to learn, so that certain subgroups of students, such as racial and ethnic minority students or students with a disability or limited English proficiency, are not systematically excluded or disadvantaged by the test or the test-taking conditions (APA, 2001). APA ethical guidelines state that psychologists "use assessment methods that are appropriate to an individual's language preference and competence, unless the use of an alternative language is relevant to the assessment issues" (APA, Standard 9.02[c], 2002).

Internet-Based Psychological Testing

The Internet contains a variety of psychological services for both professionals and consumers including information banks and resources, psychological information, self-help sites, and now, psychological testing. The use of personal computers for psychological testing is not a new procedure; however, Internet-based psychological testing has brought about ethical concerns from professionals. Along with professional psychological tests, a huge number of mostly unre-searched, popular psychological tests related to different diagnostic areas are available on the Internet, including tests of intelligence, aptitudes, personality, emotional states, attitudes, inter-personal relationships, vocational interests, and more. Although Internet-based testing has several advantages, including highly accessible tests, convenience, speed, almost immediate and errorless scoring, and cost effectiveness (Barak, 1999), the nature of Internet-based psychologi-cal tests makes them quite questionable in terms of ethical standards. The following are examples of potential ethical problems (Barak & English, 2002):

- The lack of a clearly defined professional relationship
- The use of tests or test information by unqualified persons
- The possibility of using tests that have not been developed under appropriate scientific procedures or by qualified persons
- The possible lack of full information on reliability, validity, and other important information on tests
- The limited ability to use professional judgment in the interpretation of tests
- The use of outdated or obsolete tests
- The limited ability to explain test results to test takers
- The problem of test takers' consent
- The problem of ensuring confidentiality of individuals' test results.

Although numerous researchers have addressed concerns related to offering psychologi-cal assessment over the Internet, specific ethical codes related to Internet testing have not yet been proposed. Internet-related ethical guidelines are available today from the APA (http://www.apa.org/ethics/code2002.html) and the National Board for Certified Counselors (http://www.nbcc.org/depts/ethicsmain.htm), yet both fail to specifically address the issue of psy-chological testing on the Internet. Until the appropriate ethical codes are developed, it is impor-tant for psychological service providers to be aware of the issues involved in order to make better professional and ethical judgments in either using or recommending the use of Internet-based psychological tests.

SUMMARY

The use of tests in education and psychology has faced a number of challenges in recent years. Tests have been viewed as invading the privacy of the people who take them, as forcing people to reveal information about themselves that proves detrimen-tal, and as exposing people to unnecessary psycho-logical risks. The most strident criticism of tests has been that they are biased against minority groups and women. Both the courts and government agen-cies have taken an active role in controlling the use and abuse of tests. The psychological profession in general and testing companies in particular have attempted to reduce possible harmful side effects of testing programs, both by setting standards for appropriate test use and by reducing bias in the scores. Because tests can help to achieve many indi-vidual and social benefits, in the form of better deci-sions, it is important that tests be used wisely and carefully. When tests are used properly for their intended purposes, they can be a powerful ally in improving the human condition.

QUESTIONS AND EXERCISES

1. Why do professional organizations such as the American Counseling Association and the American Psychological Association have published codes of ethics? Why do both of these codes have entire subsections devoted specifically to testing?

2. The Joint Committee on Testing Practices has identified the most likely areas for misuse in the administration of standardized tests. Identify and explain the three most likely areas of misuse presented in this chapter.

3. What is meant by the phrase *validity of clinical opinion*?

4. Truth in testing laws have had a profound impact on the manner in which standardized tests are developed and administered. What is the major objective of such legislation? How has this legislation changed the ways in which tests are administered today?

5. Briefly distinguish between privacy and confidentiality. How serious is the problem of invasion of one's privacy? What controls are in place to ensure test takers' right to privacy?

6. Examiners who routinely test people afforded special protections under the law (e.g., children and youth, cultural minorities, people with disabilities) must be able to distinguish among several related terms: consent, coconsent, and assent. Briefly explain how these three terms are similar and how they are different.

7. What is meant by the term *unified validity*? How does the definition of this term differ from that of other types of validity used previously in this book?

8. Some potential situations involve the use of tests where the rights of one individual or group come into conflict with the rights of another individual or group. Identify two such situations and list the factors that support the claims of each side in the argument.

9. What are the potential ethical dilemmas associated with Internet-based psychological tests? What ethical codes would you suggest to appropriately deal with these dilemmas?

SUGGESTED READINGS

Dawes, R. M., Faust, D., & Meehl, P. E. (1989). Clinical versus actuarial judgment. *Science, 243,* 1668–1674.

Eyde, L. D., Robertson, G. J., Krug, S. E., Moreland, K. L., Robertson, A. G., Shewan, C. M, et al. (1993). *Responsible test use: Case studies for assessing human behavior.* Washington, DC: American Psychological Association.

Grodin, M. A., & Glantz, L. H. (1994). *Children as research subjects: Science, ethics, and law.* New York: Oxford University Press.

Impara, J. C., & Plake, B. S. (1995). Comparing counselors', school administrators', and teachers' knowledge in student assessment. *Measurement and Evaluation in Counseling and Development, 28,* 78–87.

Keith-Spiegel, P., & Koocher, G. P. (Eds.). (1995). *Ethics in psychology: Professional standards and cases.* Hillsdale, NJ: Erlbaum.

Matarazzo, J. D. (1990). Psychological assessment versus psychological testing. *American Psychologist, 45,* 999–1017.

Messick, S. (Ed.). (1995). Values and standards in performance assessment: Issues, findings, and viewpoints [Special issue]. *Educational Measurement: Issues and Practice, 14*(3).

The National Commission for the Protection of Human Subjects of Biomedical and Behavioral Research. (1979). *The Belmont report: Ethical principles and guidelines for the protection of human subjects of research.* Washington, DC: National Institutes of Health.

CHAPTER 15

Principles of Test Development

Introduction
Suggestions for Writing Objective Test Items
    General Principles for Objective Items
    Writing True–False Items
    Writing Multiple-Choice Items
    Writing Matching Items
Preparing the Objective Test for Use
Scoring the Objective Test
    Correction for Guessing

Using Item Analysis to Improve Objective Tests
    Simplified Procedures for Conducting Item Analyses
    More Formal Item Analysis Procedures
Writing Essay Test Items
    Writing Essay Questions
    Preparing the Essay Test
    Scoring Essay Items
Summary
Questions and Exercises
Suggested Readings

INTRODUCTION

In the earlier chapters in this book we discussed the properties that a good test should have. But how are those properties achieved? How does one write the items that go into good tests of achievement or of cognitive ability? Chapters 10, 11, and 12 offered some suggestions for preparing performance assessments; measures of interest, personality, and adjustment; and measures of attitudes and opinions. In this chapter we will look at some of the principles that lead to good test items for measures of achievement and ability. The principles we discuss apply both to tests that an individual teacher might prepare to assess student achievement and to standardized tests. The only real difference between the two applications is in the resources that are available.

In the section of Chapter 5 on content validity we examined the definition of the domain that the test should cover. In this chapter we assume that the task of preparing the test blueprint has already been accomplished and that we know what types of items we will need and how many of each type should be prepared. Our presentation will focus on achievement testing of the objectives from the test blueprint given in Chapter 5, but the same general principles apply to cognitive ability items. Because objective tests are the most widely used forms in standardized testing programs and are popular with teachers, we will focus most of our attention on writing and analyzing items for these tests, those in which the examinees select the best answer from among a set of alternatives. The chapter concludes with some guidelines for writing good essay test items.

SUGGESTIONS FOR WRITING OBJECTIVE TEST ITEMS

General Principles for Objective Items

In this section we discuss suggestions and recommendations that apply to writing all types of objective test items, often called **select-response items.** Many of these principles also apply to essay questions and other forms of test items where the examinees create their own responses. Special issues in the writing of these **produce-response items** are discussed at the end of this chapter.

1. *Keep the reading difficulty and vocabulary level of the test item as simple as possible.* It is best to avoid complex sentence structure or unnecessarily difficult words that can prevent students from showing what they know about the content the item is intended to assess. When technical vocabulary has been emphasized in a course and knowledge of that vocabulary is one of the objectives of instruction, it may appropriately be used, but obscure general vocabulary should be avoided. In the example given here, which was written for eighth graders, the sentence posing the item is unnecessarily wordy and complex, and the words *promiscuous, pernicious,* and *deleterious* are unnecessarily difficult for this grade level. (For each example, the correct answer is underlined. For true–false items, T indicates true and F indicates false.)

EXAMPLE

Poor: The promiscuous use of sprays, oils, and antiseptics in the nose during acute colds is a pernicious practice because it may have a deleterious effect on:

A. the sinuses.
B. red blood cells.
C. white blood cells.
D. the olfactory nerve.

Better: Which of the following may result from the frequent use of sprays, oils, and antiseptics in the nose during a bad cold?

A. Spreading of the infection to the sinuses.
B. Damage to the olfactory nerve.
C. Destruction of white blood cells.
D. Congestion of the mucous membranes in the nose.

2. *Be sure each item has a correct or best answer on which experts would agree.* Ordinarily, statements of a controversial nature do not make good objective items, although there are instances when knowledge of different viewpoints on controversial issues may be important. When this is the case, the item should clearly state whose opinion or what authority is to be used as the basis for the answer. The student should not be placed in the position of having to endorse a particular opinion or viewpoint as an indisputable fact. When the objective requires that the student marshal evidence for or against a controversial topic, the appropriate approach is to use an essay question.

EXAMPLE

Poor: T F Alcoholism is a disease.

Better: T F According to your textbook, alcoholism is a disease.

3. *Be sure each item deals with an important aspect of the content area, and not with trivia.* Sometimes teachers and other test constructors try to increase the difficulty of an item by basing it on obscure or trivial details, such as the content of a footnote or an isolated fact from a table. The first example that follows, written for an eighth-grade health test, asks for a trivial detail, the knowledge of which could not possibly make any difference in an eighth grader's level of competence in health. Example 2 consists of a statement of little importance, lifted from the textbook. Any student would know that it was true whether or not they were familiar with the course content. The only way that someone would get this item incorrect would be from thinking it was so obvious that it must be a trick question.

EXAMPLE 1

Poor: In 2000, the death rate from accidents of all types per 100,000 population in the 15–24 age group was:

    A. 59.0.
    B. 59.1
    C. 59.2.
    D. 59.3.

Better: In 2000, the leading cause of death in the 15–24 age group was from:

    A. respiratory diseases.
    B. cancer.
    C. accidents.
    D. rheumatic heart disease.

EXAMPLE 2

Poor: T F The manufacture of prescription drugs is a highly scientific industry.

4. *Be sure each item is independent.* The answer to one item should not be required as a condition for solving the next item. Every student should have a fair chance at each item on its own. In the example shown next, the person who does not know the answer to the first item is unlikely to get the second one correct except by a lucky guess.

EXAMPLE

Poor:

1. Scurvy is caused by the lack of:

    A. vitamin A.
    B. vitamin B_1.
    C. vitamin B_{12}.
    D. vitamin C.

2. A good source of this vitamin is:

    A. orange juice.
    B. cod-liver oil.
    C. liver.
    D. whole rice.

It is also important to make sure that the statement of one question does not provide the answer to another question. For example, if the stem of the second item had been "A good source of vitamin

C is," and the order of the two items had been reversed, it is quite likely that many more students would have correctly identified the cause of scurvy. When it is necessary to include both items in the test, the effect of one item on the other can be minimized by putting the items on different pages.

5. *Avoid the use of trick questions.* Objective items tend to be trick items when the student has to pick one word or number out of a sentence that appears to be focusing on an entirely different point. In the poor example that follows, the item is keyed *false* because the immunizing agent for diphtheria is either a toxoid or an antitoxin, not a vaccine. However, the statement conveys the idea that the student is to react to the effectiveness of immunization procedures against diphtheria. If the purpose of the item is to test whether a student knows the correct use of the word *vaccine,* it would be better to rephrase the item as indicated in the first better alternative. However, if the purpose of the item is to test knowledge that the death rate from diphtheria has dropped during the century, the second better alternative would be a preferred rewording. Trick questions are likely to mislead the better student who attempts to focus on the meaning of the statement rather than to check each word.

EXAMPLE

Poor: T F The use of diphtheria vaccine contributed to the decline in death rate from this disease during the 20th century.

Better: T F The immunizing material used to prevent diphtheria is called a vaccine.

Better: T F Immunization caused the death rate from diphtheria to decline during the 20th century.

6. *Be sure the problem posed is clear and unambiguous.* This is a general admonition, somewhat like "Go forth and sin no more!" and it may be just as ineffective. However, it is certainly true that ambiguity of statement and meaning is the most pervasive fault in objective test items. Let us look at two examples of this problem.

EXAMPLE 1

Poor: T F Diabetes develops after 40.

The statement is keyed true. But what does it mean? Does it mean only after 40 years of age or does it mean more frequently after 40? What does *develop* mean in this context? You can obtain data on the relative frequency of diagnosis of diabetes in people of different ages, but the time of diagnosis and the time of development are not the same. To which type of diabetes is the item writer referring, diabetes mellitus, diabetes insipidous, or some other form? Items such as this one are likely to trouble the student who knows the most, and not the less informed student. The item cannot be revised to make it an adequate item and should not be included in the test.

EXAMPLE 2

Poor: Which of the following substances is most essential to human life?

A. protein
B. water
C. vitamins
D. minerals

The keyed answer to the question is B, but all of the substances are essential to human life. To answer the question, the examinee has to guess what the item writer meant by "most essential."

In this question, the item writer was trying to determine whether the students knew that healthy people could survive for a fairly long period of time without food but could survive for only a few days without replenishing water lost from the body. The revised question tests for this knowledge with greater clarity.

EXAMPLE 2, REVISED

Better: A healthy person is marooned on a deserted island. To survive, the person needs almost immediately to find a source of:

A. protein to maintain body cells.
B. water to drink.
C. vitamins to maintain body metabolism.
D. carbohydrates or fats to supply energy.

With these six general points in mind, we turn our attention to guidelines for writing items in the various formats commonly used for objective tests.

Writing True–False Items

True–false tests owe much of their popularity to objectivity in scoring and ease of construction. Their use also permits the inclusion of a larger number of items on a test than do other item formats. Despite these advantages, the true–false test is not considered to be a sound method of assessing student performance, because it is hard to write items that are neither too difficult nor too easy or items that are not so ambiguous or tricky that they provide a poor assessment of knowledge. This approach is appropriate for only a limited range of objectives, and in many fields there are no statements, except for the trivial, that can be said to be unambiguously true or false.

The true–false item is best suited to knowledge that is categorical—for example, bacteria are either pathogenic or nonpathogenic and diseases are either communicable or noncommunicable. It is possible to write reasonable true–false items around this type of knowledge. But only a small fraction of the knowledge in any field is of this type, and much that fits the pattern is relatively unimportant. Because the statement that constitutes an item typically appears in isolation, with no frame of reference, judgments about truth or falsity are difficult.

Another problem with true–false items is that a student has a 50% chance of getting the item correct by guessing. For this reason, this format yields less accurate information per item about a student's knowledge than do other forms of objective items. As a result, a large number of items are needed to provide a precise appraisal of each student's competence.

Suggestions for Writing Better True–False Items

Though the true–false item format has serious limitations and its use is not recommended, there are some rules that, when applied, can result in better true–false items for people who insist on using them. True–false items are rarely found on professionally developed tests (however, note the exception to this statement for the lower levels of the ITBS Reading test described in Chapter 9).

1. *Ensure that the item is unequivocally true or false.* Each statement should be true enough or false enough that experts would unanimously agree on the answer. Many statements cause problems because the well-informed student can build a case for why any statement is true or why it is false. Consider the following:

EXAMPLE

Poor: T̲ F Penicillin is an effective drug for the treatment of pneumonia.

Better: T̲ F Penicillin is an effective drug for the treatment of streptococcal pneumonia.

Although the item in the first alternative is keyed *true*, the student with the most knowledge about penicillin will know that this antibiotic is more effective against certain types of pneumonia than others. Such a student might mark the statement false because it is not equally true in all cases. The revised statement removes the ambiguity.

2. *Avoid the use of specific determiners or qualified statements.* Statements that include such words as *all, never, no, always,* and other all-inclusive terms represent such broad generalizations that they are likely to be false. Qualified statements involving such terms as *usually, sometimes, under certain conditions,* and *may be* are likely to be true. Testwise examinees know this and will use such cues to get credit for knowledge they do not possess, thereby reducing the validity of the test scores as an indication of knowledge.

EXAMPLE

Poor: T F̲ All bacteria cause disease.

Better: T̲ F Pathogenic bacteria are parasites.

3. *Avoid ambiguous and indefinite terms of degree or amount.* Expressions such as *frequently, greatly, to a considerable degree,* and *in most cases* are not interpreted in the same way by everyone who reads them. When the student is left to guess what the item writer had in mind, the result is likely to be frustration and poor measurement. In the poor example that follows, the students may be troubled by the word *frequently* because drying as a method of preserving food is used extensively today only for certain fruits.

EXAMPLE

Poor: T̲ F Drying is frequently used to preserve foods.

Better: T̲ F Fruits can be preserved by drying.

4. *Avoid the use of negative statements, and particularly double negatives.* It has been known for many years (Wason, 1961; Zern, 1967) that the time needed to answer a negatively stated item is greater than that needed for an equivalent positively stated item. Furthermore, more errors are made in response to negatively phrased items. That is, students tended to miss items because they had trouble with the wording rather than because they did not possess the information required to answer correctly.

Both Wason and Zern used pairs of statements such as "36 is not an even number" and "36 is an odd number." The negative statement requires an involved, reverse process of reasoning to untangle its meaning and is semantically more difficult. In addition, students under the time pressure of the examination can easily overlook the negative. Double negatives present even greater problems of interpretation.

EXAMPLE 1

Poor: T F̲ Resistance to smallpox obtained through the use of smallpox vaccine is not called active immunity.

Better: T F̲ Resistance to smallpox obtained through the use of smallpox vaccine is called passive immunity.

EXAMPLE 2

Poor: T̲ F Tuberculosis is not a noncommunicable disease.

Better: T̲ F Tuberculosis is a communicable disease.

5. *Limit true–false statements to a single idea.* Complex statements that include more than one idea are difficult to read and understand. A statement that contains one true idea and one false idea is usually inappropriate because it is likely to be more a measure of test-taking skills than of true knowledge of the target subject matter. Complex statements may be used if the student's attention is directed toward the one part of the statement that he or she is to judge to be true or false.

EXAMPLE

Poor: T F̲ Bleeding of the gums is associated with gingivitis, which can be cured by the sufferer by daily brushing of the teeth.

Better: T F̲ Daily brushing of the teeth will cure gingivitis.

6. *Make true and false statements approximately equal in length.* There is a tendency for true statements to be longer than false ones. Generally, the greater length of true statements results from the need to include qualifications and limitations to make the statement unequivocally true. An occasional long, true statement will not cause a problem if it is matched by an occasional long, false one, and if there is no generally consistent difference in length between the two categories of statements.

7. *Include approximately the same number of true statements as false ones.* Teachers are sometimes tempted to include more true statements than false ones because of their concern that students will remember false statements and therefore be learning course content that is wrong. A problem arises when students discover this tendency and learn to answer true to statements they are in doubt about.

Variations in the Format of True–False Items

Several variations in the format of true–false items have been suggested as ways of improving them. Most of these variations endeavor to accomplish one or more of the following: (1) reduction in the ambiguity of the items, (2) reduction of the effects of guessing on the scores, and/or (3) providing more specific information about how much a student knows. The four most frequently used variations are described below.

1. *Underlining a word or clause in the statement.* This variation is the simplest one, and it is used to reduce ambiguity by focusing the attention of the examinee on the most important part of the statement.

EXAMPLES

1. T̲ F Malaria is transmitted by the <u>Anopheles</u> mosquito.
2. T F̲ If foods are frozen, harmful bacteria in them will be <u>killed</u>.

The instructions for such items should clearly indicate that the student is to judge the truth or falsity of the underlined portion in relation to the rest of the statement. Underlining also permits the use of more complex statements.

2. *Requiring students to correct false statements.* A student who correctly marks a statement *false* may have made a lucky guess or may have chosen the answer on the basis of misinformation. For example, for the item "Insulin is secreted by the pituitary gland," a student could indicate

that it is false, thinking that insulin is secreted by the adrenal glands. In this case, incorrect information leads to a correct answer. To make sure that the student knows the facts underlying a false statement—and to reduce guessing—give the student instructions to correct all statements that are marked false. The above example can be corrected by changing "insulin" to one of the pituitary hormones, by changing "is secreted" to "is not secreted," or by changing "the pituitary gland" to "an endocrine gland" or "the pancreas." Because there may be many ways to make the statement correct, it is advisable to underline the key word or words in all statements, both true and false, when this variation is used. The part of the statement that is underlined should be the specific content that the teacher is trying to appraise. Thus, in this example, a teacher trying to determine whether students knew the name of a hormone secreted by the pituitary gland should underline the word "insulin." Likewise, a teacher interested in determining whether students knew the name of the gland that secretes insulin should underline "the pituitary gland."

3. *Basing true–false items on specific stimulus material provided for the student.* True–false items tend to be most effective and most useful when they are based on specific stimulus material such as a chart, map, graph, table, or reading passage. In this situation, the examinees are instructed to respond to the item only in terms of the given material, providing them with a frame of reference that is better defined. This type of true–false item can be effectively used to appraise comprehension, interpretation, extrapolation, and logical reasoning, if appropriate stimulus material is used and the items are written to elicit these abilities, as the example shows.

EXAMPLE

Directions: The pie graph below shows how each dollar is spent for medical care. Look at the graph carefully. Statements are given following the graph.

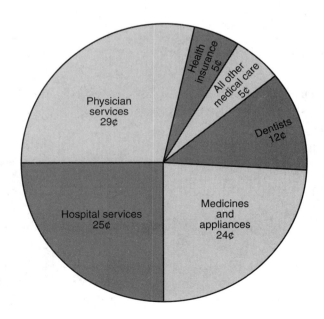

Read each statement carefully.

Mark T if the data in the graph support the statement.

Mark F if the data in the graph contradict the statement or no data are provided in the graph to either support or contradict the statement.

(T) 1. More of the medical-care dollar is spent for physicians' services than for any other single category of the expense.

(F) 2. Few Americans have health insurance.

(F) 3. Americans spend 24 cents out of every dollar they make on medicines and appliances.

(T) 4. Hospital and physicians' services together account for slightly more than half of the money spent for medical care.

(T) 5. Less money is spent on dental care than on physicians' services.

(T) 6. About 25% of the medical-care dollar is spent on hospital services.

This form of item is sometimes made more complex by requiring the student to answer in four or five categories such as *definitely true, probably true, insufficient data to determine whether it is true or false, probably false,* and *definitely false.* In this format, the item becomes a multiple-choice item rather than a true–false item.

4. *Grouping short, true–false items under a common question or statement heading.* Two examples of this variation are given here.

EXAMPLES

Directions: Place a T in front of each choice that is a correct answer to the question. Put an F in front of each choice that is NOT a correct answer to the question.

A. Which of the following diseases are caused by viruses?

(T) 1. chicken pox	(T) 5. measles
(F) 2. diphtheria	(T) 6. mumps
(T) 3. influenza	(F) 7. tuberculosis
(F) 4. malaria	(F) 8. typhoid fever

B. A 14-year-old girl ate the following food during a 24-hour period:

Breakfast	Lunch	Dinner
Cup of black coffee	Glass of Coca-Cola (8 oz) Hamburger (4 oz) with bun French fried potatoes (20 pieces)	Roast beef (9 oz) Mashed potatoes (1/2 cup) Glass of milk (8 oz) Apple pie (1 piece)

In which of the following was her diet deficient?

(T) 1. calcium	(F) 5. niacin
(F) 2. calories	(F) 6. protein
(F) 3. carbohydrates	(T) 7. vitamin A
(T) 4. iron	(T) 8. vitamin C

The format of this variation looks like a multiple-choice item, but the task for the student is to judge whether each choice is true or false in relation to the original question; therefore, it is basically a series of true–false items. The variation can be an efficient way to test for simple applications and for knowledge of categories, classifications, or characteristics. It is particularly effective for in-depth testing of a specific part of a topic. The format reduces the reading load for the student, and the question serves as a frame of reference for judging truth or falsity and removes some of the ambiguity of true–false statements. An alternative to this approach is to have the students place a check mark next to the statements that are true and to leave the others unmarked.

Writing Multiple-Choice Items

The multiple-choice item is the most flexible of the objective item types. It can be used to appraise the achievement of any of the educational objectives that can be measured by a paper-and-pencil test, except those relating to skill in written expression, originality, and the ability to organize a response. An ingenious and talented item writer can construct multiple-choice items that require not only the recall of knowledge but also the use of skills of comprehension, interpretation, application, analysis, or synthesis to arrive at the correct answer.

Unfortunately, not all multiple-choice items are of high quality, because it takes a great deal of time and skill to write good items. One of the important characteristics of the multiple-choice item is that single options can be altered or replaced. The test author, by changing distractors, has flexibility in adjusting the difficulty of the test item. Tests can then be constructed for optimum difficulty level, thus maximizing the capacity to differentiate between those taking the test.

The multiple-choice item consists of two parts: the **stem,** which presents the problem, and the list of possible answers or options. In the standard form of the item, one of the options is the correct or best answer and the others are **foils** or **distractors.** The stem of the item may be presented either as a question or as an incomplete statement. The form of the stem seems to make no difference in the overall effectiveness of the item, as long as the stem presents a clear and specific problem to the examinee.

The number of options used in the multiple-choice item differs from test to test, and there is no real reason why it cannot vary for items in the same test. An item must have at least three answer choices, or options, to be classified as a multiple-choice item, and the typical pattern is to have four or five answer choices, to reduce the probability of guessing the answer. A distinction should be made between the number of options presented for a multiple-choice item and the number of *effective,* or *functioning,* options that the item has. In the poor example that follows, written for the eighth-grade test on health that provided our example for content validity, the item will really function as a two-choice item because no one is likely to choose option A or D. The revised item still presents four answer choices but is now more likely to function as a four-option item because options A and D have been made more reasonable.

EXAMPLE

Poor: About how many calories are recommended daily for a 14-year-old girl who is 62 in. tall, weighs 103 lb, and is moderately active?

A. 0
B. 2,000
C. 2,500
D. 30,000

Better: About how many calories are recommended daily for a 14-year-old girl who is
62 in. tall, weighs 103 lb, and is moderately active?

A. 1,500
B. 2,000
C. 2,500
D. 3,000

The revised item will probably be more difficult than the original one because the options are closer in value, so those who do not know the answer will be guessing among four choices rather than two.

The difficulty of a multiple-choice item depends on the cognitive processes required by the item, as well as the closeness of the options. Consider the set of three items shown in the next example, all relating to the meaning of the term *fortified food.* We can predict that Version 1 will be relatively easy, Version 2 somewhat more difficult, and Version 3 still more difficult. In Version 1, the stem is a direct copy of the textbook definition of *fortified food,* and the distractors are not terms used to indicate the addition of nutrients to foods. The difference between Versions 1 and 2 is that the stem of Version 2 recasts the textbook definition into a novel form and calls for a different mental process than Version 1 does. The difference between Versions 2 and 3 is in the closeness of the options.

EXAMPLES

1. When a nutrient has been added that is not present in natural food, the food is said
   to be:

   A. fortified.
   B. processed.
   C. pasteurized.
   D. refined.

2. When milk processed for sale has had vitamin D concentrate added to provide at
   least 400 U.S.P. units per quart, the carton can then legally state that the milk is:

   A. fortified.
   B. processed.
   C. pasteurized.
   D. refined.

3. When milk processed for sale has had vitamin D concentrate added to provide at
   least 400 U.S.P. units per quart, the carton can then legally state that the milk is:

   A. fortified.
   B. enriched.
   C. irradiated.
   D. restored.

Suggestions for Writing Better Multiple-Choice Items

The construction of good tests requires the allocation of an adequate amount of time, proper planning, adherence to a set of well-recognized rules for item construction, and practice. Commercial test publishers retain groups of experienced item writers who generate large numbers of high-quality items for use in tests such as the ACT Assessment and the SAT. But individual teachers and researchers often need to prepare their own multiple-choice items. We can do nothing about your timeliness or planning for writing test items, but if you use the following rules for writing better multiple-choice items, the tests you prepare will be improved.

1. *Be sure the stem of the item clearly formulates a problem.* The stem should be worded so that the examinee clearly understands what problem or question is being asked before reading the answer choices. Look at the poor example that follows. When you finish reading the stem, you know only that the item is related to a part of the pancreas. You have no idea what the problem is until you read each of the options. The answer choices that are provided are heterogeneous in content; that is, one relates to structure, one to function, one to permanence, and one to location. The poor item is really nothing more than four true–false items with the words "The cell islets of the pancreas" in common. The revised item provides both a clearly formulated problem in the stem and a more homogeneous set of answer choices.

EXAMPLES

Poor: The cell islets of the pancreas:

    A. contain ducts.
    B. produce insulin.
    C. disappear as one grows older.
    D. are located around the edge of the pancreas.

Better: The cell islets of the pancreas secrete the substance called:

    A. trypsin.
    B. insulin.
    C. tryptophan.
    D. adrenaline.

2. *Include as much of the item as possible in the stem, and keep options as short as possible.* In the interests of economies of space and reading time and of having a clear statement of the problem, try to word and arrange the item so that the answer choices can be kept relatively short. If the same words or phrases are repeated in all or most of the options, as in the poor example given next, rewrite the stem to include the repetitious material. Answer choices that are long in relation to the stem frequently occur because of failure to formulate a problem clearly in the stem.

EXAMPLE

Poor: The term "empty-calorie" food designates:

    A. a food that has few essential nutrients but high caloric value.
    B. a food that has neither essential nutrients nor caloric value.
    C. a food that has both high nutritive value and high caloric value.
    D. a food that has high nutritive value but low caloric value.

Better: The term "empty-calorie" applies to foods that are:

    A. low in nutrients and high in calories.
    B. low in both nutrients and calories.
    C. high in both nutrients and calories.
    D. high in nutrients and low in calories.

3. *Include in the stem only the material needed to make the problem clear and specific.* Items with long, wordy stems containing material that is irrelevant to the problem are likely to reduce the

effectiveness and efficiency of the test. First, the unnecessary material increases the amount of reading needed for an item; it is then more difficult to separate generalized skill in reading from knowledge of the subject matter. Second, superfluous material increases reading time at the expense of answering time, making the test inefficient because fewer items can be included on the test for a given amount of testing time. The first three sentences in the following example clearly are unnecessary for defining the problem for the examinee.

EXAMPLE

Poor: Cells of one kind belong to a particular group performing a specialized duty. We call this group of cells a tissue. All of us have different kinds of tissues in our bodies. Which of the following would be classified as epithelial tissue?

A. tendons
B. adenoids and tonsils
C. mucous membranes
D. cartilage

Better: Which of the following would be classified as epithelial tissue?

A. tendons
B. adenoids and tonsils
C. mucous membranes
D. cartilage

If the purpose of the test is to appraise whether the examinee can differentiate those data necessary to solve the problem or support an argument from those that are either unnecessary or irrelevant, then one would have to include extra data in posing the problem. In such an instance, though, the extra material would be central to the process being measured and, therefore, would not be irrelevant.

4. *Use the negative only sparingly in an item.* Just as was true for true–false items, negatively stated multiple-choice items increase the reading difficulty of an item and require the student to perform more difficult reasoning tasks. Negative items also provide little information about exactly what the examinee knows.

At times it is important to test whether the examinee knows the exception to a general rule or can detect errors. For these purposes, a few items with the words *not* or *except* in the stem may be justified, particularly when overinclusion is a common error. When a negative word is included in a stem, it should be underlined or capitalized to call the examinee's attention to it.

The poor example that follows was written to measure whether students knew the function of the semicircular canals, but the item as written does not measure this aspect of the students' knowledge. The revised example measures the objective more directly. There are two reasons why the second better example shows a more appropriate use of the negative stem: (1) The most common error made by students about the duties of the Food and Drug Administration is the inclusion of meat inspection, a duty of the Department of Agriculture, and (2) it would be difficult to get three plausible misleads if the item were stated in a positive form.

EXAMPLES

Poor: Which of the following structures of the ear is NOT concerned with hearing?

A. eardrum
B. oval window

C. semicircular canals

D. cochlea

Better:

1. Which one of the following structures of the ear helps to maintain balance?

   A. eardrum

   B. oval window

   C. semicircular canals

   D. cochlea

2. Which of the following activities is NOT the responsibility of the U.S. Food and Drug Administration?

   A. inspection of warehouses storing food for interstate shipment

   B. inspection of slaughterhouses that ship meat across state lines

   C. initiation of court action to remove unhealthful food from the market

   D testing samples of foods for interstate sale

5. *Use novel material in formulating problems that measure understanding or ability to apply principles.* Most locally constructed tests place too much emphasis on rote memory and neglect measurement of the ability to use information. The multiple-choice item is well adapted to measuring simple recall, but a novel situation must be presented to the examinee if more than rote memory is to be required to answer the question. The second and third examples of items assessing knowledge of fortified foods on page 449 illustrate how you can move away from the form in which the material was originally presented to test comprehension rather than recall. Two examples are given here to illustrate how an item can be structured to appraise the ability to use information.

EXAMPLES

Rote memory 1: Which of the following foods will yield the largest number of calories when metabolized in the body?

   A. 1 gram of fat

   B. 1 gram of sugar

   C. 1 gram of starch

   D. 1 gram of protein

Application: Which of the following would result in the greatest reduction of calories if it were eliminated from the daily diet?

   A. 1 tablespoon of butter

   B. 1 tablespoon of granulated sugar

   C. 1 tablespoon of mashed potato

   D. 1 boiled egg

Rote memory 2: Death from pneumonia and influenza is most frequent among:

   A. infants and aged people.

   B. infants and elementary schoolchildren.

   C. teenagers and aged people.

   D. teenagers and young adults.

Interpretation: Look at the following graph, which shows, by age group, the death rate from Disease X.

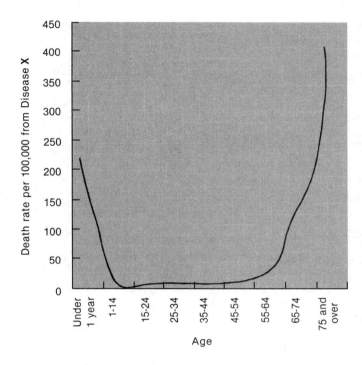

Which of the following diseases could be Disease X?

    A. pneumonia
    B. cancer
    C. tuberculosis
    D. heart disease

Note that it is important to refer to the disease by a letter that is not used for any of the response alternatives.

    6. *Be sure that there is one and only one correct or clearly best answer.* In the typical multiple-choice item, the examinee is instructed to choose one and only one answer. Having instructed the examinee to choose *the* answer that is best, the test maker is obligated to provide one and only one best answer for each item. Although this provision may seem obvious, many items on locally constructed tests either have two or more equally good answers or no good answer. In the following example, option B is keyed as the correct answer but there is also a large element of correctness for options C and E. The revised version eliminates this fault, but the item may now be too easy.

EXAMPLE

Poor: A color-blind boy inherits the trait from a:

    A. male parent.
    B. female parent.
    C. maternal grandparent.
    D. paternal grandparent.
    E. remote ancestor.

Better: A color-blind boy most probably inherited the trait from his:

A. father.

B. mother.

C. paternal grandfather.

D. paternal grandmother.

In addition to making sure that there is only one correct answer, the item writer should make sure that the keyed answer is unequivocally the best. It is the item writer's responsibility to use the very best scholarship, as well as his or her skill in phrasing the stem and answer choices, to produce a problem and answer with which experts in the field will agree.

7. *Be sure wrong answers are plausible.* One of the major advantages of the multiple-choice item is its capacity to require the examinees to select the correct answer from among three, four, or five choices, thus reducing the chance of their guessing the correct answer. However, the wrong alternatives must be attractive to examinees who are lacking in knowledge about the material the item is intended to assess. Therefore, the incorrect answer choices should be logically consistent with the stem and should represent common errors made by students in a particular grade or at a particular ability level.

In the first poor example that follows, Options A and C are compounds, not elements, and are thus inconsistent with the stem. In the second poor example, Options C and D are very implausible.

EXAMPLES

Poor: Which of the following elements is found in proteins but not in carbohydrates or fats?

A. carbon dioxide

B. oxygen

C. water

D. nitrogen

Poor: The gas formed in the cells after the oxidation of food, and taken to the lungs and expelled is:

A. oxygen.

B. carbon dioxide.

C. helium.

D. chlorine.

One good way to develop plausible distractors, particularly with items that measure quantitative concepts and skills, is to determine what answer a student would get by making a particular error at some point in analyzing or solving the problem. It is sometimes possible to identify specific informational or procedural deficiencies in this way.

8. *Be sure no unintentional clues to the correct answer are given.* Inexperienced test constructors frequently give away the correct answer to an item or give clues that permit the examinee to eliminate one or more of the incorrect answer choices from consideration. Items that contain irrelevant clues or specific determiners, correct answers that are consistently longer than incorrect answers, or grammatical inconsistencies between the stem and the wrong alternatives tend to be easier than items without these faults. To the extent that there are differences among examinees

in their awareness of these clues, what is being measured by the items changes and the validity of the test is compromised.

Examples of items containing some types of unintentional clues are given here. Item 1 is an example of a "clang association," that is, a repetition of a word, phrase, or sound in the keyed answer and in the stem. Item 2 contains specific determiners that have the same effect in multiple-choice options as in true–false statements. In Item 3, the keyed answer is much longer than the other options. Item 4 is an example of a grammatical inconsistency; the word "a" in the stem implies a singular word, but Options A and C are both plural. The revised items show how each of these faults can be corrected to make the items more effective in measuring knowledge rather than testwiseness.

EXAMPLES

Clang Association

Poor:

1. The function of the platelets in the blood is to help in:
    A. carrying oxygen to the cells.
    B. carrying food to the cells.
    C. clotting of the blood.
    D. fighting disease.

Better:

1. Which of the following structures in the blood helps in forming blood clots?
    A. red blood cells
    B. lymphocytes
    C. platelets
    D. monocytes

Specific Determiners

Poor:

2. Which of the following is characteristic of anaerobic bacteria?
    A. They never live in soil.
    B. They can live without molecular oxygen.
    C. They always cause disease.
    D. They can carry on photosynthesis.

Better:

2. The one characteristic that distinguishes all anaerobic bacteria is their ability to:
    A. withstand extreme variation in air temperature.
    B. live without molecular oxygen.
    C. live as either saprophytes or parasites.
    D. reproduce either in living cells or nonliving culture media.

Length Clues

Poor:

3. The term side effect of a drug refers to:
    A. additional benefits from the drug.
    B. the chain effect of drug action.

C. the influence of drugs on crime.

D. any action of the drug in the body other than the one the doctor wanted the drug to have.

Better:

3. Which of the following, if it occurred, would be a side effect of aspirin for a man who had been taking two aspirin tablets every 3 hours for a heavy cold and slight fever?

A. normal body temperature
B. reduction in frequency of coughing
C. easier breathing
D. ringing in the ears

Grammatical Inconsistency

Poor:

4. Penicillin is obtained from a:

A. bacteria.
B. mold.
C. coal tars.
D. tropical tree.

Better:

4. Penicillin is obtained from:

A. bacteria.
B. molds.
C. coal tars.
D. tropical trees.

9. *Use the option "none of these" or "none of the above" only when the keyed answer can be classified unequivocally as correct or incorrect.* This option can be appropriately used by experienced test writers on tests of spelling, mathematics, and study skills. In these types of tests an absolutely correct answer can be given. On other types of tests, where the student is to choose the best answer and where the keyed answer is the best answer, but not necessarily absolutely correct, the use of "none of these" or "none of the above" is inappropriate.

The option "none of the above," if used, works better when the stem is stated as a question rather than a sentence to be completed. An incomplete sentence seldom works because "none of the above" seldom completes the stem grammatically. An example of this is illustrated in the following item, which appeared on a 10th-grade biology test.

EXAMPLE

Poor: Of the following, the one that is never a function of the stem of plants is:

A. conduction.
B. photosynthesis.
C. support.
D. food storage.
E. none of the above.

Not only is the option "none of the above" grammatically inconsistent with the stem, but it is also logically inconsistent with the stem. Option E does not name a function of the plant, and the double negative effect of the option and the "never" in the stem makes comprehension of the meaning of the item difficult. There is no way of revising the item to make it better because any function of a plant is performed by the stem in some plants.

If "none of these" or its equivalent is used as an option in items requiring quantitative solutions or in spelling tests, it should be used as frequently for the correct option as any other answer choice and the stem of the item should be phrased as a question. On such tests, the option functions best if it is used as the correct answer on some of the easier items at the beginning of the test to reinforce the instruction that "none of the above" is sometimes the correct answer.

The example given next represents a poor use of the "none of the above" option in an item calling for a numerical answer, because only approximations are given rather than exact quantities. Option B is keyed as the correct answer, but Option E is better because the estimates of the blood volume for an average adult range from a low of 10 pints to a high of 16 pints. In addition, this item may be assessing knowledge that in most cases would be judged trivial.

EXAMPLE

Poor: How many pints of blood does a normal human adult of average weight have?

A. 3 pints
B. 13 pints
C. 30 pints
D. 50 pints
E. none of the above

Better: Approximately what percentage of the body weight of a healthy human adult is blood?

A. 3% to 5%
B. 8% to 9%
C. 12% to 15%
D. 20% to 25%

10. *Avoid the use of "all of the above" in the multiple-choice item.* This type of distractor is often used either when only three options can easily be generated and a fourth option is needed or when there is an easily obtained list of characteristics or traits of something and it is difficult to come up with three incorrect distractors. In this latter case, it is easy to list three of the characteristics along with an "all of the above" statement. Usually, when the option "all of the above" is used on teacher-made tests, it is the correct answer. Items using this option tend to be easy because the examinees will be led to the correct answer even though they have only partial information. Look at the poor example that follows. Assume that the examinees have been instructed to mark only one answer and that John knows that both age and weight are used to compute basal energy requirements but does not know that height is also part of the computation. He will certainly mark D for his answer; thus, he gets credit for having complete information even though he does not. In the revised version, the examinee must have full information to arrive at the keyed answer. The option "all of the above" is much more effective if it is used in a variation of the standard form, the complex multiple-choice item, described in the next section.

EXAMPLE

Poor: Which of the following factors must be considered in computing basal energy requirements?

A. age
B. height
C. weight
<u>D</u>. all of the above

Better: Which of the following factors must be considered in computing basal energy requirements?

A. weight only
B. age only
C. height and weight only
D. age and weight only
<u>E</u>. age, height, and weight

Variations in the Format of Multiple-Choice Items

A number of variations of the standard multiple-choice item have been suggested. One commonly used variation is the matching item, discussed in a separate section. In this section, we discuss two other variations that are sometimes used.

1. *Complex multiple-choice items.* This variation, which is sometimes called the multiple-multiple-choice item, gets its name from the format and the combinations of options used as answer choices. It is most effective when it is used to appraise knowledge of or ability to apply or interpret multiple causes, effects, functions, or uses. The following example illustrates a poor use of the complex multiple-choice item, and several faults of item construction. Although there are multiple signs of impaired circulation, the options are short; therefore, the knowledge could be tested more efficiently in the usual multiple-choice format. The technical problems with the item are as follows: (1) No specific problem is presented to the examinee; (2) Signs 1, 2, and 3 are used in all the answer choices so that the student is required only to determine whether Signs 4 and 5 are correct; (3) the method of presenting choices (contrast between Option C and Options B and D) is varied, which creates unnecessary difficulty for the student; and (4) Options B and C are identical.

EXAMPLE

Poor: If a bandage or cast on the arm is too tight, it might interfere with the circulation in the arm. Signs of interference with circulation include:

1. cold.	3. numbness.	5. loss of motion.
2. blanching.	4. swelling.	

<u>A</u>. all of these
B. 1, 2, 3, and 4
C. all except 5
D. 1, 2, 3, and 5

The following example illustrates an effective use of the item type, because it requires the examinee to discriminate between both the kind of food and the kind of commerce that come under the jurisdiction of the Food and Drug Administration. This type of item is both more difficult and more discriminating than the typical form of multiple-choice item that tests for the same knowledge. It is also more difficult to write good items in this format.

EXAMPLE

Effective: Look at each of the food processing or producing activities below.

1. A housewife makes jellies and sells them in her home town.
2. A butcher makes scrapple and pork sausage and sells them only in the state of Maryland.
3. A food processor makes jellies in California and sells them in New York.
4. A slaughterhouse in Chicago ships meats to all 50 states.
5. A citrus grower produces oranges in Florida and ships them to all eastern states.

Which of the activities would be subject to the regulations and supervision of the U.S. Food and Drug Administration?

    A. 2 and 4 only
    B. 3 and 5 only
    C. 3, 4, and 5 only
    D. 1, 3, and 5 only
    E. all of them

    2. *Paired statements as stimuli.* This format is an efficient and effective way of measuring judgment of relative amounts or quantities, relative effects of changing conditions, or relative chronology. It preferably should be used for content having established quantitative values. For example, the use of the pair of statements, (I) *The number of hours of sleep needed by a 14-year-old boy* and (II) *The number of hours of sleep needed by a 30-year-old man* would be undesirable, because there is no empirically determined value for the number of hours of sleep required for any age group.

EXAMPLE

Directions: Items 1 through 3 are based on pairs of statements. Read each statement carefully. On your answer sheet, mark:

    A. if the amount in Statement I is greater than that in Statement II.
    B. if the amount in Statement II is greater than that in Statement I.
    C. if the amount in Statement I is equal to that in Statement II.
    D. if there is not sufficient information to determine which amount is greater.

(B) 1. I: Caloric value of 1 tablespoon of cane sugar.

     II: Caloric value of 1 tablespoon of butter.

(A) 2. I: The daily requirement of calories for a 25-year-old male lumberjack who is 73 in. tall and weighs 190 lb.

     II: The daily requirement of calories for a 25-year-old male office clerk who is 73 in. tall and weighs 190 lb.

(A) 3. I: The daily requirement of iron for a 16-year-old girl.

     II: The daily requirement of iron for a 16-year-old boy.

Writing Matching Items

The characteristic that distinguishes the matching item from the ordinary multiple-choice item is that there are several problems whose answers must be drawn from a single list of possible answers. The matching item can best be thought of as a series of multiple-choice items presented in a more efficient manner. For example, a series of stimuli is listed down the left-hand column of the test paper and a series of options is listed down the right-hand column. The student picks the option that goes with each stimulus. The matching item has most frequently been used to measure factual information such as meanings of terms, dates of events, achievements of people, symbols for chemical elements, and authors of books. Effective matching items can be constructed by basing the set of items on a chart, map, diagram, or drawing. Features of the figure can be numbered and the examinee can be asked to match names, functions, and so on with the numbers on the figure. This type of item is useful in tests dealing with study skills, science, or technology; for example, such items might require biology students to identify cell structures.

When there is a need to assess a student's ability to make associations, matching items are more efficient than a series of multiple-choice items. The major disadvantage of this approach is that it is suitable only for measuring associations and not for assessing higher levels of understanding. Another disadvantage of this method is that such a test cannot easily be machine scored, because the number of options often exceeds the five spaces allocated to each item on standard, machine-scorable answer sheets. Of course, answer sheets can be customized for this type of item, and scanners can be programmed to read answer sheets in nonstandard ways.

To be useful, matching items, like other types of test items, must be carefully constructed. Poorly constructed matching items can be superficial measurement devices and can present the examinee with a task that makes significant demands on skills that are not part of the domain the test is designed to measure. Look at the following matching exercise, which appeared on a test in health and hygiene for an eighth-grade class.

EXAMPLE

Poor: *Directions:* Place the correct letter to the left of each number. Use each letter only once.

Column I	Column II
(p) 1. Number of permanent teeth	a. Malocclusion
(i) 2. Vitamin D	b. Tear and rip food
(n) 3. Vitamin C	c. Trench mouth
(k) 4. Enamel	d. Straightening teeth
(o) 5. Bleeding gums	e. Jawbone socket
(c) 6. Vincent's angina	f. Contains nerves and blood vessels
(d) 7. Orthodontia	g. Grind food
(e) 8. Alveolus	h. Crown
(a) 9. Lower jaw protruding	i. Sunshine
(f) 10. Pulp	j. Cleaning device
(m) 11. Acid	k Hardest substance
(l) 12. Low percentage of decay	l. Primitives
(b) 13. Cuspids	m. Decay
(g) 14. Molars	n. Citrus fruits
(h) 15. Visible part of tooth	o. Gingivitis
(j) 16. Dental floss	p. Thirty-two

Note: The "correct" answers are those designated by the person who constructed the exercise.

The example illustrates some of the most common mistakes made in preparing matching items. First, the directions are vague and fail to specify the basis for matching. Second, the set of stimuli is too heterogeneous for a good matching exercise. How many answer choices in Column II are logically possible answers for the first statement in Column I? For the second? The statements in Column I have very little in common except that they relate to teeth and dental health, in general. Third, the set is too long, and the answer choices in Column II are not arranged in any systematic order. Even examinees who know the answer to a statement have to search through the entire list in Column II to find it, which is time consuming. Fourth, some of the entries are vague, for example, entries 9, 11, and 12 in Column I and entries i, l, and m in Column II. The vagueness makes it difficult to justify the answer keyed as correct; furthermore, the accuracy of number 12 can be questioned. Fifth, there are 16 statements in Column I and 16 answer choices in Column II. If the student knows 15, he or she automatically gets the 16th correct.

Suggestions for Writing Better Matching Items

Since matching items can be thought of as a condensed series of multiple-choice items, many of the same rules for writing better items apply to both. In this section, we discuss the specific rules for writing matching items.

1. *Keep the set of statements in a single matching exercise homogeneous.* The preceding example would have been better if all of the choices were parts of a tooth, diseases of the teeth and gums, or methods of promoting oral hygiene. Homogeneous choices force the student to make genuine discriminations to arrive at correct answers. If you need to test several diverse areas of content, use a separate set of stimuli and responses for each area.

2. *Keep the set of items relatively short.* Limiting the number of items to five or six makes it easier to keep the content homogeneous. Also, short sets of items put less of a clerical burden and reading load on the examinee.

3. *Have the students choose answers from the column with the shorter statements.* The reason for this suggestion is that the answer column will be read several times by the student and it takes less time to read short statements than long ones. Having the student select from the column of shorter statements helps to minimize the already important influence of reading ability on test performance.

4. *Use a heading for each column that accurately describes its content.* A descriptive heading helps to define the task for the examinee. If the test maker is unable to identify a heading that specifically defines the content, the entries are probably too heterogeneous.

5. *Have more answer choices than the number of entries to be matched, unless answer choices can be used more than once.* The larger number of answer choices reduces the influence of guessing on test scores. It also prevents students from arriving at correct answers through a process of elimination that does not require the student always to know the correct association.

6. *Arrange the answer choices in a logical order, if one exists.* Students who know the answers should be able to find them easily. Arranging names in alphabetical order or dates in chronological order reduces the time required to find the answer.

7. *Specify in the directions both the basis for matching and whether answer choices can be used more than once.* This practice will tend to reduce ambiguity and make the task more uniform for all examinees.

A variation in the matching-item format is the classification or master list. This variation can be used quite effectively to appraise application, comprehension, or interpretation. It is an efficient way of exploring the range of mastery of a concept or a related set of concepts. An illustration of this type of item is given here.

EXAMPLE

Master Matching

Instructions: Four kinds of appeals that advertisers of health and beauty products make are given below.

  A. Appeal to fear or a sense of insecurity
  B. Appeal to snobbery or identification with a particular small group or individual
  C. Appeal to a desire to be like others, that is, to join the "bandwagon"
  D. Appeal to authority

Statements 1 through 6 are advertisements of imaginary products. Read each statement carefully. For each statement, mark the letter of the appeal that is being used. Answer choices may be used more than once.

  (A) 1. Don't let iron-tired blood get you down. Keep your verve and vivacity. Take Infantol.
  (D) 2. Research shows Lucy's Little Lethal Pills are 10 times more effective than ordinary pain killers.
  (B) 3. Duchess Poorhouse, the international beauty, bathes her face twice a day with Myrtle's Turtle Oil.
  (B) 4. Men, are you tired of a woman's deodorant? Be a man. Use No-Sweat. Leave the weaker stuff to the weaker sex.
  (B) 5. At $1,629.21, the Inside Jogger is not for everyone. Only a select few can be proud owners of one! Are you one of these?
  (C) 6. Be one of the crowd. Drink and serve Popsie's Cola.

PREPARING THE OBJECTIVE TEST FOR USE

Effective assessment requires that irrelevant sources of variation in test scores be minimized. In commercially published tests we expect the quality of work, both the organization and layout of the test and the printing, to be high; that is part of what we are paying for. When tests or other assessment devices are prepared locally, the burden for ensuring quality falls on the users themselves. The most important points to consider in arranging the items of the test are discussed in the paragraphs that follow. Although these features are presented in reference to objective tests, many of the same principles apply to rating scales, attitude surveys, and other forms of assessment.

1. *Prepare more items than you will need.* Unlikely though it may seem, not every item you write will be a good one. Following the guidelines in the preceeding sections will help, but even professional item writers fail to hit the mark with about 30% of their items. Therefore, it is essential to have about half again as many items for tryout as you expect to use in the final test, which is then constructed from the best items.

2. *Proofread the items carefully.* After the items have been written, it is a good idea to set them aside for a week or two, then go back and proofread them. You will be amazed that the items which appeared so clear and straightforward when you wrote them will seem obscure a few days later. Better yet, have a colleague read the items for clarity. If someone who is knowledgeable in the subject and in testing has difficulty making sense out of the item, so will the intended examinees.

After the items have been selected, it is necessary to prepare the test itself. The following suggestions will help you achieve reliable and valid measurement by eliminating extraneous influences on test scores that may arise from the physical features of the test.

3. *Arrange items on the test so that they are easy to read.* In the interest of those taking the test, items should not be crowded together on the test paper, because spreading out the items makes them more easily read and understood. Multiple-choice items also are easier to read if each response is on a separate line. Furthermore, items should not be split between pages, because such an arrangement may confuse the examinees. If several items all refer to a single diagram or chart, try to arrange the test so that the diagram or chart and all of the items are on the same page or on facing pages, so the examinees do not have to turn pages to go from the stimulus material to the items. An alternative when it is impossible to fit the stimulus material (chart, diagram, etc.) and the questions on a single page or facing pages is to put the stimulus material on a separate sheet that is not stapled with the rest of the test. On the downside, optimum arrangement of items to facilitate an examinee's ability to read and understand the items can add to the cost of reproducing copies of the test, because more pages will be needed for each test. (It goes without saying that the print should be large enough that it is easy to read.)

4. *Plan the layout of the test so that a separate answer sheet can be used to record answers.* The use of a separate answer sheet may make the test-taking process a bit more difficult, but there is a considerable gain in ease and accuracy of test scoring. Most standardized tests require separate answer sheets at all but the lowest levels of the test, and by the third grade, most students can easily learn to use one. The ability to use a separate answer sheet is a test-taking skill that should be taught to students, and practice in the skill should be provided early. Although test scoring equipment can be expensive, the use of a machine scorer is highly recommended. Not only does machine scoring save time, it also reduces the chance of scoring errors. Even the simplest machines can score the answer sheets, capture the data, and store it on a disk. This type of equipment can greatly facilitate item analysis procedures and further analyses of the data.

5. *Group items of the same format (true–false, multiple-choice, or matching) together.* Each different kind of objective item requires a different set of directions. Grouping items of the same format together makes it possible to write a concise and clear set of directions that will apply throughout that part of the test. Each item type also requires a different response set or approach on the part of the examinees. The examinees will be better able to maintain an appropriate response set if the items of the same type are grouped together.

6. *Within item type, group together items dealing with the same content.* This practice makes the test more coherent and provides a reasonable context for the examinee. It can also help both the student and the teacher to see the student's strong and weak points.

7. *Arrange items so that difficulty progresses from easy to hard.* This practice is of particular importance on a test for which testing time is limited and some items on the test will not be attempted by all students. Those unattempted items should be the more difficult ones that examinees would have

been less likely to answer correctly even if they had reached them. On a power test on which most students answer all of the items, this arrangement can encourage students, particularly young children and less able students, by ensuring some early success. This practice may motivate them to attempt all of the items on the test rather than to give up. However, this recommendation is supported more by professional judgment than by empirical evidence.

8. *Write a set of specific directions for each item type.* A good set of directions will provide information about how the examinees are to record their answers, the basis on which they are to select their answers, and the scoring procedures that will be used. For a test made up of multiple-choice items that will not be corrected for guessing and for which separate answer sheets are used, one might use the following set of directions.

EXAMPLE

Directions: Read each item and decide which choice best completes the statement or answers the question. Mark your answers on the separate answer sheet. Do not mark them on the test itself. Indicate your answer by darkening the space next to the letter on the answer sheet that corresponds to your choice; that is, if you think that Choice B is the best answer to Item 1, darken the space next to B in the row after item 1 on your answer sheet. Your score will be the number of correct items, so it is to your advantage to respond to every item, even if you are not sure of the correct response. Be sure your name is on your answer sheet.

The following set of directions could be used for a test made up of true–false items in which answers are to be recorded on the test paper and the total score will be corrected for guessing.

EXAMPLE

Directions: Read each of the following statements carefully.

If all or any part of the statement is false, circle the F in front of the statement.

If the statement is completely true, circle the T in front of the statement.

Your score will be the number of correct answers minus the number of incorrect answers, so do not guess blindly. If you are not reasonably sure of an answer, omit the item. Be sure your name is on your test.

These instructions would have to be revised if a separate answer sheet were being used. Commercially produced answer sheets for optical scanning usually are set up so that the first answer space (A) is equated to *true* and the second space (B) represents *false.* Also, if several types of items are being used on the test, examinees should be warned at the beginning of the test that additional directions will be provided later and that they should read those instructions carefully. With inexperienced examinees, such as young children, and with novel item forms, it is often helpful to put one or two examples of how to answer the questions immediately following the directions.

9. *Be sure that one item does not provide clues to the answer of another item or items.* Unless one is very careful in assembling items for a test, the answer to an item may be given away by a previous item. All of the items that are finally selected should be carefully checked, because it is possible for a true–false or completion item to give clues to the answer of a multiple-choice item or vice versa. For example, in the example that follows, the true–false item provides a clue to the answer to the objective item.

EXAMPLE

1. <u>T</u> F The spores of the bacteria causing botulism are present in soil and air.
2. Which of the following bacteria form spores?
    A. Staphylococcus causing food poisoning
    <u>B</u>. Bacillus causing botulism
    C. Bacillus causing typhoid fever
    D. Pneumococcus causing pneumonia

10. *Be sure that the correct responses form an essentially random pattern.* Some test constructors attempt to make the job of scoring easier by establishing a regular pattern of correct answers. For example, on a true–false test, they use a repetitive pattern such as T, T, F, F, F, or on a multiple-choice test, they use a pattern such as A, C, B, D. When a pattern is used, some testwise examinees may discover the pattern and use it as a means of answering items that they really do not know. On four-option, multiple-choice tests, there is a tendency for the correct answers to appear more frequently in the second and third positions than in the first and last positions. On a multiple-choice test the correct answer should appear in each of the possible response positions about the same percentage of the time. For example, on a four-option, multiple-choice test of 50 items, the constructor might check to see that each response position contains the keyed answer in not less than 10 and not more than 15 items. With word processing equipment the task of rearranging response alternatives is easy enough that this requirement is not hard to meet. If the test is to be machine scored, there is nothing to be gained from patterning the correct answers.

SCORING THE OBJECTIVE TEST

Once the test has been constructed, reproduced, and administered, the assessment procedure is still not complete. The test must be scored, and the scores must be interpreted. The interpretation of scores in normative- and criterion-referenced frameworks was discussed in Chapter 3. However, scores can also be influenced by the errors caused by guessing. A decision needs to be made before the test is given whether scores will be corrected for guessing. Examinees should be told whether a correction will be used, because it may influence their strategy for taking the test. Measurement experts are not in complete agreement about the usefulness of the correction for guessing, but it seems to slightly improve the accuracy of measurement. The correction also is more important on item types where chance can play a larger part, such as in true–false items.

Correction for Guessing

It is well known that examinees differ in their tendencies to guess on an objective test when they are not sure of the answer. These differences in willingness to guess introduce score variations that are not related to real individual differences in achievement. The more examinees guess, the less reliable the scores will be because getting an answer right by guessing is, by definition, introducing chance or random measurement error into the scores. Differences in willingness to guess are particularly important when tests are speeded, because not everyone has enough time to finish. Under these conditions, people who guess on items when there is not enough time to answer carefully will obtain higher scores than those who leave the items blank. One reason for instructing examinees not to guess and for imposing a penalty for incorrect answers is to try to make the guessing behavior more alike for all examinees.

A Correction for Guessing Formula

One approach to dealing with the problem of guessing is to adjust scores with a correction-for-guessing formula. The most commonly used formula is based on the assumption that all incorrect responses result from guessing. Examinees are expected either to get an item correct or to omit it. The correction-for-guessing adjustment is found by subtracting from the examinee's score the number of points equal to the gain that would be expected from guessing. On a multiple-choice test with four alternatives, a person responding at random can be expected, by chance alone, to get one out of four answers correct. Therefore, for every three questions answered incorrectly, a person can be expected to get one correct by guessing. To put this logic into mathematical terms, the following equation is used:

$$\text{Corrected score} = R - \frac{W}{n-1}$$

where R is the number of items answered correctly,

W is the number of items answered incorrectly, and

n is the number of answer choices for an item.

Items for which examinees do not give an answer, that is, items they omit, do not count in this formula for guessing. On a true–false test (where there are only two possible answers), $n - 1$ in the formula becomes $2 - 1$, or 1, and the correction for guessing reduces to the number of correct answers minus the number of incorrect answers.

The two examples that follow, the first based on a true–false test and the second on a five-alternative, multiple-choice test, illustrate how the equation works. Note that the effect of guessing is assumed to be much larger on the true–false test, so the correction causes a much larger change in the person's score.

EXAMPLE 1

Student Performance

Type of Test	n	R	W	Omits
True–false	2	48	20	7

Corrected score = 48 − 20/(2 − 1) = 48 − 20/1 = 28

EXAMPLE 2

Student Performance

Type of Test	n	R	W	Omits
Multiple-choice	5	48	20	7

Corrected score = 48 − 20/(5 − 1) = 48 − 20/4 = 43

Criticisms of the Correction-for-Guessing Equation

The correction-for-guessing formula has been criticized both because its assumptions are difficult to meet and because it generally fails to do what it purports to do, which is to correct for guessing. The formula is based on the following two assumptions: (1) that all guesses are blind, with each response having an equal probability of being chosen, and (2) that every incorrect answer results from guessing—that is, the person never responds on the basis of misinformation or mismarking the answer sheet. The first assumption rejects the possibility that a student might make an educated guess based on partial information or might eliminate some options. If this happens, the probabilities in the formula change. On a four-option, multiple-choice test, the probability that a student will obtain a correct answer becomes greater than one in four. Only in a highly speeded test, where it is not possible to give a reasoned response to all questions, will examinees engage in truly blind guessing. The second assumption precludes the possibility that a person might make an incorrect response based on faulty or misunderstood knowledge. But a good item writer will construct misleads so as to attract those with partial or incorrect information.

Undercorrection. On a four-option, multiple-choice test, the formula will undercorrect to the extent that an examinee can eliminate some alternatives and then guess between the smaller number of remaining responses. Examinees are well advised to guess under these circumstances because the penalty for guessing is less than the expected increase in score that would accrue from guessing. If even one alternative can be eliminated, guessing will help the individual's score. On the other hand, persons who are not testwise are likely to be intimidated by the knowledge that the correction-for-guessing formula is being employed, and for this reason they may refrain from guessing.

Technical Factors. Another feature of the correction formula is that it does not change the rank order of students if no questions are omitted. Under these circumstances, there is a perfect correlation between raw scores and corrected scores. Only when there are omitted responses does the correlation become less than 1.0, and even then it remains in the 90s (Ebel, 1979) unless there is a great deal of variability in the number of items omitted.

Reliability and validity are only increased by correcting for guessing if there is a positive correlation between omitted responses and the raw score (Ebel, 1979). Of course, this circumstance would not normally be expected to occur because the person who works most quickly and answers the most questions is usually the more knowledgeable. Additionally, the more testwise examinees are likely both to answer more questions and also do better on the test overall.

Why the Correction-for-Guessing Equation Is Used

You might, at this point, ask why, given its shortcomings, the correction-for-guessing equation is ever employed. The motivations of those using this formula may be more related to discouraging guessing than to correcting for it. Because guessing contributes directly to error variance, it is believed that the use of this equation might increase reliability. Reliability coefficients are the most easily obtainable and objective evidence of the quality of a test, so a great deal of emphasis is placed on these indices, and even a slight increase in reliability is hailed as improvement in a test.

Guessing on a test presents the most serious problem for tests that are highly speeded or that have items with only two answer choices. The scores obtained from such tests will probably be more dependable if they are corrected for guessing. In multiple-choice tests that have four or five answer choices and liberal enough time limits to permit all or most examinees to attempt every item, a score that is simply the number of correct answers is quite satisfactory, and little or no gain is made from correcting for guessing.

USING ITEM ANALYSIS TO IMPROVE OBJECTIVE TESTS

Commercial test publishers do not rely on judgment and the skills of item writers to make final decisions about which items to include on their tests. Rather, they conduct pilot studies called **item tryouts** to get empirical evidence concerning item quality. If a test is to contain 100 items, the publisher may try out 150 to 200 items in order to be sure the final test will have the desired properties. For the tryout, several forms of the test are prepared with different subsets of items, so each item appears with every other item. Each form may be given to several hundred examinees. Although it is not necessary that the tryout sample be representative of the target population for which the test is intended, as would be necessary for a norming sample, it should include individuals who span the range and have about the same average ability as the target population. Final item selection is then based on the kind of analysis described here. Although locally produced tests seldom are pretested in this elaborate way, item analysis of the data from one administration of the test can be employed to help improve items that may be used another time.

There are several different methods of conducting an item analysis. In terms of sophistication, the methods range from those based on complex item response theory to fairly simple ones that can easily be employed by a teacher or researcher with minimal training. With the appropriate equipment and software, it is possible to set up procedures that can easily provide a wealth of item analysis information to the test constructor, with minimal effort on his or her part. Most universities and larger school districts have test scoring equipment that can perform item analyses.

Simplified Procedures for Conducting Item Analyses

The first step in performing an item analysis is the tabulation of the responses that have been made to each item of the test—that is, how many individuals got each item correct, how many chose each of the possible incorrect answers, and how many skipped the item. You must have this information for the upper and lower sections of the group, based on the total test score. From this type of tabulation, you will be able to answer the following questions about each item:

1. How difficult is the item?
2. Does the item distinguish between the higher and lower scoring examinees?
3. Is every option selected by some examinees? Or are there some options that no examinees choose?

In the following discussion, intended to illustrate the type of information provided by an item analysis, four items from a social studies test are presented, along with the analysis of responses for each item. This test was given to 100 high school seniors enrolled in a course called Current American Problems. There were 95 multiple-choice items on the test, each with four options. The highest score on the test was 85, and the lowest score was 14. The test papers were arranged in order, by the total score, starting with the score of 85 and ending with the score of 14. The top 25 papers were selected to represent the upper group (scores ranged from 59 to 85) and the last 25 papers were selected to represent the lower group (scores ranged from 14 to 34). The item analysis is based only on those in the upper and lower groups. The responses made to each item by each student in the upper and lower groups were tallied to give the frequency of choosing each option. These frequencies are shown in the columns on the right. The correct option is underlined. Each item is followed by a brief discussion of the item data.

The first thing we can learn about the test comes from the total score distribution. The test was quite difficult. The third quartile (Q_3) is located at the point where the median should be, 62% correct [(59/95) = .62]. A second indication that the test is too hard is that at least one student scored 10 points below the chance level of 24. When this happens, it is necessary to inspect the score distribution to determine whether this was an isolated case or if several other students scored well below chance. Such poor scores could result from misinformation, serious problems with several of the items, or a motivation to do poorly. When below-chance scores are encountered, the test administrator should talk to the low-scoring examinees and try to determine the cause of the poor performance. If people are taking the test with an intent to miss items, then the value of an item analysis of these responses is highly questionable. The test also shows a wide range of scores. The range is 72 points out of a possible 95, and the interquartile range is 25; therefore, the test has been successful in spreading out the students.

The difficulty of an item is defined as the proportion of examinees who answered the item correctly. The item in our first example is an easy item because everyone in the upper group and 20 students in the lower group got it correct. Since 45 of the 50 students in the analysis got the item right, the item has a difficulty of .90 (45/50). (Note that the difficulty index is really an easiness index; high values of the index mean low difficulty.)

EXAMPLE 1

"Everyone's Switching to Breath of Spring Mouthwash!" is an example of the propaganda technique called:

	Upper	Lower
A. glittering generality.	0	2
B. bandwagon.	25	20
C. testimonial.	0	2
D. plain folk.	0	1
Item omitted	0	0

Although it is quite easy, the item does differentiate in the desired direction because the incorrect answers that occurred fall in the lower group. That is, students who earned higher scores on the total test were more likely to get the item correct. The item is also good in that all of the incorrect options are functioning; that is, each incorrect answer was chosen by at least one student in the lower group. Two or three easy items like this one would be good icebreakers with which to start a test.

Our second example is a difficult but effective item, difficult because only 13 out of 50 students got it correct, and effective because all 13 students getting the item correct were in the upper group. All of the incorrect options attracted some students in the lower group, and all of the incorrect options attracted more members of the lower group than of the higher group. Incidentally, an item such as this one illustrates that blind guessing may have less effect on scores than is often supposed. When a wrong alternative is provided that is highly attractive to people who do not have the knowledge or skill required, the effect of guessing is reduced.

EXAMPLE 2

There were no federal income taxes before 1913 because prior to 1913:

	Upper	Lower
A. the federal budget was balanced.	3	5
B. regular property taxes provided enough revenue to run the government.	9	15
C. a tax on income was unconstitutional.	13	0
D. the income of the average worker in the U.S. was too low to be taxed.	0	5
Item omitted	0	0

The next example turned out to be a poor item. First, the item is very difficult; only 8 out of the 50, or 16% of the students, got it correct. Second, the item is negatively discriminating; that is, correct answers were more frequent in the lower group than in the upper group. There are two possible explanations for these results: (1) The item was ambiguous, especially for students who knew the most, or (2) the students have not learned the provisions of the Corrupt Practices Act. Two pieces of evidence point to the second as the more likely explanation. The concentration of responses of the upper group at Option A suggests misinformation, and the essentially uniform distribution of responses of the lower group indicates random guessing. To arrive at the correct answer to the item, the student would have to know (1) the limit placed on contributions to the national committee of a political party, (2) who is forbidden to make contributions, and (3) what kind of organization the National Association of Manufacturers is. One might guess that it is points one and three that are causing difficulty for the upper group.

EXAMPLE 3

Under the Corrupt Practices Act the national committee of a political party would be permitted to accept a contribution of:

	Upper	Lower
A. $10,000 from Mr. Jones.	15	6
B. $1,000 from the ABC Hat Corporation.	4	6
C. $5,000 from the National Association of Manufacturers.	2	6
D. $500 from union funds of a local labor union.	4	7
Item omitted	0	0

Our last item is of reasonable difficulty (38/50 = .76) and shows some discrimination in the desired direction (21 versus 17), but the differentiation is not very sharp. The response pattern is one that is quite common. Only two of the four choices are functioning at all. Nobody selected either Option B or C. If we wished to improve this item, we might try substituting "wages paid for easy work" for Option B and "money paid to people on welfare" for Option C. The use of the adjective "easy" in Option B (it is also in the stem) and the idea of getting money for not working in Option C might make the item more difficult and, therefore, more discriminating. (Note that a clang association, while not acceptable in the correct answer, *is* appropriate in a distractor because it will tend to attract examinees who do not have the information or skill being tested by the item, which should make the item more discriminating.)

EXAMPLE 4

The term "easy money," as used in economics, means:

	Upper	Lower
A. the ability to borrow money at low interest rates.	21	17
B. dividends that are paid on common stocks.	0	0
C. money that is won in contests.	0	0
D. money paid for unemployment.	4	8
Item omitted	0	0

More Formal Item Analysis Procedures

The informal, straightforward approach to conducting an item analysis, discussed in the previous section, has the virtue of conceptual simplicity. We discussed item difficulty as the percent of examinees who answered the item correctly, and this definition of difficulty is fully sufficient for classical item analysis. A more abstract definition is required by the item response theory approach (see Chapter 3).

The lack of a concrete discrimination index is the most important limitation of the informal procedures. We spoke of an item having a positive discrimination in the sense that more people who scored high on the test got that item right than was the case for low scorers. But for more formal situations, such as in commercial test development, it is desirable to be able to quantify an item's ability to discriminate those who possess the information from those who do not. Two methods of indicating the discriminating power of an item are often used.

The Discrimination Index

One commonly used procedure, which we will label the **discrimination index,** is readily computed from the same data layout that we used to study the functioning of our distractors. For technical reasons, this type of analysis is usually carried out on the top and bottom 27% of examinees (that is, the extreme 54% rather than the extreme 50%, as we described earlier); however, the principles are identical, regardless of the split used. When the number of examinees is small, the upper and lower groups often are defined as above and below the median. This increases the number of people participating in the analysis but may systematically reduce the discrimination index values, because the groups are less different when the middle of the distribution has not been excluded.

The discrimination index (D) is computed by subtracting the number of students who got the item correct in the lower group (N_L) from the number who got it correct in the upper group (N_U) and dividing the difference by the number in one group. The discrimination index equation is as follows:

$$D = \frac{N_U - N_L}{N_U}$$

Applying this formula to the data from our four examples produces the following values for the discrimination index:

Example 1	$D = (25 - 20)/25 = .20$
Example 2	$D = (13 - 0)/25 = .52$
Example 3	$D = (2 - 6)/25 = -.16$
Example 4	$D = (21 - 17)/25 = .16$

These results reveal several important aspects of item discrimination. First, items that are very hard (3) or very easy (1 and 4) cannot discriminate very well. In the limiting case where everyone passes the item or everyone fails it, the value of D will be exactly zero, indicating no discrimination. While having a few very easy items that do not discriminate well may be acceptable, because of their beneficial motivational properties, we would seldom want extremely hard items unless they measured achievement of a particularly critical objective. For most purposes our test will differentiate best when it contains a majority of items of moderate difficulty, because these are the items that show the best discrimination. For example, maximum discrimination of 1.00 occurs when all of the members of the upper group got the item right and all of the members of the lower group missed it.

The second point that becomes clear from our examples is that when more people in the lower group pass the item than in the upper group, the value of D will be negative. This is what we mean by a **negatively discriminating item.** Items like this are never desirable in a test because they are measuring something other than what the rest of the test is measuring. They may be measuring nothing at all, or they may be poorly stated and confusing or misleading to the more able examinees. If an item is intended to measure an important objective and is a negative discriminator, the test constructor must either correct the problems with the item or find another way to assess that objective.

In addition to having items that are positively discriminating (that is, more people in the upper group get the item right), it is also desirable to have the distractors function in a comparable way. A distractor is functioning properly (sometimes called a **positively discriminating distractor**) when more members of the lower group than the upper group choose it. This is the case in example items 1 and 2 above. More people in the lower group selected each distractor. The performance of the distractors is not as critical to the quality of the test, but the best test items will have this property.

Item-Total Score Correlations

When the tests have been machine scored and computer facilities are available, an alternative way to assess the discriminating power of the items is to compute the correlation of each item with the total score. One advantage of this method is that items may be scored right/wrong, or scores may be awarded on degree of correctness when certain complex item formats are used or when there is a bonus for rapid responding. (Both of these scoring procedures are used on the Wechsler scales, for example, although the instrument is not formally an objective test.) The item-total correlation uses all of the data rather than just the extreme cases, and the resulting correlations have the same general properties as the D index. Many of the programs that control optical scanning equipment also have item analysis options that will produce output very similar to what we have examined, but they are more likely to use the item-total score correlation than the D-index. The correlation between total score and score on an item that scored right or wrong is called the **point-biserial correlation (r_{pb}).**

Using Discrimination Indexes

The simplest way to use the discrimination index for test development is to retain the items with the highest values (e.g., over .50), to eliminate the ones with the lowest (e.g., below .20), and to consider for modification those items between these two points. Items with negative discrimination values should, of course, be rejected or modified so they discriminate properly. In trying to determine why an item has a low index, look first at item difficulty. Items that are too easy or too hard are almost always poor discriminators. Sometimes an item is a poor discriminator even though the computed difficulty might be in an acceptable range, such as when two of four options are completely implausible, leaving the correct answer and one functioning distractor. Even if the item is so difficult that only a few students know the correct answer, many more students will get the correct answer by guessing, because they need only to guess between the two plausible responses. Of course, the test maker also needs to determine whether the item is flawed in some other way and if its construction violates the rules of good item writing. It is also important to see that all of the distractors are functioning effectively. Distractors that are not plausible make items too easy, and those that are too closely related to the correct answer make an item too difficult. This possibility of manipulating item difficulty by modifying the distractors is an advantage of multiple-choice tests.

WRITING ESSAY TEST ITEMS

The major advantage of the produce-response or essay type of question lies in its potential for measuring examinees' abilities to organize, synthesize, and integrate their knowledge; to use information to solve novel problems; and to demonstrate original or integrative thought. To accomplish these assessment objectives, each item must be carefully crafted to require the student to display these abilities. Merely posing a question in a form where examinees must write out their answers does not ensure that these abilities will be assessed.

Look at the following two essay questions:

EXAMPLE 1

What methods have been used in the United States to prevent and control communicable diseases?

EXAMPLE 2

Examine the data in the table shown below.

Causes of Death and Rate of Death from Each Disease at the Beginning and End of the 20th Century in the U.S.

Cause of Death	Rate of Death per 100,000 People	
	1900	2000
1. Pneumonia	175.4	21.8
2. Diarrhea and enteritis	139.9	1.5
3. Diseases of the heart	137.4	399.9
4. Cancer	64.0	185.6
5. Diphtheria	40.3	0.01

Explain how changes in knowledge, medical practices, and conditions of life in the United States during the 20th century account for changes in death rates shown in this table.

To answer the question in Example 1, examinees need only recall and write down information presented in the textbook or in class. No higher mental processes are required. The question in Example 2, on the other hand, requires that the examinees recall information about the characteristics and about the methods of transmission of each disease. They must then relate these to such things as immunization, chemotherapy, improvements in sanitation, and increased longevity.

Essay exams present two difficulties. First, factual knowledge may be confounded with the ability to organize and synthesize an answer. The student who knows more facts will often produce an answer that looks superior, even when originality is missing. Second, it takes much more time to think out an answer and compose a written response than it does to select an answer from a set of alternatives. Thus, differences in performance can depend on ability to write quickly and in correct form as much as on abilities the examiner wishes to assess. Also, fewer questions can be asked, making it more difficult to achieve content validity.

Several variations in the testing environment have been proposed to combat these problems. Although each presents its own difficulties, one or another may be appropriate in certain circumstances. The alternatives include the following:

1. *The "open-book" examination.* In this format students are allowed to use their textbook or class notes to assist in answering questions. This is one way to reduce the effect of differences in knowledge. The drawback of this method is that less able students are likely to use too much time trying to look up material during the test while the more able students will devote most of their time to composing their answers. Thus, students who rely on their book or notes may feel they have even less time than if the exam were a "closed-book" one.

2. *The "take-home" exam.* This variant removes the time pressure from testing by allowing each examinee to work as long as he or she wishes (or has the time to). However, this format sacrifices test security. There is no way to know for certain that each examinee worked independently. Particularly in this age of Internet information, allowing students to work in a completely unsupervised environment invites abuse.

3. *Study questions.* One strategy that combines features of both the open-book and take-home exams is to give students a list of study questions from which the examination questions will be drawn. The students might be given 8 or 10 questions and told the exam will contain three of them. This approach has the advantage that students can take as much time as they wish to prepare for the exam and use whatever resources are available to them, but they must produce their answers under supervision.

4. *Cheat sheets.* A variation on the open-book exam that reduces the problem of dependence on the textbook is to allow each student to bring to the exam one piece of paper with as many facts, procedures, or other information as desired. This approach, which can be used with objective tests as well as essay tests, can work particularly well in courses where formulas constitute a large part in the subject matter and the instructor does not wish to require that students memorize the formulas. If test security is an issue (for example, the same exam will be used for different sections of the course) it is a good idea to collect the cheat sheets with the exam papers to prevent students from writing the questions down to serve as study aids for students in other sections.

Writing Essay Questions

Here are some general guidelines for writing good essay questions.

1. *Know what mental processes you want to assess before starting to write the questions.* Persons constructing essay tests must understand fully the kinds of responses that represent the abilities they

wish to assess before they can determine the kinds of stimulus materials needed to elicit those responses. For example, if you wish to use an essay question to evaluate eighth graders' ability to think critically about health information, you might identify as evidence of critical thinking the abilities to evaluate the adequacy of an authority, to recognize bias or emotional factors in a presentation, to distinguish between verifiable and unverifiable data, to evaluate the adequacy of data, to check assertions against other known data, and to determine whether the data support the conclusion. Once you have decided that these are the competencies you wish to test, you can select, adapt, or create stimulus materials and tasks that will require the examinee to display these abilities.

2. *Use novel material or novel organization of material in phrasing the questions.* In general, we want essay questions to test the examinees' ability to *use* their information. To determine whether they can do this, we must put them in situations where they must do more than merely reproduce the material presented in class or in the textbook. Far too often, essay questions are of the form "List the factors that led to the Japanese attack on Pearl Harbor" or "What are the ways in which AIDS can be transmitted?" Both questions require the examinee to reproduce information, but not to do anything with it, and the instructional objectives implied by both questions could be much more efficiently assessed using multiple-choice questions. Good essay questions, like the one given earlier in Example 2, are difficult to write.

3. *Start essay questions with phrases such as "Compare," "Contrast," "Give original examples of," "Explain how," "Predict what would happen if," "Criticize," "Differentiate."* The use of words or phrases such as these, when combined with novel material, will help present the examinees with tasks requiring them to select, organize and apply information. Don't start essay questions with words such as "What," "When," "Who," or "List" because such words lead to tasks requiring only the reproduction of facts.

4. *Write essay questions in such a way that the task is clearly and unambiguously defined for the examinees.* We want each examinee's score to reflect how well this individual can do the specified task, not how well he or she can figure out what the task is. A question such as "Discuss the organizations that contribute to the health of a community" is global, vague, and ambiguous. What is meant by the word "discuss"? Does it imply listing organizations and what they do; criticism and evaluation of their activities; identifying gaps in the organizational structure? Are examinees to consider only government organizations or the whole gamut of public and private organizations that contribute to the health of a community? What does "contribute to the health of a community mean"? Does it mean enforcement of health regulations, treatment and prevention of illness, or sponsorship of education and research? A better way to phrase the question so that each examinee will interpret it the same way is given in the following example:

EXAMPLE

Using tuberculosis as an example, describe how each of the following organizations could be expected to contribute to the prevention of the disease or the cure or care of persons with the disease.

    a. Local and state health departments
    b. The United States Public Health Service
    c. The Department of Agriculture
    d. The National Tuberculosis Association
    e. The American Public Health Association

In this form the question provides a more common basis for response without sacrificing the freedom of the student in answering the question.

5. *A question dealing with a controversial issue should ask for and be evaluated in terms of the presentation of evidence for a position, rather than the position taken.* Many issues that confront individuals and society have no generally agreed-on answers. Yet understanding issues like these constitutes much of what is genuinely vital in education. In controversial areas, it is inappropriate to demand that students accept a specific conclusion or solution. However, it is reasonable to assess them on how well they know, can marshal, and can utilize the evidence on which a specific conclusion is based. The question "What laws should Congress pass to assure adequate medical care for all citizens of the United states?" is ambiguous and has no generally accepted answer. However, one might reasonably expect examinees to respond to a question such as the following: "It has been suggested that the cost of all medical care provided by physicians and the cost of all prescription medications be borne by funds provided by the federal government. Do you agree or disagree? Support your position with facts and logical arguments."

6. *Adapt the length and complexity of the questions and the expected answers to the maturity level of the examinees and the testing situation.* Older, more sophisticated examinees can be expected to comprehend and answer more complex questions. Also, in testing situations where time is not a factor, we may expect examinees to display more sophisticated thinking.

Preparing the Essay Test

Once you have written good test items there are several things you should do to assure that your test will function the way you want it to. Following these guidelines will help eliminate some common but unwanted effects on test scores.

1. *Be sure there are not too many or too lengthy questions for the examinees to answer in the time available.* The number of questions that can be included in an essay test depends on the length and complexity of the answers expected, the maturity of the students, and the testing time. An essay test should not be an exercise in writing speed. The examinees should have time to think out and compose their answers. The more complex the question, the longer it will take to answer. The more experienced the examinees, the more quickly they can be expected to work on problems of a given complexity. It is not uncommon for teachers to expect students to answer three to five moderately complex essay questions and 40 to 50 multiple-choice questions in an hour of testing. A test of this length might be appropriate for a college class, but for most middle and high school students it would be too long, thus emphasizing speed rather than proficiency. You should allow about 15 minutes for students to answer each reasonably complex essay question that calls for synthesis and organization. About 45 to 60 seconds is a reasonable time allotment for each multiple-choice question.

2. *If several essay questions are being given, have a range of complexity and difficulty in the questions.* Most classroom tests are given for the purpose of differentiating among students in their degree of mastery of the course material. If all of the questions are difficult enough to challenge the most able students, some of the less proficient may be unable to produce a satisfactory answer to any question. On the other hand, if all the questions are relatively easy, we will not measure the full capacity of the more able students. By providing a range of difficulty, the test will have questions appropriate for all examinees.

3. *In most circumstances, all examinees should be required to answer the same questions.* In most classes the same objectives are applied to all students. Allowing students a choice of which questions to answer reduces the common basis for differentiating among individuals. Comparing the quality of Student A's answer to Question 1 with Student B's answer to Question 2 introduces an additional source of subjectivity and measurement error into the assessment. In large national testing programs where students can be expected to have experienced different curricula, allowing a choice of questions may be appropriate, but it usually reduces the quality of measurement within a class.

4. *Write a general set of directions for the entire test.* Instructors often introduce an essay test with the simple instruction "Answer the following questions." This statement is not adequate to inform the examinees of the nature of their task. A good set of directions should specify (a) the general plan the student should use in taking the test; (b) the form in which the answers should be written, that is, connected prose or outline; (c) the general criteria that will be used to evaluate the answers; (d) the time available for completing the test; and (e) the point value for each question or portion of a question.

Scoring Essay Items

One of the drawbacks of the essay test is that there is much real work left to do after the test has been given. Adequate appraisal with an essay test requires not only a good set of items but also sound and consistent judgment of the quality of the answers. Variations in scoring from item to item and from examinee to examinee contribute to error in the measurement of competence. The following guidelines will help you to do the best job possible in evaluating student responses:

1. *Decide in advance what qualities are to be considered in judging the adequacy of an answer to each question. If more than one distinct quality is to be appraised, evaluate each one separately.* For example, you may wish to evaluate spelling and grammar as well as knowledge and organization in judging the overall quality of student responses. These are quite different competencies and should be appraised separately. Of course, when spelling and grammar will be evaluated, the students should be apprised of the fact in the directions for the test.

2. *Prepare an answer guide or model answer showing what points should be covered to receive full credit.* This practice will help you maintain a consistent set of standards across papers. It is particularly important if scoring will extend over several days.

3. *Read all answers to one question before going on to the next one.* This practice accomplishes two purposes: (1) The grader can maintain a more uniform set of standards across all papers and (2) the grader is less likely to be influenced in judging the quality of the answer to one question by comparing it to how well the student answered the previous question.

4. *After scoring the answers to one question for all papers, shuffle the papers before starting to score the next question.* It is hard to avoid comparing one student's answer to the answers given by the students whose papers were scored immediately before it. An average student who has the misfortune of having his or her paper scored right after that of the most able student in the class is likely to suffer by the comparison. By shuffling the papers, the order in which papers appear changes from item to item.

5. *Grade the papers as nearly anonymously as possible.* The less you know about *who* wrote an answer, the more objective you can be in judging *what* was written. The criteria of quality

for answers to essay questions should be the same for all examinees. Teachers sometimes object to this guideline because they wish to adjust standards for different ability levels. Adjustments for individual differences should *not* be made during scoring; these should made at an earlier point where objectives, content, and learning experiences can be differentiated. If teachers have different objectives or expectations for some students than for others, different tests should be prepared.

6. *Write comments and correct errors in the answers to essay questions.* It is a long-established principle that a test is most effective as a motivational and learning device when students get prompt specific information about their strengths and weaknesses. Teachers who make tallies of the common types of comments and errors will also gain information about the effectiveness of their teaching.

SUMMARY

Writing good test items is a learnable skill. In this chapter we have reviewed the principles that apply to all good test items. These include (1) keeping reading level and vocabulary appropriate to the purpose of the test, (2) making sure each select-response item has one best answer, (3) making sure the content is important, (4) keeping items independent, (5) avoiding trick questions, and (6) making sure the item poses a clear problem.

Although they are of limited value, true–false questions are popular. Special points to keep in mind in writing true–false items include (1) ensure that each statement is unequivocally true or false, (2) avoid specific determiners, (3) avoid ambiguous terms of amount, (4) avoid negative statements, (5) limit each item to a single idea, (6) make true and false statements approximately equal in length, and (7) have about the same number of true statements as false ones. Four modifications of the general true–false format include (1) underlining the important concept in the statement—to reduce ambiguity, (2) requiring examinees to correct false statements, (3) basing several statements on a single set of stimulus material, and (4) grouping several short statements under a common heading.

Multiple-choice items provide much more flexibility in the objectives that can be measured. Items in this format generally require examinees to read a stem that poses a problem and select the best answer from among three to five alternatives. Principles to be fol-

lowed in writing good multiple-choice items include (1) be sure the stem formulates a clear problem, (2) include as much of the item in the stem as possible to reduce reading load, (3) include only necessary material in the item, (4) avoid negatively worded items, (5) use novel material to assess comprehension and application objectives, (6) be sure there is only one correct answer, (7) be sure wrong answers are plausible, (8) avoid unintentional clues to the correct answer, and (9) use sparingly the "none of these" and "all of these" response alternatives. The complex multiple-choice item and the paired statements format are alternative forms of the multiple-choice item.

Matching items are a special case of the multiple-choice format in which several item stems share a set of response alternatives. Good matching items should involve homogeneous sets of statements and relatively short answers. Examinees should choose their answers from the shorter statements, and each column should have a heading that clearly identifies its content. There should be more response alternatives than statements, the responses should be arranged in a logical order, and directions should include the basis for matching.

When preparing a test, you should (1) write more items than you intend to use, (2) proofread the items carefully, (3) arrange the items in a readable form, (4) plan a layout that enables you to use separate answer sheets, (5) group items by format and by content, (6) arrange items by difficulty, (7) prepare specific directions for each type of item, (8) make sure one item does not give away the answer to another, and (9) make sure there is no systematic pattern to the correct answers.

One feature of all select-response tests is that some examinees will get some items correct by guessing. Guessing reduces the reliability of measurement because it introduces random error into the scores. A correction for guessing sometimes is applied to test scores by subtracting an estimate of how many answers examinees got right by guessing from their total score. The value of a correction for guessing is questionable.

Commercial test publishers evaluate their items before a test is released for public use. This is done with item analysis, a procedure that involves checking the difficulties of the items to ensure that they are in the desired range and examining the ability of items to discriminate between higher scoring and lower scoring examinees. For most purposes, a good test item will be moderately difficult and have a discrimination index value of about .50 or higher. Item analysis is also used to make sure all of the distractors are functioning as they should.

Essay questions ordinarily should be used only to assess objectives that require organization or originality. In writing essay questions you should follow these general guidelines: (1) know what mental processes you want to assess before writing the items, (2) use novel material, (3) start the question with words such as "compare" or "explain how," (4) make the task clear and unambiguous, (5) phrase questions relating to controversial material so as to have the examinees defend their positions, and (6) adapt length and complexity of questions to the abilities of the examinees. In preparing the test, (1) be sure there are not too many questions for the time allowed, (2) have a range of complexity in the different questions, (3) require all examinees to answer the same questions, and (4) prepare a good set of directions for the test. When scoring essays, (1) decide in advance what the characteristics of a good answer are, (2) prepare a model answer, (3) read all answers to one question before scoring the next one, (4) shuffle the papers between scoring different questions, (5) grade the papers anonymously, and (6) write corrections and comments on the papers.

QUESTIONS AND EXERCISES

1. Why do people who construct tests for their own local use so often use poor test development procedures?

2. What are the requirements for good test construction?

3. Under what circumstance would a criterion-referenced test be more appropriate than a norm-referenced test?

4. A teacher writes 10 objectives for a biology class and, for each objective, writes five items. An objective is considered mastered if a student correctly answers four out of five items. What is the most appropriate label for this approach to testing?

5. Present arguments both for using criterion-referenced tests and for not using them.

6. In a junior high school, one teacher takes complete responsibility for preparing the common final examination for all the classes in general science. This teacher develops the examination without consulting the other teachers. What advantages and disadvantages do you see in this procedure? How could it be improved?

7. One objective that is often proposed for the social studies program in secondary schools is to increase the students' critical reaction to the news in different news media. How could the formulation of this objective be improved so that progress toward it could be measured?

8. Look at the blueprint for the examination on a unit on health that appears in the Preparing a Test Blueprint section in Chapter 5. For which

of the cells in this blueprint would it be appropriate to use either recall or selection exercises? What factors influenced your decisions?

9. Construct four multiple-choice items designed to measure understanding or application in some subject area with which you are familiar.

10. Write a series of true–false items to assess the same outcomes used in Question 9. Which approach seemed to assess student knowledge most effectively?

11. Prepare a short, objective test for a small unit that you are teaching or taking. Indicate the objectives that you are trying to evaluate with each item.

12. For which of the following tests would correcting scores for guessing be justified? Give the reason or reasons for your decision.
    a. A 100-item, true–false test. All students answered all questions.
    b. A 70-item, multiple-choice test of spatial relations. Each item has five answer choices. For each item, one or more answer choices may be correct. All students answered all questions.
    c. A 50-item, multiple-choice test with four answer choices for each item, one of which is the keyed answer. Only 40% of the examinees completed all items.
    d. A 60-item, multiple-choice test with four answer choices for each item, one of which is the keyed answer. Ninety percent of the students answered all items.

13. A college professor has given an objective test to a large class, scored the papers, and entered the scores in the class record book. What additional steps might the professor take before returning the papers to the students? Why?

14. Collect five examples of poor items you have seen on tests. Indicate what is wrong with each item.

SUGGESTED READINGS

Albanese, M. A. (1988). The projected impact of the correction for guessing on individual scores. *Journal of Educational Measurement, 25,* 149–157.

Albanese, M. A., & Sabers, D. L. (1988). Multiple true–false items: A study of interitem correlations, scoring alternatives, and reliability estimation. *Journal of Educational Measurement, 25,* 111–123.

Bennett, R. E. & Ward, W. C. (1993). *Construction versus choice in cognitive measurement: Issues in constructed response, performance testing, and portfolio assessment.* Mahwah, NJ: Erlbaum.

Berk, R. A. (Ed.). (1984). *A guide to criterion-referenced test construction.* Baltimore: Johns Hopkins University Press.

Gronlund, N. E. (1982). *Constructing achievement tests.* Upper Saddle River, NJ: Prentice Hall.

Harper, A. E., Jr., & Harper, E. S. (1990). *Preparing objective examinations.* New Delhi: Prentice Hall of India.

Hopkins, K. D., Stanley, J. C., & Hopkins, B. R. (1990). *Educational and psychological measurement and evaluation* (7th ed.). Upper Saddle River, NJ: Prentice Hall.

Linn, R. L., & Gronlund, N. E. (2000). *Measurement and evaluation in teaching* (8th ed.). Upper Saddle River, NJ: Merrill/Prentice Hall.

Mager, R. F. (1975). *Preparing instructional objectives* (2nd ed.). Belmont, CA: Fearon.

Nitko, A. J. (2003). *Educational assessment of students* (4th ed.). Upper Saddle River, NJ: Merrill/Prentice Hall.

Osterlind, S. J. (1989). *Constructing test items.* Boston: Kluwer.

Thissen, D., Steinberg, L., & Fitzpatrick, A. R. (1989). Multiple-choice models: The distractors are also part of the item. *Journal of Educational Measurement, 26,* 161–176.

Wainer, H. (1989). The future of item analysis. *Journal of Educational Measurement, 26,* 191–208.

Percent of Cases Falling Below Selected Values on the Normal Curve

Deviation in Standard Deviation Units	Cases Falling Below (%)	Deviation in Standard Deviation Units	Cases Falling Below (%)	Deviation in Standard Deviation Units	Cases Falling Below (%)
+3.50	99.98	2.05	97.98	.85	80.23
3.40	99.97	2.00	97.72	.80	78.81
3.30	99.95	1.95	97.44	.75	77.34
3.20	99.93	1.90	97.13	.70	75.80
3.10	99.90	1.85	96.78	.65	74.22
3.00	99.87	1.80	96.41	.60	72.57
2.95	99.84	1.75	95.99	.55	70.88
2.90	99.81	1.70	95.54	.50	69.15
2.85	99.78	1.65	95.05	.45	67.36
2.80	99.74	1.60	94.52	.40	65.54
2.75	99.70	1.55	93.94	.35	63.68
2.70	99.65	1.50	93.32	.30	61.79
2.65	99.60	1.45	92.65	.25	59.87
2.60	99.53	1.40	91.92	.20	57.93
2.55	99.46	1.35	91.15	.15	55.96
2.50	99.38	1.30	90.30	.10	53.98
2.45	99.29	1.25	89.44	.05	51.99
2.40	99.18	1.20	88.49	0.00	50.00
2.35	99.06	1.15	87.49	−.05	48.01
2.30	98.93	1.10	86.43	−.10	46.02
2.25	98.78	1.05	85.31	−.15	44.04
2.20	98.61	1.00	84.13	−.20	42.07
2.15	98.42	.95	82.89	−.25	40.13
2.10	98.21	.90	81.59	−.30	38.21

(continued)

Deviation in Standard Deviation Units	Cases Falling Below (%)	Deviation in Standard Deviation Units	Cases Falling Below (%)	Deviation in Standard Deviation Units	Cases Falling Below (%)
−.35	36.32	−1.65	4.95	−2.85	0.22
−.40	34.46	−1.70	4.46	−2.90	0.19
−.45	32.64	−1.75	4.01	−2.95	0.16
−.50	30.85	−1.80	3.59	−3.00	0.13
−.55	29.12	−1.85	3.22	−3.10	0.10
−.60	27.43	−1.90	2.87	−3.20	0.07
−.65	25.78	−1.95	2.56	−3.30	0.05
−.70	24.20	−2.00	2.88	−3.40	0.03
−.75	22.66	−2.05	2.02	−3.50	0.02
−.80	21.19	−2.10	1.79		
−.85	19.77	−2.15	1.58		
−.90	18.41	−2.20	1.39		
−.95	17.11	−2.25	1.22		
−1.00	15.87	−2.30	1.07		
−1.05	14.69	−2.35	0.94		
−1.10	13.57	−2.40	0.82		
−1.15	12.51	−2.45	0.71		
−1.20	11.51	−2.50	0.62		
−1.25	10.56	−2.55	0.54		
−1.30	9.68	−2.60	0.47		
−1.35	8.85	−2.65	0.40		
−1.40	8.08	−2.70	0.35		
−1.45	7.35	−2.80	0.26		
−1.50	6.68				
−1.55	6.06				
−1.60	5.48				

References

Aamodt, M. G., Bryan, D. A., & Whitcomb, A. J. (1993). Predicting performance with letters of recommendation. *Public Personnel Management, 22,* 81–100.

Achenbach, T. M. (1991). *Manual for the Child Behavior Checklist and 1991 Profile.* Burlington, VT: University Associates in Psychiatry.

Acklin, M. W., McDowell, C. J., II, Verschell, M. S., & Chan, D. (2000). Inter-observer agreement, intraobserver reliability, and the Rorschach comprehensive system. *Journal of Personality Assessment, 74,* 15–47.

Adjutant General's Office, Personnel Research Section. (1952). *A study of officer rating methodology, validity and reliability of ratings by single raters and multiple raters* (PRS Report No. 904). Washington, DC: Author.

Adjutant General's Office, Personnel Research Section. (1953). *Survey of the aptitude for service rating system at the U.S. Military Academy, West Point, New York.* Washington, DC: Author.

Allen, W. B. (1988). Rhodes handicapping, or slowing the pace of integration. *Journal of Vocational Behavior, 33,* 365–378.

Allport, G. W. (1937). *Personality: A psychological interpretation.* New York: Holt, Rinehart and Winston.

Allport, G. W. (1955). *Becoming.* New Haven, CT: Yale University Press.

Allport, G. W., & Odbert, H. S. (1936). Trait-names, a psycholexical study. *Psychological Monographs, 47* (No. 211).

American Association on Mental Retardation. (1992). *Mental retardation: Definition, classification, and systems of supports* (9th ed.). Washington, DC: Author.

American Counseling Association. (1995). *Code of ethics and standards of practice.* Alexandria, VA: Author.

American Educational Research Association, American Psychological Association, & National Council on Measurement in Education. (1999). *Standards for educational and psychological testing.* Washington, DC: American Psychological Association.

American Psychological Association. (1954). *Technical recommendations for psychological tests and diagnostic techniques.* Washington, DC: Author.

American Psychological Association. (1992). *Ethical principles of psychologists and code of conduct.* Washington, DC: Author.

American Psychological Association. (2001). *Appropriate use of high-stakes testing in our nation's schools.* Washington DC: Author.

American Psychological Association. (2002). *Ethics code.* Available at http://www.apa.org/ethics/

Americans with Disabilities Act, 42 U.S.C.12101 (1990).

Ames, C., & Archer, J. (1988). Achievement goals in the classroom: Students' learning strategies and motivation processes. *Journal of Educational Psychology, 80,* 260–267.

Anastasi, A. (1988). *Psychological testing* (6th ed.). New York: Macmillan.

Anghoff, W. H. (1988). Validity: An evolving concept. In H. Wainer & H. Braun (Eds.), *Test validity* (pp. 19–32). Hillsdale, NJ: Erlbaum.

Banaji, M. R. (2001). Implicit attitudes can be measured. In H. L. Roediger, III, & J. S. Nairne (Eds.), *The nature of remembering: Essays in honor of Robert G. Crowder* (pp. 117–150). Washington, DC: American Psychological Association.

Barak, A. (1999). Psychological applications on the Internet: A discipline on the threshold of a new millennium. *Applied and Preventive Psychology, 8,* 231–246.

Barak, A., & English, N. (2002). Prospects and limitations of psychological testing on the Internet. *Journal of Technology in Human Services, 19* (2/3), 65–89.

Baxter, J. C., Brock, B., Hill, P. C., & Rozelle, R. M. (1981). Letters of recommendation: A question of value. *Journal of Applied Psychology, 66,* 296–301.

Belk, M. S., LoBello, S. G., Ray, G. E., & Zachar, P. (2002). WISC-III administration, clerical, and scoring errors made by student examiners. *Journal of Psychoeducational Assessment, 20,* 290–300.

Berk, R. A. (1980). A consumer's guide to criterion-referenced test reliability. *Journal of Educational Measurement, 17,* 323–349.

Berk, R. A. (1984). Selecting an index of reliability. In R. A. Berk (Ed.), *A guide to criterion-referenced test construction* (pp. 231–266). Baltimore: Johns Hopkins University Press.

Bersoff, D. N. (1981). Testing and the law. *American Psychologist, 36,* 1047–1056.

Birns, B. (1965). Individual differences in human neonates' responses to stimulation. *Child Development, 36,* 249–256.

Blatchford, C. H. (1970). *Experimental steps to ascertain reliability of diagnostic tests in English as a second language.* Unpublished doctoral dissertation, Teachers College, Columbia University, New York.

Bloom, B. S. (Ed.) (1956). *Taxonomy of educational objectives, Handbook I: Cognitive domain.* New York: Longman, Green.

Boake, C. (2002). From the Binet-Simon to the Wechsler-Bellevue: Tracing the history of intelligence testing. *Journal of Clinical and Experimental Neuropsychology, 24,* 383–405.

Borsboom, D., & Mellenbergh, G. H. (2002). True scores, latent variables and constructs: A comment on Schmidt and Hunter. *Intelligence, 30,* 505–514.

Boswell, J. (1988). *The kindness of strangers: The abandonment of children in western Europe from late antiquity to the Renaissance.* New York: Pantheon.

Boyle, G. J. (1989). Confirmation of the structural dimensionality of the Stanford-Binet Intelligence Scale (4th ed.). *Personality and Individual Differences, 10,* 709–715.

Bracken, B. A. (1991). Multidimensional self concept validation: A three instrument investigation. *Journal of Psychoeducational Assessment, 9,* 319–328.

Bracken, B. A. (1992). *Multidimensional Self Concept Test Examiner's Manual.* Austin, TX: PRO-ED.

Bracken, B. A., & McCallum, R. S. (1998). *The Universal Nonverbal Intelligence Test.* Itasca, IL: Riverside.

Brennan, R. L. (1984). Estimating the dependability of the scores. In R. A. Berk (Ed.), *A guide to criterion-referenced test construction* (pp. 292–334). Baltimore: Johns Hopkins University Press.

Brodsky, S. L. (1991). *Testifying in court: Guidelines and maxims for the expert witness.* Washington, DC: American Psychological Association.

Brody, N. (2003). Construct validation of the Sternberg Triarchic Abilities Test: Comment and reanalysis. *Intelligence, 31,* 319–329.

Browder, Diane M. (2001). *Curriculum and assessment for students with moderate and severe disabilities.* New York: Guilford.

Brown v. Board of Education of Topeka, Kansas, 347 U.S. 483 (1954).

Brown, V. L., Cronin, M. E., & McEntire, E. (1994). *Test of Mathematical Abilities* (2nd ed.). Austin, TX: PRO-ED.

Bruininks, R. H., Thurlow, M. L., & Gillman, C. J. (1987). Adaptive behavior and mental retardation. *The Journal of Special Education, 21,* 69–88.

Bruininks, R. H., Woodcock, R., Weatherman, R., & Hill, B. (1996). *Scales of Independent Behavior–Revised.* Chicago: Riverside.

Buhler, R. A. (1953). *Flicker fusion threshold and anxiety level.* Unpublished doctoral dissertation, Columbia University, New York.

Burks, H. F. (1977). *Burks Behavioral Rating Scales: Preschool and Kindergarten Edition.* Los Angeles: Western Psychological Services.

Butcher, J. N., & Rouse, S. V. (1996). Personality: Individual differences and clinical assessment. *Annual Review of Psychology, 47,* 87–111.

Butcher, J. N., & Williams, C. L. (1992a). *Essentials of MMPI-2 and MMPI-A Interpretation.* Minneapolis: University of Minnesota Press.

Butcher, J. N., & Williams, C. L. (1992b). *The Minnesota Multiphasic Personality Inventory–Adolescent.* Minneapolis: University of Minnesota Press.

Caldwell-Andrews, A., Baer, R. A., & Berry, D. T. (2000). Effects of response sets on NEO PI-R scores and their relations to external criteria. *Journal of Personality Assessment, 7,* 472–478.

Campbell, D. T., & Fiske, D. W. (1959). Convergent and discriminant validation by the multitrait-multimethod matrix. *Psychological Bulletin, 56,* 81–105.

Campbell, J. P., Dunnette, M. D., Arvey, R. D., & Hellervik, L. V. (1973). The development and evaluation of behaviorally based rating scales. *Journal of Applied Psychology, 57,* 15–22.

Cannell, J. J. (1988). Nationally normed elementary achievement testing in America's public schools: How all 50 states are above the national average. *Educational Measurement: Issues and Practice, 7*(2), 5–9.

Carroll, J. B. (1993). *Human cognitive abilities: A survey of factor-analytic studies.* Cambridge, MA: Cambridge University Press.

Cattell, R. B. (1950). *Personality: A systematic, theoretical, and factual study.* New York: McGraw-Hill.

Cheung, F. M., Leung, K., Zhang, J., & Sun, H. (2001). Indigenous Chinese personality constructs: Is the five factor model complete? *Journal of Cross Cultural Psychology, 32,* 407–433.

Civil Rights Act, 42 U.S.C. 2000e et seq. (1964).

Cohen, J., & Cohen, P. (1983). *Applied multiple regression for the behavioral sciences* (2nd ed.). Hillsdale, NJ: Erlbaum.

Cohen, R. J., & Swerdlik, M. E. (1999). *Psychological testing and assessment: An introduction to tests and measurements* (4th ed.). Mountain View, CA: Mayfield.

Cole, N. S., & Moss, P. A. (1989). Bias in test use. In R. L. Linn (Ed.), *Educational measurement* (3rd ed., pp. 201–220). New York: Macmillan.

Comprehensive Test of Basic Skills technical bulletin. (1990). Monterey, CA: McGraw-Hill.

Comrey, A. L., & Lee, H. B. (1992). *A first course in factor analysis*. Hillsdale, NJ: Erlbaum.

Connolly, A. J. (1988). *KeyMath–Revised: A diagnostic inventory of essential mathematics*. Circle Pines, MN: American Guidance Service.

Connolly, A. J. (1997). *Manual for Keymath–Revised*. Circle Pines, MN: American Guidance Service.

Conoley, J. C., & Impara, J. C. (Eds.). (1995). *The twelfth mental measurements yearbook*. Lincoln, NB: Buros Institute of Mental Measurements.

Conoley, J. C., & Kramer, J. J. (Eds.). (1989). *The tenth mental measurements yearbook*. Lincoln, NE: Buros Institute of Mental Measurements.

Conoley, J. C., Kramer, J. J., & Mitchell, J. V., Jr. (Eds.). (1988). *Supplement to the ninth mental measurements yearbook*. Lincoln, NE: Buros Institute of Mental Measurements.

Cook, T. D., & Campbell, D. T. (1979). *Quasi-experimentation: Design and analysis issues for field settings*. Chicago: Rand McNally.

Costa, P. T., & McCrae, R. R. (1992a). The five factor model and its relevance to personality disorders. *Journal of Personality Disorders, 6,* 343–359.

Costa, P. T., & McCrae, R. R. (1992b). *Professional Manual: Revised NEO Personality Inventory (NEO PI-R) and NEO Five-Factor Inventory (NEO-FFI)*. Odessa FL: Psychological Assessment Resources Inc.

Cramer, P. (1999). Future directions for the Thematic Apperception Test. *Journal of Personality Assessment, 72,* 74–92.

Cronbach, L. J. (1971). Test validation. In R. L. Thorndike (Ed.), *Educational measurement* (2nd ed., pp. 443–507). Washington, DC: American Council on Education.

Cronbach, L. J. (1988). Five perspectives on validation argument. In H. Wainer & H. Braun (Eds.), *Test validity* (pp. 3–17). Hillsdale, NJ: Erlbaum.

Cronbach, L. J., & Gleser, G. C. (1965). *Psychological tests and personnel decisions*. Champaign, IL: University of Illinois Press.

Cunningham, W. A., Preacher, K. J., & Banaji, M. R. (2001). Implicit attitude measures: Consistency, stability, and convergent validity. *Psychological Science, 12,* 163–170.

Dahlstrom, W. G. (1992). Comparability of two-point high-point code patterns from original MMPI norms to MMPI-2 norms for the restandardization sample. *Journal of Personality Assessment, 59,* 153–164.

Dana, R. H. (1990). Cross-cultural and multi-ethnic assessment. In J. N. Butcher & C. D. Spielberger (Eds.), *Recent advances in personality assessment* (Vol. 8, pp. 1–26). Hillsdale, NJ: Erlbaum.

Darlington, R. B. (1990). *Regression and linear models*. New York: McGraw-Hill.

Das, J. P., & Naglieri, J. A. (2001). The Das-Naglieri Cognitive Assessment System in theory and practice. In J. J. C. Andrews, D. H. Saklofske, & H. L. Janzen (Eds.), *Handbook of psychoeducational assessment* (pp. 33–63). San Diego: Academic Press.

Das, J. P., Naglieri, J. A., & Kirby, J. R. (1994). *Assessment of cognitive processes: The PASS theory of intelligence*. Boston: Allyn and Bacon.

Davis, D. E., & Hays, L. W. (1997). An examination of the clinical validity of the MCMI-III Depressive Personality Scale. *Journal of Clinical Psychology, 53,* 15–23.

Dawes, R. M., Faust, D., & Meehl, P. E. (1989). Clinical versus actuarial judgement. *Science, 243*(4899), 1668–1674.

Debra P. v. Turlington, 78-892 Civ. T-C (M.D. Fla. July 12, 1979), at 2380.

DeFruyt, R., Mervielde, I, Hoekstra, H. A., Hans, A., & Rolland, J. P. (2000). Assessing adolescents' personality with the NEO PI-R. *Assessment 7,* 329–345.

Deutsch, M. (1975). Equity, equality and need: What determines which value will be used as the basis of distributive justice. *Journal of Social Issues, 31,* 137–149.

Digman, J. M. (1990). Personality structure: Emergence of the five-factor model. *Annual Review of Psychology, 41,* 417–440.

Dretzke, B. J., & Heilman, K. A. (1998). *Statistics with Microsoft Excel*. Upper Saddle River, NJ: Prentice Hall.

DuBois, P. H. (1970). *A history of psychological testing*. Boston: Allyn and Bacon.

Duff, F. L. (1965). Item subtlety in personality inventory scales. *Journal of Consulting Psychology, 29,* 565–570.

Dunn, L. M., & Dunn, L. M. (1981). *Peabody Picture Vocabulary Test–Revised: Manual for Forms L and M*. Circle Pines, MN: American Guidance Service.

Dunn, L. M., & Dunn, L. M. (1997). *Peabody Picture Vocabulary Test–III examiners manual*. Circle Pines, MN: American Guidance Service.

Dwyer, K. P. (1997). IDEA amendments become law. *Communique, 25*(2), 1–4.

Dyer, F. J., & McCann, J. T. (2000). The Millon clinical inventories: Research critical of their forensic application and Daubert criteria. *Law and Human Behavior, 24,* 487–497.

Ebel, R. L. (1979). *Essentials of educational measurement* (3rd ed.). Upper Saddle River, NJ: Prentice Hall.

Education of the Handicapped Act Amendments, 20 U.S.C. 1400 (1986).

Educational Testing Service, Test Collection. (1975–1995). *Tests in Microfiche Annotated Bibliography* (Set A–Set U). Princeton, NJ: Author.

Educational Testing Service, Test Collection. (1987). *Directory of selected national testing programs*. Phoenix, AZ: Oryx Press.

Edwards, A. L. (1957). *Techniques of attitude scale construction*. New York: Appleton.

Embretson (Whitely), S. (1983). Construct validity: Construct representation versus nomothetic span. *Psychological Bulletin, 93,* 179–197.

Enright, B. E. (1983). *Enright Diagnostic Inventory of Basic Arithmetic Skills*. North Billerica, MA: Curriculum Associates.

Epstein, S. (1983). Aggregation and beyond: Some basic issues on the prediction of behavior. *Journal of Personality, 51,* 360–392.

Equal Employment Opportunity Commission, U.S. Civil Service Commission, U.S. Department of Labor, & U.S. Department of Justice. (1978, August). Uniform guidelines on employee selection procedures, 43 *Fed. Reg.* 166, 38290–38309.

Exner, J. E. (1974). *The Rorschach: A comprehensive system*. Oxford, UK: Wiley.

Exner, J. E. (1993). *The Rorschach: A comprehensive system: Volume 1. Basic foundations* (3rd ed.). New York: Wiley.

Exner, J. E., & Exner, D. E. (1972). How clinicians use the Rorschach. *Journal of Personality Assessment, 36,* 403–408.

Eysenck, H. J., & Rachman, S. (1965). *The causes and cures of neurosis: An introduction to the modern behavior therapy based on learning theory and principles of conditioning*. San Diego: Knapp.

Fabiano, E. (1989). *Index to tests used in educational dissertations*. Phoenix, AZ: Oryx Press.

Family Educational Rights and Privacy Act, 20 U.S.C. 241 (1974).

Federal Policy for the Protection of Human Subjects: Notices and Rules, 45 C.F.R. 46 (1991). *Federal Register* 166, 38290–38309. Washington, DC: U.S. Government Printing Office.

Fehrmann, P. G., & O'Brien, N. P. (2001). *Directory of test collections in academic, professional, and research libraries*. Chicago: Association of College and Research Libraries.

Feifer, S.G., & DeFina, P.A. (2000). *The neuropsychology of reading disorders: Diagnosis and intervention workbook*. Middleton, MD: School Neuropsychology.

Feldt, L. S., & Brennan, R. L. (1989). Reliability. In R. L. Linn (Ed.), *Educational measurement* (3rd ed., pp. 105–146). New York: Macmillan.

Feldt, L. S., Forsyth, R. A., Ansley, T. N., & Alnot, S. D. (1993). *Iowa Tests of Educational Development, Forms K and L*. Chicago: Riverside.

Flanagan, D. P., Andrews, T. J., & Genshaft, J. L. (1997). The functional utility of intelligence tests with special education populations. In D. P. Flanagan, J. L. Genshaft, & P. L. Harrison (Eds.), *Contemporary intellectual assessment: Theories, tests, and issues*. New York: Guilford.

Flanders, N. (1970). *Analyzing teacher behavior*. Menlo Park, CA: Addison-Wesley.

Flynn, J. R. (1984). The mean IQ of Americans: Massive gains 1932 to 1978. *Psychological Bulletin, 95,* 29–51.

Flynn, J. R. (1998). WAIS-III and WISC-III gains in the United States from 1972 to 1995: How to compensate for obsolete norms. *Perceptual & Motor Skills, 86,* 1231–1239.

Forsyth, R. A., Ainsley, T. N., Feldt, L. S., & Alnot, S. D. (2001). *Iowa Tests of Educational Development, Form A*. Itasca, IL: Riverside.

Foster, S. L., Bell-Dolan, D. J., & Burge, D. A. (1988). Behavioral observation. In A. S. Bellack & M. Hershon (Eds.), *Behavioral assessment: A practical handbook* (pp. 119–160). New York: Pergamon.

Fredericksen, J. R., & Collins, A. (1989). A systems approach to educational testing. *Educational Researcher, 18*(9), 27–32.

Fredericksen, N. (1986). Construct validity and construct similarity: Methods for use in test development and test validation. *Journal of Multivariate Behavioral Research, 21,* 3–28.

Fredericksen, N., Mislevy, R. J., & Bejar, I. I. (1993). *Test theory for a new generation of tests*. Hillsdale, NJ: Erlbaum.

Gallatin, J. (1982). *Abnormal psychology: Concepts, issues, trends*. New York: Macmillan.

Garb, H. N. (1994). Social and clinical judgment: Fraught with error? *American Psychologist, 49,* 758–759.

Gardner, H. (1983). *Frames of mind: The theory of multiple intelligences*. New York: Basic Books.

Gerbing, D. W., & Tuley, M. R. (1991). The 16PF related to the Five-Factor Model of Personality: Multiple-indicator measurement versus the a priori scales. *Multivariate Behavioral Research, 26,* 271–289.

Glass, G. V. (1977). Integrating findings: The meta-analysis of research. *Review of Research in Education, 5,* 351–379.

Glutting, J., Adams, W., & Sheslow, D. (2000). *WRIT: Wide Range Intelligence Test manual*. Wilmington, DE: Wide Range.

Goldman, B. A., & Busch, J. C. (1978). *Directory of unpublished experimental mental measures: Vol. 2*. New York: Human Sciences Press.

Goldman, B. A., & Busch, J. C. (1982). *Directory of unpublished experimental mental measures: Vol. 3*. New York: Human Sciences Press.

Goldman, B. A., & Mitchell, D. F. (1990). *Directory of unpublished experimental mental measures: Vol. 5*. Dubuque, IA: Wm. C. Brown.

Goldman, B. A., & Osborne, W. L. (1985). *Directory of unpublished experimental mental measures: Vol. 4*. New York: Human Sciences Press.

Goldman, B. A., & Sanders, J. L. (1974). *Directory of unpublished experimental mental measures: Vol. 1*. New York: Behavioral Publications.

Gottfredson, G. D., & Holland, J. L. (1989). *Dictionary of Holland occupational codes* (2nd ed.). Odessa, FL: Psychological Assessment Resources.

Gottfredson, G. D., & Holland, J. L. (1996). *Dictionary of Holland occupational codes* (3rd ed). Odessa, Fl: Psychological Assessment Resources.

Gottfredson, L. S. (1997). Why g matters: The complexity of everyday life. *Intelligence, 24*, 79–132.

Gottfredson, L. S. (2003). Dissecting practical intelligence theory: Its claims and evidence. *Intelligence, 31*, 343–397.

Gottfredson, L. S., & Sharf, J. C. (1988). Fairness in employment testing [Special issue]. *Journal of Vocational Behavior, 33*(3), 225–477.

Greenspan, S. R., & Granfield, J. M. (1992). Reconsidering the construct of mental retardation: Implications of a model of social competence. *American Journal of Mental Retardation, 96*, 442–453.

Greenwald, A. G., McGhee, D. E., & Schwartz, J. L. K. (1998). Measuring individual differences in cognition: The Implicit Association Test. *Journal of Personality and Social Psychology, 74*, 1464–1480.

Greenwald, A. G., & Nosek, B. A. (2001). Health of the Implicit Association Test at age 3. *Zeitschrift fur Experimentelle Psychologie, 48*, 85–93.

Griggs v. Duke Power Company, 401 U.S. 424 (1971).

Groth-Marnat, G. (1999). *Handbook of psychological assessment* (3rd ed.). New York: Wiley.

Guadalupe Organization v. Tempe Elementary School District, E.D. Ariz. (1972).

Guilford, J. P. (1985). The structure-of-intellect model. In B. B. Wolman (Ed.), *Handbook of intelligence* (pp. 225–266). New York: Wiley.

Hammill, D. D., Brown, L., & Bryant, B. R. (1992). *A consumer's guide to tests in print* (2nd ed.). Austin, TX: PRO-ED.

Hammill, D. D., & Larsen, S. C. (1996). *Test of Written Language—Third Edition*. Austin, TX: PRO-ED.

Hansen, J. C., & Campbell, D. P. (1985). *The Strong manual* (4th ed.). Palo Alto, CA: Consulting Psychologists Press.

Harari, O., & Zedeck, S. (1973). Development of behaviorally anchored scales for the evaluation of faculty teaching. *Journal of Applied Psychology, 58*, 261–265.

Harcourt Brace. (1996). *Stanford Achievement Test Series* (9th ed.). Orlando FL: Author.

Harcourt Brace. (2000). *Metropolitan Achievement Tests* (8th ed.). Orlando, FL: Author.

Harmon, L. W., Hansen, J. C., Borgen, F. H., & Hammer, A. L. (1994). *Strong Interest Inventory: Applications and technical guide*. Stanford, CA: Stanford University Press.

Hathaway, S. R., & McKinley, J. C. (1940). A multiphasic personality schedule (Minnesota): I. Construction of the schedule. *Journal of Psychology, 10*, 249–254.

Hathaway, S. R., & McKinley, J. C. (1989). *The Minnesota Multiphasic Personality Inventory II*. Minneapolis: University of Minnesota Press.

Heiman, G. W. (2000). *Basic statistics for the behavioral sciences* (3rd ed.). Boston, MA: Houghton Mifflin.

Hepner, J. C. (1988). *ETS test collection cumulative index to tests in microfiche, 1975–1987*. Princeton, NJ: Educational Testing Service.

Herman, K., & Samuels, R. (1985). *Computers: An extension of the clinician's mind—A sourcebook*. Norwood, NJ: Ablex.

Herrnstein, R. J., & Murray, C. (1994). *The bell curve: Intelligence and class structure in American life*. New York: The Free Press.

Hersen, M., & Bellack, A. S. (Eds.). (1988). *Dictionary of behavioral assessment techniques*. New York: Pergamon.

Heuchert, J. W., Parker, W. D., Stumpf, H., & Myburgh, C. P. (2000). The five factor model of personality in South African college students. *The American Behavioral Scientist, 44*, 112–125.

Hildebrand, D. K., & Ledbetter, M. F. (2001). Assessing children's intelligence and memory: The Wechsler Intelligence Scale for Children–Third Edition and the Children's Memory Scale. In J. J. C. Andrews, D. H. Saklofske, & H. L. Janzen (Eds.), *Handbook of psychoeducational assessment*. (pp. 13–32). San Diego: Academic Press.

Hobson v. Hansen, 269 F. Supp. 401 (D. D. C. 1967), aff'd sub nom. *Smuck v. Hobson*, 408 F.2d 175 (D.C. Cir. 1969).

Holland, J. L. (1985). *Making vocational choices: A theory of vocational personalities and work environments* (2nd ed.). Upper Saddle River, NJ: Prentice Hall.

Holland, J. L. (1997). *Making vocational choices: A theory of vocational personalities and work environments* (3rd ed.). Odessa, FL: Psychological Assessment Resources.

Holland, J. L., Powell, A. B., & Fritzsche, B. A. (1997). *Self-Directed Search (SDS) professional user's guide*. Odessa, FL: Psychological Assessment Resources.

Hunt, E. (1987). Science, technology, and intelligence. In R. R. Ronning, J. A. Glover, J. C. Conoley, & J. C. Witt (Eds.), *The influence of cognitive psychology on testing and measurement: The Buros-Nebraska symposium on measurement and testing* (Vol. 3, pp. 11–40). Hillsdale, NJ: Erlbaum.

Hyman, I. E., Jr., & Kleinknecht, E. (1998). False childhood memories: Research, theory, and applications. In L. M. Williams & V. L. Banyard (Eds.) *Trauma and memory* (pp. 175–188). Thousand Oaks, CA: Sage.

Impara, J. C., & Plake, B. S. (Eds.). (1998). *The thirteenth mental measurements yearbook*. Lincoln, NE: Buros Institute of Mental Measurements.

Jaeger, R. M. (1989). Certification of student competence. In R. L. Linn (Ed.), *Educational measurement* (3rd ed., pp. 545–572). New York: Macmillan.

Jensen, A. R. (1982). The chronometry of intelligence. In H. J. Eysenck (Ed.), *A model for intelligence*. New York: Springer.

Jensen, A. R. (1991). General mental ability: From psychometrics to biology. *Diagnostique, 16,* 134–144.

Jensen, A. R. (1993). Spearman's hypothesis tested with chronometric information-processing tasks. *Intelligence, 17,* 47–77.

Jensen, A. R. (1998). *The g factor*. Westport, CT: Praeger.

Johansson, C. B. (1991). *Career Assessment Inventory: Vocational version*. Minneapolis: National Computer Systems.

Johnson, O. G. (1976). *Tests and measurements in child development: Handbook II*. San Francisco: Jossey-Bass.

Johnson, O. G., & Bommarito, J. W. (1971). *Tests and measurements in child development: A handbook*. San Francisco: Jossey-Bass.

Kaiser, H. F. (1958). The varimax criterion for analytic rotation in factor analysis. *Psychometrika, 23,* 187–200.

Kaufman, A. S. (1990). *Assessing adolescent and adult intelligence*. Boston: Allyn and Bacon.

Kaufman, A. S. (1994). *Intelligent testing with the WISC-III*. New York: Wiley.

Kaufman, A. S., & Kaufman, N. L. (1983). *Kaufman Assessment Battery for Children: Interpretive manual*. Circle Pines, MN: American Guidance Service.

Kaufman, A. S., & Kaufman, N. L. (1985). *Kaufman Test of Educational Achievement (K-TEA)*. Circle Pines, MN: American Guidance Service.

Kaufman, A. S., & Kaufman, N. L. (1990). *Kaufman Brief Intelligence Test*. Circle Pines, MN: American Guidance Service.

Kaufman, A. S., & Kaufman, N. L. (1998). *Manual for the Kaufman Test of Educational Achievement—Comprehensive Form*. Circle Pines, MN: American Guidance Service.

Kaufman, J. C., & Kaufman, A. S. (2001). Time for the changing of the guard: A farewell to short forms of intelligence tests. *Journal of Psychoeducational Assessment, 19,* 245–267.

Keiser, R. E., & Prather, E. N. (1990). What is the TAT? A review of ten years of research. *Journal of Personality Assessment, 52,* 309–320.

Kelly, J. G. (1966). Ecological constraints on mental health services. *American Psychologist, 21,* 535–539.

Kelly, J. G. (1986). Context and process: An ecological view of the interdependence of practice and research. *American Journal of Community Psychology, 14,* 581–590.

Kennard, B. D., Stewart, S. M., Silver, C. H., & Emslie, G. J. (2000). Neuropsychological abilities and academic gains in learning disabled children: A follow-up study over an academic school year. *School Psychology International, 21,* 172–176.

Keyser, D. J., & Sweetland, R. C. (1984). *Test critiques*. Kansas City, MO: Test Corporation of America.

Kirk, R. E. (1999). *Statistics: An introduction* (4th ed.). Fort Worth, TX: Harcourt Brace.

Knouse, S. B. (1989). Impression management and the letter of recommendation. In R. C. Giacalone & P. Rosenfeld (Eds.), *Impression management in the organization*. Hillsdale, NJ: Erlbaum.

Kramer, J. J., & Conoley, J. C. (Eds.). (1992). *The eleventh mental measurements yearbook*. Lincoln, NE: Buros Institute of Mental Measurements.

Lambert, N., Leland, H., & Nihira, K. (1993). *AAMR Adaptive Behavior Scale—School Edition* (Revised). Austin, TX: PRO-ED.

Landy, F. J., Shankster, L. J., & Kohler, S. S. (1994). Personnel selection and placement. In L. W. Porter & M. R. Rosenzweig (Eds.), *Annual Review of Psychology, 45,* 261–269.

Larry P. et al. v. Wilson Riles et al. No. C 71–2270. United States District Court for the Northern District of California, San Francisco, October 1979, slip opinion.

Lester, P. A., & Bishop, L. K. (1997). *Handbook of tests and measurement in education and the social sciences*. Lancaster, PA: Technomic Publishing Company.

Levy, P., & Goldstein, H. (1984). *Tests in education: A book of critical reviews*. London: Academic Press.

Lilienfeld, S. O., Wood, J. M., & Garb, H. N. (2000). The scientific status of projective techniques. *Psychological Science in the Public Interest, 1*(2), 1–66.

Loehlin, J. C. (1992). *Latent variable analysis*. Hillsdale, NJ: Erlbaum.

Lonner, W. J. (1985). Issues in testing and assessment in cross-cultural counseling. *The Counseling Psychologist, 13,* 599–614.

Lord, F. M., & Novick, M. R. (1968). *Statistical theories of mental test scores.* Reading, MA: Addison-Wesley.

Lundy, A. (1988). Instructional set and thematic apperception test validity. *Journal of Personality Assessment, 52,* 309–320.

Maddox, T. (1997). *Tests: A comprehensive reference for assessments in psychology, education and business* (4th ed.). Austin, TX: PRO-ED.

Markwardt, F. C. (1989). *Peabody Individual Achievement Test–Revised.* Circle Pines, MN: American Guidance Service.

Markwardt, F. C. (1997). *Peabody Individual Achievement Test–Revised.* Circle Pines, MN: American Guidance Service.

Marston, D. B. (1989). A curriculum-based measurement approach to assessing academic performance: What it is and why do it? In M. R. Shinn (Ed.), *Curriculum-based measurement: Assessing special children* (pp. 18–78). New York: Guilford.

Matarazzo, J. D. (1990). Psychological assessment versus psychological testing. *American Psychologist, 45,* 999–1017.

Mather, N., & Gregg, N. (2001). Assessment with the Woodcock-Johnson-III. In J. J. C. Andrews, D. H. Saklofske, & H. L. Janzen (Eds.). *Handbook of psychoeducational assessment* (pp. 133–165). San Diego: Academic Press.

McCarney, S. B., & Leigh, J. (1990). *Behavioral Evaluation Scale–II (BES–II).* Columbia, MO: Hawthorne Educational Services.

McClelland, D. C., Atkinson, J. W., Clark, R. A., & Lowell, E. L. (1953). *The achievement motive.* New York: Appleton-Century-Crofts.

McClendon, M. J. (1994). *Multiple regression and causal analysis.* Itasca, IL: Peacock.

McClung, M. S. (1979). Competency testing programs: Legal and educational issues. *Fordham Law Review, 47,* 652.

McCrae, R. R., & Costa, P. T. (1992). Discriminant validity of NEO-PIR facet scales. *Educational and Psychological Measurement, 52,* 229–237.

McCrae, R. R., & Costa, P. T. (1997). Personality trait structure as a human universal. *American Psychologist, 52,* 509–516.

McGrew, K. S., Ittenbach, R. F., Bruininks, R. H., & Hill, B. K. (1991). Factor structure of maladaptive behavior across the lifespan of persons with mental retardation. *Research in Developmental Disabilities, 12,* 181–199.

McLoughlin, J. A., & Lewis, R. B. (2001). *Assessing students with special needs.* Upper Saddle River, NJ: Merrill/Prentice Hall.

McNulty, J. L., Graham, J. R., Ben-Porath, Y. S., & Stein, L. (1997). Comparative validity of MMPI-2 scores of African American and Caucasian mental health center clients. *Psychological Assessment, 9,* 463–470.

Meehl, P. E. (1986). Causes and effects of my disturbing little book. *Journal of Personality Assessment, 50,* 370–375.

Merrell, K. W. (1999). *Behavioral, social, and emotional assessment of children and adolescents.* Mahwah, NJ: Erlbaum.

Messick, S. (1980). Test validity and the ethics of assessment. *American Psychologist, 35,* 1012–1027.

Messick, S. (1988). The once and future issues of validity: Assessing the meaning and consequences of measurement. In H. Wainer & H. Braun (Eds.), *Test validity* (pp. 33–45). Hillsdale, NJ: Erlbaum.

Messick, S. (1989). Validity. In R. L. Linn (Ed.), *Educational measurement* (3rd ed., pp. 13–103). New York: Macmillan.

Messick, S. (1993). *Foundations of validity: Meaning and consequences in psychological assessment.* Princeton, NJ: Educational Testing Service.

Messick, S. (1995). Validity of psychological assessment: Validation of inferences from persons' responses and performances as scientific inquiry into score meaning. *American Psychologist, 50,* 741–749.

Miller, G. A. (1984). The test. *Science 84: Fifth Anniversary Issue, 5*(9), 55–60.

Miller, M. D. (1992). Review of Comprehensive Test of Basic Skills. In J. J. Kramer & J. C. Conoley (Eds.), *The eleventh mental measurements yearbook* (pp. 217–220). Lincoln, NE: Buros Institute of Mental Measurements.

Millon, T. (1990). *Toward a new personology.* New York: John Wiley.

Millon, T., Millon, C., & Davis, R. (1994). *Millon Clinical Multiaxial Inventory–III manual.* Minneapolis, MN: National Computer Systems.

Mischel, W. (1968). *Personality and assessment.* New York: Wiley.

Mischel, W. (1993). *Introduction to personality* (5th ed.). New York: Harcourt Brace Jovanovich.

Mitchell, J. V., Jr. (Ed.). (1985). *The ninth mental measurements yearbook.* Lincoln, NE: Buros Institute of Mental Measurements.

Moreland, K. L., Eyde, L. D., Robertson, G. J., Primoff, E. S., & Most, R. B. (1995). Assessment of test user qualifications: A research-based measurement procedure. *American Psychologist, 50,* 14–23.

Morreau, L. E., & Bruininks, R. H. (1991). *Checklist of adaptive learning skills*. Chicago: Riverside.

Murphy, K. R., & Davidshofer, C. O. (2001). *Psychological testing: Principles and applications*. (5th ed.). Upper Saddle River, NJ: Prentice Hall.

Murphy, L. L., Plake, B. S., Impara, J. C., & Spies, R. A. (2002). *Tests in print* (6th ed.). Lincoln, NE: Buros Institute of Mental Measurements.

Murray, H. A. (1943). *Thematic Apperception Test manual*. Cambridge, MA: Harvard University Press.

The National Commission for the Protection of Human Subjects of Biomedical and Behavioral Research. (1979). *The Belmont report: Ethical principles and guidelines for the protection of human subjects of research*. Washington, DC: National Institutes of Health.

National Education Association. (1967). Report to parents. *NEA Research Bulletin, 4*(5), 51–53.

Newmark, C. S. (Ed.). (1996). *Major psychological assessment instruments* (2nd ed.). Boston: Allyn and Bacon.

Nickerson, R. S. (1989). New directions in educational assessment. *Educational Researcher, 18*(9), 3–7.

Nihira, K., Leland, H., & Lambert, N. (1993). *AAMR Adaptive Behavior Scales–Residential and Community* (2nd ed.). Austin, TX: PRO-ED.

Nitko, A. J. (1984). Defining "criterion-referenced test." In R. A. Berk (Ed.), *A guide to criterion-referenced test construction* (pp. 8–28). Baltimore: Johns Hopkins University Press.

Nunnally, J. C., & Bernstein, I. H. (1994). *Psychometric theory*. New York: McGraw-Hill.

Nyborg, H., & Jensen, A. R. (2001). Occupation and income related to psychometric g. *Intelligence, 29*, 45–56.

O'Brien, N. P. (1988). *Test construction: A bibliography of selected resources*. New York: Greenwood.

Osgood, C. E., Suci, G. J., & Tannenbaum, P. H. (1957). *The measurement of meaning*. Urbana, IL: University of Illinois Press.

Page, E. B. (1994). Computer grading of student prose, using modern concepts and software. *Journal of Experimental Education, 62*, 127–142.

Paris, S. G. (2000). Trojan horse in the schoolyard: The hidden threats in high-stakes testing. *Issues in Education, 6*(1,2), 1–16.

Parker, K. (1983). A meta-analysis of the reliability and validity of the Rorschach. *Journal of Personality Assessment, 47*, 227–231.

PASE v. Hannon, 506 F. Supp. 831 (N.D. Ill., 1980).

Peres, S. H., & Garcia, J. R. (1962). Validity and dimensions of descriptive adjectives used in reference letters for engineering applicants. *Personnel Psychology, 15*, 279–286.

Perlmutter, B. F., Touliatos, J., & Holden, G. W. (Eds.). (2001). *Handbook of family measurement techniques: Vol. 3, Instruments & index*. Thousand Oaks, CA: Sage.

Petrill, S. A., Rempell, J., Oliver, B., & Plomin, R. (2002). Testing cognitive abilities by telephone in a sample of 6- to 8-year-olds. *Intelligence, 30*, 353–360.

Piedmont, R. L., & Chae, J. (1997). Cross-cultural generalizability of the five factor model of personality: Development and validation of the NEO PI-R for Koreans. *Journal of Cross-Cultural Psychology, 28*, 131–155.

Piedmont, R. L., McCrae, R. R., Riemann, R., & Angleitner, A. (2000). On the invalidity of validity scales: Evidence from self-reports and observer ratings in volunteer samples. *Journal of Personality and Social Psychology, 78*, 582–593.

Pinchak, B. M., & Breland, H. M. (1974). Grading practices in American high schools: National longitudinal study of the high school class of 1972. *Education Digest, 39*, 21–23.

Plake, B. S., & Impara, J. C. (Eds.). (1999). *Supplement to the thirteenth mental measurements yearbook*. Lincoln, NE: Buros Institute of Mental Measurements.

Plake, B. S., & Impara, J. C. (Eds.). (2001). *The fourteenth mental measurements yearbook*. Lincoln, NE: Buros Institute of Mental Measurements.

Plake, B. S., Impara, J. C., & Spies, R. A. (Eds.). (2003). *The fifteenth mental measurements yearbook*. Lincoln, NE: Buros Institute of Mental Measurements.

Porter, T. B. (1995). Basic considerations in informed consent in research. *Clinical Research and Regulatory Affairs, 12*, 95–109.

The Psychological Corporation. (1995). *Stanford Diagnostic Reading Test* (4th ed.). San Antonio, TX: Author.

The Psychological Corporation. (1999). *Wechsler Abbreviated Scale of Intelligence (WASI)*. San Antonio, TX: Author.

Ree, M. J., & Earles, J. A. (1992). Intelligence is the best predictor of job performance. *Current Directions in Psychological Science, 1*, 86–89.

Reynolds, C. R., & Kamphaus, R. W. (1992). *Behavior assessment system for children*. Circle Pines, MN: American Guidance Service.

Riverside Publishing Company. (2003). *Iowa Tests of Basic Skills*. Chicago: Author.

Robinson, J. P., Athanasion, R., & Head, K. B. (1969). *Measures of occupational attitudes and occupational characteristics*. Ann Arbor, MI: University of Michigan.

Robinson, J. P., Rusk, J. G., & Head, K. B. (1968). *Measures of political attitudes*. Ann Arbor, MI: University of Michigan.

Robinson, J. P., & Shaver, P. R. (1973). *Measures of social psychological attitudes* (rev. ed.). Ann Arbor, MI: University of Michigan.

Rogers, C. R. (1951). *Client centered therapy: Its current practice, implications and theory.* Boston: Houghton Mifflin.

Rogers, R., Salekin, R. T., & Sewell, K. W. (1999). Validation of the Millon Clinical Multiaxial Inventory for Axis II disorders: Does it meet the Daubert standard? *Law & Human Behavior, 23,* 425–443.

Rogers, T. B. (1995). *An introduction: The psychological testing enterprise.* Pacific Grove, CA: Brooks/Cole.

Roid, G. H. (2003). *Stanford-Binet Intelligence Scales* (5th ed.). Itasca, IL: Riverside.

Rosenbaum, B. L. (1971). *An empirical study of attitude toward invasion of privacy as it relates to personnel selection.* Unpublished doctoral dissertation, Teachers College, Columbia University, New York.

Rotatori, A. F. (1994). Test review: Multidimensional Self Concept Scale. *Measurement and Evaluation in Counseling and Development, 26,* 265–267.

Rubin, D. B. (1988). Discussion. In H. Wainer & H. Braun (Eds.), *Test validity* (pp. 241–256). Hillsdale, NJ: Erlbaum.

Runyon, R. P., Coleman, K. A., & Pittenger, D. J. (2000). *Fundamentals of behavioral statistics* (9th ed.). New York: McGraw-Hill.

Ryanen, I. A. (1988). Commentary of a minor bureaucrat. *Journal of Vocational Behavior, 33,* 379–387.

Sackett, P. R., Schmitt, N., Ellingson, J. E., & Kabin, M. B. (2001). High-stakes testing in employment, credentialing, and higher education. *American Psychologist, 56,* 302–318.

Safford, P. L., & Safford, E. J. (1996). *A history of childhood and disability.* New York: Columbia University, Teachers College Press.

Salvia, J., & Ysseldyke, J. E. (2000). Assessment (8th ed.). Boston: Houghton Mifflin.

Sattler, J. M. (2001). *Assessment of children: Cognitive applications* (4th ed.). San Diego: Author.

Sattler, J. M. (2002). *Assessment of children: Behavioral and clinical applications* (4th ed). San Diego: Author.

Scandell, D. J. (2000). Development and initial validation of validity scales for the NEO-Five Factor Inventory. *Personality and Individual Differences, 29,* 1153–1162.

Scannell, D. P., Haugh, O. M., Loyd, B. H., & Risinger, C. F. (1993). *Tests of achievement and proficiency, Forms K and L.* Chicago: Riverside.

Scannell, D. P., Haugh, O. M., Loyd, B. H., & Risinger, C. F. (1996). *Tests of Achievement and Proficiency, Form M.* Itasca, IL: Riverside.

Schinka, J. A., Kinder, B. N., & Kremer, T. (1997). Research validity scales for the NEO PI-R: Development and initial validation. *Journal of Personality Assessment, 68,* 127–138.

Schmidt, F. L. (1988a). The problem of group differences in ability test scores in employment selection. *Journal of Vocational Behavior, 33,* 272–292.

Schmidt, F. L. (1988b). Validity generalization and the future of criterion-related validity. In H. Wainer & H. Braun (Eds.), *Test validity* (pp. 173–189). Hillsdale, NJ: Erlbaum.

Schmidt, F. L., & Hunter, J. E. (1981). Employment testing: Old theories and new research findings. *American Psychologist, 36,* 1128–1137.

Schmidt, F. L., & Hunter, J. E. (1992). Development of a causal model of processes determining job performance. *Current Directions in Psychological Science, 1,* 89–92.

Schmidt, F. L., Hunter, J. E., Pearlman, K., & Hirsh, H. R. (1985). Forty questions about validity generalization and meta-analysis. *Personnel Psychology, 32,* 697–798.

Schneider, A. (2000, June 30). Why you can't trust letters of recommendation. *The Chronicle of Higher Education,* pp. A14–A16.

Schultz, D. P., & Schultz, S. E. (1996). *A history of modern psychology* (6th ed.). Fort Worth, TX: Harcourt Brace Jovanovich.

Schutte, J. W. (2000). Using the MCMI-III in forensic evaluations. *American Journal of Forensic Psychology, 19*(2), 5–20.

Seguin, E. O. (1866). *Idiocy and its treatment by the physiological method.* New York: Wood.

Shaffer, T. W., Erdberg, P., & Haroian, J. (1999). Current nonpatient data for the Rorschach, WAIS-R, and MMPI-2. *Journal of Personality Assessment, 73,* 305–316.

Sharf, J. C. (1988). Litigating personnel management policy. *Journal of Vocational Behavior, 33,* 235–271.

Shaw, M. E., & Wright, J. W. (1967). *Scales for the measurement of attitudes.* New York: McGraw-Hill.

Shepard, L. A. (1984). Setting performance standards. In R. A. Berk (Ed.), *A guide to criterion-referenced test construction* (pp. 169–198). Baltimore: Johns Hopkins University Press.

Shepard, L. A. (1989). Identification of mild handicaps. In R. L. Linn (Ed.), *Educational measurement* (3rd ed., pp. 545–572). New York: Macmillan.

Shepard, L. A. (1993). Evaluating test validity. In L. Darling-Hammond (Ed.), *Review of research in education* (Vol. 19, pp. 405–450). Washington, DC: American Educational Research Association.

Simpson, R. L. (1990). *Conferencing parents of exceptional children* (2nd ed.). Austin, TX: PRO-ED.

Siskind, G. (1966). "Mine eyes have seen a host of angels." *American Psychologist, 21,* 804–806.

Snow, R. E., & Lohman, D. F. (1989). Implications of cognitive psychology for educational measurement. In R. L. Linn (Ed.), *Educational measurement* (3rd ed., pp. 263–331). New York: Macmillan.

Spangler, W. D. (1992). Validity of questionnaire and TAT measures of need for achievement: Two meta-analyses. *Psychological Bulletin, 112,* 140–154.

Sparrow, S. S., Balla, D. A., & Cicchetti, D. V. (1984a). *Vineland Adaptive Behavior Scales.* Circle Pines, MN: American Guidance Service.

Sparrow, S. S., Balla, D. A., & Cicchetti, D. V. (1984b). *Vineland Adaptive Behavior Scales: Interview Edition, Expanded Form.* Circle Pines, MN: American Guidance Service.

Sparrow, S. S., Balla, D. A., & Cicchetti, D. V. (1984c). *Vineland Adaptive Behavior Scales: Survey Form.* Circle Pines, MN: American Guidance Service.

Sparrow, S. S., Balla, D. A., & Cicchetti, D. V. (1985). *Vineland Adaptive Behavior Scales: Classroom Edition Form.* Circle Pines, MN: American Guidance Service.

Stanford Diagnostic Mathematics Test (3rd ed.). (1984). San Antonio, TX: Psychological Corporation.

Sternberg, R. J. (1985). *Beyond IQ: A triarchic theory of intelligence.* Cambridge, England: Cambridge University Press.

Sternberg, R. J. (2003). Issues in the theory and measurement of successful intelligence: A reply to Brody. *Intelligence, 31,* 331–337.

Stiggins, R. J., Frisbie, D. A., & Griswold, P. A. (1989). Inside high school grading practices: Building a research agenda. *Educational Measurement: Issues and Practices, 8*(2), 5–14.

Stumpf, S. E. (1994). *Philosophy: History & problems* (5th ed.). New York McGraw-Hill.

Subkoviak, M. J. (1984). Estimating the reliability of mastery–non-mastery classifications. In R. A. Berk (Ed.), *A guide to criterion-referenced test construction* (pp. 267–291). Baltimore: Johns Hopkins University Press.

Sweet, S. A. (1999). *Data analysis with SPSS.* Needham Heights, MA: Allyn and Bacon.

Sweetland, R. C., & Keyser, D. J. (Eds.). (1986). *Tests: A comprehensive reference for assessments in psychology, education and business* (2nd ed.). Kansas City, MO: Test Corporaton of America.

Swenson, L. C. (1993). *Psychology and law for the helping professions.* Pacific Grove, CA: Brooks/Cole.

Tansy, M., & Miller, J. A. (1997). The invariance of the self-concept construct across White and Hispanic student populations. *Journal of Psychoeducational Assessment, 15,* 4–14.

Taylor, H. C., & Russell, J. T. (1939). The relationship of validity coefficients to the practical effectiveness of tests in selection: Discussion and tables. *Journal of Applied Psychology, 23,* 565–578.

Terman, L. M., & Merrill, M. A. (1960). *Stanford-Binet Intelligence Scale: Manual for the third revision, Form L-M.* Boston: Houghton Mifflin.

Thissen, D. (1990). Reliability and measurement precision. In H. Wainer (Ed.), *Computer adaptive testing: A primer* (pp. 161–186). Mahwah, NJ: Erlbaum.

Thorn, A. R., & Mulvenon, S. W. (2002). High-stakes testing: An examination of elementary counselors' views and their academic preparation to meet this challenge. *Measurement & Evaluation in Counseling & Development, 35,* 195–207.

Thorndike, R. L. (1982). *Applied psychometrics.* Boston: Houghton Mifflin.

Thorndike, R. L., & Hagen, E. P. (1993). *Cognitive Abilities Test.* Chicago: Riverside.

Thorndike, R. L., Hagen, E. P., & Sattler, J. M. (1986a). *Guide for administering and scoring the Stanford-Binet Intelligence Scale: Fourth Edition.* Chicago: Riverside.

Thorndike, R. L., Hagen, E. P., & Sattler, J. M. (1986b). *Stanford-Binet Intelligence Scale* (4th ed.). Chicago: Riverside.

Thorndike, R. L., Hagen, E. P., & Sattler, J. M. (1986c). *The Stanford-Binet Intelligence Scale: Fourth edition. Technical manual.* Chicago: Riverside.

Thorndike, R. L., & Thorndike, R. M. (1994). Reliability in educational and psychological measurement. In T. Husen & N. Postlethwaite (Eds.), *International encyclopedia of education* (2nd ed., pp. 4981–4995). New York: Pergamon Press.

Thorndike, R. M. (1990a). *A century of ability testing.* Chicago: Riverside.

Thorndike, R. M. (1990b). Would the real factors of the Stanford-Binet (fourth edition) please come forward? *Journal of Psychoeducational Assessment, 8,* 412–435.

Thorndike, R. M. (1999a). IRT and intelligence testing: Past, present, and future. In S. E. Embretson and S. L. Hershberger (Eds.), *The new rules of measurement: What every psychologist and educator should know* (pp. 17–35). Mahwah, NJ: Erlbaum.

Thorndike, R. M. (1999b). Review of the twelfth mental measurements yearbook. *Journal of Psychoeducational Assessment, 17,* 50–56.

Thorndike, R. M. (2001). Reliability. In B. Bolton (Ed.), *Handbook of measurement and evaluation in rehabilitation* (3rd ed., pp. 29–48). Gaithersburg, MD: Aspen.

Thorndike, R. M. (2003, September 18). *Unrestricted factor analysis of the Stanford-Binet Intelligence Scale, fifth edition.*

Paper presented at the annual meeting of the Society for Multivariate Experimental Psychology, Keystone, CO.

Thorndike, R. M., & Dinnel, D. L. (2001). *Basic statistics for the behavioral sciences*. Upper Saddle River, NJ: Merrill/Prentice Hall.

Thurstone, L. L. (1938). Primary mental abilities. *Psychometric Monographs*, No. 1.

Thurstone, L. L. (1947). *Multiple factor analysis*. Chicago: University of Chicago Press.

Topping, G. D., & O'Gorman, J. G. (1997). Effects of faking set on validity of the NEO-FFI. *Personality and Individual Differences, 23,* 117–124.

Touliatos, J., Perlmutter, B. F., & Holden, G. W. (Eds.). (2001). *Handbook of family measurement techniques: Vol. 2, Abstracts*. Thousand Oaks, CA: Sage.

Touliatos, J., Perlmutter, B. F., & Straus, M. A. (Eds.). (2001). *Handbook of family measurement techniques: Vol. 1, Abstracts*. Thousand Oaks, CA: Sage.

U.S. Department of Education. (1983). *A nation at risk: The imperative for school reform*. Washington, DC: Author.

U.S. Department of Health and Human Services. (1993). *Protecting human research subjects: Institutional Review Board guidebook*. Washington, DC: U.S. Government Printing Office.

U.S. Department of Labor. (1992). *Dictionary of occupational titles* (4th rev. ed.). Washington, DC: U.S. Government Printing Office.

U.S. Department of Labor (2000–2001). *Occupational outlook handbook*. Washington, DC: U.S. Government Printing Office.

U.S. Employment Service. (1967). *Manual for the General Aptitude Test Battery, Section III: Development*. Washington, DC: U.S. Department of Labor.

Vincent, K. R., & Harman, M. J. (1991). The Exner Rorschach: An analysis of its clinical validity. *Journal of Clinical Psychology, 47,* 596–599.

Wainer, H. (1990). *Computer adaptive testing: A primer*. Mahwah, NJ: Erlbaum.

Wainer, H., & Mislevy, R. J. (1990). Item response theory, item calibration and proficiency estimation. In H. Wainer (Ed.), *Computer adaptive testing: A primer* (pp. 65–102). Mahwah, NJ: Erlbaum.

Wald, A. (1950). *Statistical decision function*. New York: Wiley.

Wason, P. (1961). Response to affirmative and negative binary statements. *British Journal of Psychology, 52,* 133–142.

Watson v. Fort Worth Bank and Trust, U.S. Sup. Ct., No. 86–6139 (June 1988).

Wechsler, D. (1944). *The measurement of adult intelligence* (3rd ed.). Baltimore, MD: Williams & Wilkens.

Wechsler, D. (1981a). *Wechsler Adult Intelligence Scale–Revised*. San Antonio, TX: Psychological Corporation.

Wechsler, D. (1981b). *WAIS-R manual*. San Antonio, TX: Psychological Corporation.

Wechsler, D. (1989a). *Wechsler Preschool and Primary Scale of Intelligence–Revised*. San Antonio, TX: Psychological Corporation.

Wechsler, D. (1989b). *WPPSI-R manual*. San Antonio, TX: Psychological Corporation.

Wechsler, D. (1991a). *Wechsler Intelligence Scale for Children–Third Edition*. San Antonio, TX: Psychological Corporation.

Wechsler, D. (1991b). *WISC-III manual*. San Antonio, TX: Psychological Corporation.

Wechsler, D. (1997). *Wechsler Adult Intelligence Scale–Third Edition*. San Antonio, TX: Psychological Corporation.

Wechsler, D. (2002). *WPPSI-III manual*. San Antonio, TX: Psychological Corporation.

Weeks, Z. R., & Ewer-Jones, B. (1991). *The psychoeducational assessment of children* (2nd ed.). Boston: Allyn and Bacon.

White House. (1991, February 4). *The national education goals: A second report to the nation's governors*. Washington, DC: Author.

Wiederholt, J. L., & Bryant, B. R. (1992). *Gray Oral Reading Test* (3rd ed.). Austin, TX: PRO-ED.

Willett, J. B. (1988). Questions and answers in the measurement of change. In E. Z. Rothkopf (Ed.), *Review of research in education* (Vol. 15, pp. 345–422). Washington, DC: American Educational Research Association.

Wilson, P. L., (1998). Multidimensional Self-Concept Scale: An examination of grade, race and gender differences in third through sixth grade student's self-concepts. *Psychology in the Schools, 35,* 317–326.

Winter, D. G., John, P., Stewart, A. J., Klohnen, E. C., & Duncan, L. E. (1998). Traits and motives: Toward an integration of two traditions in personality research. *Psychological Review, 105,* 230–250.

Witt, J. C., Elliott, S. N., Kramer, J. J., & Gresham, F. M. (1994). *Assessment of children: Fundamental methods and practices*. Madison, WI: Brown & Benchmark.

Wood, J. M., Garb, H. N., Lilienfeld, S. O., & Nezworski, M. T. (2002). Clinical assessment. *Annual Review of Psychology, 53,* 519–543.

Woodcock, R. W. (1991). *Woodcock language proficiency battery–Revised, English form*. Chicago, IL: Riverside.

Woodcock, R. W. (1998). *The Woodcock Reading Mastery Tests–Revised*. Circle Pines, MN: American Guidance Service.

Woodcock, R. W., & Mather, N. (1989). *Woodcock-Johnson tests of achievement: Standard and supplemental batteries.* Chicago, IL: Riverside.

Woodcock, R. W., McGrew, K. S., & Mather, N. (2001). *Woodcock-Johnson III.* Itasca, IL: Riverside.

Yang, J., Bagby, R. M., & Ryder, A. L. (2000). Response style and the revised NEO Personality Inventory: Validity scales and spousal ratings in a Chinese psychiatric sample. *Assessment, 7,* 389–402.

Ysseldyke, J. E., Algozzine, B., & Thurlow, M. L. (1992). *Critical issues in special education.* Boston, MA: Houghton Mifflin.

Ysseldyke, J. E., & Christenson, S. L. (1993). *The Instructional Environment System–II.* Longmont, CO: Sopris West.

Ysseldyke, J. E., Christenson, S. L., & Kovaleski, J. F. (1994). Identifying students' instructional needs in the context of classroom and home environments. *Teaching Exceptional Children, 26,* 37–41.

Ysseldyke, M. E., Thurlow, M. L., & Erickson, R. N. (1994). *Possible sources of data for post-school level indicators.* Minneapolis, MN: University of Minnesota, College of Education and Human Development, National Center on Educational Outcomes.

Zern, D. (1967). Effects of variations in question phrasing on true-false answers by grade-school children. *Psychological Reports, 20,* 527–533.

Author Index

Aamodt, M. G., 365, 397
Achenbach, T. M., 408
Acklin, M. W., 339
Adams, W., 266, 287
Ainsley, T. N., 295
Albanese, M. A., 480
Alexander, L., 21
Allport, G., 341
Alnot, S. D., 295
Amaya, M., 433
Ames, C., 186, 195
Anastasi, A., 21, 195, 434
Andrews, T. J., 415
Angleitner, A., 347, 362
Angoff, W. H., 108, 179, 195
Archer, J., 186, 195
Archer, P., 397
Arvey, R. D., 382
Athanasion, R., 209, 216
Atkinson, J. W., 175

Baer, R. A., 347
Bagby, R. M., 347
Balla, D. A., 383, 398, 407
Banaji, M. R., 395, 397
Barak, A., 437
Barrios, B. A., 325
Baxter, J. C., 365
Beere, C. A., 216
Belk, M. S., 129, 144, 286
Bellack, A. S., 208, 215
Ben-Porath, Y. S., 350
Bennett, R. E., 480
Berk, R. A., 136, 139, 192, 325, 480
Berry, D. T., 347
Bersoff, D. N., 401
Binet, A., 12, 239, 240, 241, 247, 252
Bishop, L. K., 209, 216
Blatchford, C. H., 136, 139
Blixt, S. L., 144
Bloom, B. S., 5, 236
Boake, C., 242, 286
Bommarito, J. W., 209, 215

Bond, L., 286
Borgen, F. H., 329, 362
Borich, G., 325
Borsboom, D., 181, 195
Boyle, G. J., 253
Bracken, B., 264, 286, 351, 352
Braswell, J. S., 216
Breland, H. M., 230
Brennan, R. L., 136, 139, 140, 144
Bridgeford, N. J., 237
Brock, B., 365
Brodsky, S. L., 420
Brody, N., 245, 286
Browder, D. M., 411, 412, 415
Brown, L., 215
Brown, V. L., 410
Bruininks, R. H., 377, 379, 383, 398, 406, 407
Bryan, D. A., 365, 397
Bryant, B. R., 215, 410
Burks, H. F., 408
Buros, O., 5, 211, 215
Busch, J. C., 209, 215
Butcher, J., 346, 350

Caldwell-Andrews, A., 347
Campbell, D. T., 176, 182, 195
Campbell, J. P., 382
Cannell, J., 298, 306
Carroll, J. B., 244, 255, 286
Cattell, R., 243, 342, 347
Chan, D., 339
Cheung, F. M., 346
Christenson, S. L., 412
Cicchetti, D. V., 383, 398, 407
Clark, R. A., 175
Cohen, J., 167
Cohen, P., 167
Cohen, R. J., 21
Cole, N. S., 190, 427
Coleman, K. A., 57
Conoley, J. C., 211, 215
Cook, T. D., 182, 195

Costa, P., 342, 343, 344, 346, 347
Cramer, P., 341, 362
Cronbach, L. J., 21, 179, 180, 188, 189, 190, 195, 434
Cronin, M. E., 410
Cunningham, W. A., 395, 397

Dahlstrom, W. G., 350
Dana, R. H., 420
Darlington, R. B., 167
Das, J. P., 245, 246, 262, 286
Davidshofer, C. O., 21, 190
Davis, D. E., 356
Davis, R., 353
Dawes, R. M., 421, 438
DeFina, P. A., 409
DeFruyt, R., 346
Deutsch, M., 188, 195
Digman, J. M., 342
Dinnel, D. L., 25, 47, 57
Downey, R. G., 398
Dretzke, B. J., 57
DuBois, P. H., 2, 3, 21
Duff, F. L., 348
Duncan, L. E., 341
Dunn, L. M., 266
Dunnette, M. D., 382
Dwyer, K. P., 401

Earle, R. B., 216
Earles, J. A., 242, 281, 287
Ebbinghaus, H., 2
Ebel, R. L., 195
Edwards, A. L., 387, 397
Egan, O., 397
Ellingson, J. E., 157, 189, 196
Elliott, S. N., 412
Embretson, S. E., 108
Embretson (Whitely), S., 183, 195
Emslie, G. J., 409
English, N., 437
Erdberg, P., 421
Esquirol, J. E., 400

Evertson, C. M., 325
Ewer-Jones, B., 408
Exner, D. E., 339
Exner, J. E., 339, 362
Eyde, L. D., 418, 419, 438
Eysenck, H. J., 286

Fabiano, E., 215
Faust, D., 421, 438
Fechner, G., 2
Fehrmann, P. G., 210, 215
Feifer, S. G., 409
Feldt, L. S., 139, 140, 144, 295
Finch, F. L., 311, 325
Fiske, D. W., 176
Fitzpatrick, A. R., 480
Fitzpatrick, R., 325
Flanagan, D. P., 415
Flynn, J. R., 87, 108
Forsyth, R. A., 295
Fredericksen, N., 195, 429
Freud, S., 337
Frisbie, D. A., 230, 237
Fritzsche, B. A., 337

Gallatin, J., 400
Galton, F., 3, 241
Garb, H. N., 337, 339, 340, 362, 421
Garber, H. L., 287
Garcia, J. R., 365
Gardner, E. F., 196
Gardner, H., 246
Garner, W. R., 21
Genshaft, J. L., 415
Gerbing, D. W., 347
Gillman, C. J., 406
Glantz, L. H., 438
Glass, G. V., 193
Gleser, G. C., 434
Glutting, J., 266, 287
Goldman, B. A., 209, 215
Goldstein, H., 212, 216
Gottfredson, G. D., 362
Gottfredson, L. S., 21, 242, 245, 281, 287, 428
Graham, J. R., 350
Granfield, J. M., 406, 407
Greenspan, S. R., 406, 407
Greenwald, A. G., 394, 397
Gregg, N., 287

Gregory, R. J., 21, 287
Gresham, F. M., 412
Griswold, P. A., 230, 237
Grodin, M. A., 438
Grommon, A. H., 216
Gronlund, N. E., 237, 480
Groth-Marnat, G., 339, 362
Guilford, J. P., 5, 287
Gullickson, A. R., 236

Haertel, E., 196
Hagen, E. P., 247, 258, 265, 267, 287
Hall, B. W., 306
Hambleton, R. K., 196
Hammer, A. L., 329, 362
Hammill, D. D., 215, 410
Haney, W., 21
Hans, A., 346
Hansen, J. C., 329, 362
Harari, O., 382
Harmon, L. W., 329, 340, 362
Haroian, J., 421
Harper, A. E., Jr., 480
Harper, E. S., 480
Hartigan, J. A., 21
Hastings, J. T., 236
Hathaway, S. R., 347, 349, 350, 353
Haugh, O. M., 296
Hays, L. W., 356
Head, K. B., 209, 216
Heilman, K. A., 57
Heiman, G. W., 57
Hellervik, L. V., 382
Hepner, J. C., 215
Herman, K., 360
Herrnstein, R. J., 242, 280, 287
Hersen, M., 208, 215
Hershberger, S. L., 108
Hess, R. J., 217
Heuchert, J. W., 346
Hildebrand, D. K., 258, 287
Hill, B. K., 406, 407
Hill, P. C., 365
Hirsh, H. R., 193, 196, 280
Hoekstra, H. A., 346
Holden, G. W., 209, 216
Holland, J. L., 330, 336, 337, 362
Holland, P. W., 108
Hoover, H. D., 108
Hopkins, B. R., 480

Hopkins, K. D., 236, 480
Horn, J. L., 243, 244, 287
Howard, G. S., 21
Hunt, E., 241
Hunter, J. E., 193, 196, 242, 280, 281, 287
Hyman, I. E., Jr., 321, 325

Impara, J. C., 207, 215, 216, 438
Ittenbach, R. F., 406

Jaeger, R. M., 63, 108, 413
James, H. T., 21
Jarjoura, D., 144
Jensen, A., 240, 241, 242, 262, 281, 287
Johansson, C., 336
John, P., 341
Johnson, O. G., 209, 215
Johnson, T. F., 217
Jones, L. V., 21

Kabin, M. B., 157, 189, 196
Kamphaus, R. W., 408
Kane, M. T., 144
Kaufman, A. S., 129, 144, 243, 266, 287, 406, 410
Kaufman, J. C., 266, 287
Kaufman, N. L., 266, 287, 406, 410
Keith-Spiegel, P., 438
Kennard, B. D., 409
Keyser, D. J., 212, 215, 216
Kinder, B. N., 347
Kirby, J. R., 245, 246, 286
Kirk, R. E., 57
Kleinknecht, E., 321, 325
Klohnen, E. C., 341
Knouse, S. B., 364, 365, 397
Kohler, S. S., 373, 374, 383, 397
Kolen, M. J., 108
Koocher, G. P., 438
Kramer, J. J., 211, 412
Kremer, T., 347
Krug, S. E., 216, 438
Kubiszyn, T., 325

Lahey, M. A., 398
Lake, D. G., 216
Lambert, N., 383, 397, 398, 407
Landy, F. J., 373, 374, 383, 397

Larsen, S. C., 410
Ledbetter, M. F., 258, 287
Leigh, J., 408
Leland, H., 383, 397, 398, 407
Lester, P. A., 209, 216
Leung, K., 346
Levy, P., 212, 216
Lewis, R. B., 409
Likert, R., 388
Lilienfeld, S. O., 339, 340, 362, 421
Linn, R. L., 21, 144, 185,
    237, 480
Lippmann, W., 5
Livingston, S. A., 108
LoBello, S. G., 129, 144, 286
Lohman, D. F., 287
Lonner, W. J., 420
Lord, F. M., 144
Lowell, E. L., 175
Loyd, B. H., 296
Lundy, A., 341

Madaus, C. F., 236
Maddox, T., 208
Mager, R. F., 480
Mangen, D. J., 217
Markwardt, F. C., 410
Marston, D. B., 411
Matarazzo, J. D., 420, 438
Mather, N., 259, 287, 410
Mauser, A. J., 216
McCallum, R. S., 264, 286
McCarney, S. B., 408
McClelland, D. C., 175
McClendon, M. J., 167
McClung, M. S., 413
McCrae, R. R., 342, 343, 344, 346,
    347, 362
McDowell, C. J., 339
McEntire, E., 410
McGhee, D. E., 394, 397
McGrew, K. S., 259, 287, 406, 410
McKinley, J. C., 347, 349, 350, 353
McLoughlin, J. A., 409
McNulty, J. L., 350
Meehl, P. E., 421, 438
Mehrens, W. A., 306
Mellenbergh, G. H., 181, 195
Merrell, K. W., 415
Merrill, M., 247

Mervielde, I., 346
Messick, S., 179, 180, 181, 182,
    183, 184, 185, 186, 187, 188,
    189, 196, 427, 428, 438
Michell, J., 108
Miles, M. B., 216
Miller, D. C., 216
Miller, G. A., 416
Miller, J. A., 352
Millon, C., 353
Millon, T., 353, 362
Mischel, W., 359
Mislevy, R. J., 141, 144
Mitchell, J. V., Jr., 209, 211, 216
Moreland, K. L., 418, 419, 438
Morreau, L. E., 377, 379, 383, 398
Morrison, E. J., 325
Morrison, R. L., 398
Moss, P. A., 190, 427
Most, R. B., 418, 419
Mulvenon, S. W., 435
Murphy, K. R., 21, 190
Murphy, L. L., 207, 216
Murray, C., 242, 280, 287
Murray, H. A., 340
Myburgh, C. P., 346

Naglieri, J. A., 245, 246, 262, 286
Newmark, C. S., 287
Nezworski, M. T., 421
Nickerson, R. S., 310
Nihira, K., 383, 397, 398, 407
Nitko, A. J., 108, 315, 325, 480
Nosek, B. A., 394, 397
Novick, M. R., 144
Nyborg, H., 287

O'Brien, N. P., 209, 210, 215, 216
Odbert, H. S., 341
O'Gorman, J. G., 347
Oliver, B., 204
Osborne, W. L., 209
Osgood, C. E., 393
Osterlind, S. J., 480
Ostrow, A. C., 217
Otis, A., 4

Page, E. B., 199
Paris, S. G., 435
Parker, K., 340

Parker, W. D., 346
Pearlman, K., 193, 196, 280
Pearson, K., 3
Peres, S. H., 365
Perlmutter, B. F., 209, 216
Petersen, N. S., 108
Peterson, W. A., 217
Petrill, S. A., 204
Piedmont, R. L., 347, 362
Pinchak, B. M., 230
Pinel, P., 400
Pittenger, D. J., 57
Plake, B. S., 207, 216, 438
Plomin, R., 204
Popham, W. J., 237
Porter, T. B., 425
Porteus, S. D., 4
Powell, A. B., 337
Preacher, K. J., 395, 397
Primoff, E. S., 418, 419

Raven, J. C., 262
Ray, G. E., 129, 144, 286
Ree, M. J., 242, 281, 287
Rempell, J., 204
Reynolds, C. R., 408
Rice, J. M., 2
Riemann, R., 347, 362
Risinger, C. F., 296
Robertson, A. G., 438
Robertson, G. J., 418, 419, 438
Robinson, J. P., 209, 216
Rogers, C. R., 351
Rogers, T. B., 21, 239, 434
Rogosa, D. R., 144
Roid, G. H., 253, 255, 287, 405
Rolland, J. P., 346
Rorschach, H., 338
Rosenbaum, B. L., 424
Rotatori, A. E., 352
Rouse, S. V., 346, 350
Rozelle, R. M., 365
Rubin, D. B., 108, 186, 196
Runyon, R. P., 57
Rusk, J. G., 209, 216
Russell, J. T., 434
Ryder, A., 347

Saal, F. E., 398
Sabers, D. L., 480

Sackett, P. R., 157, 189, 196
Safford, E. J., 399, 400, 415
Safford, P. L., 399, 400, 415
Salvia, J., 414, 415
Samuels, R., 360
Sanders, J. L., 209
Sattler, J. M., 243, 247, 252, 258, 265, 287, 415
Savard, J. G., 217
Scandell, D. J., 347
Scannell, D. P., 296
Schinka, J. A., 347
Schmidt, F. L., 193, 196, 242, 280, 281, 287, 429
Schmitt, N., 157, 189, 196
Schneider, A., 365
Schnur, R., 217
Scholl, G., 217
Schultz, D. P., 400
Schultz, S. E., 400
Schwartz, J. L. K., 394, 397
Seguin, E., 400
Shaffer, T. W., 421
Shama, D. B., 144
Shankster, L. J., 373, 374, 383, 397
Sharf, J. C., 21, 428, 433
Shaver, P. R., 209, 216
Shaw, M. E., 209, 216
Shepard, L. A., 63, 108, 179, 180, 181, 183, 184, 189, 196, 221, 408
Sheslow, D., 266, 287
Shewan, C. M., 438
Silver, C. H., 409
Simon, T., 239, 247
Simpson, R. L., 404
Skinner, B. F., 352
Slavin, R. E., 237
Snow, R. E., 287
Spangler, W. D., 341
Sparrow, S. S., 383, 398, 407
Spearman, C., 4, 240, 241, 242, 247

Spies, R. A., 207, 216
Stanley, J. C., 480
Stein, L., 350
Steinberg, L., 480
Stern, W., 240
Sternberg, R. J., 244, 245, 287
Stewart, A. J., 341
Stewart, S. M., 409
Stiggins, R. J., 230, 237
Straus, M. A., 209, 216
Strong, E. K., 4
Stumpf, H., 346
Subkoviak, M. J., 136
Suci, G. J., 393
Sun, H., 346
Sweet, S. A., 57
Sweetland, R. C., 212, 215, 216
Swenson, L. C., 416
Swerdlik, M. E., 21

Tannenbaum, P. H., 393
Tansy, M., 352
Taylor, H. C., 434
Terman, L., 4, 247, 252
Terwilliger, J. S., 237
Thissen, D., 140, 144, 480
Thorn, A. R., 435
Thorndike, E. L., 3, 100, 240, 244, 246, 255
Thorndike, R. L., 108, 144, 247, 258, 265, 267, 287, 316
Thorndike, R. M., 2, 3, 21, 25, 47, 57, 100, 108, 144, 211, 239, 253, 255, 316
Thurlow, M. L., 406
Thurstone, L. L., 4, 5, 100, 240, 241, 287, 393
Topping, G. D., 347
Touliatos, J., 209, 216
Tuley, M. R., 347

Urbina, S., 21

Valette, R. M., 217
Verschell, M. S., 339
Vincent, K. R., 340
Vold, D. J., 21

Wainer, H., 105, 108, 141, 144, 480
Wald, A., 434
Wall, J., 217
Ward, W. C., 480
Weatherman, R., 407
Weber, E., 2
Wechsler, D., 129, 241, 242, 243, 255, 262, 406
Weeks, Z. R., 408
Whitcomb, A. J., 365, 397
Whitely, S., 183
Wiederholt, J. L., 410
Wigdor, A. K., 21
Willett, J. B., 144
Williams, C. L., 350
Wilson, J., 144
Wilson, P. L., 352, 362
Winter, D. G., 341
Witmer, L., 400
Witt, J. C., 412
Wood, J. M., 339, 340, 362, 421
Woodcock, R. W., 259, 287, 407, 410
Wright, J. W., 209, 216

Yang, J., 347
Yen, W. M., 108
Yerkes, R., 4
Ysseldyke, J. E., 412, 414, 415

Zachar, P., 129, 144, 286
Zedeck, S., 382
Zhang, J., 346
Zieky, M. J., 108

Subject Index

Page numbers followed by a "t" indicate tables; numbers followed by an "f" refer to figures.

AAMRA Adaptive Behavior
  Scales, 407
Abbreviated individual tests,
  265–266
Ability continuum
  related to scores, 38f
Ability, estimating, 105
Abscissa, 34
Absent scales, 377
Abstract/visual reasoning, 252
Abstract/visual reasoning tests
  Stanford-Binet Intelligence Scale,
    249–250
Absurdities tests, 249
Academic achievement tests, 232
Academic progress, reporting,
  227–231
Accountability, age of, 6
Achievement decisions, relative, 62
Achievement tests, 60, 340. *See also*
  Standardized achievement tests
  academic, 232
  college-level, 295–298
  criterion-referenced standardized,
    303–304
    problems with, 304–305
  diagnostic, 302–303
  group standardized, 291–294
  individually administered,
    294–295
  problem with administration of,
    298–300
  secondary school, 295–298
Active inference, 179
Adaptive behavior, 406–407
Adaptive Behavior Scales, 383–384
Adjustment, 326–361
Adjustment assessment, 337–358
Administration, 206
Administrative indexes, 333–336
Adverse impact, 433
Affective assessment measures, 225
Affiliation, 340, 341

Age equivalent, 69, 239
Age norms, 65t, 69–70
  girls for height, 70f
Age of accountability, 6
Age score, 69
Aggression, 340
Aggressive personality disorder,
  354t
Alcohol dependence, 355
Alternation ranking, 384
Ambiguity, 370
Ambiguous statements, with writing
  true–false items, 444
American College Testing Program
  (ACT), 5, 232, 298
American Educational Research
  Association (AERA), 19
  standards, 128
American Psychological Association
  (APA), 19 standards, 128
Americans with Disabilities Act of
  1990 (PL 101-336), 401
Analogic reasoning, 265
Anchors, 389
Anonymous grading
  of essay tests, 477
Answers
  to essay questions, 477
  to test items, 440
  for writing matching items, 461
Antisocial personality disorder, 354t
Anxiety, 18, 355
Appropriate reference groups
  norms for, 202
Aptitude test, 61, 238–284
Area conversion, 79–84
Area normalizing transformations, 79
Arithmetic mean, 40
  computer applications, 40–42
Armed Services Vocational Aptitude
  Battery (ASVAB), 281
Army Alpha, 4
Army Beta, 4

Army standard (AGCT) scores, 84
  percentiles and normal curve, 83f
Artificiality of conventional cognitive
  tests, 307–308
Artistic themes, 330, 332t
Assent, 426
Assessing products, 309
Assessment instruments
  packaged with curricular
    materials, 223–224
  types of, 223–224
Assessment processes of children
  with disabilities, 403–405
Attention, 245, 259
Attenuation, due to unreliability, 135
Attitude rating scale, 390–395
  alternative formats, 393
  example of, 392f
  implicit attitudes, 394–395
  item analysis, 391–392
  item selection, 389–391
  reliability of, 393
  semantic differential, 393–394
Attitude scales
  summative, 388–389
Attitudes, 363–395
  measuring, 386–395
Attributes
  determining operations to isolate
    and display, 11–13
  identifying and defining, 10–11
  quantifying, 13–14
  relevant, 15
  selection of, 14–15
Autonomy, 425–426
Average, 229
Average general intelligence
  frequency distribution, 283t
Avoidant personality disorder, 354t

Bar graph, 34
Base rate, 167, 434
  prediction, 170–174

Basic Interest Scales, 332, 332t
Bead memory, 251–252
Behavior, 313
    adaptive, 406–407
    categories, 323–324
    isolated, 324
    rater focusing on, 382
    records of, 322
    representing personality
        attributes, 319–320
    theory of human, 175
Behavior Assessment for
    Children (BASC), 408
Behavior Evaluation Scale II, 408
Behavioral and socioemotional
    functioning, 407–408
Behavioral approaches
    to personality assessment,
        352–358
Behavioral statements, 377
Behavioral theories, 338
Behaviorally disturbed, 408
Bell curve, 47, 48f
The Bell Curve, 242, 280
Beneficence, 427
Bias, 190–191, 323, 386, 432–434
Binet's theory, 239–240
Binet-Simon scales, 3–4, 239–240
Bipolar-manic, 355
Block design, 257
Borderline disorders, 354
Brown v. Board of Education, 402
Burks Behavioral Rating Scales, 408
Buros Institute, Web site, 211–212

California Achievement Test
    (CAT), 291
California Test Bureau (CTB), 267
Career Assessment Inventory
    (CAI), 336
Carroll's three-stratum theory, 244
Cattell-Horn theory, 243–244
Central tendency, 36–43
Change sensitive scores, 255
Characteristic curve, 101
Characteristics, 313
Cheat sheets, 474
Checklist of Adaptive Living
    Skills, 379f
Checklists, 313–314

Child Behavior Checklist, 408
Children. *See also* Disabled children
    equal treatment of, 402
Chinese competitive examinations
    for civil service positions, 2
Civil Rights Act of 1964
    (PL 88-352), 432
Civil service positions
    Chinese competitive
        examinations, 2
Clang association, 455
Classification decisions, 7
Classroom instructional decisions,
    222–225
Clerical perception, 278
Clinical opinion, validity of, 420–421
Clinical personality disorders scales,
    353–354
Clinical scales, 348
Clinical Syndromes Scales, 355
Clues, 464
Coconsenter, 426
Coding, 257
Coefficient alpha, 118
    computer application, 120
Cognitive abilities, 239–246
    assessment in disabled children,
        405–406
    general, 280–284
    nonverbal measures of, 262–265
Cognitive Abilities Test (CogAT),
    105, 267, 267f, 268f, 269–271,
    269t, 270f, 270t
Cognitive Assessment System (CAS),
    259–260
Cognitive processes, 148
Cognitive tests, artificiality, 307–308
College Entrance Examination Board
    (CEEB) scores, 84
    percentiles and normal curve, 83f
College Level Examination Program
    (CLEP), 297–298
College-level achievement tests,
    295–298
College, premature decision
    making, 232
Common factor analysis, 240
Competence
    comprehensive model of
        general, 407f

environmental, 406
    professional, ethics of, 419–421
    social, 406
Competency testing, minimum,
    412–414, 418f, 428
Competitive examinations
    Chinese, for civil service
        positions, 2
Complex multiple-choice items,
    458–459
Componential subtheory, 245
Comprehension tests, 249
Comprehensive model of general
    competence, 407f
*Comprehensive Reference for
    Assessments in Psychology, Education
    and Business,* 208
Comprehensive Test of Basic Skills
    (CTBS), 291
Compulsive personality disorder, 354t
Computer adaptive testing, 104
    reliability of, 139–142
Computer scoring, 198–199
Computerized scoring and
    interpretation, 360–361
Computerized test interpretation,
    199–200
Concentration, 18
Concurrent validity, 158
Confidentiality, 423–424
Conscientious rating, 367
Consequential basis of test
    interpretation, 186–187
Consequential basis of test use,
    187–189
Constant error, 115
Construct, 10
    external theory of, 183–184
    internal theory of, 183–184
Construct underrepresentation, 182
Construct validity, 175
    centralized view of, 182–183
    of score-based inferences,
        181–182
    threats to, 181–182
    as whole validity, 181–184
Constructed-response items, 149
Construct-irrelevant test variance, 182
Construct-related evidence of
    validity, 174–178

Consumer's Guide to Tests in Print, 212
Content, of test items, 441
Content areas, relative emphasis
    of, 149
Content-related validity, 155
Contextual subtheory, 244
Controversial issues in writing essay
    test items, 476
Convenience, 360
Conventional cognitive tests, 308
Conventional themes, 331, 332, 332t
Convergent validity, 177
Conversion hysteria, 348
Converted standard scores, 77
Copying, 250
Correct response
    probability of, 141f
Correction-for-guessing, 465–467
Correlation between variables
    effects of unreliability on,
        134–135
Correlation coefficient, 51
    computer applications, 53–54
    distribution of scores, 52f
    prediction of, 169f
Correlations, predictions about,
    176–178
Course content, 147
Covert characteristics, 369–370
Criterion, 157
    problem of, 158–159
Criterion measure
    availability, 160
    bias, 160
    convenience, 160
    qualities desired, 159–160
    relevance, 160
Criterion-referenced evaluation,
    62–64, 154, 315
Criterion-referenced reports, 92–96
Criterion-referenced skills
    analysis, 93f
Criterion-referenced standardized
    achievement tests, 303–304
    problems with, 304–305
Criterion-referenced tests, 60
    domains in, 61–62
    reliability of, 135–139
    validity for, 192–193
Criterion-related validity, 157

Critical incidents, 382
Crystallized intelligence, 243
Cube design, 264
Cumulative frequency, 33
Cumulative frequency curve, 35
    computer applications, 35–36
    mathematics test, 36f
Cumulative frequency
    distributions, 33
    mathematics test, 33t
Curricular decisions, 7, 233–234
Curricular validity, 413
Curriculum-based assessment,
    410–411
Curriculum-based measurement
    (CBM), 410–411
Curve. *See also* Normal curve
    bell, 47, 48f
    characteristic, 101
    cumulative frequency, 35
        computer applications, 35–36
    information function, 141–142
    item characteristic, 101f,
        103f, 104f
    item information, 142f
Cutting score, 170

Das-Naglieri Cognitive Assessment
    System, 259–260
Das-Naglieri PASS model, 245–246
Databases, 213
Day-by-day instructional decisions,
    225–227
Debasement, 355
Debra P. v. Turlington, 413
Debriefing, 426
Deception, 426
Decisions
    classification, 7
    classroom instructional, 222–225
    curricular, 7, 233–234
    day-by-day instructional, 225–227
    educational, 218–235
    instructional, 7
    mastery, 62, 192
    measurement, 8–9
    personal, 7
    placement, 7, 219–222
        how made, 221–222
    political, 234–235

premature
    college, 232
    public, 234–235
    relative achievement, 62
    selection, 7, 232–233
    types of, 7–8
    values, 8–9, 219
Definition, 14, 15
Delusional disorder, 355
Dependent personality disorder, 354t
Depression, 348
Descriptive information,
    errors in, 431
Desirability, 355
Determiners, 455
Developmental standard scores
    (DSS), 68–69
    comparison of, 86t
Deviations, 45
Diagnostic achievement tests,
    302–303
*Dictionary of Behavioral Assessment
    Techniques,* 208
Dictionary of Occupational Titles, 337
Difference scores
    nature of, 132f
    reliability of, 131–133, 133t
Differential Aptitude Tests
    (DAT), 193
Difficult-to-evaluate products, 309
Digits, memory for, 252
Dignity, respect for, 423–432
Directions
    for essay tests, 477
    for test taking, 464
*Directory of Selected National Testing
    Programs,* 209
*Directory of Test Collections in
    Academic Professional and Research
    Libraries,* 210
*Directory of Unpublished Experimental
    Mental Measures,* 209
Disabled children
    assessment of, 399–415
        current and emerging issues in,
            412–414
        major domains, 405–409
        outcomes based, 414
        traditional academic
            eligibility meeting, 404

follow-up evaluations, 404–405
historical care of, 399–400
legislation covering, 401–403
Disclosure, 355
Disclosure, Desirability, and
    Debasement scales, 356
Discriminant validity, 178
Discrimination, 6, 102
Discrimination factor, 365
Discrimination index, 471
    using, 472–473
Dissent, 426
Dissertation Abstracts International, 213
Distractors, 448
Distribution
    shape of, 42–43
    variability, 45f
Distributive justice, 428
Documentation, 360
Domain-referenced tests, 60
Domain score, 136
Drug dependence, 355
Dynamic theories, 337
Dysthymia, 355

Ecological assessment, 411–412
Economy, 197–198
Education for All Handicapped
    Children Act of 1975 (PL 94-142),
    220, 401
Education Index, 213
Education, planning future,
    231–235
Educational decisions, 218–235
Educational measurement
    battery period, 5–6
    boom period, 4–5
    early period, 3–4
    era of brass instrument
        psychology, 3
    laboratory period, 3
    period of criticism and
        consolidation, 5
    second period of criticism, 6
Educational records, privacy of, 402
Educational Resources Information
    Center Clearinghouse on
    Assessment and Evaluation
    (ERIC/AE), 208

Educational Testing Service (ETS),
    208, 297
Efficiency, 360
Effort, 367
Eighth grade health, final
    examinations, 150t
Elementary and Secondary
    Education Act of 1965, 6
Emotional disturbance, 222, 408
Emotional reaction to person being
    rated, 368
Empirical predictions, 360
Empirical scale construction,
    329, 347
Empirical validity, 157
Employee performance appraisal, 378f
Enright Diagnostic Inventory of Basic
    Arithmetic Skills, 410
Enterprising themes, 331, 332, 332t
Environmental competence, 406
Equation building, 251–252
Equivalent test forms, 105–106
Error, 314. *See also* Standard error
    of estimate; Standard error
    of measurement
    constant, 115
    in descriptive information, 431
    generosity, 372, 385
    of measurement, 110
Essay test items
    writing, 473–478
        suggestions for, 474–478
Essay tests
    anonymous grading, 477
    preparation for, 476–477
E-testing, 203–204
Ethics, 416–438
Ethnic minorities, 16–17
Examiners, age and educational level
    of, 152
Excel
    arithmetic mean, 40–42
    central tendency, 42–43
    coefficient alpha, 120
    correlation coefficient, 53–54
    frequency distribution, 27–28
    grouped frequency distribution,
        31–33, 35f
    histogram, 34–35
    linear transformation, 80–81

median, 38
percentile rank, 73–76
percentiles, 39–40
regression, 165
standard scores, 78–79
Experiential subtheory, 244–245
Experimental treatments, 427
    prediction about response to, 178

Face validity, 157
Factor analysis, 176, 342
Facts, 8–9
Fair use, 19
Fairness, 190–191
    standards for, 422
False negatives, 434
False positives, 434
Family Educational Rights and
    Privacy Act of 1974 (PL 93-380),
    402, 435
Feminists, 16–17
Finger dexterity, 278
Fluid intelligence, 243
Focused test, 60t
Foils, 448
Forced-choice format, 385–386
    disadvantages of, 386
Form perception, 277
Formative evaluation, 60, 222
Formula, for guessing
    correction, 466
Free association phase, 338
Frequency distribution
    computer application, 27–31
    mathematics test, 29t
    preparation of, 27–33
Full-scale intelligence (FSIQ),
    242, 254t
Functional systems, 245

The g Factor, 242
Gardner's proposal, 246
General-ability tests, 246–266
General Aptitude Test Battery (GATB),
    5, 276–279, 282f, 284f, 289t
General cognitive ability, 280–284
General intelligence, 240
General occupational themes,
    330–331
Generosity error, 372, 385

Grade equivalents, 65–69, 88
  comparison of, 86t
Grade norms, 65–69, 65t
Grades
  anonymous, 477
  assigning, 230
  importance of, 230–231
Graduate Record Exams (GRE),
  105, 280
Graphic representation, 34–36
  computer applications, 34–35
Graphic scales, 376–377
Gray Oral Reading Test-Third
  Edition, 410
GRE, 105, 280
Griggs v. Duke Power Company, 432
Group
  level on trait, 125–126
  variability of, 125
Group general-ability tests, 266–273
Group item analysis, 96f
Group standardized achievement
  tests, 291–294
Grouped frequency distribution,
  28–33
  computer application, 28–33
Grouped frequency distribution scores
  mathematics test, 30t
*Guadalupe Organization v. Tempe
  Elementary School District,* 402
Guessing
  correction for, 465–466
    criticism of, 466–467

Halo effect, 318, 372–373
*Handbook of Tests and Measurement
  in Education and the Social
  Sciences,* 209
High-stakes testing, 435–436
Histogram, 34–35
  mathematics test, 34t
Histrionic personality disorder, 354t
Hit rate, 171, 434
Hobson v. Hansen, 402
Holland occupational themes, 331f
Homogeneous statements for writing
  matching items, 461
Humanistic theories, 338
  disabilities, 400
Hypochondriasis, 348

Hypomania, 348
Hypothesis testing, 180

Ideology, 186
Idiosyncrasies, 371–372
Implicit attitudes rating scale, 394–395
Inconsistency, sources of, 111–112
Independent ratings, pooling from
  several raters, 381
Individual scores, interpretation of,
  49–50
Individual item analysis, 95f
Individualization, 360
Individualized education program
  (IEP), 220, 401
Individually administered
  achievement tests, 294–295
Individuals, variation due to, 114
Individuals with Disabilities
  Education Act (IDEA) of 1990
  (PL 101-476), 401
Inference, 25
  active, 179
  interpretive, 179
  score-based, construct validity,
    181–182
  statistical, 46
Information function curves, 141–142
Informed consent, 425–426
Inquiry phase, 338
Instructional decisions, 7
Instructional Environment
  System–II, 412
Instructional validity, 413
Instructions for test administration,
  201–202
Intelligence, 10
  assessment in disabled children,
    405–406
  average general, frequency
    distribution, 283t
  crystallized, 243
  fluid, 243
  full-scale, 242
  general, 240
  performance, 242
  theory of multiple, 246
  verbal, 242
Intelligence quotient (IQ), 87,
  240, 248

Intelligence tests, litigation
  concerning, 402
Interest measures, 327–337
  problems with, 358–359
Interest tests, 327
Interests, 326–361
Internal consistency reliability,
  117–120
Internet, 213
  Buros Institute, 211–212
  psychological testing, 436–437
Interpretation, 19
Interpretive inference, 179
Interquartile range, 44, 391
Interval scale, 26
Investigative themes, 330, 332t
Iowa Tests of Basic Skills–Form A
  (ITBS-Form A), 85t, 91, 126, 291,
  292f–293f, 410
  school average norms, 97t
  vocabulary test, 126t
Iowa Tests of Educational
  Development (ITED), 295–297,
  296f
Isolated behavior, determining
  significance of, 324
Item analysis
  attitude rating scale, 391–392
  procedures for conducting,
    468–471
Item characteristic curve, 101f,
  103f, 104f
Item information, 140
  curves, 142f
  function, 141
Item response theory (IRT), 65,
  100–101, 126
  test, 141
Item sampling, 234
Item selection, attitude rating scale,
  389–391
Item trace line, 101
Item tryouts, 468
Items, appropriate level of difficulty
  for, 153–156

Jensen's theory, 241–242
Job successes, two-by-two
  tables of, 167t
Jobs, profile correlations for, 283t

Kappa statistic, 317
Kaufman Assessment Battery for
  Children (K-ABC), 406
Kaufman Brief Intelligence Test
  (K-BIT), 266
Kaufman Test of Educational
  Achievement (K-TEA),
  294, 410
Kindness, 385
Knowledge-acquisition
  components, 245
Kuder-Richardson Formula-20,
  119, 129t
Kuder-Richardson Formula-21,
  119

Lake Wobegon effect, 298
Language assessment, written,
  409–410
Language minorities, 16–17
Language usage, 276
Larry P. et al. v. Wilson Riles et al.,
  402–403
Latent trait theory, 100–101
Learning disability, classification,
  221–222
Least restrictive environment
  (LRE), 401
Length clues, 455–456
Letters of recommendation, 364–366
Likert scale, 388
Linear conversion, 79
Linear transformation, 79, 82
  computer applications, 80–81
Litigation concerning disabilities,
  402–403

Mainstreaming, 220–221
Major depression, 355
Manual dexterity, 278
Masculinity-feminity, 348
Mastery decisions, 62, 192
Mastery frame of reference, 63
Mastery test of English
  construction, 137f
Matching items
  writing, 459–462
    suggestions for, 461–462
Math assessment in disabled
  children, 409–412

Mathematics test
  cumulative frequency curve, 36f
  cumulative frequency
    distributions, 33t
  frequency distribution, 29t
  grouped frequency distribution
    scores, 30t
  histogram, 34t
  scatterplot, 50f
  sixth-grade scores, 23t–24t
Matrices, 250
Matrix format, 262–263
Matrix sampling, 106
Mazes, 258, 265
Mean
  arithmetic, 40
    computer applications,
      40–42
Measurement
  current issues in, 15–19
  decisions, 8–9
  error, 110
  fundamental issues in, 1–21
  history of, 2–6
  numbers, 22–57
  problems with, 14–15
  scales of, 25–33
  steps in, 9–15
Measurement operation, variation
  due to, 114
Mechanical reasoning, 275
Median, 37–38
  computer application, 38
Median rating, 390–391
Medical training, 429
Memory for digits, 252
  for objects, 252
  for sentences, 251
Mental abilities, primary, 240
Mental ability tests, 232
Mental age, 87, 239, 247
Mental Measurements Yearbook
  (*MMY*), 5, 208, 211, 212, 213
Messick's unified theory of validity,
  185–189
Meta-analyses, 280
Meta-analysis, validity generalization,
  193–194
Metacomponents, 245
Method covariance, 178

Metropolitan Achievement Tests
  (MAT), 291
Millon Clinical Multiaxial
  Inventory–III (MCMI–III), 353
  profile sheet, 357f
  scales, 356, 359
Millon Clinical Personality Disorders
  Behavioral Characteristics, 354t
Millon Clinical Personality
  patterns, 353t
Minimum competency testing,
  412–414, 418f, 428
Minnesota Multiphasic Personality
  Inventory (MMPI), 5, 347–348
  clinical scales of, 348–350
Minnesota Multiphasic Personality
  Inventory–2 (MMPI-2),
  349–350, 359
Minnesota Multiphasic Personality
  Inventory–Adolescent
  (MMPI-A), 350
Minorities, 16–17
  discrimination, 6
  language, 16–17
  motivation of, 16
Modal interval, 37
Mode, 37
Monasteries caring for persons with
  disabilities, 400
Motivation of minority groups, 16
Motor coordination, 278
MTMM correlation matrix,
  176–177, 177f
Multidimensional Self-Concept Scale
  (MSCS), 351–352
Multiple abilities tests, 273–279
Multiple-choice items
  writing, 448–459
  suggestions for, 449–458
  variations in format, 458–459
Multiple intelligences, theory of, 246
Multiple observers
  advantages of, 316
  reliability of, 316–317
Multitrait multimethod (MTMM)
  correlation matrix, 176–177, 177f

Narcissistic personality disorder, 354t
National Commission for the
  Protection of Human Subjects of

Biomedical and Behavioral Research, 427
National Council on Measurement in Education (NCME), 19
Negative statements
   writing multiple-choice items, 451
   with writing true-false items, 444–445
Negatively discriminating item, 472
Negativistic personality disorder, 354t
Neuropsychological functioning, assessment of, 408–409
Neuroticism, extraversion, and openness (NEO) Personality Inventory, 342–347, 344f, 359
   adjective checklist correlates, 345t–346t
Nonlinear transformation, 79–84
Nonverbal IQ, 254t
Norm group, 62, 65
Normal curve, 47
   Army standard (AGCT) scores, 83f
   percent of cases falling below selected values, 481–482
   percentile points, 75f
   standard score scales in relation to, 83f
Normal curve equivalents, 81–82
   and percentile ranks and stanines, 82t
Normal distribution, 47, 48f
   standard deviation, 48f
Normalizing transformations, 79–84
Normative comparisons, 17–18
Normative scores, relative information, 98–99
Norm-referenced assessment, 315
Norm-referenced evaluation, 64–84
Norm-referenced tests, 61
   domains in, 61–62
Norms, 207
   cautions in using, 98–100
   interchangeability of, 84–87
   types of, 65t
Novel material
   writing multiple-choice items, 452
Numbers, 13
Numerical ability, 276

Numerical reasoning, 274
Nutritional status, 18

Object assembly, 257
Object memory, 265
Objective test items, writing, 440–462
Objective tests
   preparing for use, 462–465
   scoring of, 465–467
   using item analysis to improve, 468–473
Objectives, 223
Objects, memory for, 252
Observations
   cost of, 323
   lack of opportunity to, 368–369
   length of time for, 320
   organization of, 321–322
Observed score, 110
Observers
   multiple
      advantages of, 316
      reliability of, 316–317
   problems fitting into setting, 323
   training of, 320–321
Occupational scales, 329–331
Occupational themes, Holland, 331f
Ogive, 35
Open book tests, 474
Operational definition, 12
Oral tests, 224–225
Ordinal scale, 26
Ordinate, 34
Otis-Lennon School Ability Test, 267

Paired statements, 459
Paper folding and cutting, 250
Paper-and-pencil tests, 224
Par, performance in relation to, 228–229
Paranoia, 348
Paranoid disorders, 354
Parents in Action Special Education v. Hannon (PASE v. Hannon), 403
Patterns analysis, 249–250
Peabody Individual Achievement Test (PIAT), 294, 410
Peabody Picture Vocabulary Test–Third Edition (PPVT-III), 266

People, 100
   changes in testing, 111
Percentages, 376
Percentile norms, 65t, 70–76
Percentile rank, 71, 71t
   comparison of, 86t
   computer applications, 73–76
   determining, 71t
Percentiles, 39
   Army standard (AGCT) scores, 83f
   calculation of, 71t
   comparison of, 86t
   computer application, 39–40
   standards score scales in relation to, 83f
Perceptual organization score, 258
Perceptual speed and accuracy, 275
Perfection, performance in relation to, 228
Performance, 13
   assessment of, 315–318
   evaluation, 307–324
      cognitive tasks, 310
Performance appraisal, employee, 378f
Performance assessment, 225
Performance assessment exercise, mathematics, 311f–312f
Performance components, 245
Performance intelligence (PIQ), 242
Performance scale, 256
Performance tests, 225
   scoring of, 310–311
Personal decisions, 7
Personal Style Scale, 333, 333t
Personality, 326–361
   learning from others, 364–386
Personality assessment, 337–358
   behavioral approaches, 352–358
   dynamic approaches to, 338–341
   humanistic approaches, 351–352
   trait approaches, 341–350
Personality disorder
   aggressive, 354t
   antisocial, 354t
   avoidant, 354t
   compulsive, 354t
   dependent, 354t
   histrionic, 354t
   narcissistic, 354t

negativistic, 354t
schizoid, 354t
self-defeating, 354t
Personality disorders scales, clinical, 353–354
Personality measures, problems with, 358–359
Personality tests, 327
Phrases, for writing essay test items, 475
Picture arrangement, 256
Picture completion, 256
Pilot training, 158f
PL 88-352, 432
PL 93-380, 402, 435
PL 94-142, 220, 401
PL 101-336, 401
PL 101-476, 401
Placement decisions, 7, 219–222
how made, 221–222
Placement sequence, referral to, 403
Planning, 245, 259
Planning, attention, simultaneous processing, and successive processing (PASS) theory, 245–246
Plato, 239
Plausible answers, writing multiple-choice items, 454
Point-biserial correlation, 472
Political decisions, 234–235
Population, 46
Positive, maximizing, 430–431
Positively discriminating distractor, 472
Post-traumatic stress disorder, 355
Potential, performance in relation to, 229–230
Power, 340, 341
Power test, 262
Practical reliability, 129
Practicality, 124
Precision, 112
Prediction, 174
about response to experimental treatments, 178
making, 160–161
Prediction interval, 173
Predictive validity, 157
Predictor, 54

Premature decision making, college, 232
Prereferral intervention, 403
Present scales, 377
Primary language not English, 402
Primary mental abilities, 240
Privacy, 423–424
invasion of, 17
Problems, clear posing of, 442
Process assessment, 313–315
Processing speed score, 258
Produce-response, 149
Produce-response items, 440
Product
assessment of, 315–318
evaluation of, 225, 307–324
cognitive tasks, 310
Professional competence, ethics of, 419–421
Professional responsibility, 421–422
Professional training, ethics of, 417–419
Proficiency tests, 232
Profile narrative report, 91
Profiles, 88–92
Projective hypothesis, 338
Proofreading, 463
Psychasthenia, 348
PsychLit, 213
Psychodiagnostic procedures, proficiency in, 417
Psychological Abstracts, 213
Psychological Corporation Assessment Center, 203
Psychometric theories, 241
Psychometrics, grounded in, 419
Psychopathic deviate, 348
Public decisions, 234–235

Q sort, 386
Quadrants, 50
Qualified statements with writing true–false items, 444
Quality, 10
Quantitative reasoning, 251–252
Quartiles, 44
computer applications, 44
Quotients, 87–88

Racial bias, litigation concerning, 402
Range, 44
Ranking procedures, 384–385
Rater
ability to rate accurately, 368
biases, 371–372
education for, 380–381
focusing on behaviors, 382
input from, 382
selection of, 380
Rating
improving accuracy of, 379–383
improving effectiveness of, 374–379
problems obtaining, 367–374
selecting qualities for, 381
Rating effectiveness, factors limiting, 372
Rating instruments, refinements in, 374
Rating procedures for special situations, 383–386
Rating scales, 314–315, 366
construction of, 382
Ratio IQ, 248
Ratio scale, 26
Raven's Progressive Matrices, 262–263, 263f
Raw scores, 67
Reading assessment, in disabled children, 409–412
Reading difficulty of test items, 440
Reading tests
scatterplot, 50f, 161f
scatterplot scores, 161f
sixth-grade scores, 23t–24t
Realistic themes, 330, 332t
Real-life situations, 322
Reasoning
abstract/visual, 252
analogic, 265
mechanical, 275
numerical, 274
quantitative, 251–252
verbal, 252, 274
Recommendation, letters of, 364–366
Records
of behavior, 322
educational, privacy of, 402

Reference groups, 50
  norms for, 202
Referrals for special education
  services, 404
Regression, computer application,
  165–166
Regression equation, 160
Regression line, 161, 162f
  finding, 163–164
Relationship, measures of, 50–55
Relative achievement decisions, 62
Reliability, 54, 109–144, 206
  attitude rating scale, 393
  comparison of methods, 121–122
  of computer adaptive testing,
    139–142
  as consistency, 110–112
  of criterion-referenced tests,
    135–139
  of difference scores, 131–133,
    133t
  estimating, 128
  evidence of, 202
  factors affecting, 125–130
  internal consistency, 117–120
  low, 373
  minimum level of, 130–131
  of multiple observers, 316–317
  overlapping with validity,
    191–192
  practical, 129
  split-half, 117
  theoretical *versus* practical
    reliability, 128–130
  variation in, 121t
  ways of expressing, 112–113
  ways to assess, 113–121
Reliability coefficient, 112–113,
  124–125, 129t
Reliability data, interpretation of,
  122–124
Reliability diagonals, 177
Repetition of measurement,
  114–115
Resemblance judgments, 379
Response categories, refinements in,
  376–377
Response options, 374
Response sets, 358
Retesting with same test, 114–115

Revised NEO Personality Inventory
  (NEO PI-R), 342–347, 344f, 359
  adjective checklist correlates,
    345t–346t
Rights, respect for, 423–432
Rival hypothesis, 184
Rorschach Inkblot Test, 338, 339f
Routine test use, practicality in,
  197–217
Rubric, 199

Safety, 309
Samples, limited, 111–112
Scales, 13, 24, 25, 207
Scales of Independent
  Behavior–Revised, 407
Scatterplots, 50, 161f
  mathematics test, 50f
Schizoid personality disorder, 354t
Schizophrenia, 348
Schizotypal disorders, 354
Scholastic Aptitude Test (SAT), 5,
  105, 172f, 232, 280
School average norms, 97–98
Scientific responsibility, 421–422
Score-based inferences, construct
  validity, 181–182
Score interval, 28
Score profile, 88–92
Scores. *See also* Difference scores;
  Test scores
  ability continuum, 38f
  age, 69
  Army standard (AGCT), 84
  percentiles and normal curve, 83f
  change sensitive, 255
  College Entrance Examination
    Board (CEEB), 84
  percentiles and normal curve, 83f
  converted standard, 77
  correlation coefficient, 52f
  cutting, 170
  developmental standard, 68–69
    comparison of, 86t
  domain, 136
  features facilitating use of, 201–203
  giving meaning to, 58–106
  individual, interpretation of,
    49–50
  lists of students, 89f

nature of, 58–62
normative, relative information,
  98–99
observed, 110
processing speed, 258
raw, 67
spread of, 25
standard age, 248
true, correlation between, 134f
universal scale, 105
Scoring, 206
Scoring essay items, 477–478
Scoring keys, 201–202
Screening for disabilities, 403
Secondary school achievement tests,
  295–298
Selection decisions, 7, 232–233
Selection ratio, 167, 434
Select-response items, 103, 149, 440
Self-concept, 351, 352f
Self-defeating personality
  disorder, 354t
Self-determination, 425–426
Self-Directed Search (SDS), 336–337
Self-help skills, 406–407
Self-perception, 351
Semi-interquartile range, 44
Sentences, memory for, 251
Severe Clinical Syndromes
  Scales, 355
Severe Personality Disorders Scales,
  354–355
Short statements for writing
  matching items, 461
Short-term memory tests, 251–252
Simultaneous processing, 245, 262
Single-item scales, 389–390
Sixteen Personality Factor
  Questionnaire (16PF), 342
Skewed, 42–43, 43f
Social adjustment, 375
Social competence, 406
Social consequences, 187–189
Social desirability, 358
Social introversion, 348
Social responsibility, 427–432
Social themes, 331, 332t
Socioemotional functioning, 407–408
Somatoform, 355
Sources of Test Information, 209, 210

Spatial aptitude, 277
Spatial memory, 264–265
Spatial relations, 275
Spearman-Brown prophecy
  formula, 117
Spearman's g, 240
Specimen set, 210
Speech and language disabilities, 405
Speed test, 262
Spelling tests, 59t, 276
  sixth-grade scores, 23t–24t
Spencer, Herbert, 239
Split-half reliability, 117
SPSS
  arithmetic mean, 40–42
  central tendency, 42–43
  coefficient alpha, 120
  correlation coefficient, 53–54
  frequency distribution, 27–28
  grouped frequency distribution, 32
  histogram, 34–35
  linear transformation, 80–81
  median, 38
  percentile rank, 73–76
  percentiles, 39–40
  standard scores, 78–79
Standard age score (SAS), 248
Standard deviation, 45–46
  computer application, 47
  interpreting, 45–49
Standard error of estimate, 171,
  172f, 173f
Standard error of measurement, 112,
  122–124, 122f, 123t
Standardization, 360
Standardized achievement tests, 223,
  288–305
  distinctive features of, 288–289
  grade ranges covered by, 291t
  interpreting, 300–302
  norms, 289
  objectives, 289
  types of, 290–291
  uses of, 290
Standard score norms, 65t, 76–79
Standard score scales, 76
Standard scores, 49–50
  comparison of, 86t
  computer applications, 78–79
Standards, 421–422

Standards for Educational and
  Psychological Testing, 19,
  421–422, 436
Stanford-Achievement Test (SAT),
  291, 410
Stanford Diagnostic Mathematics
  Test, Fourth Edition, 302
Stanford Diagnostic Reading Test,
  303, 410
Stanford-Binet Intelligence Scale, 4,
  87, 213
  abstract/visual reasoning tests,
    249–250
  organization of, 252–253
  subtests of, 249
  verbal reasoning tests, 249
Stanford-Binet Intelligence Scale
  (SB5), 253–255, 405
Stanford-Binet Intelligence
  Scale–Fourth Edition (SB-IV)
  247–253
Stanines, 82–83
  percentiles and normal curve, 83f
Statistical inference, 46
Statistical theory, 4
Statistical validity, 157
Statistics, 25
Stem, 448, 450
Sternberg's triarchic theory, 244–245
Stimulus variables, 374
  refinements in presenting,
    374–375
Strong-Campbell Interest Inventory
  (SCII), 327
Strong Interest Inventory (SII),
  327–336
  long-term stability of, 335t
  reliability and validity of, 335
  sample profile form from, 334f
Strong Vocational Interest Blank
  (SVIB), 327, 328
Structural theories, 241
Student profile chart, 90f
Study questions, 474
Subdivided tests, 116–120
Subjectivity, 323
Subscore intercorrelations, evidence
  of, 202
Successive processing, 245, 262
Summative attitude scales, 388–389

Summative evaluation, 60, 222
Summative rating, 388
Supply-response, 149
Symbol search, 258
Symbolic memory, 264
Systematic observation, 318–324
  advantages and disadvantages of,
    322–323
  conducting, 319–322
  disadvantages of, 323–324

Table of specifications, 147–156
Take-home exams, 474
Tasks, 100
  changes in testing, 111
Teacher-made assessment
  instruments, 224–225, 226–227,
  226f
Test administration, features
  facilitating, 200–201
Test bias, litigation concerning, 402
Test blueprint, 147–156
Test Collection Catalog, 209
Test construction, standards
  for, 422
Test content, 147
Test Critiques, 212
Test data
  beneficiaries of, 423–424
  personal, 424–425
  use of, 424
Test development, principles of,
  439–480
Test documentation, standards
  for, 422
Test evaluation, standards for, 422
Test interpretation, features
  facilitating, 201–203
Test items, 152
  layout on page, 201
Test layout, 463
Test of Mathematical
  Abilities–Second Edition, 410
Test of Written Language–Third
  edition, 410
Test relationship to other variables,
  evidence of, 202–203
Test–Retest, 129t
Test scores
  descriptive information, 431

ethics of, 420
frames of reference, 59–61
generalization layers, 191f
as indicators, 430–431
questions to ask about, 22–25
related to other factors, 431
Test takers, rights and
responsibilities of, 18–19
Test use, adverse consequences of, 187
Tests
aids to interpreting results, 205
alternate forms of, 115
controversial issues in, 432–437
critics' opinions of, 211–212
distribution of, 153
getting information about,
207–214
guides for evaluating, 204–207
guides for use of, 203
information about, 205
length of, 127–128
parallel forms, 115–116, 119
practical issues related to, 197–217
research on, 212–214
single-administration methods,
116–120
social benefits of, 428–429
standards for, 422
Tests and Measurements in Child
Development, 209
Tests in Education, 212
Tests in Microfiche, 208, 209, 210
Tests in Print, 207, 212, 213
Tests of Achievement and Proficiency
(TAP), 166, 172f, 297
Thematic Apperception Test (TAT),
340–341
sample card, 340f
Theoretical reliability versus practical
reliability, 128–130
Theory, 186
Theory of human behavior, 175
Theory of multiple intelligences, 246
Thought disorder, 355
Three-stratum theory (Carroll's), 244
Thurstone scaling, 393
Thurstone's primary mental abilities,
240–241
Times direction, 360
of difference, 130t

Trait, covertness of, 369–370
Trait names, 375
Trait theories, 337
Transitory product, 309
Trick questions, 442
True–false items
writing, 443–448
unequivocally, 443–444
variations in format, 445–446
True score, 110
correlation between, 134f
Truth in testing, 434–435
T-scores, percentiles and normal
curve, 83f
Two-factor theory, 240

Undercorrection, 467
Unified theory of validity (Messick's),
185–189
Unified validity, 428
Uniform standard of reference,
370–371
Universal Nonverbal Intelligence Test
(UNIT), 264–265
Universal scale score, 105
Unreliability, effects on correlation
between variables, 134–135

Validation, as scientific enterprise,
179–181
Validity, 109–110, 124, 145–194,
205–206, 355, 360. See also
Construct validity
of clinical opinion, 420–421
concurrent, 158
construct-related evidence of,
174–178
content for measures of
aptitude/performance, 156
content-related, 155
content-related evidence of,
147–156
convergent, 177
for criterion-referenced tests,
192–193
criterion-related, 157
criterion-related evidence of,
157–174
curricular, 413
discriminant, 178

empirical, 157
face, 157
facets of, 185t
instructional, 413
Messick's unified theory of,
185–189
predictive, 157
questionable, 373–374
statistical, 157
unified, 428
unified view of, 179–185
Validity coefficients, interpretation
of, 164–170
Validity diagonals, 177
Validity generalization, 281
Validity theory and test bias,
190–191
Value implications, 186–187
Values, 430
decisions, 8–9, 219
Variability, measures of, 43–44
Variables, correlations between, 55t
Variance, 45
Variance components, 139
Verbal aptitude, 276
Verbal comprehension, 258
Verbal intelligence (VIQ),
242, 254t
Verbal reasoning, 252, 274
Verbal relations tests, 249
Verbal scale, 256
Vineland Adaptive Behavior
Scales, 407
Vocabulary level of test items, 440
Vocabulary routing test, 253
Vocabulary tests, 249
Vocational criteria, predicting, 164t

Washington Assessment of Student
Learning (WASL), 6
Watson v. Fort Worth Bank and
Trust, 433
Web site, Buros Institute, 211–212
Wechsler Abbreviated Scale of
Intelligence (WASI), 266
Wechsler Adult Intelligence
Scale–Third Edition
(WAIS-III), 255
Wechsler-Bellevue Intelligence
Scale, 5

Wechsler Intelligence Scale for Children–Third Edition (WISC-III), 129, 255
Wechsler Intelligence Scale for Children–Fourth Edition (WISC-IV), 258
Wechsler intelligence scales, 255–258, 405–406
Wechsler Preschool and Primary Scale of Intelligence–Third Edition (WPPSI-III), 255
Wechsler's theory, 242–243
Wide Range Intelligence Test (WRIT), 266
Wisdom, limits of, 431–432
Women, discrimination, 6

Woodcock-Johnson Psycho-Educational Battery–Third Edition, 259, 260t–261t, 295, 410
Woodcock Language Proficiency Battery–Revised, 410
Word spelling tests, 59t
World knowledge, scale of, 100, 100f
World War I, 3–4
Writing essay test items, 473–478
  suggestions for, 474–478
Writing matching items, 459–462
  suggestions for, 461–462
Writing multiple-choice items, 448–459
  suggestions for, 449–458
  variations in format, 458–459

Writing true–false items, 443–448
  unequivocally, 443–444
  variations in format, 445–446
Written language assessment in disabled children, 409–412

Young children, observations of, 322–323

Z-scores, 49–50, 51, 82
  computer application, 78–79
  percentiles and normal curve, 83f